Mastering™ HTML and XHTML

Deborah S. Ray and Eric J. Ray

ISBN: 0-7821-4141-2   1,136 pages   US $49.99

Mastering HTML and XHTML is the most complete, up-to-date book on the core language of the Web. You'll learn everything you need to know about coding web pages in both HTML and XHTML, the latest, more powerful version of HTML. But it doesn't stop there. You also get practical instruction in complementary web technologies such as JavaScript, CSS, and Dynamic HTML, along with a Masters Reference that makes it easy to find the information you need. Tying it all together is the authors' expert guidance on planning, developing, and maintaining effective, accessible websites.

XML Processing with Perl™, Python, and PHP

Martin C. Brown

ISBN: 0-7821-4021-1   448 pages   US $49.99

XML Processing with Perl, Python, and PHP teaches you to reap the special advantages of processing your XML with these and four other scripting languages. Choose the language that makes the most sense for you and move ahead. With this book's help, you'll master the execution of remote procedures, the internal modeling of XML data, the exporting of internal data into XML, and the conversion of XML to formats as varied as SQL, HTML, and proprietary configuration schemes. Application-specific examples keep you focused on the real world; at the same time, the scripting techniques you'll learn all rise above specific applications. Like XML data, they're flexible, and they'll serve you well in whatever context you're working.

D0370050

PERL™, CGI, AND JAVASCRIPT® COMPLETE, 2ND EDITION

SYBEX®

SAN FRANCISCO ► LONDON

Associate Publisher: Joel Fugazzotto

Acquisitions Editor: Denise Santoro Lincoln

Developmental Editor: Carol Henry

Production Editor: Susan Berge

Compilation Editors: Andy Lester, Dave Taylor

Technical Editor: Charlie Hornberger

Copyeditor: Tiffany Taylor

Compositors: Rozi Harris, Bill Clark, Interactive Composition Corporation

Proofreaders: Emily Hsuan, Darcey Maurer, Laurie O'Connell, Nancy Riddiough, Monique van den Berg

Indexer: Nancy Guenther

Book Designer: Maureen Forys, Happenstance Type-o-Rama

Cover Designer: DesignSite

Cover Photographer: The Image Bank

Library of Congress Card Number: 2003101652

ISBN: 0-7821-4213-3

CONTENTS AT A GLANCE

CONTENTS

INTRODUCTION

*P*erl, CGI, and JavaScript Complete, 2nd Edition is a one-of-a-kind computer book—valuable both for the breadth and quality of its content and for its low price. This compilation of information from some of Sybex's very best books provides comprehensive coverage of Perl, CGI, and JavaScript, indispensable scripting languages for anyone interested in creating dynamic, interactive websites. This book, unique in the computer book world, was created with several goals in mind:

- ▶ To offer a thorough guide covering all the most important features and uses of the Perl, JavaScript, and CGI languages—at an affordable price

- ▶ To acquaint you with some of our best authors, their writing styles and teaching skills, and the level of expertise they bring to their books—so that you can easily find a match for your interests and needs

Thus you can see that this book is designed to provide you with all the essential information you'll need to get the most from your study of scripting and website creation. At the same time, *Perl, CGI, and JavaScript Complete, 2nd Edition* will invite you to explore the even greater depth and wider coverage of material in the source books as well as other Sybex titles by the same authors.

If you have read other software development books, you have seen that there are many possible approaches to the task of creating and transforming web pages. Frankly, it seems there are as many programming styles as there are programmers! The books from which *Perl, CGI, and JavaScript Complete, 2nd Edition* was compiled represent this range of approaches. From the quick, concise *No Experience Required* style to the extremely thorough *Mastering* style, these books also address readers at various levels of computer experience. As you read through various chapters of this book, you'll be able to quickly identify which approach and level of expertise works best for you. You'll also see what these books have in common: a commitment to clarity, accuracy, and practicality.

You'll find in these pages ample evidence of the high quality of Sybex's authors. Unlike publishers who produce "books by committee," Sybex authors are encouraged to write in individual voices that reflect their own experience with the evolution of the computing technology. Nearly every book represented here is the work of a single writer or a pair of close collaborators. When Eric Herrmann, for example, says, "Personally, I am not a big fan of most HTML editors because I think they try to do too much . . . ," you know you are getting the benefit of *his* direct experience.

In adapting the various source materials for inclusion in *Perl, CGI, and JavaScript Complete, 2nd Edition*, the revisers and compilation editors preserved these individual voices and perspectives. Chapters were edited to update technological issues, minimize duplication and coverage of nonessential information, and revise the cross-referencing so you can easily follow a topic across chapters. Some sections have also been edited for length in order to include as much updated, relevant, and important information as possible.

Who Can Benefit from This Book?

Perl, CGI, and JavaScript Complete, 2nd Edition is designed to meet the needs of a wide range of web page and website developers, ranging from the hobbyist experimenting with JavaScript to the professional working with 500+ line Perl-based CGI tools. Therefore, although you certainly can read this book from beginning to end, not all of you will need to read every chapter. The table of contents and the index will guide you to the subjects you're looking for. You'll find everything from an overview of JavaScript and how it fits into a web page, to the subtle but important nuances of security in a Perl-based CGI program, as well as extensive examples of working with the Document Object Model from within JavaScript.

Even if you have only a little familiarity with programming, this book will get you started working with Perl and CGI programming. Starting in Chapter 8, you'll find step-by-step instructions for the creation of your first simple CGI program; then you can slowly build up to more complex and useful software as you progress through the rest of the book. If your interests are in JavaScript as a way to add pizzazz to your web pages, start at the very beginning of the book to learn all about this powerful addition to basic HTML.

Intermediate users with a background in software development, perhaps even some experience in Java or Perl, will find useful nuggets of information throughout this book. And for you advanced "bitheads," this book will be useful as a reference work on all three of the technologies.

How This Book Is Organized

Perl, CGI, and JavaScript Complete, 2nd Edition begins with four chapters on JavaScript fundamentals. This section of the book is designed to teach you the basics of the JavaScript language. You'll see how JavaScript lets you interact with the elements of the Document Object Model, and you'll get up and running with your own JavaScript programs.

Next come three chapters focused on more-advanced JavaScript concepts. They explore some of the more practical uses of JavaScript within a Web context, focusing on validating and processing forms, exploiting cookies, and achieving graceful interaction between JavaScript and CGI programs.

In Chapters 8 through 13, the focus switches to Perl and CGI programming. You'll learn how to write your first program, how to debug Perl programs, and how to use Perl and CGI in the real world (such as dealing with files, bringing your counter to the Web, and running your counter). You'll also learn how to create and process HTML forms with Perl, and how Perl lets you work within the world of Unicode.

Chapter 14 begins the section of the book where the real Perl fun begins! You'll learn how to create a cool guestbook for your website and monitor website activity. You'll also learn all about e-mail programs and protocols, and Unix and Windows e-mail solutions for your Perl programs. This section of the book also demonstrates interaction with databases using Perl, showing you how to create a database table and import data. You'll get an introduction to the SQL language, and instructions for creating an Internet connection to a database. The final chapter tells you how to utilize Perl's support for XML solutions.

At the end of the book you'll find three appendixes that provide comprehensive JavaScript and Perl references. The JavaScript objects, Perl functions, and Perl module references found in this section are essential resources to learning and working with JavaScript, CGI, and Perl.

A Few Typographic Conventions

Within each chapter, the figures, tables, and code listings have all been renumbered to match their new chapter numbers. For example, Chapter 3 in this book was originally Chapter 10 in the book from which it was excerpted, so all of the numbers have been converted to reflect the Chapter 3 numbering (for example, Figure 10.1 is now Figure 3.1).

When you notice the ➥ arrow in a line of code, it's indicating that the line has been broken to fit the printed page. When you type this at your own computer, make sure that you end up with the continued line appended to the end of the preceding line.

This typeface is used to identify code elements, Internet URLs, and filenames and paths. **Boldface** is used to indicate key parts of a code listing, and occasionally keyboard input. *Italic* represents placeholders such as *file* and *object*.

You'll find these types of special notes throughout the book:

TIP

Tips tell you about quicker and smarter ways to accomplish a task. These Tips have been accumulated by the authors after many hours working with the specific technologies/languages.

NOTE

Notes usually represent alternate ways of accomplishing a task or some important additional information.

WARNING

Warnings are significant instructions that will save you from disaster. When you see a Warning, do pay attention to it.

YOU'LL ALSO SEE SIDEBAR BOXES LIKE THIS

These sidebars provide added explanations of special topics that are referred to in the surrounding discussions and that you may want to explore further. Sidebars may also provide notes on minor enhancements that were made to a chapter brought over from its original book.

For More Information

Visit the Catalog at the Sybex website, www.sybex.com, to learn more about all the books contributing to *Perl, CGI, and JavaScript Complete, 2nd Edition*. That's also where you'll find the supporting code for each chapter. Look for the Download link on the *Complete* book's Catalog page.

We hope you enjoy this *Perl, CGI, and JavaScript Complete, 2nd Edition* collection and find it useful. Good luck in your programming and website development endeavors!

Chapter 1

LEARNING THE FUNDAMENTALS

Imagine being able to create interactive multimedia adventure games that anyone can play over the World Wide Web. Imagine being able to create animated product catalogs that not only help your customers find the products they want but enable them to purchase them using secure online payment systems. Imagine being able to create database applications for use by your company's sales force from one end of the country to another via the company's intranet. With JavaScript, you no longer have to imagine—you can do it all.

JavaScript is the powerful programming language for the Web that not only enables the development of truly interactive web pages, but also is the essential glue that integrates *HTML*, *XML*, *Java applets*, *ActiveX Controls*, *browser plug-ins*, *server scripts*, and other web *objects*, permitting developers to create *distributed applications* for use over the Internet and over corporate *intranets* as well.

Adapted from *Mastering JavaScript Premium Edition*
by James Jaworski
ISBN 0-7821-2819-X

If the terms in the preceding paragraphs are a bit confusing to you, you've come to the right place to begin your involvement with JavaScript and the world of interactive web page development. In this chapter, I will provide the background information you need to begin mastering the JavaScript language. I'll begin with the concepts that are essential to understanding the operation of the Web.

NOTE

JavaScript is supported by Netscape Navigator, Microsoft Internet Explorer, Mozilla, Chimera, Sun's HotJava, Opera Software's Opera Browser, and other browsers. As such, it is an important tool for both current and future web development. Throughout the JavaScript sections of this book, we will emphasize the scripting capabilities provided by Navigator 6 and 7 (JavaScript 1.5) and Internet Explorer 6 (JScript 5.6). The other JavaScript-capable browsers take their lead from Navigator and Internet Explorer, but may not fully support all of the features of JavaScript 1.5 or JScript 5.6. For instance, the Opera 5 browser claims to support "most" of the JavaScript 1.4 core.

THE WEB

The Web is one of the most popular services provided via the Internet. At its best, it combines the appeal of exploring exotic destinations with the excitement of playing a video game, listening to a music CD, or even directing a movie, and you can do it all by means of an intuitive, easy-to-use, graphical user interface. Probably the most appealing aspect of the Web, however, is the fact that it isn't just for spectators. Once you have some experience with web *authoring tools* (and even something as simple as Notepad or SimpleText can be a web authoring tool), you can publish yourself—and offer over the Web anything you want to make available, from your company's latest research results to your own documentary on the lives of the rich and famous.

To many people, the most familiar element of the Web is the *browser*. A browser is the user's window to the Web, providing the capability to view web documents and access web-based services and applications. The most popular browsers are Netscape's Navigator and Microsoft's Internet Explorer, the last few versions of which support JavaScript. Both browsers are descendants of the Mosaic browser, which was developed by a team of programmers, notably including Marc Andreessen, at the National Center for Supercomputing Applications (NCSA), located at the University of Illinois, Urbana-Champaign. Mosaic's slick graphical user interface (GUI, pronounced "gooey") helped transform the Web from a research tool to the global publishing medium it is today.

Today's web browsers have gone far beyond Mosaic's GUI features with multimedia capabilities and browser-based implementations of software runtime environments such as Java and JavaScript. These programming languages make it possible to develop web documents that are highly interactive, meaning they do more than simply connect you to another web page elsewhere on the Internet. *Web documents created with JavaScript contain programs*—which you, as the user of a browser, run entirely within the context of the web pages that are currently displayed. This is a major advance in web publishing technology. It means, for one thing, that you can run web-based applications without having to install additional software on your machine.

To publish a document on the Web, you must make it available to a web *server*. Web servers retrieve web documents in response to browser requests and return the documents to the requesting browsers. Web servers also provide gateways that enable browsers to access web-related applications, such as database searches and electronic payment systems.

The earliest web servers were developed by CERN and NCSA. These servers were the mainstay of the Web throughout its early years. Lately, commercial web servers, developed by Netscape, Sun Microsystems, Microsoft, and other companies, have become increasingly popular on the Web, and the open-source Apache web server is still the most widely used according to many surveys. These servers are designed for higher performance and to facilitate the development of complex web applications. They also support the development of server-based applications using languages such as Perl, Java, Visual Basic, and JavaScript. Code written in these languages can be integrated very tightly with the server, with the result that server-side programs are executed very efficiently.

Because the Web uses the Internet as its communication medium, it must follow Internet communication *protocols*. A protocol is a set of rules governing the procedures for exchanging information. The Internet's *Transmission Control Protocol* (TCP) and *Internet Protocol* (IP) enable worldwide connectivity between clients and servers. Layered atop the TCP/IP protocols for communication across the Internet, the Web also uses its own protocol, called the *Hypertext Transfer Protocol* (HTTP), for exchanges between browsers and servers. Browsers use HTTP to request documents from servers, and servers use it to return requested documents to browsers. Figure 1.1 shows an analogy between the English language and telephony protocols over the phone system on one hand, and HTTP and TCP/IP over the Internet on the other hand. Browsers and servers communicate via HTTP over the Internet the same way an American and an Englishman would communicate via English over a phone system.

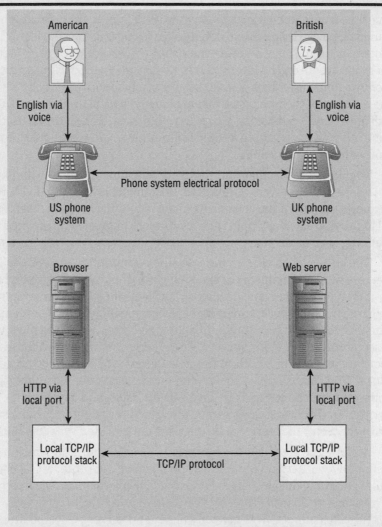

FIGURE 1.1:   Browsers and servers communicate via HTTP over the Internet the same way an American writer and a British editor communicate via English over a phone system.

THE HYPERTEXT MARKUP LANGUAGE

The Hypertext Markup Language (HTML) is the *lingua franca* of the Web. It is used to create web pages and is similar to the codes used by some word processing and document layout programs.

HTML uses ordinary text files to represent web pages. The files consist of the text to be displayed and the *tags* that specify *how* the text is to be displayed. For example, the following line from an HTML file shows the text of a title between the appropriate title tags:

```
<TITLE>Mastering JavaScript</TITLE>
```

The use of tags to define the elements of a web document is referred to as *markup*. Some tags specify the title of a document; others identify headings, paragraphs, and hyperlinks. Still others are used to insert forms, images, multimedia objects, and other features in web documents.

NOTE

This book assumes that you have a working knowledge of HTML. This section briefly reviews the important aspects of the language. If you have not used HTML, you should also check out the links to HTML tutorials and reference information located on this book's web page at www.sybex.com.

Tags always begin with a left angle bracket (<) and end with a right angle bracket (>). The name of the tag is placed between these two symbols. Usually, but not always, tags come in pairs, to surround the text that is marked up. Such tags are referred to as *surrounding* tags. For example, HTML documents begin with the <HTML> tag and end with the </HTML> tag. The first tag of a pair of tags is the *beginning* or *opening* tag, and the second tag of the pair is the *ending* or *closing* tag. The ending tag has the same name as the beginning tag except that a / (forward slash character) immediately follows the <.

Other tags, known as *separating* tags, do not come in pairs, and have no closing tags. These tags are used to insert such things as line breaks, images, and horizontal rules within marked-up text. An example of a separating tag is <HR>, which inserts a horizontal rule (a line) across a web page.

Both surrounding and separating tags use *attributes* to specify properties of marked-up text. These attributes and their *attribute values*, if any, are included in the tag. For example, you can specify a horizontal rule 10 pixels high and the entire width of the browser window using the following tag:

```
<HR SIZE="10">
```

This tag contains a SIZE attribute that is assigned an attribute value of 10.

NOTE

Attributes and attribute values are placed in the opening tag of a pair of surrounding tags and don't have to be repeated when the tag is closed—for example, <P ALIGN="center">info</P>.

Listing 1.1 contains a sample HTML document that illustrates the use of tags in marking up a web page. Figure 1.2 shows how Netscape Navigator displays this HTML document. The <HTML> and </HTML> tags identify the beginning and end of the HTML document. The document contains a head, identified by the <HEAD> and </HEAD> tags, and a body, identified by the <BODY> and </BODY> tags. The document's head contains a title that is marked by the <TITLE> and </TITLE> tags. (The title appears at the top of the Navigator window.)

NOTE

You can download the file for Listing 1.1, ch01-01.htm, from the Sybex website, on the product page for this book.

Listing 1.1: Example HTML Document (ch01-01.htm)

```
<HTML>
<HEAD>
<TITLE>This text is the document's title.</TITLE>
</HEAD>
<BODY>
<H1 ALIGN="CENTER">This is a centered heading.</H1>
<P>This is the first paragraph.</P>
<P>This is the second paragraph.</P>
<HR SIZE="10">
<P ALIGN="CENTER">This paragraph is centered and
    below the horizontal rule.</P></BODY>
</HTML>
```

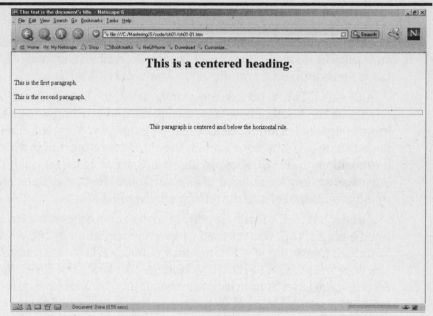

FIGURE 1.2:   A browser display of the HTML document shown in Listing 1.1

Here are a few items to notice in this listing:

▶ The document's body contains a Heading 1 that is marked by the
<H1> and </H1> tags. The opening <H1> tag uses the ALIGN
attribute to center the heading.

▶ Two paragraphs immediately follow the heading. These paragraphs are marked by the paragraph tags <P> and </P>.

▶ Following these two paragraphs is a horizontal rule with its SIZE
attribute set to 10.

▶ The last element of the document's body is a paragraph that
uses the ALIGN attribute to center the paragraph.

The Development of HTML and XHTML

HTML was originally developed by Tim Berners-Lee at CERN. Since
then, it has evolved through several major revisions. Each revision adds
new tags that increase the expressive power of the language. For example,
HTML 2 added the capability to include forms within web documents,
and HTML 3.2 added tags for tables and tags that support the use of
JavaScript and Java.

NEW

As of this writing, HTML 4.01 is the latest official version of the HTML language; and a hybrid of XML and HTML, called Extensible Hypertext Markup Language (XHTML), is beginning to gain popularity. HTML 4 adds support for international text, greater accessibility, more flexible tables, generic objects, printing, and advanced style sheets.

Although HTML is periodically standardized, the language continues to grow as the result of new tags, attributes, and attribute values that browser developers introduce. Because Netscape and Microsoft hold the largest share of the browser market, they have taken the lead in defining new additions to HTML. These additions are not part of the official HTML language, so they are referred to as *extensions*. Most extensions are eventually integrated into the official version of HTML.

Although HTML 4 is the current standard, some believe its days are numbered. XHTML was released as a recommendation by the World Wide Web Consortium (W3C) in January 2000. XHTML is essentially a simple reformulation of HTML to be more like XML, the *Extensible Markup Language*. Simplicity and extensibility are XHTML's primary advantages over HTML. XHTML removes the flexible coding supported by HTML. This makes XHTML simpler and easier to parse, allowing XHTML parsers to be quicker and smaller. Because XHTML is an XML application, it is easily extended. New tags and attributes can be defined and added to those that are defined in the standard. Much of XHTML is identical to HTML, however, and the changes—to force paired tags, for example—are pretty easy: The <HR> tag referenced earlier would be written as <hr size="10" />. Notice that XHTML tag and attribute names are always lowercase, and that all attribute values must be in quotes.

Even though XHTML is the logical successor to HTML, there is no need to convert all your web pages to the new standard. If you do, you'll find that some of your pages won't be rendered correctly by non-XHTML capable browsers. In addition, the document object models supported by current browsers are HTML based, although theoretically they should also work with XHTML implementations. Even though Navigator 6 and 7 and Internet Explorer 5 provide XML support, their primary capabilities and features still center around HTML.

Cascading Style Sheets

Style sheets provide the capability to control the way HTML elements are laid out and displayed. For example, you can use style sheets to control the color, font, and spacing used with different HTML elements. Support for Cascading Style Sheets (CSS) was developed by the W3C and introduced with HTML 3.2, and additional CSS support was added in HTML 4. *Cascading* refers to the capability to use multiple levels of style sheets for a document where one level of style can be used to define another.

Two levels of CSS have been defined. CSS1 is a simple style sheet mechanism that allows basic styles (for example, fonts, colors, and spacing) to be associated with HTML elements. CSS1 is an outgrowth of HTML 3.2 and is supported by Internet Explorer 3 (and later), Navigator 4 (and later), and other browsers. CSS2 builds on CSS1 to add support for media-specific style sheets, content positioning, downloadable fonts, table layout, internationalization, automatic counters and numbering, and other capabilities.

In addition to CSS1 and CSS2, Navigator 4 introduced JavaScript Style Sheets (JSS). JSS is similar to CSS1 and makes styles available as JavaScript properties, although few developers, if any, use JSS, given the predominance of Internet Explorer on the Web.

HELPER APPLICATIONS

Most graphical web browsers provide support for viewing images in common graphics formats, such as Graphics Interchange Format (GIF) and Joint Photographic Experts Group (JPEG). Some can even play audio files. However, most browsers do not provide much more than that in terms of multimedia features. Instead of building larger, more complicated browsers to handle many different file formats, browser developers use *helper applications*. When a browser encounters a file type that it does not know how to handle, it searches its list of helper applications to see if it has one that can deal with the file. If a suitable helper is found, then the browser executes the helper and passes it the name of the file to be run. If an appropriate helper cannot be found, then the browser prompts the user to identify which helper to use or to save the file for later display.

External Viewers and Plug-Ins

Early helper programs operated independently of the web browser. These programs, referred to as *external viewers*, were executed separate from the browser and created their own windows to display various types of files. Netscape and Microsoft developed the capability for their second-generation browsers to use *plug-in* or *add-in modules*, which not only execute automatically when needed but display their output in the browser window. Since then, numerous companies have developed plug-in modules to support everything from the three-dimensional worlds created by the Virtual Reality Modeling Language (VRML) to CD-quality audio and a variety of streaming video formats.

Plug-in modules are generally quicker to load and more efficient than external viewers. Because they execute with the browser, they can be accessed from within the browser environment. Netscape lets you control plug-in modules from Java and JavaScript code via its LiveConnect toolkit. Microsoft provides a similar capability through its Internet Explorer Object Model.

Using MIME Types to Identify Helpers for File Formats

So far, I've described how browsers use helper applications to display different types of files, but how does a browser know which helpers to use for a given file? The answer lies in MIME types and sometimes in filename suffixes.

Multipurpose Internet Mail Extensions (MIME) was originally developed as a standard for including different types of files in electronic mail. It was subsequently adopted for web servers and browsers to identify the types of files referenced in a web page.

MIME identifies file types using a *type/subtype* naming scheme. Examples of common MIME types are text/plain, text/html, image/gif, and video/quicktime. The first component of a MIME type identifies the general type of a file, and the second part identifies the specific type within the general category. For example, the text/plain and text/html types both belong to the text category, but they differ in their subtypes. Table 1.1 lists some common MIME types.

TABLE 1.1:   Example MIME Types

MIME TYPE	DESCRIPTION
text/plain	Generic ASCII text file
text/html	Text file containing HTML
image/gif	Image in Graphics Interchange Format
image/jpeg	Image in Joint Photographic Experts Group format
audio/x-wav	File containing sounds stored in the Windows audio file format

TABLE 1.1 continued: Example MIME Types

MIME TYPE	DESCRIPTION
video/mpeg	Video in the Moving Pictures Experts Group format
video/quicktime	Video in the Apple QuickTime format
application/octet-stream	Raw (unformatted) stream of bytes
application/x-javascript	File containing JavaScript source code

Web servers contain configuration files that match file extensions with their MIME types. For example, files that end with the extension .htm or .html are associated with the text/html MIME type, and files that end with .jpg, .jpe, or .jpeg are associated with the image/jpeg MIME type.

Browsers also contain configuration information about MIME types. This information is used to map MIME types to the helper application that displays files of that type.

When a browser requests a file from a web server, the server uses the filename's extension to look up the file's MIME type if it's not already specified by the program generating the material. The server can also try to guess the type of file from its contents if there is no filename extension, or simply assign a MIME type if the file is being generated by the server on-the-fly. The server then identifies the file's MIME type to the browser. The browser uses the file's MIME type to determine which helper application, if any, is to be used to display the file. If the file is to be displayed by an external viewer, the browser waits until the file has been completely received before launching the viewer. If the file is to be displayed by a plug-in, the browser launches the plug-in and passes the file to the plug-in as the file is received. This process enables the plug-in to begin displaying the file before it is fully loaded (or *stream* it), which is an important capability of audio- and video-intensive applications.

UNIFORM RESOURCE LOCATORS (URLS)

A *Uniform Resource Locator (URL)* is the notation used to specify the address of an Internet file or service.

A URL always contains a *protocol identifier,* such as http or ftp, and often a host name, such as home.netscape.com, www.microsoft.com, and ftp.cdrom.com, which appear in the previous examples. The most commonly used protocol identifiers are http and ftp, but if you examine the Protocol Helpers section of your browser's Preferences menu (sometimes reached from Tools or another top level menu), you will find support for older, more obscure identifiers such as wais and gopher. The protocol identifier is also referred to as a *scheme.* When you write a web (HTTP) URL, the protocol identifier is followed by :// and then the host name of the computer to which the protocol applies. (In URLs, pathnames are written using forward slash [/] characters rather than backslash [\] characters.) For example, to access the main home page of Microsoft on the host named www.microsoft.com, you would use the URL http://www.microsoft.com. To access the root directory of the File Transfer Protocol (FTP) server hosted by ftp.cdrom.com, you would use the URL ftp://ftp.cdrom.com.

In addition to the host name, the URL can specify the pathname and filename of a file to be accessed by adding a single / character followed by the name. For example, the Internet book area on the Sybex website is located in the Internet subdirectory of the directory sybexbooks.nsf on Sybex's web server's root directory. The URL for this area is therefore http://www.sybex.com/sybexbooks.nsf/Internet/.

NOTE

URLs can also contain additional addressing components, such as a port name before the path and filename and a file offset after the filename.

THE *FILE* PROTOCOL IN URLs

Your browser can use the file protocol to access files located on your local machine. Suppose the file test.htm was located on your Windows desktop. The path to this file would be c:\windows\desktop\test.htm. To open the file with your browser, you would use the following URL: file://localhost/C|/WINDOWS/Desktop/test.htm.

The host name localhost in the previous URL refers to the local filesystem and can be omitted safely. However, you should retain

CONTINUED ➡

the slash following `localhost`. The previous URL could be thus be written as follows: `file:///C|/WINDOWS/Desktop/test.htm`.

Note that in both examples the `C:` drive designation is written as `C|` instead. If you are using a Macintosh or Unix browser, this format might vary slightly. On a Mac, for example, a file reference might appear more akin to `file://localhost/Users/demo/Desktop/test.htm`.

THE HYPERTEXT TRANSFER PROTOCOL (HTTP)

HTTP is the protocol used for communication between browsers and web servers. HTTP uses a request/response model of communication. A browser establishes a connection with a server and sends a URL request to the server. The server processes the browser's request and sends a response back to the browser.

A browser connects with a web server by establishing a TCP connection, by default at port 80 of the server. You can specify server ports other than 80; for instance, to connect to port 8234 on the `www.fictionalhost.com` server, the URL would be `http://www.fictionalhost.com:8234/`. This port is the address at which web servers "listen" for browser requests. Once a connection has been established, a browser sends a request to the server. This request specifies a request method; the URL of the document, program, or other resource being requested; the HTTP version being used by the browser; and other information related to the request.

Several request methods are available. GET, HEAD, and POST are the most commonly used:

GET   Retrieves the information contained at the specified URL. You can also use this method to *submit* data collected in an HTML *form* (the topic of Chapter 5, "Processing Forms") or to invoke a Common Gateway Interface (CGI) program (discussed in the next section). When the server processes a GET request, it delivers the requested information (if it can be found). The server inserts at the front of the information an HTTP header that provides data about the server, identifies any errors that occurred in processing the request, and describes the type of information being returned as a result.

HEAD   Similar to the GET method, except that when a web server processes a HEAD request, it returns only the HTTP header data and not the information that was the object of the request. The HEAD method is used to retrieve information about a URL without actually obtaining the information addressed by the URL.

POST   Informs the server that the information appended to the request is to be sent to the specified URL. The POST method is typically used to send form data and other information to CGI programs. The web server responds to a POST request by sending back header data followed by any information generated by the CGI program as a result of processing the request.

NEW

The current version of HTTP is HTTP 1.1. It incorporates performance, security, and other improvements to the original HTTP 1. A new version of HTTP, referred to as HTTP-NG, is currently being defined. (The *NG* stands for *next generation*.) The goal of HTTP-NG is to simplify HTTP and make it more extensible. However, little progress has taken place over the past few years, and the project may be considered dead.

COMMON GATEWAY INTERFACE PROGRAMS

The *Common Gateway Interface* (CGI) is a standard that specifies how web servers can use external programs. Programs that adhere to the CGI standard are referred to as *CGI programs*. These programs can be used to process data submitted with forms, to perform database searches, and to support other types of web applications, such as clickable image maps.

A browser request for the URL of a CGI program comes about as the result of a user clicking a link, requesting the output of a CGI program (for example, many sites have their default home page generated by a CGI program rather than as a static HTML page), or submitting a form. The browser uses HTTP to make the request. When a web server receives the request, the web server executes the CGI program and also passes it any data that was submitted by the browser. When the CGI program performs its processing, it usually generates data in the form of a web page, which it returns via the web server to the requesting browser.

The CGI standard specifies how data may be passed from web servers to CGI programs and how data should be returned from CGI programs to the web server. Table 1.2 summarizes these interfaces. In Chapter 5 and Chapter 7, "Interfacing JavaScript with CGI Programs," you'll study CGI and learn how to create CGI programs.

TABLE 1.2: CGI Summary

METHOD OF COMMUNICATING	INTERFACE	DESCRIPTION
Command-line arguments	Web server to CGI program	Data is passed to the CGI program via the command line that is used to execute the program. Command-line arguments are passed to CGI programs as the result of ISINDEX queries.
Environment variables	Web server to CGI program	A web server passes data to the CGI program by setting special *environment variables* that are available to the CGI program via its environment
Standard input stream	Web server to CGI program	A web server passes data to a CGI program by sending the data to the standard character input stream associated with the CGI program. The CGI program reads the data as if a user manually entered it at a character terminal.
Standard output stream	CGI program to web server	The CGI program passes data back to the web server by writing the data to its standard output stream. The web server intercepts this data and sends it back to the browser that made the CGI request.

JAVA APPLETS

The Java language, developed by Sun Microsystems, Inc., has realized tremendous popularity. Although it was originally developed as a language for programming consumer electronic devices, Java has increasingly been adopted as a hardware- and software-independent platform for developing advanced web applications. Java can be used to write stand-alone applications, but a major reason for its popularity is that you can also develop Java programs that can be executed by a web browser.

Java programs that can be executed by the web browser are called *applets* rather than applications, because they cannot be run outside the browser's window without a separate viewer or helper application. (*Application* usually implies a complete, stand-alone program.) Programmers create Java applets using built-in programming features of the Java Developer's Kit (JDK). Web pages, written in HTML, reference Java applets using the <APPLET> or <OBJECT> tag, much as images are referenced using the <IMG> tag. When a browser loads a web page that references a Java applet, the browser requests the applet code from the web server. When the browser receives the applet code, it executes the code and allocates a fixed area of the browser window. This area is identified by attributes specified with the <APPLET> tag. The applet is not allowed to update the browser display or handle events outside its allocated window area.

By way of comparison, JavaScript provides access to the entire web page, but is a much smaller, lighter-weight programming language that also doesn't support many of the more advanced object-oriented programming features of Java. Netscape Navigator and Microsoft Internet Explorer provide the capability for JavaScript scripts to load Java applets, access Java objects, and invoke their methods.

ACTIVEX—MICROSOFT OBJECTS

ActiveX is Microsoft's approach to executing objects other than Java applets in Internet Explorer. The name *ActiveX* was used to make it seem like a new and innovative technology. However, ActiveX is nothing more than Component Object Model (COM) objects that can be downloaded and executed by Internet Explorer. COM traces its origin back to the Object Linking and Embedding (OLE) technology of Microsoft Windows 3.1.

COM objects are instances of *classes* (object types) that are also organized into *interfaces*. Each interface consists of a collection of *methods* (functions). COM objects are implemented inside a *server* (dynamic-link libraries, operating system service, or independent process) and are accessed via their methods. The *COM library* provides a directory of available COM objects. Over the years since Windows 3.1, many software components have been developed as COM objects.

ActiveX components are COM objects that implement a specific type of interface. They are important in that they provide a means for the large base of COM objects to be reused within Internet Explorer. They also allow older languages, such as C++ and C, to be used to build components for web applications.

Although ActiveX components allow the use of legacy software in Internet Explorer, they also present some drawbacks. The most significant drawback is that ActiveX is only supported by Internet Explorer 4 and later—no other browser (including earlier versions of Internet Explorer) can use ActiveX. ActiveX has also been criticized for its poor security. An ActiveX component is not required to behave in a secure manner like a Java applet or JavaScript script. In fact, it has been demonstrated that ActiveX components can be used to steal or modify sensitive information or completely wipe out a user's system. Microsoft has countered this vulnerability by allowing ActiveX components to be digitally signed. This does not prevent ActiveX components from violating security, but, in some cases, a signature can be used to determine whether a particular website is responsible for causing damage.

ActiveX components are useful in intranet applications where all users of a particular company are required to use Internet Explorer and the components are signed by the company or a trusted developer. Because the Internet Explorer Object Model allows ActiveX components to be accessed from JavaScript, JavaScript scripts can be used to integrate the ActiveX components into the intranet applications.

A BRIEF HISTORY OF JAVASCRIPT

Often, one programming language evolves from another. For example, Java evolved from C++, which evolved from C, which evolved from other languages. Similarly, Netscape originally developed a language called *LiveScript* to add a basic scripting capability to both Navigator and its web-server line of products; when it added support for Java applets in its release of Navigator 2, Netscape replaced LiveScript with JavaScript. Although the initial version of JavaScript was little more than LiveScript renamed, JavaScript has been subsequently standardized through the European Computer Manufacturing Association (ECMA) and is now also referred to as ECMAScript (formally ECMA-262).

NOTE

Although JavaScript bears the name of Java, JavaScript is a very different language that is used for a very different purpose.

JavaScript supports both web browser and server scripting. Browser scripts are used to create dynamic web pages that are more interactive, more responsive, and more tightly integrated with plug-ins, ActiveX components, and Java applets. JavaScript supports these features by providing special programming capabilities, such as the ability to dynamically generate HTML and to define custom event-handling functions.

You include JavaScript scripts in HTML documents via the HTML <SCRIPT> tag. When a JavaScript-capable browser loads an HTML document containing scripts, it evaluates the scripts as they are encountered. The scripts may be used to create HTML elements that are added to the displayed document or to define functions, called *event handlers*, that respond to user actions, such as mouse clicks and keyboard entries. Scripts can also be used to control plug-ins, ActiveX components, and Java applets.

Microsoft implemented its version of JavaScript, named JScript, in Internet Explorer 3. The scripting capability of Internet Explorer 3 is roughly equivalent to Navigator 2. Netscape introduced JavaScript 1.1 with Navigator 3 and JavaScript 1.2 with Navigator 4. JavaScript 1.1 added a number of new features, including support for more browser objects and user-defined functions. JavaScript 1.2 added new objects, methods, properties, and support for style sheets, layers, regular expressions, and signed scripts.

Microsoft introduced its ECMAScript-compliant version of JScript in Internet Explorer 4. JScript is tightly coupled to Internet Explorer and allows almost all HTML elements to be scripted. Microsoft also included server-side JavaScript support with its Internet Information Server (IIS). It later developed a more general approach to server-side scripting with its Windows Script Host and remote scripting technologies. Remote scripting allows Internet Explorer to remotely execute scripts on a server and receive the server script outputs within the context of a single web page.

Netscape and Microsoft submitted their scripting languages to the ECMA for standardization. ECMA released the Standard ECMA-262 in June of 1997. This standard describes the ECMAScript language, which is a consolidation of the core features of JavaScript and JScript.

Updated versions of this standard were released in June 1998 (Revision 2) and December 1999 (Revision 3). ECMA also released ECMA-290 in June 1999. ECMA-290 covers the development of reusable components in ECMAScript.

Microsoft worked closely with the ECMA and updated Internet Explorer 4 and JScript (JScript 3.1) to achieve ECMAScript compliance. Navigator achieved ECMAScript compliance with JavaScript 1.3, which is supported in Navigator 4.06 through 4.7.

Internet Explorer 5 introduced JScript 5, which provides additional scripting capabilities, such as the try - catch statement. This statement provides advanced error handling support and is included in ECMAScript Revision 3. Internet Explorer 5.5 was introduced after ECMAScript Revision 3 and provides full Revision 3 support. Navigator 6.0 and later supports JavaScript 1.5, which is fully compliant with ECMAScript Revision 3.

While Netscape and Microsoft were busy introducing new versions of their browsers and scripting languages, Opera Software (www.opera-software.com) launched another JavaScript-compatible browser. In addition, Sun jumped into the JavaScript field with its HotJava browser. HotJava 3.0 is ECMAScript compliant. Other browser developers followed by developing JavaScript-capable browsers of their own.

Another JavaScript-related standardization effort was initiated by the W3C to standardize the basic objects made available by browsers when processing HTML and XML documents. This effort resulted in a specification known as the Document Object Model (DOM) Level 1. It provides a standard set of objects for representing HTML and XML documents, a standard model of how these objects can be combined, and a standard interface for accessing and manipulating them. The DOM is like an application programming interface (API) for HTML and XML documents. However, the DOM is not a complete API, in that it does not specify the events that occur when a user interacts with an HTML or XML document (and methods for handling them). Version 6 and 7 of Navigator and version 5 of Internet Explorer support the DOM.

Today, the latest version of JavaScript is 1.5, but the additions to JavaScript in version 1.4 and 1.5 are unlikely to influence your day-to-day web development: Runtime errors are reported differently, regular expressions have been enhanced, functions can be conditionally declared, and named read-only constants are now supported. Netscape Navigator 6 and later, Microsoft Internet Explorer 6.0 and later, and Mozilla all support JavaScript 1.5.

Java Servlets and JavaServer Pages

Sun Microsystems developed the Java Servlet API as an extension to the standard Java specification; it provides a way to write modules that run within a server to handle requests in a client-server architecture. You can think of servlets as applets that run on the server side rather than the client side. The fundamental Servlet API isn't tied to the HTTP protocol, but the API does have a framework specifically tailored to handling HTTP requests. A number of different vendors have products that implement the Servlet API, so if you write a web-based application using it, you won't necessarily be tied to a single vendor's products. Although there can be performance benefits to using servlets over a typical CGI script, perhaps the most attractive feature of using servlets is the full access to the rest of Java's standard APIs (for instance, the JDBC API, which provides a standard interface for connection to a variety of SQL database stores). If your project will reuse or interface with other modules of Java code, you should consider using this technology instead of standard CGI techniques.

JavaServer Pages (JSP) technology is an extension to Servlets that specifies ways to dynamically author HTML and XML pages. JSPs are particularly suited to situations where you need to change certain aspects of a page's content but can use a template to provide the basic format and structure of the page. For instance, an application that needs to display invoices online to users might use an Invoice template that defines fonts, tables, and headers and footers, but might rely on application logic to fill in the line items and dollar amounts.

NOTE

The Tomcat Server is an open-source reference implementation of the Servlet and JSP technologies that runs on Windows and a variety of Unix platforms. You can download it free from http://jakarta.apache.org/tomcat/.

ASP, Windows Scripting Host, and Remote Scripting

Microsoft's Active Server Pages (ASP) is a server-side scripting environment that is similar to JSP. You can use it to include server-side scripts and ActiveX components with HTML pages. The combined HTML and script file is stored as an ASP file. When a browser requests the ASP file from your web server, the server invokes the ASP processor. The ASP processor reads the requested file, executes any script commands, and sends the processed results as a web page to the browser. ASP pages can also invoke ActiveX components to perform tasks, such as accessing a database or performing an electronic commerce transaction. Because ASP scripts run on the web server and send standard HTML to the browser, ASP is browser independent.

Microsoft introduced ASP with IIS version 3. It also works with later versions of IIS, Personal Web Server for Windows 95, and Peer Web Server for Windows NT Workstation.

As a result of the success of ASP, Microsoft developed Windows Script Host (WSH), a technology that allows scripts to be run on Windows 95, 98, ME, NT 4, 2000, and Windows XP. WSH is language independent and supports JScript, VBScript, and other languages. It lets you execute scripts from the Windows desktop or a console (MS DOS) window. WSH scripts are complete in themselves and do not need to be embedded in an HTML document. WSH is an exciting technology in that it extends the capabilities of JScript beyond the Web to the Windows desktop and operating system. You can use WSH scripts to replace MS DOS scripts and take full advantage of the Windows GUI, ActiveX, and operating system functions in JScript scripts.

NOTE

WSH can be freely downloaded from Microsoft's website at http://msdn .microsoft.com/scripting/.

NOTE

If you want to use a web server other than Microsoft's IIS, you can use the Sun ONE Active Server Pages component (http://wwws.sun.com/software/ chilisoft/) to deploy ASP on the Apache, Sun ONE, or Zeus web server on a variety of non-Windows platforms, including Linux.

Microsoft's latest addition to scripting technology is referred to as *remote scripting*. Remote scripting enables client-side scripts running on Internet Explorer to execute server-side scripts, running on IIS. Internet Explorer and IIS can perform simultaneous processing and communicate with each other within the context of a web page, allowing the page to be dynamically updated with server information without having to be reloaded. This process frees the user from having to reload a web page during the execution of a web application and provides for a higher degree of interaction between the browser and web server. For example, with remote scripting, a web server can validate form data and provide the user with feedback while the user is still filling out the form.

Remote scripting allows browser/server communication to be accomplished in either a synchronous or asynchronous manner. When synchronous communication is used, a client-side script executes a server-side script and waits for the server-side script to return its result. When asynchronous communication is used, the client-side script executes the server-side script and then continues with its processing without waiting for the server-side script to finish. You can find more information about remote scripting at Microsoft's Developer Network site: http://msdn.microsoft.com/scripting/.

ANOTHER SERVER-SIDE SCRIPTING SOLUTION: PHP

In addition to the popular ASP solution from Microsoft, an alternative server-side solution is offered by PHP, an open-source solution that is included with the Apache web server, among others. There are lots of good online references to PHP, but the best place to start is http://www.php.net/.

XML AND XSL

One of the most powerful features of Navigator 6 and 7 and Internet Explorer 5 and 6 is their support for the Extensible Markup Language (XML). These browsers can display XML files directly. Moreover, they allow XML files to be scripted using JavaScript and JScript much as HTML files are scripted.

XML documents are similar to HTML documents in their use of tags and attributes to mark up text. However, XML differs from HTML in that it does not define a fixed set of markup tags. Instead, XML lets you define the tags and attributes of customized markup languages. For example, you could use XML to define a product catalog and then display the catalog directly with an XML-capable browser. You could customize the way the catalog is displayed using CSS or the Extensible Style Language (XSL). You could also translate the XML to HTML in a format specified by an XSL style sheet.

NOTE

The XML 1.0 specification is available at www.w3.org/TR/REC-xml. The XSL specification is available at www.w3.org/TR/xsl/. The XSL Transformations specification is available at www.w3.org/TR/xslt.

XSL is to XML as CSS is to HTML. XSL is a language for expressing style sheets. It is organized into two parts: the XSL Transformations language (XSLT) and a vocabulary (expressed in XML) for specifying formatting semantics. XSLT lets you specify how an XML document of one type can be transformed into a document with another set of markup tags. XSLT can also be used to specify how XML documents should be translated into HTML. The second part of XSL, the formatting language, lets you specify how XML documents should be rendered for a variety of display media, such as the Web and printed documents.

NOTE

XML documents can also be formatted using CSS.

INTRANETS, EXTRANETS, AND DISTRIBUTED APPLICATIONS

For the last few years, corporations have been deploying pure TCP/IP networks internally to take advantage of the full range of standards-based services provided by the Internet. These "company-internal internets" have become known as *intranets*. Intranets may be private networks that are physically separate from the Internet, internal networks that are separated from the Internet by a firewall, or simply a company's internal extension of the Internet.

Companies deploy intranets so that they can make internal services available to their workers using popular Internet tools and technologies. E-mail, web browsing, and web publishing are the most popular of these services. Many companies make web servers available for their employees' intranet publishing needs. These intranet web servers allow departments, groups, and individuals within a company to conveniently share information while usually limiting access to the information published on the intranet to company employees.

The popularity of intranets as a way of communicating and of sharing information within a company has brought about a demand for more powerful and sophisticated intranet applications. The eventual goal is for the intranet to provide a common application framework from which a company's core information processing functions can be implemented and accessed. Sun, Microsoft, and other web software providers are focusing on the intranet as the primary application framework for the development of business software.

Because of its client/server architecture and user-friendly browser software, the Web is the perfect model for implementing these common intranet application frameworks. The approach taken by Netscape, Microsoft, and other web software developers is to use the web browser as the primary interface by which users connect to the intranet and run intranet and extranet applications. These applications are referred to as *distributed applications,* because their execution is distributed in part on the browser (via JavaScript, Java, ActiveX, XML, and other languages), in part on the server (via CGI programs and JavaScript and Java server-side programs), and in part on database and other enterprise servers.

Distributed intranet and extranet applications use HTML, JavaScript, Java, XML, and other languages for programming the browser-based user interface portion of the distributed application. They also use Perl, Java, Visual Basic, and other languages to perform server-side programming.

In some distributed application development approaches, Java is seen as a key technology for developing the components of distributed applications, and JavaScript is seen as the essential glue that combines these components into fully distributed web-based intranet and extranet applications. Other approaches rely less on JavaScript and more on Java.

WHAT'S NEXT

This chapter covered the concepts that are essential to understanding the operation of the Web. You learned about web development languages such as HTML, XML, Java, and JavaScript. You also have been introduced to related web technologies such as HTTP, CGI, Java Servlets, JSP, ASP, and remote scripting. You should have a basic understanding of how these elements work together when you're developing web applications.

In Chapter 2, you'll begin the exciting process of learning to use JavaScript to write sample client-side scripts. You'll begin doing some actual programming using JavaScript. If you've never done any programming, you should read the material carefully—it introduces fundamental programming concepts that are used throughout this book.

Chapter 2
Working with JavaScript

JavaScript started as LiveScript, a scripting language Netscape developed. Independently, Sun Microsystems had developed Java (formerly Oak), as a language to control consumer electronic devices. Because of its power and efficiency, Java found a home on the Internet as a language for small programs called *applets*.

Along the way, Netscape and Sun joined forces to embed a Java *Virtual Machine* in web browsers. In a move to take advantage of marketing serendipity, Netscape changed the LiveScript name to JavaScript, and the rest is history. JavaScript resembles Java syntactically, but there are significant differences. JavaScript was designed to control the way the entire HTML-generated web page is rendered as well as its response to user input. Java applets, on the other hand, are restricted to a specific, autonomous region of a web page. Because applets execute within this isolated "sandbox," they are permitted a wider range of operations than is available in JavaScript.

Updated from *Dynamic HTML: Master the Essentials*, by Joseph Schmuller
ISBN 0-7821-2277-9

In its effort to gain a firm foothold on the Web, Microsoft developed its own flavor of JavaScript and called it JScript. Microsoft's implementation has a few enhancements designed to take advantage of Internet Explorer (IE). It quickly became evident to web designers and programmers, however, that the differences between JavaScript and JScript required developers in many instances to write two or more scripts to accomplish the same task, each variation addressing the needs of specific browsers. To help simplify things, the European Computer Manufacturing Association (ECMA) standards body drafted the ECMAScript standard (see Chapter 1, "Learning the Fundamentals," for a more comprehensive history of JavaScript). In most respects, today's web browsers conform to the standard, making it easier to write scripts that will run compatibly on many different vendors' browsers. Throughout the book, you will see references to ECMAScript; where relevant, we'll highlight persisting differences between JavaScript and JScript.

JavaScript Syntax

In JavaScript, a line ends with a semicolon. Thus, JavaScript has no need for a line continuation character: Until it encounters a semicolon, most JavaScript interpreters consider everything to be part of one line.

The other scripting language possibility in IE is VBScript, a language based heavily on Visual Basic. However, it's only supported within the Microsoft browser, so in the interest of cross-platform and cross-browser compatibility, almost all web developers focus on JavaScript as their scripting language of choice.

If you know VBScript, it's interesting to consider how JavaScript differs. A couple of differences have already been mentioned, but here are some others:

▶ A procedure in VBScript is either a function (if it returns a value) or a subroutine (if it doesn't). In JavaScript, on the other hand, every procedure is a function, whether it returns a value or not. In a JavaScript function, curly brackets surround the code: The left curly bracket ({) follows the function's argument list, and the right curly bracket (}) is the last character in the function. Here's what the format looks like:

```
function functionName(argument1, argument2) {
    statement 1;
```

```
        statement 2;
            .
            .
            .
        statement n;
    }
```

▶ If you're used to programming in VBScript, you've probably adopted a loose outlook about uppercase and lowercase letters. VBScript is *case-insensitive*, meaning that index and INDEX are equivalent. JavaScript, however, is *case-sensitive*, so that index and INDEX are most decidedly *not* the same.

▶ In JavaScript, you indicate a one-line comment with two slashes: //. JavaScript ignores anything on the same line that follows the two slashes. You can also have a comment that spans more than one line. A multiline comment begins with /* and ends with */.

VARIABLES

Here are some rules to follow when you name variables in JavaScript:

▶ The name must start with an alphabetic character (a–z or A–Z) or an underscore (_).

▶ The rest of the name can contain any letter, any digit, or an underscore.

▶ A variable's name can't contain a space or other punctuation (except underscores).

▶ Avoid JavaScript *reserved words* as the names of variables.

A Word about Reserved Words

Reserved words are set aside for a particular purpose, and therefore shouldn't be used for variable names. Here are the reserved words:

abstract	boolean	break	byte	case
catch	char	class	const	continue
debugger	default	delete	do	double
else	enum	export	extends	false

final	finally	float	for	function
goto	if	implements	import	in
instanceof	int	interface	long	native
new	null	package	private	protected
public	return	short	static	super
switch	synchronized	this	throw	throws
transient	true	try	typeof	var
void	volatile	while	with	

NOTE
The names of built-in functions and objects are also reserved.

Creating Variables

JavaScript programmers typically use variables without declaring them, although, strictly speaking, this isn't good programming practice. To declare a variable explicitly, use var. Explicit declaration helps avoid conflicts in variable creation.

This example uses var to declare variables in a script for animation:

```
var glblTimer;
var glblAnimationStartedFlag = 0;
```

As you can see, two uses of var are possible: A *declaration* declares the variable; *initialization* declares the variable and sets an initial value. When possible, initialization is good programming practice, particularly when you're declaring flag or counter variables.

Also notice the glbl prefix. Although it isn't required, I use it to indicate that a variable's scope is global. Functions throughout a SCRIPT element can refer to a global variable. To make a variable global, you declare it prior to any function. A local variable, on the other hand, is created inside the body of a function, and only that function can refer to it.

To shorten the number of lines in your script, JavaScript allows you to declare more than one variable with a single var statement, and even tuck variable initializers into the declaration statement:

```
var x, y = 3, z;
```

Variable Types

Because JavaScript is a *loosely typed* language, you don't have to specify the type of data a JavaScript variable will hold when you declare it.

JavaScript has three types of variables:

▶ *Numeric variables* contain numbers: `var numberOfWords=78`.

▶ *String variables* contain text between quotation marks: `var myName = "Joseph"`.

▶ *Boolean variables* contain one of two possible logic values: `true` or `false`.

JavaScript treats the reserved word `null` as an empty variable.

When you put data into a variable, in effect you define it to be a numeric, a string, or a boolean. In a script, you can put different types of data into a variable at different times, thus changing that variable's subtype. You have to be careful when you do this, however, because you can get unexpected results. Here's an example:

```
var numFirst = 17,
var numSecond = 76;
var numSum;
numSum = numFirst + numSecond;
```

These lines of code result in 93 as the value for numSum. If you keep the value of numSecond as is and change the type of numFirst to a string, however,

```
varNumFirst = "17";
```

then

```
numSum = numFirst + numSecond;
```

gives the string "1776" as the value for numSum. Why? That last expression for numSum now sees the string "17" as the value for numFirst and automatically turns numSecond into the string "76". In that context, the +, which added the two numbers in the first numSum expression, becomes the concatenation operator.

NOTE

Concatenation describes the linking of two or more strings. The + operator can act as the addition operator for a set of numeric variables, but it will act as the concatenation operator if one variable is a string.

A Word about Numbers

JavaScript has one type of numeric variable, logically named the numeric. This type holds both integers and floating-point numbers. The numbers can be in scientific notation, like 8.765e15 or 6.54e-19. Numbers can also be octal (base 8) or hexadecimal (base 16). If the JavaScript interpreter encounters a number with a leading 0, it interprets it as a base 8 number. If the interpreter encounters a number with a leading 0 followed by an x, it interprets it as a hexadecimal.

A Word about Strings

Inside a string, you can place special characters that tell the JavaScript interpreter to perform specific actions or to interpret a character in a special way. For example, you can add a long string to a text area, like this:

```
function info(event){
textArea = document.forms[0].elements["textareaEventInfo"];
textArea.value = "target: " + event.target.name + "\n"
    + "which: " + event.which + "\n"
    + "modifiers: " + event.modifiers + "\n"
    + "type: " + event.type + "\n"
    + "screenX: " + event.screenX + "\n"
    + "screenY: " + event.screenY + "\n"
    + "pageX: " + event.pageX + "\n"
    + "pageY: " + event.pageY;
}
```

The special character here is "\n", which tells the interpreter to move to the next line in the text area before displaying the next part of the string. Of course, if the output will be interpreted by a web browser as HTML, don't forget to also include <BR> tags, or for XHTML, <br /> tags.

The backslash (\) is the signal for the advent of a special character. Sometimes the backslash indicates that a punctuation mark used for one purpose should be interpreted another way. For example, if you want to include a double quote as part of a string (and not as the beginning or end of a string), precede it with a backslash. Table 2.1 shows the JavaScript special characters.

TABLE 2.1:   JavaScript Special Characters

Symbol	What It Is
\\	Backslash
\'	Single quote

TABLE 2.1 continued: JavaScript Special Characters

Symbol	What It Is
\"	Double quote
\b	Backspace
\f	Form feed
\n	New line
\r	Carriage return
\t	Tab
\v	Vertical tab

CREATING OBJECTS

JavaScript enables you to create new objects. You use the reserved word new to do this. The format is

```
var variableName = new ClassName;
```

This code tells the JavaScript interpreter that you're creating a new instance of ClassName and you're calling it variableName. In JavaScript, strings, numbers, and arrays are objects. When you create a new instance of one of these types, as in

```
var stringName = new String("DHTML Master the Essentials");
```

it's the same as

```
var stringName = "DHTML Master the Essentials";
```

Sometimes you have no choice but to use new, as in the next section.

CREATING ARRAYS

Sometimes you want to refer to a set of items that are similar in some way, and you'd like to be able to refer to them as "the first one," "the second one," and so forth, without giving each item a unique name. In these cases, the *array* is the appropriate structure to use.

Simple Arrays

As an example of how JavaScript handles arrays, consider the array called SportNames, which holds the names of sports in this order: "Baseball", "Basketball", "Bowling", "Football", "Hockey", "Soccer", and "Track". I've put this array into Table 2.2. As you can see, the index corresponds to the row, and you begin numbering indices from 0 rather than from 1 (this is called *zero-based indexing*).

TABLE 2.2: The SportNames Array

INDEX	SPORT
0	"Baseball"
1	"Basketball"
2	"Bowling"
3	"Football"
4	"Hockey"
5	"Soccer"
6	"Track"

NOTE

In JavaScript 1, position 0 holds the length of the array, and the first item goes into position 1. In JavaScript 1.1 (and later) and in JScript, you put the first item in position 0.

With this array, you refer to "Baseball" as `sportNames[0]` and to "Football" as `sportNames[3]`. (Note the use of square brackets, rather than parentheses, as in VBScript.)

In JavaScript (beginning with version 1.1), an array is an object. Every array is an instance of the `Array` class. As you saw in the preceding section, you use the reserved word new to create a new instance of a class. Thus, you would create the `sportNames` array object with the statement

```
var sportNames = new Array(7);
```

NOTE

It's customary in JavaScript to begin object names with lowercase letters.

This code creates the array and inserts the items:

```
var sportNames = new Array(7);
sportNames[0] = "Baseball"
sportNames[1] = "Basketball"
sportNames[2] = "Bowling"
sportNames[3] = "Football"
```

```
sportNames[4] = "Hockey"
sportNames[5] = "Soccer"
sportNames[6] = "Track"
```

JavaScript's built-in `Array` object gives you another way to initialize an array:

```
var sportNames = new Array("Baseball", "Basketball",
    "Bowling", "Football", "Hockey", "Soccer", "Track");
```

It also gives you another way to refer to an array-item. These two expressions

```
sportNames[3]
sportNames["Football"]
```

are equivalent. With a string index, as in the second expression, the array-item becomes a property of the `sportNames` object. So the statement

```
sportNames.Football
```

is equivalent to the other two. This statement, however,

```
sportNames.3
```

generates an error.

Complex Arrays

To carry the example forward, suppose you add a column to the table—a column that denotes whether the sport is in the Olympics. Table 2.3 shows the layout.

TABLE 2.3:   Expanding the SportNames Array

Index	Sport	Olympic Sport?
0	"Baseball"	Yes
1	"Basketball"	Yes
2	"Bowling"	No
3	"Football"	No
4	"Hockey"	Yes
5	"Soccer"	Yes
6	"Track"	Yes

You can represent this kind of table in a *multidimensional* array. A JavaScript multidimensional array is an array of arrays. To make a two-dimensional array out of Table 2.3, you can consider each row as an array, and then combine those arrays into another array:

```
var baseball = new Array("Baseball", "Yes");
var basketball = new Array("Basketball", "Yes");
var bowling = new Array("Bowling", "No");
var football = new Array("Football", "No");
var hockey = new Array("Hockey", "Yes");
var soccer = new Array("Soccer", "Yes");
var track = new Array("Track", "Yes");
var sportNames = new Array(baseball, basketball, bowling,
basketball, bowling, football, hockey, soccer, track);
```

In this array, you'd refer to "Bowling" as sportNames[2][0]. Note the syntax of the two sets of brackets. The statement sportNames[2,0] generates an error.

Array Methods

The Array object provides a number of methods, the most common of which are the following:

- ▶ toString() returns a string version of the array. Array elements are separated by commas.

- ▶ join(separator) returns a string that holds all the array items, with the value of separator as the separator between consecutive elements.

- ▶ reverse() reverses the order of the array items.

- ▶ sort() sorts the array items.

JavaScript Operators

JavaScript contains a full set of operators for comparisons, logical operations, and arithmetic. Table 2.4 shows the comparison operators.

TABLE 2.4: JavaScript Comparison Operators

Operator	Name
==	Equality
!=	Inequality
<	Less Than
>	Greater Than

TABLE 2.4 continued: JavaScript Comparison Operators

Operator	Name
<=	Less Than Or Equal To
=>	Greater Than Or Equal To

Notice that the Equality comparison operator (==) is different from the symbol (=) that assigns a value to a variable. Table 2.5 presents the JavaScript logical operators, and Table 2.6 presents the arithmetic operators.

TABLE 2.5: JavaScript Logical Operators

Operator	What It Means
!	NOT
&&	AND
||	OR

TABLE 2.6: JavaScript Arithmetic Operators

Operator	Name
+	Addition
−	Subtraction
*	Multiplication
/	Division
%	Modulus
++	Increment
−−	Decrement
−	Negation

Each of the last three operators is a *unary* operator: an operator that works on one entity. The expression `variableName++` is equivalent to

```
variableName = variableName + 1;
```

and `variableName--` is equivalent to

```
variableName = variableName - 1;
```

NOTE

JavaScript also has a set of bitwise logical operators. You'll probably have little use for them, so we won't cover them much in this book.

Assignment Operators

The equal sign (=) is the JavaScript assignment operator. You can combine this operator with arithmetic and logic operators, as Table 2.7 shows.

TABLE 2.7: Combining the Assignment Operator with Arithmetic and Logic Operators

COMBINATION	WHAT IT MEANS
x += y	x = x + y
x -= y	x = x - y
x *= y	x = x * y
x /= y	x = x / y
x %= y	x = x % y
x |= y	x = x | y
x &= y	x = x & y

PROGRAM FLOW

JavaScript gives you a number of ways to choose an alternative when your script encounters a choice point.

switch

JavaScript's `switch` is analogous to the C language `case` statement. It enables your program to perform a test and then, based on the result, pick one of several possible paths, called *cases*. Within each path, you can have a number of lines of code. When the program finishes going through the code for that path, your program exits the `switch` if it encounters a `break` statement; otherwise it drops through into the next possible code block, possibly going through them all if you're unlucky. The moral: Make sure you religiously include `break` statements with the `switch` structure.

Imagine an expression called `testExpression` with the possible values `"baseball"`, `"football"`, `"basketball"`, and `"hockey"`. The `switch` would look like this:

```
switch(testExpression) {
    case "baseball" :
        statement 1;
        statement 2;
        statement 3;
        break;
    case "football" :
        statement 4;
        statement 5;
        break;
    case "basketball" :
        statement 6;
        statement 7;
        statement 8;
        statement 9;
        break;
    case "hockey" :
        statement 10;
        break;
    default :
        statement 11;
        break;
}
```

Note the final case, `default`, which executes if `textExpression` isn't one of the indicated values.

What happens if you don't include `break`? All the statements that follow the matching `case` will execute until a `break` statement is encountered, even though they're within different cases.

You'll work through an exercise with `switch` later in this chapter.

if

JavaScript's `if` statement is straightforward:

```
if (conditional expression) {
    statement 1;
    statement 2;
}
```

If the conditional expression evaluates to true, `statement 1` and `statement 2` execute. If not, they don't.

else

`else` extends the `if` statement. It specifies code to execute if the conditional expression evaluates to false:

```
if (conditional expression) {
    statement 1;
    statement 2;
}
else {
    statement 3;
    statement 4;
}
```

Another Kind of *if*

Sometimes a program has to set the value of a variable as the result of evaluating a conditional expression. Here's a shorthand way to do this:

```
minimum = (a < b? a : b)
```

If the conditional expression evaluates to true, `minimum` is set as the value of a. If the conditional expression evaluates to false, `minimum` is set as the value of b. This succinct fragment sets `minimum` to the lesser of a and b.

MAKING CODE REPEAT

JavaScript provides a set of options for making code repeat.

for

The `for` loop is a fundamental way to make code repeat. Here's the format:

```
for (starting expression; conditional expression;
update expression) {
    code that runs while the conditional expression
evaluates to true
}
```

Here, for example, is a for example:

```
<HTML>
<HEAD>
<SCRIPT TYPE="text/javascript" LANGUAGE="javascript1.3">
function forExample() {
    for (i = 0; i < 10; i++) {
        document.forms[0].elements[0].value += "\n" +
            "the value of i is: " + i;
    }
}
</SCRIPT>
<TITLE>Sample JavaScript Function</TITLE>
</HEAD>
<BODY onload="forExample()">
<FORM>
<TEXTAREA ROWS="15" COLS="30">
</TEXTAREA>
</FORM>
</BODY>
</HTML>
```

If you were to open this file (we'll call it forExample.html for future reference) in Navigator or in IE, you would see this in the TEXTAREA:

```
the value of i is: 0
the value of i is: 1
the value of i is: 2
the value of i is: 3
the value of i is: 4
the value of i is: 5
the value of i is: 6
the value of i is: 7
the value of i is: 8
the value of i is: 9
```

As you can see, the for loop stops executing when i gets to 10 because the conditional expression i < 10 is no longer true.

NOTE

If the expression document.forms[0].elements[0].value looks strange to you, don't be too concerned; we'll cover it again in Chapter 4, "Working with Objects."

while

The while loop is another frequently used way of repeating code. The general format is

```
while (conditional expression) {
    code that executes while the
    conditional expression is true
}
```

To produce the same output as in the for example, the SCRIPT should look like this if you're using while:

```
<SCRIPT TYPE="text/javascript" LANGUAGE="javascript1.3">
var i = 0;
function whileExample() {
    while (i < 10) {
        document.forms[0].elements[0].value += "\n" +
            "the value of i is: " + i;
        i++;
    }
}
</SCRIPT>
```

And change the <BODY> tag to:

```
<BODY onload="whileExample()">
```

do while

The do while loop, new in JavaScript 1.2, guarantees that code will execute at least once. In this loop, the conditional expression appears after the code to be executed:

```
do {
    code to execute
}
while (conditional expression)
```

The code in do executes, and control then moves to while. If the conditional expression evaluates to true, control moves back to do. The process continues until the conditional expression evaluates to false.

To use this type of loop to produce the output in the for example, the SCRIPT is as follows:

```
<SCRIPT TYPE="text/javascript" LANGUAGE="javascript1.3">
var i=0;
function dowhileExample() {
```

```
do {
    document.forms[0].elements[0].value += "\n" +
        "the value of i is: " + i;
    i++;
}
while (i < 10)
}
```

Change the <BODY> tag to:

```
<BODY onload="dowhileExample()">
```

A Special *for* Loop

JavaScript provides for...in, a for loop that enables you to examine the properties of an object or the elements of an array. The format is

```
for property in object {
    code to execute
}
```

To show you how this loop works, here's an exercise that combines some of the knowledge you've acquired in this chapter. You'll create a page that IE and Navigator can both open. The particular browser that opens it will determine the page heading. The script uses the for...in loop to access the properties of the browser's window object, and the document.write method displays those properties and any defined values.

In your text editor, create a page called forinExample.htm. In the HEAD element, create a SCRIPT, and in the SCRIPT element type

```
function forinExample() {

}
```

The first part of the function is a switch statement. The test expression for the switch is the window.navigator.appName property. The switch statement works in conjunction with the case statement, covered previously. It evaluates an expression and attempts to match it to a set of case labels. (Browser objects are discussed in more detail in Chapter 4.) This property holds a string that indicates which browser opened the page. The case statements use the document.write method to put an appropriate header on the web page:

```
switch (window.navigator.appName) {
    case "Microsoft Internet Explorer" :
        document.write("<CENTER><H1>IE Window Object
```

```
Properties</H1><HR></CENTER><BR>");
        break;
    case "Netscape" :
        document.write("<CENTER>
        ➥<H1>Navigator Window Object
Properties</H1><HR></CENTER><BR>");
        break;
}
```

Next, you set up the for...in loop that accesses the window object's properties and displays them on the page:

```
var property;

for (property in window) {
    document.write("The " + property +
        " of this window is: " +
        window[property] + "<BR>")
}

}
```

The expression window[property] takes advantage of the JavaScript equivalence between object.property and the array reference object ["property"] that I mentioned earlier in the section on arrays. Notice that you use the concatenation operator along with the HTML <BR> tag. This is like concatenating "\n" at the end of a string—it causes the next result to appear on the next line in the display.

Add the appropriate HTML:

```
<TITLE>Accessing the Window Object</TITLE>
</HEAD>
<BODY onload="forinExample()">
</BODY>
</HTML>
```

In the <BODY> tag, the inline call to forinExample() starts things off when the page loads.

Figure 2.1 shows this page in IE, and Figure 2.2 shows the page in Navigator.

Note the different headings in the pages. Also, you can see how the properties of the window object differ between the two browsers. Not all the properties have values, but it's still an instructive exercise.

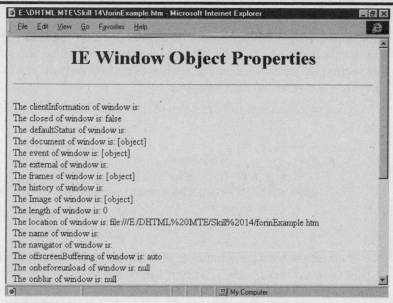

FIGURE 2.1: forinExample.htm in IE shows the properties of the IE window object.

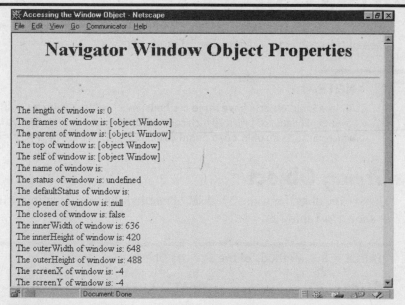

FIGURE 2.2: forinExample.htm in Navigator shows the properties of the Navigator window object.

break and *continue*

JavaScript provides mechanisms for getting out of a loop and for advancing to the next iteration of a loop. The break statement, which you saw in the section on switch, immediately moves control outside of a loop. continue moves to the next iteration.

A quick modification to forExample.htm provides an example of continue:

```
function forExample() {
    for (i = 0; i < 10; i++) {
        if (i % 2 == 0) { continue; }
        document.forms[0].elements[0].value += "\n" +
            "the value of i is: " + i;
    }
}
```

The if statement tests the remainder of dividing i by 2. If the remainder is 0, continue advances to the next iteration of the for loop. The net effect is to display only odd values of i.

BUILT-IN OBJECTS

In JavaScript, String, Date, and Math are objects built into the language. Each of these objects provides useful methods.

NOTE

All JavaScript objects have three methods: eval, which evaluates a string of JavaScript code; toString, which converts an object to a string; and valueOf, which converts an object to a primitive value.

The *String* Object

The String object provides a full set of methods for manipulating strings, as shown in Table 2.8.

TABLE 2.8: Methods of the String Object

METHOD	WHAT IT DOES
anchor(name)	Turns the string into an HTML anchor tag, using name as the anchor's name.
big()	Changes the string's text to a big font.

TABLE 2.8 continued: Methods of the String Object

METHOD	WHAT IT DOES
blink()	Changes the string's text to a blinking font.
bold()	Changes the string's text to a bold font.
charAt(index)	Finds the character in the string at the (zero-based) index position.
fixed()	Changes the string's text to a fixed-pitch font.
fontcolor(color)	Changes the string's text to a specified color.
fontsize()	Changes the string's text to a specified size.
indexOf(character,from)	Searches the string for the first occurrence of character, returning its position in the string. You can optionally start the search at from.
italics()	Changes the string's text to italics.
lastIndexOf(character,from)	Searches backward through the string to find the last occurrence of character.
link(href)	Turns the string into an HTML link tag, with href as the anchor name.
small()	Changes the string's text to a small font.
split(sep)	Returns an array created by splitting the string into separate sections at each occurrence of the string sep.
strike()	Changes the string's text to a strikethrough font.
sub()	Changes the string's text to a subscript font.
substring(start,finish)	Returns a substring of the string beginning at start and ending at finish.
sup()	Changes the string's text to a superscript font.
toLowerCase()	Changes the string's text to lowercase.
toUpperCase()	Changes the string's text to uppercase.

How do you use these methods? Here's an exercise to show you. You'll create a JavaScript function that incorporates some of these methods and uses the document.write() method to display the results on a web page.

In your text editor, create a SCRIPT element that initializes a new string:

```
<SCRIPT TYPE="text/javascript" LANGUAGE="javascript1.3">
var s = new String("DHTML Master the Essentials");
```

Next, start a function called `stringThings` that takes an argument called `stringName`. This argument will hold a string:

```
function stringThings(stringName) {
```

Eventually, you'll call `stringThings` with s as the argument.

Have the first line of the function use `document.write()` to display the string:

```
document.write(stringName + "<BR>");
```

Now add three lines. The first italicizes the string,

```
document.write(stringName.italics() + "<BR>");
```

the second makes it bold,

```
document.write(stringName.bold() + "<BR>");
```

and the third shows how you can put methods together to produce a composite result:

```
document.write(stringName.bold().italics().fontsize(25) +
    "<BR>");
```

That last line makes the string bold and italic, and gives it a font size of 25 points.

Now let's turn the string into an array. This line breaks the string wherever a space occurs and displays the resulting segments as the items in an array:

```
document.write(stringName.split(" ") + "<BR>");
```

This line forms the array and sorts the array-items:

```
document.write(stringName.split(" ").sort() + "<BR>");
```

This line forms the array and reverses the order of the array-items:

```
document.write(stringName.split(" ").reverse() + "<BR>");
```

Finally, add a line that returns and displays a substring. This expression gives you a surprising result, as you'll see in a moment:

```
document.write(stringName.substring(1,4) + "<BR>");
```

Finish the function and the `SCRIPT` element:

```
}
</SCRIPT>
```

Add this HTML:

```
<TITLE>String Things</TITLE>
```

```
</HEAD>
<BODY onload="stringThings(s)">
</BODY>
</HTML>
```

The in-line function call in <BODY> activates `stringThings()` when the page opens. It calls the function with s as the argument, and s is the newly created string `"DHTML Master the Essentials"`.

Listing 2.1 shows the whole `stringThings.htm` file.

Listing 2.1: *stringThings.htm*

```
<HTML>
<HEAD>
<SCRIPT TYPE="text/javascript" LANGUAGE="javascript1.3">
var s = new String("DHTML Master the Essentials");
function stringThings(stringName) {
    document.write(stringName + "<BR>");
    document.write(stringName.italics() + "<BR>");
    document.write(stringName.bold() + "<BR>");
    document.write(stringName.bold().italics().fontsize(25)
    + "<BR>");
    document.write(stringName.split(" ") + "<BR>");
    document.write(stringName.split(" ").sort() + "<BR>");
    document.write(stringName.split(" ").reverse() +
    "<BR>");
    document.write(stringName.substring(1,4) + "<BR>");
}
</SCRIPT>
<TITLE>String Things</TITLE>
</HEAD>
<BODY onload="stringThings(s)">
</BODY>
</HTML>
```

Figure 2.3 shows the page in IE. (It looks the same in Navigator.)

Note the lines that display arrays. In each array, the items appear in a comma-delimited list. The last line shows that surprising result I mentioned. With the arguments to `substring` set at 1 and 4, you would expect the function to return HTML. Instead, it returns HTM.

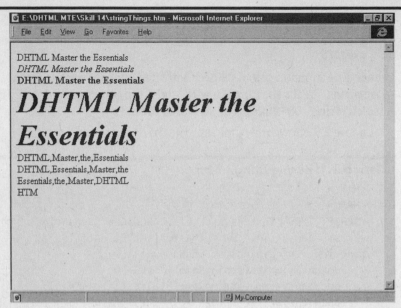

FIGURE 2.3:   `stringThings.htm` in IE shows the results of applying String methods.

NOTE

You can see a quirky little difference between IE and Navigator if you go into the `stringThings.htm` file and delete + "`<BR>`" from the final `document.write()`. You can reopen the page in IE and see all the `document.write()` results displayed, or you can reopen the page in Navigator and see that the final `document.write()` doesn't appear.

The *Math* Object

The JavaScript `Math` object has methods you can use to build calculations into your scripts. Table 2.9 shows these methods.

TABLE 2.9:   Methods of the Math Object

METHOD	RETURNS...
`abs()`	A number's absolute value
`acos()`	A number's arc cosine in radians
`asin()`	A number's arc sine in radians

TABLE 2.9 continued: Methods of the Math Object

Method	Returns...
atan()	A number's arc tangent in radians
ceil()	The given number with all fractional values removed, plus one if the fractional value is greater than zero. That is, ceil(1.03) = 2, whereas ceil(1.00) = 1
cos()	A number's cosine
exp()	e to a specified power
floor()	The given number with all fractional values removed. floor(1.93) = 1
log()	A number's natural logarithm
max()	The larger of two numbers
min()	The lesser of two numbers
pow()	The value of a base to a specified power
random()	A pseudo-random number between 0 and 1
round()	A number rounded to the nearest integer round(1.3) = 1, round(1.50001) = 2
sin()	A number's sine
sqrt()	A number's square root
tan()	A number's tangent

Here are some examples that show how to use these methods:

```
var x, y, z;
y = Math.sqrt(x);
z = Math.pow(x,y);
x = Math.random();
```

The Math object has some useful properties—constants that can come in handy. Table 2.10 presents these properties.

TABLE 2.10: Properties of the Math Object

Property	Meaning	Approximate Value
E	Base of natural logarithms	2.718
LN2	Natural logarithm of 2	0.693
LN10	Natural logarithm of 10	2.302

TABLE 2.10 continued: Properties of the Math Object

PROPERTY	MEANING	APPROXIMATE VALUE
LOG2E	Logarithm of e to base 2	1.442
LOG10E	Logarithm of 10 to base 2	0.434
PI	Ratio of circumference of a circle to its diameter	3.1416
SQRT1_2	Square root of .5	0.707
SQRT2	Square root of 2	1.414

The *Date* Object

The JavaScript Date object gives you capabilities for working with times and dates. Table 2.11 shows its methods.

TABLE 2.11: Methods of the Date Object

METHOD	WHAT IT DOES
getDate()	Returns the day of the month in the Date object
getDay()	Returns the day of the week
getHours()	Returns the hours
getMinutes()	Returns the minutes
getMonth()	Returns the month
getSeconds()	Returns the seconds
getTime()	Returns the complete time
getTimeZoneOffset()	Returns the number of hours' difference between Greenwich Mean Time and the time zone in the computer running the script
getYear()	Returns the year
parse()	Returns the number of milliseconds between the date and January 1, 1970 00:00:00
setDate()	Sets the Date object's day of the month
setHours()	Sets the hours
setMinutes()	Sets the minutes
setMonth()	Sets the month

TABLE 2.11 continued: Methods of the Date Object

METHOD	WHAT IT DOES
setSeconds()	Sets the seconds
setTime()	Sets the complete time
setYear()	Sets the year
toGMTString()	Changes the Date object's date into a string in Greenwich Mean Time
toLocalString()	Changes the Date object's date into a string
UTC()	Returns a date in terms of the number of milliseconds since January 1, 1970 00:00:00

ALERTING, CONFIRMING, AND PROMPTING

We end this discussion of JavaScript with a look at three boxes JavaScript provides for communicating with the user. These boxes are analogous to VBScript's MsgBox.

The first, alert, presents a message and a button, as shown in Figure 2.4. This is produced with the JavaScript:

```
alert("Here we are, at the end of Skill 14");
```

FIGURE 2.4: The JavaScript alert box presents a message and a button referencing Skill 14 from *Dynamic HTML: Master the Essentials*.

The second box, confirm, presents a message and two buttons, as shown in Figure 2.5. This is produced with the following code:

```
confirm("Are you aware that we are almost finished?");
```

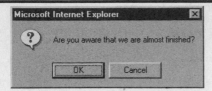

FIGURE 2.5: The confirm box presents a message and two buttons.

Finally, as shown in Figure 2.6, the prompt box presents a message, a text box for user entry, two buttons, and a wide area. This is produced with

```
prompt("Which Skill was your favorite?");
```

FIGURE 2.6: The prompt box presents a question, a text area for user data entry, and two buttons.

SUMMARY

JavaScript is a very rich scripting language. It provides a wealth of control structures, operators, built-in functions, objects, and flexibility. Some say that if you learn JavaScript, you'll have a leg up if you then try to learn Java. I'm not sure this is true, but one thing's certain: Mastering JavaScript will give you control over objects that bring a web page to life.

NOTE

For more information about the Netscape version of JavaScript, visit http://devedge.netscape.com/. For more information about the Microsoft version, visit http://msdn.microsoft.com/.

WHAT'S NEXT

Chapter 3 takes the concepts you've learned here and shows you how to integrate them into web pages that respond dynamically to user actions. You'll see how to turn your site from a bunch of underlined hyperlinks into an application with more of a "user interface."

Chapter 3
Adding JavaScript

U sing JavaScript, you can add some pizzazz to your pages, taking them from ho-hum pages to ones that react to user actions, process and check information that users provide, and even deliver information appropriate to each user. With the increasingly sophisticated nature of the Web, you often need these kinds of attractions to hold users' attention and to keep them coming back. What's more, JavaScript allows you to include useful capabilities, such as tracking users' visits and keeping other sites from "framing" your material.

In this chapter, we'll continue to explore JavaScript, discussing what it is and how to use it; and, with some examples, we'll show you how to include JavaScript in your HTML and XHTML documents. We'll begin with simple scripts and then build on them. We'll concentrate on basic JavaScript capabilities as introduced in the earlier versions of JavaScript-compatible browsers—a good compromise between high functionality and broad browser acceptance.

Adapted from *Mastering HTML and XHTML*, by Deborah S. Ray and Eric J. Ray
ISBN 0-7821-4141-2

TIP

For more information about JavaScript, see *Mastering JavaScript Premium Edition*, by James Jaworski, published by Sybex.

What Is JavaScript?

Initially created by Netscape and now an industry-wide standard, JavaScript is a scripting language that vaguely resembles Sun's Java programming language. Most popular browsers, starting with Netscape Navigator 2 and Internet Explorer (IE) 3, support JavaScript. Microsoft's JScript and the international standard, ECMAScript, are also similar to JavaScript—similar enough that we'll refer to all these scripting languages as *JavaScript*. Table 3.1 shows which browsers support which versions of JavaScript.

TABLE 3.1: Browser Support for JavaScript

JavaScript Version	Netscape Navigator	Opera	Internet Explorer
JavaScript 1.0, JScript 1.0	2.0 and higher	3.0 and higher	3.0 and higher
JavaScript 1.1	3.0 and higher		
JavaScript 1.2, JScript 3.0	4.0–4.05		4.0 and higher
JavaScript 1.3	4.06–4.75	4.0 and higher	
JavaScript 1.4, JScript 5.0	5.0*	5.0 and higher	5.0 and higher
JavaScript 1.5	6.0		6.0 and higher

*JavaScript 1.4 was part of Netscape Navigator 5, which was not released.

TIP

Microsoft also supports VBScript, a competing scripting approach. We recommend JavaScript (or the Microsoft equivalent, JScript) for most purposes, however, because JavaScript is much more widely supported on a variety of platforms.

JavaScript is powerful enough to be truly useful, even though it isn't a full-fledged programming language. What's more, JavaScript is relatively easy and fun to use. Be careful, though, because JavaScript can cause problems with accessibility for both visually impaired visitors and those who use older technology. JavaScript use can also irritate visitors. For example, the event handlers discussed later in this chapter often violate visitor expectations and make the visitor's experience less predictable, which can often have negative effects.

JavaScript is simpler and less sophisticated (therefore less complex) than a "real" programming language. Nonetheless, in order to work with JavaScript, you need to be familiar with the following terms and concepts:

Object An *object* is a thing—a check box on a form, the form itself, an image, a document, a link, or even a browser window. Some objects are built into JavaScript and are not necessarily part of your web page. For example, the Date object provides a wide range of date information. You can think of objects as the nouns in the JavaScript language.

Property A *property* describes an object. Properties can be anything from the color to the number of items, such as radio buttons, within an object. When users select an item in a form, they change the form's properties. You can think of properties as the adjectives in the JavaScript language.

Method A *method* is an instruction. The methods available for each object describe what you can do with the object. For example, using a method, you can convert text in an object to all uppercase or all lowercase letters. Every object has a collection of methods that act on that object, and every method belongs to at least one object. You can think of methods as the verbs in the JavaScript language.

Statement A *statement* is a JavaScript language sentence. Statements combine the objects, properties, and methods (nouns, adjectives, and verbs). Many of the statements for JavaScript are remarkably natural in their structure and terminology.

Function A *function* is a collection of statements that performs an action or actions. Functions contain one or more statements and can therefore be considered the paragraphs of the JavaScript language.

Event An *event* occurs when something happens on your page, such as the page being loaded, a user submitting a form, or the mouse cursor being moved over an object.

Event Handler   The browser launches an *event handler* based on the occurrence of a specific event. For example, the onmouseover event handler performs an action when the user moves the mouse pointer over the object. You can think of an event handler as posing questions or directing the action of a story.

Variable   A *variable* stores data temporarily (usually until the user closes the page or moves to a new page). Each variable is given a name so that you can refer to it in your code.

Let's look at some JavaScript code. Once you can identify the pieces, JavaScript is as easy to read as HTML or XHTML code:

```
<!DOCTYPE html PUBLIC ".//W3C/DTD XHTML 1.0 Transitional//EN"
   "http://www.w3.org/TR/xhtml1/DTD/xhtml1-transitional.dtd">
<html xmlns="http://www.w3.org/1999/xhtml">
<head>
   <title>The Basic Page</title>
</head>
<body>
   <h1>Welcome!</h1>
   <a href="http://www.nytimes.com/"
      onmouseover="window.status='The latest news!';
        return true;"
      onmouseout="window.status=''; return true;">
   Read the New York Times online</a>
</body>
</html>
```

In the preceding code, note the following JavaScript elements:

Object	window is a JavaScript object.
Property	status is a JavaScript property.
Statement	return true is a JavaScript statement.
Event handler	onmouseover and onmouseout are both JavaScript events that can be tied to specific handlers.

WARNING

Although we often use extra spaces, indents, and line breaks for readability in our printed code, do not insert any additional spaces or line returns in your JavaScript code. Make sure that each JavaScript statement is on a single line, and allow the text to wrap without a line return. JavaScript sees line returns as JavaScript characters and adds them to your code (which will often make the code nonfunctional). It's fine to use line returns at the actual end of a line of code, before you start the next line, but not in the middle of a line of code.

If you test the previous code in a browser, you'll see the message *The latest news!* appear in the status bar at the bottom of the browser window when you roll the mouse cursor over the Read The New York Times Online link, and disappear when you roll the mouse cursor off the link.

NOTE

The JavaScript discussed in this chapter is exclusively client-side JavaScript. This means the user's browser does the work, and the server is not involved. Although server-side JavaScript exists, it is outside the scope of this book and, frankly, is rare nowadays.

ADDING JAVASCRIPT TO YOUR DOCUMENT

You can add JavaScript to your page in three ways:

- ▶ Embed the JavaScript in the page.
- ▶ Place the JavaScript in the document head.
- ▶ Link to JavaScript stored in another file.

TIP

The options for placing JavaScript closely resemble the options for placing style sheets, and you'll find them familiar if you've worked with Cascading Style Sheets (CSS) in the past.

Table 3.2 describes the elements and attributes you use to add JavaScript to your documents.

TABLE 3.2:   Elements and Attributes Used to Add JavaScript

ITEM	TYPE	DESCRIPTION
script	Element	Identifies the script section in the document.
language= "javascript"	Attribute of script	Specifies the scripting language (and, optionally, version).
src="url"	Attribute of script	Optionally specifies the location of an external script.

TABLE 3.2 continued: Elements and Attributes Used to Add JavaScript

ITEM	TYPE	DESCRIPTION
type="text/javascript"	Attribute of script	Provides the script MIME type; required.
noscript	Element	Provides content for non-script-capable browsers.
<!-- //-->	Comment markup	Hides the contents of the script from non-script-capable browsers. Note that this differs from comment markup used for style sheets.

Embedding JavaScript

If you're adding a fairly short JavaScript, your best bet is to embed it in the HTML or XHTML document in the code the JavaScript affects. For example, JavaScript that adds the current date to your document is a few lines long, so you can easily embed the script in your document.

Embedding works like this: When users open your page, their browsers read your source document line by line. If your code includes JavaScript within the document body, the browser performs the actions as it reads the page. For example, if the body element includes JavaScript, the first task the browser completes is running the script. Or, if you include JavaScript in the first actual text of the document, the browser runs the script as soon as it gets to the text.

Let's embed a JavaScript that prints the current time and date as the page loads. The JavaScript statement—in this case, the whole script—is `document.write(Date())`. Here are the steps:

TIP

As in other chapters, we're using XHTML as the sample code; however, the examples and steps work just as well if you use HTML.

1.   Start with the following XHTML code:

```
<!DOCTYPE html PUBLIC
    "-//W3C/DTD XHTML 1.0 Transitional//EN"
"http://www.w3.org/TR/xhtml1/DTD/
➥xhtml1-transitional.dtd">
<html xmlns="http://www.w3.org/1999/xhtml">
<head>
    <title>The Date Page</title>
```

```
    </head>
    <body>
        <h1>Welcome!</h1>
    </body>
    </html>
```

2. Add an introductory sentence:

```
    <body>
        <h1>Welcome!</h1>
        <p>Today's date is:    </p>
    </body>
```

3. Add script tags where you want the script:

```
    <p>Today's date is:
        <script>
        </script>
    </p>
```

4. Add the type attribute to specify the script's MIME type, and the language attribute to specify that the scripting language is JavaScript:

```
    <p>Today's date is:
        <script type="text/javascript" language="javascript">
        </script>
    </p>
```

5. Add comment lines to hide the script from browsers that do not recognize scripting. Include standard comment markup (<!--and -->), and preface the closing comment markup with // to hide the comment close from the JavaScript interpreter; if you don't, you'll get an error. The complete comment looks like this:

```
    <p>Today's date is:
        <script type="text/javascript" language="javascript">
            <!--
            // -->
        </script>
    </p>
```

6. Add the actual JavaScript statement:

```
    <script type="text/javascript" language="javascript">
        <!--
            document.write(Date());
        // -->
    </script>
```

That's it! The resulting page looks like this:

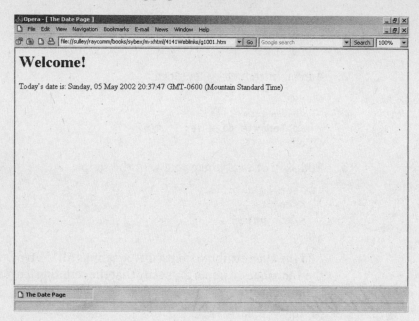

Using this method, the initial *Today's date is:* text appears in all browsers, regardless of whether they support JavaScript. Browsers that don't support JavaScript display *Today's date is:* and a blank. To hide the text from browsers that don't support JavaScript, simply remove the text from the p element and replace the JavaScript statement as shown in the following code:

```
<script type="text/javascript" language="javascript">
   <!--
      document.write("Today's date is: " + Date());
   // -->
</script>
```

This way, users will either see the JavaScript or not see it, but they won't see a lead-in with an unfulfilled promise. You get the same effect in JavaScript-capable browsers and nothing at all in non-JavaScript browsers.

You're not restricted to a single JavaScript statement, and you can embed several statements throughout the page source. The additional statements in the following code display information about the user's browser in the document:

```
<body>
   <h1>Welcome!</h1>
```

```
<p><script type="text/javascript" language="javascript">
<!--
   document.write("Today\'s date is: " + Date());

   // -->
</script></p>
<p><script type="text/javascript" language="javascript">
   <!--
      document.write("You appear to be using " +
         navigator.appName + " version " +
         navigator.appVersion + ".")
   // -->
</script></p>
</body>
```

In this script, the JavaScript is interpreted line by line as it appears in the source. In the new statement, the text strings, such as *You appear to be using*, are combined with properties of the navigator object—that is, with characteristics of the browser—to display the line shown. See Appendix A for a full rundown of objects, including the navigator object, and their properties. The resulting page from this example looks like this:

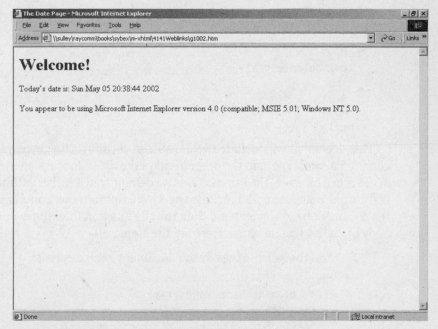

Embedding is a great way to start adding JavaScript to your page. You can use this technique alone or combine it with others.

TIP

If you choose to embed the JavaScript, you'll need to provide for older browsers that don't support it, or, more likely, for visitors who have chosen to disable it. See the section "Providing for Older Browsers" later in this chapter.

Adding a JavaScript Function in the Head

If you repeatedly use specific JavaScript procedures within documents, consider placing a JavaScript function in the document head element. Collecting individual statements in one place creates a function; creating functions in the head element is convenient and easy to troubleshoot, and it reduces the amount of code to manage and download to users' browsers.

In the following examples, we'll show you how to add JavaScript statements to the document head. Here's the code to start with:

```
<!DOCTYPE html PUBLIC "-//W3C/DTD XHTML 1.0 Transitional//EN"
    "http://www.w3.org/TR/xhtml1/DTD/xhtml1-transitional.dtd">
<html xmlns="http://www.w3.org/1999/xhtml">
<head>
    <title>The Date Page</title>
</head>
<body>
    <h1>Welcome!</h1>
    <p>
    </p>
</body>
</html>
```

This document will include two JavaScript sections. One displays the current date and time, and the other displays the name and version number of the user's browser—the same actions we demonstrated earlier within the body of the document. You include the JavaScript function command in the document head element and then run the function from the document body by calling just its name. Here are the steps:

1. Add the script tags to the document head element:

```
<head>
    <title>The Date Page</title>
    <script>
    </script>
</head>
```

2. Add the `type` attribute to specify that the script is a JavaScript, and the `language` attribute to specify that the scripting language is JavaScript:

```
<head>
    <title>The Date Page</title>
    <script type="text/javascript" language="javascript">
    </script>
</head>
```

3. Add comment markup (`<!-- //-->`) to hide the script from other browsers. Don't forget the slashes:

```
<head>
    <title>The Date Page</title>
    <script type="text/javascript" language="javascript">
        <!--
        // -->
    </script>
</head>
```

Remember, you're putting the script in the document head, so by itself it will not display anything in the browser window. You have to place instructions in the document body to do anything with the script.

4. To make a function out of the JavaScript statement that displays the date, you name the statement and place it in inside curly brackets (a.k.a. *braces*: { }). In this example, the name is `printDate`. Add the keyword `function`, the function name (including a set of parentheses), and the braces.

```
<head>
    <title>The Date Page</title>
    <script type="text/javascript" language="javascript">
        <!--
        function printDate() { }
        // -->
    </script>
</head>
```

TIP

If a function needs parameter values, they're usually inserted in these parentheses. For consistency, even functions without parameters, like this one, include parentheses in their names.

5. Add the JavaScript statement within the braces. Use the same code you used in the document body a few pages ago (remember, we have to wrap lines to fit them on the printed page; you should type the JavaScript function all on one line):

```
<head>
    <title>The Date Page</title>
    <script type="text/javascript" language="javascript">
        <!--
            function printDate() {
                document.write("Today's date is: "
                    + Date());
            }
        // -->
    </script>
</head>
```

6. To *call* (which means to activate or run) the function from the document body, add another set of script tags within the body tags:

```
<body>
    <h1>Welcome!</h1>
    <p>
        <script type="text/javascript"
            language="javascript">
            <!--
            // -->
        </script>
    </p>
</body>
```

7. Add printDate(), which is the name you gave the function, within the tags:

```
<body>
    <h1>Welcome!</h1>
    <p>
        <script type="text/javascript"
            language="javascript">
            <!--
                printDate()
            // -->
        </script>
    </p>
</body>
```

Now your code looks like Listing 3.1.

Listing 3.1: Including JavaScript in the *head* Element

```
<!DOCTYPE html PUBLIC "-//W3C/DTD XHTML 1.0 Transitional//EN"
    "http://www.w3.org/TR/xhtml1/DTD/xhtml1-transitional.dtd">
<html xmlns="http://www.w3.org/1999/xhtml">
<head>
    <title>The Date Page</title>
    <script type="text/javascript" language="javascript">
    <!--
        function printDate() {
            document.write("Today's date is: " + Date());
        }
    // -->
    </script>
</head>
<body>
    <h1>Welcome!</h1>
    <p><script type="text/javascript" language="javascript">
    <!--
        printDate()
    // -->
    </script></p>
</body>
</html>
```

TIP

If you separate the JavaScript into its own section, enclose it within comment markup: `<!--` and `//-->`. Not all browsers can interpret JavaScript, and the comment markup instructs these browsers to ignore the JavaScript section. JavaScript-enabled browsers will see past the comments and recognize the script element.

WARNING: COMMENTS MAY NOT WORK IN XHTML IN THE FUTURE

The traditional practice of using the comment element (`<!-- -->`) to hide scripts from browsers that do not support JavaScript may not work in the future in XHTML, because XML parsers may silently remove the contents of comments—that is, your script!

CONTINUED ➥

There are two possible solutions:

▶ Use external scripts (which is recommended for XHTML). (See the section "Linking JavaScript.")

▶ Wrap the content of the script in a CDATA-marked section, which defines the content of the script as data an XML parser will not parse. For example:

```
<script>
  <![CDATA[
     ...script content ...
  ]]>
</script>
```

Of course, it's the rare browser that knows how to handle XML CDATA sections, although further support for XML is likely in upcoming browser versions. It will remain a conundrum for the developer, however, because it's difficult to balance writing to the latest browsers and ensuring compatibility with the earliest. At least the comment element used in HTML documents should not be affected.

Linking JavaScript

If you plan to use script functions in several documents, consider placing them in a separate file and referring to that file from your document. You can build, test, and store working JavaScript code in one location and use it in several web pages. You can also share this code with others who can link it into their documents.

TIP

Linking JavaScript is preferable, if possible, because it eases management issues and helps you reuse the code effectively.

The linked document is simply a text file that includes all your variable definitions and functions. You can even copy the functions from the headers of your existing documents if you want. If this document also includes variables and functions that you don't need for the web page, the browser uses what it needs as the variables and functions are called by the JavaScript code in the document.

To continue with our date example, you can create a `functions.js` document that contains the following text:

```
function printDate() { document.write(Date()) }
```

This linked document does not require any special headings or elements—so it doesn't need comment markup or script tags. An external JavaScript file is a text document whose only content is JavaScript code (similar to an external style sheet, which is a text document with only style definitions). It doesn't require any HTML or XHTML code, but simply includes the definitions for the variables and functions. You can then link to the script with the following code from the document head element (including all the surrounding tags):

```
<head>
    <title>The Date Page</title>
    <script src="functions.js" type="text/javascript"
        language="javascript">
    </script>
</head>
```

Now, by including this reference to your external script document, using the appropriate URL for the `src` attribute, you can access any functions included in this external script from any document you create by using the same function call you would use if the script were embedded.

You can include as many functions or variable definitions in your external script document as you like. Alternatively, you can reference multiple external scripts by including additional `script` elements.

Providing for Older Browsers

As you add JavaScript to your pages, it's good form to accommodate browsers in which JavaScript is disabled or unavailable, as well as older browsers that cannot interpret JavaScript. If you include JavaScript in the head element or if you link the JavaScript from a separate document, you've already provided for older browsers because these don't show up in the document body.

However, if you embed the JavaScript, you must make sure the script doesn't show up as horribly rendered HTML on the web page. The best way to accommodate older browsers is to make sure text that is dependent on the JavaScript functionality (such as *Today's date is*) is part of the

JavaScript block. Recall from Listing 3.1 that the embedded code looks like this:

```
<script type="text/javascript" language="javascript">
  <!--
      document.write("Today's date is: " + Date());
  // -->
</script>
```

To give additional information to non-JavaScript browsers (rather than just hiding information from them), you can also use the `noscript` element and include alternative text. For example, if you have a form that uses JavaScript to validate input, you can add a statement to the top of the form, within a `noscript` element, that warns users of non-JavaScript browsers that their responses won't be validated and that they should be particularly careful to proofread their responses. In the following example, the JavaScript-enabled browser displays only the *Personal Information Form* heading, followed by *Please enter your name and address below*:

```
<h2>Personal Information Form</h2>
<noscript>
  <p>Please be very careful to proofread your responses.
     If any information is incorrect (particularly your
     e-mail address), we won't be able to contact you.</p>
</noscript>
Please enter your name and address below:<br />
```

Other browsers will also display the *Please be very careful* text.

Using the `noscript` element is a convenient way to deal with a small amount of JavaScript or JavaScript that isn't essential to the content of your document. If you have more complex JavaScript applications on your page, you'll need to identify users' browsers and automatically direct them to the correct page. In that case, instead of putting content within the `noscript` tags, you create a separate page for users without JavaScript. To do this, you need a script to perform browser detection, and at least two different versions of the page (one for users with JavaScript enabled and one for users without JavaScript).

TIP

See HotScripts on the Web at www.hotscripts.com for server-side means of identifying browsers and redirecting them appropriately.

ADDING EVENT HANDLERS

JavaScript relies heavily on event handlers, which are invoked in response to what is happening (the page loading into the browser, for example) or what a visitor is doing on the page—moving the mouse, clicking a button, or selecting options on a form—and then do whatever you tell them to do in each instance. For example, with the onmouseover and onmouseout event handlers, you can change the information in your status bar, flash an alert box, or change an illustration.

TIP

JavaScript provides a variety of event handlers that let you tie events to specific sections of your script. In this chapter, we discuss only a couple of them, but the principles used apply to all event handlers. Appendix A explains all of them.

Using *onmouseover* and *onmouseout* Events

You commonly use an onmouseover event with the anchor element (a) to provide additional information about a link. The onmouseout event generally undoes what the onmouseover event does.

Using these event handlers, you can, among other things, implement timed status bar events, swap images, and alert users. We'll show you how in the next few sections. But first, let's look at how to add the onmouseover and onmouseout event handlers.

TIP

Neither IE 3 or earlier nor Netscape Navigator 2 or earlier recognizes the onmouseout event. If your visitors use these browsers (which is unlikely), consider using a separate function to clear the status bar.

Let's add the onmouseover and onmouseout event handlers to display a new message in the status bar and then remove it. This technique is handy for displaying information in the status bar that is more descriptive than the URL the browser automatically displays there. Here are the steps:

1. Start with a document that includes a link:

```
<!DOCTYPE html PUBLIC
    "-//W3C/DTD XHTML 1.0 Transitional//EN"
    "http://www.w3.org/TR/xhtml1/DTD/
    ➥xhtml1-transitional.dtd">
```

```
<html xmlns="http://www.w3.org/1999/xhtml">
<head>
   <title>Status Bar</title>
</head>
<body>
   <h1>Welcome!</h1>
   <a href="http://www.nytimes.com/">
      Visit the New York Times.</a>
</body>
</html>
```

2. Add the onmouseover event handler to the a element:

```
<a href="http://www.nytimes.com/" onmouseover="">
   Visit the New York Times.</a>
```

3. Add window.status= to the event handler. The window
   .status property specifies what appears in the status bar:

```
<a href="http://www.nytimes.com/"
   onmouseover="window.status=''">
   Visit the New York Times.</a>
```

4. Add the text that will appear in the status bar, enclosed
   in single quotes (' '). You use single quotes because the
   window.status statement is enclosed in double quotes, and
   you must nest unlike quotes within each other:

```
<a href="http://www.nytimes.com/"
   onmouseover="window.status='The latest news!'">
   Visit the New York Times.</a>
```

5. Add a semicolon (to indicate the end of the statement), and
   add return true to the end (just before the closing quotes).
   This tells the JavaScript interpreter that the action is complete,
   and to do it:

```
<a href="http://www.nytimes.com/"
   onmouseover="window.status='The latest news!';
      return true;">
   Visit the New York Times.</a>
```

If you try this example, you'll see that the *The latest news!* statement
appears in the browser status bar after you move the cursor over the
link. The statement stays in the status bar, which probably isn't what you
want. To restore the status bar after the cursor moves away from the link,
add the onmouseout event handler:

```
<a href="http://www.nytimes.com/"
   onmouseover="window.status='The latest news!';
```

```
    return true;"
onmouseout="window.status=''; return true;">
Visit the New York Times.</a>
```

COMMENTS IN JAVASCRIPT

Add comments (notes to yourself, not just comment markup) to your JavaScript to track what the script does. Comments are useful for future reference and helpful to people with whom you share your JavaScript functions. Comments in JavaScript are preceded by two forward slashes: //. You need to add these slashes at the beginning of each comment line, as in the following code segment:

```
<script type="text/javascript" language="javascript">
<!--
function checkOut() {
 // The following loop rejects the survey if any
 // fields were not filled out
 for (x=0; x<document.survey.elements.length;x++){
     if (document.survey.elements[x].value == "") {
        alert("Sorry, you forgot one of the required
             fields. Please try again.")
        break;  }  }
 return false;
 if (document.survey.firstname.value.length <= 2) {
    alert("Please enter your full first name.")
    return false;  }  }
//-->
</script>
```

ADDING A LITTLE EXCITEMENT TO THE PAGE LOAD

Just as events can respond to a user's mouse actions, events can occur when the page loads or unloads. However, anything time consuming (such as playing a sound) or intrusive (such as displaying a welcome alert) can irritate users far more than impressing them with your technical skills. We suggest that you perform actions with onload or onunload event handlers only if users expect them in the context of the page or for other reasons, such as the example of breaking out of frames, later in this chapter.

Swapping Images

You can use the onmouseover and onmouseout event handlers to change linked images when the mouse cursor moves over them. These are often called *rollovers*.

WARNING

This technique works only with Netscape Navigator 3 or later and IE 4 or later. Older browsers don't recognize images as objects.

To change an image when the mouse moves over it, you need an HTML element (often an anchor, a) and two versions of the image: the standard presentation and the highlighted presentation. When the page initially loads, the standard image is visible. Then, when the mouse moves over the image, the highlighted image replaces the standard image. When the mouse cursor moves away again, the images change back. Conceptually, the process is the same as changing the status bar text in the preceding example; however, instead of changing the status bar, you swap images.

To set up images to swap, you first need a pair of images that are precisely the same size but visually different. (If the images are different sizes, the process works but looks bad to users.)

Next, you need a link using an image in your document. The img element must also have a name attribute so the JavaScript can identify and refer to it. Let's use the following sample document:

```
<!DOCTYPE html PUBLIC "-//W3C/DTD XHTML 1.0 Transitional//EN"
    "http://www.w3.org/TR/xhtml1/DTD/xhtml1-transitional.dtd">
<html xmlns="http://www.w3.org/1999/xhtml">
<head>
    <title>Image Swap</title>
</head>
<body bgcolor="#ffffff" text="#000000" link="#0000ff"
    vlink="#800080" alink="#ff0000">
    <center>
        <a href="http://www.example.com/">
            <img src="image1.gif" width="50" height="10"
                border="0"
                name="catbtn" id="catbtn" alt="catbtn" /></a>
    </center>
</body>
</html>
```

Two images, cleverly titled image1.gif and image2.gif, are available to swap within the img element. To identify the image, you refer to it by name (here, `catbtn`) and `src`, which is a property of the `catbtn` image object. For example, to change the image (but not change it back), you can use a statement such as the following:

```
onmouseover="catbtn.src='image2.gif'; return true;"
```

In the context of the `img` element set to `image1.gif`, the onmouseover statement looks like this:

```
<a href="http://www.example.com/"
    onmouseover="catbtn.src='image2.gif'; return true; ">
<img src="image1.gif" width="50" height="10" border="0"
    name="catbtn" id="catbtn" alt="catbtn" /></a>
```

Triggering this statement changes the source (`src`) property of the object named `catbtn` to `image2.gif`.

Similarly, to change the image back when the cursor moves away, use an `onmouseout` statement with the opposite image setting, as shown here:

```
<a href="http://www.example.com/"
    onmouseover="catbtn.src='image2.gif'; return true;"
    onmouseout="catbtn.src='image1.gif'; return true;">
<img src="image1.gif" width="50" height="10" border="0"
    name="catbtn" id="catbtn" alt="catbtn" /></a>
```

The complete code for simple image swapping with two images is shown in Listing 3.2. Note that this is just a contrived example. If you enter this code in a text editor, it will work only if you have two images titled `image1.gif` and `image2.gif`.

Listing 3.2: Simple Image Swapping with Two Images

```
<!DOCTYPE html PUBLIC "-//W3C/DTD XHTML 1.0 Transitional//EN"
    "http://www.w3.org/TR/xhtml1/DTD/xhtml1-transitional.dtd">
<html xmlns="http://www.w3.org/1999/xhtml">
<head>
    <title>Image Swap</title>
</head>
<body bgcolor="#ffffff" text="#000000" link="#0000ff"
      vlink="#800080" alink="#ff0000">
    <center>
        <a href="http://www.example.com/"
           onmouseover="catbtn.src='image2.gif'; return true;"
           onmouseout="catbtn.src='image1.gif'; return true;">
        <img src="image1.gif" width="50" height="10" border="0"
           name="catbtn" id="catbtn" alt="catbtn" /></a>
```

```
        </center>
      </body>
      </html>
```

For a series of images, you use a series of if statements in a function to make the changes. Using if statements keeps your code easier to read and makes it easier to change your script later. You can add more statements to reshuffle images in different contexts by adding a function like this in the head section of your document:

```
function imagereplacer(place) {
    if (place==1) document.catbtn.src="image2.gif";
    if (place==2) document.catbtn.src="image1.gif";  }
```

The if statements check for the value of place and change the image accordingly. You call this function from the body of your document. Instead of writing the full imagereplacer function in the a element, you put just the function name in the attribute value, with the desired setting for place in the parameter parentheses, as shown here:

```
<a href="http://www.example.com/">
    <img src="image1.gif" width="50" height="10" border="0"
        onmouseover="imagereplacer(1)" alt="catbtn"
        name="catbtn"
        id="catbtn" onmouseout="imagereplacer(2)" />
</a>
```

If you want to do more—such as change the image *and* change the status bar, or if you have several different cases you want to handle without writing if statement after if statement—you can use a special JavaScript keyword, switch, as shown here:

```
function imagereplacer(place) {
    switch (place) {
        case(1): document.catbtn.src="image2.gif";
            window.status="Second Image";
            break;
        case(2): document.catbtn.src="image1.gif";
            window.status="First Image";
            break;  }  }
```

Using this technique, you can list all the options. Similar to the previous if statements, the switch statement lists each option and the action to take, but with switch it's easier to perform multiple or complex actions. In a switch statement, each option is a case. In this example, the first line calls the function and includes the number for the variable place. You use place in the switch statement, which has two cases. If place is equal to one, use case(1), which sets the source property for the image named catbtn (catbtn.src) to image2.gif.

TIP
If you're using objects, methods, properties, or event handlers from early versions of JavaScript, you don't need to add the version to the language attribute. However, if you're using expanded capabilities from later versions— as you'll do with the switch statement here—and functions are defined in the document, include the version number within the attribute; for example, language="javascript1.5".

The change from the if-statement imagereplacer function to the case-statement version requires no changes within your document body. When you put JavaScript functions in the document head, you can make changes without editing all the elements in your code.

WARNING
It's important to test your JavaScript code in as many browsers as possible. The code in Listing 3.2 works in both Netscape Navigator 3 and later and IE 4 and later. However, the code using the switch statement works in IE 4 and later, but only in Netscape Navigator 6 and later.

Using *onclick* and *onchange* Event Handlers

In addition to onmouseover and onmouseout event handlers, you can use onclick and onchange event handlers, which are activated when users click an object or a button or change a form field, respectively. Including these event handlers is similar to using the onmouseover and onmouseout event handlers. You can use the onchange or onclick event handler to set link destinations in forms, among other things.

Alerting Users with *onclick*

A handy use for the onclick event is an alert box, which is a small dialog box that contains a message and an OK button. For example, an alert could be an expanded note about the object, such as *Come to this page for more news on this year's programs!*

At its simplest, you can combine an event handler (to start the process) with an alert, like this:

```
<img src="infolink.jpg" alt="link"
    onclick="alert('Visit NYT!'); return true;" />
```

Users see the accompanying dialog box and must click OK to proceed. Alerts can be quite irritating, however, so use them with care. For example, you can combine the alert with form-validation information and base the alert box on the user's form responses.

Setting Link Destinations in Forms

One of the handiest JavaScript functions is setting link destinations in forms to direct users to information based on their selections in the form. For example, if a form contains a Course Offered selection list, users can choose courses that interest them, and you can programmatically set the destination of a jump to meet the needs of the selections. You can also use JavaScript to set destinations so that when a user clicks buttons or performs other actions on the page, the script opens new pages—just as traditional links would. This technique can add visual interest to your pages as well as let you interactively produce new pages for your users.

Minimally, to set destinations and activate links, use the `onclick` event handler, as shown here:

```
<form>
    <input type="radio" name="lesson" value="Lesson 1"
      onclick="self.location='lesson1.html'" />
    Lesson 1: Getting Started
</form>
```

The `self.location='lesson1.html'` entry opens the file `lesson1.html` in the same window when a user clicks the radio button. If you want the document to open in a separate window, the process is similar. For example, to open `lesson1.html` in another frame, called `main`, you can use the following:

```
<input type="radio" name="lesson" value="Lesson 1"
  onclick="parent.main.location='lesson1.html'" />
    Lesson 1: Getting Started
```

TIP

The `parent.main.location` object name refers to the `parent` document. In this example, that would be the frameset document; this name then refers to the `main` object (frame) within the frameset, then the `location` property of the frame.

A single jump can also lead to a variable destination—the document opened depends on the user's selection from a list. Say your document contains catalog information, such as pictures, product descriptions, and prices. A user clicks a category to open the correct page of your catalog. Users might also select activities from a list such as this:

```
<form>
    <select name="Activity"
            onchange="setLink(this.selectedIndex)">
        <option>Hiking</option>
        <option>Camping</option>
        <option selected="selected">Mountain</option>
        <option>Sailing</option>
        <option>Winter</option>
    </select>
</form>
```

The onchange event handler passes information to a function called setLink. The selectedIndex property is the position in the list (starting with zero of the current selection in the list). So, this.selectedIndex is the numeric value that represents the position in the current list of the value selected.

A relatively simple function setLink, located in the document head, assigns the final URL to the page properties and loads the new URL:

```
<script type="text/javascript" language="javascript">
    <!--
    function setLink(num) {
        if (num = 0) { self.location="hiking.html"   }
        if (num = 1) { self.location="camping.html"   }
        if (num = 2) { self.location="mountain.html"  }
        if (num = 3) { self.location="sailing.html"   }
        if (num = 4) { self.location="winter.html"    }  }
    //-->
</script>
```

With this type of scripting, it's easier to figure out what's going on, to make changes later, and to accommodate unique, nonsequential names, such as newmountainbikes.html or augustactivities.html.

Using the *onsubmit* Event Handler

One of the most common uses for the onsubmit event handler is validating form input. You can verify that users fill in required fields, that they make required selections, or that they fill in an appropriate combination of fields. Suppose you provide a form that lets users purchase T-shirts. You can use JavaScript to verify that users include their mailing address, provide a credit card number, and specify a color. If you lack any of this input from users, you won't be able to complete the order.

The following examples, based on the TECHWR-L general information form, show a couple of approaches to form validation. These examples assume a form with `name="survey"`. If your form is named differently, please adjust accordingly. You can also substitute `form[0]` for the name of the first form within your page.

You can use the following generic script to loop through your form and check for forgotten or omitted values:

```
<script type="text/javascript" language="javascript">
   <!--
   function checkOut() {
      for (x = 0; x < document.survey.elements.length; x++) {
         if (document.survey.elements[x].value == "") {
            alert("Sorry, you forgot one of the required
                  fields. Please try again.")
            break; } }
      return false; }
   //-->
</script>
```

To check your form, use `onsubmit="checkOut(this.form)"` in your form element. The script looks through each of the fields in your form to see whether any are completely empty; if there's an empty field, an alert appears with the *Sorry...* text, and then the function completes.

TIP

For a more sophisticated (and user-friendly) solution, consider making the script report back to the user which field was not completed. Your users will thank you.

If some fields need to be filled and some don't, or if you need to check specific values, you can handle these situations. For example, to ensure that the first name field (called `firstname`) is filled out and not too short (fewer than two characters), add the following `if` statement to the script:

```
if (document.survey.firstname.value.length <= 2) {
   alert("Please enter your full first name.")
   return false; }
```

The complete script looks like this:

```
<script type="text/javascript" language="javascript">
   <!--
   function checkOut() {
      for (x = 0; x < document.survey.elements.length; x++) {
         if (document.survey.elements[x].value == "") {
```

```
            alert("Sorry, you forgot one of the required
                fields. Please try again.")
            break; } }
    return false;
    if (document.survey.firstname.value.length <= 2) {
        alert("Please enter your full first name.")
        return false; } }
//-->
</script>
```

You can continue adding other conditions in the same way.

One of the more complex validation problems involves e-mail addresses. Although more complex scripts are available, you'll probably find that a basic check to ensure the address includes something, an @ sign, and something else (like kelly@somewhere) will suffice:

```
<script type="text/javascript" language="javascript">
    <!--
    function checkOut() {
        for (x = 0; x < document.survey.elements.length; x++){
            if (document.survey.elements[x].value == "") {
                alert("Sorry, you forgot one of the required
                    fields. Please try again.")
                break; } }
        return false;
        if (document.survey.firstname.value.length <= 2){
            alert("Please enter your full first name.")
            return false }
        if (document.survey.emailaddr.value.indexOf('@')==-1 ){
            alert("Please correct your email address. It
                should look like you@domain.com")
        return false } }
//-->
</script>
```

This addition verifies that the address contains an @ and that something after the @ exists. If you need more comprehensive validation, check out the scripts at JavaScript.com.

Using the *onload* Event Handler

The onload event handler is activated when a document loads in a web browser. After a user clicks a link (or follows a bookmark, or whatever), the new page is transferred from the server and loaded into the browser. The onload event handler is activated as soon as the necessary functions and the opening body element load.

You can use this event handler to play a sound file or to launch annoying pop-up ads, but you can also use it for more practical purposes. For example, if you have a website that does not use frames, you might want to use an `onload` event handler to ensure that your pages are not loaded into frames. In other words, if you are in charge of the ASR Outfitters website, you would not want to be "framed," as shown in Figure 3.1.

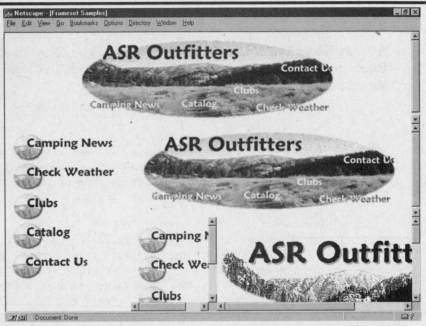

FIGURE 3.1:   You can use event handlers to keep from being "framed," as ASR Outfitters is here.

In this example, you first check the `location` property of the `window` object to see whether it is top, meaning it is not embedded in a frameset. If the property is not top, the JavaScript function resets the `location` property to make it top.

To use an `onload` event handler, you must do two things:

▶ Create the function you want to use.

▶ Add the `onload` event handler to the opening body element.

As you have done previously, you create the script in the document head. Here's how:

1. In an HTML or XHTML document, add the `script` element and comment lines in the document head:

```
<!DOCTYPE html PUBLIC
    "-//W3C/DTD XHTML 1.0 Transitional//EN"
"http://www.w3.org/TR/xhtml1/DTD/
➡xhtml1-transitional.dtd">
<html xmlns="http://www.w3.org/1999/xhtml">
<head>
    <title>Framed Document</title>
    <script type="text/javascript" language="javascript">
        <!--
        //-->
    </script>
</head>
<body>
    <h1>Framed Document</h1>
    <p>Content goes here</p>
</body>
</html>
```

2. Name the function `breakFrames` and add the needed braces:

```
<script type="text/javascript" language="javascript">
    <!--
    function breakFrames() {  }
    //-->
</script>
```

3. Add the `if` statement to determine whether the document is within a frameset:

```
<script type="text/javascript" language="javascript">
    <!--
    function breakFrames() {
        if (window.top.location != window.self.location){}
    //-->
</script>
```

4. Add the action to be performed when the `if` statement is true (that is, when the document is included in frames):

```
<script type="text/javascript" language="javascript">
    <!--
    function breakFrames() {
        if (window.top.location != window.self.location )
```

```
{ window.top.location = window.self.location }
    //-->
</script>
```

5. Add a `return true` statement. Again, this serves to tell the JavaScript interpreter that the function is done:

```
<script type="text/javascript" language="javascript">
    <!--
    function breakFrames() {
        if (window.top.location != window.self.location )
{ window.top.location = window.self.location }
        return true;  }
    //-->
</script>
```

6. With this `breakFrames` script in the document head, now you need to call the script from within the body element to execute the entire function. Add an `onload` statement to the body element:

```
<body onload="breakFrames()">
```

Listing 3.3 shows the complete code.

Listing 3.3: JavaScript Using an `onload` Event Handler

```
<!DOCTYPE html PUBLIC
    "-//W3C/DTD XHTML 1.0 Transitional//EN"
  "http://www.w3.org/TR/xhtml1/DTD/xhtml1-transitional.dtd">
        <html xmlns="http://www.w3.org/1999/xhtml">
<head>
    <title>Framed Document</title>
    <script type="text/javascript" language="javascript">
        <!--
    function breakFrames() {
        if (window.top.location != window.self.location)
{ window.top.location = window.self.location }
        return true;  }
        //-->
    </script>
</head>
<body onload="breakFrames()">
    <h1>Framed Document</h1>
    <p>Content goes here</p>
</body>
</html>
```

With the event handler and script in place, your document will break out of any frameset in which it appears (including your own, of course).

Tracking Users with Cookies

Cookies are objects you can use to store information about users of your site, and that you can access with JavaScript. You can think of cookies as high-tech nametags that identify your browser and pass along a little other information to a server computer. For example, if you visit the Amazon.com website using your Opera browser and purchase a book there, the Amazon .com server deposits a cookie on your computer. The next time you visit that site with that browser, the server looks for the cookie so it can identify you. The cookie on your computer is matched to information about you that is stored on the server, such as the information you provided and the books you purchased. In this case, cookies can help make subsequent visits easier, because users don't have to reenter information.

Although the security risk to users is minor, many people are (understandably) sensitive about having information stored about them and read by other computers. For that reason, browsers now offer users a lot of control over how cookies are handled. Early versions of Netscape Navigator simply accepted all cookies. Now, most browsers that recognize cookies have an option to warn users when a cookie is created and give users the option to accept or reject individual cookies, or to reject cookies that are not coming from the same site you are browsing.

TIP

Most browsers include options for handling cookies. In Netscape Navigator, select Edit ➢ Preferences ➢ Advanced to specify how you want the browser to handle cookies. In IE, go to Tools ➢ Internet Options ➢ Privacy for cookie options. The default in both browsers is to enable cookies, so you need to change the options only if you want to disable cookies, or if you want to receive a message before allowing a cookie to be placed in your computer.

Either way, the cookie information is not public property; the cookie stores information for you only, and not for public broadcast. Additionally, the cookie generally just contains information to identify you to the server, and then the server associates that information ("aha, it's Jane Doe, back for more books") with your address and book-purchasing history, for example. When the server asks your browser for the cookie, it can only see and read the cookie it deposited, not other cookies, files, or information.

You can track users to your website using two types of cookies:

▶ *Session cookies*, which endure only until a user closes the browser

▶ *Persistent cookies*, which endure until the expiration date you set

Session Cookies

Suppose you want to keep some information about a user's browsing session, such as the pages browsed or the products viewed. You can do so using session cookies. This JavaScript not only records the user's session information, but also sends a message to the user when he or she arrives at and exits your site.

TIP

This example shows some of the capabilities and power of cookies. It's also likely to irritate some users. Even if they know that cookies can be set and used, they probably don't want to be overtly reminded of the fact.

To implement session cookies, first create an empty cookie when the page loads. Start with a functional document, such as the following:

```
<!DOCTYPE html PUBLIC "-//W3C/DTD XHTML 1.0 Transitional//EN"
    "http://www.w3.org/TR/xhtml1/DTD/xhtml1-transitional.dtd">
<html xmlns="http://www.w3.org/1999/xhtml">
<head>
    <title>ASR Outfitters Cookie Form</title>
</head>
<body>
    Cookie Bearing Document
</body>
</html>
```

Now, follow these steps:

1. Add a function to the document head element that sets the document cookie to the local time and date:

```
<script type="text/javascript" language="javascript">
    <!--
    function homeMadeCookies() {
        var gotHere = new Date();
        document.cookie = gotHere.toLocaleString()  }
    // -->
</script>
```

2. Initialize the cookie from the `onload` event handler:

```
<body onload="homeMadeCookies()">
```

The `onload` event handler starts the function called `home-MadeCookies`, which creates and places a value into the variable `gotHere`. From that information, the next line converts the GMT time to local time and stores that in `document.cookie`.

3. By setting up a second function, you can display a message when the user leaves. The `fareWell` function looks like this:

```
function fareWell() {
    var timedVisit = new Date();
    var tempTime = timedVisit.toLocaleString();
    alert("You got here at: " + document.cookie +
            " and now it's: " + tempTime + ".  " +
            "Thank you for visiting our site.");  }
```

4. By adding an `onunload` event handler to the body element, you can display the farewell message:

```
<body onload="homeMadeCookies()" onunload="fareWell()">
```

The `fareWell` entry uses an alert to display a brief—cookie-based—message thanking the user, as shown in Figure 3.2.

FIGURE 3.2:   You can use cookies to produce alerts specific to the user's situation.

Persistent Cookies

You can also store information in cookies for a period of time. You use persistent cookies when you want to store information and use it in the future. For example, if a user fills out a form that includes his or her name and other personal information, you want to keep that information and use it when the user visits in the future. This is, for example, how the Amazon.com site tracks your visits and seems to know things about you during subsequent visits.

Here are some facts you should know about persistent cookies:

▶ A browser retains a limited number of cookies. Older cookies are discarded to make room for new ones.

▶ A cookie cannot be larger than 4KB.

▶ You can have only 20 cookies per domain, per user.

These restrictions may not seem limiting at first, but they become so when the demand for feedback increases. Unlike session cookies, persistent cookies need an expiration date. After the cookie expires, a former user is treated as a new user.

TIP

Matt's Script Archive includes a section titled HTTP Cookie Library that provides an excellent overview of the subject, pointers to many important resources, and a helpful list of FAQs. You'll find all this material online at www.scriptarchive .com/faq/cookielib.html. Also see www.cookiecentral.com/faq/ for lots of good information.

WHAT'S NEXT

In this chapter, we introduced you to JavaScript and showed you some of the most basic (and useful) JavaScript functions. As you can see, JavaScript offers a variety of useful applications and can help you create cutting-edge documents. From here, you can wander to several chapters. Here's what we recommend:

▶ See Chapter 4 for lots more information about working with objects.

▶ See Chapter 5 for a more in-depth treatment of JavaScript and Forms.

- ▶ See Chapter 6 for a more comprehensive discussion of JavaScript and Cookies.

- ▶ Appendix A offers a comprehensive guide to JavaScript, which you can use to expand on the basics in this chapter.

TIP

You'll find lots of scripts available for public use on the Web. For starters, go to `javascript.internet.com`. You could also search for "JavaScript" at `www.yahoo.com`, `www.google.com`, or other search services, or visit `www.javascript.com`.

Chapter 4

WORKING WITH OBJECTS

O ne of the most important features of JavaScript is that it is an object-based language. This fact simplifies the design of JavaScript programs and enables them to be developed in a more intuitive, modular, and reusable manner.

This chapter describes JavaScript's support of objects and object-based programming. It introduces the JavaScript object model and summarizes the predefined JavaScript objects supported by both Internet Explorer and Netscape Navigator. It also shows how to create your own object types. When you finish this chapter, you'll be able to define and use objects in your web pages.

Adapted from *Mastering JavaScript Premium Edition* by James Jaworski
ISBN 0-7821-2819-X

WHAT ARE OBJECTS?

Objects are entities that exist in the real world of people, places, and things. But they also exist in the cyber world of computers and networking. Examples of real-world objects include you, the book you are reading, and the lamp that you use to provide you with light. Examples of cyber-world objects are the web pages you create and the individual HTML elements they contain. I will discuss these types of objects in relation to JavaScript.

An object consists of two things:

▶ A collection of *properties* that contain data

▶ *Methods* that enable operations on the data contained in those properties

When you view something as an object, you look at it in terms of its properties and methods. Table 4.1 identifies some of the properties and methods that could apply to the example objects mentioned in the previous paragraph.

TABLE 4.1:   Examples of Objects, Properties, and Methods

OBJECT	PROPERTIES	METHODS
You (real-world object)	height	eat()
	weight	exercise()
	hairColor	grow()
This book (real-world object)	pages	turnPageForward()
	currentPage	turnPageBackward()
		goToPage()
A lamp (real-world object)	onOffState	turnOn()
		turnOff()
A web page (cyber-world object)	title	open()
	bgColor	close()
	links	write()
An HTML button (cyber-world object)	name	setLabel()
	value	

You've already seen several examples of JavaScript objects. You've used the document object and its write() method in many of the scripts in previous chapters. You've also used the alert() method of the window object to display messages to the user. The fields of a form are also objects. You've seen how the value property of a field can be used to test and set the field's value. By the time you finish this chapter, you will have encountered all the predefined JavaScript objects supported by both Internet Explorer (IE) and Navigator and learned how to create objects of your own.

What Is Object-Oriented Programming?

The field of software engineering has evolved over the 50 or so years of the computer's existence. This evolution has brought about different approaches and strategies to the task of creating high-quality software while minimizing development time and costs. The most successful development approach currently in use is the *object-oriented* approach. Object-oriented programming (OOP) *models* the elements of a software application as objects—object types are named, their properties are identified, and their methods are described. Once an object type is defined, it can be used to create specific instances of other objects of that type and to construct other, more complex object types.

NOTE
An object type is referred to as a *class* in object-oriented languages such as Java and C++.

Object Types and Instances

An *object type* is a template from which specific objects of that type are created. It defines the properties and methods common to all objects of that type. For example, let's consider a person's mailing address as an object type. I'll name it MailAddress and give it the properties streetAddress, city, state, and postalCode. I'll also define changeAddress() as a method for changing one person's address and findAddress() as a method for finding out another person's address. (Don't worry about how I'm doing this—you'll learn that later. For this explanation, focus on what's being done.)

When I define the `MailAddress` object type, I haven't specified anyone's address. I've only developed a template for the creation of an address—kind of like a blank Rolodex card. The address type can be *instantiated*, which is the programming term for creating a specific *instance* of that type of object; in this case, it would mean creating a specific person's address record. This is similar to producing a Rolodex card, filling it in, and sticking it in the Rolodex. The capability to define an object type from which specific object instances can then be created is a basic but important feature of object-oriented software development.

Creating Object Types

Although the definition and instantiation of object types is a basic feature of object-oriented languages, it is not the only feature these languages provide. The ability to use object types to define *other* object types is what really gives OOP its power. You can do this in two major ways: through *object composition* and *inheritance*.

Object Composition

One approach to developing object types is to define primitive object types that serve as simple building blocks from which more complex types can be composed. This approach is referred to as *object composition*. Consider the process of building a house. Somebody must make the boards, nails, and glass panes that are used as the basic building blocks for constructing most homes. These building objects are assembled into more complex objects such as doors, windows, and prefabricated walls. These more complex objects are then, in turn, assembled into larger objects that eventually are integrated into a finished home. In the same way that these simple objects are used to construct a wide variety of different homes, simple object types are used in programming to create more complex object types that are eventually integrated into a final software application. For example, the `MailAddress` object can be used to create an employment application form, which is itself used to create a personnel database system.

Object composition is closely related to and depends on the capability to support *object re-use*. When an object type is defined, it is often desirable that it be defined in such a way that it can be reused in other software applications. This reuse simplifies the development of other applications, and leads to cost and schedule savings. The reuse of software objects is just as important as the reuse of technology in other engineering disciplines.

Encapsulation: Packaging Objects   Software objects are reusable when they follow certain design principles. One of the most important principles is *encapsulation*: the packaging of an object's properties and methods into a container with an appropriately defined interface. The object's interface must provide the methods and properties that enable the object to be used in the intended manner and must do it without providing methods or properties that would allow the object to be misused. If this abstract description is difficult to fathom, consider the interface of an automobile. Auto designers provide standardized steering, braking, and throttling capabilities in all cars, because these capabilities are basic to driving. However, no automobile manufacturer provides drivers with the capability to manually control the firing of spark plugs from the dashboard. Even if drivers were provided with this capability, they more than likely could not use it to any advantage.

Modularity and Information Hiding   Encapsulation depends on two important concepts for its success. The first concept, *modularity*, refers to an object's being complete in and of itself and not accessing other objects outside their defined interfaces. Modular objects are said to be *loosely coupled*, which means dependencies between objects are minimized, and internal changes to an object do not require changes in other objects that make use of the object. The second concept, *information hiding*, refers to the practice of limiting information about an object to that required to use the object's interface. It is accomplished by removing information about the internal operation of an object from the object's interface.

Inheritance: A Hierarchical Approach to Object Design

The second major way of constructing object types from other object types is through *inheritance*. In this approach, higher-level, more abstract object types are defined, and from these defined objects, lower-level, more concrete object types are derived. When a lower-level object type is created, it identifies one or more higher-level object types as its *parent* type. The *child* type inherits all the properties and methods of its parents. This approach eliminates the need to redefine these properties and methods. The child type is free to redefine any of the methods that it inherits or to add new properties and methods. Thus the child type can tailor its inherited characteristics to new situations.

As an example, consider the various types of objects that can be constructed to implement a scrolling marquee. At the highest level, you can construct a `GenericMarquee` that has the basic properties `scrolledText` and `scrollRate` and provides basic methods, such as `startScrolling()` and `stopScrolling()`. From this generic marquee, you can create more complex marquees. For example, you can construct `HorizontalMarquee` and `VerticalMarquee` object types that add the property `scrollDirection` to those inherited from `GenericMarquee`. These, in turn, can be further refined into marquees that use colored text and backgrounds—you can add the properties `textColor` and `backgroundColor` and the methods `randomTextColor()` and `randomBackgroundColor()`.

Using inheritance, more sophisticated, tailored object types can be created from those that are already defined. You do so by adding the properties and methods needed to differentiate the new objects from their parents. Once a useful object type is created, you can reuse it many times to create several child objects and numerous generations of offspring.

Classification and Inheritance   OOP languages, such as Java and C++ (but not JavaScript), refer to an object's type as its *class* and provide the capability to develop child classes from parent classes using inheritance. The resulting class structure is called a *classification scheme*. The classification schemes that result from object-oriented development mimic those that are fundamental to the way human beings acquire and organize knowledge. For example, we develop general class names, such as *animal*, that we use to refer to large groups of real-world objects. We then develop names of subclasses, such as *mammal*, *bird*, and *reptile*, which we use to refine our concept of animal. We continue to develop more detailed classes that differentiate between objects of the same class. Developers of object-oriented programs carry out the same sort of classification process.

Single and Multiple Inheritance   Part of the reason inheritance is a successful approach to object development is that it mimics the way we acquire and organize knowledge—it is therefore *intuitive* to us. In addition, inheritance is *efficient*, because it only requires you to define the properties and methods that are unique for an object's type.

Some languages, notably Java, enforce a more restricted form of inheritance, known as *single inheritance*. Single inheritance requires that a child class have only one parent. However, a parent may have multiple children. Because a child class inherits its properties and methods from a single parent, it is an exact duplicate of its parent before it adds its own unique properties and methods.

Other languages, notably C++, support *multiple inheritance*. As you might expect, multiple inheritance allows child classes to inherit their properties and methods from more than one parent class. Multiple inheritance is much more powerful than single inheritance, because it allows independent—but complementary—branches of the class structure to be fused together into a single branch.

Multiple inheritance does, however, introduce some difficulties with respect to name resolution. Suppose that class C is the child of both class A and class B. Suppose also that class A and B define different save() methods. Which of these two methods is inherited by class C? How does the compiler determine which method to use for objects of class C? Although it is possible to develop naming schemes and compilers that resolve naming difficulties resulting from multiple inheritance, these solutions often require a significant amount of additional compilation and runtime processing.

Polymorphism: Many Methods with the Same Name   Although it may seem undesirable to have many methods with the same name, the capability to do so is a feature of OOP. *Polymorphism* is the capability to take on different forms. It allows an object type to define several different implementations of a method. These methods are differentiated by the types and number of parameters they accept. For example, you can define several different print() methods, each of which is used to print objects of different object types. You can define other print() methods that take a different number of parameters. The interpreter, compiler, or runtime system selects the print() method that is most appropriate for the object being printed. Polymorphism allows the programmer to use a standard method, such as print(), to perform a particular operation and to define different forms of the method to be used with different parameters. This approach promotes standardization and reusable software and eliminates the need to come up with many slightly different names to distinguish the same operation being performed with different parameters.

JavaScript's Object-Based Programming Features

In the previous section, you learned about the capabilities that are common to OOP languages. JavaScript does not support several of the capabilities described, but Java does support them. It is worth your while to become familiar with the OOP capabilities described in the preceding section. That way, you'll be ready to eventually begin learning how Java applets can be integrated with JavaScript scripts. In this section, you'll learn which OOP capabilities JavaScript supports and how they are used to develop object-based JavaScript programs.

JavaScript does not support the basic OOP capabilities of encapsulation and information hiding. However, this is not as bad as it first appears. JavaScript is a scripting language, not a full programming language. The features it does provide are geared toward letting you quickly and easily generate scripts that execute in the context of a web page or a server-side application.

JavaScript supports the development of object types and the instantiation of these types to create object instances. It provides great support for object composition, but only fair support for modularity and object reuse. Table 4.2 summarizes JavaScript's object-based programming capabilities.

TABLE 4.2: JavaScript's Object-Based Programming Capabilities

CAPABILITY	DESCRIPTION
Classification	Because JavaScript supports inheritance, you can use it to develop a hierarchy of object types.
Encapsulation	Because JavaScript lacks information-hiding capabilities, you cannot use it to develop encapsulated object types. Any method or property that is defined for a type is always directly accessible.
Information hiding	JavaScript does not provide any capabilities to support information hiding.
Inheritance	An object type can extend and inherit the properties and methods of another object type.
Modularity	JavaScript code can be defined in a modular fashion, but JavaScript does not provide any features that enforce modular software development.
Object composition	Object types can be defined in terms of other predefined or user-defined object types.

TABLE 4.2 continued: JavaScript's Object-Based Programming Capabilities

Capability	Description
Object instantiation	Object types are instantiated using the new operator to create specific object instances.
Object reuse	JavaScript software can be reused via the SRC attribute of the SCRIPT tag. Software can be made available for reuse via the Internet.
Object types	JavaScript supports both predefined and user-defined object types. However, JavaScript does not provide capabilities for type enforcement. You can assign an object of any type to any variable.
Polymorphism	JavaScript supports polymorphism using the arguments array for function definitions.

Although JavaScript does not provide all the features of full OOP languages, it does provide a suite of object-based features that are specially tailored to browser and server scripting. These features include a number of predefined browser and server objects and the capability to access related objects through the properties and methods of other objects. If this seems abstract, don't worry—you'll see several concrete examples of these features throughout this chapter.

THE JAVASCRIPT OBJECT MODEL

JavaScript supports a simple object model that is supported by a number of predefined objects. The *JavaScript object model* centers around the specification of object types that are used to create specific object instances. Object types under this model are defined in terms of properties and methods:

- *Properties* are used to access the data values contained in an object. Properties, by default, can be updated as well as read, although some properties of the predefined JavaScript objects are read-only.

- *Methods* are functions used to perform operations on an object. Methods can use the object's properties to perform these operations.

NOTE

This chapter describes the JavaScript object model as introduced in JavaScript 1.2 and as implemented in all recent releases of both Netscape Navigator and IE. Each of these browsers also provides browser-specific objects, methods, and properties.

Using Properties

You access an object's properties by combining the object's name and its property name as follows:

objectName.propertyName

For example, the background color of the current web document is identified by the bgColor property of the predefined document object. To change the background color to white, you can use the following JavaScript statement:

```
document.bgColor="white"
```

This statement assigns the string "white" to the bgColor property of the predefined document object. Listing 4.1 shows how you can use this statement in an example script. Figure 4.1 shows the web page the script produces. Several buttons are displayed with the names of different colors. When you click a button, the button's onClick event handler changes the background of the document by setting the document.bgColor property.

Listing 4.1: Using JavaScript Properties

```
<HTML>
<HEAD>
<TITLE>Using Properties</TITLE></HEAD>
<BODY>
<H1>Using Properties</H1>
<FORM>
<P><INPUT TYPE="BUTTON" NAME="red" VALUE="Red"
  ONCLICK='document.bgColor="red"'></P>
<P><INPUT TYPE="BUTTON" NAME="white" VALUE="White"
  ONCLICK='document.bgColor="white"'></P>
<P><INPUT TYPE="BUTTON" NAME="blue" VALUE="Blue"
  ONCLICK='document.bgColor="blue"'></P>
</FORM>
</BODY>
</HTML>
```

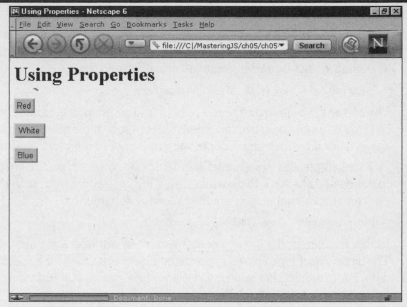

FIGURE 4.1: Using properties to change background colors (Listing 4.1)

Using Methods

You access an object's methods in the same manner as its properties:

```
objectName.methodName(parameterList)
```

The parameters, if any, are separated by commas. The parentheses must be used even if no parameters are specified. The following is an example of a method invocation:

```
r=Math.random()
```

The random() method of the predefined Math object is invoked. This method returns a random floating-point number between 0 and 1. The number is then assigned to the r variable.

You have been using the methods of predefined JavaScript objects since your first script in Chapter 3, "Adding JavaScript." You've used the write() method of the document object to generate HTML entities that are written to the current document. You've also used the alert() method of the window object to display pop-up dialog boxes. In the next section, you'll be introduced to some of the objects that are automatically created by JavaScript-capable browsers. Later in this chapter, all the predefined JavaScript objects will be introduced in summary form.

Creating Instances of Objects

You create instances of objects of a particular object type using the new operator. You've previously used the new operator to create array objects. The same syntax is used to create objects of other types:

```
variable = new objectType(parameters)
```

The objectType(parameters) portion of the previous statement is referred to as the *constructor*. Some object types have more than one constructor. Constructors differ in the number of parameters they allow.

For example, Date is a predefined JavaScript object type. To create an instance of Date with the current date and time and assign it to the currentDate variable, you use the following statement:

```
currentDate = new Date()
```

In this statement, the Date() constructor does not take any parameters. The Date object type also lets you create object instances for a specified date. For example, the following statement creates an instance of Date for January 1, 2005:

```
currentDate = new Date(2005,0,1)
```

The constructor used in the previous statement, Date(2005,0,1), takes three parameters. The Date object type provides other constructors in addition to the ones described in this section. (The Date object type is formally introduced later in this chapter in the section "The Date Object.")

BROWSER OBJECTS

When a web page is loaded by a JavaScript-capable browser, the browser creates a number of JavaScript objects that provide access to the web page and the HTML elements it contains. These objects are used to update and interact with the loaded web page. Table 4.3 identifies these objects and summarizes their use.

TABLE 4.3: Browser Objects

Object	Use
anchor object	To access the target of a hypertext link.
anchors array	To access all anchor objects within a document.
applet object	To access a Java applet.

TABLE 4.3 continued: Browser Objects

Object	Use
applets array	To access all applets in a document.
area	To access an area within a client-side image map.
button	To access a form button that is not a Submit or Reset button.
checkbox	To access a check box of a form.
document	To access the document currently loaded into a window. A document refers to an HTML document that provides content (that is, one that has HEAD and BODY tags).
elements array	To access all form elements (fields or buttons) contained within a form.
embed object	To access an embedded object.
embeds array	To provide access to all embedded objects in a document.
event object	To access information about the occurrence of an event. The event object provides information about a specific event.
Event object	To access information about the occurrence of an event. The Event (capitalized) object provides constants that are used to identify events.
fileupload	To access a file upload element of a form.
form object	To access an HTML form.
forms array	To access all forms within a document.
frame object	To access an HTML frame.
frames array	To access all frames within a window.
hidden	To access a hidden field of a form.
history	To maintain a history of the URLs accessed within a window.
image object	To access an image embedded in an HTML document.
images array	To access all image objects within a document.
link object	To access a text- or image-based source anchor of a hypertext link. IE combines the link object with the anchor object.
links array	To access all link objects within a document.
location	To represent a URL. It can be used to create a URL object, access parts of a URL, or modify an existing URL.
mimeType object	To access information about a particular MIME type supported by a browser.
mimeTypes array	An array of all mimeType objects supported by a browser. IE provides tacit support for mimeTypes, returning an empty array.

TABLE 4.3 continued: Browser Objects

Object	Use
navigator	To access information about the browser that is executing a script.
password	To access a password field of a form.
plugin object	To access information about a particular browser plug-in.
plugins array	An array of all plug-ins supported by a browser. IE provides tacit support for plugins, returning an empty array.
radio	To access a set of radio buttons of a form or to access an individual button within the set.
reset	To access a Reset button of a form.
screen	To access information about the size and color depth of a user's screen.
select option	To access a select list of a form. The option object accesses the elements of a select list.
submit	To access a Submit button of a form.
text	To access a text field of a form.
textarea	To access a text area field of a form.
window	To access a browser window or a frame within a window. The window object is assumed to exist and does not require the window prefix when you refer to its properties and methods.

Table 4.3 summarizes the predefined objects created by a JavaScript-capable browser when a web page is loaded. JavaScript also supports object types that are independent of the web page that is loaded. These objects are described in the "Other Predefined Object Types" section later in this chapter.

The Browser Object Hierarchy

Your browser creates the objects presented in Table 4.3 as the results of web pages you design. For example, if you create a web page with three forms, then the forms array will contain three form objects corresponding to the forms you have defined. Similarly, if you define a document with seven links, then the links array will contain seven link objects that correspond to your links.

The browser objects are organized into a hierarchy that corresponds to the structure of loaded web documents and the current state of the browser. This hierarchy is referred to as an *instance hierarchy*. The window and navigator objects are the highest-level objects in this hierarchy.

The *window* Object

The window object represents a browser window, and it has properties that are used to identify the objects of the HTML elements that form that window. For example, the frames array is a property of a window object. If the window uses the FRAMESET tag to define multiple frames, then the frames array contains the frame object associated with each frame. The window's location property refers to the location object that contains the URL associated with the window. The window's screen property can be used to obtain the user's screen dimensions and color depth. Refer to Table 4.3 for more about the window object's properties.

NOTE

IE combines the link and anchor objects. Both links and anchors can be accessed via the anchors array.

The *navigator* Object

The navigator object, like the window object, is a top-level object in the browser hierarchy. The navigator object describes the configuration of the browser being used to display a window. Two of its properties, mimeTypes and plugins, contain the list of all MIME types and plug-ins supported by the browser—unless you're running IE, that is. IE returns empty arrays for the mimeTypes and plugins properties and instead uses the embeds property to access the objects that have been embedded using EMBED. To be maximally confusing, Netscape Navigator does not support the embeds property.

Hierarchical Object Identifiers

Because your browser organizes the various objects of a web page according to the instance hierarchy described in the previous section, a hierarchical naming scheme is used to identify these objects. For example, suppose an HTML document defines three forms, and the fifth element of the second form is a radio button. You can access the name of this radio button using the following identifier:

```
document.forms[1].element[4].name
```

This identifier refers to the name of the fifth element of the second form of the current document. (Remember that array indices begin at 0.) You can display this name using the following statement:

```
document.write(document.forms[1].element[4].name)
```

NOTE

You do not have to identify the window object when you refer to the current window's properties and methods—your browser assumes the current window object by default. There is one exception, however: In event-handling code, the current document object is assumed by default.

In most cases, you can refer to a property or method of a browser-created object by starting with document and using the property names of the objects that contain the object (such as links, anchors, images, and forms) to identify the object within the instance hierarchy. When you have named the object in this fashion, you can then use the object's property or method name to access the data and functions defined for that object.

Listing 4.2 provides an example of using hierarchical names to access the elements defined within a web document. The document defines a number of functions in the document head. It begins by invoking the open() method of the window object to open a second browser window. This second window is assigned to the outputWindow variable and is used to write the description of the objects defined for the HTML document shown in Listing 4.2. The open() method takes two parameters: the URL of the document to be loaded in the window and a window name. Because you don't want to load a document at another URL, set the URL parameter to a blank string.

Listing 4.2: Using Hierarchical Object Identifiers

```
<HTML>
<HEAD>
<TITLE>Using Hierarchical Object Identifiers</TITLE>
<SCRIPT LANGUAGE="JavaScript"><!--
outputWindow = open("","output")
```

```
function setupWindow() {
 outputWindow.document.write(
  "<HTML><HEAD><TITLE>OutputWindow</TITLE></HEAD><BODY>")
}
function describeBrowser() {
 outputWindow.document.write("<H2>Browser Properties</H2>")
 outputWindow.document.write(navigator.appCodeName+" ")
 outputWindow.document.write(navigator.appName+" ")
 outputWindow.document.write(navigator.appVersion+"<BR>")
 outputWindow.document.write(navigator.mimeTypes.length+
  " MIME types are defined.")
 outputWindow.document.write(navigator.plugins.length+
" plug-ins are installed.")
}
function describeWindow() {
 outputWindow.document.write("<H2>Window Properties</H2>")
 outputWindow.document.write("Frames: "+frames.length+"<BR>")
 outputWindow.document.write("URL: "+location.href+"<BR>")
}
function describeDocument() {
 outputWindow.document.write("<H2>Document Properties</H2>")
 describeLinks()
 describeForms()
}
function describeLinks(){
 outputWindow.document.write("<H3>Links</H3>")
 outputWindow.document.write("This document contains "
  +document.links.length+" links:<BR>")
 for(i=0;i<document.links.length;++i)
  outputWindow.document.write(document.links[i].href+"<BR>")
}
function describeForms() {
 outputWindow.document.write("<H3>Forms</H3>")
 for(i=0;i<document.forms.length;++i) describeForm(i)
}
function describeForm(n) {
 outputWindow.document.write("Form "+n+" has "
  +document.forms[n].elements.length+" elements:")
 for(j=0;j<document.forms[n].elements.length;++j)
  outputWindow.document.write(" "
   + document.forms[n].elements[j].name)
 outputWindow.document.write("<BR>")
}
```

```
function finishWindow() {
 outputWindow.document.write("<FORM><INPUT Type='button'
➡Value='Close Window' onClick='window.close()'></FORM>")
 outputWindow.document.write("</BODY></HTML>")
}
// --></SCRIPT></HEAD>
<BODY>
<H1>Using Hierarchical Object Identifiers</H1>
<P><A HREF="http://www.javascript.com/">Link to
  JavaScript web site.</A></P>
<P><A HREF="http://home.netscape.com/">Link
to Netscape's home
 page.</A></P>
<FORM>
<P><INPUT TYPE="TEXT" NAME="textField1"
 VALUE="Enter text here!"></P>
<P><INPUT TYPE="CHECKBOX" NAME="checkbox1"
 CHECKED="CHECKED">I'm checkbox1.</P>
<P><INPUT TYPE="CHECKBOX" NAME="checkbox2">I'm
checkbox2.</P>
<INPUT TYPE="SUBMIT" NAME="submitButton" VALUE="Click here!">
</FORM>
<SCRIPT LANGUAGE="JavaScript"><!--
setupWindow()
describeBrowser()
describeWindow()
describeDocument()
finishWindow()
// --></SCRIPT>
</BODY>
</HTML>
```

The setupWindow() function generates the head of the second document and its opening BODY tag. It uses the outputWindow variable to select the second window as the target for writing. This function and other functions in the script write their output using statements of the form

```
outputWindow.document.write()
```

These statements tell JavaScript to write to the document object of the window object identified by the outputWindow variable.

The describeBrowser() function displays some of the navigator object's properties to the second window. It also uses the outputWindow variable to select this window. It displays the appCodeName, appName, and appVersion, and uses the length property of the mimeTypes and plugins arrays to determine the number of MIME types and plug-ins supported by the browser.

The describeWindow() function displays some properties of the original (first) window. It displays the number of frames defined by the window and the URL of the document loaded into the window. Because the window does not define any frames, the length of the frames array is 0. The href property of the window's location object gets the text string corresponding to the URL. The URL displayed when you execute the script will be different depending on the directory from which you run this chapter's files.

The describeDocument() function displays some of the properties associated with the current document in the second window. It invokes the describeLinks() and describeForms() functions to perform this processing.

The describeLinks() function uses the length property of the links array to identify the number of links contained in the document. It then executes a for loop to display the URL associated with each of these links. The href attribute of the link object gets the text string corresponding to the URL.

The describeForms() function uses the length property of the forms array to iterate through the document's links and display each one. The displayForm() function displays each form.

The displayForm() function uses the length property of the elements array of each form object to identify the number of elements contained in a form. It takes a single parameter, identified by the n variable. This parameter identifies the index into the forms array of the form object being displayed. The name of each field element is displayed by referencing the name property of each object contained in the elements array of each form object identified in the forms array. This is a good example of using hierarchical object naming to access the low-level elements of an HTML document.

The finishWindow() function appends the following HTML to the body of the document displayed in the second window:

```
<FORM>
<INPUT Type='button' Value='Close Window'
 onClick='window.close()'>
</FORM>
</BODY>
</HTML>
```

The form is used to create a button labeled Close Window, which closes the second window. The `onClick` attribute of the `INPUT` tag is assigned the event-handling code, `window.close()`, which closes the window when the button is clicked. The `window` object should be explicitly referenced in event handlers to ensure that the current window is closed and not the current document. The `</BODY>` and `</HTML>` tags are used to end the displayed document.

The main body of the HTML document defines two links: one to the useful `Javascript.com` website and one to Netscape's home page. The document then defines a form with four elements: a text field, two check boxes, and a Submit button.

The script contained in the main body of the document invokes the `setupWindow()`, `describeBrowser()`, `describeWindow()`, `describe-Document()`, and `finishWindow()` functions to display the contents of the first window in the second window referenced by the `outputWindow` object. This script is placed at the end of the document so that the various HTML elements of the document are defined when the script is invoked.

A second window is created to display the document's properties. The web browser displays this second window as shown in Figure 4.2. Figure 4.3 shows the original document.

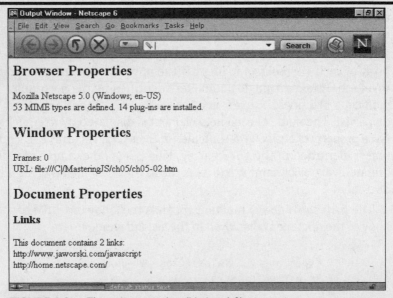

FIGURE 4.2:   The output window (Listing 4.2)

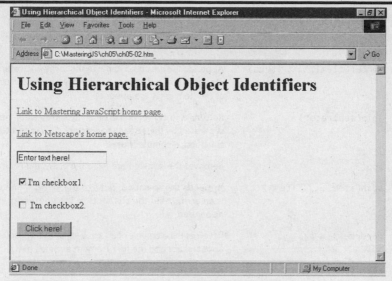

FIGURE 4.3:   The original document window (Listing 4.2)

OTHER PREDEFINED OBJECT TYPES

In addition to the predefined browser objects discussed in earlier sections, JavaScript provides general-purpose object types that support common operations. These object types are defined by the ECMAScript specification and are described in the following sections. Some earlier browsers do not support all the properties and methods of these objects.

The *Array* Object

The Array object allows arrays to be accessed as objects. As discussed in Chapter 2, "Working with JavaScript," the ECMAScript specification defines two properties for the Array object: length and prototype. The length property identifies the length of an array. The prototype property is supported by all object types; it allows additional properties and methods to be defined for an object type. (This property is covered in the "Adding Properties and Methods to an Object Type" section later in this chapter.)

ECMAScript defines the Array methods shown in Table 4.4.

TABLE 4.4: Methods of the Array Object

METHOD	DEFINITION
concat(item1, ..., itemn)	Appends the specified items to the array and returns the modified array. If an item is an array, then the elements of the item array are appended.
join(separator)	Returns a string version of an array. Array elements are separated by the *separator* string. If no separator is specified, a comma is used.
pop()	Removes the last element from the array and returns it.
push(item1, ..., itemn)	Appends the specified items to the array. If an item is an array, then the elements of the item array are appended.
reverse()	Reverses the elements of an array—that is, the last element appears first and the first element appears last.
shift()	Removes the first element from the array and returns it.
slice(start, end)	Returns an array consisting of all elements beginning with the index *start* and ending at the index *end*. If *end* is omitted, then all elements from *start* to the end of the array are returned.
sort(comparisonFunction)	Sorts the elements of an array according to a comparison function. If no comparison function is specified, the array elements are sorted in dictionary order. If a comparison function is specified, it should take two parameters, p1 and p2, and return a negative integer if p1 is less than p2, zero if p1 equals p2, and a positive integer if p1 is greater than p2.
splice(start, deleteCount, item1, ..., itemn)	Replaces the *deleteCount* elements of the array starting at array index *start* with *item1*, ..., *itemn*.
toLocaleString()	Returns a string version of an array. Array elements are separated by locale-specific separators.
toString()	Returns a string version of an array. Array elements are separated by commas.
unshift(item1, ..., itemn)	Prepends the items (in order) to the front of the array.

Listing 4.3 illustrates the use of some of the listed methods. It creates an array of integers 0 through 10 and applies the toString(), join(':'), reverse(), and sort() methods to it. Figure 4.4 shows the results.

Listing 4.3: Using the Methods of the *Array* Object

```html
<HTML>
<HEAD>
<TITLE>Using Arrays</TITLE>
<SCRIPT LANGUAGE="JavaScript"><!--
// --></SCRIPT></HEAD>
<BODY>
<H1>Using Arrays</H1>
<SCRIPT LANGUAGE="JavaScript"><!--
myArray = [0, 1, 2, 3, 4, 5, 6, 7, 8, 9, 10]
document.write("myArray: "+myArray+"<P>")
document.write("myArray.toString(): "+
    myArray.toString()+"<P>")
document.write("myArray.join(':'): "+myArray.join(':')+"<P>")
document.write("myArray.reverse(): "+myArray.reverse()+"<P>")
document.write("myArray.sort: "+myArray.sort())
// --></SCRIPT>
</BODY>
</HTML>
```

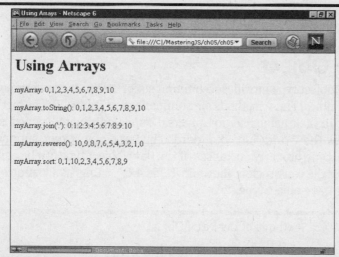

FIGURE 4.4:   The results of applying array methods (Listing 4.3)

NOTE

IE and Navigator provide browser-specific Array methods in addition to those in the ECMAScript specification.

The *Boolean* Object

The `Boolean` object allows Boolean values to be accessed as objects. It supports the `prototype` property and the `toString()` and `valueOf()` methods. The `toString()` method returns the string equivalent of a Boolean value. The `valueOf()` method returns `true` or `false` depending on the value of the underlying object.

You create `Boolean` objects by identifying their value as an argument to the constructor:

```
myBoolean   = new Boolean(false)
yourBoolean = new Boolean(true)
```

Why would you want to create a `Boolean` object instead of just setting a variable to `true` or `false`? By creating a `Boolean` object, you can use the `toString()` and `valueOf()` methods. Although this may not seem to be much of an added capability, when you get to the `Date` object, you'll be able to appreciate the advantages of working with objects instead of primitive values.

Note that you can also call `Boolean` as a function:

```
booleanValue = Boolean(1)
```

This is equivalent to calling the `ToBoolean()` function.

The *Date* Object

The `Date` object type provides a common set of methods for working with dates and times. These methods are summarized in Table 4.5. The methods with *UTC* in their name refer to Universal Time Coordinated, which is the time set by the World Time Standard. The `Date` object type supports the `prototype` property. Instances of the `Date` object type can be created with any of the constructors shown in Table 4.6. Listing 4.4 illustrates the use of the `Date` object type.

TABLE 4.5: Methods of the Date Object

Method	Description
getDate()	Returns or sets the day of the month of the Date object.
getUTCDate()	
setDate(date)	
setUTCDate(date)	

TABLE 4.5 continued: Methods of the Date Object

METHOD	DESCRIPTION
getDay()	Returns the day of the week of the Date object.
getUTCDay()	
getHours()	Returns or sets the hour of the Date object.
getUTCHours()	
setHours (hours [, min, sec, ms])	
setUTCHours (hours [, min, sec, ms])	
getMilliseconds()	Returns or sets the milliseconds value of the Date object.
getUTCMilliseconds()	
setMilliseconds(ms)	
setUTCMilliseconds(ms)	
getMinutes()	Returns or sets the minutes of the Date object.
getUTCMinutes()	
setMinutes (min [, sec, ms])	
setUTCMinutes (min [, sec, ms])	
getMonth()	Returns or sets the month of the Date object.
getUTCMonth()	
setMonth(month [, date])	
setUTCMonth (month [, date])	
getSeconds()	Returns or sets the seconds of the Date object.
getUTCSeconds()	
setSeconds(sec [, ms])	
setUTCSeconds(sec [, ms])	
getTime()	Returns or sets the time of the Date object.
setTime(time)	
getTimeZoneOffset()	Returns the time zone offset (in minutes) of the Date object.
getYear()	Returns or sets the year of the Date object. The full year methods use four-digit year values.
getFullYear()	
getUTCFullYear()	
setYear(year)	
setFullYear (year [,month, date])	
setUTCFullYear (year [,month, date])	

TABLE 4.5 continued: Methods of the Date Object

METHOD	DESCRIPTION
toGMTString()	Converts a date to a string in Internet GMT (Greenwich Mean Time) format.
toLocaleString()	Converts a date to a string in *locale* format, which means the format commonly used in the geographical region in which the user is located.
toLocaleDateString()	
toLocaleTimeString()	
toString()	Returns a string value of a Date object.
toDateString()	
toTimeString()	
valueOf()	Returns the number of milliseconds since midnight on January 1, 1970.
toUTCString()	Returns a string that represents the time in UTC.
parse()	Parses the given date string and returns an instantiated object for the specified date.

TABLE 4.6: Date Constructors

CONSTRUCTOR	DESCRIPTION
Date()	Creates a Date instance with the current date and time.
Date(dateString)	Creates a Date instance with the date specified in the date-String parameter. The format of the dateString is month day, year hours:minutes:seconds.
Date(milliseconds)	Creates a Date instance with the specified number of milliseconds since midnight January 1, 1970.
Date(year, month, day, hours, minutes, seconds, milliseconds)	Creates a Date instance with the date specified by the year, month, day, hours, minutes, seconds, and milliseconds integers. The year and month parameters must be supplied. If other parameters are included, then all preceding parameters must be supplied.

Listing 4.4: Using the *Date* Object

```
<HTML>
<HEAD>
<TITLE>Using the Date Object Type</TITLE>
</HEAD>
```

```
<BODY>
<H1>Using the Date Object Type</H1>
<SCRIPT LANGUAGE="JavaScript"><!--
currentDate = new Date()
with (currentDate) {
 document.write("Date: "+(getMonth()+1)+"/"
  +getDate()+"/"+getFullYear()+"<BR>");
 document.write("Time: "+getHours()+":"+getMinutes()+":"
  +getSeconds())
}
// --></SCRIPT>
</BODY>
</HTML>
```

The previous document uses the methods of the Date object type to write the current date and time to the current document object. The currentDate variable is assigned a new Date object that is created using the new operator and the Date() constructor. A with statement makes the object stored with currentDate the default object for object references. The two write() method invocations use the getMonth(), getDate(), getFullYear(), getHours(), getMinutes(), and getSeconds() methods to access the various components of a Date object. Figure 4.5 shows the web page generated by Listing 4.4.

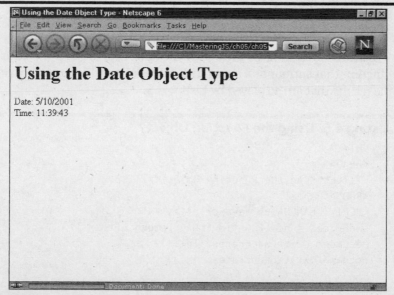

FIGURE 4.5:   Using the Date object type (Listing 4.4)

The *Function* Object

The Function object allows functions to be accessed as objects. You can use it to dynamically create and invoke a function during a script's execution. The ECMAScript specification identifies the length and prototype properties. The length property identifies the number of parameters defined for a function. Navigator and IE define the arguments and caller properties. The arguments property is an array that identifies the arguments passed to a function when it is invoked. The caller property identifies the function that invoked a particular function. Navigator also defines the arity property, which is identical to the length property.

The ECMAScript specification defines the toString(), apply(thisArg, argArray), and call(thisArg, arg1, ..., argn)() methods. The toString() method returns a string representation of the function. The apply() method invokes the function on the object specified by thisArg with the arguments contained in argArray. The call() method is similar to the apply() method, but it passes the arguments individually.

You create Function objects by supplying the function's parameters and body to the Function() constructor:

```
variable = new Function("p1", "p2", ..., "pn", "body")
```

The opening and closing brackets ({ and }) of the function body are not specified. The following function returns $x^2 + y^2$:

```
myFunction = new Function("x", "y", "return x*x + y*y")
```

Listing 4.5 illustrates the use of the Function object. It creates a function that surrounds a string with braces ([and]). Figure 4.6 shows the results that are displayed by Listing 4.5.

Listing 4.5: Using the *Function* Object

```
<HTML>
<HEAD>
<TITLE>Using the Function Object</TITLE>
<BODY><H1>
<SCRIPT LANGUAGE="JavaScript"><!--
addBraces = new Function("s","return '['+s+']'")
document.write(addBraces("This"))
document.write(addBraces("is"))
```

```
document.write(addBraces("a"))
document.write(addBraces("test."))
// --></SCRIPT>
</H1></BODY>
</HTML>
```

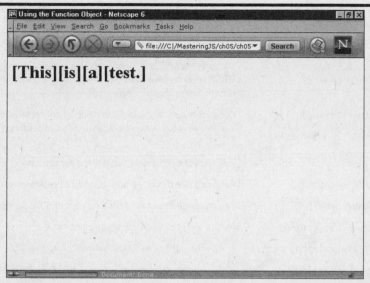

FIGURE 4.6: The results of the dynamically created function (Listing 4.5)

The *Global* Object

The ECMAScript specification defines the Global object to associate an object with the globally accessible variables and functions defined in earlier versions of JavaScript. Navigator and IE implement the Global object but do not allow it to be explicitly created (via new Global()) or referenced (via Global.). Instead, its properties and methods are referenced directly as global variables and functions.

The ECMAScript specification defines three constant properties: undefined, NaN, and Infinity. The undefined constant identifies a variable that does not have a defined value. The NaN constant means *not a number*. The Infinity property represents positive infinity. Methods defined for the Global object are shown in Table 4.7.

TABLE 4.7:   Methods of the Global Object

METHOD	DEFINITION
decodeURI(uri)	Performs the opposite transformation of the encodeURI() function.
decodeURIComponent (uriComponent)	Performs the opposite transformation of the encodeURI- Component() function.
encodeURI(uri)	Converts the *uri* into an encoded URI using UTF-8 encoding.
encodeURIComponent (uriComponent)	Converts the *uriComponent* into an encoded URI using UTF-8 encoding. Assumes that the argument is a component of a URI rather than a complete URI.
escape(string)	Converts the *string* into a new string where certain characters are converted into escape sequences in accordance with RFC 1738.
eval(x)	Evaluates and returns the value of the expression *x*.
isFinite(number)	Returns true if *number* is finite and false otherwise.
isNaN(number)	Returns true if *number* is not a number and false otherwise.
parseFloat(string)	Parses the *string* as a floating-point value.
parseInt(string, radix)	Parses the *string* as an integer of base *radix*.
unescape(string)	Converts a string encoded by escape() back to its original value.

You can use these methods to support numerical tests and URI encoding/ decoding in accordance with industry standard Request for Comments (RFC) documents 1738 and 2396. (If you're interested, you can read all the RFCs online at http://www.rfc-editor.org/.)

NOTE

The escape() and unescape() methods were removed in the ECMAScript 3 specification. Older browsers may continue to support these methods for some time, but you should update your scripts so that they do not rely on these deprecated functions.

The *Math* Object

The Math object provides a standard library of mathematical constants and functions. The constants are defined as properties of Math and are listed in Table 4.8. The functions are defined as methods of Math and are summarized in Table 4.9. Specific instances of Math are not created because Math is a built-in object and not an object type. Listing 4.6 illustrates the use of the Math object; Figure 4.7 shows the web page it generates.

TABLE 4.8: Math Properties

PROPERTY	DESCRIPTION
E	Euler's constant
LN2	The natural logarithm of 2
LN10	The natural logarithm of 10
LOG2E	The base 2 logarithm of e
LOG10E	The base 10 logarithm of e
PI	The constant π
SQRT1_2	The square root of ½
SQRT2	The square root of 2

NOTE

The values of the reciprocal properties (such as Math.SQRT1_2 and 1/Math.SQRT2) should be equal. However, because of round-off error, in practice these values will be slightly different.

TABLE 4.9: Math Methods

METHOD	DESCRIPTION
abs(x)	Returns the absolute value of x.
acos(x)	Returns the arc cosine of x in radians.
asin(x)	Returns the arc sine of x in radians.
atan(x)	Returns the arc tangent of x in radians.
atan2(x,y)	Returns the angle of the polar coordinate corresponding to (x,y).
ceil(x)	Returns the least integer that is greater than or equal to x.
cos(x)	Returns the cosine of x.
exp(x)	Returns e^x.
floor(x)	Returns the greatest integer that is less than or equal to x.

TABLE 4.9 continued: Math Methods

METHOD	DESCRIPTION
log(x)	Returns the natural logarithm of x.
max(x,y)	Returns the greater of x and y. If more than two arguments are supplied, the method returns the greatest of all the arguments.
min(x,y)	Returns the lesser of x and y. If more than two arguments are supplied, the method returns the least of all the arguments.
pow(x,y)	Returns x^y.
random()	Returns a random number between 0 and 1.
round(x)	Returns x rounded to the closest integer.
sin(x)	Returns the sine of x.
sqrt(x)	Returns the square root of x.
tan(x)	Returns the tangent of x.

NOTE

Although the ECMAScript specification suggests that implementations should use IEEE 754 standard arithmetic for the functions in Table 4.9, it doesn't require them to do so. You may find slight variations in the results returned depending on the approximation algorithms used.

Listing 4.6: Using the *Math* Object

```
<HTML>
<HEAD>
<TITLE>Using the Math Object</TITLE>
</HEAD>
<BODY>
<H1>Using the Math Object</H1>
<SCRIPT LANGUAGE="JavaScript"><!--
document.write(Math.PI+"<BR>")
document.write(Math.E+"<BR>")
document.write(Math.ceil(1.234)+"<BR>")
document.write(Math.random()+"<BR>")
document.write(Math.sin(Math.PI/2)+"<BR>")
document.write(Math.min(100,1000)+"<BR>")
// --></SCRIPT>
</BODY>
</HTML>
```

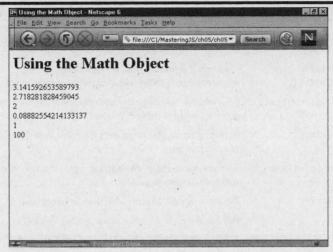

FIGURE 4.7: Example of using the Math object (Listing 4.6)

The *Number* Object

The Number object type allows numbers to be treated as objects. The ECMAScript specification defines the Number properties shown in Table 4.10.

TABLE 4.10: Number Properties

PROPERTY	DEFINITION
MAX_VALUE	The maximum possible numeric value.
MIN_VALUE	The minimum possible numeric value.
NaN	Not a number.
NEGATIVE_INFINITY	Negative infinity.
POSITIVE_INFINITY	Positive infinity.
prototype	The prototype property supported by all object types.

NOTE

The preceding properties are used to identify numbers as having special characteristics. They are not normally used in scripts. Instead, use the properties and methods of the Global object.

The ECMAScript specification defines the Number methods shown in Table 4.11.

TABLE 4.11:   Number Methods

METHOD	DEFINITION
toExponential (fractionDigits)	Converts the number into an exponential string representation with the specified number of fraction digits.
toFixed(fractionDigits)	Converts the number into a string representation with the specified fixed number of fraction digits.
toLocaleString()	Returns a string that represents the number in a locale-specific format.
toPrecision(precision)	Converts the number into a string representation with the specified numerical precision.
toString(radix)	Returns a string that represents the number in base *radix*.
valueOf()	Returns the numeric value of the Number object.

Instances of the Number object are created by supplying a numeric value to the Number() constructor:

```
myNumber = new Number(123.456)
```

The *Object* Object

The Object object is the base object from which all other objects are derived. Its properties and methods are available to other object types. The Object object supports the prototype and constructor properties. The constructor property identifies the name of the object's constructor.

The Object object supports the methods shown in Table 4.12.

TABLE 4.12:   Methods of the Object Object

METHOD	DEFINITION
hasOwnProperty (propertyName)	Returns a Boolean value indicating whether the object has the specified property.
isPrototypeOf(object)	Returns a Boolean value indicating whether the object is a prototype of the other object.
propertyIsEnumerable (precision)	Returns a Boolean value indicating whether the object has the specified property and the property is enumerable.
toLocaleString()	Returns a string representation of the object in a locale-specific format.
toString()	Returns a string representation of the object.
valueOf()	Returns the object upon which the method is invoked.

You can create Object objects by supplying a number, string, Boolean value, or function in the Object() constructor. However, this is rarely done. Instead, it is better to use the constructor of the specific object type (that is, Number(), String(), Boolean(), or Function()).

The *String* Object

The String object type allows strings to be accessed as objects. It supports the length and prototype properties. The length property identifies the string's length in characters.

The String object type provides a set of methods for manipulating strings. The methods defined in the ECMAScript specification are summarized in Table 4.13. Any JavaScript string value or variable containing a string value can use these methods. Both Netscape and IE define String methods in addition to those contained in Table 4.13.

TABLE 4.13: String Methods

METHOD	DESCRIPTION
charAt(index)	Returns a string that consists of the character at the specified index of the string to which the method is applied.
charCodeAt(index)	Returns the Unicode encoding of the character at the specified index.
concat(s1, ..., sn)	Concatenates the specified strings to the string upon which the method is invoked, and returns the new string.
fromCharCode(codes)	Creates a string from a comma-separated sequence of character codes.
indexOf(pattern)	Returns the index of the first string specified by the pattern parameter that is contained in a string. Returns -1 if the pattern is not contained in the string.
indexOf(pattern, startIndex)	Same as the previous method, except searching starts at the position specified by *startIndex*.
lastIndexOf(pattern)	Returns the index of the last string specified by the *pattern* parameter that is contained in a string. Returns -1 if the pattern is not contained in the string.
lastIndexOf(pattern, startIndex)	Same as the previous method, except searching starts at the position specified by *startIndex*.
localeCompare(s)	Compares the string with the string *s* using a locale-specific comparison. Returns 0 if the strings are equivalent and a non-zero numeric value if the strings are not equivalent.

TABLE 4.13 continued: String Methods

Method	Description
match(regExp)	Matches the string against the specified regular expression.
replace(searchValue, replaceValue)	Replaces *searchValue* with *replaceValue* and returns the result. Refer to Appendix A.
search(regExp)	Searches the string for the specified regular expression and returns the index of where it is found. Refer to Appendix A.
slice(start, end)	Returns a substring starting from character position *start* and running to, but not including, character position *end* (or through the end of the string if *end* is undefined).
split(separator, limit)	Separates a string into an array of substrings based on the *separator*. If *limit* is specified, then the array is limited to the number of elements given by *limit*.
substring(startIndex)	Returns the substring of a string beginning at *startIndex*.
substring(startIndex, endIndex)	Returns the substring of a string beginning at *startIndex* and ending at *endIndex*.
toLowerCase()	Returns a copy of the string converted to lowercase.
toLocaleLowerCase()	Returns a copy of the string converted to lowercase using a locale-specific transliteration.
toString()	Returns the string value of the object.
toUpperCase()	Returns a copy of the string converted to uppercase.
toLocaleUpperCase()	Returns a copy of the string converted to uppercase using a locale-specific transliteration.
valueOf()	Returns the string value of the object.

Listing 4.7 illustrates the use of the String object type. The script in the document body begins by defining the function displayLine(), which displays text followed by the BR tag. The displayLine() function displays several text strings that are modified using sample string methods. Figure 4.8 shows the web page generated by Listing 4.7.

Listing 4.7: Using the *String* Object

```
<HTML>
<HEAD>
<TITLE>Using the String Object Type</TITLE>
</HEAD>
```

```
<BODY>
<SCRIPT LANGUAGE="JavaScript"><!--
function displayLine(text) {
  document.write(text+"<BR>")
}
s = new String("This is a test of the JavaScript "
    +"String methods.")
displayLine('s = '+s)
displayLine('s.charAt(1) = '+s.charAt(1))
displayLine('s.charCodeAt(1) = '+s.charCodeAt(1))
displayLine('s.indexOf("is") = '+s.indexOf("is"))
displayLine('s.lastIndexOf("is") = '+s.lastIndexOf("is"))
displayLine('s.substring(22,32) = '+s.substring(22,32))
displayLine('s.toLowerCase() = '+s.toLowerCase())
displayLine('s.toUpperCase() = '+s.toUpperCase())
split = s.split(" ")
for(i=0; i<split.length; ++i)
  displayLine('split['+i+'] = '+split[i])
// --></SCRIPT>
</BODY>
</HTML>
```

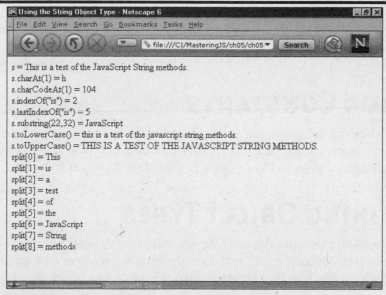

FIGURE 4.8: Using the String object (Listing 4.7)

Creating *String* Objects

You can create `String` objects in the same manner as other JavaScript objects, using the new operator. For example, you can assign the variable `text` the string `"I am a string"` using the following statement:

```
text = new String("I am a string")
```

This statement is equivalent to the following:

```
text = "I am a string"
```

Regular Expressions and the *RegExp* Object

Support for *regular expressions* was introduced in JavaScript 1.2. Regular expressions are string expressions that describe a pattern of characters. They provide a powerful capability for finding patterns in text strings and performing search and replace operations on text. Regular expressions use a very compact, powerful, but somewhat arcane syntax. In JavaScript, regular expressions are implemented using the RegExp object.

NOTE
Although regular expressions were not included in the basic ECMAScript specification, they are included in ECMAScript 2, which should parallel JavaScript 2.0.

COLOR CONSTANTS

JavaScript defines a number of color constants you can use with methods and functions that take color parameters. Some of these color constants are red, orange, yellow, green, blue, white, black, and brown.

DEFINING OBJECT TYPES

JavaScript provides the capability for you to define your own object types and create specific object instances. To create a new object type, you simply define a function that constructs specific instances of the object type.

Essentially, this constructor function does two things:

▶ It assigns values to the object type's properties.

▶ It identifies other functions to be used as the object type's methods.

As an example of defining a new object type, let's create the Table object type. You'll use this object type to create simple tables using JavaScript and write them to the current document.

NOTE

The function used as a constructor of an object type must have the same name as the object type.

Identifying and Assigning Properties

The first thing you need to do is identify the properties of the Table object type. The number of rows and columns in the table are obvious properties with which to start. Let's name these properties Table.rows and Table.columns. You also need to define a property to store the elements of the table. Call this property Table.data and let it be an array of the following length:

```
Table.rows * Table.columns
```

Because HTML allows some table cells to be designated as header cells, also define the property Table.header as an array of the same length, where each element is a Boolean value indicating whether a table cell is a header cell. Finally, define a Table.border property that identifies the border width of the table.

The following code shows how the table constructor is defined using these items:

```
function Table(rows,columns) {
  this.rows = rows
  this.columns = columns
  this.border = 0
  this.data = new Array(rows*columns)
  this.header = new Array(rows*columns)
}
```

As you can see, the Table() constructor takes the parameters rows and columns and assigns them to this.rows and this.columns. The this prefix is a special keyword that refers to the current object. For example, the statement this.rows = rows assigns the value stored in the rows parameter to the rows property of the current object. Similarly, this.columns = columns assigns the columns parameter to the columns property of the current object. You didn't have to name the parameters to the Table() constructor rows and columns—they could have been named x and y. However, it is common to name parameters after the object type properties to which they are assigned.

The border property of the current object is set to the default value of 0. This results in the creation of a borderless table. As mentioned earlier, the data and header properties are each assigned an array of size rows * columns.

To create an object that is an instance of the Table object type, you use the new operator in conjunction with the Table constructor. For example, the following statement creates a table of three rows by four columns and assigns it to the t variable:

```
t = new Table(3,4)
```

Defining Methods

So far, you've defined the properties of the Table object type. However, you need to define some methods to update the values of the data, header, and border properties and to write the Table object to a document object.

You define methods by assigning the name of an already defined function to a method name in an object type constructor. For example, suppose the Table_setValue() function is defined as follows. This function sets the value of the table cell at the specified row and column parameters to the value parameter:

```
function Table_setValue(row,col,value) {
  this.data[row*this.columns+col]=value
}
```

You can use the previously defined Table_setValue() function as the setValue() method of the Table object type by including the following statement in the Table constructor:

```
this.setValue = Table_setValue
```

Note that trailing parentheses are not used in the previous statement. The new Table constructor is as follows:

```
function Table(rows,columns) {
  this.rows = rows
  this.columns = columns
  this.border = 0
  this.data = new Array(rows*columns)
  this.header = new Array(rows*columns)
  this.setValue = Table_setValue
}
```

An example of invoking the setValue() method for the Table object stored in the t variable follows:

```
t.setValue(2,3,"Hello")
```

This statement sets the table data value at row 2 and column 3 to "Hello".

Definition of the *Table* Object

Listing 4.8 provides a complete definition of the Table object. Note that functions must be defined before they can be assigned to a method name.

Listing 4.8: Definition of the *Table* Object (*table.js*)

```
function Table_getValue(row,col) {
  return this.data[row*this.columns+col]
}
function Table_setValue(row,col,value) {
  this.data[row*this.columns+col]=value
}
function Table_set(contents) {
  var n = contents.length
  for(var j=0;j<n;++j) this.data[j]=contents[j]
}
function Table_isHeader(row,col) {
  return this.header[row*this.columns+col]
}
function Table_makeHeader(row,col) {
  this.header[row*this.columns+col]=true
}
function Table_makeNormal(row,col) {
  this.header[row*this.columns+col]=false
}
```

```
function Table_makeHeaderRow(row) {
 for(var j=0;j<this.columns;++j)
  this.header[row*this.columns+j]=true
}
function Table_makeHeaderColumn(col) {
 for(var i=0;i<this.rows;++i)
  this.header[i*this.columns+col]=true
}
function Table_write(doc) {
 doc.write("<TABLE BORDER="+this.border+">")
 for(var i=0;i<this.rows;++i) {
  doc.write("<TR>")
  for(var j=0;j<this.columns;++j) {
   if(this.header[i*this.columns+j]) {
    doc.write("<TH>")
    doc.write(this.data[i*this.columns+j])
    doc.write("</TH>")
   }else{
    doc.write("<TD>")
    doc.write(this.data[i*this.columns+j])
    doc.write("</TD>")
   }
  }
  doc.writeln("</TR>")
 }
 doc.writeln("</TABLE>")
}
function Table(rows,columns) {
 this.rows = rows
 this.columns = columns
 this.border = 0
 if(rows * columns > 0) {
  this.data = new Array(rows*columns)
  this.header = new Array(rows*columns)
 }else{
  this.data = new Array(1)
  this.header = new Array(1)
 }
 this.getValue = Table_getValue
 this.setValue = Table_setValue
 this.set = Table_set
 this.isHeader = Table_isHeader
```

```
    this.makeHeader = Table_makeHeader
    this.makeNormal = Table_makeNormal
    this.makeHeaderRow = Table_makeHeaderRow
    this.makeHeaderColumn = Table_makeHeaderColumn
    this.write = Table_write
}
```

Listing 4.8 adds the getValue(), set(), isHeader(), makeHeader(), makeNormal(), makeHeaderRow(), makeHeaderColumn(), and write() methods to the table definition introduced in the previous section. The getValue() method returns the data value stored at a specified row and column. The set() method stores an array of values as the contents of a table. The makeHeader() and makeNormal() methods identify whether a cell should or should not be a header cell. The makeHeaderRow() and makeHeaderColumn() methods designate an entire row or column as consisting of header cells. The write() method writes a table to a document object.

Using the *Table* Object

Listing 4.9 provides an example of the use of the Table object. The document's body contains a script that creates, initializes, and displays a three-row by four-column Table object. Using the SRC attribute of the SCRIPT tag, it includes the table.js file presented in the previous section. It begins by creating a Table object and assigning it to the t variable. It then creates an array named contents that contains a list of values. The set() method is invoked to assign the contents array to the cells of the table stored at t. The table's border property is set to four pixels, and the cells of column 0 are designated as header cells. Finally, the write() method writes the table to the current document object. Figure 4.9 shows the web page resulting from the script in Listing 4.9.

Listing 4.9: Using the *Table* Object

```
<HTML>
<HEAD>
<TITLE>Defining Object Types</TITLE>
<SCRIPT LANGUAGE="JavaScript" SRC="table.js"><!--
// --></SCRIPT>
</HEAD>
<BODY>
<H1>Defining Object Types</H1>
<SCRIPT LANGUAGE="JavaScript"><!--
t = new Table(3,4)
```

```
contents = new Array("This","is","a","test",
    "of","the","table","object.",
    "Let's","see","it","work.")
t.set(contents)
t.border=4
t.makeHeaderColumn(0)
t.write(document)
// --></SCRIPT>
</BODY>
</HTML>
```

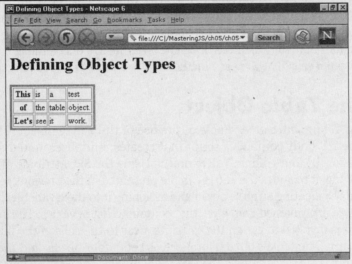

FIGURE 4.9:   An example table (Listing 4.9)

Adding Properties and Methods to an Object Type

Object types that can be instantiated with the new operator are referred to as *instantiable* object types. They include all user-defined object types and most of the predefined object types. Examples of object types that are not instantiable are Math and Global. JavaScript provides the capability to add properties and methods to already defined instantiable object types via the prototype property.

For example, suppose you want to add a background color attribute to the Table object type defined in the previous section. You can add the new attribute with the following statement:

```
Table.prototype.bgColor = "cyan"
```

This statement uses the `prototype` property of the `Table` object type to create a new property called `bgColor` to represent the background color of the table.

Now that you've defined the `bgColor` property, you should create an additional method called `colorWrite()` that writes a table using the `bgColor` property. The following function performs this processing:

```
function Table_colorWrite(doc) {
  doc.write("<TABLE BORDER="+this.border+" BGCOLOR="
      +this.bgColor+">")
  for(var i=0;i<this.rows;++i) {
   doc.write("<TR>")
   for(var j=0;j<this.columns;++j) {
    if(this.header[i*this.columns+j]) {
     doc.write("<TH>")
     doc.write(this.data[i*this.columns+j])
     doc.write("</TH>")
    }else{
     doc.write("<TD>")
     doc.write(this.data[i*this.columns+j])
     doc.write("</TD>")
    }
   }
   doc.writeln("</TR>")
  }
  doc.writeln("</TABLE>")
}
```

You can use this `Table_colorWrite()` function as the `colorWrite()` method by including the following statement in your script:

```
Table.prototype.colorWrite=Table_colorWrite
```

Listing 4.10 updates the script from Listing 4.9 to use the new `bgColor` property and the `colorWrite()` method. Figure 4.10 shows the web page that results from Listing 4.10. Note that you do not have to modify the original `table.js` file that is included via the SRC attribute.

TIP

Always create an object of the object type being modified before using the object type's prototype property. This will ensure that any new properties and methods are added correctly.

Listing 4.10: Updating an Object Type Definition

```
<HTML>
<HEAD>
<TITLE>Updating Object Types</TITLE>
<SCRIPT LANGUAGE="JavaScript" SRC="table.js"><!--
// --></SCRIPT>
</HEAD>
<BODY>
<H1>Updating Object Types</H1>
<SCRIPT LANGUAGE="JavaScript"><!--
function Table_colorWrite(doc) {
 doc.write("<TABLE BORDER="+this.border+" BGCOLOR="
     +this.bgColor+">")
 for(var i=0;i<this.rows;++i) {
  doc.write("<TR>")
  for(var j=0;j<this.columns;++j) {
   if(this.header[i*this.columns+j]) {
    doc.write("<TH>")
    doc.write(this.data[i*this.columns+j])
    doc.write("</TH>")
   }else{
    doc.write("<TD>")
    doc.write(this.data[i*this.columns+j])
    doc.write("</TD>")
   }
  }
  doc.writeln("</TR>")
 }
 doc.writeln("</TABLE>")
}

t = new Table(3,4)
Table.prototype.bgColor="cyan"
Table.prototype.colorWrite=Table_colorWrite
contents = new Array("This","is","a","test","of",
    "the","table","object.",
  "Let's","see","it","work.")
t.set(contents)
t.border=4
t.makeHeaderColumn(0)
t.colorWrite(document)
```

```
// --></SCRIPT>
</BODY>
</HTML>
```

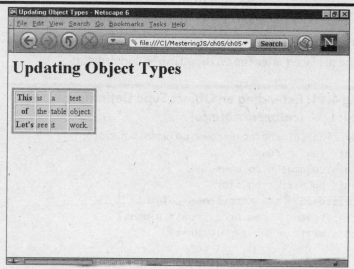

FIGURE 4.10:   Table with a background color (Listing 4.10)

EXTENDING OBJECT TYPES

In the previous example, you customized the Table object by adding a new method to its prototype. JavaScript also provides the capability to extend an object type and create a new object type that has all the properties and methods of the extended object type in addition to new properties and methods of its own.

Extending object types is easy with JavaScript. For example, suppose you've defined an object type A and you want to extend it with object type B. All you have to do is insert the following statement after B's definition:

```
B.prototype = new A;
```

This statement tells JavaScript that the A object type is to be used as the prototype for defining the B object type.

Extending *Table* with *ColoredTable*

To see how easy it is to extend an object type, let's extend the Table object type with a new object type named ColoredTable. The ColoredTable object type adds a bgColor property and redefines the write() method to display the table's background color. Listing 4.11 shows the `ColoredTable` object's definition. The `ColoredTable` constructor is redefined to add the bgColor argument. Note that the `write()` method is redefined as the `Table_colorWrite()` function from Listing 4.10. The `ColoredTable` is identified as extending `Table` via the following line:

```
ColoredTable.prototype = new Table;
```

This line is placed after the `ColoredTable` constructor.

Listing 4.11: Extending an Object Type Definition (*coloredtable.js*)

```
function ColoredTable(rows,columns,bgColor) {
 this.rows = rows
 this.columns = columns
 this.bgColor = bgColor
 this.data = new Array(rows*columns)
 this.header = new Array(rows*columns)
 this.write = Table_colorWrite
 }


ColoredTable.prototype = new Table;

function Table_colorWrite(doc) {
 doc.write("<TABLE BORDER="+this.border+" BGCOLOR="
    +this.bgColor+">")
 for(var i=0;i<this.rows;++i) {
  doc.write("<TR>")
  for(var j=0;j<this.columns;++j) {
   if(this.header[i*this.columns+j]) {
    doc.write("<TH>")
    doc.write(this.data[i*this.columns+j])
    doc.write("</TH>")
   }else{
    doc.write("<TD>")
    doc.write(this.data[i*this.columns+j])
    doc.write("</TD>")
   }
  }
  doc.writeln("</TR>")
 }
 doc.writeln("</TABLE>")
 }
```

Listing 4.12 shows how to use the ColoredTable object. Note that table.js and coloredtable.js must be included in the document. The page that it generates is similar to that shown in Figure 4.10.

Listing 4.12: Extending an Object Type Definition

```
<HTML>
<HEAD>
<TITLE>Extending Object Types</TITLE>
<SCRIPT LANGUAGE="JavaScript" SRC="table.js"><!--
// --></SCRIPT>
<SCRIPT LANGUAGE="JavaScript" SRC="coloredtable.js"><!--
// --></SCRIPT>
</HEAD>
<BODY>
<H1>Extending Object Types</H1>

<SCRIPT LANGUAGE="JavaScript"><!--
t = new ColoredTable(3,4,"yellow")
contents = new Array("This","is","a","test","of",
    "the","table","object.",
  "Let's","see","it","work.")
t.set(contents)
t.border=4
t.makeHeaderColumn(0)
t.write(document)
// --></SCRIPT>
</BODY>
</HTML>
```

DELETING PROPERTIES AND METHODS

You can use the delete operator to delete an element of an array, or to delete a property or method of a user-defined object. Its syntax is as follows:

```
delete arrayName[arrayIndex]
delete objectName.propertyName
delete objectName.methodName
```

For example, suppose the myTable variable refers to a Table object. The following statement deletes the header property of the object referenced by myTable:

```
delete myTable.header
```

There are few occasions in which it is desirable to delete a property or method of an existing object. As such, the delete operator is rarely used in this way.

The *event* Object

Now that you know what objects are, let's go over the properties of the event object. An instance of the event object is created whenever an event occurs during the execution of a script. Navigator and IE each define a different set of properties for the event object. Both browsers use the type property to identify the type of event that occurred and the screenX and screenY properties to identify the screen location at which the event occurred. Navigator and IE also implement some similar properties with different names, as summarized in Table 4.14.

TABLE 4.14:   Similar Navigator and IE Event Properties

Navigator Property	IE Property	Description
pageX, pageY	clientX, clientY	The location of the event relative to the web page
target	srcElement	The event source
which	button	The mouse button associated with the event
key	keyCode	The Unicode character code of the character corresponding to the key press
modifiers	altKey, ctrlKey, shiftKey	The state of the Alt, Control, or Shift key

What's Next

This chapter has described JavaScript's support of objects and object-based programming. It introduced the JavaScript object model and summarized the predefined JavaScript objects. It also showed you how to create your own objects and methods.

Chapter 5 concentrates on using HTML forms to capture user input. If you need to build a site that responds to more than just user clicks, this is an important topic. You can use your knowledge of JavaScript's interaction with forms to make your site far more straightforward for the user, particularly when user-entered data needs to be validated, or to avoid creating a form that has needlessly tedious and repetitive fields.

Chapter 5
PROCESSING FORMS

Forms provide you with an important capability for web page development: They allow you to gather information from individuals who browse your web pages. This is especially important if you use your website to advertise or sell products. Forms provide a full range of graphical user interface (GUI) controls, and they automatically submit the data they collect to your web server. This data can then be processed by CGI programs, server-side scripts built using JavaServer Pages (JSP), server-side JScript scripts written as Microsoft's Active Server Pages (ASP), PHP scripts embedded within other web pages, or other types of server-side scripts.

JavaScript provides a number of features you can use to enhance the forms you develop for web applications. These features let you validate form data before it is submitted to your server and exercise greater control of the interaction between your forms and web users.

Adapted from *Mastering JavaScript Premium Edition* by James Jaworski
ISBN 0-7821-2819-X

This chapter introduces the form object and discusses the JavaScript objects associated with form fields and GUI controls. It shows how to use the properties and methods of these objects, and how to handle form-related events. When you finish this chapter, you will know how to use JavaScript to create forms that perform local processing, and you will be able to use these forms to communicate with CGI programs.

THE *FORM* OBJECT

JavaScript provides the form object to enable your scripts to interact with and exercise control over HTML forms. The form object is accessed as a property of the document object. Your browser creates a unique form object for every form that is contained in a document. These objects can be accessed via the document.forms[] array.

The form object is important because it provides you with access to the forms contained in your documents and allows you to respond to form-related events. Table 5.1 lists the properties of the form object that are supported by both Internet Explorer and Netscape Navigator. These properties provide access to a form's attributes and let you work with a form's fields and GUI controls. The form object provides two common methods, submit() and reset(), that are used to submit a form or reset a form's entries to their default values. (The events that forms handle are covered in Chapter 3 in the section "Adding Event Handlers," and in the section "Using Form Event Handlers" later in this chapter.)

TABLE 5.1:   Properties and Objects of the form Object

PROPERTY	DESCRIPTION
acceptCharset	Provides access to a list of the supported character sets for the current form element
action	Provides access to the HTML ACTION attribute of the <form> tag
button	An object representing a button GUI control
checkbox	An object representing a check box field
elements	An array containing all the fields and GUI controls included in a form
encoding	Provides access to the HTML ENCTYPE attribute of the <form> tag
enctype	Provides access to the HTML ENCTYPE attribute of the <form> tag
fileUpload	An object representing a file-upload form field

TABLE 5.1 continued: Properties and Objects of the form Object

PROPERTY	DESCRIPTION
hidden	An object representing a hidden form field
length	Provides access to the length of the elements array
method	Provides access to the HTML METHOD attribute of the <form> tag
name	Identifies the name of the form (from the NAME attribute of the <form> tag)
password	An object representing a password field
radio	An object representing a radio button field
reset	An object representing a reset button
select	An object representing a selection list
submit	An object representing a submit button
target	Provides access to the HTML TARGET attribute of the <form> tag
text	An object representing a text field
textarea	An object representing a text area field

ACCESSING FORMS WITHIN JAVASCRIPT

Because form objects are considered properties of documents, you access them by referencing the documents within which they are contained. If you name a form when you create it, you can access the form by its name. Forms are named using the form's NAME attribute. For example, if you create a form named employeeData, you can access its method property using employeeData.method.

You can also use the document object's forms property to access the forms contained in a particular document. The forms property is an array that contains an entry for each form contained in a document. Suppose the employeeData form is the third form contained in the document loaded into the current window. You can access the form's method property using document.forms[2].*method* or document.forms["employeeData"].*method*.

Accessing Form Elements

A form can contain a wide variety of fields and GUI controls. These form components are referred to as *elements* of the form and are objects in their own right. Table 5.2 lists the objects that may be contained in a form.

TABLE 5.2:   Objects that May Be Contained in a Form

Object	Description
button	A general-purpose button
checkbox	A clickable field that allows multiple selections from within a group
FileUpload	A field that allows a user to specify a file to be submitted as part of the form
hidden	A field that may contain a value, but is not displayed within a form
password	A text field in which the user-entered value isn't displayed on the screen (although it's transmitted back to the server in the clear)
radio	A clickable field that allows only a single selection from within a group
reset	A button that is used to reset the contents of a form to the default state
select	A list from which individual list items may be selected
submit	A button that is used to submit the data entered into a field
text	A single-line field for entering text
textarea	A multiline field for entering text

If the elements of a form are named using an HTML NAME attribute, you can access the element using this name. For example, suppose you have a form named form1 that contains a text field named uid. You can access the value of this field using form1.uid.value.

In most cases, you access the elements of a form using the form object's elements array property. This array contains an object for each element of a form. Suppose the uid field of the form1 form is the seventh element defined in the form. You can access the value of the uid field using form1.elements[6].value or form1.elements["uid"].value.

The objects described in Table 5.2 reference the elements of a form and have properties and methods of their own. Most of these objects have the name, type, and value properties. The name property provides access to the button's NAME attribute. The type property identifies the object's type. The `value` property identifies the object's value. Tables 5.3 and 5.4 summarize the objects' properties and methods.

TABLE 5.3: Properties of Form Elements

Object	Property	Description
button	name, type, value	
checkbox	checked	Identifies whether the check box is currently checked
	defaultChecked	Identifies whether the check box is checked by default
	name, type, value	
FileUpload	name, type, value	
hidden	name, type, value	
password	defaultValue	Identifies the object's default value
	name, type, value	
radio	checked	Identifies whether the radio button is currently checked
	defaultChecked	Identifies whether the radio button is checked by default
	name, type, value	
reset	name, type, value	
select	length	Identifies the length of the select list
	name, type	Provides access to the object's NAME attribute
	options	An array that identifies the options supported by the select list
	selectedIndex	Identifies the first selected option within the select list
submit	name, type, value	
text	defaultValue	Identifies the default text to be displayed in the text field
	name, type, value	
textarea	defaultValue	Identifies the default text to be displayed in the text area field
	name, type, value	

TABLE 5.4:   Methods of Form Elements

OBJECT	METHOD	DESCRIPTION
Button	click()	Simulates the button being clicked
Checkbox	click()	Simulates the check box being clicked
FileUpload	select()	Selects the input area of the file upload field
Hidden	None	
Password	select()	Highlights the text displayed in the password field
Radio	click()	Simulates the clicking of the radio button
reset	click()	Simulates the clicking of the reset button
select	None (other than blur() and focus())	
submit	click()	Simulates the clicking of the submit button
text	select()	Highlights the text in the text field
textarea	select()	Highlights the text in the text area

NOTE

All form elements have the form property. This property references the form in which the element is contained. All form elements except the hidden element provide the handleEvent() method for directly invoking the element's event handlers.

NOTE

All of the objects in Table 5.4 have the blur() and focus() methods. The blur() method removes focus. The focus() method gives focus. Table 5.4 lists the objects' methods beyond blur() and focus().

Listing 5.1 shows how you can access the individual forms and form elements in multiform documents. It creates the three-form document shown in Figure 5.1. When you click the Submit button on the first form, the onSubmit() handler invokes the displayFormData() function. Note that it does so in the context of a return statement. This causes the form submission to be aborted when displayFormData() returns a false value. This is always the case because displayFormData() always returns false.

Listing 5.1: Accessing the Elements of a Form (*formacc.htm*)

```
<HTML>
<HEAD>
<TITLE>Multiform Document Example</TITLE>
<SCRIPT LANGUAGE="JavaScript"><!--
function displayFormData() {
 win2.open("","window2")
 win2.document.open("text/plain")
 win2.document.writeln("This document has "+
  document.forms.length+" forms.")
 for(i=0;i<document.forms.length;++i) {
  win2.document.writeln("Form "+i+" has "+
   document.forms[i].elements.length+" elements.")
  for(j=0;j<document.forms[i].elements.length;++j) {
   win2.document.writeln((j+1)+" A "+
    document.forms[i].elements[j].type+" element.")
  }
 }
 win2.document.close()
 return false
}
// --></SCRIPT>
</HEAD>
<BODY>
<H1>Multiform Document Example</H1>
<FORM ACTION="nothing" onSubmit="return displayFormData()">
<H2>Form 1</H2>
<P>Text field: <INPUT TYPE="TEXT" NAME="f1-1"
  VALUE="Sample text"></P>
<P>Password field: <INPUT TYPE="PASSWORD" NAME="f1-2"></P>
<P>Text area field:
<TEXTAREA ROWS="4" COLS="30"
  NAME="f1-3">Write your novel here.</TEXTAREA></P>
<P><INPUT TYPE="SUBMIT" NAME="f1-4" VALUE="Submit">
<INPUT TYPE="RESET" NAME="f1-5"></P>
</FORM>
<HR>
<FORM>
<H2>Form 2</H2>
<P><INPUT TYPE="CHECKBOX" NAME="f2-1" VALUE="1"
   CHECKED> Check me!</P>
<P><INPUT TYPE="CHECKBOX" NAME="f2-1" VALUE="2">
  No. Check me!</P>
```

```
<P><INPUT TYPE="CHECKBOX" NAME="f2-1" VALUE="3">
  Check all of us!</P>
<P><INPUT TYPE="RADIO" NAME="f2-2" VALUE="1">AM</P>
<P><INPUT TYPE="RADIO" NAME="f2-2" VALUE="2" CHECKED>PM</P>
<P><INPUT TYPE="RADIO" NAME="f2-2" VALUE="3">FM</P>
<INPUT TYPE="FILE" NAME="f2-3">
</FORM>
<HR>
<FORM>
<H2>Form 3</H2>
<INPUT TYPE="HIDDEN" NAME="f3-1">
<SELECT NAME="f3-2" SIZE="4">
<OPTION VALUE="">Item 1</OPTION>
<OPTION VALUE="">Item 2</OPTION>
<OPTION VALUE="" SELECTED>Item 3</OPTION>
<OPTION VALUE="">Item 4</OPTION>
<OPTION VALUE="">Item 5</OPTION>
</SELECT>
</FORM>
</BODY>
</HTML>
```

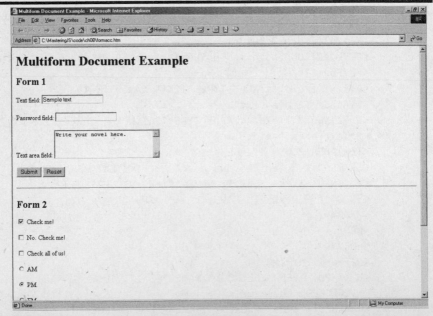

FIGURE 5.1:   A multiform document (Listing 5.1)

NOTE

You can access the file for Listing 5.1, `formacc.htm`, and all the code listings in this *Complete* book, from the Sybex website link for this book at `http://www.sybex.com`.

The `displayFormData()` function creates and opens a separate window and assigns the `window` object to the `win2` variable. It then opens the window's document with a text/plain MIME type. It uses the `forms` array of the first window's `document` object to determine how many forms are contained in the document. It then writes this information to the document contained in `win2`. Next, it identifies the number of elements in each form using the `length` property of the form's `elements` array. Finally, it displays the `type` property of each form element via `win2`, as shown in Figure 5.2.

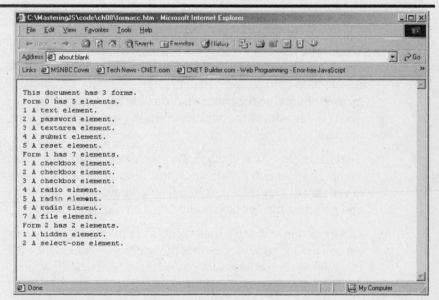

FIGURE 5.2:   A summary of the contents of the multiform document (Listing 5.1)

USING FORM EVENT HANDLERS

JavaScript's ability to handle form-related events is a powerful tool for customizing form behavior. It allows you to control the user's interaction with your forms and to process form data as the user enters it. It also lets you process form data locally at the user's browser, reducing the load on your communication bandwidth and on your web server.

Form event handlers respond to events that indicate the user has performed an input action, such as filling in a text field, clicking a button, or submitting a form. These event handlers check the data entered by the user and then either prompt the user to correct any errors or provide the user with other feedback about the data that was entered. You can also use form event handlers to adaptively present new forms to a user based on the user's response to prior forms.

Responding to User Actions

Event handling in general, and form event handling in particular, are introduced in Chapter 3, "Adding JavaScript." If you have not already read Chapter 3, you would do well to review that material before continuing with this chapter.

Most form events fall into the following categories:

Clicks and Checks   These are the most common types of form events. A user clicks a button or checks a check box to provide information or to perform an action. These events are handled by event-handling functions that provide feedback to the user about the results of the actions taken in response to the click or check.

Text Changes   Text changes are another common type of form event. The user enters data into a text field or text area, an event is generated, and the event handler validates the user's entry and performs further processing based on the user's input.

List Selection   When a user selects an item from a selection list, event-handling code verifies that the selection is consistent with other inputs and performs any processing indicated by the selection.

Change of Focus   Change-of-focus events occur when a form element, such as a text field or selection list, receives or loses the current input focus. These events usually do not require special event handing. However, JavaScript provides the capability to do so when required.

Form Submission and Reset   These events are generated when a user clicks a submit or reset button. Form-submission events are typically handled by validating all the data entered by the user, performing any local processing on that data, and then forwarding the data to a CGI program or other server-side script.

Because we covered form event handling in Chapter 3, I won't bore you with more trivial examples. Instead, let's use JavaScript's event-handling capabilities to create a form-based Hangman game—something that is impossible to do in HTML alone.

If you're not already familiar with Hangman, here's a short description: You try to guess an unknown word by guessing letters one at a time. You are initially presented with a word pattern in which each letter of the word to be guessed is represented by an underscore (_) character. This pattern indicates how many letters are in the word, but nothing more. When you guess a letter that is in the word, the underscore(s) representing that letter are replaced by the letter you guessed correctly, thus showing you where the letter appears in the word. You continue to guess until you run out of guesses or until you guess all the letters of the word.

Your status in terms of guesses is depicted in a gallows, which is why it's called Hangman. Each time you guess incorrectly, a "body part" is added to the victim. You are allowed only seven incorrect guesses (head, upper and lower torso, two arms, two legs) before the game is over. Although somewhat morbid, Hangman is an engaging game and makes for a great JavaScript example.

Before you learn how the game is implemented using form event handling, you should play a few games. Start the game by opening hangman .htm from your browser. You can find this file on the Sybex website for this book at http://www.sybex.com. At startup, the game presents the display shown in Figure 5.3. Play the game by clicking the buttons labeled A through Z. If you guess correctly, the game will display the position of the letter in the Word To Guess text field, as shown in Figure 5.4. If you guess incorrectly, a part of the body will be hung in the gallows, as shown in Figure 5.5. If you continue to guess incorrectly, your effigy will be hung, an alert dialog box (see Figure 5.6) will tell you that you lost, and the game will start again. If you are clever enough to guess the word before you are hung, an alert dialog box will tell you that you won, and the game will start over. Clicking the Start Again button immediately restarts the game with a new word to guess.

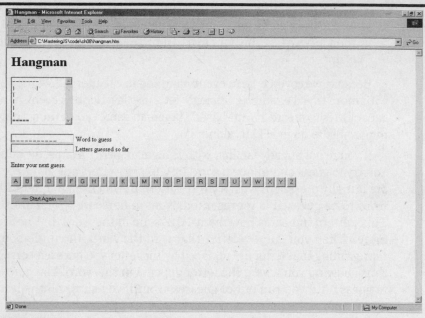

FIGURE 5.3:   The Hangman opening display (Listing 5.2).

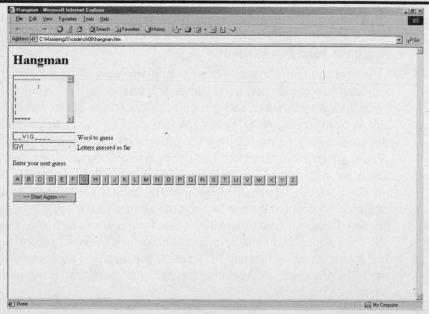

FIGURE 5.4:   You guessed correctly (Listing 5.2).

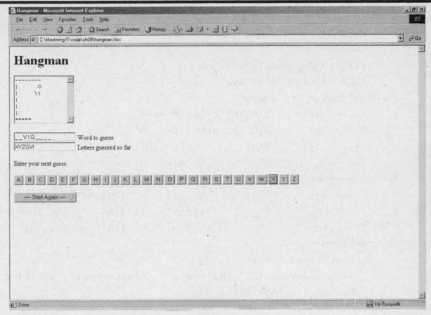

FIGURE 5.5: You guessed incorrectly (Listing 5.2).

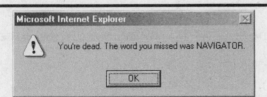

FIGURE 5.6: You're hung (Listing 5.2).

NOTE

If you try to modify any of the form's text fields, an alert message will tell you not to mess with that field. Try it to see what happens.

Listing 5.2 shows the contents of the hangman.htm file. This file is fairly long, but don't worry; I'll go over it one small piece at a time. The file contains two scripts: one in the document head and one in the document body. I'll begin with the script in the document head because that's the part your browser processes first.

Listing 5.2: A JavaScript Hangman Game (*hangman.htm*)

```
<HTML>
<HEAD>
<TITLE>Hangman</TITLE>
<SCRIPT LANGUAGE="JavaScript"><!--
gallows = new Array(
"-----\n|         |\n|\n|\n|\n|\n=====",
"-----\n|         O\n|\n|\n|\n|\n=====",
"-----\n|         O\n|         |\n|\n|\n|\n=====",
"-----\n|         O\n|        \\\|\n|\n|\n|\n=====",
"-----\n|         O\n|        \\\|/\n|\n|\n|\n=====",
"-----\n|         O\n|        \\\|/\n|         |\n|\n|\n=====",
"-----\n|         O\n|        \\\|/\n|         |\n|    /\n|\n=====",
"-----\n|         O\n|        \\\|/\n|         |\n|    / \\\\n|
➥\n=====")
guessChoices = new
  Array("JavaScript","Navigator","LiveConnect","LiveWire")
function startAgain() {
 guesses = 0
 max = gallows.length-1
 guessed = " "
 len = guessChoices.length - 1
 toGuess =
    guessChoices[Math.round(len*Math.random())].toUpperCase()
 displayHangman()
 displayToGuess()
 displayGuessed()
}
function stayAway() {
 document.game.elements[3].focus()
 alert("Don't mess with this form element!")
}
function displayHangman() {
 document.game.status.value=gallows[guesses]
}
function displayToGuess() {
 pattern=""
 for(i=0;i<toGuess.length;++i) {
  if(guessed.indexOf(toGuess.charAt(i)) != -1)
   pattern += (toGuess.charAt(i)+" ")
  else pattern += "_ "
 }
```

```
     document.game.toGuess.value=pattern
     }
     function displayGuessed() {
      document.game.guessed.value=guessed
     }
     function badGuess(s) {
      if(toGuess.indexOf(s) == -1) return true
      return false
     }
     function winner() {
      for(i=0;i<toGuess.length;++i) {
       if(guessed.indexOf(toGuess.charAt(i)) == -1) return false
      }
      return true
     }
     function guess(s){
      if(guessed.indexOf(s) == -1) guessed = s + guessed
      if(badGuess(s)) ++guesses
      displayHangman()
      displayToGuess()
      displayGuessed()
      if(guesses >= max){
      alert("You're dead. The word you missed was "+toGuess+".")
       startAgain()
      }
      if(winner()) {
       alert("You won!")
       startAgain()
      }
     }
     // --></SCRIPT>
     </HEAD>
     <BODY>
     <H1>Hangman</H1>
     <FORM NAME="game">
     <PRE>
     <TEXTAREA NAME="status" ROWS="7" COLS="16"
      ONFOCUS="stayAway()"></TEXTAREA>
     </PRE><P>
     <INPUT TYPE="TEXT" NAME="toGuess"
      ONFOCUS="stayAway()"> Word to guess<BR>
     <INPUT TYPE="TEXT" NAME="guessed"
      ONFOCUS="stayAway()"> Letters guessed so far<BR>
```

```
<P>Enter your next guess.</P>
<INPUT TYPE="BUTTON" VALUE=" A " ONCLICK="guess('A')">
<INPUT TYPE="BUTTON" VALUE=" B " ONCLICK="guess('B')">
<INPUT TYPE="BUTTON" VALUE=" C " ONCLICK="guess('C')">
<INPUT TYPE="BUTTON" VALUE=" D " ONCLICK="guess('D')">
<INPUT TYPE="BUTTON" VALUE=" E " ONCLICK="guess('E')">
<INPUT TYPE="BUTTON" VALUE=" F " ONCLICK="guess('F')">
<INPUT TYPE="BUTTON" VALUE=" G " ONCLICK="guess('G')">
<INPUT TYPE="BUTTON" VALUE=" H " ONCLICK="guess('H')">
<INPUT TYPE="BUTTON" VALUE=" I " ONCLICK="guess('I')">
<INPUT TYPE="BUTTON" VALUE=" J " ONCLICK="guess('J')">
<INPUT TYPE="BUTTON" VALUE=" K " ONCLICK="guess('K')">
<INPUT TYPE="BUTTON" VALUE=" L " ONCLICK="guess('L')">
<INPUT TYPE="BUTTON" VALUE=" M " ONCLICK="guess('M')">
<INPUT TYPE="BUTTON" VALUE=" N " ONCLICK="guess('N')">
<INPUT TYPE="BUTTON" VALUE=" O " ONCLICK="guess('O')">
<INPUT TYPE="BUTTON" VALUE=" P " ONCLICK="guess('P')">
<INPUT TYPE="BUTTON" VALUE=" Q " ONCLICK="guess('Q')">
<INPUT TYPE="BUTTON" VALUE=" R " ONCLICK="guess('R')">
<INPUT TYPE="BUTTON" VALUE=" S " ONCLICK="guess('S')">
<INPUT TYPE="BUTTON" VALUE=" T " ONCLICK="guess('T')">
<INPUT TYPE="BUTTON" VALUE=" U " ONCLICK="guess('U')">
<INPUT TYPE="BUTTON" VALUE=" V " ONCLICK="guess('V')">
<INPUT TYPE="BUTTON" VALUE=" W " ONCLICK="guess('W')">
<INPUT TYPE="BUTTON" VALUE=" X " ONCLICK="guess('X')">
<INPUT TYPE="BUTTON" VALUE=" Y " ONCLICK="guess('Y')">
<INPUT TYPE="BUTTON" VALUE=" Z " ONCLICK="guess('Z')"><P>
<INPUT TYPE="BUTTON" NAME="restart"
 VALUE="---- Start Again ----"
 ONCLICK="startAgain()">
<SCRIPT LANGUAGE="JavaScript"><!--
startAgain()
// --></SCRIPT>
</FORM>
</BODY>
</HTML>
```

The script defines two arrays: gallows and guessChoices; and eight functions: startAgain(), stayAway(), displayHangman(), display-ToGuess(), displayGuessed(), badGuess(), winner(), and guess(). Each of these is discussed in the following paragraphs.

The *gallows* Array

This array contains eight string entries that correspond to the eight states the gallows pole can be in: empty, head hanging, head and upper torso hanging, and so on. The strings may look cryptic, because a new line is represented by the newline character (\n) and a backslash is represented by a pair of backslashes (\\). These are the standard escape characters used by JavaScript, Java, C, and C++. Try decoding and drawing each of the strings in the gallows array to get a better feel for how these escape characters are used.

The *guessChoices* Array

This array contains four words, which are the words that the user is required to guess. One word from this array is randomly selected for each play of the game. You can add or replace the words contained in this array to tailor Hangman to your own word list.

The *startAgain()* Function

This function starts and restarts the Hangman game. It initializes variables used by the program and then invokes the functions required to display the hangman, show the word to be guessed, and display the letters that the user has already guessed. The guesses variable keeps track of how many incorrect guesses the user has made. It is used to select which element of the gallows array is to be displayed. The max variable determines how many guesses the user can make before being hung. The guessed variable is initialized to " " (one space) to indicate that the user has not yet guessed any letters.

NOTE

The value " " is used instead of "" (no space) because the indexOf() method of the string object behaves differently for the value "" than it does for any specific value.

   The len variable is used to calculate the maximum array subscript of the guessChoices array. The toGuess variable is set to a randomly selected word in the guessChoices array. This word is then converted to uppercase. The displayHangman() function displays the hangman figure in the status text area. The displayToGuess() function displays the word being guessed in the toGuess text field. The displayGuessed() function displays the letters guessed by the user in the guessed text field. When the game is first started or restarted, the displayGuessed() function is used to blank out the guessed text field.

The *stayAway()* Function

This function is called by the onFocus event handlers associated with the text fields; it warns the user not to edit the contents of the fields. Note that it moves the input focus to the A button before it displays the alert box.

The *displayHangman()* Function

This function displays the hangman character figure in the status text area. It does so by setting the value property of the status field of the current document's game form to the gallows array entry corresponding to the number of incorrect guesses.

The *displayToGuess()* Function

This function displays a word pattern based on the word to be guessed and the letters the user has currently guessed. If a user has guessed a letter of the word, that letter is displayed. Otherwise, an underscore character is displayed in place of the letter. The function loops through each letter of the word contained in toGuess and uses the string object's indexOf() method to determine whether that letter is contained in the guessed string. The word pattern is then written to the toGuessed text field.

The *displayGuessed()* Function

This function writes the value of the guessed variable to the guessed text field to inform the user of the letters they have tried. The guessed variable is updated each time a user makes a new letter guess.

The *badGuess()* Function

This function returns true if the letter represented by the s parameter is not in the word contained in the toGuess variable, and false otherwise. It is used to determine whether the user has guessed a letter in the word.

The *winner()* Function

This function checks each letter in the word in the toGuess variable and returns false if any letter is not in the string contained in the guessed variable. It returns true otherwise. It is used to determine whether the user has correctly guessed all letters of the toGuess word.

The *guess()* Function

This function is invoked whenever the user clicks a button with a letter from A through Z. It is invoked by the button's onClick event handler and passes the letter associated with the button via the s parameter.

Here's how it works:

1. The guess() function checks to see if the letter is currently in the list of letters the user has already guessed, and adds the letter to the list if it is not.

2. It checks to see if the letter is an incorrect guess, and increments the guesses variable accordingly.

3. It invokes the appropriate functions to redisplay the form's text fields.

4. It checks to see if the user has run out of guesses; if so, it alerts the user that they have been hung.

5. It invokes the winner() function to determine if the user has correctly guessed all letters of the toGuess word; if so, it tells the user that they have won.

The form displayed by the browser is named game. It contains the text area named status, the text fields named toGuess and guessed, the buttons labeled A through Z, and the Start Again button. Each element performs event handling that supports the processing of the Hangman game. This event handling is as follows:

status, *toGuess*, **and** *guessed*   These fields handle the onFocus event by invoking the stayAway() function to tell the user not to mess with the field's contents.

A through Z   These buttons handle the onClick event by invoking the guess() function and passing as a parameter the letter associated with the button.

Start Again   This button invokes the startAgain() function to reinitialize the game's variables and restart the game.

The script contained in the document body contains the single statement startAgain(), which initializes the variables used in the game and displays the contents of the form's text fields.

Client-Side Form Processing

The Hangman game in the preceding section is a great example of the power of local form processing. However, unless your sole purpose in web programming is to entertain those who browse your web page, you'll probably want to use forms to return data to your web server. This brings up an important question: Which processing should be performed locally via browser-side scripts, and which should be performed on the server? For the most part, this question is easy to answer: "If it can be performed on the browser, do it." It's a pretty good rule of thumb. However, as with most rules of thumb, some cases create exceptions.

For example, if you don't want anyone to know how you process the form data, don't do it locally on the browser. Anyone can figure out your processing approach by examining your JavaScript code. Another consideration is performance. If your web application requires a time- or resource-intensive computation, you can avoid upsetting your user by having the data sent back to your high-performance server for processing. A third issue is whether you can be 100 percent sure that every visitor will have a sufficiently capable JavaScript-enabled browser—what happens to your form processing if their browser ignores all the event handlers? All that said, forms processing is short and quick in most cases, and no noticeable impact is made on browser performance.

WORKING WITH CGI SCRIPTS

Before the advent of JavaScript, the data that forms collected from users was submitted to Common Gateway Interface (CGI) programs. The CGI programs performed all processing on the form data, and sent the results of that processing back to the browser for display to users. In this section, I'll show how to use JavaScript scripts to communicate with CGI programs on the server. More importantly, I'll show how to use JavaScript to perform local processing of form data before sending the data to CGI programs.

Sending Form Data to a CGI Program

When a form sends data to a CGI program, it uses either the GET or POST method. You specify this method by either setting the METHOD attribute of the form to "GET" or "POST" or specifying the appropriate method in the FORM tag on the page. If you use the GET method, the form encodes and appends its data to the URL of the CGI program. When a web server receives the encoded URL, it passes the form data to the CGI program via an *environment* variable. If you use the POST method, the web server passes the form's data to the CGI program via the program's standard input. The POST method is preferred over the GET method both because of data-size limitations associated with URLs (a max of 1024 characters of data) and because the POST method hides the data from the user. The form object's method property allows a form's method to be set within JavaScript.

A form's ACTION attribute specifies the URL of the CGI program to which a form's data is to be sent. The form object's action property lets you set or change this URL within JavaScript. Doing so allows a script to send a form's data to one of several CGI programs, depending upon the form's contents as entered by a user. For example, you can use a general-purpose form to collect information about users interested in your product line and then process that data in different ways, depending upon the demographic data supplied by the user.

In most cases, form data is encoded using the URL encoding scheme identified by the following MIME type: application/x-www-form-urlencoded. However, it is likely that another scheme will become popular over time, because of its support for file uploads:

```
multipart/form-data encoding
```

This encoding scheme is discussed in RFC 1867, which can be found at the URL www.jaworski.com/javascript/rfc1867.txt. The form object's encoding property identifies the encoding scheme specified by the form's ENCTYPE attribute. You can also use the encoding property to change this attribute.

NOTE

An RFC (Request for Comments) is a document used to describe a particular aspect of the Internet, such as a protocol standard or a coding scheme.

Performing Local Form Processing

Having covered the basic form properties that control a form's interaction with a CGI program, let's investigate how JavaScript can be used to locally process a form's data and then send the processed data to the web server. When a form is submitted, either as the result of a user clicking a submit button or the invocation of a form's submit() method, all the data in the form's fields is sent to the web server. This approach is both inefficient and undesirable, because you can use JavaScript to preprocess a form's data.

The secret to using JavaScript to send processed form data to CGI programs is to use a *summary form* to hold the data that is the result of local form processing. Once a form's data has been initially processed, it is put into a summary form; then the summary form is sent to the CGI program for any additional processing that is required. Listing 5.3

illustrates this concept. A web page is designed with two forms. The first form, shown in Figure 5.7, is visible to the user and is used to collect raw input data. It provides the user with four selection lists from which to select a type of automobile.

Listing 5.3: Using a Summary Form to Support Local Processing (*orderform.htm*)

```
<HTML>
<HEAD>
<TITLE>Submitting the results of local
 form processing</TITLE>
<SCRIPT LANGUAGE="JavaScript"><!--
function processOrder() {
 order = ""
 order += document.orderForm.model.selectedIndex
 order += document.orderForm.doors.selectedIndex
 order += document.orderForm.color.selectedIndex
 sel = document.orderForm.accessories
 for(i=0;i<sel.length;++i)
  if(sel.options[i].selected) order += i
 document.submitForm.result.value = order
 document.submitForm.submit()
 return false
}
// --></SCRIPT>
</HEAD>
<BODY>
<H1>Select your next car:</H1>
<PRE>Model       Doors   Color    Accessories</PRE>
<FORM ACTION="" NAME="orderForm"
 ONSUBMTT="return processOrder()">
<SELECT NAME="model" SIZE="3">
<OPTION>Big Blob</OPTION>
<OPTION>Wild Thing</OPTION>
<OPTION>Penny Pincher</OPTION>
<OPTION>Class Act</OPTION>
</SELECT>
<SELECT NAME="doors" SIZE="3">
<OPTION>2 doors</OPTION>
<OPTION>4 doors</OPTION>
</SELECT>
<SELECT NAME="color" SIZE="3">
```

```
<OPTION>red</OPTION>
<OPTION>white</OPTION>
<OPTION>blue</OPTION>
<OPTION>black</OPTION>
<OPTION>brown</OPTION>
<OPTION>silver</OPTION>
<OPTION>pink</OPTION>
</SELECT>
<SELECT NAME="accessories" SIZE="3" MULTIPLE="MULTIPLE">
<OPTION>air conditioning</OPTION>
<OPTION>CD player</OPTION>
<OPTION>bigger engine</OPTION>
<OPTION>fancy dashboard</OPTION>
<OPTION>leather seats</OPTION>
</SELECT>
<P>
<INPUT TYPE="SUBMIT" NAME="order"
 VALUE="I'll take it!"></P>
</FORM>
<FORM ACTION="http://www.jaworski.com/cgi-bin/echo.cgi"
      METHOD="GET" NAME="submitForm">
<INPUT TYPE="HIDDEN" NAME="result">
</FORM>
</BODY>
</HTML>
```

When the first form is submitted, the onSubmit event handler invokes the processOrder() function as the argument of a return statement. If the function returns false, the form is not submitted; but if it returns true, the form *is* submitted to the server. Because processOrder() *always* returns false, the form will never be submitted. Instead, process-Order() fills in the invisible field in the second form and submits the second form to a CGI program located on my web server. This CGI program is located at the URL www.jaworski.com/cgi-bin/echo.cgi. It merely echoes back any form fields that it has received from the browser. Figure 5.8 provides an example of the CGI program's output.

I'll summarize what I've covered so far. The first form gathers automobile selection data from the user. When the first form is submitted, process-Order() is invoked to process this data locally on the user's browser. processOrder() then inserts the processed data into the second form (named submitForm) and submits the second form to my web server. The web server then echoes the form fields back to the browser.

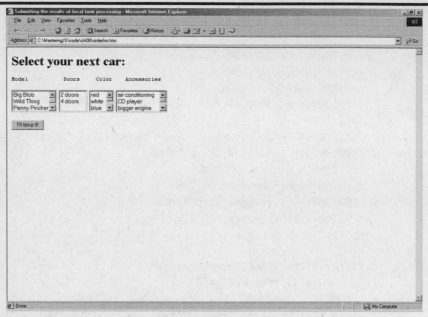

FIGURE 5.7:   The form presented to the user (Listing 5.3)

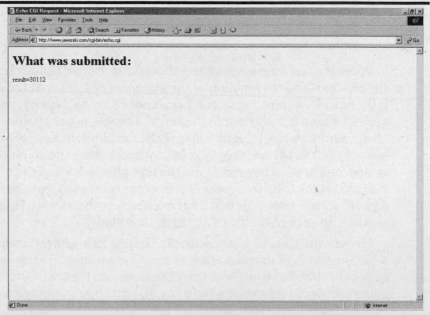

FIGURE 5.8:   The form data echoed by the web server (Listing 5.3)

The processing performed by processOrder() is quite simple, but it illustrates how locally processed form data can be sent to a web server. Here are the steps:

1. processOrder() begins by setting the order variable to a string that contains the indices of the list items selected in the model, doors, and colors selection lists. Each of these three lists is a single-selection list.

2. For each item in the multiple-selection accessories list, processOrder() checks to see if the item has been selected, and appends the index of each selected accessories item to the string stored in the order variable.

3. The processOrder() function sets the invisible results field of submitForm to the value stored in order. By doing so, it places all of the first form's results into a single field in submitForm.

4. The processOrder() function invokes the submit() method of submitForm to send the result field to my web server.

Although you may not be impressed by the complexity of the processing performed by processOrder(), you should realize the value of the approach it takes. This approach allows you to design your forms so that they are most appealing to your end users. When the user submits a filled-out form, you can process the form's results and send the results to your web server in whatever format is most efficient for your CGI or other server-side programs.

TIP

The only caution I'll add is that your server-side CGI still must be capable of handling unprocessed data, in case you are visited by someone with an older browser or with a special browser adapted for surfers with visual impairment or other accessibility concerns. One solution, of course, is to kick back the information with a "please upgrade your browser" message, but because the goal is to sell cars, that's probably not the ideal strategy. This issue points to a dilemma facing website designers who seek to have maximum processing on the page itself, and there's no perfect solution. You'll need to have a good understanding of your site's visitors and make sure their needs are met as best possible.

What's Next

This chapter introduced the form object and discussed the JavaScript objects associated with form fields and GUI controls. You've learned how to work with the properties and methods of these objects, and how to handle form-related events. In the next chapter, you'll see how to enhance your forms by using hidden form fields and cookies.

From a web server's standpoint, each request received for a page or CGI is from a new user; nothing in the request tells the server what the user entered in an HTML form three pages back. So, in Chapter 6 we'll discuss ways to individually identify users, and how to pass along important data between visits to different HTML forms. This is a key concept in developing a web application.

Chapter 6
USING HIDDEN FIELDS AND COOKIES

The Web was originally designed to be *stateless*, in the sense that all web servers would process URL requests in the same manner, independent of any previous requests. This design enabled the first web servers to be fast and efficient by not requiring them to maintain information about the browsers requesting URLs. Browsers also operated in a stateless fashion, processing new URL requests independently of previous requests.

The stateless design of the Web works well in most cases. When a browser requests a particular web page, the web server that provides that page serves it up to the browser the same way every time. Similarly, all web browsers requesting a particular web page always request that page in the same way. However, in some situations you *want* the processing of one web page to be dependent on the processing of previous pages. For example, you may want to enable a user to complete a series of forms in which the user's responses to the first form determine which forms are

Adapted from *Mastering JavaScript Premium Edition*
by James Jaworski
ISBN 0-7821-2819-X

provided next. For example, you may want to create a form that collects general information about the user, such as name and address, and link it to subsequent forms to collect more information. However, those forms will vary, depending on what country the user has entered in the first form.

A number of capabilities have been successively introduced to enable web applications to be built on the stateless design of the Web. *Hidden form fields* were introduced first, followed by HTTP *cookies*. These capabilities allow CGI programs to maintain information about individual web browsers. With JavaScript's support of browser-side scripting, the use of hidden fields and cookies can be taken to new levels.

In this chapter, you'll learn how to use hidden fields and cookies to maintain browser state information and how you can use this information in your scripts to develop more capable and powerful web applications. When you've finished this chapter, you'll be able to read and update hidden fields and cookies using JavaScript, and locally implement on the browser side much of the complex state-related processing that would otherwise be performed by server-side CGI programs.

MAINTAINING STATE INFORMATION

To gain a greater understanding of the problem of maintaining state information, let's explore the example discussed in this chapter's introduction. Suppose you want to develop a web page that presents a related series of forms to a user as follows:

Form 1   Collects the user's name, address, phone number, and e-mail address

Form 2   Asks the user which of your products they currently use

Form 3   Asks the user to evaluate the products they use

Say the user receives the first form, fills it out, and submits it. It goes to a CGI program located on your web server. This CGI program processes the form's data and sends the second form to the user. The user fills out the second form and submits it. It goes to the same or perhaps a different CGI program on your server. When this CGI program receives the second form's data, it has no way of knowing that the second form's data is related to the data of the first form. Therefore, it cannot combine the results of the two forms in its database. The same problem occurs with the CGI program that receives the third form's data.

There is a workaround to this problem. You can have users enter a small piece of common information, such as their e-mail address, in all three forms. When the second and third forms are submitted to your web server, a CGI program can combine their data based upon the common e-mail address. This workaround allows your CGI programs to continue to operate in a stateless manner. However, your users suffer by having to re-enter their e-mail address in all three forms. Although this may not seem to be much of an inconvenience, it is noticeable, and it detracts from the appeal of your forms.

It would be even better if your CGI program could remember the e-mail address entered on the first form and attach it to the second and third forms that it sends to your browser. Hidden form fields (discussed next) were added to HTML to provide CGI programs with this specific capability.

Using Hidden Form Fields

Hidden form fields are text fields that are not displayed and cannot be modified by a user. Forms with hidden fields are usually generated by CGI programs as the result of processing data submitted by other forms.

In most cases, a CGI program sets a hidden field to a particular value when the server sends a form to a browser. When a user fills out and submits a form containing a hidden field, the value originally stored in the field is returned to the server. The server uses the information stored in the hidden field to maintain state information about the user's browser. To see how this works, let's examine how hidden fields can be used in the three-form example discussed in the previous section.

When a user fills out the name and address information and submits form 1, the CGI program on your server processes the form data by creating a record in a database and sending form 2 back to the user. However, instead of sending a static form 2, it dynamically *generates* a form 2 that contains a hidden field, with the field's value set to the e-mail address submitted in the first form. It might look like this in the HTML source:

```
<input type="hidden" name="email" value="someone@somewhere">
```

When the user fills out and submits form 2, the hidden field (still with the user's e-mail address) is sent to your CGI program. Your CGI program can now relate the data of the second form with that of the first because they both have the same value in the e-mail address field (even though the user did not have to retype their e-mail address in the second form). The same process is carried out for the third form, after which the CGI program sends back a web page to the user, thanking him or her for filling out the forms.

WARNING

Although hidden form fields aren't displayed in a browser's main window, that doesn't mean the data in these fields is completely inaccessible to the user. For instance, most browsers have a "view source" feature that displays a page's raw HTML code, including all hidden field values. Furthermore, a nefarious user could write a client-side script that substitutes different values for hidden fields the CGI is expecting. Many Internet security alerts have resulted from CGI programs' blind acceptance of hidden fields' values.

JavaScript and Hidden Form Fields

At this point, you are probably wondering what any of this has to do with JavaScript. JavaScript's browser-side programming features take full advantage of and enhance the capabilities provided by hidden fields. With JavaScript, you can eliminate the need to send three forms back and forth between the user's browser and your CGI programs. A JavaScript script can perform the processing of all three forms locally on the user's browser and then consolidate the forms' results before sending them to a CGI program.

To see how JavaScript can use hidden fields to implement the three-form customer survey, open the survey.htm file with your browser. (To download this book's code, go to the book's product page at http://www.sybex.com/.) This survey file uses the hidden form control.htm. Your browser will display the first form of a three-form series, as shown in Figure 6.1. Fill out this form and click the Next button. Make sure you fill in the E-mail Address field; otherwise, you will receive the alert message shown in Figure 6.2.

FIGURE 6.1:   The first form of the customer survey asks the user to enter general name and address information. (Listing 6.3)

FIGURE 6.2:   If the user skips the E-mail Address field, the form validation alert notifies the user that this information is necessary. (Listing 6.3)

After you click the Next button, the form shown in Figure 6.3 is displayed. This form asks you to identify which products you use. Click the check box of at least one of these fictitious products.

NOTE
If you do not select at least one of the four products, the third part of the form will be skipped.

After you click the Next button of the second form, the third form is displayed, as shown in Figure 6.4. The third form asks you to evaluate the products you selected in the second form. Use the radio buttons to perform your product evaluation.

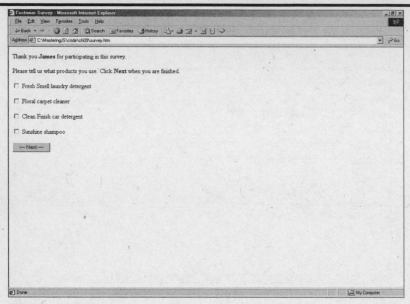

FIGURE 6.3: The second form of the customer survey asks users what products they use. (Listing 6.4)

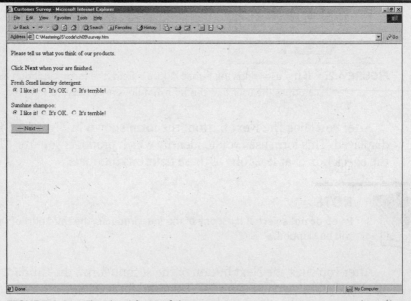

FIGURE 6.4: The third form of the customer survey asks customers how they like the products. (Listing 6.5)

When you click the Next button on the third form, all the values from the three forms are collectively sent to the CGI program located at www.jaworski.com/cgi-bin/thanks.cgi. This CGI program reads these values and then sends back the thank-you message shown in Figure 6.5.

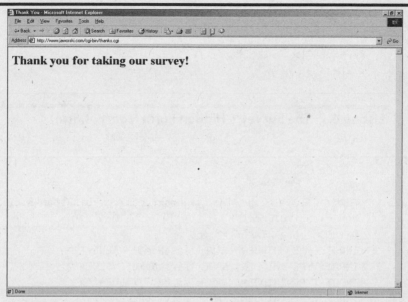

FIGURE 6.5:   The thank-you message is displayed after the user completes the survey.

The processing performed in the example all takes place on the user's browser. A CGI program is not required until after all three forms have been filled out. The values of these forms are stored in a separate, invisible form that consists entirely of hidden fields. As the user completes each form, the values of the current form are stored in the hidden fields of the invisible form. When the user has completed the third form (or completed the second form without checking any products), the result is submitted to the CGI program. This approach is much more efficient than having a CGI program process the results of each form separately.

The survey.htm file shown in Listing 6.1 defines a two-frame set. The first frame loads the file form1.htm (Listing 6.3) and the second frame loads control.htm (Listing 6.2). The BORDER attribute of the frame set is set to 0 to avoid displaying a distracting border between frames.

Listing 6.1: Defining the Survey's Frame Set (*survey.htm*)

```
<HTML>
<HEAD>
<TITLE>Customer Survey</TITLE>
</HEAD>
<FRAMESET COLS="*,10" BORDER="0">
<FRAME SRC="form1.htm">
<FRAME SRC="control.htm">
</FRAMESET>
</HTML>
```

Listing 6.2: The Survey's Hidden Form (*control.htm*)

```
<HTML>
<HEAD>
</HEAD>
<BODY>
<FORM ACTION="http://www.jaworski.com/cgi-bin/thanks.cgi"
 NAME="controlForm"
 METHOD="post" TARGET="_top">
<INPUT TYPE="HIDDEN" NAME="lastName" VALUE="">
<INPUT TYPE="HIDDEN" NAME="firstName" VALUE="">
<INPUT TYPE="HIDDEN" NAME="street" VALUE="">
<INPUT TYPE="HIDDEN" NAME="city" VALUE="">
<INPUT TYPE="HIDDEN" NAME="state" VALUE="">
<INPUT TYPE="HIDDEN" NAME="country" VALUE="">
<INPUT TYPE="HIDDEN" NAME="zip" VALUE="">
<INPUT TYPE="HIDDEN" NAME="phone" VALUE="">
<INPUT TYPE="HIDDEN" NAME="email" VALUE="">
<INPUT TYPE="HIDDEN" NAME="products" VALUE="">
<INPUT TYPE="HIDDEN" NAME="evaluation" VALUE="">
</FORM>
</BODY>
</HTML>
```

Listing 6.3: The First Form of the Survey (*form1.htm*)

```
<HTML>
<HEAD>
<TITLE>Customer Survey: General Information</TITLE>
```

```
<SCRIPT LANGUAGE="JavaScript"><!--
function processForm1() {
 form1 = document.forms["formOne"]
 if(form1.email.value=="")
  alert("You must fill in your e-mail address!")
 else {
  controlForm = parent.frames[1].document.controlForm
  controlForm.lastName.value=form1.lastName.value
  controlForm.firstName.value=form1.firstName.value
  controlForm.street.value=form1.street.value
  controlForm.city.value=form1.city.value
  controlForm.state.value=form1.state.value
  controlForm.country.value=form1.country.value
  controlForm.zip.value=form1.zip.value
  controlForm.phone.value=form1.phone.value
  controlForm.email.value=form1.email.value
  location.href="form2.htm"
 }
}
// --></SCRIPT>
</HEAD>
<BODY>
<P>Dear Valued Customer:</P>
<P>Thank you for participating in our survey. Please fill out
 the following general information and then click <B>Next</B>
 to continue with the survey.</P>
<FORM ACTION="" NAME="formOne">
<P>Last name: <INPUT TYPE="TEXT" NAME="lastName">
 First name: <INPUT TYPE="TEXT" NAME="firstName"></P>
<P>Street address:
<INPUT TYPE="TEXT" SIZE="50" NAME="street">
 </P>
<P>City: <INPUT TYPE="TEXT" NAME="city">
 State/Province: <INPUT TYPE="TEXT" NAME="state"></P>
<P>Country: <INPUT TYPE="TEXT" NAME="country">
 Postal code: <INPUT TYPE="TEXT" NAME="zip"></P>
<P>Phone number: <INPUT TYPE="TEXT" NAME="phone"></P>
<P>E-mail address: <INPUT TYPE="TEXT" SIZE="30" NAME="email">
 </P>
<P></P>
<INPUT TYPE="BUTTON" NAME="next" VALUE="---- Next ----"
 onClick="processForm1()">
```

```
</FORM>
</BODY>
</HTML>
```

The `control.htm` file defines a form with 11 hidden fields. Because all of the form's fields are hidden, the form is not displayed. These fields are filled in with the data collected by the three visible forms that are displayed to the user.

The form's NAME attribute is set to `"controlForm"`. This setting allows the form to be referenced by name by the JavaScript code that executes with the forms contained in the first frame. (See Chapter 5, "Processing Forms," for more information about accessing form values within JavaScript.)

The form's ACTION attribute is set to the URL of the target CGI program, and its METHOD attribute is set to `"post"`. When the form is submitted, this CGI program receives the data that has been stored in the hidden fields and returns a thank-you message to the user. The form's TARGET attribute is `"_top"`. This value causes the thank-you message to be displayed in the full window occupied by `survey.htm` rather than in the frame occupied by `control.htm`.

The `form1.htm` file displays the form shown in Figure 6.1 in the first frame of the frame set. It contains a single script that defines the `process-Form1()` function. This function handles the onClick event generated when the user clicks the Next button. It sets the form1 variable to document `.forms["formOne"]` so that it can be used as a shortcut (to avoid having to retype the document prefix). It then checks to see if the email field is blank. If it is blank, it displays an alert dialog box to the user; otherwise, it continues on with its processing. The controlForm variable is used as a shortcut to the hidden form stored in the second frame. All the fields from form1 are then copied into the hidden fields of controlForm. Finally, the form2.htm (Listing 6.4) file is loaded into the first frame, and formTwo replaces formOne.

Listing 6.4: The Second Form of the Survey (*form2.htm*)

```
<HTML>
<HEAD>
<TITLE>Customer Survey: Product Usage</TITLE>
<SCRIPT LANGUAGE="JavaScript"><!--
function processForm2() {
  controlForm = parent.frames[1].document.controlForm
  form2 = document.forms["formTwo"]
```

```
   products = ""
   if(form2.laundry.checked) products += "1"
   if(form2.carpet.checked) products += "1"
   if(form2.car.checked) products += "1"
   if(form2.shampoo.checked) products += "1"
   controlForm.products.value=products
   location.href="form3.htm"
}
// --></SCRIPT>
</HEAD>
<BODY>
<SCRIPT LANGUAGE="JavaScript"><!--
var s = "<P>Thank you <B>"
s += parent.frames[1].document.controlForm.firstName.value
s += "</B>"
document.write(s)+
document.writeln("for participating in this survey.</P>")
// --></SCRIPT>
<P>Please tell us what products you use. Click <B>Next</B>
  when you are finished.</P>
<FORM NAME="formTwo">
<P><INPUT TYPE="CHECKBOX" NAME="laundry">
  Fresh Smell laundry detergent</P>
<P><INPUT TYPE="CHECKBOX" NAME="carpet">
  Floral carpet cleaner</P>
<P><INPUT TYPE="CHECKBOX" NAME="car">
  Clean Finish car detergent</P>
<P><INPUT TYPE="CHECKBOX" NAME="shampoo">
  Sunshine shampoo</P>
<P></P>
<P><INPUT TYPE="BUTTON" NAME="next"
  VALUE="---- Next ----" onClick="processForm2()"></P>
</FORM>
</BODY>
</HTML>
```

The form2.htm file displays the form shown in Figure 6.3. It contains two scripts—one in the document head and the other in the document body. The script in the document body is executed when the web page is generated. This script is used to insert the first name of the user into the text that is displayed above the form. The script in the document head defines the processForm2() function. This function handles the onClick event that is generated when the user clicks the Next button. It sets the hidden products field of controlForm based on the products the user has checked. It then loads form3.htm (Listing 6.5) as the replacement for form2.htm in the first frame.

Listing 6.5: The Third Form of the Survey (*form3.htm*)

```
<HTML>
<HEAD>
<TITLE>Customer Survey: Product Evaluation</TITLE>
<SCRIPT LANGUAGE="JavaScript"><!--
function usesProducts() {
 productsUsed =
  parent.frames[1].document.controlForm.products.value
 usage = new Array(productsUsed.length)
 productsInUse=false
 for(i=0;i<usage.length;++i) {
  if(productsUsed.charAt(i)=="0") usage[i]=false
  else{
   usage[i]=true
   productsInUse=true
  }
 }
 return productsInUse
}
function askAboutProducts() {
 document.writeln
  ('<P>Please tell us what you think of our products.</P>')
 document.writeln
  ('<P>Click <B>Next</B> when your are finished.</P>')
 document.writeln('<FORM NAME="formThree">')
 if(usage[0]){
  document.writeln('<P>Fresh Smell laundry detergent:<BR>')
  document.writeln('<INPUT TYPE="RADIO" NAME="laundry"')
  document.writeln('VALUE="like" CHECKED> I like it!')
  document.writeln('<INPUT TYPE="RADIO" NAME="laundry"')
  document.writeln('VALUE="ok"> It\'s OK.')
  document.writeln('<INPUT TYPE="RADIO" NAME="laundry"')
  document.writeln('VALUE="dislike"> It\'s terrible!')
  document.writeln('</P>')
 }
 if(usage[1]){
  document.writeln('<P>Floral carpet cleaner:<BR>')
  document.writeln('<INPUT TYPE="RADIO" NAME="carpet"')
```

```
    document.writeln('VALUE="like" CHECKED> I like it!')
    document.writeln('<INPUT TYPE="RADIO" NAME="carpet"')
    document.writeln('VALUE="ok"> It\'s OK.')
    document.writeln('<INPUT TYPE="RADIO" NAME="carpet"')
    document.writeln('VALUE="dislike"> It\'s terrible!')
    document.writeln('</P>')
  }
  if(usage[2]){
    document.writeln('<P>Clean Finish car detergent:<BR>')
    document.writeln('<INPUT TYPE="RADIO" NAME="car"')
    document.writeln('VALUE="like" CHECKED> I like it!')
    document.writeln('<INPUT TYPE="RADIO" NAME="car"')
    document.writeln('VALUE="ok"> It\'s OK.')
    document.writeln('<INPUT TYPE="RADIO" NAME="car"')
    document.writeln('VALUE="dislike"> It\'s terrible!')
    document.writeln('</P>')
  }
  if(usage[3]){
    document.writeln('<P>Sunshine shampoo:<BR>')
    document.writeln('<INPUT TYPE="RADIO" NAME="shampoo"')
    document.writeln('VALUE="like" CHECKED> I like it!')
    document.writeln('<INPUT TYPE="RADIO" NAME="shampoo"')
    document.writeln('VALUE="ok"> It\'s OK.')
    document.writeln('<INPUT TYPE="RADIO" NAME="shampoo"')
    document.writeln('VALUE="dislike"> It\'s terrible!')
    document.writeln('</P>')
  }
  document.writeln('<P></P><P>')
  document.writeln('<INPUT TYPE="BUTTON" NAME="next"')
  document.writeln('VALUE="---- Next ----" ')
  document.writeln(' onClick="processForm3()"></P>')
  document.writeln('</FORM>')
}
function processForm3() {
  controlForm = parent.frames[1].document.controlForm
  form3 = document.forms["formThree"]
  evaluation = ""
  for(i=0;i<form3.elements.length-1;++i)
    if(form3.elements[i].checked)
      evaluation += form3.elements[i].value + " "
  controlForm.evaluation.value=evaluation
  controlForm.submit()
}
```

```
// --></SCRIPT>
</HEAD>
<BODY>
<SCRIPT LANGUAGE="JavaScript"><!--
if(usesProducts()) askAboutProducts()
else parent.frames[1].document.controlForm.submit()
// --></SCRIPT>
</BODY>
</HTML>
```

The form3.htm file, unlike form1.htm and form2.htm, consists almost entirely of JavaScript code. Most of the code is contained in the script located in the document's head. A small script is contained in the document's body. This script invokes the usesProducts() function to determine whether the user checked any products when they filled out formTwo. If the user checked at least one product, the askAboutProducts() function is invoked to generate formThree. Otherwise, the controlForm is submitted as is, without the user having to fill in formThree.

The script in the document head defines three functions: uses-Products(), askAboutProducts(), and processForm3:

The *usesProducts()* Function   This function checks the hidden products field of controlForm to determine what products the user checked when filling in formTwo. It initializes the usage array based on this information. It sets productsInUse to true if the user has checked any products in formTwo, and to false otherwise. It then returns this value as a result.

The *askAboutProducts()* Function   This function generates the HTML content of formThree. It creates a short text introduction to the form, generates the <form> tag, and generates a set of three radio buttons for each product the user selected in formTwo. It then generates a Next button for the form, setting the form's onClick event handler to processForm3(). Finally, it generates the closing </form> tag.

The *processForm3()* Function   This function handles the onClick event generated when the user clicks the Next button after filling out formThree. It summarizes the radio buttons checked by the user and stores this summary in the hidden evaluation field of controlForm. It then submits the data contained in controlForm.

USING COOKIES

Hidden form fields were introduced to enable CGI programs to maintain state information about web browsers. They work well in situations in which the state information is to be maintained for a short period of time, as is the case when a user fills out a series of forms. However, hidden fields do not allow state information to be maintained in a *persistent* manner. That is, hidden fields can only be used on a page containing a form that encompasses the hidden fields. When a user leaves that page or exits the browser, the information contained in a hidden form field is lost forever.

Netscape developed the *cookie* as a means to store state-related and other information in a persistent manner. The information stored in a cookie is maintained between browser sessions; it survives when the user turns off their machine, because it's written to a cookie file on the local client system. Cookies allow CGI and other programs to store information on web browsers for significantly longer time periods.

NOTE
Cookies are supported by Netscape Navigator, Internet Explorer (IE), Mozilla, Safari, and most other major browsers.

A cookie usually consists of information sent by a server-side program in response to a URL request from the browser. The browser stores the information in the local cookie file (the cookie jar) according to the URL of the CGI program sending the cookie. This URL may be generalized, based on additional information contained in the cookie.

When a browser requests a URL from a web server, the browser first searches the local cookie files to see if the URL of any of its cookies matches the URL being requested. The browser then sends the information contained in the matching cookie or cookies to the web server as part of the URL request. Cookies provide CGI programs with the capability to store information on browsers. Browsers return this information to CGI programs when they request the URL of the CGI program. CGI programs update cookies when they respond to browser URL requests. In this manner, a CGI program can use browsers to maintain state information and have the browsers return this information whenever the user invokes the CGI program.

To get a better feel for how cookies work, let's revisit the three-form example introduced earlier in this chapter. The goal is to implement a sequence of forms in which each form expands upon the information gathered in previous forms. In order to do this, a CGI program must be able to relate the data received in later forms with that received in earlier forms. The solution is for the CGI program to identify related forms using data that is common to these forms. A person's e-mail address is a common example of this identifying data.

Cookies provide a persistent mechanism for storing identifying data. When a browser submits formOne to a CGI program, the CGI program responds by sending formTwo to the browser. A cookie containing the user's e-mail address accompanies this second form. When the browser submits formTwo, it returns any cookies that match the CGI program to which the form is submitted. This causes the user's e-mail address to be returned with the submitted formTwo data. The CGI program then sends formThree to the browser. When the user submits formThree, the browser again checks the local cookie file and sends any related cookies.

Cookies are obviously more powerful than hidden form fields. Because cookies can persist between browser sessions, you can use them to store permanent user data, such as identification information (e-mail address) and preferences (frames, background colors, and so on), as well as state information (the current page in an online book).

WARNING

Cookies are less visible to the end user than are the values of hidden fields, but that doesn't mean cookies are completely invisible. Most often, the cookies are stored in a file that is easily readable by anyone with access to the computer on which the browser is run. Even if the client computer's hard disk isn't accessible, the cookies are still sent over the network and, if unencrypted, can be intercepted by anyone with a network sniffer. You should never store sensitive information, such as user accounts and passwords, in cookies.

How Is Information Stored in a Cookie?

A cookie is created when a CGI program includes a Set-Cookie header as part of an HTTP response. This response is generated when a browser requests the URL of the CGI program. The syntax of the Set-Cookie header is the following:

```
Set-Cookie: NAME=VALUE
[; expires=DATE][; path=PATH][; domain=DOMAIN_NAME][; secure]
```

The *NAME=VALUE* field (discussed next) is required. The other fields are optional; however, they should all appear on the same line as the Set-Cookie header.

NOTE

More than one Set-Cookie header may be sent in a single HTTP response.

When a browser sends matching cookies back to a web server, it sends an HTTP request header in the following format:

```
Cookie: NAME1=VALUE1; NAME2=VALUE2; ... NAMEN=VALUEN
```

NAME1 through *NAMEN* identify the cookie names, and *VALUE1* through *VALUEN* identify their values.

The *NAME=VALUE* Field

This field contains the essential data being stored in a cookie. For example, when used to store my e-mail address, it could appear as email=jamie@jaworski.com. A semicolon, comma, or white-space character is not allowed in the *NAME=VALUE* string, per the cookie specification. Applications are free to develop their own encoding schemes for these strings or can use the HTTP standard of %20 for spaces.

The *expires=DATE* Field

This field specifies the expiration date of a cookie. If it is omitted, the cookie expires at the end of the current browser session. The date is specified in the following format:

```
Weekday, DD-Mon-YY HH:MM:SS GMT
```

Weekday is the day of the week, *DD* is the day of the month, *Mon* is the first three letters of the month, *YY* is the year (for example, 02), *HH* is hours, *MM* is minutes, and *SS* is seconds. The GMT time zone is always used. The example date

```
Monday, 20-Sep-10 12:00:00 GMT
```

represents noon GMT on September 20, 2010.

Although cookies store the year in a two-digit year format, no year 2000 (Y2K) problem is associated with them. Browsers accept the year 10 as the year 2010. If cookies are still around in the middle of the twenty-first century, browsers of that era will need to be updated to support dates in the later part of that century. Cookies that specify long-term user preferences should specify an expiration date of several years to help ensure that the cookies are available as needed in the future. Cookies that specify short-term state information should expire in days, at which point the expired (stale) cookies are automatically destroyed.

The *path=PATH* Field

This field specifies a more general path for the URL associated with a cookie. For example, suppose the URL of a CGI program is www.courseone .com/masterjs/js-examples/ch06/test.asp. The *path* of that CGI program is /masterjs/js-examples/ch06/. In order to associate a cookie with all of my CGI programs in this example, I could set path=/masterjs.

The *domain=DOMAIN_NAME* Field

When a cookie is stored in the local filesystem, it is organized by the URL of the CGI program that sent the cookie. The domain field specifies a more general domain name to which the cookie should apply. For example, suppose the URL of the CGI program that sends a cookie has the domain athome.jaworski.com. A domain=jaworski.com field in a cookie associates that cookie with all hosts in the jaworski.com domain, not just the single host athome.jaworski.com. The domain field cannot be used to associate cookies with top-level domains.

The *secure* Field

If the secure field is specified, a cookie is sent over only a secure communication channel (HTTPS servers).

NOTE

You can find Netscape's original documentation on cookies at http:// wp.netscape.com/newsref/std/cookie_spec.html.

Using JavaScript with Cookies

Cookies provide a powerful feature for web application development, but using them with CGI programs can be somewhat messy. You have to design your programs to send cookies via the HTTP response header and to receive cookies via the HTTP request header. Although this is not difficult to implement, it means more processing is performed on the server and not on the browser.

JavaScript, on the other hand, can take full advantage of cookies by reading and setting them locally on the browser, eliminating the need for the cookies to be processed by CGI programs. A JavaScript script can then forward any information the CGI program requires to perform its processing. By using JavaScript to maintain cookies and perform as much processing as possible on the browser, CGI programs can be greatly simplified and in some cases eliminated.

You set the cookie associated with a document using the document's `cookie` property. When you set a cookie, you must provide the same cookie fields that would be provided by a CGI program. For example, consider the following statements:

```
email="jamie@jaworski.com"
expirationDate="Thursday, 01-Dec-11 12:00:00 GMT"
document.cookie="email="+email+";expires="+expirationDate
```

These statements set the value of the cookie property of the current document to the string `"email=jamie@jaworski.com; expires=Thursday, 01-Dec-11 12:00:00 GMT"`. Note that the `expires` field is required to keep the cookie from expiring after the current browser session. You can also use `domain`, `path`, and `secure` fields when a `cookie` property is set.

When the value of the cookie is retrieved using the following statement, `cookieString` is assigned the value `"email=jamie@jaworski.com"`:

```
cookieString=document.cookie
```

If multiple cookies were set for the current document, `cookieString` would contain a list of semicolon-separated *name=value* pairs. For example, consider the following statements:

```
email="jamie@jaworski.com"
firstName="Jamie"
lastName="Jaworski"
expirationDate="Thursday, 01-Dec-11 12:00:00 GMT"
document.cookie="email="+email+";expires="+expirationDate
document.cookie="firstName="+firstName
 +";expires="+expirationDate
document.cookie="lastName="+lastName+
  ";expires="+expirationDate
cookieString=document.cookie
```

The value of `cookieString` includes the *name=value* pairs of the `email`, `firstName`, and `lastName` cookies. This value is `"email=jamie@jaworski .com; firstName=Jamie; lastName=Jaworski"`.

To get a feel for how you access cookies via JavaScript, run the file `cooktest.htm` shown in Listing 6.6. It displays the form shown in Figure 6.6. This form allows you to enter the text of a cookie and then set the cookie by clicking the Set Cookie button. The new value of the cookie is displayed at the top of the web page.

Listing 6.6: A Cookie Test Program (*cooktest.htm*)

```
<HTML>
<HEAD>
<TITLE>Cookie Test</TITLE>
<SCRIPT LANGUAGE="JavaScript"><!--
function updateCookie() {
 document.cookie=document.form1.cookie.value
 location.reload(true)
}
// --></SCRIPT>
</HEAD>
<BODY>
<SCRIPT LANGUAGE="JavaScript">
 document.write("Your current cookie value is: '"+
   document.cookie+"'")
</SCRIPT>
<FORM ACTION="" NAME="form1">
<P>Enter new cookie: <INPUT TYPE="TEXT" SIZE="60"
 NAME="cookie"></P>
<INPUT TYPE="BUTTON" NAME="setCookie" VALUE="Set Cookie"
 onClick="updateCookie()">
</FORM>
</BODY>
</HTML>
```

To see how this script works, enter the cookie shown in Figure 6.7 and click the Set Cookie button. The new cookie is displayed, as shown in Figure 6.8. Experiment with this program by entering cookies with different or no expiration dates, terminating your browser, and restarting it to see which cookies persist between browser sessions.

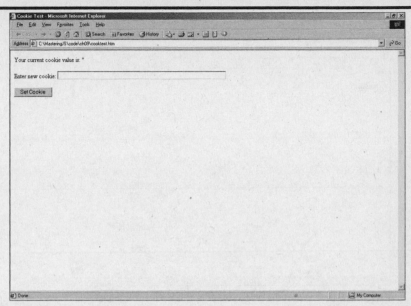

FIGURE 6.6: The cookie test program's opening screen tells the user the current cookie value and prompts them to enter a new cookie. (Listing 6.6)

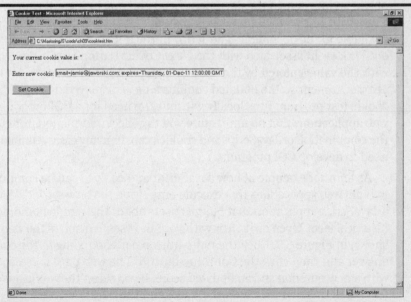

FIGURE 6.7: An example of how to enter the text of a cookie. (Listing 6.6)

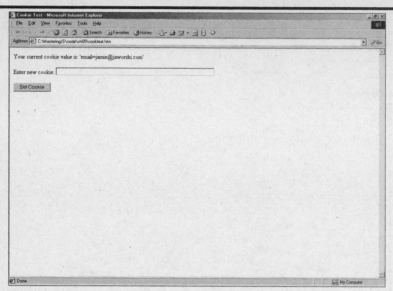

FIGURE 6.8:   When the page reloads, the new cookie is displayed. (Listing 6.6)

The cookie test program is very simple. This attests to the power and flexibility with which JavaScript supports cookies. The program consists of two scripts: one in the document head and one in the document body. The script in the document body displays the current cookie values available to the document. The script in the document head handles the onClick event associated with the Next Cookie button by setting a cookie with the value entered by the user. It then reloads the current cooktest .htm document so the updated cookie value is displayed. Note that the cookie test program runs locally without the need for a CGI program. For web applications that do not require you to collect information from users, the combination of JavaScript and cookies can, in many cases, eliminate the need to develop CGI programs.

As another example of how JavaScript and cookies can be combined to build web applications that execute entirely on the browser, let's develop a JavaScript application that quizzes users about their understanding of historical facts. Open quiz.htm with your browser; it displays the web page shown in Figure 6.9. Click the radio button corresponding to the correct answer and then click the Continue button. The web page is redisplayed with a new question and an updated score. If you select the wrong answer, you are notified with an alert message, and the question is redisplayed. When you have successfully answered all the questions in the quiz, you will be congratulated with the web page shown in Figure 6.10.

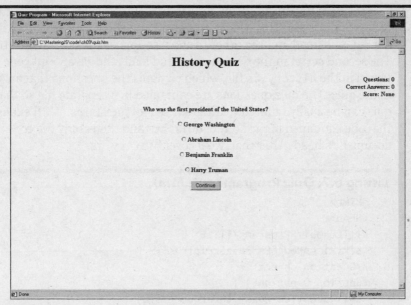

FIGURE 6.9:   The quiz program's opening display lists a quiz question and a group of possible answers. (Listing 6.7)

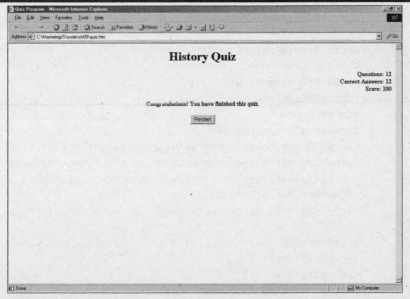

FIGURE 6.10:   The quiz program's final display tells users how well they scored. (Listing 6.7)

The `quiz.htm` file is shown in Listing 6.7. It consists almost entirely of JavaScript code. This code is organized into three scripts: two in the document's head and the other (a short script) in the document's body. The second script in the document's head loads the JavaScript code contained in the `history.js` file, which contains the questions that are used in the quiz. The quiz questions are contained in a separate file so that the quiz can be easily tailored to different sets of questions. We'll examine the code contained in the body of `quiz.htm` and then study the code in the document's head. After that, we'll cover `history.js`.

Listing 6.7: Quiz Program (*quiz.htm*)

```
<HTML>
<HEAD>
<TITLE>Quiz Program</TITLE>
<SCRIPT LANGUAGE="JavaScript"><!--
//Question object
function Question() {
 this.question=Question.arguments[0]
 var n=Question.arguments.length
 this.answers = new Array(n-2)
 for(var i=1; i<n-1; ++i)
  this.answers[i-1]=Question.arguments[i]
 this.correctAnswer=Question.arguments[n-1]
}
function readCookie() {
 currentQuestion=0
 numberOfQuestions=0
 correctAnswers=0
 score="None"
 cookie=document.cookie
 currentQuestion=getNumberValue(cookie,"currentQuestion")
 numberOfQuestions=getNumberValue(cookie,"numberOfQuestions")
 correctAnswers=getNumberValue(cookie,"correctAnswers")
 if(numberOfQuestions>0)
  score=Math.round(correctAnswers*100/numberOfQuestions)
}
function getNumberValue(s,n) {
 s=removeBlanks(s)
 var pairs=s.split(";")
 for(var i=0;i<pairs.length;++i) {
  var pairSplit=pairs[i].split("=")
```

```
  if(pairSplit[0]==n) {
   if(pairSplit.length>1) return parseInt(pairSplit[1])
   else return 0
  }
 }
 return 0
}
function removeBlanks(s) {
 var temp=""
 for(var i=0;i<s.length;++i) {
  var c=s.charAt(i)
  if(c!=" ") temp += c
 }
 return temp
}
function askNextQuestion() {
 document.writeln("<H4 ALIGN='CENTER'>"
  +qa[currentQuestion].question+"</H4>")
 displayAnswers()
}
function displayAnswers() {
 document.writeln('<FORM NAME="answerForm">')
 for(var ii=0;ii<qa[currentQuestion].answers.length;++ii) {
  document.writeln('<H4 ALIGN="CENTER">')
  document.writeln('<INPUT TYPE="RADIO" NAME="answer"> ')
  document.writeln(qa[currentQuestion].answers[ii])
  if(ii+1==qa[currentQuestion].answers.length) {
   document.writeln('<BR><BR><INPUT TYPE="BUTTON"')
   document.writeln('NAME="continue" VALUE="Continue" ')
   document.writeln(' onClick="checkAnswers()">')
  }
  document.writeln('</H4>')
 }
 document.writeln('</FORM>')
}
function checkAnswers() {
 var numAnswers=qa[currentQuestion].answers.length
 var correctAnswer=qa[currentQuestion].correctAnswer
 for(var jj=0;jj<numAnswers;++jj) {
  if(document.answerForm.elements[jj].checked) {
   if(jj==correctAnswer){
    correct()
```

```
        break
      }else{
        incorrect()
        break
      }
    }
    if(jj==numAnswers){
     incorrect()
     break
    }
  }
}
function correct() {
 ++currentQuestion
 ++numberOfQuestions
 ++correctAnswers
 updateCookie()
 location.reload(true)
}
function incorrect() {
 ++numberOfQuestions
 updateCookie()
 alert("Incorrect!")
 location.reload(true)
}
function updateCookie() {
 document.cookie="currentQuestion="+currentQuestion
 document.cookie="numberOfQuestions="+numberOfQuestions
 document.cookie="correctAnswers="+correctAnswers
}
function endQuiz() {
 document.cookie="currentQuestion=0"
 document.cookie="numberOfQuestions=0"
 document.cookie="correctAnswers=0"
 document.writeln('<FORM NAME="finishedForm">')
 document.write("<H4 ALIGN='CENTER'>")
 document.write
    ("Congratulations! You have finished this quiz.")
 document.write('<BR><BR><INPUT TYPE="BUTTON" ')
 document.writeln('NAME="restart" VALUE="Restart" ')
 document.writeln(' onClick="restartQuiz()">')
 document.writeln("</H4>")
```

```
      document.writeln('</FORM>')
   }
   function restartQuiz() {
      location.reload(true)
   }
   // --></SCRIPT>
   <SCRIPT LANGUAGE="JavaScript" SRC="history.js"><!--
   // --></SCRIPT>
   </HEAD>
   <BODY>
   <SCRIPT LANGUAGE="JavaScript"><!--
   readCookie()
   document.writeln("<H1 ALIGN='CENTER'>"+pageHeading+"</H1>")
   document.writeln("<P ALIGN='RIGHT'><B>Questions: "
    +numberOfQuestions+"<BR>")
   document.writeln("Correct Answers: "+correctAnswers+"<BR>")
   document.writeln("Score: "+score+"</B></P>")
   if(currentQuestion >= qa.length) endQuiz()
   else askNextQuestion()
   // --></SCRIPT>
   </BODY>
   </HTML>
```

The Code in the Document Body

The code in the body of quiz.htm is very short. The readCookie() function is invoked to read the cookies associated with the document and use the cookie's *name=value* pairs to initialize the script's variables to the current state of the quiz. The cookies contain the number of the current question, the number of questions asked so far, and the number of correct answers. Next, the script creates a document heading based on the value of the pageHeading variable. (The pageHeading variable is initialized in history.js.)

The number of questions asked, number of correct answers, and quiz score are then displayed. The script checks to see if the value of currentQuestion is equal to or greater than the length of the qa array. (The qa array is also defined in history.js; it is used to store all of the quiz's questions and answers.) If the currentQuestion variable is greater than or equal to the length of the qa array, all questions have been asked, and the endQuiz() function is invoked to end the quiz. Otherwise, the askNextQuestion() function is invoked to present the user with another question.

The Code in the Document Head

The first script in the head of quiz.htm defines 12 functions:

The *Question()* Function   This function is used in history.js to create Question objects. It uses the arguments property of the function object to determine how many arguments were passed in the Question() invocation. The first argument is the text of the question. The last argument is an integer that identifies the correct answer. All arguments between the first and the last define the answers to a question.

The *readCookie()* Function   This function reads the cookies of the current document and sets the currentQuestion, numberOfQuestions, and correctAnswers variables. It then uses these values to calculate the value of the score variable.

The *getNumberValue()* Function   This function is used by readCookie() to parse the cookie string s and return the value associated with a particular name n. It does this by removing all blanks from s and then splitting s by means of the field separator (;). Having separated the string into name=value fields, it then separates these fields using =. It checks to see if the name component of the split field matches n, and returns the value associated with the name as an integer. If the name does not have a value, it returns 0.

The *removeBlanks()* Functions   This function removes all blanks contained in a string and returns this value as a result.

The *askNextQuestion()* Function   This function displays the current question in a centered Heading 4. It then invokes displayAnswers() to display the possible answers associated with this question.

The *displayAnswers()* Function   This function displays the possible answers of the current question as a form. A radio button is displayed with each answer. A Continue button follows the answers. The Continue button's onClick event handler is set to the checkAnswers() function.

The *checkAnswers()* Function   This function is invoked when a user answers a question and clicks the Continue button. It determines how many answers are associated with a question and then determines whether the radio button of each answer is checked. When it finds a checked button, it determines whether the checked button is the correct answer. If the answer is correct, it invokes the `correct()` function; otherwise, it invokes the `incorrect()` function. If no radio buttons have been clicked, the `incorrect()` function is invoked.

The *correct()* Function   This function increments the `currentQuestion`, `numberOfQuestions`, and `correctAnswers` variables, and invokes `updateCookie()` to write the values of these variables to the document's cookie jar. It then reloads the `quiz.htm` file to process the next question.

The *incorrect()* Function   This function increments the `numberOfQuestions` variable and invokes `updateCookie()` to write the value of this variable to the document's cookie jar. It then reloads the `quiz.htm` file to reprocess the same question.

The *updateCookie()* Function   This function uses the document's cookie jar to temporarily store the program's state while the `quiz.htm` file is reloaded. It stores the values of the `currentQuestion`, `numberOfQuestions`, and `correctAnswers` variables.

The *endQuiz()* Function   This function ends the quiz by setting the document's cookies back to their initial state. It then displays a form that congratulates the user for finishing the quiz, and displays a Restart button so the user can restart the quiz if they wish. The `onClick` event handler for the Restart button is `restartQuiz()`.

The *restartQuiz()* Function   This function handles the clicking of the Restart button by reloading the `quiz.htm` file so the quiz can be restarted.

The Source File

The `history.js` file (Listing 6.8) is easy to understand. It defines the `pageHeading` variable that displays the heading on each quiz page. It then creates the `qa` array. Each element of `qa` is a `Question` object, and 12 questions are defined. Feel free to add your own questions or delete the ones that I've created—you can change the content of the quiz by modifying `history.js`. You can also substitute your own question file for `history.js` by modifying the SRC attribute value of the second script block in `quiz.htm`.

Listing 6.8: Quiz Questions (*history.js*)

```
//Heading displayed on the quiz page
pageHeading="History Quiz"
//Questions
qa = new Array()
qa[0] = new Question("Who was the first president" +
    " of the United States?",
 "George Washington",
 "Abraham Lincoln",
 "Benjamin Franklin",
 "Harry Truman",
 0)
qa[1] = new Question("When did Columbus discover America?",
 "1249",
 "1942",
 "1492",
 "1294",
 2)
qa[2] = new Question("Who commanded the Macedonian army?",
 "Napoleon",
 "Alexander the Great",
 "Cleopatra",
 "George Patton",
 1)
qa[3] = new
  Question("Where did Davy Crockett lose his life?",
 "The Spanish Inquisition",
 "The Alamo",
 "Miami, Florida",
 "On the Oregon Trail",
 1)
qa[4] = new
  Question("Who was the first man to walk on the moon?",
 "Louis Armstrong",
 "Buzz Armstrong",
 "Jack Armstrong",
 "Neil Armstrong",
 3)
qa[5] = new Question("Who wrote <I>The Scarlet Letter</I>?",
 "Michael Crichton",
 "Ernest Hemingway",
```

```
  "Nathaniel Hawthorne",
  "Charles Dickens",
  2)
qa[6] = new Question("Eli Whitney invented:",
  "Mad Cow's Disease",
  "the Cotton Gin",
  "whisky",
  "the automobile",
  1)
qa[7] = new
  Question("Who was known as the King of the Fauves?",
  "Salvatore Dali",
  "Henri Matisse",
  "Pablo Picasso",
  "Vincent Van Gogh",
  1)
qa[8] = new Question("Who discovered the force of gravity?",
  "Isaac Newton",
  "Galileo",
  "Copernicus",
  "Albert Einstein",
  0)
qa[9] = new Question("Who created HTML?",
  "Tim Berners-Lee",
  "Marc Andreessen",
  "Bill Gates",
  "Jim Barksdale",
  0)
qa[10] = new
  Question("Leonardo da Vinci was born in Greece.",
  "True",
  "False",
  1)
qa[11] = new Question("Louisiana was purchased from France.",
  "True",
  "False",
  0)
```

This example shows how JavaScript can use cookies to create a complex web application without the use of a CGI program. All the cookie processing is performed locally on the browser.

Comparison: Cookies versus Hidden Form Fields

Now that you've learned how both hidden fields and cookies can be used to maintain state information, you may wonder which one you should use and when. In general, cookies are the preferred option because they allow persistent storage of state information, and hidden fields do not. However, cookies may not be the right choice for all applications. Table 6.1 summarizes the trade-offs between cookies and hidden fields.

TABLE 6.1:   Cookies versus Hidden Fields

Trade-Off	Cookies	Hidden Fields
Ease of use	Requires cookie string parsing	Requires form setup and access
Browser support	Navigator, IE, other browsers	Almost all browsers
Server support	May not be supported by some servers	Supported by all servers
Performance	Slower—requires disk I/O	Faster—implemented in RAM
Persistent storage	Supported	Not supported
Availability	Maximum cookie storage may be reached	No practical storage limitation

Both cookies and hidden fields are easy to use; however, both also have some coding overhead associated with them. Cookie strings need to be parsed when they are read. Hidden fields require invisible forms to be set up. As far as ease of use is concerned, I prefer cookies, because all the setup processing is performed in JavaScript.

Although cookies are supported by Navigator, IE, and other browsers, they are not supported by all browsers. On the other hand, hidden fields are supported by all HTML 2-compatible browsers, which encompasses all modern browsers available for any computing platform.

Not all web servers support cookies, although they do support hidden form fields. Cookies are not as performance-efficient as hidden fields because cookie operations require disk I/O to the local cookie file. However, in most applications, this performance difference is not noticeable.

Cookies provide persistent storage. That is their biggest advantage and why they were developed in the first place. If you require persistent storage, you have to use cookies.

Cookies may not always be available to your scripts. The cookie specification states that a browser cannot claim to be cookie-capable unless it provides a minimum cookie storage capacity of 300 (currently, this limit is not a problem for most browsers). However, with the increase in cookie popularity, it could be an issue in the future. In addition, most browsers limit the number of cookies that can be stored for a given domain. Netscape Navigator 4 has a 20-cookie-per-domain limit, and IE 3 has a single-cookie-per-domain limit. Also keep in mind that most recent browsers, including IE 5 and later versions, as well as Netscape 7, have preference settings that permit users to block all attempts to save cookies on the client system. By contrast, hidden fields do not have any practical limits.

What's Next

In this chapter, you learned how to use hidden fields and cookies to maintain browser state information. You learned how JavaScript enhances the capabilities that both hidden fields and cookies provide by maximizing local processing and reducing the need for CGI programming.

Chapter 7 goes into detail about how CGI scripts work on the web server end to process form data and create truly dynamic websites. Learning the details here will make it easier for you to understand how CGI scripts work, and perhaps even more importantly, how to diagnose problems when they occur.

Chapter 7

INTERFACING JAVASCRIPT WITH CGI PROGRAMS

The Common Gateway Interface (CGI) is the standard for communication between web servers and server-side web programs. Apache, Netscape, Microsoft, and just about all other web servers support CGI. Thus, for the most part, web application designers can develop server-side programs that will work regardless of the particular type of web server used at a website. If you want to write a server-side program that will have the greatest portability, then develop it as a CGI program or a Java servlet.

In this chapter, you'll learn how CGI programs work. We'll cover the types of web applications in which CGI programs are used. On the one hand, you'll learn how to interface JavaScript scripts with CGI scripts; on the other hand, you'll learn how to use CGI programs to generate JavaScript code. When you finish this chapter, you'll know how to combine JavaScript scripts with CGI programs in your web applications.

Adapted from *Mastering JavaScript Premium Edition* by James Jaworski
ISBN 0-7821-2819-X

WHEN TO USE CGI PROGRAMS

When you're creating a web application, you should perform as much processing as is reasonably possible on the browser, rather than on the server, to conserve precious communication bandwidth and server-processing resources. Any processing that is performed locally reduces the load on your web server.

However, for some web applications, server-side processing is essential. These applications include any that collect and store data about multiple users (for example, online registration forms and customer surveys). Applications that require significant database support (for example, large catalogs and search engines) also fall into this category.

CGI programs provide the interface between web browsers and online databases. Any web application that requires server-side storage or access to non-web resources is a potential candidate for the use of a CGI program.

HOW CGI PROGRAMS WORK

CGI programs (also referred to as CGI scripts) are the standard interface for communication between web servers and external programs. The CGI specification identifies how data is to be passed from a web server to a CGI program, and back from the CGI program to the web server.

NOTE
Refer to Chapter 5, "Processing Forms," for a discussion and examples of using CGI programs with forms.

The following points summarize how the CGI works:

▶ A browser requests a CGI program by specifying the program's URL. The request arises as the result of the user's submitting a form, clicking a link, or typing the CGI script's URL directly into the browser.

▶ When a web server receives a URL request, it determines whether the URL refers to a CGI program. Most web servers identify CGI programs by their location or by their filename extension. For example, all files in the path /cgi-bin/ or with the extensions .cgi or .pl may be considered CGI programs by the server.

▶ When a web server identifies a request for a CGI program, it executes the CGI program as a separate process and passes any data included in the URL to the program.

▶ The CGI program performs its processing and returns its output to the web server. The conventions defined by the CGI specification determine how CGI programs receive data from and return data to web servers. These conventions are described in the following sections.

The overall process is depicted in Figure 7.1.

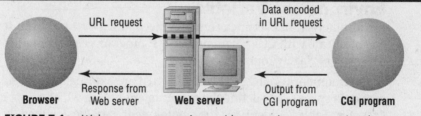

FIGURE 7.1: Web servers communicate with external programs using the conventions of CGI.

Getting Data from the Web Server

When a CGI program is executed, one of its first tasks is to determine what data was passed to it by the web server. This data may be passed in the following ways:

▶ Command-line arguments

▶ Environment variables

▶ The program's standard input data stream

Almost all programming languages support command-line arguments and the standard input stream. Environment variables are less commonly used outside of web applications. The following subsections describe when and how CGI programs receive data via each of these mechanisms.

Command-Line Arguments

Command-line arguments are parameters that are passed to programs via the command line used to execute the program. For example, the following command line executes the search program and passes it the string news as an argument:

```
search news
```

HTTP ISINDEX queries are the means of passing data to CGI programs as command-line arguments. CGI programs read the command-line arguments via the mechanisms provided by the programming language in which they are written. For example, the C programming language provides the argc and argv variables for accessing command-line arguments. The Perl programming language provides the @ARGV array for the same purpose.

Environment Variables

Environment variables are a common mechanism by which web servers communicate with CGI programs. All CGI programs can receive data from web servers via environment variables.

Environment variables are variables that are external to a program's own data space. They define the environment within which a program executes. Table 7.1 identifies the environment variables defined by CGI version 1.1. The most important are CONTENT_LENGTH, which identifies the number of bytes passed via standard input, and PATH_INFO and QUERY_STRING, which identify data passed via extra path information or a query string.

TABLE 7.1: Environment Variables Used by CGI

ENVIRONMENT VARIABLE	DESCRIPTION
AUTH_TYPE	The authentication scheme used to validate the user requesting access to a web page.
CONTENT_LENGTH	The number of characters that have been passed via standard input.
CONTENT_TYPE	The MIME type associated with the data available via standard input.
GATEWAY_INTERFACE	The version of the CGI specification supported by the server.
HTTP_*	The contents of the various HTTP headers received by the web server. HTTP_ is prepended to the name of the header. For example, the ACCEPT header is represented by the HTTP_ACCEPT environment variable, and the USER_AGENT header is represented by the HTTP_USER_AGENT variable.
PATH_INFO	The extra path information added to the URL of the CGI program.

TABLE 7.1 continued: Environment Variables Used by CGI

ENVIRONMENT VARIABLE	DESCRIPTION
PATH_TRANSLATED	The full path name translated from the URL by the web server.
QUERY_STRING	The query string portion of the URL (that is, the portion of the URL after the ? character).
REMOTE_ADDR	The IP address of the host associated with the requesting browser.
REMOTE_HOST	The name of the host associated with the requesting browser. If the server does not have this information (typically because it isn't set to do reverse DNS lookups), it leaves this variable unset, and the CGI application should look to REMOTE_ADDR to identify the client.
REMOTE_IDENT	The verified username associated with the requesting browser (if the HTTP server and remote host support the IDENT identification mechanism).
REMOTE_USER	The name of the user associated with the requesting browser. This variable is set only if the script is protected by HTTP authentication.
REQUEST_METHOD	The method associated with the browser request: GET, POST, HEAD, and so on.
SCRIPT_NAME	The path and name of the CGI program.
SERVER_NAME	The name of the web server host.
SERVER_PORT	The HTTP port number (usually 80) used by the web server.
SERVER_PROTOCOL	The name and version of the protocol used by the requesting browser to submit the request.
SERVER_SOFTWARE	The name and version number of the web server software.

The environment variables shown in Table 7.1 are available to any CGI program regardless of whether the program was executed as the result of an ISINDEX query, a form submission, or the clicking of a hyperlink.

Many programming languages provide special mechanisms for accessing environment variables. For example, Perl provides the $ENV array, and C provides the getenv() library function. Because the capability to read environment variables is important for any nontrivial CGI programs, it should be a primary consideration when selecting a CGI programming language.

TIP

Some web servers, such as Netscape servers, define server-specific environment variables in addition to those defined by the CGI. If you want your CGI programs to be portable between web servers, you should not use these server-specific environment variables.

Reading Query String Data   When data is passed to a CGI program via the QUERY_STRING environment variable, the data is encoded using the following conventions. These coding conventions are referred to as *URL encoding*:

▶ Spaces are replaced by plus (+) signs.

▶ Any other nonalphanumeric or non-ASCII characters may be replaced by character codes of the form %*xx* (with the *xx* being replaced by two hexadecimal digits). For example, %2a is used to encode a plus sign.

CGI programs must decode the data passed via the QUERY_STRING variable. They do so by replacing plus signs with spaces, and sequences of the form %*xx* with their character equivalent. This process is known as *URL decoding*.

NOTE

JavaScript provides the escape() and unescape() functions to support URL encoding and decoding. The escape() function takes a single string parameter and returns a URL-encoded version of the string. The unescape() function takes a single string parameter and returns the URL-decoded version of the string.

Form Data Coding   In addition to query string encoding, you can use other application-specific codings. For example, form data is encoded as a sequence of *name=value* pairs separated by ampersands (&); *name* is replaced by the form field's name attribute and *value* is replaced by the field's value when submitted by the user. Any equal signs or ampersands appearing in the data are encoded using the %*xx* hexadecimal coding scheme covered in the previous section.

When the form uses the GET method, form data is passed to CGI programs via the QUERY_STRING environment variable. When the form uses the POST method, form data is passed to the CGI programs via standard input. The use of standard input is covered later in this chapter.

CGI programs should decode form data by using the ampersands to separate the query string into *name=value* pairs, using the equal signs to separate the *name* and *value* portions, and then decoding the *name* and *value* portions using the URL decoding conventions.

NOTE

If a query string does not have data in the form of *name=value* pairs, then most web servers assume the requested URL is an `ISINDEX` query, and pass the query string as a command-line argument.

Reading Extra Path Data   Extra path information is data that is added to a URL as additional path information following the path to the CGI program. The extra path information is passed to a CGI program using the PATH_INFO environment variable. For example, in the following URL

```
http:/www.jaworski.com/cgi-bin/echo-query.cgi/extra/path/info
```

the path `/extra/path/info` that follows `echo-query.cgi` would be passed to the echo-query program via PATH_INFO as `"/extra/path/info"`. Extra path information is an easy way to send fixed information to CGI programs. It is generally used with nonform URLs.

TIP

If you intend to use extra path information to send data to CGI programs, you should use URL encoding to ensure that the data is correctly processed by web browsers and servers.

The Standard Input and Output Streams

Standard input refers to the keyboard input received by character-mode programs, such as non-graphical DOS programs and Unix and Windows NT command-line programs. Similarly, *standard output* typically refers to the visible output produced by these programs: characters that are displayed on the console monitor (in this context, normally the *server's* console window, not the user's).

NOTE

The physical console of olden days has been replaced by a command-line console window on modern windowing systems.

In addition to treating users' input and output in standard ways, most operating systems have the capability of allowing command-line programs to run in an environment where the user's keyboard and display monitor can be *simulated.* This means input other than the user's keyboard input (for instance, a query string or extra path information in a URL, or data from a browser form) can be *redirected* to a program *as* standard input. The program can process the data regardless of the fact that the data came from some source other than the standard source (keyboard input). Similarly, a program's output can be redirected by a server to the user's browser as though it were standard output to the server's own console display. Web servers use this redirection capability to process posted form data, as shown in Figure 7.2.

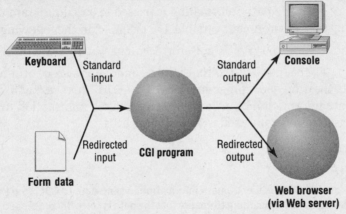

FIGURE 7.2:   Web servers redirect the standard input and output streams of CGI programs to support browser/CGI program communication.

When the POST method is used to submit a form, the form's data is sent by the web server to a CGI program as standard input to the CGI program. When a web server creates a process to execute a CGI program, it redirects the form's data to the standard input stream of the CGI program. This data appears to a CGI program as if it was typed by a user at a keyboard.

The output of the CGI program is returned to the web server so it can be redirected to the user's browser. By redirecting standard input and output, the web server allows CGI programs to be designed using the simple character-stream approach common to DOS and Unix programs. Almost all programming languages provide capabilities to read data from the standard input stream and write data to the standard output stream.

Sending Data Back to the Web Server

A CGI program returns data to the requesting browser via the web server. In all cases, it returns the data by writing it to the standard output stream. The output of the CGI program must begin with a header line, followed by a blank line, and then by the data to be displayed by the browser. The header line usually consists of a Content-type header that specifies the MIME type of the data returned by the CGI program. In most cases, the MIME type will be text/html, as shown in the following example:

```
Content-type: text/html

<HTML>
<HEAD>
<TITLE>CGI Results</TITLE>
</HEAD>
<BODY>
<H1>It worked!</H1>
</BODY>
</HTML>
```

The header line does not have to be a Content-type header; a CGI program can instead return a Location header that specifies the name of a URL to be loaded. For example, consider the following program output. The Location header specifies that the results.htm file located at the partial URL /javascript/results.htm is to be returned as the result of the CGI program's execution:

```
Location: /javascript/results.htm
blank line
```

TIP

When using a Location header, be sure to follow it by a single blank line, even if the header is the entirety of your script.

Using Nonparsed Header Programs

As mentioned in the previous section, CGI programs normally return data to the requesting browser via the web server, which takes care of providing all the required HTTP headers. However, CGI programs can bypass the web server and return data directly to the requesting browser. Of course, when you do this, your CGI program is responsible for providing all the required headers.

CGI programs that bypass the web server and return data directly to web browsers are referred to as *nonparsed header programs*. Most web servers require nonparsed header CGI programs to begin with the characters nph– (*nph* followed by a hyphen) to help servers differentiate between regular CGI programs and nonparsed header programs..

You should almost never use nonparsed header programs. By going through the web server, your CGI programs can be designed much more simply and easily. The only time it makes sense to bypass the web server is when your CGI program returns a large amount of data and you don't want the server to delay transmission of the data to the browser.

The General Design of a CGI Program

Now that you've learned how CGI programs receive data from and return data to web servers, we'll cover the general design of typical CGI programs. Most CGI programs are *transaction oriented*. They receive input data from a browser, perform processing based on the data received from the browser, and return the results of the processing to the browser. The way a CGI program reads and processes its data depends on the way requested by a browser.

ISINDEX Queries

The CGI program looks for input data by checking its command-line arguments. If it does not have any data, then it returns a web page containing an ISINDEX tag to the requesting browser. This result allows the user to submit data to the CGI program. If the CGI program does contain data in its command-line arguments, then it decodes the data using URL decoding, processes the ISINDEX query, and sends the results of the query to the requesting browser.

Form Processing

CGI programs that process form data access it in different ways depending on whether the form is submitted using the GET or POST method. If the form is submitted via the GET method, then the form data is read from the QUERY_STRING variable. If the form is submitted via the POST method, then the form data is read from the standard input stream.

When the form data has been read, it is decoded and processed. The data returned by the CGI program can consist of other forms, other web pages, or files of other MIME types.

Server-Side Image-Map Queries

CGI programs that process image-map queries read the coordinates of the user's click from the QUERY_STRING environment variable. These programs perform their processing based on the coordinates of the click and a map file. The map file associates image regions with URLs.

The particular map file to be used can be specified as extra path information. The image-map program returns the URL associated with the coordinates of the user's click.

Using Custom Hyperlinks to Invoke CGI Programs

Some CGI programs may be invoked as the result of the user clicking a hyperlink. Data may be passed to the CGI program via a query string or extra path information contained in the URL. The CGI program uses command-line arguments and environment variables to access this data. It performs its processing and then returns its output to the browser.

A SHELL SCRIPT EXAMPLE

By now, you are probably anxious to see an example of a CGI program. Listing 7.1 provides a CGI script written in Bourne Shell, the Unix command shell. Don't worry if you don't understand everything shown; the script only uses the echo and cat commands. The first line of the script identifies the file as a shell script. The second line writes the Content-type header to standard output. The third line writes the required blank line to standard output. Subsequent lines write an HTML document to standard output.

Listing 7.1: The *echo-query* Script

```
#!/bin/sh
echo "Content-type: text/html"
echo
echo "<HTML>"
echo "<HEAD>"
```

```
echo "<TITLE>Echo CGI Request</TITLE>"
echo "</HEAD>"
echo "<BODY>"
echo "<H1>CGI Request</H1>"
echo "<H2>Command Line Arguments</H2>"
echo "<P>Number of command line arguments: $#</P>"
echo "<P>Command line arguments: "$*"</P>"
echo "<H2>Environment Variables</H2>"
echo "<PRE>"
echo AUTH_TYPE = $AUTH_TYPE
echo CONTENT_LENGTH = $CONTENT_LENGTH
echo CONTENT_TYPE = $CONTENT_TYPE
echo GATEWAY_INTERFACE = $GATEWAY_INTERFACE
echo HTTP_ACCEPT = $HTTP_ACCEPT
echo HTTP_USER_AGENT = $HTTP_USER_AGENT
echo PATH_INFO = $PATH_INFO
echo PATH_TRANSLATED = $PATH_TRANSLATED
echo QUERY_STRING = $QUERY_STRING
echo REMOTE_ADDR = $REMOTE_ADDR
echo REMOTE_HOST = $REMOTE_HOST
echo REMOTE_IDENT = $REMOTE_IDENT
echo REMOTE_USER = $REMOTE_USER
echo REQUEST_METHOD = $REQUEST_METHOD
echo SCRIPT_NAME = $SCRIPT_NAME
echo SERVER_NAME = $SERVER_NAME
echo SERVER_PORT = $SERVER_PORT
echo SERVER_PROTOCOL = $SERVER_PROTOCOL
echo SERVER_SOFTWARE = $SERVER_SOFTWARE
echo "</PRE>"
echo "<H2>Standard Input</H2>"
cat -
echo "</BODY>"
echo "</HTML>"
```

The first part of the document identifies the command-line arguments passed to the CGI program. The $# variable identifies the number of command-line arguments, and the $* variable identifies the values of these arguments.

The second part of the returned document identifies the environment variables passed to the CGI program. These variables are referenced by prepending a $ to the name of the environment variable.

The last part of the returned document identifies the data sent to the CGI program via the standard input stream. The `cat` command reads `CONTENT_LENGTH` characters from standard input and writes them to standard output.

NOTE

You can access the `echo-query` program shown in Listing 7.1 via the URL `http://www.jaworski.com/cgi-bin/echo-query.cgi`.

To use the `echo-query` script, you need to either create an HTML document to access the script's URL or enter the URL directly in your web browser. Listing 7.2 provides such a document as an example of how easily you can interface to a CGI script on the server. It contains a link to `echo-query` with both extra path information and a query string appended.

If you open `cgi-test.htm` with your browser, you will see the web page displayed in Figure 7.3. Figure 7.4 shows the web page that is returned if you click the link to the CGI program. Note the value of the `QUERY_STRING` and `PATH_INFO` variables.

TIP

The `echo-query` script is a useful tool for testing your links in order to see how the data they encode is passed to a CGI program.

Listing 7.2: Accessing the *echo-query* Script (*cgi-test.htm*)

```
<HTML>
<HEAD>
<TITLE>CGI Test</TITLE>
</HEAD>
<BODY>
<A HREF="http://www.jaworski.com/cgi-bin/echo-query.cgi/
➥extra/path/info?f1=v1&f2=v2">
Click here to access echo-query</A>
</BODY>
</HTML>
```

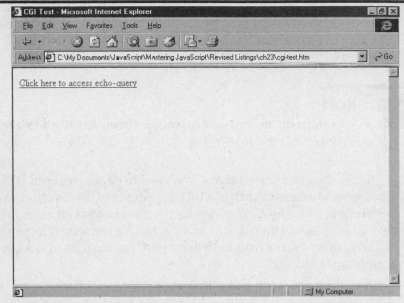

FIGURE 7.3: The web page generated by `cgi-test.htm` (Listing 7.2)

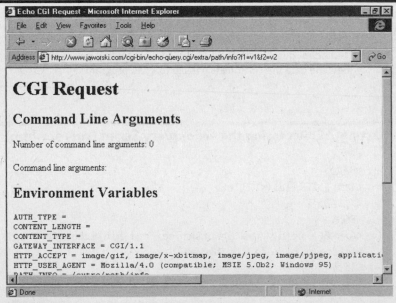

FIGURE 7.4: The results returned by `echo-query` (Listing 7.2)

INTERFACING JAVASCRIPT SCRIPTS WITH CGI SCRIPTS

JavaScript scripts can use CGI programs to access online databases, to access Internet services, or to perform other types of server-side processing. The interface between a JavaScript script and a CGI program is through the CGI program's URL. Scripts can use the URL to invoke a CGI program and pass data to it as a query string or extra path information. If a CGI program is accessed via an HTML form, then the form's data can be used to control the CGI program's behavior.

The js2cgi.htm file, shown in Listing 7.3, demonstrates how you can access CGI programs via JavaScript. If you open js2cgi.htm with your browser, it will generate the HTML form shown in Figure 7.5. If you fill out the form and click the Submit button, your form data will be sent to the add2db.cgi CGI program at the URL http://www.jaworski.com/cgi-bin/add2db.cgi, and the web page shown in Figure 7.6 will be displayed.

Listing 7.3: Interfacing JavaScript with a CGI Program (js2cgi.htm)

```
<HTML>
<HEAD>
<TITLE>JavaScript to CGI Communication</TITLE>
<SCRIPT LANGUAGE="JavaScript"><!--
function sendToCGI() {
 results=""
 surveyForm=window.document.survey
 for(var i=0;i<surveyForm.length-1;++i)
  if(surveyForm.elements[i].checked)
    results+=i%6
 window.location.href=
   "http://www.jaworski.com/cgi-bin/add2db.cgi?"+results
}
// --></SCRIPT>
</HEAD>
<BODY BGCOLOR="white"">
<H1 ALIGN="CENTER">Product Survey</H1>
<P ALIGN="CENTER">Please complete the following survey and
click the Submit button when finished.</P>
```

```
<FORM NAME="survey">
<P><B>General feeling toward product:</B><BR>
<INPUT TYPE="radio" NAME="g1"> Strongly like<BR>
<INPUT TYPE="radio" NAME="g1"> Like<BR>
<INPUT TYPE="radio" NAME="g1"> Neither like nor dislike<BR>
<INPUT TYPE="radio" NAME="g1"> Dislike<BR>
<INPUT TYPE="radio" NAME="g1"> Strongly dislike<BR>
<INPUT TYPE="radio" NAME="g1" CHECKED> No opinion<BR>
</P>
<P><B>Product quality:</B><BR>
<INPUT TYPE="radio" NAME="g2"> Very high quality<BR>
<INPUT TYPE="radio" NAME="g2"> High quality<BR>
<INPUT TYPE="radio" NAME="g2"> Average quality<BR>
<INPUT TYPE="radio" NAME="g2"> Poor quality<BR>
<INPUT TYPE="radio" NAME="g2"> Very poor quality<BR>
<INPUT TYPE="radio" NAME="g2" CHECKED> No opinion<BR>
</P>
<P><B>Product pricing:</B><BR>
<INPUT TYPE="radio" NAME="g3"> Price is very high<BR>
<INPUT TYPE="radio" NAME="g3"> Price is high<BR>
<INPUT TYPE="radio" NAME="g3"> Price is about right<BR>
<INPUT TYPE="radio" NAME="g3"> Price is low<BR>
<INPUT TYPE="radio" NAME="g3"> Price is very low<BR>
<INPUT TYPE="radio" NAME="g3" CHECKED> No opinion<BR>
</P>
<P><B>Purchase plans:</B><BR>
<INPUT TYPE="radio" NAME="g4"> Plan to purchase<BR>
<INPUT TYPE="radio" NAME="g4"> May purchase<BR>
<INPUT TYPE="radio" NAME="g4"> May purchase if price is
 lowered<BR>
<INPUT TYPE="radio" NAME="g4"> May purchase if quality is
 improved<BR>
<INPUT TYPE="radio" NAME="g4"> Do not plan to purchase<BR>
<INPUT TYPE="radio" NAME="g4" CHECKED> No opinion<BR>
</P>
</TABLE>
<INPUT TYPE="BUTTON" VALUE="Submit"
 onClick="sendToCGI()">
</FORM>
</BODY>
</HTML>
```

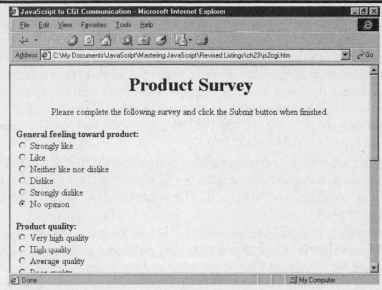

FIGURE 7.5:   Using JavaScript to process a form's data and send it to a CGI program (Listing 7.3)

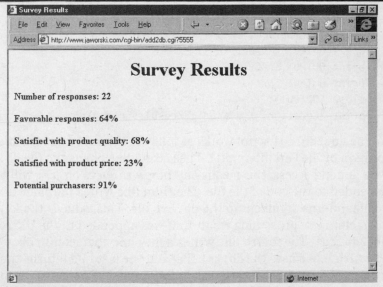

FIGURE 7.6:   The survey results are displayed using JavaScript generated by a CGI program. (Listing 7.5)

The js2cgi.htm file consists of an HTML form with four sets of radio buttons. The user clicks the radio buttons to fill out the product survey. The sendToCGI() function handles the onClick event of the Submit button by determining which buttons were selected and creating a four-character text string (stored in the results variable) that summarizes the form's data. For example, suppose a user selected the third value of the first set of radio buttons, the fourth value of the second set, the first value of the third set, and the last value of the last set. The value of the results variable would be 2305.

The value of the results variable is appended to the URL of the CGI program as a query string, and the href property of the current window's location object is set to the URL. This causes the URL of the CGI program to be requested.

When the web server receives the URL request for add2db.cgi, it executes the Perl script shown in Listing 7.4. Because the query string passed by js2cgi.htm is a single value and not a *name=value* pair, the web server assumes the request is an ISINDEX query and passes the data contained in the URL's query string as a command-line argument.

Listing 7.4: A Perl Program that Stores the Form Data on the Server (add2db.cgi)

```perl
#!/usr/bin/perl
open (OUTPUT, ">>db.txt");
print OUTPUT @ARGV;
print OUTPUT "\n";
close (OUTPUT);
print "Location: /javascript/results.htm\n\n";
```

The add2db.cgi script works as follows: The first line identifies the location of the Perl interpreter. The second line opens the file db.txt with append access; this means anything written to db.txt will be appended to the end of the file. The third line writes the value of the command-line argument to the db.txt file. This value is the four-character form processing result that was appended to the URL of add2db.cgi. The fourth line writes a new line character to db.txt. The fifth line closes the db.txt file, and the last line returns the file located at http://www.jaworski.com/javascript/results.htm as the result of the CGI program's processing. Figure 7.6 shows how results.htm is displayed.

RETURNING JAVASCRIPT FROM CGI PROGRAMS

One of the more powerful techniques of integrating client-side JavaScript scripts with CGI programs is to use CGI programs to return JavaScript code. In doing so, your web applications become more dynamic and efficient by allowing browsers to perform some of the CGI program's processing. Instead of responding with a static web page, your CGI programs can perform the minimum amount of server-side processing and return a JavaScript script that completes the application processing on the browser.

The following example shows how you can use CGI programs to return JavaScript code. This example builds on the add2db.cgi example of the previous section.

In the last line of Listing 7.4, the results.htm file is returned to complete the processing of add2db.cgi. Listing 7.5 shows the contents of results.htm. It contains two scripts in the document head. The first script includes JavaScript code from the URL http://www.jaworski.com/cgi-bin/getdb.cgi—but this is the URL of a CGI program. Listing 7.6 shows the source code of getdb.cgi.

Listing 7.5: Displaying the Results of the Product Survey (results.htm)

```
<HTML>
<HEAD>
<TITLE>Survey Results</TITLE>
<SCRIPT LANGUAGE="JavaScript"
 SRC="http://www.jaworski.com/cgi-bin/getdb.cgi"><!--
// --></SCRIPT>
<SCRIPT LANGUAGE="JavaScript"><!--
function displayResults() {
 var n=r[24]
 var favorable=(r[0]+r[1])/n
 favorable=Math.round(favorable*100)
 var quality=(r[6]+r[7]+r[8])/n
 quality=Math.round(quality*100)
 var price=(r[14]+r[15]+r[16])/n
 price=Math.round(price*100)
 var purchase=(n-r[22])/n
 purchase=Math.round(purchase*100)
```

```
document.write("<P><B>Number of responses: "+n+"</B></P>")
writeResult("Favorable responses: ",favorable)
writeResult("Satisfied with product quality: ",quality)
writeResult("Satisfied with product price: ",price)
writeResult("Potential purchasers: ",purchase)
}
function writeResult(s,n) {
 document.write("<P><B>"+s+n+"%</B></P>")
}
// --></SCRIPT>
</HEAD>
<BODY>
<H1 ALIGN="CENTER">Survey Results</H1>
<SCRIPT LANGUAGE="JavaScript"><!--
displayResults()
// --></SCRIPT>
</BODY>
</HTML>
```

Listing 7.6: A CGI Script that Returns Its Results as JavaScript (*getdb.cgi*)

```
#!/usr/bin/perl
print "Content-type: application/x-javascript\n\n";
print "r= new Array(";
open (INPUT,"db.txt");
@totals=(0,0,0,0,0,0,0,0,0,0,0,0,0,0,0,0,0,0,0,0,0,0,0,0);
$num=0;
while(<INPUT>) {
 $num++;
 chop;
 $line=$_;
 for($i=0;$i<4;$i++){
  $n=substr($line,$i,1);
  $totals[6*$i+$n]++;
 }
}
for($i=0;$i<24;$i++){
 print $totals[$i];
 print ",";
}
print $num;
print ")\n";
```

Because the output of getdb.cgi is crucial to the operation of results .htm, let's examine the operation of getdb.cgi before continuing with the discussion of results.htm. The file getdb.cgi is a Perl script that summarizes the data contained in db.txt and returns its results as a JavaScript array. Recall that each line of db.txt is a four-digit value that describes the data entered into the form shown in Listing 7.3. The getdb.cgi script reads through db.txt and counts how many times radio buttons 1 through 6 are selected for survey topics 1 through 4. This results in a 24-value array. A twenty-fifth value is added that identifies the number of lines in db.txt. getdb.cgi performs its processing as follows:

Line 1   Identifies the location of the Perl interpreter.

Line 2   Identifies the MIME type of the data returned by getdb .cgi as application/x-javascript. Note that a blank line follows the Content-Type header.

Line 3   Returns the beginning of a JavaScript array definition that is assigned to variable r.

Lines 4–6   Open db.txt for input, initialize the @totals array to 0, and set $num to 0.

Lines 7–15   Loop through db.txt and read each line. $num counts the number of lines read. $totals[6*$i+$n] counts the number of times radio button $n is selected for topic $i.

Lines 16–19   Print the values of $totals to the JavaScript output.

Lines 20–21   Add the number of lines in db.txt as the twenty-fifth value of the r array.

Getting back to results.htm, the second script contains two functions: displayResults() and writeResult(). The first, displayResults(), performs further processing on the r array to summarize and display the results of the survey. It sets n to r[24], which is the number of lines in db.txt. It then calculates the percentage of favorable responses, the percentage of responses in which the product quality and price were acceptable, and the percentage of respondents who are potential purchasers. These results are then displayed using the writeResult() function.

WHAT'S NEXT

In this chapter, you learned how CGI programs work and saw the types of web applications in which CGI programs are used. You learned how to interface JavaScript scripts with CGI scripts and how to use CGI programs to generate JavaScript code.

Next, we begin our exploration of Perl. Chapter 8 introduces some basic concepts of Perl programming. Although it's possible to write CGI scripts in most any computer language, Perl is the language most often used. When you see how easy it is to process text and files in Perl, you'll begin to see why the language is so popular among web programmers.

Chapter 8

INTRODUCING PERL AND CGI

The Internet has become—perhaps arguably—the most important communication medium in the world. There is virtually no argument, however, about the World Wide Web. It is the Internet's most important channel of communication. If you want to deal with the Net, pretty soon you'll have to deal with the Web.

In this part of the book, you'll learn about one of the most important aspects of the Web. The *Common Gateway Interface* (CGI) and applications written in the Perl programming language give you the tools to create dynamic, informative web pages, with which you can fashion a website that your visitors will find truly useful and worth revisiting.

A good website is not just a collection of pretty pictures. It has to *do* something. With Perl and CGI, you can make it do just that.

Updated from *Perl CGI Programming: No Experience Required*, by Erik Strom

ISBN 0-7821-2157-8

WHY PERL AND CGI?

A web page is a text document that is formatted with a set of commands—a programming language, if you will—called the *Hypertext Markup Language* (HTML). The name is descriptive: HTML is a markup language; that is, it controls the way a document looks. HTML instructions tell a web browser, such as Netscape's Navigator or Microsoft's Internet Explorer, how it should go about displaying the page on-screen. But HTML by itself has practically no facilities for making a web page do things. You have to rely on other means for that.

Java has been used to create dynamic web pages, as have proprietary languages such as Microsoft's VBScript and Netscape's JavaScript. Today, however, the Perl programming language is hands-down the most popular method of making a web page do something, mainly because Perl is freely available and will run on every computer platform that can host a web server. Coupled with the CGI, Perl is used on the vast majority of websites to create web pages that have to do more than sit there and look pretty.

Long before Java, there was CGI. CGI is the most common method for passing information from an HTML document to a program that can process the information. CGI doesn't care what browser you're using; even nongraphical Lynx-type software will work.

Unlike Java and its more proprietary cousins, CGI is not a programming language, nor does it load itself onto the visitor's machine to run. CGI is, as its name suggests, an interface—a set of rules. It resides on the web server computer, providing a way for the page to communicate in a rough fashion with the server. CGI allows you to write programs to deal with the page in *any* language—including Perl.

PERL'S ANCIENT HISTORY

There is only one reason that Perl programs—or *scripts*, which is a lexical convention that will be explained shortly—are so universal in Web programming: Until the last few years, virtually every web server in existence was running on a Unix system, and Perl is among the most useful of Unix tools. The first Hypertext Transfer Protocol (HTTP) servers were written for Unix, too, and were freely distributed among system administrators who wanted to try out the Web. CGI was developed as a standard of communication on these systems. In a sense, Perl, HTTP, and CGI all became standards for doing web work (see Figure 8.1).

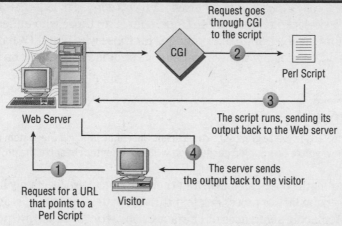

FIGURE 8.1:   The HTTP-CGI-Perl connection

The beauty of standards is that they usually transcend the platforms on which they originated. The number of non-Unix web servers and websites on the Internet increases every day. Yet the HTTP-CGI-Perl connection remains the same because it was lifted intact into the newer platforms.

Unix is, in a very large sense, an operating system written by and, most importantly, for programmers. It really was never intended for humans to use easily, which is why so many people have gone to such extraordinary lengths to make Unix more friendly, with X Windows and various other graphical interfaces. These interfaces require tremendous amounts of processing power, so in many cases system designers have given up and relegated bare-bones Unix to the background, running it on the system server and hanging Macintoshes or other workstations running Windows on the network for users.

The beauty of Unix for those who have taken the time to learn it is in the rich set of software tools it provides. Unadorned Unix is like a box of wonderful Swiss Army knives; with any one of them, you can carve any masterpiece your imagination can conjure. Perl is one of the most useful of those Swiss Army knives.

We Owe It All to Larry Wall: A History of Perl

Larry Wall is a linguist-turned-programmer who released Perl 1.0 in 1987, while attempting a sticky project for Unisys. *Perl* has many reverse acronyms. The most commonly accepted is *Practical Extraction and Report Language*, although Unix wags have come up with many earthier descriptions, such as *Pathologically Eclectic Rubbish Lister*. Perl was derived in large part from sed and awk—jackhammers of the Unix toolbox for those who understand them, unintelligible command programs for those who don't. (What can one say about a program whose most famous error message is awk: bailing out near Line 1?)

NOTE

The Perl language grew out of the classic Unix philosophy: If the system doesn't allow you to do your job easily, then write another tool to solve the problem.

The strengths of sed and awk, and their offspring Perl, lie mainly in their built-in capabilities for processing text through pattern-matching, searching for and replacing sequences of characters—or *strings*—in entire groups of files, and the use of Unix's obscure yet extremely powerful regular expressions, which are discussed in full in Chapter 12, "Creating HTML Forms with Perl."

REGULAR EXPRESSIONS: BANE AND BOON

Regular expressions are among the most useful—and most difficult to master—tools in the Unix array. You can think of them as super-charged search-and/or-replace operations. Whereas most any text editor will let you find phrases and replace them with other phrases throughout a file, regular expressions add a great deal of power to the operation. For example, you can use regular expressions to look for strings at the beginning or end of a line, or in a word, or for a specific number of occurrences.

But it's not easy. A Perl regular expression that swaps the first two words in a line of text looks like this:

```
s/^(\S+)\s+(\S+)/$2 $1/;
```

Doesn't make much sense, does it? But that could be a useful operation.

We'll defer a full explanation of regular expressions until Chapter 12. For now, let's just say that you will find many uses for them.

The bedrock of Unix is the C programming language (most of it is written in C); but C, in its position at the foundation of the operating system, adheres to the minimalist philosophy of Unix, which means you often have to write scads of C code to accomplish relatively simple tasks. A trivial search-and-replace operation on a text file, written in C, requires you to at least scan the file character by character and could easily grow from a simple subroutine into an entire application (see Figure 8.2). But the same operation can be accomplished in a few lines of Perl code (see Figure 8.3).

```
WebPage - [C:\usr\erik\PERL-CGI\ADDGUEST.CPP]
File  Edit  Search  Window  Help

    ZeroMemory (&GuestEntry, sizeof (GUEST_ENTRY));      // Hose out the structure.

    char*   INFO_ARRAY [] =
    {
        GuestEntry.FirstName,
        GuestEntry.LastName,
        GuestEntry.City,
        GuestEntry.State,
        GuestEntry.Country,
        GuestEntry.EMail,
        GuestEntry.Comments,
        NULL
    };

    char*   o;                      // Couple of pointers for string manipulation.
    char*   p = buf;
    int     n = 0;                  // Counter.

    while ((o = strchr (p, '&')) != NULL)
        {
        *o = NULL;                  // End the substring here.
        strcpy (INFO_ARRAY [n++], p);   // Copy the data into the correct spot.
        p = ++o;                    // Get the next one.
        }
```

FIGURE 8.2:   An example of code written in C++

```
WebPage - [C:\usr\erik\PERL-CGI\addguest.pl]
File  Edit  Search  Window  Help

    @InfoArray = split (/&/, $post_info);

# Go through each element in @InfoArray, split off the
# "variable=" part, then translate pluses into spaces and
# any escaped hex chars back into their real character values.

    for ($n = 0; @InfoArray[$n]; $n++)
        {
        ($dummy, $temp) = split (/=/, @InfoArray[$n]);
        $temp =~ tr/+/ /;
        $temp =~ s/%([\dA-Fa-f][\dA-Fa-f])/pack ("C", hex ($1))/eg;
        @InfoArray [$n] = $temp;
        }

# Now we'll check to see if we have anything to write
# to the guest book.  We need a first or last name, at
# least; otherwise, we'll jump around the routines that
# write this stuff to the guest book file.

    if ((length (@InfoArray[$FirstNameIndex]) != 0)
        || (length (@InfoArray [$LastNameIndex]) != 0))
        {

        # Tack the current time to the end of the array.
```

FIGURE 8.3:   An example of code written in Perl

TIP

Perl is a challenge to learn, but it is infinitely more efficient for the programmer (read: "fewer lines of code") and easier to use than C.

Unix programmers snapped up Perl as a tool of choice almost immediately for doing tasks ranging from quick and dirty to horribly complex. Because you can call most of the standard Unix system services from a Perl script, including the internetworking functions, you probably could write an entire operating system in it. It would be very slow, but it would run a computer. To this day, almost every serious Unix systems programmer works with Perl almost daily. It's just too useful for programmers to ignore.

As of this writing, Perl is at version 5.8. You may hear about development of the next generation, Perl 6, which is shaping up to be a huge overhaul of the language. Don't worry, however, that your Perl 5 programs will become obsolete; Perl 5 will be around for a long time.

Perl and the World Wide Web

Perl has become popular for web work because it is an *interpreted* language, like the first versions of BASIC, rather than a *compiled* language, such as C or C++. The essential difference between a compiled and interpreted application is that a compiled program has been translated into the machine language of the computer on which it will run by another program called a *compiler*. The translated, or compiled, file will run all by itself. An interpreted program, on the other hand, is translated and run on the fly by a program called an *interpreter.*

Compiled programs, because they consist of machine-language instructions, generally run faster. But for the same reason, they are not portable from one computer platform to another. Code compiled for a Sun box or a Macintosh won't run on an Intel-based PC because the different processors that power these machines all speak radically different tongues. Your program would have to be recompiled for the target machine before it would work. It might even have to be rewritten.

There are no such restrictions on interpreted Perl code. All you need is some version of the Perl interpreter—called `perl`—on the target computer. Perl interpreters have been ported to every popular computer platform, from Sun to Alpha to Apple to Intel and more, and with very few exceptions your Perl programs should transport unchanged into every environment.

This feature won't sound important to novice programmers. However, porting C code even between the different flavors of Unix is an art that not many people have the patience or skill to do full time. It is tedious, difficult, and time-consuming. The capability to develop and test code on one computer and then simply drop it into another, as you can do with Perl, is a boon cherished by all professional programmers.

Perl programs are not compiled, which is why we refer to them as *scripts*. Like shell scripts in Unix or batch and command files on Windows, Perl programs are just text files that run through an application to process their commands. Perl programs are still programs, with all the power and versatility the word implies.

BUILDING A PERL SCRIPT

Now that you have a little background, you'll write your first Perl program. It's a simple example that gives you the basic idea of how a Perl script is written and run. All of the subsequent examples will build on this one.

USING EXISTING PERL SCRIPTS

Perl scripts are simply text files you can create using your favorite text editor. Perl is the language of choice for CGI developers because of its ease of use on Unix machines. Its popularity, which may be one reason you bought this book, also has other benefits, including a huge body of existing code. Most of it is free, which means you can drop it into your web server and run it, regardless of the operating system that powers your computer. Most of that code was written, tested, and debugged by Unix programmers who had their own websites to maintain. The primary source for existing Perl code is the Comprehensive Perl Archive Network (CPAN). Visit www.cpan.org, or the searchable search.cpan.org. You can also find lots of stuff in USENET—go to comp.lang.perl.misc. Or try one of the web search engines such as Yahoo!.

So it makes sense for you to be running Perl on your website, if only from the standpoint of the effort you want to put into writing software. If you have a task to perform and someone else has already written the code to perform it—and has no compunctions about your using it—then why shouldn't you avoid reinventing wheels?

First Things First: Perls before Code

You can't do anything without the Perl language interpreter. Make sure you have a copy of it before you go further.

TIP

You can get Perl for Windows by pointing your web browser to http://www .activestate.com. For Unix sources, visit http://www.cpan.org. Perl for the Macintosh (pre OS X) is available at http://www.macperl.org. If you're running a Macintosh with OS X, it already has a Unix-based Perl installed.

Installing the Perl interpreter can be as simple as running a setup program or as complicated as extracting the source code and compiling it yourself. Fortunately, Perl is included in many Unix distributions. If that's the case on your system, obviously you don't have to do anything. The Perl installer for Windows can be downloaded for no cost from ActiveState.

COMPILING YOUR OWN PERL INTERPRETER...

Compiling the Perl source code yourself is the method preferred by Unix system administrators. Because the most freely available C code for Perl was written primarily for Unix systems, it compiles easily most of the time.

Compiling the code for Windows is possible, but the process is beyond the scope of this book. The latest versions of the most popular C/C++ development packages available for Windows— Visual C++ from Microsoft and Borland C++ for Windows from Borland International—both contain quirks that prevent a straightforward compilation of the Perl source code. Unless you want to change the functionality of Perl (which is an exercise of dubious logical value) and devote hours to debugging someone else's code, you're much better off using whatever executable files you can find for the operating system you're using.

Loading the Interpreter

Regardless of your operating system, once you have the Perl interpreter, you're ready to go. On Unix, things will be a little easier if you put the Perl interpreter in a subdirectory included in your PATH environment string, which is a system variable that maps out where the operating system should look when you type the name of a program at the command line. In other words, if you have loaded PATH by typing **PATH=/usr/bin;/usr/me;/pub/local/etc** at the command line and you then enter **perl**, the operating system will look in each of those directories for Perl before it gives up and complains that the command couldn't be found. The same is true in Windows.

Note that in Windows, the directories in PATH are separated by semicolons (;) and the directory delimiter is a backslash (\), but in Unix they are separated by colons (:) and the directory delimiter is a forward slash (/). You'll need to adjust accordingly if you're a Unix user. Keep this in mind as you work through the examples in this chapter.

TIP

The setup program for the Windows Perl at www.activestate.com will ask if you want Perl to be added to your PATH. If you answer affirmatively, the change will take place the next time to restart your computer.

As we discussed earlier, Perl scripts are simple text files that you can create using your favorite text editor. To put together your first Perl program, start that text editor now and enter the following lines:

```
#!/usr/bin/perl

print "Hello World!", "\n";

# End hello.pl
```

NOTE

The first line in the program begins with Perl's comment character (#), and the interpreter will ignore it. However, it must contain the path to your Perl interpreter. If your system's Perl interpreter is not in /usr/bin, change the path to the correct subdirectory.

That's fairly easy. We'll explain what's going on in the next section; for now, save the file as hello.pl and close your text editor.

Running the "Hello" Example

hello.pl is about as tiny as programs get, both in the writing and in the execution. It is intended to be run from the command line, which means the shell in Unix, the console command processor in Windows NT/2000/XP, or CMD.EXE or COMMAND.COM in Windows 95/98/ME.

TIP

We'll use the term *command line* frequently, so to avoid the confusion of having to refer to both operating system methods, we'll henceforth refer to the Unix shell and the Windows console as the command line. Also, because Perl adheres to the Unix convention of specifying path names with the forward slash (/) rather than Microsoft's backslash (\), we will adhere to it, too, in the text of our examples. Remember the difference when you're typing commands in the Windows console.

Open a command-line window. Because Perl is an interpreted language, you won't be running your first Perl program directly: You have to run perl with your Perl program as an argument to it. If, when you installed the Perl software on your system, you did as we suggested and put it somewhere in your PATH, then you can simply type

```
perl hello.pl
```

Otherwise, you have to type in the full path to perl followed by the name of your program. For example, if you installed Perl in /myprogs/perl, and that subdirectory is not in your PATH environment variable, type

```
/myprogs/perl hello.pl
```

When you run the program, the result should look something like Figure 8.4. Notice that the program prints "Hello, World!" with a line-feed, which advances the cursor to the beginning of the next line, to the screen. Congratulations! You are now a Perl programmer.

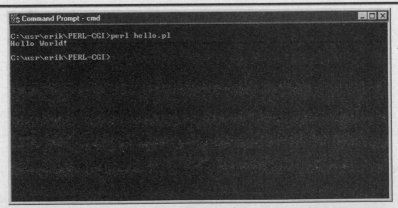

FIGURE 8.4:   The results of running your first Perl program

How Perl Programs Run

In a technical sense, the Perl interpreter is a language compiler that doesn't write its translated output to a file on the disk. Its "output file" is called *standard output*, or *stdout* in systems parlance, but most of the time this is the screen.

If a program name is given on the command line, the interpreter first checks the validity of each line, dumping out error messages for incorrect code and stopping if it finds any. If your program passes muster, the interpreter executes each line of code. One of the convenient aspects of doing it this way is that you find out immediately if your program does something wrong—and programs inevitably do. Most developers work on windowed systems, and they run the text editor with their Perl program code in one window and keep the command-line screen in another (see Figure 8.5). It is then easy to pop from window to window, writing and fixing code in the text editor and testing the code from the command line. With Perl, you get all your errors at once, and that speeds up the coding process. With a compiled language such as C or C++, you have to write the code, compile it, fix any errors that have cropped up in the compilation, compile it again, link it to the external libraries it needs, and then run it and see what errors occur there.

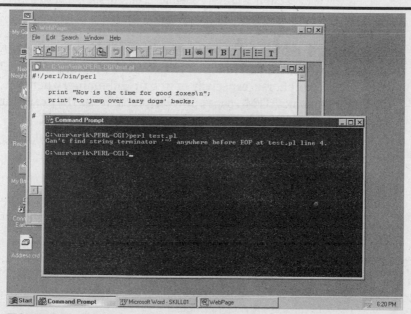

FIGURE 8.5: The two-window debugging process

Dissecting the "Hello" Example

We have briefly covered the first line in the program. We'll now take apart this line, #!/usr/bin/perl, piece by piece:

 # (Pound Sign)   This is Perl's comment character, which means that anything following it up to the end of the line is ignored by the interpreter. You can document your program on comment lines, so that others (or you, after you haven't touched the program in a few months) can understand what is being accomplished in the code.

! **(Exclamation Point)**   This first comment line is a special case. Unix reads to the exclamation point (!) and recognizes it as an instruction to the shell (a command for the command line). Strictly speaking, it tells the shell to run the Perl interpreter with the program code as its input.

NOTE

Note that this first line is only required if you want to execute your Perl scripts without calling the interpreter directly, by typing hello.pl at the command prompt, as opposed to /usr/bin/perl hello.pl. However, the convention is still to have this line in every program, if only to show that your .pl file is a standalone program, and not a library of routines.

The Heart of the Program: *print*

You use only one real Perl function in this short program—print. This function is a workhorse, especially in web programming, where you will use Perl to construct HTML pages. You will probably use the print function in every program you write.

Later we'll go into a detailed description of how print works, because it can do a lot. For now, let's look at what it does in hello.pl:

```
print "Hello, World!", "\n";
```

The unadorned print, as you have used it in the example program, takes a list of strings (text enclosed by quotation marks) as its *arguments*, or *parameters*.

TIP

We'll use the terms *argument* and *parameter* interchangeably in reference to the data you use with Perl functions.

In this case, you are telling print that you want it to print the phrases *Hello World!* and \n to the screen. Notice that the two phrases, which are the print function's arguments, are separated by a comma. It is also important that the line ends with a semicolon, which acts as a statement terminator. All statements in Perl must end with the semicolon; the interpreter will complain if you forget to do this, and it's usually the first thing you will do wrong.

The Strange \n

"Hello World!" is easy enough to figure out, but what is this \n? C-language programmers and others who are familiar with Unix conventions know this as the *newline* character. If you've never seen it before, remember the backslash (\) that precedes the n: It is called an *escape* character because it gives a special meaning to the character that follows it. The \n specifically refers to the line-feed character, with a value of 10 in the ASCII character set.

The line-feed is the standard line ender in Unix; the Windows convention is to end each line with a carriage return *and* a line-feed, which in a Perl print command would be set up as \r\n. However, the Perl interpreter knows what operating system it's running on, and it makes allowances for these differences. For now, whether you compose your code on Unix or Windows, you can use \n as a line ender.

Table 8.1 lists some other Perl escaped characters.

TABLE 8.1: Some of the Perl Special Characters

CHARACTER STRING	DOES THIS
\n	Newline or line-feed
\r	Carriage return
\t	Tab
\f	Form-feed
\b	Backspace
\033	ASCII 27 (Escape) in octal
\x1B	Same in hexadecimal
\cD	Ctrl+D
\\	Backslash
\"	Double quote
\'	Single quote

NOTE

Table 8.1 doesn't list all of the Perl special escaped characters. These are just the most common.

The escaped double quote (\") can be confusing. You use it when you want to use the double quote character in a string, rather than use it to *delimit* the string. For example, the Perl code

```
print "Hello World!", "\n";
print "\"Hello World\"", "\n";
```

results in the following output to the screen:

```
Hello, World!
"Hello, World!"
```

Perl also allows a construct to keep you from loading your strings with backslashes. You can use q/*STRING*/ and qq/*STRING*/ too, where *STRING* is the phrase enclosed between the slashes.

VARIABLES, SCALARS, AND LISTS IN PERL

The code you've written so far is simple. Let's make it a bit more complicated—and therefore useful—by introducing three new concepts:

- ▶ **Variable**—Data stored in specific memory location
- ▶ **Scalar**—A single variable that defines either numeric or string (character) data
- ▶ **List**—A number of scalars stored sequentially in one variable

Perl Variables: What's in a Name?

The capability to store data in locations that have specific names lies at the heart of any useful programming language. Moving data to a specific spot in memory and being able to recall it by name (or location) at a later time is known as working with *variables*. If you have done any programming, you are familiar with the concept of variables. However, the conventions used in Perl can be a little weird for the uninitiated, so if you're thinking of skipping this section, please don't.

Storing data in a variable is as straightforward as picking a name and setting it equal to a value. Complex programming languages such as C have lots of rules for what types of data can be stored where; for example, in C, integers have to go into int variables; strings of characters are stored as char arrays; and so forth. Variables must be declared and given types before they can be used.

Perl, despite all it owes to C, plays fast and loose with those rules. In Perl, you declare a variable merely by using it, which helps to make the Perl development process somewhat quicker and easier than programming in C.

WARNING

The rules of good, structured programming apply to Perl as they do to any other language: Make your Perl code readable by using lots of comments. Just because a language allows a fast and loose form of variable declaration is no excuse for writing spaghetti code.

Introducing Scalars

The most fundamental data items in Perl are called *scalars*. The word can be intimidating to beginners because its meaning is not immediately apparent. A scalar is nothing more than a single piece of data. Scalars differ from another fundamental Perl data type, which is the *list* (defined in the "Perl Lists" section). Perl regards numeric and string data as scalar values, and, in most cases, it's pretty good at telling the difference between the two and acting properly.

NOTE

In most programming languages, strings are simply strings of characters. "Now is the time for all good folks to come to the aid of their party" is a string. Notice that it is enclosed in quotes. This is important in Perl.

The important thing to remember about scalar variables is that they always begin with a dollar sign ($). You can call them anything you want, just never forget the dollar sign.

WARNING

Perl is a case-sensitive language, which means it distinguishes between upper- and lowercase letters in names. Thus, it will regard $VariableName and $variablename as two different scalar variables.

You can create a second version of hello.pl to illustrate the concept of storing data in scalar variables. Type the following lines into your text editor and save the file as hello2.pl:

```
#!/usr/bin/perl

# hello2, a slightly more sophisticated "Hello World"

$Hello = "Hello, World";      # String variable
$TimeAround = 2;              # Numeric variable

print $Hello, " for the ", $TimeAround, "nd time!\n";""

# End hello2.pl
```

Now run the program as you did the one you created earlier. You'll see this result on your screen:

```
Hello, World for the 2nd time!
```

Notice that you were able to set the two variables, $Hello and $Time-Around, to two unrelated types. Yet the print function knew what to do with them and assembled the resulting output string flawlessly. print is even smarter than we've made it appear here; the line could have been written to include the variables in one long string argument, such as the following:

```
print "$Hello for the ${TimeAround}nd time!";
```

The important thing to note here is that TimeAround is enclosed in curly braces to set it off from the nd. But print has no trouble culling the variables from the other parts of the string and behaving properly.

This shorthand capability is one of Perl's great strengths, as you will see when you begin to write more complicated programs. However, brevity in code is not necessarily an ideal to strive for, unless it directly leads to more efficient code. Writing a program that is clear and understandable is much more important.

Perl Lists

You have learned so far that scalar variables handle and store individual pieces of data. But what if you have a collection of related data? It would be convenient to store all of it in a variable.

Perl lists do just that. Lists are similar to arrays in many other programming languages, where the variable name defines a starting point (index 0) and the members are stored consecutively. You increase the index and add it to the starting point to arrive at the array member you want.

NOTE

A Perl *list* is the equivalent of an *array* in Visual Basic, C++, and many other languages. We'll use the terms interchangeably.

The C language requires that all members of the array be of the same type, which really only means they are all the same size. Perl doesn't care about type. Any old thing can go into a list—strings, numbers, characters—and they all happily coexist.

What's in a List?

List notation in Perl is as specific as scalar notation. List names begin with the @ character; after that, you can call them anything you want.

Setting a list equal to something, or loading it with data, is a bit more complex, but we can make it understandable with a few examples. An array of numbers is set up like this:

```
@Numbers = (1, 2, 3, 4, 5, 6);
```

You now have an array of six consecutive numbers called @Numbers. In Perl, as in many other languages, arrays start at position 0, so if you set a scalar variable to the value of the first member of @Numbers

```
$OneNumber = $Numbers[0];
```

then $OneNumber equals 1.

Notice that the notation changed a little in the last line: You refer to the first element of @Numbers with a dollar sign in front of it. But isn't that how you note a *scalar* value? Yes, it is. The notation is correct because if just one member of a list is a scalar, you must use the dollar sign in front of it. The *subscript,* which is the part of $Numbers[0] enclosed in brackets, is where you tell Perl which member of the array you want.

STREAMLINED PERL

Here's a handy Perl shortcut. Because the members of the array are consecutive numbers, you could have initialized it like this:

```
@Numbers = (1..6);
```

It's the same as specifying each of the numbers from 1 to 6, as far as Perl is concerned.

Lists of Strings

When you load strings into an array, they need to be distinguished somehow. The Perl convention departs slightly from what you have learned so far, which is to enclose strings of characters in double quotes. You can do this with lists, but it is considered more correct to delimit lists of strings with single quotes ('). Table 8.2 illustrates some of the things you can do with arrays.

TABLE 8.2:   Perl List Examples

INITIALIZATION	COMMENT
@list = (4..8);	Same as @list = (4,5,6,7,8)
@list1 = ('red', 'green', 'blue');	Array of names of colors
@list2 = (1, 'yellow', @list1);	Same as @list2 = (1, 'yellow', 'red', 'green', 'blue');
@list3 = ();	Empty list
@list4 = (0,1, @list3, 3);	Same as @list4 = (0,1,3);

Perl lists have numerous other features, but we'll save those for when we approach more complex programming topics. For now, you should know what a list is, how to initialize it, and how to access one of its members.

PERL AND THE COMMON GATEWAY INTERFACE

You've learned a little about the Perl programming language. Now let's see how it fits into the Web. CGI is the key; it has been used for many years as a facility for passing information from a web page to a program that can process the information.

Despite what many programmers put on their resumes, CGI is not a programming language. It is, as the name states explicitly, an *interface*. It allows you to write a program that takes all its input from an HTTP request (usually from a web browser posting from an HTML web page) and do something with that input. You can regard CGI as a kind of pipeline between your web page and a Perl program (see Figure 8.6): Whatever is entered on the page is available to your program through CGI.

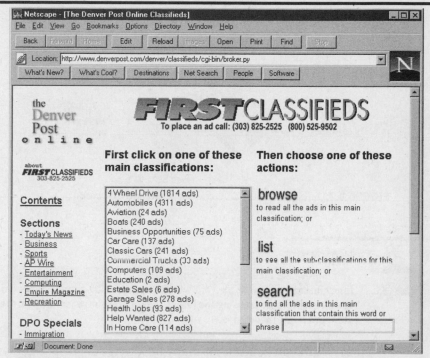

FIGURE 8.6: A search phrase or a list selection entered in this form will be processed by a Perl program through CGI.

HTML is quite good at describing how a web page should look in a browser, but the language itself has virtually no facilities for processing information or even making rudimentary decisions. When you run a Perl program from the command line, it takes its input, generally, from you, at your keyboard; and it sends its output, generally, back to you, at the screen. CGI reroutes those standard conventions. The user types information into a web page, which is sent by the user's browser to your web server, which then passes it to the Perl program as input. Then, CGI sends your program's output back to the web server. If the output happens to be formatted correctly in HTML, the server puts it out as an HTML document to whatever browser is connected to it. In other words, a `print` statement from within your Perl program prints to the web server, not the screen (see Figure 8.7).

The Difference Between Standard and CGI Output

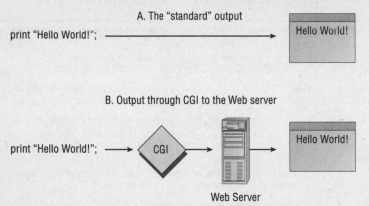

FIGURE 8.7: The difference between standard and CGI output

WARNING

Some browsers include extensions written to HTML that support all kinds of fancy interpretation. In the real world, however, you cannot depend on your website visitors' possessing the latest and greatest browsers with all their non-standard HTML extensions.

This is a difficult concept for many neophytes to grasp, but it is the foundation of using CGI as a pipeline between Perl and HTML. You can draw a web page from a Perl program. And, because Perl is a fully functional programming language, rather than a markup language such as HTML, you can decide within your program what to draw based on what has been entered in the page and sent to you.

Of course, this facility isn't limited to Perl. You can interface with CGI using any program written in any language (provided, of course, that it will run on your computer). Indeed, there may be occasions when you need the brute force of C/C++ or some other high-level compiled language to tackle a process that would bring your web server to its knees if the program were written in Perl. For example, a program that does a lot of heavy number crunching would be much faster in C or C++ than in Perl. Those occasions will be rare, however. Most of what you need to do can be accomplished more easily from a Perl script than from a compiled program. Additionally, your Perl program won't have to be rewritten and recompiled if you move to another operating system or computer platform.

What Is CGI?

Common Gateway Interface probably doesn't mean much to you. But without it, there would be no reason to talk about Perl and web pages, because there would be no way to link the two.

CGI as a concept has been applied to many systems other than links between web servers and application programs. For example, it would provide a clean and near-universal interface for database servers and their clients without the barriers introduced by proprietary systems. Software manufacturers sometimes seem to worry about making sure that you only do business with them, but a "common gateway" from one system to another provides a standard of sorts to which the manufacturers have to adhere; if they can't deal with it, no one will buy their applications.

For now, anyone who knows what you're talking about when you say *CGI* will assume that you're talking exclusively about web applications. In that context, without the Web, there would be no CGI. And without the Internet, there would be no Web.

CGI: The Force Behind the Web

Where HTML gives the Web its look, CGI makes it functional. It is what its name implies: a common gateway between the web server and applications that can be useful to the server, but doesn't run as a part of it. CGI is the only way the server can communicate with these other applications, such as a database.

NOTE

Keep in mind that no support exists for CGI outside of HTTP servers. In other words, CGI only works with HTTP servers. Its uses outside that realm have been interesting, but strictly marginal.

A Common Gateway

In technical terms, a *gateway* is an interface or an application that allows two systems to pass information between them. For example, all modern e-mail server applications, from Unix sendmail to Windows Exchange, use the Simple Mail Transfer Protocol (SMTP). These programs speak the common language of SMTP, and act as gateways between computers on the Internet to allow mail to be sent and received. (You'll learn more about sendmail in Chapter 16.)

Likewise with your web server: It doesn't know Perl from Adam, but through the mechanism of CGI it can handle requests from clients, or visitors to your site, and pass the results back. Because the server is only following a set of rules for passing information, it does not know or care what you use in the background to process what it sends you. The functions are independent of one another. Thus, you can write CGI programs in any programming language. The only requirement is that the information you send back must be formatted in a way the server recognizes.

TIP
You can find a great deal of information on the formal CGI specification at
http://www.w3.org/CGI/.

The CGI Environment

MS-DOS, Unix, and, to a limited extent, Windows users should be at least a little familiar with the concept of *environment variables.* For example, as we discussed earlier in the chapter, on both MS-DOS and Unix, an environment variable called PATH stores the list of directories through which the operating system will search when you type a program name on the command line.

To the operating system, whether it's Windows or Unix, the *environment* is a block of memory where variable names can be stored as string values, such as

```
PATH=c:/bin;c:/usr/bin;c:/usr/local/bin
```

Taking this example further, whenever the user refers to %PATH% (on Windows) or $PATH (on Unix), the operating system substitutes

```
c:/bin;c:/usr/bin;c:/usr/local/bin
```

Remember that in Unix, you use colons instead of semicolons to separate directories in the PATH.

The web server fills in a standard list of environment variables when it runs; it fills in others when requests are made of it. In the simplest sense, this is how CGI gets information between the server and your program (see Figure 8.8).

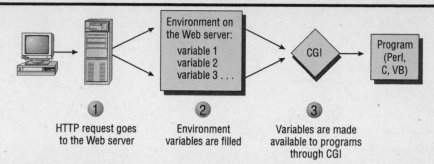

FIGURE 8.8: The web server, CGI, and the environment

WHAT'S NEXT

In this chapter, you learned about the different ways of making dynamic content on your website, and about Perl's many strengths. You were also introduced to some of the basics building blocks of Perl syntax, including strings, scalars, and arrays, and you created a simple "Hello, World" program.

In Chapter 9, you'll examine the mechanics of writing a program. You'll learn about the tools to make programming easier and then put together these basics into your first working Perl CGI program.

Chapter 9

WRITING YOUR FIRST PROGRAM

Introductions are important. You can describe someone with words, but a real introduction should be done in person. This chapter provides a personal introduction to Perl 5. You will meet Perl 5 through two programs. The first program, which shows your system configuration variables, demonstrates the simplicity of Perl 5. The second program illustrates Perl 5's most recent application, which is CGI programming. These two programs represent the minor poles of Perl 5: system administration and Internet programming. One program is five lines long; the other program is more than 75 lines. You'll see that Perl 5 is a programming language for a myriad of uses.

This chapter begins with some background on Perl 5 and explains what type of programming language Perl is. It then progresses rapidly through running and editing Perl 5 programs. In the final sections of the chapter, you'll work through a CGI program example. When you're finished with this chapter, you'll have some useful Perl 5 programs and you'll understand how to edit and run Perl 5 programs on your own computer and over the Internet.

Updated from *Mastering Perl 5*, by Eric C. Herrmann
ISBN 0-7821-2200-0

Introducing Perl 5

Perl 5 is the most powerful, easy to use, and full-featured programming language available today. That's my opinion, so let me tell you why I think Perl 5 is the best.

Perl was written by a linguist (not a computer scientist) named Larry Wall. Larry built Perl to evolve over time, as a language does. Traditional programming languages evolve slowly and at some point stop changing. Perl, like a spoken language, evolves quickly to meet each new generation's needs.

The Evolution of Perl

Perl stands for Practical Extraction and Report Language. Perl's original purpose was to generate reports that tracked errors and corrections to a software development project that involved multiple types of machines and spanned the United States.

The distribution of Perl 5 has always been freely available on the Internet, and that distribution includes the source code. Distributing a language interpreter's source code is a bold and uncommon move. It means anyone can modify the language to meet individual needs and goals.

Perl attracted the attention of Unix system administrators, who needed a language that was easier to use than the C programming language and more powerful than scripting languages such as Bourne and C-shell. Unix system administrators and others contributed to the language, updating it and submitting free scripts that made their jobs easier. Originally, most Perl users were Unix system administrators and other people with similar needs, who used Perl's text-processing power to generate reports and write scripts that aided in the configuration and monitoring of Unix systems.

In 1994, the World Wide Web became a new and powerful influence on the jobs of Unix system administrators. They turned to Perl as their tool to help them with their new web tasks. As they built new tools, they continued their practice of sharing those tools.

When new users of the Web wanted to create dynamic web pages through CGI programming, they were generally working on a Unix web server. Perl was freely available on those Unix web servers, and users started using Perl for their CGI applications. Because Perl was built to process text, and much of CGI programming is processing user input and returning HTML text pages, Perl was a natural fit for this new programming environment.

These new users of Perl continued the tradition of sharing their programs freely throughout the Internet. In the middle 1990s, Perl continued to evolve and went through a major maturation stage with revision five, called Perl 5. Perl 5 is a total rewrite of the original Perl, with many new features. Perl 5 is not just Perl any more than C++ is just C.

Perl was always designed to run on any computer, but because it usually ran on a Unix computer, it had (and still has) a decidedly Unix flavor. In the later half of the 1990s, applications and versions of Perl targeted toward Windows programming environments began to appear. Today, Windows versions of Perl 5 are freely available and are distributed with the main Perl 5 distribution. The programs presented in this book were first run on a Windows computer and then tested on a Unix computer, if necessary.

Perl 5 today is easy to use, and thousands of free CGI, system administrative, and text processing programs written in Perl are available on the Internet. With the addition of references and objects to Perl 5, the language has matured into part of the mainstream programming world.

A Perl Program

As I said at the beginning of this chapter, the best way to introduce you to Perl 5 is with some Perl code. Listing 9.1 is a little program that lets you see some information about your computer.

Listing 9.1: Environment Variables

```
1. #!/usr/local/bin/perl
2. foreach $key (keys %ENV){
3.    print qq|The value of $key is $ENV{"$key"} \n|;
4. }
```

TIP

The program shown in Listing 9.1 is available from this Complete book's page on the Sybex website, www.sybex.com, as are all the examples in this book that are drawn from *Mastering Perl 5* chapters. However, I recommend typing in most of the listings, except the long ones. The act of typing in a program can help you remember what you just read about it. It's easy to go to sleep while reading a technical book. So, here's your opportunity to get some Dilbert-type exercise—make those finger muscles humongous!

The output from Listing 9.1 is shown in Figure 9.1. If you have Perl 5 installed on your computer, you can run this program and see the environment variables on your computer.

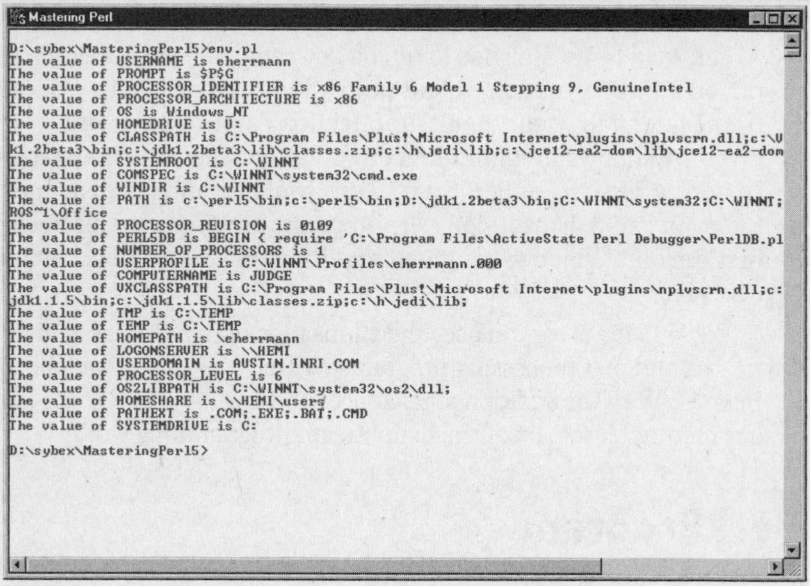

FIGURE 9.1:   Running a Perl program to get environment variables

Environment variables are created each time you run a program. An environment variable contains information about the services, hardware, and data available to your program. The environment variables available to your program vary based on where the program is executed. For example, the environment variables available from an MS-DOS window, a Unix command shell, or a CGI program are different. As you can see in Figure 9.1, environment variables include things like your username, your processor's type, and the name of your operating system.

If you don't have Perl 5 installed yet, see Chapter 8. If you don't know how to run this program from your computer, don't worry. You'll learn how to run Perl programs in this chapter. If you don't know what I meant when I said you could run this program "without compiling it," let me explain that Perl 5 is an interpreted language, which means it is not compiled to a binary executable. The difference between an interpreted language and a binary executable is important to Perl programmers, so we will explore those concepts in the next section.

Perl as an Interpreted Language

Perl 5 is an interpreted language. Programs are usually run in one of two forms: as binary executables or as interpreted. *Binary executables* are programs that have been compiled and linked into a format that can run on a computer without the compiler or linker present. *Interpreted programs*, on the other hand, require the interpreter to be installed on the computer they are running on. But this explanation doesn't make much sense without definitions of the terms *compiler*, *linker*, and *interpreter*.

A *compiler* takes the code you type into a file, like the code in Listing 9.1, and converts it into a series of ones and zeros, or binary numbers, that your computer understands. However, the compiled program is only a small piece of an overall binary executable. Modern programs use preexisting library routines to add, subtract, print output, and get input. These library routines are like pieces of a puzzle that need to be linked together with the newly compiled program to create a binary executable. This is the job of the *linker*. A compiled language, such as C, requires you to install a compiler and linker on your computer. You then compile and link your program, which can be a lengthy and painful process. The result of this process, however, is a binary executable program that runs without the compiler and linker.

A program written in an interpreted language, such as Perl 5, is converted to machine-readable format when the program is run. This means that it does not go through the standard compilation and linking process that binary executables do. Interpreted programs run the code that is in a file just as you see it, as in Listing 9.1. The steps required to run a program—converting the programming language to machine-readable format and then linking in other library routines—still occur. These steps take place when your interpreted program begins execution, and are handled by the *interpreter*. For this reason, the interpreter that converts your program must be installed wherever your program runs, which has two main effects.

First, because your program is converted into machine format at the moment it is run, that machine format is more likely to be compatible with the machine it is running on. This is one of the primary features of Perl 5: In contrast to binary executable programs, your Perl 5 programs are likely to run on any platform without modifications. Because binary executables usually contain operating system–specific information, you usually must compile and link a version of your program for every version of each operating system you want your program to run on.

NOTE

Binary executable programs usually need to be run on a computer that has the same operating system and operating system version as the one on which it was compiled and linked. Different versions of the same operating system are sometimes but not always compatible. Different operating systems such as Unix, Windows, and the Macintosh operating system are seldom compatible.

Second, because your program is converted to machine format when it is executed, most interpreted programs are slower than similar programs that are compiled. It takes time to convert your Perl 5 syntax to machine format. However, because Perl 5 is an extremely optimized and fast interpreted language, it isn't much slower than compiled code. For this small sacrifice in speed, you get a program that is very portable (can be run on different operating systems without modification).

Another benefit of an interpreted language is that the coding and testing process is much easier and faster. With a compiled language, you must write your code, compile it, link it, and then test it. The compiling and linking steps usually take a bit of time and sometimes create additional debugging issues unrelated to the syntax errors in your code. With Perl 5, you just write your code and test it. This process is very quick and leads to a programming paradigm called "code a little; test a little," which is an excellent way to develop programs. (*Paradigm*, by the way, just means a way of doing something; in short, a pattern or a model to follow.)

In summary, every program is eventually converted to a machine-readable format, and supporting libraries are made available for the program's use. Binary executables, such as C programs, are converted to machine format before the program is run. Interpreted programs, such as Perl 5 programs, are converted to machine format when your program starts up or sometimes as the program is run. Binary executables are typically faster than interpreted programs, but Perl 5 code usually performs well in speed performance tests against binary executables. Interpreted code is more portable than binary executable code. Finally, the code and test process for Perl 5 programs is easier and quicker than the code, compile, link, and test process necessary for binary executables.

Windows, Unix, and Perl

Perl 5, like the Java programming language, will run on a Unix, Windows, or Macintosh operating system, with little or no change required to the code you've written. This feature is called *portability*. The Java jingle of "Write once, run anywhere" also applies to Perl 5. This portability feature of Perl 5 means the beginning programming skills taught in this chapter must be taught for both the Unix and the Windows operating systems. (I will not be covering the Macintosh operating system.)

The Unix operating systems brands are too numerous to name. Some of the more widely used Unix operating systems are HP-UX, Solaris, and Linux. Perl 5 runs on all these brands of Unix without modification.

DIFFERENCES BETWEEN UNIX AND WINDOWS

The differences between the Unix and Windows operating systems can be traced back to the fundamentally different approaches taken in their development. Here's a comparison:

Windows	Unix
Initially developed by an entrepreneur	Developed by some university grad students
Developed for commercial sale	Although now developed by several vendors for commercial sale, is still available in several free varieties
Developed with one man's vision for its future	Developed by many, many contributors with a variety of visions and goals
Developed for ease of use	Developed for easy access to the operating system

Unix may be powerful, but the user interface is frequently cryptic and unknown. Windows may be weak in many areas, but the user interface is easy to learn and consistent.

As Windows moved away from the DOS interface to support the ease-of-use paradigm, its programming interface became less friendly. Unix has always supported the programming interface, and the tools to support programming have increased over the years. The programming interface is where you will notice the greatest difference between the two operating systems, but, of course, that is where you will be working. As you learn to use Perl programs, you will learn the differences between these two operating systems' programmer interface, which is the command line.

RUNNING PERL PROGRAMS

You run Perl 5 programs from either an MS-DOS window or command prompt (from a Windows computer) or the Unix command shell (if you're running the Unix operating system). Both are referred to as the *command-line interface*. In this section, you will learn the few commands that are necessary on the Windows and Unix operating systems to run Perl 5 programs (such as the one shown in Listing 9.1).

You may be thinking that if you're running Windows, you don't need to read the information about using the Unix command shell. However, if you are writing Perl scripts, some of those scripts are likely to be CGI programs that require installation on a Unix server. You'll learn more about CGI programs later in this chapter. For now, you should read the Unix command shell section so you will be prepared.

Using the Command Prompt

The Command Prompt, or MS-DOS window on some versions of Windows, is an independent window that allows you to enter MS-DOS commands from the keyboard. You open a Command Prompt window by selecting Start ➣ Programs ➣ Accessories ➣ Command Prompt (or MS-DOS Prompt), as shown in Figure 9.2.

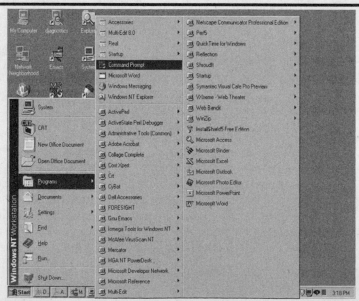

FIGURE 9.2:   Opening an MS-DOS window

When you open an MS-DOS window, your cursor is placed at the right of the command prompt (>). The *command prompt* is the keyboard interface for issuing MS-DOS commands. The command prompt, by default, displays the current working directory, as you can see in Figure 9.3.

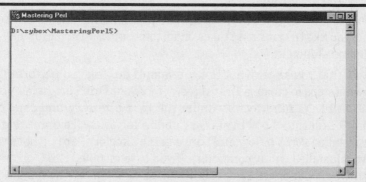

FIGURE 9.3:   The command prompt in an MS-DOS window

There are just a few commands you must know to run Perl programs from the MS-DOS window. You need to know how to view the contents of a directory, change directories, create a directory, and start a program.

Working with Directories

To view the contents of a directory, use the di r command. This command lists the directory in long format, which shows each file's eight-character filename and extension, size, last modified date, and full name. To see the directory in abbreviated format, use the command di r /W. Abbreviated format shows only the eight-character name and three-character extension of each file in the directory.

To change to a different directory, use the cd command. To tell the command which directory you want to change to, you enter a pathname as a command argument. A *pathname* is a guide to a location on your computer, including the drive, directory, and subdirectories. A *command argument* is the additional information you supply to the command that specifies how the command should operate or what the command should operate on. The cd command takes either an absolute or relative pathname as a command argument. An *absolute* pathname starts from the root of the directory tree, represented by a backslash (\), and lists the path all the way to the destination directory. A *relative* pathname starts with the current directory and lists the path from there to the one you want.

If you are not starting from the disk drive the absolute path is on, you must change to that particular disk drive. To change disk drives, type the correct disk drive letter followed by a colon and press Enter (you don't need to type the cd part). For instance, if you want to change to disk drive E, type E: and press Enter.

To create a new directory, use the mkdir command. Like the cd command, the mkdir command takes an absolute or relative pathname as its command argument.

Now that you know what the commands do, you can perform the following steps to create a Test directory for your Perl 5 programs, create an MPListings subdirectory under the Test directory, and copy the Listing 9.1 file into the MPListings subdirectory. Here, I assume that you have installed Perl 5 onto your D drive in the directory Perl5 (that's where I have it installed on my computer). If you have installed Perl 5 on another disk drive and/or directory, substitute those names in the following steps:

1. Select Start ➢ Programs ➢ Accessories ➢ Command Prompt (or MS-DOS Prompt) to bring up an MS-DOS window. This step should put you at the command prompt in a directory on the C disk drive (such as C:\WINDOWS>).

2. Move to the D disk drive by typing D: and pressing Enter. (You should press Enter after entering each command, so I won't mention it again.) When you first change to the D disk drive, you should be at the root directory, which is D:\. If you are not, change to the root directory by typing **cd **.

3. To create a Test directory with an MPListings subdirectory, type

   ```
   mkdir \Perl5\Test\MPListings
   ```

4. Copy the file that contains Listing 9.1 into the D:\Perl5\ Test\MPListings directory. You can use the copy command from the MS-DOS window, like this:

   ```
   copy environmentVariables.pl
   ➥D:\Perl5\Test\MPListings\environmentVariables.pl
   ```

   Or you can run Windows Explorer and drag-and-drop the environmentVariables.pl file into the new directory, which is the method I prefer.

In step 3, you use an absolute pathname to create the directory. This command can be executed from anywhere on the D drive. On a Windows

computer, you can create a directory node without first creating previous directory nodes. In other words, it is not necessary to create the
Test directory before you create the MPListings directory.

NOTE

A *directory node* is another name for any individual directory along a directory
path. A *directory tree* is a set of directories with a beginning node and several
nodes that are subdirectories beneath the beginning node. The beginning node
of a directory tree is called the *root node*. When you install Perl 5 into the directory D:\Perl5, the installation creates a directory tree. The root node is Perl5.
The subdirectories under the root node, such as Test, lib, html, and eg, are
branches along the Perl5 directory tree.

You can also create the directories using relative pathnames, which
looks like this:

```
>D:
>cd Perl5
>mkdir test
>cd test
>mkdir MPListings
```

Each of these commands uses a relative pathname. The pathname is relative
to the current working directory. Changing directories to the Perl5 directory
is relative to the root directory. Creating the Test directory is relative to
the Perl5 directory. Changing directories to the Test directory also is
relative to the Perl5 directory. Creating the MPListings directory is relative
to the Test directory.

Running a Program

Now you're ready to run a Perl program. To run the program shown in
Listing 9.1, follow these steps from the command prompt:

1. Change directories to the MPListings directory using an
   absolute pathname by typing

   cd \Perl5\test\MPListings

2. If you are on a Windows computer, run the program by
   typing

   perl environmentVariables.pl

You should see something on your screen similar to Figure 9.1.

Using Other Commands

There are several other commands you may find useful. If you're not using Windows 2000 or XP, the DOSKEY command will make your life easier. Every time you bring up the Command Prompt window, the first thing you should type is **DOSKEY**. The DOSKEY command tells the MS-DOS window to remember your previously typed-in commands, saving them in a previous command buffer.

With DOSKEY installed, you can use the up arrow key to display your previous commands. You can then press Enter to execute a previous command exactly as you used it last time, or you can modify a previous command to perform a similar but slightly different command. To modify a previous command, press the up or down arrow key until you see the command you want to modify; then, use the left and right arrow, Delete, Backspace, and/or regular alphanumeric keys to modify the command to perform the new operation. Once you get used to using the previous command buffer, you'll save a lot of time entering new commands.

Another command you might want to use in the MS-DOS window is rmdir, which deletes a directory. The directory must be empty before it can be deleted. Use the rmdir command with relative and absolute pathnames, the same way you use the mkdir and cd commands.

To delete a file, use the del command from the MS-DOS window, like this:

```
del fileName.pl
```

Finally, you can get additional help on MS-DOS commands by typing **help** at the command prompt.

Using the Unix Command Shell

Navigating around the Unix command shell isn't a lot different from navigating through the MS-DOS window. However, unlike with the Windows operating system, the Unix command shell is the default interface for the Unix operating system. Some Unix brands, including HP-UX and Solaris, have a more Windows-like environment, but most Unix users start out at the Unix command shell when they log on to a Unix computer.

If you are reading this section, it's probably because you need to install a CGI program on a Unix web server. Your CGI programming interface is likely through a Telnet session, which is discussed later in this chapter. The commands you use to run the program in Listing 9.1 on your Unix computer are the same commands you use to install your CGI program, and they are similar to the MS-DOS commands explained in the previous section.

Working with Unix Directories

The Unix command shell has a command prompt, much like the MS-DOS window. However, the default Unix command prompt is not the current working directory, and it may be something as simple as the right arrow (>). Figure 9.4 shows the Unix command shell. To see the current working directory on a Unix computer, use the pwd (print working directory) command.

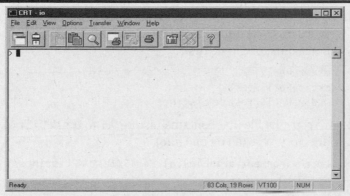

FIGURE 9.4:   The Unix command shell

To view the contents of the current directory on a Unix computer, use the ls (list) command. This command shows the contents of the directory in an abbreviated format, much like the MS-DOS dir /W command. To view more details about the files in the current working directory, add switches to the ls command (a *switch* modifies the basic behavior of a command). To view the contents of the directory in long format, use the ls -la command. These switches tell the ls command to list the directory contents in long format (l) and to list all filenames (a), including hidden files.

To change directories, use the cd command, using the same syntax as described for the MS-DOS cd command in the previous section. One difference between the two commands is the separator used in the pathname. Unix uses a forward slash (/) directory separator rather than the backslash (\) used by MS-DOS. Another difference is that unlike MS-DOS pathnames and filenames, Unix pathnames and filenames are case-sensitive. In other words, the directory test is different from the directory Test.

Let's create a Per15 test directory and an MPListings subdirectory, and then copy the program shown in Listing 9.1 into that subdirectory. Note that the Unix environment is less forgiving than the MS-DOS environment— you need to explicitly create each directory node separately. Also, unlike with Windows systems, I don't recommend creating your test directory in the Perl5 installation directory. It's a better idea to create the MPListings directory under your home directory (which is normally where you start when you log in to your Unix computer), which will probably be named after your login username on the computer. For example, on my web server, my home directory is named yawp and is located at /home/yawp. Follow these steps:

1. Create the MPListings directory node by using relative directory paths. The beginning relative path will be relative to your home directory. Type this:

   mkdir Perl5
   mkdir Perl5/test
   mkdir Perl5/test/MPListings

2. To copy the file that contains Listing 9.1 to the MPListings directory, type (all on one line)

   cp environmentVariables.pl Perl5/test/MPListings/

Running a Program under Unix

You could run the program in Listing 9.1 under Unix just as you did from the Windows operating system, like this:

   >perl environmentVariables.pl

However, this is not the preferred way of running executable programs on a Unix computer.

Unlike MS-DOS, which uses file extensions to associate a file type with a program (the file type of .PL is associated with Perl 5 executables when you install Perl 5 on a Windows computer), Unix looks for a line in the file that tells it which program to run with the executable file. Perl 5 programs that run on a Unix computer must include a line that has the path to the Perl 5 installation (as in Listing 9.1), like this:

   #!/usr/local/bin/perl

This line allows you to execute your Perl program by simply typing its name at the command prompt. However, there's one more catch: The file's permissions must have been set so that the file is, in fact, *executable*.

Unix file permissions are separated into three groups: owner, group, and world. Each group has three privileges that may be turned on or off: read access, write access, and executable access. The Unix chmod command modifies a file-access permission using a three-digit number that assigns a permissions value to the files. The possible permissions values make up a binary number, which you type in as an octal value. The possible octal numbers and their meanings are shown in Table 9.1.

TABLE 9.1: Unix Permissions

BINARY NUMBER	OCTAL NUMBER	MEANING
000	0	No permissions
001	1	Execute only
010	2	Write only
011	3	Write and execute
100	4	Read only
101	5	Read and execute
110	6	Read and write
111	7	Read, write, and execute

You set the file permissions for each group using a single octal digit to represent each group's permissions. To set the permissions to read, write, and execute for the owner and to read and execute for the group and world, combine the three permission values like this:

owner = 7, group = 5, world = 5

Therefore, to make your Perl program executable from the command line, you must change its permissions mode to executable (755) using the chmod command, like this:

```
chmod 755 filename.pl
```

CHANGING UNIX FILE PERMISSIONS FOR THE OCTAL IMPAIRED

You can also make the same file permissions change on most Unix systems by typing **chmod u+rwx,g+rx,o+rx** (user = read, write, execute; group = read, execute; other = read, execute).

To run the program shown in Listing 9.1, follow these steps from the Unix command shell:

1. Change directories to the `MPListing` directory by typing

   cd \Perl5\test\MPListings

2. Make the program executable by typing

   chmod 755 environmentVariables.pl

NOTE
Remember that Unix filenames are case-sensitive: `environmentVariables.pl` is not the same file as `EnvironmentVariables.pl`.

3. To run the program, type the name of the executable file:

   environmentVariables.pl

If this doesn't work, try including the current working directory:

./environmentVariables.pl

You should see something similar to Figure 9.1 on your screen. As with the MS-DOS window example, compiling and linking a Perl 5 program is not necessary to run the program file.

Using Other Unix Commands

The Unix commands for creating and deleting directories are the same as those used in the MS-DOS window: `mkdir` creates a directory and `rmdir` removes one. The Unix command for deleting a file is `rm`, and the command for copying a file is `cp`.

USING PROGRAMMER'S EDITORS

While you are learning Perl, you should be writing and editing the listings in this book. However, I don't recommend using just any text editor or word-processing program. If you are working on a Windows computer and using Notepad or Microsoft Word to edit your programs, you are making your job harder, not easier. If you are working on a Unix computer and using vi as your editor, you are making the same mistake. When you are writing Perl programs, you should be working in an environment that enhances your productivity. You should use an editor that understands the programming language. These types of editors are called *language-sensitive* or *programmer's* editors, and they make your programming job a lot easier.

If you're working with Unix, take a look at Vim, available at www.vim
.org/. It's an extended version of the old Unix standby editor, vi, but with
great improvements, like color highlighting. There's also a Windows
version called gvim. If you'd like a Windows editor, but without the Unix-like
keystrokes, take a look at Multi-Edit at www.multiedit.com.

Modifying a Program

The program in Listing 9.1 prints out the environment variables on your
Unix or Windows operating system. The environment variables are printed
in a seemingly random order. In this section, you will modify Listing 9.1
so it prints the environment variables in alphabetical order. This is not a
difficult task. The goal of this section is to show you how easy it is to modify
and use a Perl 5 program.

Follow these steps to edit the program:

1. Open Listing 9.1 in your editor of choice.

2. Save Listing 9.1 using a different filename. The filename can
   be anything, but it should have the extension .pl. I used the
   filename sortedEnvVars.pl.

3. Modify line 2 by inserting the word sort after the opening
   parenthesis. Make sure you leave a space between the word
   sort and the word keys, as shown here:

   ```
   foreach $key (sort keys %ENV){
   ```

4. Save your modified file.

5. Open a command-line interface window (either an MS-DOS
   window or a Unix command shell). At the command prompt,
   change directories to the same directory where you saved the
   modified file.

6. Run the modified file. If you are on a Windows computer, type

   ```
   perl sortedEnvVars.pl
   ```

   If you are on a Unix computer, type

   ```
   chmod 755 sortedEnvVars.pl
   ./sortedEnvVars.pl
   ```

Regardless of which type of computer you are using, you should see
the same information Listing 9.1 printed—but it should now be in alphabetical order, as shown in Figure 9.5.

```
Mastering Perl                                                          _ □ ×

D:\sybex\MasteringPerl5>sortedEnvVars.pl
The value of CLASSPATH is C:\Program Files\Plus!\Microsoft Internet\plugins\nplvscr
k1.2beta3\bin;c:\jdk1.2beta3\lib\classes.zip;c:\h\jedi\lib;c:\jce12-ea2-dom\lib\jce
The value of COMPUTERNAME is JUDGE
The value of COMSPEC is C:\WINNT\system32\cmd.exe
The value of HOMEDRIVE is U:
The value of HOMEPATH is \eherrmann
The value of HOMESHARE is \\HEMI\users
The value of LOGONSERVER is \\HEMI
The value of NUMBER_OF_PROCESSORS is 1
The value of OS is Windows_NT
The value of OS2LIBPATH is C:\WINNT\system32\os2\dll;
The value of PATH is c:\perl5\bin;c:\perl5\bin;D:\jdk1.2beta3\bin;C:\WINNT\system32
ROS~1\Office
The value of PATHEXT is .COM;.EXE;.BAT;.CMD
The value of PERL5DB is BEGIN { require 'C:\Program Files\ActiveState Perl Debugger
The value of PROCESSOR_ARCHITECTURE is x86
The value of PROCESSOR_IDENTIFIER is x86 Family 6 Model 1 Stepping 9, GenuineIntel
The value of PROCESSOR_LEVEL is 6
The value of PROCESSOR_REVISION is 0109
The value of PROMPT is $P$G
The value of SYSTEMDRIVE is C:
The value of SYSTEMROOT is C:\WINNT
The value of TEMP is C:\TEMP
The value of TMP is C:\TEMP
The value of USERDOMAIN is AUSTIN.INRI.COM
The value of USERNAME is eherrmann
The value of USERPROFILE is C:\WINNT\Profiles\eherrmann.000
The value of UXCLASSPATH is C:\Program Files\Plus!\Microsoft Internet\plugins\nplvs
jdk1.1.5\bin;c:\jdk1.1.5\lib\classes.zip;c:\h\jedi\lib;
The value of WINDIR is C:\WINNT

D:\sybex\MasteringPerl5>
```

FIGURE 9.5:   Sorted environment variables

UNDERSTANDING PERL SYNTAX BASICS

Now that you've run and edited a Perl 5 program, you're ready to learn what Perl expects to see in a program. Here, we'll go over some of the requirements for a program's structure and the components of a Perl 5 program.

All programs do three basic things:

► They manipulate data, which involves storing, retrieving, and modifying data.

► They perform operations (such as adding and subtracting) that modify the data structures created to receive the results of an operation.

► They jump around through branching statements. Branching statements in higher-level languages are called *loop* and *conditional statements*.

A program is made up of many variations on these three basic themes: manipulating data, operating on that data, and jumping around based on testing the contents of a piece of data. The organization of these basic structures makes a program.

Perl Program Structure

Some programming languages require your program to be in a particular format, such as data first, then subroutine declarations, and then the main program. Perl 5 forces very little program structure on you. As you will learn in more detail in later chapters, Perl 5 allows you to declare and define data and subroutines anywhere in your program.

NOTE

A *subroutine* is a reusable piece of code. It's usually given a name and then referred to as needed throughout a program. When a subroutine is called, your program jumps to the first line of the subroutine. The code in the subroutine runs to completion and then returns control to the calling statement. All subroutines in Perl 5 return a value, which may be saved into a variable. Subroutines that return a value are also called *functions*.

A subroutine or piece of data that is *declared* is named but not assigned any value. A subroutine or data item that is *defined* is assigned a value and may also be declared at the same time.

A data declaration looks like this:

```
my ($time);
```

The keyword my declares a local variable. A *variable* is a name used to store data and refer to that data. The variable in this statement is $time. (The parentheses are not required, but they are convenient if you want to create a definition list.)

A data definition looks like this:

```
my ($length) = 10;
```

This data definition stores the value 10 into the variable $length.

In addition to data and subroutine declarations and definitions, a Perl 5 program includes *statements* (both simple and complex), which you will learn about in the next section. All Perl 5 programs are part of a package. If the package is undeclared, the package name is main.

Perl Program Components

I'm not sure why every field—computer programmers, as well as doctors, lawyers, truck drivers, and so on—finds it necessary to change the English language when perfectly ordinary words would work just as well. Nevertheless, there are some terms you must understand in order to build a program. In this section, you will learn the basic terms used to describe components of Perl 5 programs.

Operators and Lvalues

An *operator* performs a function or operation on a piece of data. For example, the addition operator (+) adds two numbers together, and then assigns one value to another data object. The assignment operator (=) takes the value on the right side of the equal sign and stores it into the variable (lvalue) on the left side of the equal sign.

The term *lvalue* can be easily translated into left-hand value. It usually refers to the variable on the left side of an assignment operator. An lvalue always refers to some type of modifiable variable. The computer term for modifiable variable is *mutable*. Variables that cannot be modified are called *immutable*.

Expressions and Statements

Expression is another computer term that seems to be used to confuse the uninitiated. *Expression* in plain English means value. What's unique about an expression is that the value is usually the result of some type of operation. An expression may be an operation such as addition, the value returned from a subroutine call, or any other valid Perl 5 operation that returns a value.

A *statement* is made up of an operation and an lvalue. All Perl 5 statements end with a semicolon. (There is an exception to this rule—the semicolon on the last statement of any block, defined in the next section, is optional.) The *syntax* (format) of an assignment statement is

```
lvalue = expression;
```

For example, you might use this assignment statement:

```
$sum = $subTotal + $tax;
```

This statement adds the values in the variables $subTotal and $tax and then assigns the result to the variable $sum. Another way to say this is that the lvalue $sum is assigned the value of the expression $subTotal plus $tax.

Blocks

A *block* is a series of related program lines typically used in *control statements*, which are loop and conditional statements used to jump around in programs based on testing the contents of a piece of data. A block begins and ends with opening and closing curly braces. All Perl 5 control statements, such as if and while, must be formed as a block, like this:

```
if (conditional expression) {
    $lvalue = expression;
}
```

The block of statements may be empty, but the braces are still required.

Comments

A *comment* is any text in your program that is ignored by the computer or, rather, by the interpreter. Programmers use comments to document their programs, to make it clear to themselves and to other programmers what the code is doing. A comment in Perl 5 begins with the pound sign (#), like this:

```
# Determine whether the line from the database matches
# the search criteria
```

The pound sign tells the Perl 5 interpreter to ignore everything on the line following the pound sign. A comment can begin anywhere within a line. Everything following the pound sign on that line will be ignored. A newline character terminates the comment. Comments do not affect your code's execution or correctness in any way, but they are extremely important.

WRITING A CGI PROGRAM

CGI programming is a major application of Perl 5 programming. A CGI program runs on a web server, interfacing with both the web browser and web server. If you've never run a CGI program on your web server, you'll learn how to do so in this section. Our example uses an HTML registration form and a CGI program that reads registration data to explain the fundamentals of CGI programming.

Before we go into the details of the CGI program, we need to cover some definitions and underlying concepts of CGI programs and the environment in which they work. We'll begin with definitions of CGI, client/server model, and HTTP communications. Then we'll get to the web server, HTTP form, and CGI program for the example.

Defining CGI

CGI programs can create dynamic web pages, which are built in response to a customer profile or query. CGI programs can be obvious, like a complex shopping cart application, or completely hidden, saving or serving data but never creating a line of HTML. CGI stands for Common Gateway Interface, which is the application and interpretation of the HTTP specification. That definition may be complete, but it isn't very informative. Let's see how the terms *Common*, *Gateway*, and *Interface* actually apply.

The Common Gateway Interface is "common" to all web servers as a way for them to talk to programs that run on the server. It defines a standard set of information that the server passes to the program before it runs. This way, it doesn't matter if your program runs under Apache, IIS, or any other web server. As long as it expects the standard CGI variables to be passed, your program will work the same under all three.

The CGI acts as an *interface* between the web server and other applications on the server machine. The interface program understands the HTTP interface protocols required by the web server and can act as an interface between other computer applications and the web server.

NOTE
Accessing databases is a common CGI task. The CGI program doesn't perform the actual database tasks, but instead acts as an interface program interpreting the incoming data requests into the correct syntax for Microsoft Access, Microsoft SQL Server, Oracle, and other major database applications. When the database responds to the query, the interface program translates the response into the correct HTTP and HTML format for transmission through the web server to the web client. Accessing databases and e-mail are two of the larger interface applications of CGI programming.

A CGI program is part of the communication between a web client and a web server. This communication is a key element in the client/server interface model, which we will examine next.

Understanding the Client/Server Interface Model

The Internet is the ultimate client/server model. Your web browser (the client) communicates with your server (appropriately called a web server), which is interacting with many other services. The web browser (client) requests a resource from the web server. The client then waits for the web server to respond. This is the essence of client/server communication.

Let's use a restaurant as a client/server analogy. When you go to a busy restaurant and you don't have a reservation, you ask the maitre d' or hostess for a table. At that point, you are the *client* and the maitre d' is the *server*. You have made a request and been placed on a list to be served (seated). When your name pops to the top of the list, you are served. Your client request has been processed by the server, and the resource you requested has been allocated to you.

Now you are at your table and your waiter (or waitress) is ready to take your order. Your waiter is the server, who takes the order from you, the client. The waiter takes the order to the kitchen and gives the order to the chef. The waiter, your server, has become a client of the chef, and the chef is now the server. The server is always the process that has the resource you (the client) want. In this example, the resource you want is food. However, this resource is not directly available from your server, the waiter. The waiter passes your resource request to another server, which makes the waiter a client to the next server, the chef.

This example illustrates the power of the client/server model very well. You need a single resource: dinner. You have a single server: the waiter getting you that resource. That server is specialized, however. The server's only job is to take requests for resources and pass them on to other servers—the chef or bartender in our restaurant analogy. If your server only took care of a single client (you), your server would spend a lot of wasted time waiting for your food to be prepared and then for you to eat. Your service from this one server might be very good, but it would be expensive. Dedicated processes are always more expensive.

Instead of serving only you and wasting time while waiting for something to do, your server serves other clients, and usually stays busier but still takes good care of you. This is the power of the client/server model. The server serves multiple clients, and in a properly balanced system (which isn't necessarily easy to design), the client processes receive the resources they requested in a timely manner.

Obviously, the client and server need a way to communicate so the client can make requests and the server can respond. In the case of the web client and web server, this communication is done using HTTP, as explained in the next section.

Understanding HTTP Communications

As you have learned, a client/server communication is usually initiated by the client requesting a service. Figure 9.6 shows a simple client/server HTTP communication. If this communication were initiated from your web browser, you would only see the output shown in Figure 9.7.

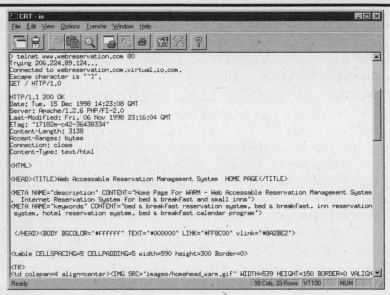

FIGURE 9.6:   HTTP client/server communication

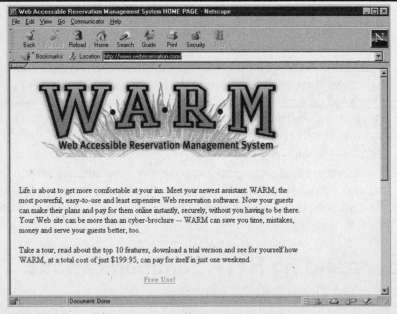

FIGURE 9.7:   Web browser client/server communication

To try this yourself, telnet to any website. (For the example shown in Figure 9.6, I used my own virtual domain so I could return a small HTML document, which makes the HTTP headers easier to see.) For example, to telnet to the Yahoo! website, you would use this command:

```
telnet www.yahoo.com 80
```

You must telnet to port 80, which is the default network port where the web server process listens for client requests. This port is similar to the radio frequency on which ham radio operators transmit and listen. The ham radio operators can transmit and receive on any frequency, but they are more likely to hear and be heard on a commonly known frequency.

To retrieve a document from the web server, you must send it an HTTP request header. In Figure 9.6, you can see the GET header on the fifth line. To retrieve the default document for the document root on a web server, issue this command:

```
GET / HTTP/1.0
```

Then press Enter twice to end the HTTP request. A blank line terminates all HTTP client/server header transmissions. This is like the ham radio operators saying, "Over" when they are finished transmitting, to tell the receiver they have switched their radio set to receive and are now listening for messages. The GET method header is the default method when requesting a URL.

If you have made a valid HTTP request header, you will receive an HTTP status response header of 200 and further information in response to your HTTP request. You can see this response on the line following the blank line after the GET request in Figure 9.6.

The web server's most common HTTP request header is the method request header. This header indicates the type of request the web client is making. The three most common method header types are GET, POST, and HEAD. The HEAD method type is primarily used by the search-bots of the major search engines like Yahoo!, Excite, Infoseek, and Lycos. Your browser commonly uses the GET and POST method headers when requesting HTML documents. As you just saw, the GET method header is generally used when you are requesting a URL. The POST method is frequently used when transferring data from the client to the server, as you'll see in the CGI program example, coming up shortly.

NOTE
Data transferred using the HTTP method GET is available to your CGI program in the environment hash %ENV using the hash key QUERY_STRING. Data transferred using the HTTP method POST is available to your CGI program in the Standard Input (STDIN) input buffer handle. The amount of data in the STDIN input buffer is available to your CGI program in the environment hash %ENV using the hash key CONTENT_LENGTH. You'll see examples of retrieving data in CGI programs in later chapters.

The web server always begins an HTTP response to the client's HTTP request with an HTTP status response header. A valid HTTP status code of 200 means the web server was able to respond correctly to the client's request.

The primary role of a CGI program is to generate and decode HTTP headers. A CGI program contains two main parts:

► Part one reads any incoming HTTP headers and data from the web client.

► Part two generates any required response from the web server.

Both parts are optional but are usually present. Each part uses the HTTP headers to communicate between the web client and the web server. Your CGI program typically responds with a Content-Type: text/html HTTP response header, which tells the browser to expect an HTML document.

The elements of client/server interaction you've learned about are used for the web browser and web server communication in our CGI program example. Now let's look at the web server configuration for CGI.

Configuring the Web Server

As you've learned, a CGI program is part of the communication between a web client and a web server. The CGI program runs on the web server, usually under a directory called cgi-bin. In this section, you will learn about the web server directories and configuration variables that are necessary for installing and running CGI programs.

The HTML page is served up by the web server to the web client from a directory tree called the document root. The *document root* is the directory path on your web server to the beginning of the HTML directory tree. The HTML directory tree is the directory and subdirectories that contain your website's HTML documents. The web server begins searching for HTML documents by prepending the document root path to the directory path given after the domain portion of the URL address.

A URL address is made up of three parts: the protocol, the domain name, and the file identifier. These parts contain the following information:

- ▶ The protocol indicates the protocol name. The web server handles protocols of type `http://`, but URL protocols also may be `ftp`, `wais`, `gopher`, `telnet`, and other types, which are handled by other server-side applications. The protocol name is not case-sensitive.

- ▶ The domain name is the name of the server your web browser is contacting. The machine Internet address is a unique series of numbers or characters. Like the protocol name, the domain name is not case-sensitive.

- ▶ The file identifier is the path (absolute or relative) to the file, beginning from the document root. The file may be any valid filename. The filename extension tells the web server what file type headers to return to the web client. The file identifier is case-sensitive.

How your web server interprets filename extensions, searches for documents, handles CGI requests, and performs other functions is determined by your web server's configuration files. These files are usually located in a configuration directory inside the server root directory tree. The server root, like the document root, is a directory path on the web server. The web server usually stores your configuration, log, and error files within the server root directory tree.

Listing 9.2 is an edited copy of a web server configuration file from one of my virtual domains. Lines 6 and 7 of Listing 9.2 show the definition of the server root and document root. On line 10 of Listing 9.2, you can see a handler defined for CGI scripts.

NOTE

A *script* is another name for a program. Scripts are usually short programs, and typically they are written in an interpreted programming language (like Perl 5) rather than a compiled language.

NOTE

The line numbers in code listings are provided for easy reference and, of course, aren't part of the code itself.

Listing 9.2: Web Server Configuration File

```
 1. ##### Apache conf file
 2. Port 80
 3. ServerAdmin webmaster@practical-inet.com
 4. ServerName www.practical-inet.com
 5.
 6. ServerRoot /virtual/customer/practical-inet.com
 7. DocumentRoot /virtual/customer/practical-inet.com/htdocs
 8.
 9. DirectoryIndex blocked.html index.html index.htm
➥index.php index.cgi home.html home.htm welcome.html
➥welcome.htm
10. AddHandler cgi-script .cgi
11.
12. UserDir disabled
13. FancyIndexing on
14. XBitHack Full
15.
16. Alias /icons/ /virtual/customer/practical-inet.com/icons/
17. ScriptAlias /cgi-bin/ /virtual/customer/
➥practical-inet.com/cgi-bin/
18.
19. AddIconByEncoding (CMP,/icons/compressed.gif)
➥x-compress x-gzip
20. AccessFileName .htaccess
21. DefaultType text/plain
22.
23. AddEncoding x-compress Z
24. AddEncoding x-gzip gz
25.
26. AddType text/html .shtml
27. AddHandler server-parsed .shtml
```

Writing the Registration Form

Using a registration form for gathering information over the Internet is another common CGI application. Figure 9.8 shows the Internet registration form you will use in this example. The source code used to generate this HTML registration form is shown in Listing 9.3.

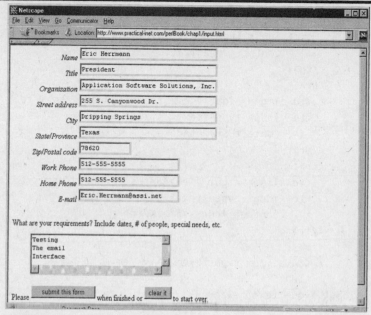

FIGURE 9.8: An HTML registration form

Listing 9.3: HTML Registration Form Source

```
<html> <head></head>
<body bgcolor="#FFFFFF" link="#808000">
<div align="left">
<form
action="http://www.practical-inet.com/cgi-bin/perlBook/
➡chap9/readInput.cgi"
method="POST">
<blockquote>
    <table border="0">
      <tr>
        <td align="right"><em>Name</em></td>
        <td><input type="text" size="35" name=
            "Contact_FullName"> </td>
      </tr>
      <tr>
        <td align="right"><em>Title</em></td>
        <td>
<input type="text" size="35" name="Contact_Title">
</td>
      </tr>
```

```
      <tr>
        <td align="right"><em>Organization</em></td>
        <td><input type="text" size="35" name=
            "Contact_Organization"> </td>
      </tr>
      <tr>
        <td align="right"><em>Street address</em></td>
        <td><input type="text" size="35" name=
            "Contact_StreetAddress"> </td>
      </tr>
      <tr>
        <td align="right"><em>Address (cont.)</em></td>
        <td><input type="text" size="35" name=
            "Contact_Address2"> </td>
      </tr>
      <tr>
        <td align="right"><em>City</em></td>
        <td>
<input type="text" size="35" name="Contact_City">
</td>
      </tr>
      <tr>
        <td align="right"><em>State/Province</em></td>
        <td>
<input type="text" size="35" name="Contact_State">
</td>
      </tr>
      <tr>
        <td align="right"><em>Zip/Postal code</em></td>
        <td>
<input type="text" size="12" maxlength="12" name=
            "Contact_ZipCode"> </td>
      </tr>
      <tr>
        <td align="right"><em>Country</em></td>
        <td><input type="text" size="25" name=
            "Contact_Country"> </td>
      </tr>
      <tr>
        <td align="right"><em>Work Phone</em></td>
        <td>
<input type="text" size="25" maxlength="25" name=
```

```
                                  "Contact_WorkPhone"> </td>
            </tr>
            <tr>
              <td align="right"><em>Home Phone</em></td>
              <td>
<input type="text" size="25" maxlength="25" name=
                  "Contact_HomePhone"> </td>
            </tr>
            <tr>
              <td align="right"><em>FAX</em></td>
              <td>
<input type="text" size="25" maxlength="25" name=
                  "Contact_FAX"> </td>
            </tr>
            <tr>
              <td align="right"><em>E-mail</em></td>
              <td>
<input type="text" size="25" name="Contact_Email"> </td>
            </tr>
            <tr>
              <td align="right"><em>URL</em></td>
              <td>
<input type="text" size="25" maxlength="25" name=
                  "Contact_URL"> </td>
            </tr>
          </table>
        </blockquote>
        <p>What are your requirements? Include dates, # of people,
          special needs, etc.</p>
        <blockquote>
          <p><textarea name="comments" rows="5" cols="35">
</textarea> <br>
          </p>
        </blockquote>
        <p>Please <input type="submit" value="submit this form">
          when finished or <input
        type="reset" value="clear it"> to start over. </p>
      </form>
      </body>
      </html>
```

When submitted, the HTML registration source from Listing 9.3 calls the CGI program `readInput.cgi`, described next.

NOTE

You will need to modify the fifth line of Listing 9.3, `action="http://www` `.practical-inet.com/cgi-bin/perlBook/chap9/readInput.cgi"`, to reflect the URL for your web server.

Creating the CGI Program

The CGI program `readInput.cgi`, shown in Listing 9.4, follows the steps that every CGI program must follow:

1. Decode any incoming data.

2. Use that data to interface with any server-side programs.

3. Return valid HTTP headers.

These three steps are the basics of any web-browser-to-web-server communication. The web browser and the web server create a classic client/server relationship, as explained earlier. The web browser, through the HTML form in Listing 9.3, calls the web server requesting the resource `readInput` `.cgi` in Listing 9.4.

NOTE

The program `readInput.cgi` teaches you Perl and CGI programming in the context of their environment instead of a simple made-for-the-book example. This makes your job a little harder at first but more rewarding in the long run. You will need to confront more new concepts, but you can rest assured that the skills you learn are practical and relevant to a real-world programming environment.

Listing 9.4: *readInput.cgi*

```
1. #!/usr/bin/perl
2.
3. %postInputs = readPostInput();
4. $dateCommand = "date";
5. $time = `$dateCommand`;
6. open (MAIL, "|/usr/sbin/sendmail -t") || return 0;
7.
8. select (MAIL);
9. print << "EOF";
```

```
10. To:    YOUR_ADDRESS\ @YOUR_DOMAIN.com
11. From: $postInputs{ 'Contact_Email'}
12. Subject: $postInputs{ 'Organization'}  Information
�th Requested
13.
14. $time
15. $postInputs{ 'Organization'}  Information Requested
16. Name: $postInputs{ 'Contact_FullName'}
17. Email: $postInputs{ 'Contact_Email'}
18. Street Address: $postInputs{ 'Contact_StreetAddress'}
19. Street Address (cont): $postInputs{ 'Contact_Address2'}
20. City: $postInputs{ 'Contact_City'}
21. State : $postInputs{ 'Contact_State'}
22. Zip: $postInputs{ 'Contact_ZipCode'}
23. Work Phone: $postInputs{ 'Contact_WorkPhone'}
24. Home Phone: $postInputs{ 'Contact_HomePhone'}
25. FAX: $postInputs{ 'Contact_FAX'}
26. Email: $postInputs{ 'Contact_Email'}
27. Comments: $postInputs{ 'comments'}
28.
29.
30. EOF
31. close(MAIL);
32. select (STDOUT);
33. printThankYou();
34.
35. sub readPostInput(){
36.     my (%searchField, $buffer, $pair, @pairs);
37.     if ($ENV{ 'REQUEST_METHOD'} eq 'POST'){
38.        read(STDIN, $buffer, $ENV{ 'CONTENT_LENGTH'} );
39.        @pairs = split(/&/, $buffer);
40.        foreach $pair (@pairs){
41.            ($name, $value) = split(/=/, $pair);
42.            $value =~ tr/+/ /;
43.            $value =~ s/%([a-fA-F0-9][a-fA-F0-9])
➤/pack("C", hex($1))/eg;
44.            $name =~ tr/+/ /;
45.            $name =~ s/%([a-fA-F0-9][a-fA-F0-9])
➤/pack("C", hex($1))/eg;
46.            $searchField{ $name} = $value;
47.        }
48.    }
```

```
49.     return (%searchField);
50. }
51.
52. sub printThankYou(){
53. print << "EOF";
54. Content-Type: text/html
55.
56. <HTML>
57. <HEAD>
58. <TITLE>THANK YOU FOR FOR YOUR REQUEST</TITLE>
59. </HEAD>
60. <BODY>
61. <TABLE CELLSPACING=2 CELLPADDING=2 border=0 width=600>
62. <TR><th><BR>
63. <center>
64. <FONT SIZE=+3><B>Thank You
$postInputs{ 'Contact_FullName'}  </b></font>
65. </center><BR><BR>
66.
67. <CENTER><B><FONT SIZE=+1>
68. <P>For submitting your information.
We will get back with you shortly.
69. </P>
70. </FONT></B><CENTER>
71. </th>
72. </table>
73. </BODY>
74. </HTML>
75.
76. EOF
77. }
```

Before you can test this example, you need to know how the installation of a CGI program works. In the next section, you will learn how and where to install your CGI programs.

Installing CGI Programs

To install the HTML registration form shown in Listing 9.3, you must know the document root and the script alias. The script alias identifies the CGI program's directory tree for the web server. The web server will look only within the CGI program directory tree for CGI programs. In Listing 9.2, the script alias is on line 17:

```
ScriptAlias /cgi-bin/
➡/virtual/customer/practical-inet.com/cgi-bin/
```

The HTML registration form must be installed into a directory under your web server's document root. Each web server's document root is unique. Your web server probably has a FAQ (Frequently Asked Questions) list, telling you where to install HTML files. If it doesn't, you'll need to get this information from your web administrator.

Copy the program in Listing 9.3 to your web server using FTP, placing the file into your document root. (Refer to the note that follows Listing 9.1 for a reminder about how to access copies of this chapter's listings.) Now copy the CGI program shown in Listing 9.4 to your web server's cgi-bin directory.

WARNING

Whenever you copy files between a Windows and a Unix computer with FTP, be sure to set the transfer mode to ASCII. Unix and Windows use different characters to determine the end of a line. If you copy a program from Windows to Unix in the default binary mode, your program may not work.

Next, if you are on a Unix web server, you must set the correct file permissions on the files. As explained earlier, file permissions tell the Unix operating system who can read, write, and/or execute a file. Your HTML file's permissions should be set to owner = 6, group = 4, world = 4. These settings give you permission to read and write to the file; the group and world get read access to the file. Use the chmod command like this:

```
chmod 644 register.html
```

Your CGI program's permissions should be set to owner = 7, group = 5, world = 5. These settings give you permission to read, write, and execute the file; the group and world get read and execute access to the file. Use the chmod command like this:

```
chmod 755 readInput.html
```

To test the installation of your CGI program, execute it from the command line, as you learned earlier in this chapter in the section "Using the Unix Command Shell." If you have problems, see Chapter 10, "Debugging Your Programs," for information.

To test your HTML installation, in your web browser, enter the URL of your web server followed by the filename of the installed HTML file as the location, like this:

```
http://www.yourDomain.com/registration.html
```

Now that you have a working CGI program installed on your web server, let's dissect that program and get a better understanding of how Perl 5 and CGI programs work.

Understanding How a CGI Program Works

You've learned about the client/server interface model, and you put together a CGI application. Now it's time to see how the programming code works. As we work through the code, you'll come across many types of Perl 5 constructs that will probably be new to you. Don't worry if this material is not crystal clear right now—this is just a quick-start example to show you the power of Perl 5 and make you eager to learn the details you need to know to write your own programs.

First, your web browser requests a resource from the web server. This happens when you click the Submit This Form button (in the form shown earlier in Figure 9.8), which has the web browser call the CGI program identified by the action attribute of the HTML registration form tag. The web browser then generates an HTTP method request header. The method type for the HTML registration form in Listing 9.3 is POST, which is also an attribute of the HTML form tag. Here is that HTML form tag from Listing 9.3:

```
<form action="http://www.practical-inet.com/cgi-bin/
➡perlBook/readInput.cgi" method="POST">
```

This tag means the data submitted by the form will be available for your CGI program through Standard Input (also known as the special variable STDIN), just as though you fed the data to your program right from the command prompt except that the data contains special encoding for data submitted through web forms.

Now that the web browser has sent the web server an HTTP request header, the web server decodes and responds to the web client's request. The web server decodes the HTTP request header and determines by looking at the file extension that it must pass the request to a CGI program.

The web server activates the CGI program readInput.cgi. The first thing the CGI program does is read the input data sent by the HTML form. It does so on line 3 of Listing 9.4:

```
%postInputs = readPostInput();
```

This is a subroutine call, which means the program jumps to line 35 of Listing 9.4 and continues execution from there:

```
sub readPostInput(){
```

The subroutine `readPostInput` is made up of the block of statements that begins with the opening curly brace on line 35 and continues to the closing curly brace of line 50. The subroutine `readPostInput` verifies that the request header `method` was `POST` on line 37 and then reads the data from the HTML form on line 38 into the variable `$buffer`.

```
if ($ENV{ 'REQUEST_METHOD'} eq 'POST'){
    read(STDIN, $buffer, $ENV{ 'CONTENT_LENGTH'} );
```

The CGI input is passed from the web browser to the web server in URL-encoded `name/value` pairs. Each `name/value` pair is directly associated with the HTML form `input` tag. Each HTML form `input` tag has `name` and `value` attributes. The name should be set inside the HTML file. Look back at Listing 9.3 and notice that each HTML form `input` tag contains a `name` attribute that is set to some unique name, as in these two examples:

```
<Input type="text" size="35" name="Contact_FullName">
<input type="text" size="35" name="Contact_Title">
```

The value is set by the user's input. When the user clicks on the HTML form's Submit button, the browser collects all the data associated with the HTML input tags and URL-encodes the data. This URL encoding converts some characters for safe transfer over the Internet and associates each name and value attribute with an equal sign. Each `name/value` pair is separated from the next `name/value` pair by an ampersand (&).

Line 39 of Listing 9.4 separates the name/value pairs into an array named `@pairs`:

```
@pairs = split(/&/, $buffer);
```

The array is then URL-decoded from lines 42 through 45 and saved into a Perl 5 hash named `%searchField`.

```
$value =~ tr/+/ /;
$value =~ s/%([a-fA-F0-9][a-fA-F0-9])/pack("C", hex($1))/eg;
$name =~ tr/+/ /;
$name =~ s/%([a-fA-F0-9][a-fA-F0-9])/pack("C", hex($1))/eg;
```

The hash is returned to the calling program on line 49:

```
return (%searchField);
```

HASHES

Associative arrays, or *hashes*, are common data structures used by Perl programmers. Unlike an array, which is a list of elements defined with a statement like

```
@myarray = ("a", "b", "c");
```

an associative array is a list of paired elements, defined like this

```
%myhash = ("a","b","c","d");
```

or this

```
%myhash = ('a' => "b", 'c' => "d");
```

You can also define an individual hash pair as needed:

```
$myhash{'a'} = "b";
```

Once your CGI program has decoded the incoming data, it can use the data as part of an interface to other programs. On line 6 in Listing 9.4, it creates a connection to the e-mail program `sendmail`:

```
open (MAIL, "|/usr/sbin/sendmail -t") || return 0;
```

The e-mail message (lines 10 through 29) is sent to the `sendmail` program via the `print` statement on line 9:

```
print << "EOF";
```

This `print` statement, using the `heredoc` operator (`<<`), sends everything from lines 10 through 29 to the file handle selected on line 8, which is connected to the `sendmail` program.

The e-mail message is sent to the e-mail address on line 10:

```
To:   YOUR_ADDRESS\@YOUR_DOMAIN.com
```

The EOF marker on line 30 ends the data transfer initiated by the `print` statement on line 9. The results of the e-mail message generated in lines 10 through 29 are shown in Figure 9.9. The connection to the `sendmail` program is closed on line 31:

```
close(MAIL);
```

On line 33, the CGI program prepares to respond with a valid HTTP response header by the subroutine call:

```
printThankYou();
```

This subroutine call jumps to line 52:

```
sub printThankYou(){
```

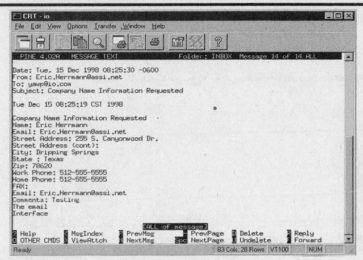

FIGURE 9.9: Registration e-mail

CGI programs are responsible for returning a valid HTTP header. Lines 54 through 57 create the required HTTP response headers:

```
Content-Type: text/html

<HTML>
<HEAD>
```

The Content-Type: text/html HTTP response header tells the web browser that the remaining data returned by the web server will be HTML text. The results are shown in Figure 9.10.

NOTE

The blank line on line 55 of Listing 9.4, following the Content-Type:text/html response header on line 54, is critical. The blank line tells the web browser (client) this is the last HTTP response header. Any data following the blank line is not part of the HTTP header traffic. Your web browser decodes the Content-Type HTTP response header to determine what type of data follows the last HTTP response header.

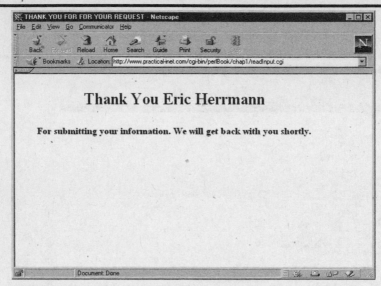

FIGURE 9.10:   Registration Thank You response

This completes the HTML communication between the web browser and web server, which I believe deserves a recap. Here are the steps involved in using our sample CGI program:

1. Your web browser, the client, through the HTML form's `action` field, submits an HTTP request header `method` of type POST (the type most frequently used when transferring data from a client to a server).

2. The web server decodes the HTTP request header and calls the CGI program identified in the HTTP request hcader.

3. The CGI program `readInput.cgi` decodes the incoming POST data.

4. The CGI program `readInput.cgi` uses the incoming data to interface with the `sendmail` program and creates an e-mail message.

5. The CGI program `readInput.cgi` completes the client/server transaction by returning an HTTP response header, which is the Thank You HTML page shown in Figure 9.10.

WHAT'S NEXT

In Chapter 10, you'll learn how to accomplish another fundamental programming task. This task helps you follow a major programming rule: Just writing the code isn't enough—it also needs to do the right thing. Making your code do the right thing is called *debugging*. Before you get frustrated because your code doesn't work, you'll learn how to fix and avoid the bugs (errors) that inevitably creep into everyone's programs.

Chapter 10
DEBUGGING YOUR PROGRAMS

When you *debug* your code, you look for coding errors and try to fix them. Inevitably, some bugs will creep into your code. You can use the techniques you'll read about in this chapter to speed up the debugging process.

Coding errors usually come in two forms: syntax errors and logic errors. When you're looking for errors in programs you typed in from this book, you can concentrate on syntax errors. *Syntax errors* are errors created when you fail to follow the required format of a Perl 5 statement. The first section of this chapter explains how to locate and fix syntax errors quickly and painlessly.

Eliminating errors is, of course, what debugging is all about. In the section on avoiding errors, you'll learn about coding practices and techniques that will help you prevent errors in your code. You'll also learn about some mistakes that are commonly made in Perl 5 programs.

Because every program has bugs, every decent language has a debugger. Perl 5 comes with a fully functional Perl debugger. In addition to the free debugger distributed with Perl 5, the builders

Updated from *Mastering Perl 5*, by Eric C. Herrmann
ISBN 0-7821-2200-0

of one of the Windows versions of Perl 5 offer a Windows Perl 5 debugger, which is also described in this chapter.

What about your CGI programs? The techniques used for standard debugging don't work as well in the CGI environment. Over the years, I've developed a few techniques to help locate CGI bugs, which you'll learn about in the final section of this chapter.

If you code, you debug. Learn the rules of debugging, and your Perl 5 coding experience will be a lot less frustrating.

HANDLING SYNTAX ERRORS

You will make all kinds of mistakes if you take my advice and type in the programs you're reading about in this book. Don't let those mistakes discourage you from typing in the programs. Not only will the typing process help you learn how to write Perl 5 programs, but it will also help you learn how to debug programs. You know the examples work, so you only need to concentrate on one kind of coding error—your typing mistakes. Once you become familiar with the typing errors you make, you'll be able to track them down quickly and correct them in your own code.

Let's begin with an example of how Perl 5 reacts when it finds a syntax error. You'll see that Perl 5's diagnostic messages are helpful, but you need to learn how to interpret them.

Pinpointing Syntax Errors

Figure 10.1 graphically illustrates the effect of just one typo in a program: a missing quotation mark. In Figure 10.1, five different error messages (eight on-screen lines) are printed for a small typing error.

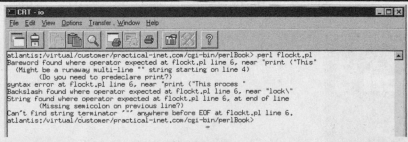

FIGURE 10.1:   Perl 5 syntax error messages

You can learn a couple of things from Figure 10.1 that will help you become better at debugging your code:

- ► One error can create multiple error messages.

- ► Those error messages usually contain the information you need to locate your problem, so don't ignore them.

The last error message in Figure 10.1 is the best clue to the problem. The Perl 5 interpreter is telling you that there is an unbalanced double quotation mark somewhere in the program. It tells you this with the message "Can't find string terminator" "anywhere before EOF at flockt.pl line 6." When you see this type of message, you know you forgot to include a closing quotation mark at the end of a string (a *string* is character data surrounded by quotation marks); you just need to locate where the missing quotation mark should be inserted. Perl 5's other messages help you pinpoint the error.

NOTE

The program used for Figure 10.1 is small, so the EOF (end of file) in the "Can't find string terminator" message references line 6. If this program was 100 lines long, with the error created on line 5, Perl 5 would continue looking for the ending quote until it reached the end of the file at line 100. The EOF condition would still occur, but it would reference line 100 instead of line 6.

NOTE

The line numbers in code listings are provided for easy reference and, of course, aren't part of the code itself.

Listing 10.1 shows the program that generated the error messages in Figure 10.1.

Listing 10.1: Missing Quote

```
1.   #!/usr/local/bin/perl
2.   use Fcntl ":flock";
3.   open (OUTFILE, ">>flockTest.txt") || die $!;
4.   # The following line generates the error!
5.   print ("Requesting Exclusive lock\n);
6.   flock(OUTFILE, LOCK_EX) || die $!;
7.   print ("This process now owns the Exclusive lock\n");
8.   $in = <STDIN>;
9.   flock(OUTFILE, LOCK_UN)|| die $!;
10.  close (OUTFILE);
```

The actual error in this small program is on line 5, where Perl 5 complains about having a bareword where an operator was expected:

```
print ("Requesting Exclusive lock\n);
```

Barewords are character strings without surrounding quotation marks and that do not begin with $, @, or %, which are the variable designators.

When you begin looking for an error, look for the obvious things first. The messages in Figure 10.1 are generated by a common syntax error made by both experienced and inexperienced programmers. This error is among the most frequently repeated syntax errors, which are listed here:

▶ Keyword misspelled, such as if as fi or elsif as elseif

▶ Semicolon missing

▶ Comma missing

▶ Parenthesis missing

▶ Curly brace (block delineator) missing

▶ Quotation mark missing

As you saw in Figure 10.1, a common syntax error (a missing quotation mark) can generate a variety of error messages. Your job as a debugger is to learn to ignore the extraneous information and focus on the important information. For example, the error messages in Figures 10.2 and 10.3 contain important debugging information.

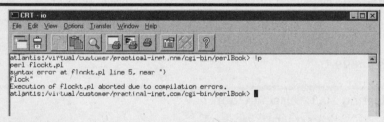

FIGURE 10.2:   A syntax error message identifying a program line

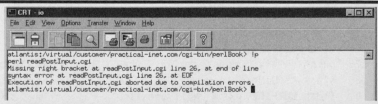

FIGURE 10.3:   Missing braces

The syntax error messages in both figures give you a good indication of the problem. In Figure 10.2, the error message tells you that you have a syntax error at line 5 near the right parenthesis. In this example, a semicolon was left off the end of the Perl 5 statement on line 4. However, the message identifies line 5. Rarely does the error message identify the correct line when you forgot a semicolon.

In Figure 10.3, the error message tells you that the program is missing a right bracket at line 26. You can believe Perl 5 when it tells you your program is missing a parenthesis or a right bracket, but again, don't believe the line number identification. Perl will match the brackets out of order until it runs out of brackets.

The lesson here is that Perl is kind enough to tell you what the problem is, but it is up to you to find the precise location. Fortunately, Perl usually gets you close enough to the real problem that you should be able to figure it out.

Whenever you see an error message that identifies a line number, you know one thing for certain: The error is not on any line *after* the line identified in the error message. You also know the error is likely to be on the line identified or on a previous line. Unfortunately, sometimes the previous line may be 100 or more lines back. Messages about syntax errors that fail to complete a Perl 5 statement—such as missing quotes, right brackets, and missing semicolons—rarely identify the correct line. Messages about syntax errors that are wholly contained within a single statement—such as misspelled keywords or improperly formed conditional expressions—usually correctly identify the line number of the error.

Understanding Error Messages

As you've seen in the examples, Perl 5 error messages usually contain the information that you need to find the error. A good programmer reads the error messages.

When you see a lot of error messages, realize that usually only the first few messages point to the real error. You should concentrate on the early messages, because the later error messages are probably a result of an earlier error. Now, you're probably thinking that I just contradicted myself, because the previous paragraph says good programmers read the messages, and this one implies that you should ignore the messages at the end of a long list of error messages. The best guideline is a balance of focusing on some of the messages and ignoring others, and achieving this balance comes only with practice.

Perl 5 has almost 500 error messages you can read at your leisure in the HTML documentation under the filename perldiag.html. You can find this file under the documentation directory of your Perl 5 installation. You don't need to read the entire list of error messages, but it is a good idea to know about this file in case you run across a message you don't understand. The following sections describe some of the error and warning messages you are likely to see early in your Perl 5 programming career.

NOTE

Warning messages appear only when you run your program with the warning switch (-w) enabled. This is a good debugging technique, as explained later in this chapter.

Syntax Errors

Syntax error messages are usually generated by the common syntax errors you just learned about. These messages are frequently interrelated and should be interpreted as Perl's best guess. Use these error messages as clues to help identify and locate the error. Syntax error messages include the following:

▶ "Missing semicolon in previous line."

▶ "Can't find terminator before EOF." This message is usually the result of a missing right bracket or quotation mark.

▶ "Might be runaway multi-line string starting on line *n*." This message usually indicates a missing quotation mark.

▶ "Missing right bracket."

Did Not Return a True Value

You can write reusable Perl 5 subroutines and include them in your main programs with the require or use keyword. Every required or used file must return a true value as the last line of the file. This means that whenever you write a program that will be included in another program using the require or use keyword, the last line of the required file must equal some value other than zero or null. Perl 5 interprets zero and null values as false. To fix this problem, add the following statement to the end of any file included in other files using the require or use statement:

```
return 1;
```

Can't Locate Function in @*INC*

Perl 5 uses the @INC array to locate library modules and files when loading subroutines. Frequently, this error occurs because you misspelled a function name. Perl 5 dutifully went looking for the misspelled function and couldn't find it.

Look carefully at the error message. If the function name is wrong, correct it. If the function name is correct, you need to modify the locations Perl is searching for library routines. You can modify the @INC array by using the push or unshift function to place the correct path into @INC. Another solution is to use the lib pragma to specify where to find the library, as in

```
use lib '/path/to/lib';
```

Panic: Some System Error

When you see an error that starts with "panic," don't panic. This is an error at the system level instead of at your code level. Several possible problems may have created this type of error. Your program may have used up all your system resources, which happens when your code doesn't release resources when it finishes using them. Perhaps you initialized a variable to a negative number and it was used as an input to a system function before the variable was properly set.

You cannot fix a system error, but it's likely you are using a reference to an invalid location in memory, building an array in an infinite loop, or using some other resource related to the error. First, determine the type of system error by looking at the panic message. Then look at your code and try to locate the sections that might affect the error identified in the panic message. If there are errors before the panic error, solve those problems first.

Missing Comma after First Argument

This error message appears when you forget to type the comma after the first argument of a function. For example, here is an error I make quite often:

```
@names = split(/:/ @nameList,3);
```

You'll learn how to use various Perl 5 functions and their arguments throughout this book.

String @*varName* Now Must Be Written as \@*varName*

You must use the escape character (\) with all literal at signs (@). This error is commonly found in Perl 4 code being upgraded to a Perl 5 installation. In the Perl 4 distribution, you could print e-mail addresses directly in your HTML code. With Perl 5, you will see an error message if you write an e-mail address like this:

```
print "mailto:Recipient@domainName.com";
```

Instead, you must write the e-mail address like this:

```
print "mailto:Recipient\@domainName.com";
```

You can also use single quotes so that the @ is not interpolated:

```
print 'mailto:Recipient@domainName.com';
```

Use of Function Is Deprecated

Deprecated means a function has been replaced with a new function or method. A deprecated function works in the currently released version of Perl 5 but may not be supported in future releases of Perl 5.

You'll see this type of warning message when your code uses a function that has been replaced with a newer function, variable, or syntax. The warning message usually includes information about how to fix the error. For example, one of the deprecated messages in the current build is "Use of implicit split to @_ is deprecated." The diagnostic message tells you to "assign the results of a split() explicitly to an array (or list)."

When the warning message isn't helpful enough, you can look up the deprecated function in the online documentation delivered with your Perl distribution. Each deprecated function or variable should have an explanation of the newer replacement function or variable.

WARNING

Don't write new code with deprecated functions. Your code and the deprecated function will work today, but your program may not run under future releases of Perl.

Use of Uninitialized Value

This warning message tells you an assignment statement uses a variable that has never been explicitly set in your program. See the "Avoiding

Misspelled Variable Names" section later in this chapter for more information about problems that can result.

qw Used Commas in List

The qw operator separates barewords in a list with white space characters (blank, tab, newline, and so on). Putting commas in lists built using the qw operator is unnecessary and creates words that include the comma symbol.

You will see this type of warning message when your code has initialized an array like this:

```
@trees = qw|Elm, Birch, Cedar, Oak|;
```

Initializing your array this way creates tree names like Elm, when you really wanted names like Elm (without the comma included as part of the name). You probably meant to initialize the array like this:

```
@trees = qw|Elm Birch Cedar Oak|;
```

Name Only Used Once: Possible Typo

Pay attention to this warning message. This error usually occurs when you misspell a variable name. Debugging misspelled variable names can be frustrating and time consuming. See the "Avoiding Misspelled Variable Names" section later in this chapter for more information about this type of error.

Found = in Conditional, Should Be ==

This is another warning message that could save you hours of debugging time. The message says a conditional expression included an assignment operator (=) instead of the equal-to Boolean operator (==). Most conditional expressions test the contents of data instead of making an assignment statement. Making an assignment in a conditional expression is not an error and usually results in a true value, but it's often not what you meant to code.

AVOIDING ERRORS

If it isn't broken, you don't have to fix it! That's pretty obvious, isn't it? You can make sure it isn't broken by taking some preventative maintenance measures in your code. Some types of errors can be avoided by setting the correct Perl command-line switch. Other errors can be avoided by following good coding practices. In this section, you will learn a few things you can do to limit the number of bugs that creep into your code and thereby reduce the amount of time you spend debugging your code.

Turning On Warning Messages

The first tip for avoiding bugs in your code doesn't even require a coding change. Whenever you change your code, always run it the first time with Perl 5 warnings enabled, like this:

```
perl -w programName.pl
```

Doing so is likely to result in a lot of warning messages being printed out. Don't ignore these messages—they tell you where to look in your code for potential problems. For example, the following types of messages, which were discussed in the previous section, appear only when you run your program with warnings enabled:

▶ Use of function is deprecated

▶ Use of uninitialized value

▶ qw used commas in list

▶ Name only used once: possible typo

▶ Found = in conditional, should be ==

Avoiding Misspelled Variable Names

One of the features of Perl 5 is the ability to declare and use variables any place in your code. Sometimes this feature introduces hard-to-find bugs. Also, Perl 5 is a case-sensitive language; if you change the case of one character in a variable name, the variables are not the same. For example, the variable names $firstName and $FirstName refer to different storage locations.

If you make a typing mistake in assigning or using a variable name, Perl 5 creates a new variable. Now your code is using the wrong variable name, and either the data you meant to use elsewhere won't be available or the data your code is now using isn't valid. You can take two simple steps to avoid this problem (and one of them isn't careful typing). One is to use the warning switch (-w), as described in the previous section.

An alternative to using the warning switch is to use the Perl 5 pragma strict. The pragma strict tells the compiler to generate three types of errors:

▶ An error for any variable used before it was declared

▶ An error if your code uses symbolic references

▶ An error if your code uses barewords

You can use the pragma strict to restrict only the use of variable names, excluding the restrictions on symbolic references and barewords, by adding the following line in your code:

```
use strict 'vars';
```

You can put this line anywhere in your code. Then all the variable names that follow this line must be declared using the keyword my or local.

You turn this restriction off by inserting this line:

```
no strict 'vars';
```

If you use the strict pragma in your code, you'll never have to debug a variable misspelling, because all variables must be declared before they can be used.

WARNING

The strict pragma can make it difficult for your code to use other modules and programs that don't follow this rule. If you have a problem using other modules, turn off strict 'vars' around the offending module and turn it back on when you need it.

Following Good Coding Practices

Following good coding practices will make it easier for you (and others) to debug your programs. Here are a few tips to get you started.

Comments

Comment your code. My first boss made me comment every single line of code I wrote. That was a bit much, but comments are very important in avoiding and removing bugs. Before you begin a new section of code, you should clearly define what you want the new section to do, and then write the code the way you described it. You'll see examples throughout this book.

Indentation

Indent your code. This is easy to do if you have a good editor. However, if you aren't using a tool that indents your code automatically, you should do it manually. Every time you open a new block of statements with a left curly brace, indent your code some common amount. I like to use three spaces, but the indentation amount doesn't really matter—just be consistent. After you close a block of statements with a right curly brace, outdent a consistent number of spaces.

Meaningful Variable Names

Use meaningful variable names. Don't create variable names of one or two characters. Use variable names that reflect the purpose of the variable. You shouldn't go overboard and make every variable half a line long, but every variable should be understandable when you try to read your own code next year (or next week).

Testing Loop and Conditional Expressions

The rule here is to build a little, test a little. Test your code as you write it. Don't wait until you're finished writing the entire program to see if it works. Test each piece as you build it. When you build a new while loop, run a couple of tests on it to make sure it stops and starts when you expect it to. As you build each new logical block of code, test it.

Beginning or End of Array Tests

Some places in code are particularly error prone. Loop indexes and any conditional expressions that check for the beginning or end of an array should be carefully tested. In your code, let Perl 5 iterate through your arrays like this

```
foreach (@array){ ...}
```

instead of explicitly indexing through the array:

```
for ($index=0; $index<$max; $index++){
    $array[$index]; ...
    }
```

When your code must explicitly use the beginning or last index, make sure you test those cases.

Positive Logic

Another way to avoid errors in conditional expressions is to use positive logic. Don't be negative! That may sound like a philosophy of life, but it should also be your programming philosophy. Every time you write a conditional expression, you have a choice of testing for the existence of some condition or testing for the absence of some condition, like this:

```
while (!red) { ...}    #negative
until (red) { ...}     #positive
```

Whenever possible, test for the presence of a condition. If you find your conditional logic checks for the negative case, take a moment to look for the positive condition. Every coin has two sides, and every conditional expression has a positive and negative solution. Sometimes the positive condition isn't practical, but that should be the exception in your code. Testing for positive logic makes your code easier to understand, and positive logic usually requires less maintenance.

Special Cases

Along with avoiding negative conditions in your conditional expressions, you should also try to avoid handling special cases. Code that works for every case except one, two, three, or more cases is prone to errors. There always seems to be one more exception. Look for the solution that doesn't require thinking in terms of the exceptions.

For example, if you are writing a program that determines when the chicken should cross the road, you might write something like this: Cross the road except when the light is red or yellow, or when there is a vehicle in the way, or when a bicycle is coming.... As you can see, the exception list can get very long. Instead, write something like this: Cross the road when the light facing you is green and the cross traffic is clear.

Avoiding Common Perl 5 Mistakes

The tips in this section relate directly to Perl 5. They help you avoid common Perl 5 programming mistakes.

String and Numeric Tests

The testing of scalar data is context-based. If you use a string operator, Perl 5 tests the data in string context. New programmers frequently test for equality using the numeric test operator (==) when they should be using the string equality operator (eq). This isn't a syntax error in Perl 5, but it is likely to produce erroneous results. Most Perl 5 operators have numeric and string counterparts. Make sure you use the correct operator for the correct data context.

List and Scalar Context

Perl 5 functions and operators perform different operations when operating in list or scalar context. The file input operator (<>) reads an entire file in list context. The same operator reads only one line in scalar context.

An array returns its size when used in scalar context, like this:

```
$size = @array;
```

In list context, an array assignment copies the entire array:

```
@arrayCopy = @array;
```

Barewords

Perl 5, like a natural language, makes a lot of decisions based on context. As explained earlier in the chapter, *barewords* are character strings that do not begin with $, @, or % characters, or have surrounding quotation marks, like this:

```
@languages = (Perl, C, C++, Fortran, Pascal);
```

Perl 5 must decide whether the bareword is a subroutine call (its first choice), a file handle, a label, or a character string. In previous versions of Perl, the default was to treat the bareword as a quoted string unless context clearly determined an alternative. In Perl 5, the bareword defaults to a subroutine call unless context determines another choice. When Perl 5 finds a bareword in your code that it cannot associate with a subroutine, file handle, or label, Perl 5 will treat the bareword as a double quoted string.

TIP

To avoid conflicts with current and future built-in subroutines, when you name file handles or labels, use only uppercase characters. Perl 5's built-in subroutines and functions are named using lowercase characters.

You should avoid using barewords in your code unless the context is obvious. I like to use barewords in initializing arrays (as shown in the previous example), because in those cases the context is obvious.

If you run your code at least once with warnings enabled (using the warning switch -w, discussed earlier in the chapter), Perl 5 will point out all the barewords in your code. You can then decide if they are errors or features.

Default Variables

Perl 5 provides default choices for many functions and operations. Use the default variables, such as $_ and ARGV, only when it is clear by context and convention that the default variables are being used. The use of the default options can make your code hard to understand, error prone, and difficult to maintain.

The *my* and *local* Keywords

Use the keyword my to declare your variables. Using the keyword local creates a variable whose scope includes any called subroutines. If you create a variable with the keyword local and then call a subroutine, the subroutine may overwrite the variable or the main routine may overwrite the subroutine's variable, like this:

```
...
local $myTemp = 15;
local $yourTemp = 20
doSomething ();
...
sub doSomething () {
    $yourTemp = True;
    while ($yourTemp){
        $myTemp++;
        if ($myTemp == 10){
            $yourTemp = 0;
        }
    }
}
```

There is no way to determine what the real intent of this code might have been, but the calling routine has modified the initial value of $myTemp, and the value of $yourTemp was modified in the subroutine. If the declarations in both the calling routine and the subroutine had used my instead of local, the subroutine variables $myTemp and $yourTemp would not have been affected by and would not have interfered with the calling routine's variables.

In short, never use local. When you declare your variables, use my.

Global Variables versus Parameters

It seems easier to not pass your variables to your subroutine explicitly. If you don't declare a variable using my, it is global in scope and can be seen by any subroutine you call, as you saw in the example in the previous section.

Using global variables creates code that is hard to modify and has unusual side effects throughout the program. When you call a subroutine, pass the data to the subroutine explicitly:

```
my $myVar=15;
my $yourVar=0;
doSomething($myVar, $yourVar);
...
sub doSomething {
    my($myVar, $yourVar)=@_;
...
}
```

Now an action taken in the subroutine affects only the subroutine. Your subroutine can explicitly return any data it wants to make available to the calling program.

Loop Variable Modification

The foreach statement creates an optional loop variable when processing arrays and lists. The loop variable is a reference to the actual array or list variable. If you modify the loop variable, you are also modifying the actual value. This is a nice feature if you understand it, but it's a surprise to many programmers who expect the loop variable to be a temporary location.

HANDLING RUNTIME ERRORS

If you try to run your program and Perl tells you your program didn't compile, then you have a syntax error, as discussed earlier in this chapter. When your code runs but produces the wrong results, you have a runtime error. This section focuses on runtime errors, which usually take a little more work to fix than syntax errors.

When you don't have a debugger handy, use print statements or some other type of error message to tell you what went wrong with your code. You'll learn about using debuggers a little later in the chapter. Here, we'll look at some other debugging techniques.

Using the System Error Variable

When you perform any system functions, such as opening a file, a special variable ($!) contains information about any failure conditions. This variable always contains the last system error message, which means you should only check it if the last operation you performed failed.

Perl provides two functions, die and warn, that work hand in hand with the system error message variable ($!). Both the die and the warn functions will print the filename and line number in the file where the error occurred or the contents of the specified print list (any data you want printed when your program stops).

The die function causes your program to stop executing, or die. The syntax of the die function to output the filename and line number is

```
die print_list;
```

To output only the contents of print_list, include a newline character (\n) at the end of print_list:

```
die "print_list" . "\n";
```

The following form uses the die function with the system error message variable to output the filename and line number:

```
die $!;
```

In some cases, you want your program to continue executing but you still need an error message printed to the screen. In those cases, use the warn function, which has the same syntax as the die function.

```
warn print_list;
```

I like to use a combination of the system error message variable and the die or warn function whenever I call a system function. Listing 10.2 (a program named (errorMessage.pl) demonstrates how to use these functions with system calls, and Figure 10.4 shows the output.

Listing 10.2: The System Error Message

```
1.  #!/usr/local/bin/perl
2.  open (FH,"<t.t") || warn "$!\n";
3.  open (FH,"<t.t") || warn $!;
4.  print "after warn\n";
5.  open (FH,"<t.t") || die $!;
6.  print "after die";
```

```
Select Mastering Perl                                         _ □ ×

D:\sybex\MasteringPerl5>perl errorMessage.pl
No such file or directory
No such file or directory at errorMessage.pl line 2.
after warn
No such file or directory at errorMessage.pl line 4.

D:\sybex\MasteringPerl5> ▮
```

FIGURE 10.4:   Using the system error message variable

Although Listing 10.2 is a contrived example, it illustrates the easiest mechanism for calling die or warn. The OR operator (||) after the open call activates the die or warn function only if the return value from the open function is false.

Line 2 of Listing 10.2 illustrates the use of the warn function with a newline character in the print list. As you can see in Figure 10.4, the first error message does not include any file information. Line 5 of Listing 10.2 illustrates the result of the die function. Line 6 never executes, because the die function stops execution of the errorMessage.pl program.

Inserting *print* Statements

One of the most common methods of debugging a program is to insert print statements throughout the program. The print statement can be a simple statement identifying that you reached a particular location in your code. More frequently, however, the print statement includes variable names that tell you the current state of your program.

I used to insert print statements and then remove them. Then I had to rewrite them the next time a new bug appeared. There is an easier way. Every time you add a debug print statement, use an if $DEBUG clause:

```
print "some Debug Info \n" if $DEBUG;
```

You must initialize the $DEBUG variable at the front of your program, like this:

```
$DEBUG=1 if $ARGV[0]=~/^-D(ebug)?/i;
```

This statement sets the variable $DEBUG to 1 only if the first argument from the command line is –d (uppercase or lowercase), followed by an optional ebug. Now, when you need to debug your code, you can add print statements and leave them in your code. The only time they will execute is when you add a -Debug argument after your program name, as follows:

```
perl errorMessage.pl –d
```

WARNING

Make sure the –d comes after errorMessage.pl, rather than before it; otherwise, Perl will think the –d is a flag for Perl.

Searching for Bugs

When you have a large program with a runtime error, just finding the bug can be a real pain. When trying to locate bugs in a large program, I use a method called *binary search*. The binary search method looks in only half the code at one time. For example, here are the steps for using this method with a 100-line program:

1. Copy the last 50 lines to a temporary file and then delete them from your program. (You may need to leave in closing braces or other required statements.)

2. Rerun your program. If the error disappears, the problem is in those last 50 lines of your program; otherwise, it is in the first 50 lines. Let's assume the problem is in the last 50 lines of code.

3. Take the half of the code with the error in it and return it to the main program. Now your main program has lines 1 through 75, and your temporary program has lines 76 through 100.

4. Rerun your program. If the error is still missing, you now know it is in the last 25 lines.

5. Add half of the last 25 lines back in and rerun your program. If the error shows up, you know the problem is between lines 76 and 87.

6. Repeat this process until you have identified the exact line that contains the error. You can find the error because you have a much smaller area in which to look.

The ultimate way to find bugs is with a debugger. In the next section, you'll learn about the Perl 5 debugger and a commercial Windows-based debugger.

USING A DEBUGGER

A *debugger* is a tool that allows you to execute your code one or more lines at a time. Every debugger should let you view variables and set *breakpoints*, which stop execution of your code at predetermined locations. Perl 5 comes with a debugger that performs these basic functions and more. Here, we'll look at the Perl 5 debugger, including how to use it with the Emacs editor in an interactive window. Then I'll tell you about the ActiveState Windows debugger, which I use to debug my code.

Running the Perl Debugger

The Perl debugger is available with all Perl 5 distributions at no charge. To start the Perl 5 debugger, you must be at the command prompt. From the command prompt, enter:

```
Perl -d filename.pl
```

The debugger will be invoked on the file you designated. If your program has syntax errors, Perl will exit with an error message (remember that Perl 5 first compiles your program before running it). You will need to use one of the debugging techniques discussed earlier in this chapter to fix the syntax error before starting the debugger.

NOTE

The examples shown in this section use the DOS command window, but these commands also work from the Unix command shell.

If your program is syntactically correct, you will see a beginning debugger screen, which should look like the one shown in Figure 10.5. You can see the debug prompt, DB<1>, on the last line of the opening window.

NOTE

Notice in Figure 10.5 that the debugger says "Emacs support available." Many of the commands you will learn here work both from your Emacs editor and the command line.

```
Mastering Perl - perl -d slices.pl                              _ □ ×

D:\sybex\MasteringPerl5>perl -d slices.pl

Loading DB routines from perl5db.pl version 1.0401
Emacs support available.

Enter h or 'h h' for help.

main::(slices.pl:1):       @digits = (11..21);
  DB<1>
```

FIGURE 10.5:   The Perl 5 debugger window

Getting Help

The second line printed by the Perl debugger tells you how to get help.
Because your DOS command window on a Windows computer may not
have a scroll bar, the first thing you need to be aware of is how to get help
about help. If you type **h** at the debug prompt, you'll get a listing of debugging commands. To get an expanded list of the debugging commands,
type in **h h** at the debug prompt. Figure 10.6 shows an example of what
you will see.

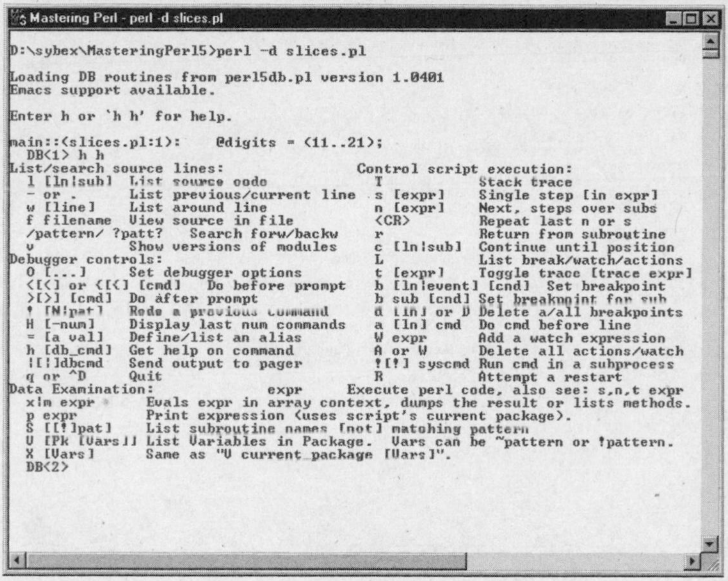

FIGURE 10.6: The Perl 5 debugger's help information

The help function from the DOS command window provides further
help for additional commands. To get help on a particular command, type
h *command* (where *command* is a help command) at the debug prompt. If you
type **h o**, you get a screen full of information about the various debugger
options. Other requests for help repeat a one-line help statement, which is
the same information as shown in Figure 10.6.

Displaying Source Code

If you're not looking at the help messages, then you probably want to look
at your code. The two commands I most frequently use to view my source

code in the Perl debugger are list (1) and window (w). These two commands tell the debugger to show you your source code.

As shown in Figure 10.7, you can type 1 from the debug prompt to list the next 10 lines of your program. Each time you enter 1, the next 10 lines of your source code are printed. The 1 command starts displaying from the last displayed line. For example, if line 50 is the last displayed line and you enter 1, lines 51 through 60 will be displayed.

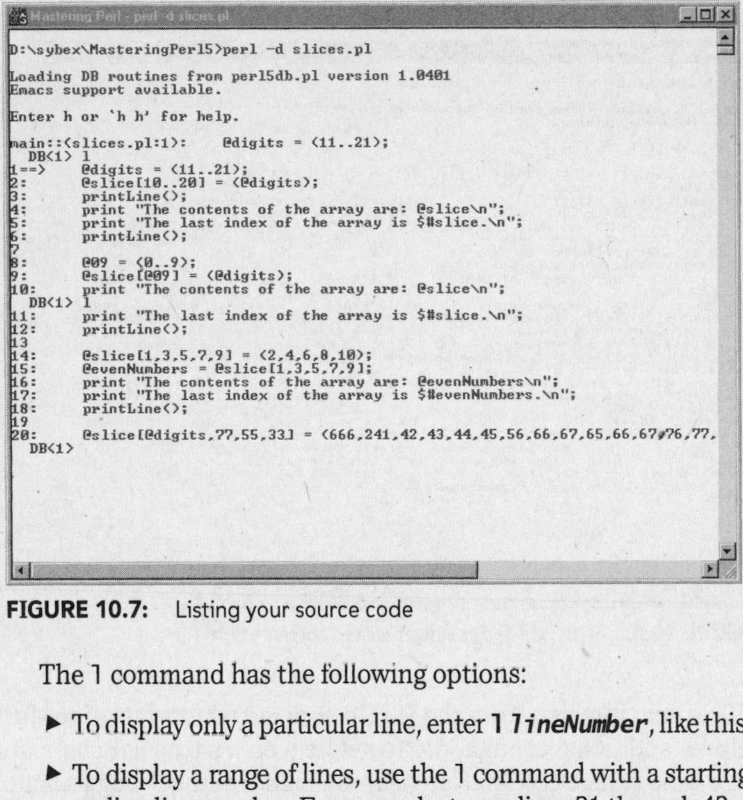

FIGURE 10.7:   Listing your source code

The 1 command has the following options:

▶ To display only a particular line, enter 1 *lineNumber*, like this: 1 8.

▶ To display a range of lines, use the 1 command with a starting and ending line number. For example, to see lines 21 through 42, enter 1 21–42. Alternatively, you can enter the starting line number, a plus sign, and then the number of additional lines you would like. For example, to see line 15 and the following 20 lines, enter 1 15+20.

▶ To list the contents of a subroutine, type 1 followed by the subroutine name: 1 *subName*.

When I'm debugging, I usually like to see a few lines surrounding the current line. The w command shows a few lines before the current line and a few lines after the current line. You can also use the w command with a line number to show the lines surrounding a particular location. Figure 10.8 shows an example of each of these forms of the command.

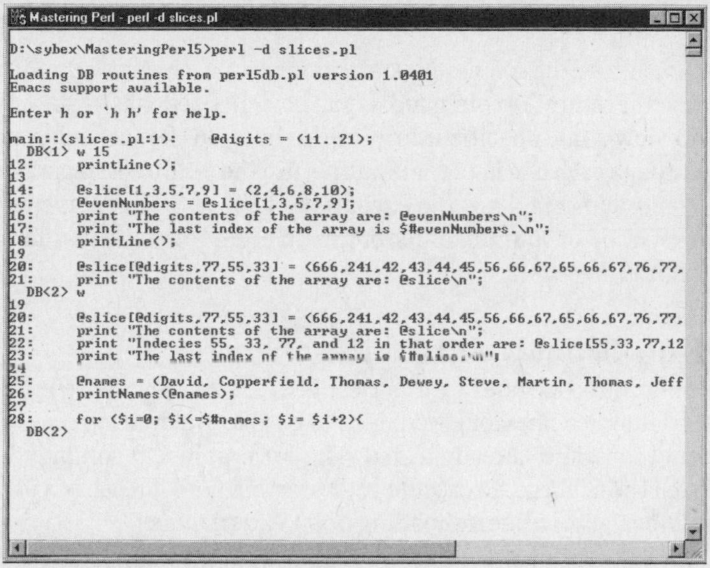

FIGURE 10.8: Using the window (w) command

Executing Your Code

The purpose of a debugger is to give you control over the execution of your program. The following are the primary commands for executing your code one or a few lines at a time:

▶ To execute one line of code at a time, use the step (s) command. To execute the next statement in your program, at the debug prompt, type **s** and then press Enter. Then you can press Enter again to continue stepping through your code. The step command shows you the sequential execution of your code. If your code calls a subroutine, you will step into that subroutine, which you can continue to execute one statement at a time.

▶ To execute the next line of code, stepping over any subroutine calls, use the next (n) command. When you are stepping through your code, you frequently know whether a subroutine works. If you want to sequentially execute your code but do not want to enter a subroutine, use the next command.

► To execute until the next program interrupt, use the continue (c) command. The continue command tells the debugger to execute your code until it finds a breakpoint. Your code will execute to completion unless you have set breakpoints to interrupt your program. Setting breakpoints is described in the next section.

► To execute the remaining statements in the current subroutine, use the return (r) command. If you have stepped into a subroutine to view some specific information, but you don't need to step through each line in the subroutine, use the return command. This command completes the execution of the subroutine and stops execution of your program on the first Perl 5 statement after the subroutine call.

Setting Breakpoints

Executing your code one line at a time gets old very fast. When your code is several hundred lines long, you need to be able to skip the pieces of your program that you've already tested. The breakpoint (b) command allows you to tell the debugger to execute your program until it reaches a particular line number, subroutine, or loading of an external file.

To set a breakpoint at a particular line, enter **b *lineNumber***, like this: b 8. To execute until you reach that line, type **c** at the debugger prompt. Your program will execute up to but not including the breakpoint line.

Conditional breakpoints stop execution of your program only when a specific condition is met. The syntax of conditional breakpoints is as follows:

```
B lineNumber condition
```

The condition may be any expression. The breakpoint will stop execution of your program only if the condition evaluates to true. Figure 10.9 shows an example of a breakpoint set on line 8 with this conditional statement:

```
($slice[10] == 11)
```

This means to stop execution of the program when the tenth element of the slice array is equal to 11. The breakpoint is set in the middle of Figure 10.9 and looks like this:

```
b 8 $slice[10]==11
```

To show all the breakpoints you have active in your debugging session, type **L**. To delete all your breakpoints, type **D**. To delete an individual breakpoint, type **d** followed by the line number of the breakpoint: d 8.

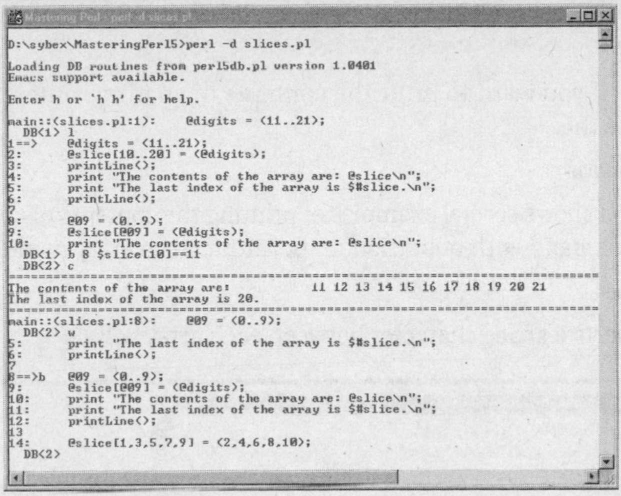

FIGURE 10.9: Setting a conditional breakpoint

I like to include external program files into my code using the `require` command (the `require` command includes subroutines into a program from other files on the hard disk). Frequently, I need to set breakpoints in these required files. You cannot set a breakpoint in a required file unless you are currently executing in the required file. The easiest way to stop your code at a required file is with the breakpoint on load command:

```
b load filename
```

For example, if the required filename is `readPostInput.cgi`, the breakpoint on load command looks like this:

```
b load readPostInput.cgi
```

The breakpoint command also accepts a subroutine name as a breakpoint value. When you use the breakpoint command with a subroutine name, your program will stop on the first executable line of the subroutine. Breakpoints on subroutine names may also be conditional, as follows:

```
b readPostInput $DEBUG == 1
```

This conditional breakpoint will stop here only if the variable `$DEBUG` is equal to 1.

Viewing Program Data

Once you've stopped your program using the step or breakpoint commands, you need to be able to look at your program's data to determine what is wrong with your code. The print (p) command prints the contents of a variable or expression. The syntax of the p command is as follows:

p *expression*

For example, if you want to print the contents of an array, enter the command like this:

p *@arrayName*

Figure 10.10 shows several examples of printing the contents of an array. Notice the command with quotation marks around the array name:

p "@slice"

This form inserts a space character between each array cell.

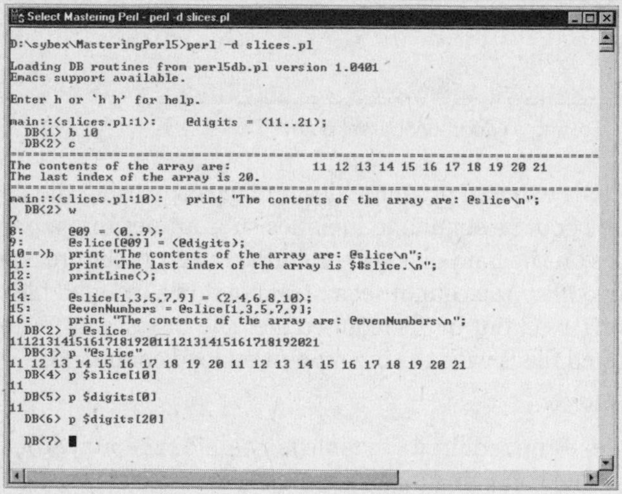

FIGURE 10.10:   Printing the contents of arrays

Quitting the Debugger

You will find your debugging sessions are interactive with your programming sessions. Your programming development cycle will begin to resemble the following: Build a little, test a little, debug a little, fix a little, build a little.... Quite often, the test-a-little, debug-a-little, and fix-a-little cycles take a lot more time than the build-a-little portion.

Once you have located your coding error in the debugger, there is usually no reason to continue running your program. You exit the debugger by entering the quit (q) command. Once you exit the debugger, you will most likely open your favorite editor and modify your program based on the information gathered during your debugging session. After you have made your changes, test your code to see if you have really fixed the error.

As you get more experienced with programming and debugging, you should explore the debug commands in more detail. The commands you have learned here are the basic ones you will use with almost every debugging session.

Running the ActiveState Windows Debugger

The Perl debugger has everything you need in a debugger, but it lacks a little in ease of use. Because I spend a good portion of my day writing and debugging code, I use the ActiveState debugger, shown in Figure 10.11. This tool is not free, but it is well worth the cost. This debugger enhances the built-in Perl debugger with an intuitive and easy-to-use interface.

TIP

The ActiveState debugger is available at www.activestate.com. You can run an evaluation copy on your computer at no cost. Instructions for integrating the ActiveState debugger with the Multi-Edit editor are available at the ActiveState website.

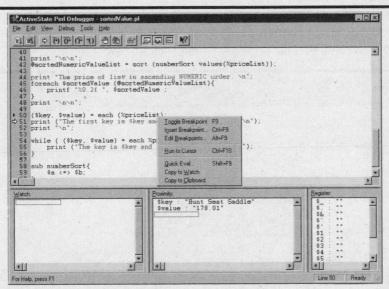

FIGURE 10.11: The ActiveState Windows debugger

The toolbar buttons and menus across the top of the window allow you to manage your debugging session. From left to right, the buttons perform the following operations: continue, quit, show the next statement, step, step over, step out of, run to cursor, insert breakpoint, and delete all breakpoints. As you can see, these operations are similar to (if not the same as) the free Perl 5 debugger operations.

The right three buttons on the top toolbar (excluding the help button) activate the bottom three windows of the ActiveState debugger:

▶ The Watch window shows the values of variables you have explicitly requested.

▶ The Proximity window shows the values of scalar variables surrounding the current execution point of your program. (The current execution point is also called the *instruction pointer location*.)

▶ The Registry window shows the contents of the Perl 5 special variables that are relevant to the current instruction pointer.

If you right-click with your mouse, you bring up the pop-up menu also shown in Figure 10.11. (This pop-up menu is the interface I most frequently use.) One of the options on this menu is Quick Eval. Selecting that option brings up the QuickEval window, shown in Figure 10.12. The QuickEval window allows you to view data and evaluate Perl 5 expressions. Note that to evaluate or view the contents of an array, as shown in Figure 10.12, you must surround the array name with quotation marks. If you evaluate an array without surrounding quotation marks, then the size of the array is returned.

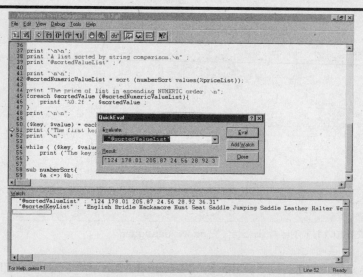

FIGURE 10.12: Evaluating data

Figure 10.12 also shows the Watch window fully expanded at the bottom of the screen. You can add variables to the Watch window through the QuickEval window. Once a variable is added to the Watch window, its current value is displayed throughout your program's execution.

Here, you've learned about just a few of the main features of the Active-State debugger. The user interface is intuitive, and as you work with it, you will learn about the other capabilities of this debugger.

DEBUGGING CGI PROGRAMS

Debugging CGI programs usually involves creative use of `print` statements. Here are the three basic steps for the CGI programmer:

1. Make sure your code is syntactically correct.

2. Test your code with sample data.

3. Print the data sent to your CGI program using a debugging interface subroutine.

Make sure your CGI program compiles without syntax errors before you begin debugging it through your web server. If you are running the program on a Unix computer, make sure the file permissions are set to 755. Then test the program by running it from the command line.

After you know your program does not have any syntax errors, you can move on to the next steps. The following sections explain the techniques I use to debug my CGI programs and include some examples.

Running the Program with Test Data

If the program is free of syntax errors, I run it with special test data. This step is critical, because most CGI programs require external data sent via a web page. If this method does not solve the problem, then I modify my CGI program to show the data it is receiving and add `print` statements as necessary, as described in the next section.

To test my CGI program, I first create a file of debug information. This file should contain data already in the format your CGI program expects. The file shown in Listing 10.3 is a debug data file I used to debug an online reservation program. You then include the debug file in your CGI program using the `require` command, an example of which follows the listing.

This mechanism of testing a CGI program allows you to load and run your program from the command line using your favorite debugger interface, which is much easier than trying to debug blindly based only on your web browser's output.

Listing 10.3: Debug Data

```
%lodgingInfo = (
'ARRIVAL_DATE' => "10/6/98",
'ROOM_PREFERRENCE' => "Red River",
'LENGTH_OF_STAY' => 4,
'PAYMENT_METHOD' => "Credit Card",
'NAME' => "Eric C. Herrmann",
'ADDRESS' => "255 S. Canyonwood Dr.",
'CITY' => "Austin",
'STATE' => "Texas",
'ZIP' => "78620",
'TELEPHONE' => "512-442-2991",
'EMAIL' => "yawp\@io.com",
'OCCASION' => "20th Wedding Anniversary",
'SPECIAL_REQUEST' => "It would be really nice if you would
➥do something very nice and let us take the raft down
➥the creek",
'NUMBER_IN_PARTY' => 2,
'UID' => 62878766310,
'PAYMENT_METHOD' => "onLine",
) ;
$ENV{ 'QUERY_STRING'} ="UID=  14fa7198.49.249.718";
return 1;
```

When I want to test a CGI program I insert a line like this:

```
require "debugConstants.cgi" if $DEBUG:
```

Notice that the last line of Listing 10.3 returns a 1. If the last line of a required file does not return a true value, your program will fail.

Adding *print* Statements

If I need to do further debugging of my CGI program, my next step is to modify the program to show the data it is receiving and add print statements as necessary. The first thing I modify the program to do is print the HTTP response header Content-Type: text/html. I also modify the program so that it performs this special debug function only when I send it a unique input variable.

As an example, I have modified Listing 9.4 from Chapter 9, modifying line 3 to run the `printDebug` subroutine when the input form sends the user's name as Debug, as shown in Listing 10.4.

NOTE

The subroutine `printDebug` can be inserted at any reasonable place into your code. I usually put my subroutines at the end of the file, as shown here.

Listing 10.4: Debugging CGI Programs

```perl
1. #!/usr/bin/perl
2.
# REPLACE LINE 3:
# 3. %postInputs = readPostInput();
# WITH THIS LINE:
3. printDebug() if $postInputs{ 'Contact_FullName'}
   =~ /Debug/i;
4. $dateCommand = "date";
5. $time = `$dateCommand`;
6. open (MAIL, "|/usr/sbin/sendmail -t") || return 0;
7.
8. select (MAIL);
9. print<<"EOF";
# ...lines omitted for space

sub printDebug(){
    print "Content-type: text/html\n\n";

    foreach $key (sort keys %postInputs){
      print qq|$key ==> $postInputs{ "$key"}  <br>|;
    }
    exit(1);
}
```

As shown in Figure 10.13, this approach allows you to see your incoming CGI data. If you need to see other data in the program, insert `print` statements as required.

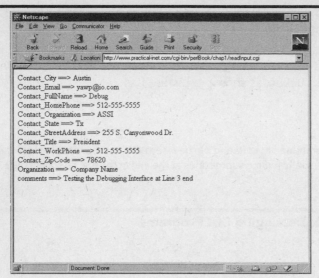

FIGURE 10.13: Viewing incoming CGI POST data

I recommend that you always print your input CGI data as your first online CGI debugging step. The input data is the most likely source of errors. Notice that the subroutine printDebug in Listing 10.4 calls the exit function after printing the input data. This prevents the remaining portion of the CGI program from running. You should comment out the exit statement if you need other parts of your CGI program to execute after you call the printDebug subroutine.

Another way to print information is by using the Data::Dumper module, available on the Comprehensive Perl Archive Network (CPAN). Printing a hash is as simple as this:

```
use Data::Dumper;
print Dumper( \%ENV ), "\n";
```

What's Next

If you've never coded with Perl before, you're now prepared to enter the Perl 5 programming world. Chapters 9 and 10 were designed to give you the foundation you need to work though the remainder of the Perl chapters with confidence. In Chapter 11, you'll learn about how to use Perl and CGI in a web server environment. You'll learn about file handling to keep track of data on your website, and how to make sure it doesn't get corrupted. You'll put all this knowledge together to make a simple web-page access counter.

Chapter 11

USING CGI IN THE REAL WORLD

Y ou are fairly well grounded by now in the processes that allow CGI to work with the World Wide Web. You can create a Perl program that draws its own web page. You are also familiar with the methods used in CGI to pass information between the web server and a CGI program.

But you haven't done anything really *useful* yet. In this chapter, you'll dive right in, take what you've learned thus far, and put it to work by creating an access counter for your website.

Updated from *Perl CGI Programming: No Experience Required*, by Erik Strom

ISBN 0-7821-2157-8

The Task: Counting Your Visitors

A popular feature among webmasters is a simple *access counter* that keeps track of every visit to the website. It displays a little message at the bottom of the home page that tells the user what number visitor they are, such as: "You are visitor No. 10,001!" See Figure 11.1 for an example of an access counter display.

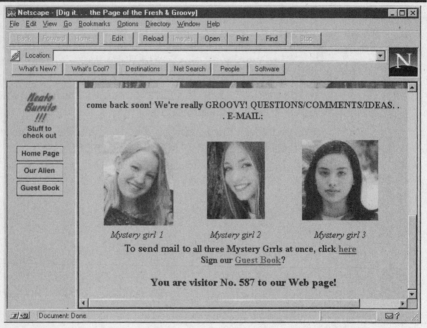

FIGURE 11.1:   An example of one of the many access counters on the Web

Such a little thing should be fairly easy to lash together, shouldn't it? Well, yes and no. It is a straightforward task, but it can't be accomplished with HTML alone. You need the power of Perl in the background to do the work for you.

How to Go About It

Creating an access counter is a programming problem—a system problem— and the best way to go about solving it is to first get up and walk away from your computer. That's right; turn the thing off if you need to. You'll be designing a system, a small and simple one, but a system nevertheless. The computer and the code are the *last* steps in the process of analyzing, designing, and implementing the solution to a problem.

NOTE

In technospeak, a *system* is nothing but the solution to a problem: It's the analysis, design, and implementation of a tool or set of tools that will do the thing you want to do. The thing might be as monumental as keeping track of the daily transactions in a stock exchange, or it might be as simple as keeping track of a website's visitors. The beginning steps are the same regardless of the complexity of the ultimate solution.

Think, Don't Code

Many programmers, especially beginners, jump right in and start coding, and refine the bugs as they go along. The problem with this approach is that it ties you inexorably to the computer and the programming tools you have at your disposal. As a result, you will end up with a solution that is entirely dependent on these tools.

It is more logical to approach a problem from a more general perspective. You have something you want to do, so how do you go about it? What, in general, do you need to do to implement a solution? We can distill this thinking phase down to three categories:

- ▶ Analysis
- ▶ Design
- ▶ Implementation

Once you have mapped out the steps needed to solve the problem, once you have identified a general approach to a solution, *then* you can identify which of your available tools you'll need to solve the problem with what you have at hand.

To begin, find a comfortable chair, take a pad and pencil with you, and begin sketching. You need to think, not code.

Analysis

The first step in your sketching process is analysis. To effectively accomplish your task (or solve your problem), you need to properly identify what needs to be done. For example (as in Figure 11.2), to count the hits on a web page, you need to:

- ▶ Store a number somewhere
- ▶ Be able to read the number
- ▶ Be able to increment it (add 1)
- ▶ Write it out to the web page
- ▶ Store the number again

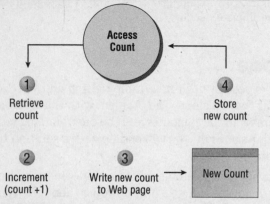

FIGURE 11.2:   The requirements of an access counter

Design

Once you have analyzed your problem, you need to begin thinking about design. For instance, the number your access counter derives must be stored in a permanent place, where you can get to it any time you need to, change it, and store it again. A file on disk is a logical candidate, because data will stay in files even when your computer is turned off, barring some catastrophe. A disk file is the first choice of most programmers for storing data gathered by a program because it's easy and relatively safe. So, let's decide to store the number in a file.

Having made that decision, you can flesh out the list of requirements from the analysis of the problem. The design of your solution, illustrated in Figure 11.3, can proceed step by step:

1.   If this is the first time the program runs, create a file and store the value 1 in it. Proceed to step 3.

2. Otherwise, open and read the file. Add 1 to the value you have read.

3. Display the new value on the web page.

4. Write the new value to the file.

5. Close the file.

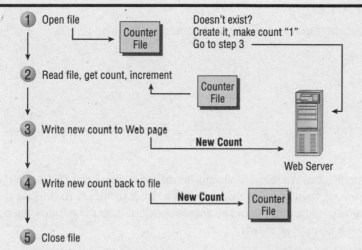

FIGURE 11.3: Opening, reading, writing, and closing the counter file

Implementation

You will implement your solution using Perl, of course, and HTML. However, the requirements of the web page access counter highlight one concept you haven't covered yet: files.

How Perl Deals with Files

You have analyzed and designed a solution for the task of putting an access counter on your web page. But the implementation step, according to the design, needs a method to store the counter in a disk file.

A disk is nothing more than a magnetic platter, very similar to a recording tape, that is capable of storing data. The low-level details of how that is accomplished aren't relevant to a discussion of files. What *is* relevant is the idea that a file is just a collection of characters. They may not be characters in forms or combinations that are meaningful to humans, as in the case of a program file. But the characters are stored (recorded) in their original sequence on the disk, and that's how you deal with them.

The concept of a file on disk was intended originally to make an analogy to paper files in a cabinet full of folders. When you want to read a file, you have to open it first. When you're done with it, you have to close it.

Files in Perl

The Perl functions that allow you to manipulate files are

- ▶ open
- ▶ close
- ▶ read
- ▶ print
- ▶ write

It's always best to learn by doing, so rather than wading into a lengthy discussion of these file functions, let's write a program to handle the rudimentary requirements of the access counter. Enter the following code, which we will analyze shortly:

```perl
#!/perl/bin/perl

# access.pl
#
# First version.  Creates or opens a file with a number
# in it, increments the number, writes it back.
    $CountFile = "counter.dat";    # Name of counter file.

# Open the file and read it.  If it doesn't exist, its
# "contents" will be read into a program variable as "0".

    open (COUNT, $CountFile);
    $Counter = <COUNT>;            # Read the first line..

# Close the file, then reopen it for output.

    close (COUNT);
    open (COUNT, ">$CountFile");

# Increment $Counter, then write it back out.  Put up a
# message with the new value.  Close the file and exit.
```

```
$Counter += 1;
print COUNT $Counter;
print "$CountFile has been written to $Counter times.\n";
close (COUNT);
```

```
#                         End access.pl
```

Save this sample code as `access.pl` and run it a few times from the command line. Figure 11.4 illustrates what you should see.

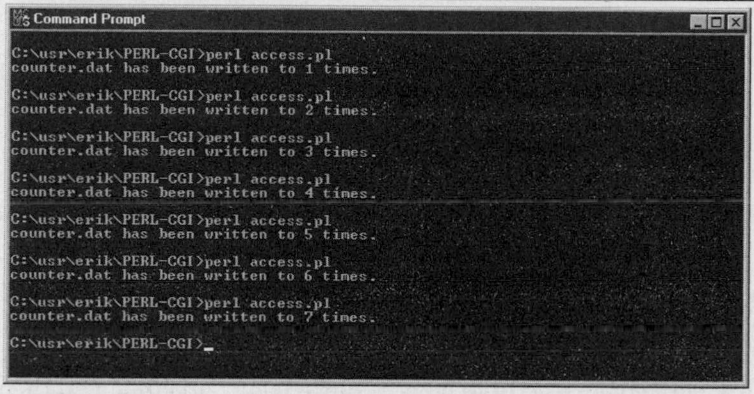

FIGURE 11.4: The results of running the simplest form of the access counter

Opening, Closing, and Writing Files

When you ran `access.pl`, you probably noticed that it uses only two of the new Perl functions listed earlier: open and close. They are all you need to do simple file manipulation.

And, as usual when using new Perl stuff, you saw some strange and unfamiliar operators. Let's dissect this program so you can see what you've done.

The first program line sets a program variable:

```
$CountFile = "counter.dat";     # Name of counter file.
```

The file's name is `counter.dat`. Of course, you can call it anything you want, within the file-naming rules of your operating system. Whatever you do, it is best to do it here, at the top of the program, and *put it in a variable*. You could have referred to `counter.dat` throughout the program, but what if you decided to change it? By putting the name in a variable, you've ensured that it only has to be changed once. Laziness and impatience win the day again.

TIP

To a Perl programmer, laziness and impatience aren't bad things. Larry Wall has often said that laziness, impatience, and hubris are the three virtues of a Perl programmer.

File Handles

The next two code lines in `access.pl` open the file and read whatever is in it.

```
open (COUNT, $CountFile);
$Counter = <COUNT>;              # Read the first line.
```

The arguments to open take the form

```
open (HANDLE, Expression);
```

where `Expression` usually is a filename or some variable that contains one. But what is this `HANDLE`?

When you open a file, you actually are instructing Perl to perform a complex series of steps. Information about the file is stored in the computer's memory, where you can deal with it if you want, and the processes that allow you to read from it and write to it are initialized. Perl then needs a way to refer to the file, so it sets up a *handle*, which you can treat as a variable name for the file. Until the file is closed and the handle is put back into circulation, you will perform all your file operations on this handle.

This line of the program shows the handle in action, and also shows a useful shortcut:

```
$Counter = <COUNT>;              # Read the first line.
```

You can read directly from a file handle by putting brackets (< >) around it, as you did with <COUNT>. Because you can be reasonably certain that `counter.dat` contains either one number or nothing, you can set the value of the `$Counter` variable to whatever you read from the file.

But what about the first time the program is run, when `counter.dat` doesn't exist yet? When you open a nonexistent filename for reading, Perl returns a `NULL` handle. So, setting a scalar variable to the handle's contents would effectively set the variable to 0.

Input, Output

The next two lines in `access.pl` are liable to be a little confusing to beginners.

```
close (COUNT);
open (COUNT, ">$CountFile");
```

Why do you `close` the file and then instantly re-open it? And why is `$CountFile` in quotes this time with a > character in front of it?

The > operator is the difference between *input* and *output* on a file in Perl. You might remember the > and < symbols as the operators for *redirection* of input and output in MS-DOS. These conventions were borrowed from Unix, so it's no wonder they're used in Perl.

When you put the greater-than sign in front of the filename parameter to open, the file is opened for output (or writing), and open will create the file if it doesn't exist or overwrite anything that is in the file. The less-than sign opens the file for input to the program (or reading), but this is so common that Perl regards less-than as the default if you leave it off. The append symbol (>>) will append anything you write to the file to what already is in the file.

So, the code snippet

```
close (COUNT);
open (COUNT, ">$CountFile");
```

creates `counter.dat` the first time you run the program, and opens it for overwriting on any subsequent runs.

REDIRECTING INPUT AND OUTPUT

Unix and Windows, as well as the Windows progenitors all the way back to the early versions of MS-DOS, interpret < and > (the greater-than and less-than signs) as special symbols. They are used to *redirect* the channels through which you normally interact with your computer (essentially the screen and the keyboard) into other places (usually files).

Normally, a command-line program expects its *input* to come from the keyboard, and it ships its *output* to the screen. However, if you were to run a program called `foo` in this manner

```
foo > bar
```

then whatever foo is supposed to print to the screen would instead be written into a file called bar, which would be created if it didn't exist already, or overwritten if it did.

Likewise, the line

```
foo < bar
```

CONTINUED ➡

would expect the information the user would normally enter through the keyboard to come from a file called bar.

One more redirection symbol combines two greater-than signs (>>) to create an *append* command. This command tacks any new data to the end of the file to its right, rather than overwriting it.

print Works with Files, Too

The last bit of code from access.pl brings up a couple of interesting new Perl concepts.

```
$Counter += 1;
print COUNT $Counter;
print "$CountFile has been written to $Counter times.\n";
close (COUNT);
```

In the first line, $Counter += 1, the += is a shortcut borrowed from the C programming language. In this example, it is identical to writing:

```
$Counter = $Counter + 1;
```

Why not simply write $Counter = $Counter + 1? For one thing, $Counter += 1 is shorter and, therefore, follows the twin precepts of laziness and impatience. However, some programmers might insist that the longer form is clearer—that is, it more clearly states the intention of the code. In the end, it's a matter of taste.

NOTE

Probably the most common criticism of C as a programming language is that its inherent economy encourages programmers to write programs that are too terse. Perl, with its roots deep in the C language, must shoulder this criticism as well.

NOTE

Perl's += operator is one of a family that includes all of the arithmetic operators used in the language. You also can use -= for subtraction, *= for multiplication, and /= for division. The number on the right side of the equation doesn't have to be 1; it can be any valid number or scalar variable.

The other line worthy of special mention in this code snippet is the second:

```
print COUNT $Counter;
```

This line brings up a feature of print that we haven't covered yet: The function presumes that its first argument is a file handle. If it's left out, print uses the current output file handle, which, unless you have done something special and specific, will be the *standard output* (the screen).

That's why there isn't a comma between COUNT and $Counter in the example. If there were, print would treat COUNT as a scalar or list variable and try to write it to the standard output, leading to strange and possibly indecipherable results. In any event, nothing would get into the file to which COUNT refers.

THE *READ* AND *WRITE* FUNCTIONS IN PERL

Perl has just about all the simple functionality you need when you're dealing with the most common manipulations on a file. The best example is the one you just finished: You were able to write a program that creates, reads, and writes to a file without once invoking the Perl functions that specifically refer to these actions (read and write).

Do you need them both? Most definitely, especially read.

In access.pl, your only responsibility was to read the first (and only) line of counter.dat into a scalar variable. There will be many occasions when you don't want to do this. You will instead want to read a chunk from the file, process the chunk, and then get another. read is the tool of choice for such operations. It expects at least three, possibly four, arguments:

```
read (HANDLE, BUFFER, LENGTH, OFFSET);
```

You know *HANDLE*; it's a file handle. *BUFFER* is a scalar variable that holds the chunk of the file you read, and *LENGTH* is the number of characters—or *bytes*—in the chunk. For example,

```
read (COUNT, $Buffer, 256);
```

reads 256 bytes into $Buffer from the file referred to by COUNT. The *OFFSET* argument is not used that often and is, therefore, optional. It tells read to load the bytes into *BUFFER* at a different starting point than the beginning.

CONTINUED ➡

The `write` function is almost never used in normal Perl file processing. `print` is preferable—and, in fact, more correct—in nearly every case. `write` is used to put formatted records into a file. It is intended to be used with reports printed on paper, so its functionality veers toward formatting headings, pages, and such.

WARNING

Putting the comma between the file handle and the first string argument to print is an easy gaffe to commit. Larry Wall placed it second in his list of common mistakes made by novices.

The remaining lines in `access.pl` write a message to the screen and close the file; nothing new here. Now you're ready to turn the program into a CGI application and bring it to the Web.

BRINGING YOUR COUNTER TO THE WEB

You have written the rudiments of a web page access counter. You also should have a fair-to-middling understanding of how files work in Perl. However, `access.pl` will only work from the command line at this point, and we want it to run on the Web. Let's make this basic program CGI-ready.

You've Been Here Before

You already know which wrappers you need to fit over a Perl program to turn it into a CGI application. Here's a recap of what your program needs to do:

- ▶ Send a proper HTTP header to the web server.

- ▶ `print` information you want displayed in HTML format.

- ▶ Send a proper HTML ender to the web server, so it knows when you're finished.

- ▶ Run the program as a URL in a web browser.

Following these rules, you can fit the wrapper over `access.pl`. Here's the wrapper code specified in `access.pl`'s `require` statement:

```
# html.pl

# Contains header and ender subroutines for setting
# up HTML documents from Perl.

# Set up a standard HTML header section with the page title
# passed on the command line.

sub HTML_Header
{
      # Put up standard HTTP opening line.
    print "Content-type: text/html", "\n\n";
      # Specify HTML document.
    print "<HTML>", "\n\n";
      # Specify header section.
    print "<HEAD>", "\n\n";
      # Put up the title line.
    print "<TITLE>", "@_", "</TITLE>", "\n\n";
      # End header section.
    print "</HEAD>", "\n\n";

}                        #    End HTML_Header.pl.

# Set up a standard HTML footer section.  At this point,
# it simply ends the BODY and HTML sections.

sub HTML_Ender
{
    print "\n", "</BODY>", "\n\n";
    print "</HTML>", "\n\n";

}                        # End HTML_Ender
1;
```

And here's `access.pl`:

```
#!/perl/bin/perl

 # access.pl
 #
 # Second version.  Creates or opens a file with a number
 # in it, increments the number, writes it back, then
 # displays the result in a message on a web page.

    # Get HTML header, ender.
    require "perl-cgi/html.pl";
```

```
      # Name of counter file.
      $CountFile = "counter.dat";
      # web page title.
      $PageTitle = "Web Page Access Counter";

   # Open the file and read it.  If it doesn't exist, its
   # "contents" will be read into a program variable as undef,
   # which is effectively zero.""

      open (COUNT, $CountFile);
      $Counter = <COUNT>;      # Read the contents.

   # Close the file, then reopen it for output.

      close (COUNT);
      open (COUNT, ">$CountFile");

   # Increment $Counter, then write it back out.
   # Put up a message with the new value.  Close the file.

      $Counter += 1;
      print COUNT $Counter;
      close (COUNT);

   # Put the result up in a standard HTML document.

      &HTML_Header ($PageTitle);         # HTTP header info.
      print "<BODY>\n";
      print "<H1>$PageTitle</H1>\n";  # Big heading.
      print "<HR>\n";                 # Draw a rule.
      print "<H3>You are visitor #$Counter ";
      print "to our Web page!</H3>\n";
      &HTML_Ender;

   #                      End access.pl
```

Save this as access.pl again, overwriting the old version, and run it, this time as a URL in your web browser. Figure 11.5 illustrates what you should see.

WARNING

Make sure the directory in which you have installed access.pl has write permission set for users coming in from the World Wide Web, or make the program put counter.dat in some other accessible directory. Otherwise, the file will never be written, and the only number of visitors you'll ever see is 1.

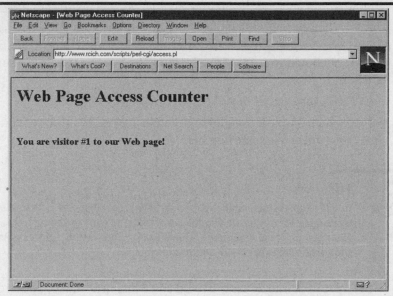

FIGURE 11.5:   The access counter moves to the Web.

Refining the Program

The access.pl program doesn't make a very spiffy home page, but all the elements are there for you to add this code to your own page. However, you'll soon be annoyed to notice that your access count is incremented every time *you* call up the page, too. If you test your web pages thoroughly—and you certainly should—the counter can be boosted to unrealistic heights in no time.

Fortunately, CGI provides a way to get around this problem. One of the environment variables available through CGI contains the IP address of the website visitor who initiated the HTTP session. If you can read that address and compare it with your own, it is a simple matter to decide whether the count should go up. Perl makes it easy for you to automate the process. Checking a visitor's IP address also provides the opportunity to introduce a new Perl concept: conditional expressions using the if statement, which we'll discuss in the next section.

To Increment or Not

Recall from Chapters 8 ("Introducing Perl and CGI") and 9 ("Writing Your First Program") that the web server fills its environment with a great deal of information about the computer that has started up an HTTP session. This information is passed along to a Perl program through CGI.

The environment variable that contains a visitor's IP address is called REMOTE_ADDR, and you can get to it by using Perl's @ENV array of environment variables:

```
$VisitorAddress = $ENV{ 'REMOTE_ADDR'} ;
```

$VisitorAddress now contains an Internet address in the form nnn.nnn.nnn.nnn, where n is some number.

TIP

Your IP address is something you should have at your disposal. On a Unix system, try running ifconfig. On Windows machines, ipconfig should tell you what you need to know. If neither of these works, your Internet Service Provider should be able to get the IP address for you.

Let's get back into access.pl and add a line near the top to store your IP address. Here's the code:

```
# Second version.  Creates or opens a file with a number
# in it, increments the number, writes it back, then
# displays the result in a message on a web page.

    # Get HTML header, ender.
    require "perl-cgi/html.pl";
    # Name of counter file.
    $CountFile = "counter.dat";
    # web page title.
    $PageTitle = "Web Page Access Counter";
    # My IP address.
    $HomeBase = "198.66.21.24";
    # Visitor's IP address.
    $VisitorAddress = $ENV{ 'REMOTE_ADDR'} ;
```

Two new variables are initialized in this revision to access.pl: $HomeBase, in which your IP address is stored, and $VisitorAddress, which pulls the visitor's IP out of the environment. As usual, you should replace the string given to $HomeBase with your own IP address.

Comparing Conditions

You should now be able to compare the incoming address with your own and decide whether the access count will be incremented. if is known as a *conditional* statement. A conditional statement allows you to compare two conditions and go in one direction or another based on the results of the comparison.

In Perl, if begins a code block similar to what you learned about with the while statement. It looks like this:

```
if (This statement is true)
    {
    Execute;
    this block;
    of code;
    }
```

The truthfulness or falseness of the statement in parentheses usually is determined by the result of an *equality*. In other words, in the statement if (1 > 2), the comparison in parentheses is false (1 is not greater than 2, at least not in this dimension), so the code block will not be executed.

Because scalar variables can contain either string or numeric information, Perl needs to know what kind of comparison is being made. As a result, two sets of operators are used to differentiate between the two types of data. Table 11.1 summarizes these *relational operators*.

TABLE 11.1:   Perl Relational Operators

NUMERIC	STRING	MEANS
==	eq	Is equal to
!=	ne	Is not equal to
>	gt	Is greater than
<	lt	Is less than
>=	ge	Is greater than or equal to
<=	le	Is less than or equal to
<=>	cmp	Not equal, signed result

IP addresses are numeric, but not in the form passed back to you in REMOTE_ADDR. You should use the string comparison operator, eq, to determine whether they match.

NOTE

IP addresses in the form nnn.nnn.nnn.nnn are set up as a convenience for humans. The address goes through a complex transformation to become a real number that is then passed to the Internet.

Change the line in access.pl that increments $Counter

```
$Counter += 1;
```

to say this:

```
if ($VisitorAddress ne $HomeBase)
    {
    $Counter += 1;
    }
```

If the visitor's address is *not equal* to your address, *then* the code adds 1 to the counter.

NOTE

Why not say if ($VisitorAddress eq $HomeBase)? Because the only time an action is required is if the two addresses are not equal. If the visitor's address is the same as yours, you don't increment the counter—you don't do anything.

Now you won't artificially boost the number of visits recorded to your web page.

RUNNING THE COUNTER

So far, you have run access.pl by typing a URL into your web browser and having it tell the web server to execute the code. Eventually, however, you will want to add this feature to your own web page, which visitors visit by typing its URL into their browsers. How do you get access.pl to run automatically?

Unfortunately, standard HTML doesn't provide a straightforward way of doing this. The only HTML method for jumping to a URL is through a hyperlink, and those usually have to be clicked, or otherwise specifically requested, by a user.

Getting around HTML

The quick and dirty way around this limitation would be to change the name of your website from, say, www.MySite.com to www.MySite.com/scripts/access.pl. That's ugly. You don't want to do that.

Some webmasters point their site URLs to an HTML document that is just a *facing page*, which puts up a "Welcome!" message and advises the visitor to click on a hyperlink to enter the site. Figure 11.6 is an example of a facing page. The "Click here to enter!" message is the hyperlink.

FIGURE 11.6:   A website facing page with a hyperlink to the real thing

The hyperlink is a URL to a Perl script that runs the access counter and also draws the entire home page. This is not a bad solution, though it requires a somewhat inelegant extra step.

Sadly, the only other solutions are based on proprietary extensions to HTML or equally proprietary graphics packages. This is such a perplexing problem that a small industry has sprung up around it—you can rent space on websites that do nothing more than keep track of your visitors and draw the count on your home page. However, we can simply use HTML frames to automate our counter.

Using Frames to Automate a URL

A few versions back, Netscape developers came up with the idea of including *frames* in the HTML, which their Navigator browser would understand. This gave the browser (and the HTML developer writing web pages for Navigator) the ability to break a web page up into different windows, each operating independently of the others. At the time, it only worked with Netscape's software, which is why you still see a lot of web pages that give you a choice between frame-capable displays and regular HTML.

Microsoft included the ability to recognize and deal with frames in its Internet Explorer browser, so the two most popular web packages on the market today will do frames. As a result, it is no longer imperative to make provisions for frame-damaged browsers, which was not the case even a few years ago. These days, the chances are extremely good that you can depend on your visitors' having the capability to display frames.

Refer back to Figure 11.1, which illustrates a home page constructed with frames. Interestingly, it also illustrates a home page with a built-in access counter. Its creator used a feature of the frame extensions that Netscape tacked on to HTML.

On a frame-capable website, you generally make the home-page HTML document the one that sets up the frames. It then calls in the actual HTML documents that make up the home page. The beauty of this setup, for our purposes, is that each frame declaration needs to know what HTML document it should call in, but the declaration effectively is in the form of a URL. The result is that you can put *any* valid URL in a frame declaration, including the path to a Perl script that will generate a number showing the hits on the website and draw the home page for you.

Figure 11.7 shows the HTML document that draws the page in Figure 11.1. Notice that the source for the frame named Main, which is the window on the right in Figure 11.1, is a URL pointing to access.pl. The remaining information is a list of arguments to access.pl. It specifies the HTML document to draw as the home page and the location of the file in which the access count is stored.

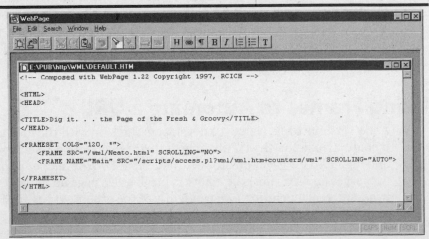

FIGURE 11.7:   This HTML code produces the web page shown in Figure 11.1.

TIP

Rather than generating HTML documents directly through strings that are printed out to the web server, it is cleaner to make your Perl program read and print each line of an actual HTML file. This approach keeps the two types of code separate, and the code bit easier to maintain. You'll learn more in Chapter 12, "Creating HTML Forms with Perl."

WHAT'S NEXT

HTML forms are the most heavily used interactive construct on the World Wide Web. In Chapter 12, you'll learn how to gather and process information sent to you through CGI from a form.

Chapter 12
CREATING HTML FORMS WITH PERL

Forms in HTML are what make the World Wide Web interactive; they make it something more than a collection of good-looking graphics. Forms are what your website visitors will use to communicate with you, the webmaster.

CGI is the heart of the communication; Perl is the brain. With these two tools, you will make your website *useful*—for both your visitors and you.

Updated from *Perl CGI Programming: No Experience Required*, by Erik Strom
ISBN 0-7821-2157-8

BUILDING AN HTML FORM

The concept of a form in the Hypertext Markup Language (HTML) is quite simple. It gives the user the capability to *enter* information, rather than just *display* it. This feature alone allows two-way communication over the Web (see Figure 12.1).

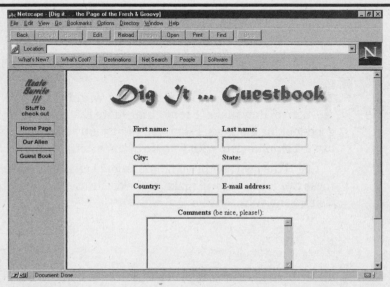

FIGURE 12.1:   Two-way communication on the Web is accomplished with forms.

HTML can't do anything with the information in a form all by itself, but it *can* send the information to something that knows how to deal with it. Through CGI, a Perl script can process the data a visitor deposits on your website and proceed according to your plan (see Figure 12.2).

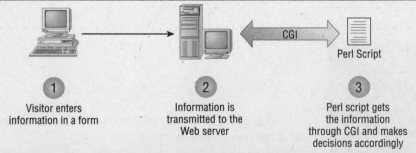

FIGURE 12.2:   Processing visitor information through CGI and Perl

This is important. Your intelligently written Perl script is capable of making decisions about how information should be digested and what to send back to the visitor as a result. Without the interaction that HTML forms allow, you would have no way of learning anything about your visitors. You'd be working in the dark.

A Simple Form

Forms in HTML are used for two purposes: collecting information and creating interactivity between the visitor and the web server. As an example of the former, you can create a small visitor information form with the following HTML code:

```
<HTML>
<HEAD>
<TITLE>Visitor Information Form</TITLE>
</HEAD>
<BODY>
<H1 ALIGN="LEFT">Visitor Information Form</H1>
<HR>
<FORM ACTION="perl.bat" METHOD="GET">
<B>
Last name: <INPUT TYPE="text" NAME="LastName" SIZE="16">
First Name: <INPUT TYPE="text" NAME="FirstName" SIZE="16">
<BR><BR>
Address: <INPUT TYPE="text" NAME="Address" SIZE="32">
City: <INPUT TYPE="text" NAME="City" SIZE="32">
<BR><BR>
State: <INPUT TYPE="text" NAME="State" SIZE="2">
<BR><BR>
<CENTER>
<INPUT TYPE="submit" VALUE="Send Information">
<INPUT TYPE="reset" VALUE="Clear Form Fields">
</CENTER>
</B>

</FORM>
</BODY>
</HTML>
```

NOTE

An *interactive* website can tailor an individual response to a visitor's input.

If you save this code as `form1.html`, you can run it in your web browser by telling the browser to open the file in whatever location you've stored it. The result should look similar to Figure 12.3.

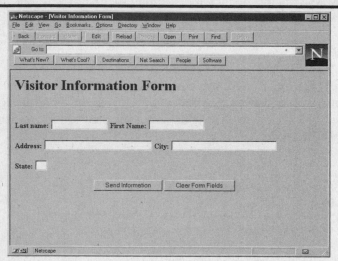

FIGURE 12.3: The first version of the visitor information form

HTML FORMS REDUX

A form is kicked off in HTML with the <FORM> statement, of course, but there is a bit more to it. Here's a brief review of the form tools used in the example:

ACTION The action the form should take when the user clicks the button given an INPUT TYPE of `submit`. This is a URL to a CGI program.

INPUT TYPE Indicates that some kind of interaction with the user, or some *input*, is expected. The type can be `checkbox`, `hidden`, `image`, `password`, `radio`, `reset`, `submit`, or `text`.

METHOD Usually GET or POST, although the default is GET if no method is given. The method determines how the form data will be sent out to a CGI application (details later in the chapter).

NAME Essentially a variable name. This string is sent to the CGI application along with the information in the field it names in the form *name=value*.

Table 12.1 lists the various input types, with details of what they do.

TABLE 12.1:   HTML Input Types

Type	Description
checkbox	An on/off checked box that is used to indicate a certain choice has been selected.
hidden	A field hidden from the user. It can be used to pass information between the browser and the web server, and then to the CGI program.
image	An inline image (such as a GIF or JPEG file) with its URL indicated by SRC=. Clicking on the image will submit the form data along with the *x-y* coordinates of where it was clicked (measured from the top-left corner of the image).
password	A one-line text field in which typed text is displayed as asterisks or some other character. Used for passwords, obviously.
radio	A radio button. Similar to a check box, but radio buttons usually are set up in groups with the same name given to each button. Only one button in the group can be on; clicking one turns off any others.
reset	A special button that resets (clears) the form. Its VALUE parameter determines what is displayed on the button.
submit	Another special button, which submits the form data to the URL specified in the form's ACTION parameter. Its VALUE parameter determines what is displayed on the button.
text	A one-line field for entering text. Its width on the screen is determined by the SIZE parameter.

Submitting the Form

form1.html uses few of HTML's tricks, just a few text input types and the submit and reset buttons. Your purpose here is not to see how great-looking forms are put together, but to learn what happens when you or one of your visitors clicks that submit button.

Two methods can be used to send out the form's data—the information entered in its fields—and these are specified in the METHOD parameter to the HTML FORM command. You have used GET in this example; the other choice is POST. The difference between them is the way they send the data. As you will see, your choice in methods will be determined by the amount of data in the form; very generally, GET is used for small amounts and POST for large amounts or when you want to hide the information from the user. Also, because the parameters in a GET are in the URL, that results page can be saved as a bookmark. Pages that you POST to cannot.

You used GET in the example for two reasons. First, it's short. Second, without even loading it on a website, you can get a visual idea of how the data is sent when you submit the form.

Let's create something to fool the browser. On Windows , if Perl is in your path (and it should be), you can create a little file called `perl.bat` that has nothing in it but the word `perl`. A shell script on Unix would accomplish the same thing. Save it in the same directory in which you put `form1.html`, and then crank up your web browser and open the file.

Fill out the form with anything that fits. Figure 12.4 illustrates some suggested bogus data.

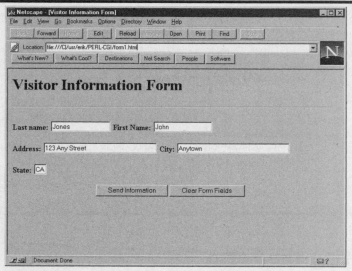

FIGURE 12.4:   The form is filled out and ready to submit.

Now, submit the form by clicking the Send Information button. Figure 12.5 illustrates what appears in Netscape Navigator's Location field when you ship this form. The "CGI" program you specified in the form's ACTION field doesn't do anything, but you can see what would be shipped to it.

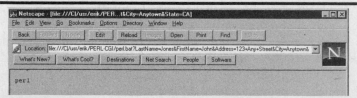

FIGURE 12.5:   The URL sent by the form in Figure 12.4

This *query string* is set up by the browser as a URL. You don't have to worry about how it's done; any browser will do it automatically. However, you *do* have to interpret it in your CGI program, so you'd better know how it's put together.

URLs and CGI

You have seen how an HTML form is built and the functions it uses to send information to the web server. The form the information takes is important, because your Perl program must be able to interpret it.

Uniform Resource Locators (URLs) were developed as a way to specify resources on the Internet with a single line of *printable* ASCII text. Notice the emphasis on *printable*—this will become important to you as you learn to decode the special characters sent in a URL. In its simplest and most familiar form, a URL gives the domain name of a website: for example, www.sybex.com.

URLs aren't limited to the Web. All the major Internet protocols, such as FTP, Gopher, WAIS, and HTTP, can read and understand a URL. They are set up in a specific way, containing:

- ▶ The protocol of the URL's server (Gopher, WAIS, HTTP, and so on)
- ▶ The server's domain name
- ▶ The server's TCP/IP port number, which, if omitted, will default to the well-known port for the service—again, Gopher, WAIS, HTTP, and so forth
- ▶ The location of the resource on the server

The URL that your browser constructed in submitting form1.html is set up in this fashion, with file:// as the protocol, and the domain name, port, and resource location all addressed in the path to perl.bat. Figure 12.6 illustrates a full URL pointing over the Internet to the same location.

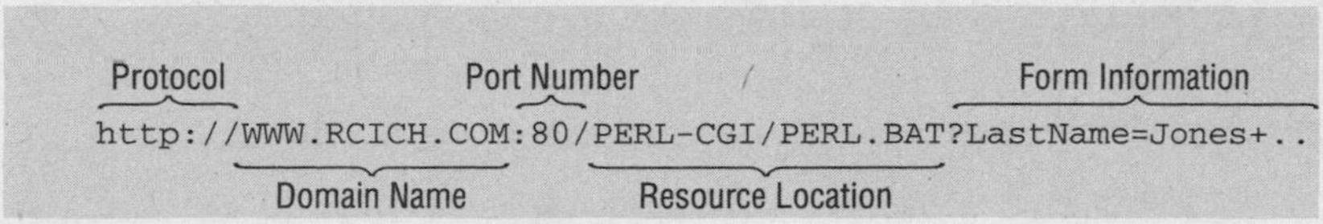

Protocol   Port Number   Form Information

http://WWW.RCICH.COM:80/PERL-CGI/PERL.BAT?LastName=Jones+..

          Domain Name   Resource Location

FIGURE 12.6:   The anatomy of a URL

Printable Characters

Like most other Internet protocols, URLs were originally designed to ensure that they could be sent via e-mail. Most older mail systems were capable of recognizing only 7-bit characters, so the characters used in a URL must conform to that limitation.

However, even some of these characters have a special meaning in a URL. For example, the ampersand (&) is used to separate the parameters in the query string. But you will encounter many occasions when you have to send ampersands and plus signs and equal signs and even 8-bit, non-ASCII characters in a URL. How can it be done?

The solution in the URL scheme of things is to *encode* these special characters in the form

    %nn

where the percent sign (%) indicates that the next two characters are the *hexadecimal value* of the actual, encoded character. A good example is the question mark (?) that begins the query string in our example:

```
perl.bat?LastName=Jones&FirstName=John&
➥Address=123+Any+Street . . .
```

Again, this character has a special meaning in the URL, because it indicates that perl.bat should be run with the arguments that follow it. If a *literal* question mark is included in any of the arguments, it is encoded as

    %26

because 26 is the hexadecimal (hex) code for a question mark in the ASCII table.

Table 12.2 shows the other printable ASCII characters that have a special meaning in a URL and, therefore, will be encoded by the browser. Any control characters that wind up in a URL will be encoded, too.

TABLE 12.2: Printable Characters Encoded in URLs

CHARACTER	HEX VALUE
Tab	09
Space	20
"	22
<	3C
>	3E

TABLE 12.2 continued: Printable Characters Encoded in URLs

CHARACTER	HEX VALUE
[	5B
\	5C
]	5D
^	5E
`	60
{	7B
|	7C
}	7D
~	7E

Because you, as the CGI programmer, are sitting at the other end of this scheme, you don't have to deal with encoding characters. The rule for you is simple: Any time you encounter a percent sign in a query string, you can assume the next two characters are the hexadecimal code of the character that is really intended to be there.

TIP

If you're worried about getting literal percent signs in a URL, don't be. They will be encoded, too.

You don't have to be too concerned with the actual ASCII values of the characters, although every programmer usually has an ASCII table handy for reference. Perl has a number of tricks for turning hexadecimal values into characters, as you'll soon see. At your end, you need to recognize an encoded character, strip off the percent sign, and send the remaining number to a Perl function that will translate it for you.

HEXADECIMAL NUMBERING: A LITTLE MATH LESSON

The *hexadecimal*, or base-16, number system is meat and potatoes to people who program for a living. This is the case primarily because it is a convenient way to represent the *binary*, or base-2, numbers that are meat and potatoes to computers.

CONTINUED ➡

Computers deal with data in *bits*, or 1s and 0s, that indicate an *on* or *off* state. The binary numbering system is especially important, because binary numbers are the only kind that computers can process at the lowest level. However, this system has only two allowable digits: 1 and 0. The *decimal* number 5 in this system is 101, because it consists of 1 of 2^0 (1), 0 of 2^1 (0), and 1 of 2^2 (4): $1 + 0 + 4 = 5$.

In the hexadecimal numbering system, there are 16 allowable digits. In decimal, 0 through 9 are the numbers you would expect. The decimal numbers 10 through 15 are represented by the characters A through F. The hex number FF is 255 in decimal, because it consists of F of 16^0 (15) and F of 16^1 (16 x 15, or 240): $15 + 240 = 255$.

Because of its binary, on-off architecture, everything on a computer at some point boils down to a power of two. When you hear technicians talking about a 32-bit microprocessor, which is what powers most PCs these days, they are referring to a processor that handles data in chunks of 32 bits. That's a maximum number of one less than 2^{32}, or a binary number consisting of 32 ones:

11111111111111111111111111111111

This number is no less intimidating in decimal: 4294967295.

The beauty of hex numbering is that each digit represents exactly four binary bits. You can't say that about decimal, where 32 bits comes out to 4-billion-something. Broken down to 4 bits per digit, the hex value of 232 − 1 is rather elegant:

```
1111 1111 1111 1111 1111 1111 1111 1111
  F    F    F    F    F    F    F    F
```

Plus, FFFFFFFF certainly is easier to keep track of than a number consisting of 32 ones.

URL Encoding with GET

The QUERY_STRING environment variable is the method of storage for the information passed from an HTML form to a CGI program through GET. When you use the GET method to pass the information, it is tacked on to the end of the URL:

```
perl.bat?LastName=Jones&FirstName=John&
  Address=123+Any+Street . . .
```

The arguments to the CGI application are separated from the application name by a question mark (?) and the URL is built in *name=value* pairs, with each pair separated from the others by an ampersand (&). Notice, too, that all the spaces in the URL have been replaced with plus signs (+). These three characters, plus the percent sign that flags any encoded characters and the equal sign that separates the *name=value* pairs, are what you'll need to deal with in your Perl-CGI script.

To get a little practice with these concepts and to learn some new concepts in Perl, you'll write a program to read the QUERY_STRING, decode it, and print all of its names and values in an HTML document. Here's the program:

```perl
#!/perl/bin/perl

# geturl.pl
#
# A little Perl script to read, decode and print the names
# and values passed to it from an HTML form through CGI.

# Get HTML header, ender, define the page title.

    require "/pub/scripts/perl-cgi/html.pl";  # Full path.
    $Title = "Get Information From A URL";

# Get the query string.

    $QueryString = $ENV{'QUERY_STRING'} ;

# Use split to make an array of name-value pairs broken at
# the ampersand character.

    @NameValuePairs = split (/&/, $QueryString);

# Put up an HTML header, page title and a rule.


    &HTML_Header ($Title);
    print "<BODY>\n";
    print "<H1>$Title</H1>\n";
    print "<HR>\n";

# Split each of the name-value pairs and print them
# on the page.

    foreach $NameValue (@NameValuePairs)
```

```
        {
        ($Name, $Value) = split (/=/, $NameValue, 2);
        print "Name = $Name, value = $Value<BR>\n";
        }

    # End the HTML document.

        &HTML_Ender;

    #   End geturl.pl
```

Store this code as `geturl.pl` in a directory from which you can run Perl scripts over the web server. Now, change the `ACTION=` string in `form1.html` to the correct path to `geturl.pl`. Also, move `form1.html` into a directory on your web server. You'll be calling it up through your website this time, rather than as a simple file in the browser.

Start your browser and connect to the website with the correct URL to `form1.html`. Fill in the form with information similar to what has been entered in Figure 12.7. This time, use some characters that will be encoded by the browser when they're shipped through CGI. When you click the Send Information button, the result should be similar to what is illustrated in Figure 12.8.

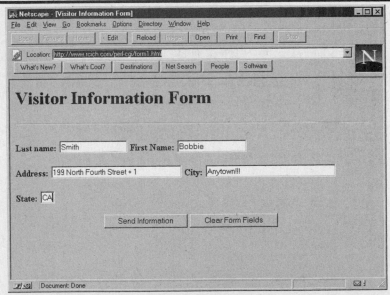

FIGURE 12.7: An information form with special characters

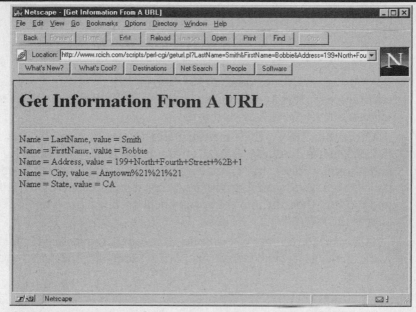

FIGURE 12.8:   What the Perl script gets from the information form

Decoding a Query String

You no doubt noticed that the information displayed by geturl.pl is full of strange encodings and separators. You'll take care of those shortly. For now, let's examine how you broke a single URL into a series of *name=value* pairs.

NOTE

The CGI module, part of Perl 5.8.0, includes a number of different functions that take care of this decoding for you.

The hero in this program is split, another workhorse Perl function that you will use again and again in your applications. split is specified this way:

```
split (/PATTERN/, STRING, LIMIT);
```

where *PATTERN* is a delimiter or point of separation, *STRING* is the string to split, and the optional *LIMIT* tells split to do no more than *LIMIT* separations.

split returns an array of strings broken at the *PATTERN*, which is eliminated in the array. *PATTERN* is always put between the forward slash (/) characters, but it can be left out. This call to split

```
@Array = split (//, $String);
```

fills @Array with the contents of $String broken out at any instance of *white space* (spaces, tabs, and line-enders). *PATTERN* also can be a regular expression, which we'll cover shortly.

Other than split, there is little in geturl.pl that you haven't seen before. You use the QUERY_STRING environment variable to obtain the URL submitted by form1.html; you break the query string into individual *name=value* pairs by using split to separate it on the ampersand character; and you split the pairs into their component parts by specifying the equal sign as the *PATTERN*.

However, the strings still contain all those URL-encoded characters, and it looks as if it will be tedious to take them out, doesn't it? Well, let's see.

THE POWER OF REGULAR EXPRESSIONS

Change the foreach loop in geturl.pl to read this way:

```
# Split, decode each of the name-value pairs and print
# them on the page.

    foreach $NameValue (@NameValuePairs)
        {
        ($Name, $Value) = split (/=/, $NameValue);
        $Value =~ tr/+/ /;
        $Value =~ s/%([\dA-Fa-f][\dA-Fa-f])/
            pack ("C", hex ($1))/eg;
        print "Name = $Name, value = $Value<BR>\n";
        }
```

If you've never worked with regular expressions, the two new lines in geturl.pl probably are among the weirdest things you've ever seen. However, install the new program, fill out form1.html in your web browser, and submit it, using all the bizarre characters you want. Your result will be what you typed in, as illustrated in Figure 12.9.

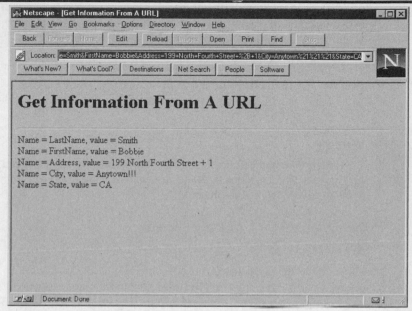

FIGURE 12.9:   All the encoded characters are translated.

Where did all the garbage go? If you had any doubts about the power of Perl, this trick should dispel them. If you have been intimidated by the perplexing and strange conventions of regular expressions, you now should feel inspired to learn them. You have accomplished *in two lines of code* what probably would have taken an entire program to do in C or C++. In Perl, you just have to learn the lingo. Let's begin by examining the two new lines in geturl.pl.

Translations, Substitutions

The first new line is fairly simple, though meaningless to the untrained eye:

```
$Value =~ tr/+/ /;
```

A couple of new Perl concepts surface in this line:

► In the expression "$String =~ /PATTERN/", the =~ operator (the match operator) is true if $String contains /PATTERN/.

► tr (the translate function) turns all characters found between the first two forward-slash characters following it into the characters between the second two slashes.

You will use the =~ operator frequently—always, in fact, when you want to change characters in a string into other characters. The specification for tr is

```
tr /SEARCH_LIST/REPLACE_LIST/
```

where *SEARCH_LIST* is the characters for which you want to search, and *REPLACE_LIST* is what their new values will be.

NOTE

There are three optional parameters to tr that go after the last slash: c, d, and s. (They stand for complement, delete, and squeeze.) You don't need them at this point, so we won't discuss them.

The line from geturl.pl that utilizes tr

```
$Value =~ tr/+/ /;
```

has the + character as its *SEARCH_LIST* and a space as its *REPLACE_LIST*. Therefore, it will go through the $Value string and replace every occurrence of the plus character (+) with a space. This approach is handy in URLs, where all spaces are designated by plus signs.

The second new line in geturl.pl is trickier:

```
$Value =~ s/%([\dA-Fa-f][\dA-Fa-f])/
➥pack ("C", hex ($1))/eg;
```

It's a little easier to understand if it is explained in the sequence of events that it kicks off.

This program line turns URL-encoded characters back into *printable* characters. Remember the *%nn* convention, in which special characters are encoded with a percent sign followed by their hexadecimal ASCII values? This is where the encoded values revert to real characters. Let's step through the program line:

► s is the Perl substitute function. Like tr, it takes everything it finds in $Value that matches the string between the first two forward slashes and replaces it with what is between the second two slashes.

► In this example, s is told to look for % followed by two characters that are either digits, designated by \d, or the characters A through F (or a through f), which are the valid hexadecimal numbers.

▶ The expression pack ("C", hex ($1)), which is specified as the *REPLACE_LIST* for s, is best understood if it is taken apart from the inside out. hex is a Perl function that expects its argument to be a hexadecimal number, and it returns a decimal number. $1 is the value found by the expression in the first set of parentheses in *SEARCH_LIST*, minus the percent sign. pack is a function that takes its second argument and "packs" it into a binary value or structure based on the template that is its first argument. In this example, the template is C, which tells pack to stuff the value in the second argument into a character.

▶ The e at the end of the line indicates to s that *REPLACE_LIST* is an expression rather than a string. Without it, every *%nn* string in $Value would be literally replaced with pack ("C", hex ($1)). The e tells s to do the replacement with the result of the expression.

▶ The g following e tells s to do a global substitution; in other words, replace every instance of *SEARCH_LIST* in $Value with what is calculated in *REPLACE_LIST*. If you left off this parameter, s would do the operation on the first occurrence and then quit.

Here's a recap of the Perl regular-expression functions we've covered so far, with their formal parameters:

▶ tr /*SEARCH_LIST*/*REPLACE_LIST*/ translates the characters specified in *SEARCH_LIST* to the corresponding characters in *REPLACE_LIST*.

▶ hex (*EXPRESSION*) interprets *EXPRESSION* as a hexadecimal number and returns the decimal value. For example, hex (10) returns 16.

▶ pack (*TEMPLATE*, *EXPRESSION*) packs *EXPRESSION* into a binary structure based on *TEMPLATE*.

YOU'RE RIGHT: REGULAR EXPRESSIONS *ARE* HARD

One of Perl's biggest strengths over bare-metal programming languages such as C and C++ comes from its ability to format text so easily. However, it uses regular expressions heavily to accomplish the formatting. Make no mistake, regular expressions are difficult.

CONTINUED ➡

But another of Perl's strengths is that you can write a workable, useful program in it without knowing every detail of the language, something you've already demonstrated in the examples you've built so far. As you gain more proficiency with Perl, your programs will utilize the knowledge you've gained, too.

You will learn about some hairy details of regular expressions in this chapter, but don't be too concerned if you don't get it right away. With practice, it'll come to you. Meanwhile, it's helpful to think of regular expressions as nothing more than a search-and-replace function on steroids.

Regular Expressions in Detail

A regular expression is used to match a pattern in a string and, possibly, replace it with another pattern. The string can match any of the alternatives of the regular expression; alternatives are separated with a vertical bar (|), are evaluated from left to right, and always stop on the first match.

The building blocks of a regular expression are the characters used to represent events or other characters:

- ▶ ^ stands for the beginning of a string.

- ▶ $ stands for the end of the string.

- ▶ \B is a non-word boundary.

- ▶ \b is a single word boundary (see \w and \W).

Regular expressions can include *quantifiers,* which tell how many times an event or string must occur:

- ▶ {*bottom, top*} (where *bottom* and *top* are numbers) means the event must occur *bottom* times and no more than *top* times.

- ▶ {*number,*} means it has to happen at least *number* times.

- ▶ {*number*} means it must occur exactly *number* times.

- ▶ * is the same as {0,}.

- ▶ + is the same as {1,}.

- ▶ ? is the same as {0,1}.

The period character, or *dot* (.), is an often-used tool because it matches *any* character except the newline. You can include specific characters in lists enclosed by square brackets; ranges are indicated with a hyphen, as in A–Z.

The backslash (\) before a character gives it a special meaning. Table 12.3 illustrates the backslashed special characters.

TABLE 12.3: Special Characters in Regular Expressions

CHARACTER	MEANING
\n	Newline
\r	Carriage return
\t	Tab
\f	Form feed
\d	A digit, or single number
\D	A non-digit
\s	White space, such as space, tab, or newline
\S	Non-white space
\w	An alphanumeric character
\W	Non-alphanumeric
\xnn	Where nn is a hex value, the character having that value
\0nn	Same as \xnn, using octal (base 8) numbers

Another convention you'll see often in regular expressions is the use of $1, $2, $3, and so on. These scalar variables correspond, left to right, to the expressions in parentheses in *SEARCH_LIST*. They're especially valuable because they maintain their value outside the regular expression. For example, the string 19 May 1997 can be split into its parts with this code snippet:

```
$string = ~ /(..) (...) (....)/;
$day = $1;
$month = $2;
$year = $3;
```

WARNING

$1, $2, and $3 are equivalent to \1, \2, and \3 in regular expressions. Keep this in mind if you mistakenly try to interpret a number literally by escaping it, and the results aren't what you expect.

EXERCISE: BUILDING YOUR WEBSITE

You've created some simple forms in this chapter. You can prepare yourself for Chapter 13, "Perl and Unicode," by expanding on them. After all, HTML forms aren't difficult to set up. It's processing the information in the forms that presents the knotty problems. Try the following:

▶ As an experiment, create some more-complex forms that use all the available HTML controls. Use radio buttons, check boxes, and the rest—it doesn't matter if you know what they'll return. Play with them and observe what comes back in the resulting URLs.

▶ Analyze the URLs created with each of the forms you create. Look at what appears on the Go To line of your web browser. Your familiarity with these conventions will be invaluable.

WHAT'S NEXT

This is enough information about regular expressions for now. You'll learn more about them as you become comfortable with what you've been exposed to so far.

In Chapter 13, you'll learn about using Perl with Unicode, which enables you to work with foreign character sets.

Chapter 13
PERL AND UNICODE

Perl is one of the few "old" languages into which support for the Unicode system has been successfully and largely transparently integrated. If you wanted to, you could write your entire Perl script using ideographs and other Unicode characters for your function and variable names—the integration is that transparent.

In this chapter, we'll look at the most important parts of the Perl language when working with Unicode data, including how to introduce Unicode characters into your strings and how to work with and manipulate Unicode characters once you have them in a Perl variable.

Adapted from *XML Processing with Perl, Python, and PHP*, by Martin C. Brown
ISBN 0-7821-4021-1

NOTE

The entire Unicode implementation within Perl is a work in progress. Perl 5.8 has greatly improved Unicode support over its introduction in version 5.6, and all the details of how Unicode support will work in Perl 6 are still under discussion. The best way to keep up to date is to read the Unicode documentation that comes with the latest Perl distribution, available in the perlunicode man page.

CORE SUPPORT

Since Perl 5.6, it's been possible to write Perl scripts entirely in Unicode. Operators, functions, and standard variables obviously retain their U.S. English heritage, but user variables and functions can use Unicode characters in their names, and you can introduce Unicode literal strings without resorting to special techniques.

To enable full Unicode support in this fashion, you must use the utf8 pragma. Doing so forces Perl to accept both string literals and symbolic names that use Unicode characters. Without the utf8 pragma in force, you can still introduce Unicode literals into your code, but you cannot use them within variable, function, and other user-definable names.

Internally, all strings are now stored in Unicode format. As a result, in addition to enabling all Perl operator functions to work with Unicode data, you can also manipulate the information character-by-character. There are no limitations in converting or combining Unicode strings into ASCII strings, because Perl makes no such distinction.

Specifying Unicode Characters and Sequences

Perl stores all strings internally in Unicode format. That means there is no special Unicode string datatype, and there are no complexities in mixing and matching ASCII and Unicode (which includes ASCII) characters into the same scalar value. For example, the assignment

```
$msg = "Hello World\n";
```

is, as far as Perl is concerned, in Unicode format.

To include a Unicode character beyond the standard ASCII into your string literals, you can do so either directly, if your editor/platform supports Unicode, or through the \x{} and \N{} escape sequences in a string. The first method, \x{}, allows you to specify the Unicode character number in hexadecimal within the braces. For example, here's how to include the Greek lowercase pi symbol into a string:

```
$note = "The value of \x{3c0} is 3.141592654";
```

The second format enables you to include the character by its Unicode name. This is a long name, usually specified in capitals, that describes the character according to its main character set and description. For example, the name for the letter A is LATIN CAPITAL LETTER A. To use this format, you must use the charnames pragma, which imports the necessary name/character tables. For example, you could change the previous example to this:

```
use charnames ':full';
$note = "The value of \N{GREEK SMALL LETTER  PI}
➡is 3.141592654";
```

Using Unicode names in this fashion is probably not the easiest way to introduce Unicode characters into your text, but it can be useful if you can remember (or work out) the description and not the corresponding number. See the charnames man page for more information about the different character classes you can import this way.

Note that as with all other escape sequences, you lose these definitions. The resulting string literal is a Unicode string, which in this case is assigned to a variable.

You can see a complete list of the Unicode character numbers and names in the file Unicode.xxx in the unicode directory within your Perl library directory. The xxx refers to the version number of the Unicode standard being used; with Perl 5.6.1, this was 3.01 (Unicode.301). Perl 5.8.0 has dropped this convention and calls the file UnicodeData.txt; you can find it in the unicore directory.

Character Numbers

The chr() and ord() functions work with Unicode values as standard. If you supply chr() with a value beyond 255, it assumes you are introducing a Unicode character and returns the value accordingly. Conversely, the ord() function translates a Unicode character back to its numerical number.

For example, this fragment introduces the ø (o with a cross) into a string:

```
$name = "Rikke J" . chr(248) . "rgensen";
```

The ord() function can be used to convert this back into a number:

```
$number = ord(substr($name, 7, 1));
```

WORKING WITH UNICODE DATA

The general rule to follow with Unicode in Perl is that a typical operator will now operate on characters (including multibyte Unicode ones) unless you've explicitly told it otherwise through use of the bytes pragma. You must take care, therefore, when you're working with characters that are potentially non-ASCII in scripts that accept data from outside sources. Most of these problems can be resolved fairly easily. For example, when looking for a specific character sequence, you must ensure that you are matching against the Unicode equivalent. Because Perl's support for Unicode character and mixed ASCII/Unicode strings is so transparent, doing so is incredibly easy.

In this section, we'll look at three areas that often catch people out: case translations, regular expressions, and character- and byte-based comparisons and calculations.

Case Translations

Unless you've used the bytes pragma (detailed in the section "Data Size Traps," later in this chapter), Perl will automatically assume you are working with Unicode data. It will change the case of a string through the \U or \L character escape or the uc(), ucfirst(), and corresponding functions, according to the Unicode lookup tables.

For ASCII data, this behavior has the expected effect. For Unicode data outside the ASCII range, it converts a character or characters to their corresponding uppercase or lowercase value as defined within the language and character set in use. For example, the following fragment creates a variable with the lowercase pi letter (π) in it and then uses uc() to obtain the uppercase letter pi (Π):

```
$lcpi = "\x{3c0}";
$ucpi = uc("\x{3c0}");
printf("%x\n",ord($lcpi));
printf("%x\n",ord($ucpi));
```

The result should be the hexadecimal values of the characters in the Unicode table, 3C0 for lowercase pi and 3A0 for uppercase:

```
$ perl piunicode.pl
3c0
3a0
```

Regular Expressions

By default, regular expressions work identically to regular expressions using ASCII characters. The regular expression system is completely Unicode character aware and will therefore match or substitute characters (not bytes) within source strings. Only two areas need special attention: the matching of non-specific Unicode characters and the use of Unicode character classes for matching.

Matching Unicode Characters

The regular expression semantics of Perl have been modified to accommodate the Unicode system so that most existing constructs will work with Unicode characters. For example, the period character (.) matches any Unicode (and therefore ASCII) character except newline (\n), as you would expect.

In addition, some new escape sequences have been introduced and existing sequences modified to handle specific Unicode and traditional instances:

- ▶ The \c sequence matches any one-byte character, including Unicode characters that can be defined within a single byte (that is, 8-bit or ASCII only).

- ▶ The \N{*NAME*} sequence explicitly matches the Unicode character defined by *NAME*.

- ▶ The \X sequence matches any Unicode sequence that would normally make up a single character, including multibyte sequences.

Thus you can match against a Unicode character sequence using \X and a non-Unicode character sequence using \c.

Unicode/Posix Classes

In addition to matching against specific characters, Perl also provides methods for matching against specific character classes. Perl supports the traditional character classes, such as \d for matching any digit and \s for matching against white space, and new sequences for matching against specific properties throughout the Unicode tables.

These sequences are defined through a series of property definitions that you can match using \p{*PROP*} and its negation, \P{*PROP*}, to select characters according to their Unicode properties. For example, the equivalent of \d across all Unicode characters (including foreign representations of numbers outside the Latin format) is \p{IsN}. The full list of these properties is too large to include here, but the basic properties (case, character, digit, and non-character) are listed in Table 13.1.

TABLE 13.1:   Standard Unicode Character-Class Properties

PROPERTY	MEANING
IsC	Other
IsCc	Other, control
IsCf	Other, format
IsCn	Other, not assigned
IsCo	Other, private use
IsCs	Other, surrogate
IsL	Letters (Perl defined)
IsLl	Letter, lowercase
IsLm	Letter, modifier
IsLo	Letter, other
IsLt	Letter, title case
IsLu	Letter, uppercase
IsM	Marks (Perl defined)
IsMc	Mark, combining
IsMe	Mark, enclosing
IsMn	Mark, non-spacing
IsN	Numbers (Perl defined)
IsNd	Number, decimal digit
IsNl	Number, letter
IsNo	Number, other
IsP	Punctuation (Perl defined)
IsPc	Punctuation, connector
IsPd	Punctuation, dash
IsPe	Punctuation, close
IsPf	Punctuation, final quote

TABLE 13.1 continued: Standard Unicode Character-Class Properties

PROPERTY	MEANING
IsPi	Punctuation, initial quote
IsPo	Punctuation, other
IsPs	Punctuation, open
IsS	Symbols (Perl defined)
IsSc	Symbol, currency
IsSk	Symbol, modifier
IsSm	Symbol, math
IsSo	Symbol, other
IsZ	Separators (Perl defined)
IsZl	Separator, line
IsZp	Separator, paragraph
IsZs	Separator, space

In addition to these broad classes, Perl also supports more familiar composite classes through both a series of Posix classes and Unicode properties. You can use the Posix classes in Perl using [:*class*:]. For example, to match digits, you use [:digit:]. To match against the Unicode equivalent, you use \p{isDigit}.

The full list of Posix character classes is given in Table 13.2. The corresponding composite Unicode properties and their Posix equivalents are listed in Table 13.3.

TABLE 13.2: Posix Character Classes

CLASS	MEANING
alnum	Any alphanumeric (equivalent to [[:alpha:][:digit:]])
alpha	Any letter (uppercase or lowercase)
ascii	Any 7-bit ASCII character (that is, those with a value between 0 and 127)
cntrl	Any control character—basically, those ASCII characters with a decimal value of less than 32, including newlines, carriage returns, and tabs
digit	Any character representing a digit (0–9)

TABLE 13.2 continued: Posix Character Classes

Class	Meaning
graph	Any alphanumeric or punctuation character
lower	Any lowercase letter
print	Any printable character (equivalent to [[:alnum:][:punct:][:space:]])
punct	Any punctuation character
space	Any white-space character (space, tab, newline, carriage return, or form feed)
upper	Any uppercase letter
word	Any identifier character—basically, alnum and the underscore
xdigit	Any hexadecimal digit (upper- or lowercase, 0–9 plus a–f)

TABLE 13.3:   Perl's Composite Unicode Properties

Property	Consists of	Posix Equivalent
IsASCII	[\x00-\x7f]	ascii
IsAlnum	[\p{IsLl}\p{IsLu}\p{IsLt}\p{IsLo}\p{IsNd}]	alnum
IsAlpha	[\p{IsLl}\p{IsLu}\p{IsLt}\p{IsLo}]	alpha
IsCntrl	\p{IsC}	cntrl
IsDigit	\p{Nd}	digit
IsGraph	[^\pC\p{IsSpace}]	graph
IsLower	\p{IsLl}	lower
IsPrint	\P{IsC}	print
IsPunct	\p{IsP}	punct
IsSpace	[\t\n\f\r\p{IsZ}]	space
IsUpper	[\p{IsLu}\p{IsLt}]	upper
IsWord	[_\p{IsLl}\p{IsLu}\p{IsLt}\p{IsLo}\p{IsNd}]	word
IsXDigit	[0-9a-fA-F]	xdigit

For more information about the other properties supported by Perl (which are subject to constant change as new languages, character sets, and

Perl composites are produced), check the Unicode documentation that comes with Perl.

Data Size Traps

One of the problems with the Unicode system is that it is possible to encode single characters into multiple bytes. Doing so can make certain operations break if you are relying on storing information within fixed-size blocks that rely on a byte, rather than a character figure.

By default, Perl now reports sizes in terms of characters where appropriate. That means strings and other textual scalars (hash keys, for example), which are internally stored in Unicode anyway, report their length in characters when tested through the length() function.

To get the byte length of a string, as opposed to the character length, you need to use the bytes pragma. The following example uses the bytes pragma without changing the behavior of the length() function; instead, to get the length in bytes, you use the version in the bytes pragma:

```
use bytes (); # Loads without enforcing byte interpretation

$charlen = length($string);
$bytelen = bytes::length($string);
```

As a general rule, outside a bytes pragma declaration, Perl assumes you are working with characters. A more explicit list of the treatment of bytes/characters outside a bytes pragma declaration is as follows:

▶ Strings and regular expression patterns may contain characters with values larger than 8 bits.

▶ Identifiers may contain alphanumeric characters, including ideographs (utf8 pragma required).

▶ Regular expressions match characters, not bytes.

▶ Character classes in regular expressions match characters, not bytes.

▶ Named Unicode properties and block ranges can be used as character classes.

▶ The regular expression metasymbol \X matches any Unicode sequence.

▶ The tr/// operator transliterates characters, not bytes.

- ▶ Case translation operators (\U, \L and uc(), ucfirst(), and so on) use the Unicode translation tables.

- ▶ Functions and operators that deal with position and length within a string use character, rather than byte positions. Exclusions are pack(), unpack(), and vec(), which traditionally work on byte- or bit-based data anyway.

- ▶ The c and C formats for pack()/unpack() do not change—they still extract byte-based information. If you want to use characters, use the U format.

- ▶ The chr() and ord() functions work on multibyte characters.

- ▶ The reverse() function in a scalar context reverses by character, rather than by byte.

UNICODE CHARACTER CONVERSIONS

There is no convenient built-in mechanism for converting a Unicode character string into a format suitable for printing on any device. The easiest way to translate something for display on a simple (non-Unicode-capable) device is probably to use tr/// to convert anything beyond the ASCII range to a question mark:

```
tr/\0-\x{10ffff}/\0-\xff?/;
```

This is not a tidy solution, and it won't help if you want to convert Unicode to Mac-Roman, for example. For those situations where you have a specific destination (or source) character set in mind, the solution is to use the Unicode::Map8 module from Gisle Aas.

In addition to supporting most of the base tables supported internally by the Unicode standard, the module also provides access to a number of other standard character tables, including Macintosh, PC code pages (starting CP, as used in DOS/Windows 3.11). It even includes some tables specific to certain fonts, including the Adobe Zapf Dingbat font that covers most of the ideographs available on Mac and Windows machines.

SUMMARY

Perl supports Unicode natively, allowing you to create Unicode-compatible strings using the same methods and techniques you would use with a normal Perl string. In addition to supporting Unicode in strings, you can also create variables, functions, and other token names using Unicode characters.

When you're working with Unicode strings, there is syntactically no difference from using ASCII strings, and methods and escape sequences let you include specific Unicode characters in a given string. Other elements of Perl also support Unicode characters, and the regular expression engine includes the capability to search and match Unicode strings for different character types, regardless of their originating language.

The only area that requires care is working with Unicode information. Standard Perl automatically returns all counts and other calculations in a Perl string using characters, rather than bytes. In most situations this behavior shouldn't cause a problem, but you should be aware of the effects and how to use the `bytes` pragma to obtain size information in strict 8-bit quantities.

WHAT'S NEXT

In the next chapter, we'll return to the web and create a guest book application, and learn about Perl's handling of different external data formats along the way.

Chapter 14
CREATING A GUEST BOOK FOR YOUR WEBSITE

O ne of the wonderful capabilities of the World Wide Web is that it can be used as a repository. Information stored anywhere can be retrieved—from anywhere—as long as it's accessible to and from the Web. Research avenues have been blown wide open by the Web.

So far, the Perl-CGI programs you've written have provided instant feedback for your visitors. But once the information has been entered and displayed, it's gone; it can't be retrieved, because it was never stored anywhere.

In this chapter you'll design a guest book web page that will allow visitors to enter pertinent details about themselves. You'll write CGI programs in Perl to get a guest book entry for a single visitor, store the entry in a disk file, and display the entire roster of visitors. You'll also learn the basics of website security and what you can do in your CGI programs to prevent visitors from inadvertently or maliciously entering data that could damage your site or your system.

Updated from *Perl CGI Programming: No Experience Required*, by Erik Strom

ISBN 0-7821-2157-8

DESIGNING THE GUEST BOOK

A good guest book design is simple, but not too simple. You want a visitor to provide enough information to benefit you and anyone who calls up the list. Conversely, most visitors won't take the time to write their autobiographies, so don't expect them to. You'll take several steps to ensure that they don't, in fact, because you don't want visitors unnecessarily eating up disk space on your website. Figure 14.1 illustrates a website with a guest book. It may look familiar, because we used it as an example in Chapter 12.

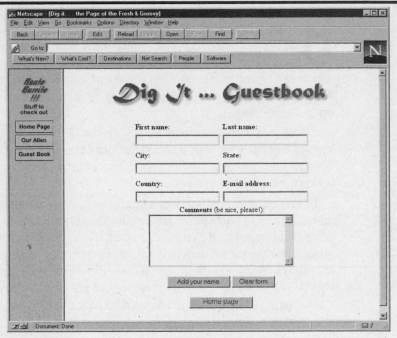

FIGURE 14.1:   An example of a guest book web page

Listing 14.1 shows the HTML source for a page similar to the one illustrated in Figure 14.1. You can call it guestbook.html. Called up in your web browser, the guest book form should look similar to that shown in Figure 14.2.

Listing 14.1: Guest Book Entry Form

```
<HTML>
<HEAD>
<TITLE>Perl-CGI Guest Book</TITLE>
</HEAD>
```

```
<BODY>
<CENTER>
<H1 ALIGN="CENTER">Perl-CGI Guest Book</H1>
<HR>

<FORM ACTION="/scripts/perl-cgi/addguest.pl" METHOD="POST">

<TABLE WIDTH="50%">

<TR>
<TD><STRONG>First name: </STRONG></TD> <TD><STRONG>
Last name: </STRONG></TD>
</TR>
<TR>
<TD> <INPUT TYPE="text" NAME="first_name" SIZE="24"
 MAXLENGTH="30"> </TD>
<TD> <INPUT TYPE="text" NAME="last_name" SIZE="24"
 MAXLENGTH="30"> </TD>
</TR>
<TR>
<TD><STRONG>City: </STRONG></TD> <TD><STRONG>
 State: </STRONG></TD>
</TR>
<TR>
<TD> <INPUT TYPE="text" NAME="city" SIZE="24"
 MAXLENGTH="30"> </TD>
<TD> <INPUT TYPE="text" NAME="state" SIZE="24"
 MAXLENGTH="30"> </TD>
</TR>
<TR>
<TD><STRONG>Country: </STRONG></TD> <TD><STRONG>
 E-mail address: </STRONG></TD>
</TR>
<TR>
<TD> <INPUT TYPE="text" NAME="country" SIZE="24"
 MAXLENGTH="30"> </TD>
<TD> <INPUT TYPE="text" NAME="email" SIZE="24"
 MAXLENGTH="72"> </TD>
</TR>
</TABLE>

<STRONG>Comments</STRONG><BR>
<TEXTAREA NAME="comments" COLS="36" ROWS="6"
></TEXTAREA>
```

```
<BR>
<P>
<INPUT TYPE="submit" VALUE="Add your name">
<INPUT TYPE="reset" VALUE="Clear form">
</P>
</FORM>
</CENTER>

</BODY>
</HTML>
```

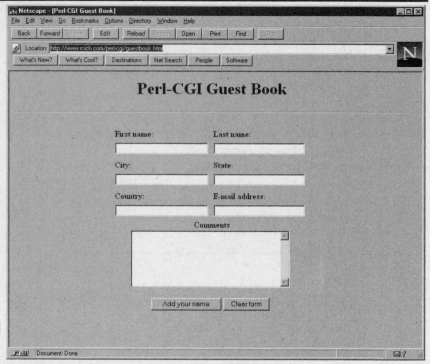

FIGURE 14.2: The entry page for your guest book

This page is a pretty good example of how tables are constructed in HTML. Notice the table declaration at the top:

```
<TABLE WIDTH="50%">

<TR>
<TD><STRONG>First name: </STRONG></TD> <TD><STRONG>
```

```
    Last name: </STRONG></TD>
  </TR>
  <TR>
  <TD> <INPUT TYPE="text" NAME="first_name" SIZE="24"
    MAXLENGTH="30"> </TD>
  <TD> <INPUT TYPE="text" NAME="last_name" SIZE="24"
    MAXLENGTH="30"> </TD>
  </TR>
  </TABLE>
```

This code sets the width of the table to 50 percent of the screen width and then formats the rows and columns for the first block of text fields, in this case for the visitor's first and last names.

TIP

It's a good idea to use percentages rather than fixed values for setting the width of a table. Your visitors will have a variety of screens, running at different resolutions. An HTML table that has its width set to a certain number of pixels will be larger or smaller, depending on the display resolution—in extreme cases, it might not even fit on the screen. Using the percentage width ensures that your tables will be sized to fit the screen proportionately, regardless of the visitor's equipment.

The text fields have been given MAXLENGTH values; these values prevent a user from entering too much data in a field. Note that the script still has to watch for too much data coming in, because a malicious user could remove the MAXLENGTH value from a private copy of the page. Still, MAXLENGTH helps most users do the right thing.

ADDING GUEST BOOK ENTRIES

Gathering and filing an entry from the guest book form is a straightforward job in Perl. Let's create a program called addguest.pl, shown in Listing 14.2.

Listing 14.2: *addguest.pl*

```
#!/usr/bin/perl

use GuestBook;

# Get the POSTed information from STDIN and put it in
# $post_info.
```

```
    read (STDIN, $post_info, $ENV { 'CONTENT_LENGTH'} );

# Split off the fields, which are delimited with '&',
# and put them in @InfoArray.

    @InfoArray = split (/&/, $post_info);

# Go through each element in @InfoArray, split off the
# "variable=" part, then translate pluses into spaces and
# any escaped hex chars back to their real character values

    for ($n = 0; $n < scalar @InfoArray; $n++)
        {
        ($dummy, $temp) = split (/=/, $InfoArray[$n], 2);
        $temp =~ tr/+/ /;
        $temp =~ s/%([\dA-Fa-f]{2})/
        ➥pack ("C", hex ($1))/eg;
        $InfoArray [$n] = $temp;
        }

# Now we'll check to see if we have anything to write
# to the guest book. We need a first or last name, at
# least; otherwise, we'll jump around the routines that
# write this stuff to the guest book file.

    if ((length ($InfoArray[$FirstNameIndex]) != 0)
            || (length ($InfoArray [$LastNameIndex]) != 0))
        {

# Tack the current time to the end of the array.


        # Put the current time in the array.
        $InfoArray[$NumEntryTime] = time();

# Pack the data into a binary structure, open the guest
# book file for appending, and write it all out to disk.

        $GuestEntry = pack ($GuestEntryStruct, @InfoArray);
        open (GUEST_LOG, ">>$GuestBookPath")
            || die "Can't open guest book: $!";
        print GUEST_LOG $GuestEntry;
```

```
        close (GUEST_LOG);
        }                        # End if ((length...)

# Finally, we put up a cute little HTML document announcing
# that everything's done, with a link to the guest book
# viewer.

    &HTML_Header ("All done!");
    print <<END_OF_BLOCK;
<BODY>
<CENTER>
<H1>Thanks for taking the time to sign
our guest book...</H1>
<HR>
Click
<A HREF="/scripts/perl-cgi/guestbook.pl">here</A>
to view the guest book.
<BR>
END_OF_BLOCK

&HTML_Ender ();

#                    End addguest.pl
```

Note the last section of code, which includes `print <<END_OF_BLOCK`. This is called a *here document;* it lets Perl print large chunks of text at once, without requiring multiple `print` statements.

You probably noticed the `use GuestBook` statement at the top of the program. This is a safer way of doing the `require` you used in previous chapters. Put this code in `GuestBook.pm` (note the pm) in the same directory as `addguest.pl`:

```
# GuestBook.pm
#
# Header file for the routines to add data to and read it
# back from the Guest Book.
#

use html;

# Some useful constants.

    # Format for pack ()
    $GuestEntryStruct        = "a30 a30 a30 a30 a30 a30 a256 l";
```

```
                    # Path to guest book file
                    $GuestBookPath          = "/pub/http/perl-cgi/ngbook.dat";

            # Indexes of elements in the packed structure.

                    $FirstName              = 0;
                    $LastName               = 1;
                    $City                   = 2;
                    $State                  = 3;
                    $Country                = 4;
                    $EMail                  = 5;
                    $Comments               = 6;
                    $NumEntryTime           = 7;
                    $NumElements            = 8;    # Number of elements
                    $GuestEntrySize         = 440;  # All the sizes added up.


            #                       End GuestBook.pm
```

Rename html.pl from Chapter 11 to give it a .pm extension. Now connect with your web server and guestbook.html. Fill out the form, as shown in Figure 14.3.

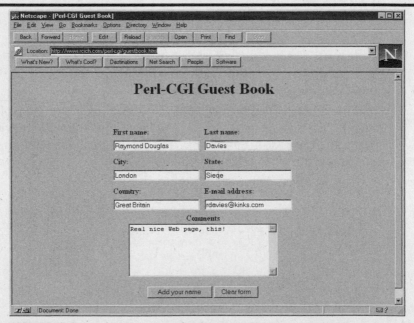

FIGURE 14.3:   A filled-out guest book entry in Netscape Navigator

Now submit the form. You'll see a page similar to the one shown in Figure 14.4.

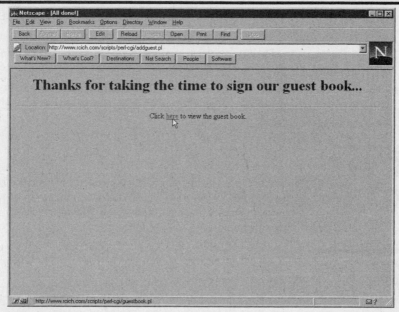

FIGURE 14.4:   The guest book entry has been filed.

Dissecting the Code

You've encountered so many new concepts in the last two files that your head may be swimming. You have a working guest book entry form and CGI back-end, so let's slow down a little and take the program apart.

The used file at the top (GuestBook.pm) contains the use that brings in the familiar subroutines of html.pl, which is now html.pm. The .pm extension for the file is a convention you'll begin following now for Perl header files that can be used over and over by many programs. This extension is used for Perl packages.

The scalar variables defined in GuestBook.pm are used not only in addguest.pl; you'll also need these variables to list the guest book entries. Rather than duplicate them in two programs, it's easier to include all of them in one file.

Note the open line:

```
open (GUEST_LOG, ">>$GuestBookPath")
            || die "Can't open guest book: $!";
```

What's this die function, and why does it follow a logical OR symbol?

This is another of Perl's many handy shortcuts. die amounts to a "bail out now!" instruction, allowing you to print an explanatory message along with it. It is used when errors are encountered—errors so bad that the program cannot continue.

You can tie many Perl functions to die with the logical OR (||) symbol. Used in this fashion, it means "do this; if it doesn't work, call die and terminate the program." In other words, if open can't create or append to the file that is its argument, control goes to die, the message is printed, and the program exits.

TIP

The Perl global variable $! always contains the value of the last system error. die understands this. If you put $! in the die function's message string, die will print a semi-explanatory message all by itself. (Sometimes you may not find the message too helpful!)

NOTE

die is probably used most often with open; if a file can't be opened, die prints a message explaining why, and exits. die's less-fanatical little brother is warn, which operates the same way with the same argument but doesn't terminate the program. Usually, if a file won't open, you want die rather than warn, because your program won't be useful if it can't use the file.

There is one unfamiliar exception: The $GuestEntryStruct appears to be a string of nonsense, but its comment line says it is a format for pack (). What could that be?

Reading and Writing Structured Data

pack and unpack are ubiquitous in programs that read and write binary data to and from disk files. They are necessary because Perl would like to believe that everything it deals with is in the form of a string. It can convert pretty easily between numbers and strings on an individual basis, but it falls apart when things get too complicated.

In the real world, programmers run into situations all the time in which they have to manipulate pieces of information that are structured in records, each of which has a fixed length and each member of which has its own fixed length. For example, if you were putting an employee-information database together, you would fashion each employee entry with a certain size for each bit of information: The name could be 32 characters; the address might be 64; the employee's age and salary could be two numeric fields, each taking 4-byte integers; and so on. The entire entry would be a record with a length equal to the combined maximum sizes of each field. Each record would fit into the same amount of space in a disk file; each record could be called into another program and manipulated, and then written back to the disk.

The file into which all these records go is called a *database*. You have created a small one: addguest.pl. Here's how pack works to make it possible.

pack and Its Many Formats

The specification for pack couldn't be simpler:

```
pack (TEMPLATE, LIST);
```

It turns *LIST* into a scalar value based on what is contained in *TEMPLATE*. However, the template is where things get hairy.

The template tells pack the type of the data in the list and its length. Table 14.1 shows a list of the pack template formats. (These formats may look strange and intimidating, but you'll generally use only a few of them—until you reach the point where they don't look so strange and intimidating anymore.)

TABLE 14.1: The pack Formats

CHARACTER	DESCRIPTION
A	ASCII string that will be padded with spaces
a	ASCII string, no space padding
B	Bit string, high- to low-order
b	Bit string, low- to high-order
C	Unsigned character
c	Signed character
d	Double-precision floating-point number
f	Single-precision floating-point number
H	Hexadecimal string, high nybble (4 bits) first
h	Hex string, low nybble first
I	Unsigned integer
i	Signed integer
L	Unsigned long integer

TABLE 14.1 continued: The pack Formats

CHARACTER	DESCRIPTION
l	Signed long integer
N	Long integer in "network" order
n	Short integer in "network" order
p	Pointer to string
X	Back up a byte
x	NULL byte
u	Uuencoded string
@	Fill with NULLs to absolute position

It would be useful for you to review the use of pack in Chapter 12, where you learned how to decode URL-encoded characters. The same translation code is in addguest.pl, so you don't have to go very far to refresh your memory:

```
$temp =~ s/%([\dA-F]{2})/pack ("C", hex ($1))/ieg;
```

Recall that the pack function in this line of code takes the number calculated by hex and turns it into a character. The "C" template tells pack to do it; the "C" isn't followed by a number, so pack does just one character. The line

```
$string = pack ("C4", 48, 49, 50, 51);
```

yields 0123 because "C4" says to act on four characters, and 48 through 51 are the decimal ASCII values of the characters (*not* numbers!) "0" through "3".

addguest.pl deals mainly with strings, so it uses the "a" template format heavily. "a*n*", where *n* is some number, sets aside the space required by the number, runs in its corresponding string from the list, and fills whatever is left with NULL characters. The line

```
$string = pack ("a8", "Now is");
```

yields "Now is\0\0" (remember, "\0" is a NULL byte) because "Now is" contains only six characters; the remainder is padded.

TIP

The "A" template format, as shown in Table 14.1, uses space characters to do the padding. This is not usually what you want to do with strings stored in a binary structure, because the spaces count as part of the string and its length. A NULL ends the string where it stands.

Inversely, a format that is too short will truncate the string passed to it. The line

```
$string = pack ("a2", "Now is");
```

will result in `"No"`.

Now, let's look at the format string in `addguest.pl` (actually, the string passed in from `GuestBook.pm`):

```
$GuestEntryStruct = "a30 a30 a30 a30 a30 a30 a256 l";
```

You should be able to decode it yourself; it sets up six 30-byte strings, followed by one of 256 bytes, and ends with a signed long integer. These correspond with the following from the guest book form:

First name

Last name

City

State

Country

E-mail address

Comments

The last field is reserved for the time of the visit, which is calculated in `addguest.pl`.

White space between format elements is ignored, so you could write

```
$GuestEntryStruct = "a30a30a30a30a30a30a256l";
```

but that's not as easy to read. The more readable your strings are, the easier it is to keep track of what they should be doing, and the less likely you are to make mistakes.

We mentioned `pack`'s companion, `unpack`, at the beginning of this section. It takes the same arguments as `pack` but works in reverse. In other words,

```
$string = pack ("a30 a30 a30 a30 a30 a30 a256 l",
                $first, $last, $city, $state, $country,
                $email, $comments, $time);
```

stuffs all those variables into `$string` in a form that is suitable for writing into a 440-byte record in a disk file (long integers are 4 bytes long). When you read it back into a program with

```
read (FILEHANDLE, $string, 440);
```

you can then invoke unpack to bring back all the data:

```
($first, $last, $city, $state,
  $country, $email, $comments, $time) =
    unpack ("a30 a30 a30 a30 a30 a30 a256 l", $string);
```

The only other unfamiliar part of addguest.pl is the function that fills the last element of the record with the time of the visit. The Perl function time returns the current time as a 4-byte-long integer measured in seconds from midnight, January 1, 1970, according to the Unix convention. This makes time—and the values it calculates—completely portable between Unix and Microsoft-powered systems.

TIP

Microsoft operating systems keep track of time based on other starting dates, which can get weird. Some Windows time functions, for example, measure time in 8-byte integers consisting of seconds dating back to the 1600s! But, again, Perl works the same no matter what system it's running on.

Before you move on to writing a Perl program to display the entries in your new guest book, take note of one feature in addguest.pl. The conditional expression

```
if ((length ($InfoArray[$FirstNameIndex]) != 0)
        || (length ($InfoArray [$LastNameIndex]) != 0))
```

tests the first- and last-name fields to ensure they contain something. If they don't, the form information is *not* written into the guest book file, and the program proceeds directly to the last display page, from which you can get the entire list of entries. That's how to get the list without adding to it: Just submit a form with nothing in the name fields.

Displaying the Guest Book

Listing the entries in your guest book file is less challenging than getting them into the file to begin with. You just do everything in reverse.

Still, you'll need to deal with some perplexing details. The steps are straightforward:

1. Set up variables to hold the information you'll read from the file. Obviously, you need to know how the variables are structured, but you took care of that in addguest.pl.

2. Open the guest book file for reading.

3. Read one record. You need to know its length, but you've taken care of that, too.

4. Format the data to your liking in HTML.

5. print it out to the web server.

6. If there are any more records in the file, go back to step 3.

7. If not, close the file.

You're finished.

Displaying the Guest Book with Perl

Save the Perl code in Listing 14.3 as guestbook.pl in a directory accessible to your CGI pipeline.

Listing 14.3: *guestbook.pl*

```perl
#!usr/bin/perl

# guestbook.pl
#
# Reads records from the guest book file specified in
# guestbook.pm, formats them in HTML and sends them
# to a web page.


use GuestBook;

    $Title = "Perl-CGI Guest Book Entries";

# Attempt to open the guest book file.  Again, this is
# a fatal error if it doesn't succeed.

    open (GUEST_LOG, $GuestBookPath) ||
        die "Can't open guest book: $!";

# Set up the HTML document.

    &HTML_Header ($Title);
    print "<BODY>\n";
```

```perl
        print "<H1 ALIGN=\"CENTER\">$Title</H1>\n";
        print "<HR>\n";

# Read records and display them in a while loop. The test
# at the top of the while block fails when all the records
# have been read.


        while (read (GUEST_LOG, $buffer, $GuestEntrySize))
            {

        # Use unpack to load the record into an array of fields
        # based on the same template we used with pack to format
        # them for the file.

            @InfoArray = unpack ($GuestEntryStruct, $buffer);

        # Loop through the elements of the array and remove any
        # NULL padding from the strings, in case this is being
        # run on a browser that prints spaces for NULLs.

            for ($n = 0; $n < ($NumElements - 1); $n++)
                {
                $InfoArray[$n] =~ s/\0//g;
                }

        # Load separate variables with the elements in
        # @InfoArray.

            ($FirstName, $LastName, $City, $State, $Country,
                $Email, $Comments, $NumAccessTime) = @InfoArray;

            print "<STRONG>Name:</STRONG><BR>\n";

            print "$FirstName $LastName<BR>\n";
            print "<STRONG>E-mail address:</STRONG><BR>\n";
            print $Email, "<BR>\n";
            print "<STRONG>From:</STRONG><BR>\n";
            print $City, " ", $State, " ", $Country, "<BR>\n";
            print "<STRONG>On:</STRONG><BR>\n";
```

```
# Set up a string time description after running the
# 4-byte time value through localtime ().

    ($sec, $min, $hour, $mday, $mon,
        $year, $wday, $yday, $isdst)
        = localtime ($NumAccessTime);

    $year += 1900;
    print "$WeekDay[$wday], $Month[$mon] $mday, ",
    print " at $hour:";
    print "0" if $min < 10;
    print "$min:";
    print "0" if $sec < 10;
    print "$sec<BR>\n";

    print "<STRONG>Comments:</STRONG><BR>\n";
    print $Comments, "<BR>\n";
    print "<HR>\n";
    }

close (GUEST_LOG);
&HTML_Footer ();

#                   End GuestBook.pl
```

Now add the following two arrays to the bottom of GuestBook.pm:

```
# Days of the week.

    @WeekDay = qw( Sunday Monday Tuesday Wednesday
                   Thursday Friday Saturday );

# Months of the year.

    @Month = qw( January February March April May
                 June July August September October
                 November December );

# End GuestBook.pm
```

Note the new qw() construct, which stands for *quote words*. It creates a list of the words extracted out of the string, using white space as the word delimiters. The following are equivalent:

```
@stooges = ( "Larry", "Moe", "Curly" );
@stooges = qw( Larry Moe Curly );
```

but the qw() version is easier to read and maintain, because you don't have to mess with the quotes and commas.

Start your web browser and connect with guestbook.html. Fill in the form a few times with bogus or real entries. You should see something similar to what is illustrated in Figure 14.5.

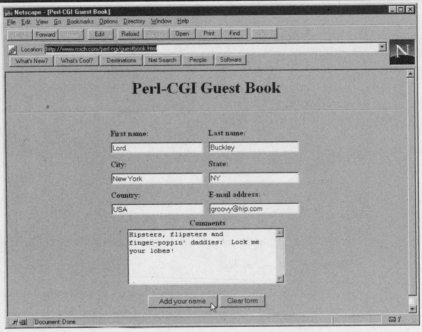

FIGURE 14.5:   Fill out the form again.

TIP

If you click your browser's Back button after submitting the form, you will go back to the form page. Click Clear Form to get a blank form and do it again.

Finally, click the link on your Thank-you page that invokes the display script (guestbook.pl). You'll see something similar to Figure 14.6.

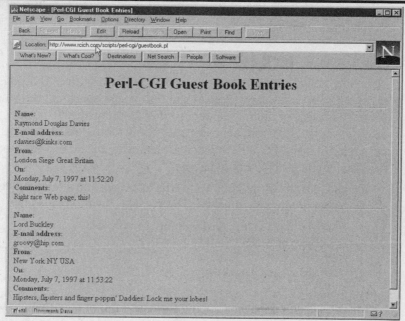

FIGURE 14.6:   Displaying the guest book entries

Dissecting the Display Program

It's exhilarating to get something to work, isn't it? Now comes the sticky part: understanding what you have done.

Actually, there isn't much in guestbook.pl that you haven't already done. The Perl read function that gets the records from the file is set up in a while loop that terminates when read reaches the end of the file:

```
# Read records and display them in a while loop. The test
# at the top of the while block fails when all the records
# have been read.

    while (read (GUEST_LOG, $buffer, $GuestEntrySize))
        {
        .
        .
        .
```

Notice that read's LENGTH parameter uses $GuestEntrySize instead of a hard-coded number; this is another example of the wisdom of placing *constant*—that is, non-variable—values in one place, where they can be changed easily. Each record read from the file is unpacked into an array, as you learned previously.

for Loops, NULLs

The code block that follows the call to unpack introduces the Perl for statement. for is similar to foreach in that it sets up a loop. But whereas foreach is ideal for pulling elements out of an array until it's empty, for provides a great deal more control over many more data structures than foreach. (Actually, for and foreach are identical; the differences described here are just de facto standard usages.)

for uses a counter variable, $n in this example, and a *terminating condition* to decide when it's finished. The for specification looks like this:

```
for (starting count; terminating condition;
➡do something with count)
    {
    Do this code block;
    }
```

for is especially good for stepping through subscripted arrays, as you do in the for block in guestbook.pl. The purpose in this example is to go through each string member of @InfoArray and strip out the trailing NULL characters used to pad them when they went through pack. The for starts the counter, $n, at 0. It terminates when $n equals $NumElements - 1, which is all the elements in the array except the last one (the long-integer value denoting the time the guest book entry was made). Each time through the loop, $n++ is executed, which increments it.

The elements go through a regular expression substitution in the body of the loop:

```
$InfoArray[$n] =~ s/\0//g;
```

The substitution operator in this case searches globally (note the g at the end) for all occurrences of \0 (the NULL character) and replaces them with nothing, which removes the NULLs from the string.

Keeping Time

The last bit of new stuff in guestbook.pl is the Perl function localtime. Four-byte integers denoting billions of seconds from some epoch, or starting date, may be meaningful to the computer as a way of telling time, but humans can't do much with them. Perl provides localtime to break the huge time values into something you can use in your programs.

localtime's specification looks like this:

```
($sec, $min, $hour, $mday, $mon, $year, $wday, $yday, $isdst)
    = localtime (time);
```

where

▶ $sec is the number of seconds past the minute

▶ $min is the number of minutes past the hour

▶ $hour is the hours past midnight

▶ $mday is the day of the month, starting from 0, not 1

▶ $mon is the numeric month, again starting from 0

▶ $year is the number of years from 1900 (such as 102 for 2002)

▶ $wday is the numeric day of the week, starting from 0

▶ $yday is the numeric day of the year

▶ $isdst is a flag indicating whether it's daylight saving time

▶ time is the 4-byte integer

localtime's return values are the impetus for the two arrays you added to GuestBook.pm. You can use the numeric values from localtime as subscripts into these arrays to pull out the real names of days of the week and months, as in guestbook.pl:

```
print "$WeekDay[$wday], $Month[$mon] $mday, ", $year + 1900;
print " at $hour:";
print "0" if $min < 10;
print "$min:";
print "0" if $sec < 10;
print "$sec <BR>\n";
```

The conditionals testing $min and $sec for values less than 10 are intended to pad them with 0s so you don't print times such as 11:6:5.

What's in a Form: Security Issues

HTML text input types and TEXTAREA fields allow a visitor to type in just about anything. This makes the HTML text types useful in terms of gathering information. However, they are also your largest window of vulnerability to attack by malicious or clumsy visitors.

There isn't much you can do about obscene or libelous entries in a guest book, unless you write your Perl script to filter out George Carlin's "seven dirty words" or some such thing. Putting a table of obscenities together might be a fascinating exercise, but, in the end, it would be a waste of time.

A bigger worry for you should be the *amount* of text a visitor can enter in one field. For example, it would be relatively simple for a visitor to crank up a file transfer and dump a few megabytes of garbage into the First Name field of your form. If you hadn't planned for that possibility, the garbage would hopelessly clog the CGI program you've hooked up to the HTML document. Assuming it made it through the Perl script without crashing it—and your web server—it would needlessly hog disk space in the guest book file. Perhaps the worst part would be when other visitors got pages of garbage instead of your guest book. A good start at limiting this sort of nonsense can be found in the text declarations in guestbook.html:

```
<TD> <INPUT TYPE="text" NAME="first_name" SIZE="24"
MAXLENGTH="30"> </TD>
```

The MAXLENGTH tag tells the browser to accept a maximum number of characters in the field. Note that the MAXLENGTH value is slightly larger than the width of the field, in case someone really does have a long first_name. But there's a great deal of difference between 30 and 30 million bytes.

Unfortunately, HTML's TEXTAREA tag, which allows the user to type in more than one line of text, has no provision for limiting the amount that goes into it. You'll fall back on a second line of defense for that: the Perl-CGI script itself.

A Last Word on Security

It's possible to enter system commands and HTML code into an HTML text field such as the ones you used in the guest book programs. Sometimes doing so can damage your system, if your Perl code takes any of the text and executes it as a system command.

It's also possible to enter a URL into one of the text fields. For example, a visitor could drop the path to a picture file into the Comments field of the guest book, as illustrated in Figure 14.7. Figure 14.8 illustrates how easy it is to do this.

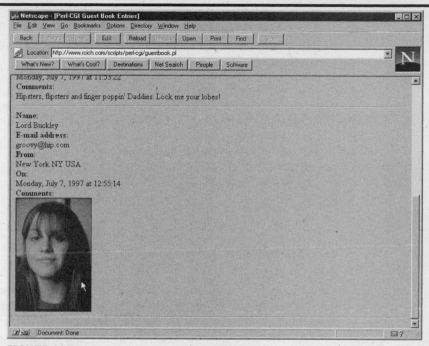

FIGURE 14.7: A picture gets into the guest book.

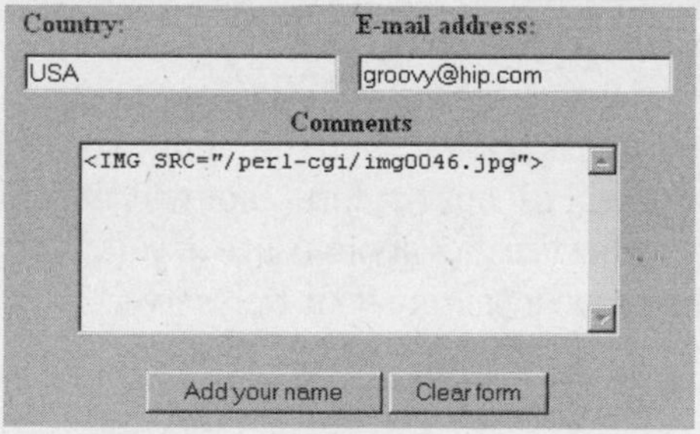

FIGURE 14.8: A URL in a form text field

The picture in Figure 14.7 certainly won't harm anything, but it could have been something not so nice. In any event, it isn't what you intended to have in the guest book.

The easiest way to guard against such intrusions is to filter out characters that obviously go into HTML code, shell commands, or URLs. Adding one small code block to addguest.pl provides the filter:

```
# Go through each element in @InfoArray, split off the
# "variable=" part, then translate pluses into spaces and
# any escaped hex chars back into their real values

for ($n = 0; $n < scalar @InfoArray; $n++)
    {
    ($dummy, $temp) = split (/=/, $InfoArray[$n], 2);
    $temp =~ tr/+/ /;
    $temp =~ s/%([\dA-Fa-f]{2})/
▶pack ("C", hex ($1))/eg;
    if ($temp =~ /[;<>&\*`|]/)
        {
        print "Illegal entry!!\n";
        exit;
        }
    $InfoArray [$n] = $temp;
    }
```

Calling exit to just exit the program is merely a suggestion; you can proceed any way you want. The point is this: There is no reason for any of the characters in the test to be in a guest book entry, and there is every reason for them to be in something you don't want. This is just one more line in your defenses.

WHAT'S NEXT

We've learned how to create a guest book to find out about your visitors. Unfortunately, not every visitor will fill out the form, nor will they fill it out cvcry time they visit. For aggregate statistics about usage of your site, you'll need a program to analyze the usage logs from your web server. Turn to the next chapter, "Monitoring Website Activity," to find out how.

Chapter 15
Monitoring Website Activity

Web server software is written to connect with literally the whole wide world. Such grand ambition may not be completely fulfilled at your website, although you certainly can give it a try. But whether large or small, heavily visited or not, your web server generates an amazing amount of information about itself and what your visitors do when they connect with your site.

As a beginning webmaster, you may not have looked at the logs created by your server or even know where the log files are. However, after completing this chapter, you will be able to find the logs—and use them to your advantage.

Updated from *Perl CGI Programming: No Experience Required*, by Erik Strom
ISBN 0-7821-2157-8

USING LOG FILES AND SIMPLE REPORTS

The logs maintained by your web server contain a voluminous amount of information, which you can use any way you like. Using a Perl script as your template, it isn't difficult to extract simple information from the log files and fashion the information into a report.

The benefits of keeping track of people who visit your website may not be immediately apparent. Also, when you consider that the standard server log records not just every visit to the site but *every transaction* made during the connection, you may begin to wonder what you're going to do with all that information.

The benefits depend on how you plan to use your website. When the World Wide Web began to become popular, most noncorporate webmasters who could afford to hang a server on the Internet were running what could be termed "vanity" websites—"Hi, welcome to my website; here are some pictures of the kids." Years later, the Web is now a vehicle for commercial enterprise, and web advertising is commonplace.

Any advertiser who wants to track visitors' marketing profiles relies on the data within the server's log files. Think about the advantage this gives you over other advertisers: Newspapers and other more traditional advertising media have to depend on surveys and polls to develop profiles of the type of person who reads a particular ad. They have to depend on the honesty of the people participating in the surveys and polls to determine who even looks at the ads. On a website, you have no such vagaries to contend with. The information is there, always at your fingertips. All you have to do is take advantage of it.

Decoding a Log File

To the uninitiated, a web server log file looks just plain weird. You'll learn in this section what each of the log entries means, and how to decode an entry. The log files are text files—you can edit them if you like, although doing so is *not* a recommended practice. You'll need to deal with a couple of formats and several log file locations, depending on the server.

TIP

By default, Internet Information Server (IIS) stores its log files in winnt\system32\ logfiles\W3SVC1 with a different file for each day. Apache, by default, puts its logging information in a file called access_log, which can be found where the HTTPD server was installed.

Getting Information from IIS Logs

Figure 15.1 shows one of IIS's log files, opened with Notepad. As you can see, it's not pretty. But all of it means something. Let's start by taking apart one line:

```
152.163.195.39, -, 6/13/97, 21:37:00, W3SVC, OWSLEY,
➡207.77.84.202, 328, 60, 29, 304, 0, GET,
➡/wml/homepage.gif, -,
```

Note that log entries span only one line; the example here is broken because that's the only way it will fit on the printed page.

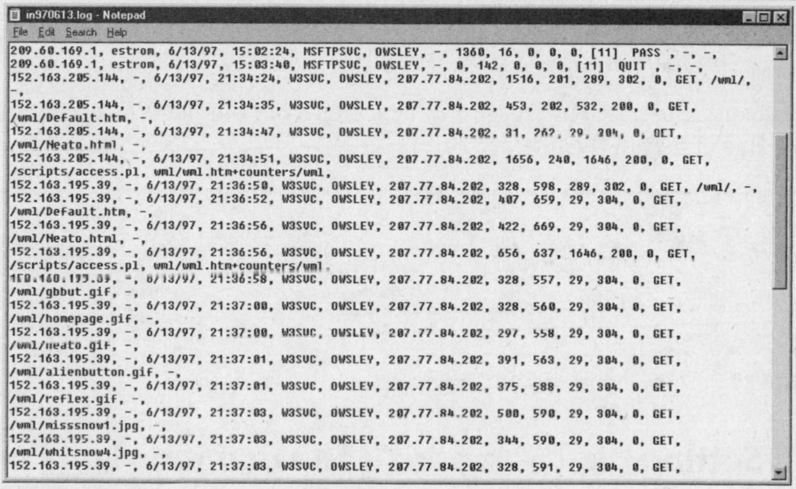

FIGURE 15.1:   The raw information in an IIS log file

Notice that each of the 15 entries is separated from the others with a comma. This is how you distinguish them; the commas are also Perl's hint for breaking out entries when you run the log information into a report.

The entries in IIS's log file are broken down this way:

- ▶ User's IP address
- ▶ Client's username, which is usually "-" in IIS
- ▶ Date of request
- ▶ Time of request
- ▶ Service name and instance (usually W3SVC1 in IIS)
- ▶ Web server's name (computer name)

- ▶ Server IP address

- ▶ Elapsed CPU time (in milliseconds) of the operation

- ▶ Number of bytes received

- ▶ Number of bytes sent

- ▶ Service status code

- ▶ Windows status code

- ▶ Operation requested

- ▶ Target of the operation

- ▶ Query string

As illustrated in Figure 15.2, each entry in our list is strung out in a line of text in the log file.

FIGURE 15.2:   The format of an IIS log file entry

Setting the "Standard": The Common Log Format

The log format used by IIS is considered nonstandard; in other words, it's something new. The "old" standard is known as the Common Log Format, and it's used by default on the Apache server.

Here's an example log entry in the Common Log Format:

```
pooky.petdance.com - - [28/Apr/2002:00:15:07 -0700]
➥"GET /weblint/ HTTP/1.1" 200 318
```

Again, keep in mind that this entry normally appears in one line but is broken here to fit on the printed page.

The entries in the Common Log Format log file are broken down this way:

- ▶ Client's IP address or hostname

- ▶ Client identity (usually -)

- ▶ Client userid (usually -)

- ▶ Date and time of request

▶ Operation requested, plus the target of the operation and the HTTP version being used

▶ HTTP response code from the server

▶ Number of bytes transferred

Figure 15.3 breaks out the components of a Common Log Format entry.

Client Name
(Not Used by
Samba Server)   Username   Time Zone   HTTP
                                                                                                                  Result Code

website.com 140.172.165.58 admin [27/Apr/1997:20:47:43 -0700] "GET \session\adminlogin HTTP/1.0" 200 160

    Client IP Address   Date and Time   Operation and Target   Bytes
                                     of Request   Requested, plus   Transferred
                                                                      HTTP Version

FIGURE 15.3:   The components of the Apache Common Log Format

NOTE

Your web server may be configured to do a *reverse DNS lookup*, in which it converts the IP address, such as 63.99.198.12, to a host name, such as www.sybex.com. A reverse lookup may cause a slowdown on the web server, so many administrators leave it turned off. Also, some IP addresses cannot be converted back to a hostname.

NOTE

Note the format of the date and time stamp: [28/Apr/2002:00:15:07 -0700]. The date and time are easily picked out, but you may not be familiar with the −0700 that ends the string. This is a time zone value, indicating the number of hours that were added to Greenwich Mean Time (GMT) to obtain the correct local time, which is displayed in the string. In this example, −0700 says to subtract seven hours (note the −) from GMT. If you know your time zones, you'll recall that Mountain Standard Time is seven hours behind GMT. If you don't know your time zones, it's easy to look them up, load them into a table, and use the table to calculate the correct zone with a Perl program. Also, all the operating systems covered by *Perl, CGI, and JavaScript Complete* can correct for daylight savings time, and the date and time stamp in the log file will reflect this correction.

Selecting Your Log Format

If you're using IIS on your website, you have two or three options for log formats. It's easy to choose the format that best suits your needs.

For Windows NT, the configuration program for the IIS web server is found in the Internet Service Manager, which can be found on NT's Start menu by choosing Programs ➢ Microsoft Internet Server. For Windows 2000 and above, go to Control Panel ➢ Administrative Tools. When you click Internet Service Manager, you'll see a window containing a list of all the Internet services running on your computer. Click the line that shows WWW under Service, and then click Properties ➢ Service Properties.

For Windows 2000 and above, the configuration program for the IIS web server is found in the Internet Services Manager, which you get to by choosing Control Panel ➢ Administrative Tools. When you click Internet Services Manager, you'll see a tree showing your server and the services running on it. Right-click on your website (probably labeled Default Web Site) and you'll get the properties for that window; the list includes all the Internet services running on your computer. Click the line that shows WWW under Service, and then click Properties ➢ Service Properties.

You will see a Web Site tab on the property sheet that appears. Click it, and it will move to the front. A window similar to the one in Figure 15.4 will be displayed.

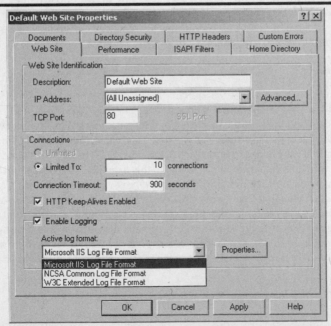

FIGURE 15.4:   The logging options for IIS on Windows 2000

Notice the Active Log Format list box under Enable Logging. If you click it, you will see three choices: Microsoft IIS, NCSA Common, and W3C Extended log formats. If you choose NCSA, IIS will begin logging entries in the NCSA Common Log Format, which is what Apache uses by default. The Microsoft IIS format (also called Standard Format under Windows NT) is what we'll be using in these examples. *Don't* use the W3C Extended log format: It allows customizations that these simple programs aren't designed to handle.

NOTE

Any changes made to the IIS web server configuration won't take effect until you stop the server and restart it. You can do this from Internet Service manager by clicking the Stop Service button on the toolbar and then clicking the Start Service button.

Click the Properties button to get to the Logging property sheet. This is where you tell IIS how to structure logging in general. The default installation sets up a directory of log files, one file for each day. The files are named in the format *SVYYMMDD*.`log`, where *SV* refers to either the IIS or NCSA log format and *YY, MM,* and *DD* are the year, month, and date, respectively. In IIS format, the server log for August 23, 1997, is named `in970823.log`. The `in` is replaced with `nc` in NCSA format, so August 23, 1997 would be `nc970823.log`.

You have several other choices if you don't like this daily logging scheme. A new log file can also be created every week, every month, or when the file reaches a size that you specify in megabytes. Click the radio button of your choice, and IIS will follow the new scheme.

TIP

If you change the IIS logging scheme, notice that the file-naming format changes, too. The current format is shown under Log File Name at the bottom of the Logging property sheet.

EXTRACTING LOG FILE INFORMATION

You have learned about the formats for web server log files and where they are kept by the various servers. Now, what can you do with all the information in the logs? Perl is especially adept at handling projects that involve processing formatted text, much more so than a lower-level compiled language such as C or C++ is. Let's see how it's done.

Using Perl to Decode a Server Log

Perl has so many facilities built into it for dealing with text—especially if the text is set up in a consistent way—that there is little reason to attempt to take a web server log file apart in any other language. First, if you know the format of the log file (and you should, on your own server), you can break a line of log entries into individual fields and store them in one line of Perl code. Let's use the example in the previous section from the IIS logs:

```
152.163.195.39, -, 6/13/97, 21:37:00, W3SVC, OWSLEY,
➥207.77.84.202, 328, 60, 29, 304, 0,
➥GET, /wml/homepage.gif, -,
```

Because the entries are separated by commas, you can use Perl's `split` function to put each entry in its own variable. (These entries were identified in the previous section, "Getting Information from IIS Logs.")

The most difficult task in creating a Perl program to extract these fields is thinking up variable names for all of them. The critical thing to remember is that the order of the variables in the call to `split` must match the order of entries in the log file line. These lines of Perl code will do it:

```
($ClientIP, $Dummy, $DateTime, $SvcName, $SrvrName,
        $SrvrIP, $CPUTime, $BytesRecv, $BytesSent,
        $SvcStatus, $NTStatus, $Operation,
        $Target, $Dummy) = split (/, /, $LogLine);
```

Remember that `split` parses the string passed to it for the pattern between the slash characters (//) in its first argument and uses the pattern as a way to break the string into components separated by the pattern. This example looks for the comma immediately followed by a space as a delimiter in the $LogLine string. Any time `split` encounters a comma and space together, it loads the text it has read previously into the next variable in the list on the left side of the equation.

Let's turn the example into a snippet of executable code as follows:

1. Load the example log file line into a local variable.

2. Process the variable with `split`, extracting each field into its own variable.

3. Print the individual values to the screen.

Enter the code in Listing 15.1 into your text editor.

Listing 15.1: Extracting Data from a Sample Log Line

```perl
#!perl/bin/perl

# Hard-code an example log line into a local variable.

    $LogLine = "152.163.195.39, -, 6/13/97, 21:37:00, W3SVC"
            .", OWSLEY, 207.77.84.202, 328, 60, 29, 304, 0"
            .", GET, /wml/homepage.gif, -";

# Extract the components using split()

    ($ClientIP, $Dummy, $Date, $Time, $SvcName,
        $SrvrName, $SrvrIP, $CPUTime, $BytesRecv,
        $BytesSent, $SvcStatus, $NTStatus,
        $Operation, $Target, $Dummy) =
     split (/, /, $LogLine);

# Print the values to the screen.
    print "Client's IP address = $ClientIP\n";
    print "Date of request = $Date\n";
    print "Time of request = $Time\n";
    print "Service name = $SvcName\n";
    print "Server name = $SrvrName\n";
    print "Server's IP address = $SrvrIP\n";
    print "Processing time = $CPUTime\n";
    print "Received $BytesRecv bytes of data\n";
    print "Sent $BytesSent bytes of data\n";
    print "Server returned status of $SvcStatus\n";
    print "Windows NT returned status code $NTStatus\n";
    print "Operation requested = $Operation\n";
    print "Target of operation = $Target\n";

# End logs.pl
```

Save this script as logs.pl and run it from the command line. Your output should look similar to Figure 15.5.

FIGURE 15.5:   An example of a simple extraction from a log file line

Dissecting the Example Code

You probably noticed one aspect of our rudimentary log entry extraction program immediately: It's ugly, at least in the way it prints the information. Don't worry: You'll learn how to pretty it up shortly. Meanwhile, let's discuss the program you have so far.

In the code line that calls `split`, notice that two variables are called `$Dummy`:

```
# Extract the components using split()

($ClientIP, $Dummy, $Date, $Time, $SvcName,
    $SrvrName, $SrvrIP, $CPUTime, $BytesRecv,
    $BytesSent, $SvcStatus, $NTStatus,
    $Operation, $Target, $Dummy) =
split (/, /, $LogLine);
```

Recall from the definition of an IIS log file entry line in the previous section that two fields are always empty and, therefore, designated with hyphens: the client's user name and the last entry in the line. The variable $Dummy is actually being filled twice, which means that after `split` is finished $Dummy will contain the value of the *last* field put in it. It really doesn't matter, because you'll ignore whatever the variable contains. That's why it's called $Dummy.

TIP

Because of the way `split` works, the second declaration of $Dummy in the list could be left out entirely. The processing of the $LogLine string would stop when `split` ran out of variables in which to place the extracted fields.

The `logs.pl` script introduces another new Perl concept: the *concatenation* operator, or dot (.). Notice the line in which `$LogFile` is given a string value:

```
# Hard-code an example log line into a local variable.

    $LogLine = "152.163.195.39, -, 6/13/97, 21:37:00, W3SVC"
            .", OWSLEY, 207.77.84.202, 328, 60, 29, 304, 0"
            .", GET, /wml/homepage.gif, -";
```

The `$LogLine` string is being set in the program rather than read from a log file, and it's long. You could have typed the whole string on one line, but it would have stretched far past the right margin of the screen. It would have looked ugly.

Perl's string concatenation operator joins two (or more) strings. In other words, given two strings

```
    $Str1 = "Now is the time ";
    $Str2 = "for all brown foxes";
```

you can combine—or *concatenate*—them into one with the dot:

```
    $Str3 = $Str1.$Str2;
```

If you print `$Str3`, you'll see

```
    Now is the time for all brown foxes
```

In the example, you need to break `$LogLine` into parts of a manageable length. Because the declaration uses the dot operator, the parts reassemble themselves.

Reading Data from a Real Log File

The example in the preceding section was just that: an example, using log data that you hard-coded into the Perl script. However, it isn't too big a job to modify the `logs.pl` script to read lines from a real log file. Let's broaden your logging experience by using the Apache server's log file from the example.

Decoding an Apache Common Log Format log entry line is nowhere near as straightforward as with IIS. Let's take another look at the previous example, refined to conform to the Apache format:

```
    140.172.165.58 - - [27/Apr/1997:20:47:43 -0700]
    "GET session/adminlogin HTTP/1.0" 200 160
```

You know enough about the individual entries by now to be able to pick them out visually. But your task at the moment is to feed them into a Perl program. Notice that entries are separated with spaces, but two of the entries—the date/time string and the operation string—contain spaces. What can you do about that?

You *could* hack together a Perl regular expression string that would extract each field intact. But the regular expression would be unintelligible to anyone but an expert in regular expressions. Why bother, when you know which fields are which to begin with?

The date/time string

```
[27/Apr/1997:20:47:43 -0700]
```

contains a single space, separating the date/time and the time zone value. The operation string

```
"GET session/adminlogin  HTTP/1.0"
```

has one space after the operation requested and two spaces after the operation target. According to the log format, these spaces will always be in the same place, so you can still use split with a simple pattern argument to split up the string. Besides, it isn't a bad idea to be able to get to these extra fields individually.

Your original Perl script, logs.pl, needs a complete rewrite, so crank up the text editor and enter the code from Listing 15.2.

Listing 15.2: Extracting Fields from an Apache Log File

```perl
#!perl/bin/perl

# logs1.pl
#
# A Perl script to read, extract, and print a log file from
# the Apache web server.
#

# Put the log file name into a local variable -- full path.

    $LogFile = "c:/logs/access.log";

# Open the file; die if that's not possible.

    open (LOG, $LogFile) or die "Can't open $LogFile: $!\n";

# Read, extract, and print each line from the log file.

    while (my $LogLine = <LOG>)
```

```
        {
# Strip out the characters we don't need.

        $LogLine =~ s/\[|\]|\"//g;
        chomp($LogLine);

# Extract the components using split()
        ($ClientIP, $Dummy, $UserName, $DateTime, $TimeZone,
            $Operation,$Target, $HTTPVers, $SrvrStatus,
            $NTStatus,$BytesXfer) = split (/ +/, $LogLine);

# Print the values to the screen.
        print "Client's IP address = $ClientIP\n";
        print "Name of user on client = $UserName\n";
        print "Date and time of request = $DateTime\n";
        print "Operation requested = $Operation\n";
        print "Operation target = $Target\n";
        print "Server returned status of $SrvrStatus\n";
        print "Windows NT returned status code $NTStatus\n";
        print "Transferred $BytesXfer bytes of data\n\n";
        } # End while (<LOG>)

    close (LOG);       # Close the log file.

 #                     End logs1.pl
```

Save the script as logs1.pl and run it from the command line. Stop it from time to time (Ctrl+S works on both Unix and Windows systems) to see what the output looks like—if the log file has many entries in it, it will roll off the screen. The output should look similar to what is illustrated in Figure 15.6.

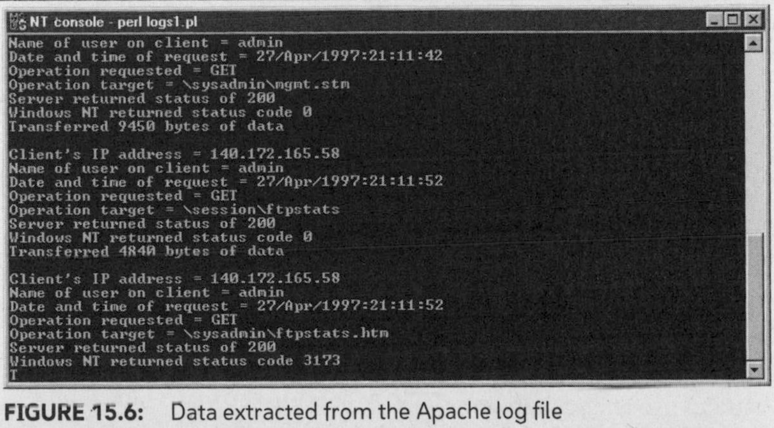

FIGURE 15.6:   Data extracted from the Apache log file

Analyzing the New Code Sample

The new Perl script, logs1.pl, mainly deals with a new format in log files. However, we need to explain a couple of new Perl goodies.

First, notice the code at the beginning of the program:

```
# Put the log file name into a local variable -- full path.

$LogFile = "c:/logs/access.log";

# Open the file; die if that's not possible.

open (LOG, $LogFile) or die "Can't open $LogFile: $!\n";
```

You store the full path to the Apache log file in a variable; doing so makes it easier to deal with and change, as you'll remember from previous chapters. The file is opened for reading (or the script dies trying) with the file handle LOG.

Next, you set up a loop that reads the log file line by line:

```
# Read, extract and print each line from the log file.

while (my $LogLine = <LOG>)
    {
```

The while statement refers to the LOG file handle enclosed in less-than and greater-than signs, which reads a line at a time into the Perl variable $LogLine until nothing is left in the file.

In the next couple of code lines, you do some simple formatting to $LogLine.

```
# Strip out the characters we don't need.

$LogLine =~ s/\[|\]|\"//g;
chomp($LogLine);
```

The string contains three characters—[ ] "—that you don't need. The substitution in the first line strips them out. If you look closely at the regular expression in the substitution, it begins to make sense: You can pick out the three characters to be stripped. All of them have special meaning in a regular expression, so they're escaped with the backslash (\); and, finally, each substitution is separated from the others with the Perl OR operator (|).

The next line calls a function you haven't seen before: chomp. It's one of those little utilities that doesn't do much, but you find yourself using it a lot. It removes any end-of-line character from the end of your string. Be sure to use chomp, and not chop.

The last line of interest in `logs1.pl` is the one that calls `split`:

```
# Extract the components using split()
        ($ClientIP, $Dummy, $UserName, $DateTime, $TimeZone,
         $Operation,$Target, $HTTPVers, $SrvrStatus,
         $NTStatus,$BytesXfer) = split (/ +/, $LogLine);
```

Notice that some new variables had to be declared to match the format of an Apache log file entry. The pattern specified for `split` has also changed. It looks a little strange, but, like the substitution done on `$LogLine`, it begins to make sense if you examine it closely. You want to break out the fields in the log entry separated by spaces. However, there are *two* spaces between the operation target and the HTTP version, as in the example used to start this section:

```
"GET session/adminlogin  HTTP/1.0"
```

A space in a regular expression [ ] will match on a space, but two spaces will constitute two matches and will thereby throw off the count of variables. Remember that `split` goes through the list of variables on the left side of the equation sequentially, throwing values into variables as it encounters matches for its pattern. Putting a plus sign after the space (+) matches on one *or more* spaces, thus ensuring that all spaces are ignored and the proper values go to the proper variables.

MONITORING ACTIVITY FROM A WEB PAGE

Your experience with web server log files now includes negotiating the formats for Microsoft's IIS and the Apache server. You may wonder what you can do with all that information. Well, this is another of those situations in which you are limited only by your imagination. You have the information, you have the tools to manipulate the information, and you have the tools to display the information any way you like.

A good place to start is a web page. You already know quite a bit about using Perl scripts to create HTML documents that can be displayed on your website through CGI. Let's use some of that knowledge to create a statistical web page that uses the information in your server log files.

Who Gets In and How Often?

With a little manipulation, you can determine the sources of hits on your website and how often they connect. You'll use the IIS log files for this example. Recall from the previous section that the default IIS log file scheme is to create a new file for each day. This scheme results in a directory full of log files, each of which you must step through to get the information for a particular day.

Here's what you'll do with the log information for each day:

▶ Identify the various IP addresses from which your website has been contacted.

▶ Count the number of IPs.

▶ Count the number of hits from each IP.

▶ Format the resulting data in an HTML document and display it in a browser.

Let's start with one file, and then build up to the entire directory. The output will go to the screen for now. Enter the code from Listing 15.3 in your text editor, ensuring that the filenames and pathnames defined at the top match valid names on your system.

Listing 15.3: Determining the Source and Frequency of Hits on Your Website

```perl
#!perl/bin/perl

# hitcnt.pl
#

# First version. Goes through a single IIS log file,
# tallying the hits and IP addresses from which they came.
# Command-line version - output to screen.

# Define path to a single log file.
    $LogDir = "c:/winnt/system32/logfiles/";
    $LogFile = "in970502.log";
    $LogPath = $LogDir.$LogFile;

# Attempt to open the log file; die if it doesn't happen.

    open (LOG, $LogPath) or die "Can't open $LogPath: $!\n";

# Loop through the log file a line at a time and extract
# the entry information.
```

```
while (<LOG>)
    {
    ($ClientIP, $Dummy, $Date, $Time, $SvcName,
        $SrvrName, $SrvrIP, $CPUTime, $BytesRecv,
        $BytesSent, $SvcStatus, $NTStatus,
        $Operation, $Target, $Dummy) =
    split (/, /);

    # Store the client IP address, increment counter.

    $NumHits{$ClientIP}++;
    } # end while (<LOG>)

close (LOG);              # Close the log file.


# Print out the results.

print "On 05/02/97:\n\n";

foreach $ip ( keys %NumHits )
    {
    print "$ip registered $NumHits{$ip} hits\n";
    }

#                    End hitcnt.pl
```

Save this Perl script as hitcnt.pl and run it from the command line. You'll see output similar to the following:

```
On 05/02/97:

153.34.183.182 registered 8 hits
207.77.84.202 registered 32 hits
208.138.70.52 registered 24 hits
131.107.3.19 registered 2 hits
152.163.207.36 registered 56 hits
```

Analyzing the First Hit Counter

The first version of hitcnt.pl is ugly in its output, as are most command-line applications. However, you have built the foundation for something much bigger.

TIP

Apache server users need to make only two small changes to get `hitcnt.pl` to work with their log files. First, of course, change the log file locations defined at the top of the program. Then change the line that calls Perl's `split` function to the same call in `logs1.pl`, the script you wrote in the previous section.

Two new Perl constructs are presented in `hitcnt.pl`: the `last` statement and hashes. A hash is a special kind of array; instead of being indexed by a number, as in `$array[4]`, the elements are indexed by a string, as in `$color{'banana'} = 'yellow'`. A hash makes simplifies tasks like counting instances of something—IP addresses, in this case. Hashes are signified by a special symbol: %.

Let's walk through the code. The client IP addresses are picked up from the log file the same way you did it in the previous section. Notice that you don't change the call to `split`:

```
while (<LOG>)
        {
        ($ClientIP, $Dummy, $Date, $Time, $SvcName,
            $SrvrName, $SrvrIP, $CPUTime, $BytesRecv,
            $BytesSent, $SvcStatus, $NTStatus,
            $Operation, $Target, $Dummy) =
            split (/,/);
```

There is one exception, however. Rather than storing the input line in a local variable, you let `split` take its data directly from the standard input (defined in Perl as `$_`). This is why `split` has only its search pattern as a parameter.

NOTE

There is no reason to call `split` with the full list of variables for an entire log file entry, because only the first variable is used in `hitcnt.pl`. However, you probably will want more than just an IP address in future versions of the script, so you might as well leave the rest of the variables.

Then you store the IP address in a hash. The index of the hash entry is the IP address, and the value of the hash entry is the number of times you've seen a given IP address:

```
$NumHits{$ClientIP}++;
```

The ++ operator says to increment the value on which it operates. The first time you find a given IP address, `$IPHash{$ClientIP}` is not defined, and it has the special value undef. Incrementing that value creates the element in the hash and gives it a value of 1. Subsequent increments will set it to 2, 3, and so on.

Finally, after the code has gone through all the records in the file, it prints out the counts based on the %NumHits hash:

```
foreach $ip ( keys(%NumHits) )
        {
        print "$ip registered $NumHits{$ip} hits\n";
        }
```

Inside the parentheses of the foreach loop is the expression keys(%NumHits), which returns a list of all the IP addresses you've seen and accumulated in the %NumHits hash. Each time through the loop, one of the keys is assigned to $ip. Then, inside the loop, the code prints the IP address and the entry in the hash for that IP address.

Counting Hits on the Entire Log Directory

You have gone through one IIS log file and extracted enough information from it to determine the number of hits from individual IP addresses in that file. With an extension to hitcnt.pl, you can extend your reach to the whole directory of IIS log files.

Perl, as usual, provides the method in a straightforward fashion. Perl can handle directories in much the same way it handles files: by opening, reading, and closing them. The main difference is that you have to use a new set of Perl functions to do the job:

- ▶ opendir, which returns a handle to the directory
- ▶ readdir, which returns the list of files in the directory
- ▶ closedir, which closes the directory handle

The specification for opendir is

```
opendir (HANDLE, PATH);
```

where HANDLE is the handle that you will use in subsequent references to the directory and PATH is the full path to the directory.

To read the directory entries, use

```
readdir (HANDLE);
```

which can fill a list variable with the contents of the directory:

```
@FileList = readdir (HANDLE);
```

WARNING

Unix and Windows directories always contain two special files designated by dots. The current directory is named . and the parent directory is . . . You will find few uses for these special files if you just want a list of filenames from a particular directory. You need to explicitly bypass them if you don't want to use them.

THE PERL-C-UNIX DIRECTORY FUNCTIONS

In addition to opendir, readdir, and closedir, there are three other Perl functions for manipulating directories:

▶ rewinddir, specified as rewinddir (*HANDLE*), which "rewinds" a directory handle back to its first entry.

▶ seekdir, specified as seekdir (*HANDLE*, *POSITION*), where *POSITION* is a place in the directory where the next readdir will take place (at the fifth or sixth filename, for example).

▶ telldir, specified as telldir (*HANDLE*), which returns the current position in the directory.

To change htcnt.pl to read and process a whole directory, you need to:

1. Get a handle for the log file directory with opendir.

2. Read all the files into an array with readdir.

3. Process the files one at a time as you did in the previous section.

The difference is that you will have more than one file to process, so the bulk of the code in hitcnt.pl can go in a foreach loop that pulls the filenames out of the array. The new program is shown in Listing 15.4.

Listing 15.4: The New Program, *htcnt.pl*

```perl
#!perl/bin/perl

# hitcnt1.pl
#
```

```
# Second version. Goes through the entire IIS log file
# directory.
# Extracts the hits and IP addresses from which they came.
# Command-line version -- output to screen.

# Define path to a log directory.

    $LogDir = "c:/winnt/system32/logfiles";

# Open the directory; die if it's not possible.


    opendir(LOGD, $LogDir) or die "Can't open $LogDir!\n";

# Get the list of log files into an array.

    @LogFiles = readdir (LOGD);

# Loop through the list, avoiding the . and .. entries.

        foreach $LogFile (@LogFiles)
            {
            if (($LogFile eq ".") || ($LogFile eq ".."))
                {
                next;
                }

        # Attempt to open the log file; die if it doesn't
        # happen.

            $LogPath = $LogDir."/".$LogFile;
            open (LOG, $LogPath) or die "Can't open $LogPath:
              $!\n";

        # Loop through the log file a line at a time and extract
        # the entry information.

            my %NumHits; # create a new hash
            while (<LOG>)
                {
                ($ClientIP, $Dummy, $Date, $Time, $SvcName,
                    $SrvrName, $SrvrIP, $CPUTime, $BytesRecv,
```

```
                    $BytesSent, $SvcStatus, $NTStatus,
                    $Operation, $Target, $Dummy) = split (/,/);

      # Store the client IP address, increment counter.

          $NumHits{$ClientIP}++;

          }                             # end while (<LOG>)

      close (LOG);                  # Close the log file.


   # Print out the results after formatting date from
   # file name.


      if ($LogFile =~ /(..)(\d\d)(\d\d)(\d\d)/)
          {
          $year = $2;
          $month = $3;
          $day = $4;
          }

      print "On $month/$day/$year:\n\n";

      foreach $ip ( keys %NumHits )
          {
          print "$ip registered $NumHits{$ip} hits\n";
          }

      print "\n";         # Extra line.

      }                             # end foreach $LogFile...

   # Close the directory.

      closedir (LOGDIR);

   #                       End hitcnt1.pl
```

Save this script as hitcnt1.pl and, again, run it from the command line. Stop the output from time to time with Ctrl+S; you should see something similar to what's illustrated in Figure 15.7.

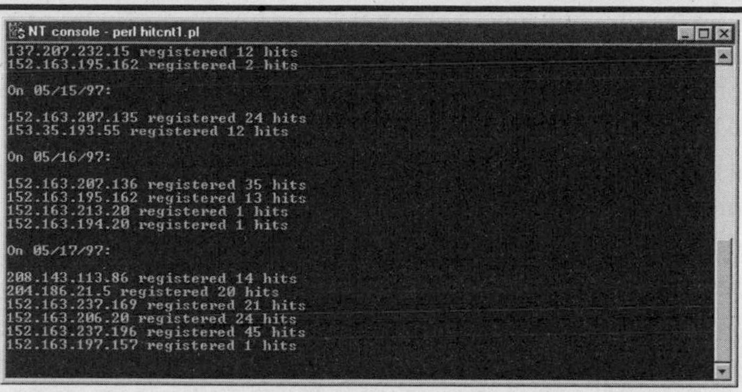

FIGURE 15.7: Counting the hits in an entire directory of log files

Analyzing the Whole-Directory Hit Counter

Despite what looks like an intimidating new program, you have added only two new features to your original hitcnt.pl. You have used Perl's directory functions to get a handle to the log file directory, and you put the code that processes the IP addresses and counts hits into a foreach loop.

The changes at the top of the program are minimal:

```
$LogDir = "c:/winnt/system32/logfiles";
opendir (LOGD, $LogDir) or die "Can't open $LogDir: $!\n";
@LogFiles = readdir (LOGD);
```

Notice that the only string constant you need to define now is the path to the log directory. The string, $LogDir, is the argument to opendir, which returns the LOGD handle. The handle is used by readdir to put all of the directory's files into @LogFiles.

There are two items of special interest at the top of the foreach loop. The first tests for the two special files present in every Windows and Unix directory:

```
foreach $LogFile (@LogFiles)
        {
        if (($LogFile eq ".") || ($LogFile eq ".."))
            {
            next;
            }
```

The filename . refers to the current directory, and .. is the parent; you don't need them in this example, so they are ignored.

How? By using the Perl next statement, which is essentially the opposite of the last statement you learned about in the previous section. Where `last` breaks *out* of the loop, `next` makes it loop again without executing any more of the subsequent code. In this example, if `$LogFile` has the value of either of the special filenames, you don't want to do anything but get the next filename.

The next code section prevents a common mistake in working with directory handles:

```
$LogPath = $LogDir."/".$LogFile;
open (LOG, $LogPath) || die "Can't open $LogPath: $!\n";
```

Notice that an entire path to the file is built into `$LogPath` by combining the directory name and the filename, because `$LogFile` will work by itself to open the file only if you have the log directory also set as your current directory. The chances of this being true every time you run `hitcnt1.pl` are slim—it's wisest to specify the full path to the file.

The last new feature in `hitcnt1.pl` makes a date out of an IIS log filename:

```
if ($LogFile =~ /(..)(\d\d)(\d\d)(\d\d)/)
    {
    $year = $2;
    $month = $3;
    $day = $4;
    }

print "On $month/$day/$year:\n\n";
```

Remember how daily IIS log names are formatted? The first two characters are `in`, followed by the two-digit year, month, and day. In other words, the log file for August 24, 1997, is named `in970824.log`. The regular expression `/(..)(..)(..)(..)/` matches each of the first four pairs of characters in the filename in order. Therefore, you can pull the year out of `$2`, the month out of `$3`, and the day out of `$4`, ignoring `$1`.

Taking the Hit Counter to the Web

You now know how to navigate through an entire directory of IIS log files and calculate and display the number of hits on each day from every IP address that has connected to your website. The last step—putting the whole thing on a web page—is the easiest.

You've already done all the hard work in reading the log files and manipulating the data. The only changes you need to make are in the `print` statements at the bottom of `hitcnt1.pl`. They need to put out HTML-formatted code now.

The HTML conversion requires a few lines of additional code. First, call in your HTML header and ender code near the top:

```
# Bring in HTML header and ender stuff.

    require "d:/pub/scripts/perl-cgi/html.pl";

# Define path to a single log file and a page title.

    $LogDir = "c:/winnt/system32/logfiles";
    $Title = "Counting Web page hits from various IPs";
```

Then, set up the header and titles for an HTML document in the program just after reading all the files in the log directory into the list:

```
# Get the list of log files into an array.

    @LogFiles = readdir (LOGD);

# Crank up a Web page.
    HTML_Header ($Title);
    print "<BODY>\n";
    print "<H1 ALIGN=\"CENTER\">$Title</H1>\n";
    print "<HR>\n";
```

Last, the portion of the script that prints the data needs a near-total rewrite:

```
if ($LogFile =~ /(..)(\d\d)(\d\d)(\d\d)/)
    {
    $year = $2;
    $month = $3;
    $day = $4;
    }

print "<H3>Date: $month/$day/$year:</H3>\n<HR>\n";
print "<TABLE WIDTH=50%>\n";

foreach $ip ( keys %NumHits )

    {
    print "<TR>\n<TD>$ip</TD>";
    print "<TD>$NumHits{$ip}</TD>\n";

    print "</TR>\n";
    }

print "</TABLE>\n<HR>\n";
```

Notice that the `print` statements format the data in HTML tables. They look better that way.

Make these changes, and then save the file as `webhit.pl` in a directory accessible to your web server through CGI. Invoke it as a URL from your web browser, and you'll see something similar to what is illustrated in Figure 15.8.

Congratulations! You've moved your hit counter to the Web.

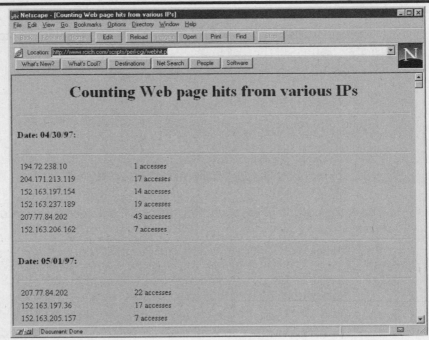

FIGURE 15.8:   The hit counter moves to the Web.

What's Next

You've undertaken a lot in this chapter. You have built, from the ground up, the capability to analyze your web server logs in a simple fashion. You have built a foundation for a full statistical analysis of your website, whether you use IIS or Apache as your server.

Let's move on to the other killer app of the Internet: e-mail. In Chapter 16, you'll learn how to send e-mail with Perl from your programs and, by extension, from CGI programs and web pages.

Chapter 16
E-Mail Solutions

Despite the popularity of the World Wide Web, e-mail is still the most commonly used application on the Internet. The SMTP protocol and the Unix `sendmail` program are well-established tools for transferring e-mail messages. The Windows mail interface has been problematic over the years, but there are now several options you can use.

In this chapter, you will learn how to apply some e-mail solutions for both Unix and Windows computers. The first two examples you'll work through require you to have a connection to a Unix `sendmail` process. I connected to my local ISP via a Telnet connection to build these examples. In the second part of this chapter, you'll learn about two Windows e-mail solutions: the Blat program and the `Mail::Sender` module. The Blat application is a Windows-only solution. The `Mail::Sender` module runs on any system with a connection to an SMTP server, which you have if you can send e-mail from your computer.

Updated from *Mastering Perl 5*, by Eric C. Herrmann
ISBN 0-7821-2200-0

An Introduction to E-Mail Programs and Protocols

SMTP (Simple Mail Transfer Protocol) is the protocol used to transmit e-mail messages across the Internet. The most popular implementation of SMTP is the `sendmail` program, which is the e-mail backbone of the Internet. SMTP and `sendmail` have been around since the 1980s. If you send e-mail, you use an SMTP server.

TIP

The full definition of the SMTP protocol can be found in RFC821. RFC stands for Request For Comments. RFCs are used as a means to document new and emerging Internet protocols. You can learn more about RFCs at `http://www.faqs.org/rfcs/`.

To communicate with an SMTP server, you must follow a specific protocol. In practice, it is not difficult to make SMTP connections. The SMTP server will reject your e-mail request if you don't talk to it correctly, but if you know the secret handshake, you can talk to any SMTP server.

The following sections provide an overview of the `sendmail` program and SMTP servers. You'll learn how to use these in Unix and Windows programs later in the chapter.

The *sendmail* Program

The `sendmail` program sends messages to one or more recipients, routing the messages over whatever networks are necessary. This use of `sendmail` makes it easy for programs like the ones presented in this chapter to offload the dirty work of delivering e-mail to the intended recipients. To use `sendmail` in this way, you simply specify the recipients of the e-mail on the command line, and read the body of the message from the standard input stream. In this mode, `sendmail` reads to the end-of-file marker or to a single line that contains the period character (.) in the leftmost column.

You can also specify recipients by including them in special headers in the message input and using the –t switch. With the –t switch, `sendmail` scans the message for recipient addresses. Each line that contains a To:, Cc:, or Bcc: will be searched for e-mail addresses. The Bcc: line, which is used as a recipient address, is deleted before the message is sent. (If you didn't remove the recipient's address, then everyone could see who got the Bcc:, and it wouldn't be a blind copy.)

SMTP Servers

An SMTP server is an instance of a mail program like sendmail that operates as a daemon listening for incoming e-mail on port 25. When operating as an SMTP server, sendmail (or any other SMTP server program) listens for incoming e-mail messages. When a message is received, the SMTP server determines the correct routing for the e-mail message by examining the e-mail headers. Local e-mail messages are delivered to their mailboxes, and remote messages are forwarded to the next SMTP server along the route to the final destination.

The SMTP server only requires that you communicate with it in a formatted manner. You don't need a special e-mail tool to talk to your SMTP server. You can use Telnet to connect to your SMTP server and send an e-mail message directly from the command line.

Figure 16.1 shows a Telnet session to an SMTP server using the Windows Telnet client. The lines that begin with three-digit numbers are responses from the mail server. All the other lines were typed directly into the Telnet window. Some Telnet clients, including the Windows client, don't normally show what you, the user, are typing in, so you may have to change a setting to make your input visible. In the case of the Windows Telnet client, run the following sequence of commands:

```
telnet
set local_echo
open mailserver.domain.com 25
```

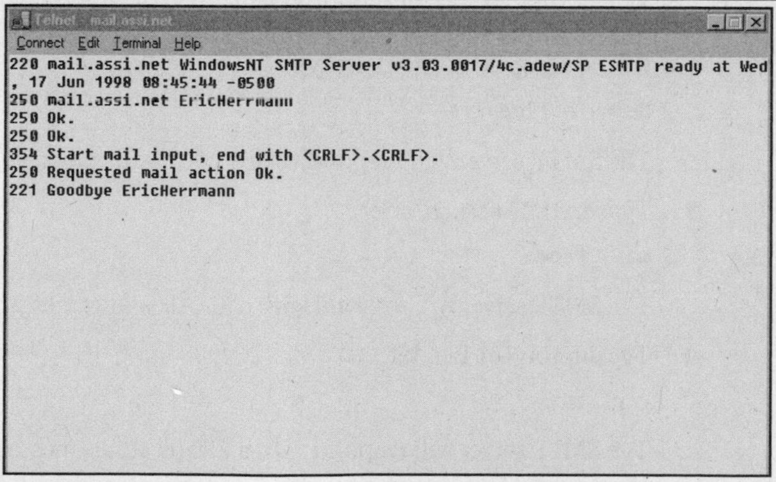

FIGURE 16.1:   A Telnet session to produce an e-mail message

The following steps show the procedure for using a Telnet session to send an e-mail message. The messages and their sequence are the same, whether you are connected to port 25 via Telnet or through a programmatic socket interface. After you issue each SMTP command, the SMTP server will respond with the appropriate status message, as shown in Figure 16.1. By following these steps in your program, you can successfully send e-mail messages from anywhere. The only difference is that in your program, you replace step 1 with a valid connection to the SMTP server:

1. From the command prompt (DOS or Unix), enter the following command, substituting the name of your SMTP server for *mail.somewhere.com*. (Press Enter after each command; SMTP commands are terminated with a newline character.)

    telnet *mail.somewhere.com 25*

    The SMTP server responds to the Telnet connection with a 220 status message.

NOTE

You must know the name of the SMTP server to which you wish to connect, because not all SMTP servers are named mail. The SMTP server's name is the name your e-mail client uses for sending e-mail. Look in the definition of the outgoing e-mail server in your favorite e-mail program; you can use that name as your SMTP server name.

2. Type the following command, substituting a computer name or something else for *YourIdentity* (any character string will be accepted as an identity):

    Helo *YourIdentity*

    The SMTP server will respond with a 250 status message.

3. Type in the From: header:

    mail from:

    The SMTP server will respond with a 250 Ok status message.

4. Type in the To: header.

    rcpt to:

    The SMTP server will respond with a 250 Ok status message.

5. Tell the SMTP server you are ready to send the e-mail message by entering the following command:

`data`

The SMTP server will respond with a 354 status message.

6. Type in additional `To:`, `From:`, `Bcc:`, `Cc:`, `Reply-To:`, `Subject:`, and other headers you want to send. When you're finished with the e-mail headers, enter a blank line. The SMTP server will not respond.

7. Type in the body of the message. When you are finished, type a dot (`.`) in the left-hand column on a line by itself, and then press Enter. The SMTP server will respond with a `250 Requested mail action Ok` message.

8. Disconnect from the SMTP server by typing:

`quit`

The SMTP server will respond with a `221 Goodbye` message.

Later in the chapter, you'll learn how to configure a Windows program, Blat, which uses the steps you just used to communicate with the `sendmail` SMTP server to send e-mail messages. The next section shows how to use the `sendmail` program from a Unix machine.

UNIX E-MAIL SOLUTIONS

From a Unix platform, you can use the `sendmail` program directly, without going through an e-mail client program such as Netscape mail, Eudora, or Outlook. The examples presented here include two common e-mail applications: one for sending and responding to an HTML registration form and one for sending personalized e-mail messages to a list of contact names.

A Registration Application

Let's begin with one of the more common uses for e-mail—transferring registration forms. This type of application includes a little HTML and CGI programming. Using an e-mail message is one of the easiest ways to process HTML form data and to notify yourself or your users of the new information.

The HTML E-Mail Form

Figure 16.2 shows an example of a registration form made up of text boxes, a pull-down menu, a text area box, and Register and Reset buttons. The form is generated by the HTML shown in Listing 16.1.

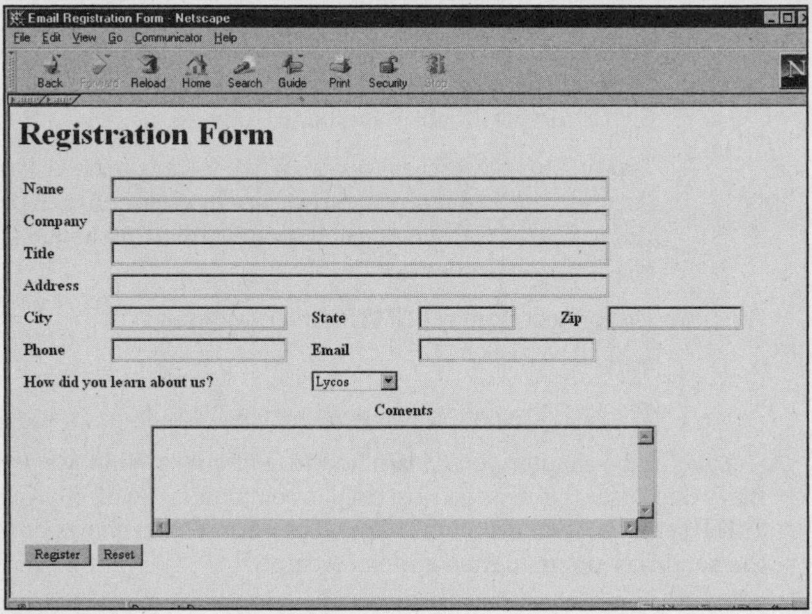

FIGURE 16.2: An e-mail registration form

Listing 16.1: An HTML E-Mail Form

```
1. <HTML>
2.   <HEAD>
3.     <TITLE>Email Registration Form</TITLE>
4.   </HEAD>
5.   <BODY>
6.     <H1>Registration Form</H1>
7.     <FORM METHOD=POST ACTION=
          "http://www.practical-inet.com/cgi-bin/perlBook
          ➥/registerEmail.cgi">
8.     <TABLE BORDER=1>
9.       <TR>
10.        <TH ALIGN="left">Name</TH>
11.        <TD COLSPAN="5">
```

```
12.          <INPUT NAME="Name" SIZE="60" TYPE="text">
13.          </TD>
14.        </TR>
15.        <TR>
16.          <TH ALIGN="left">Company</TH>
17.          <TD COLSPAN="5">
18.            <INPUT NAME="Company" SIZE="60" TYPE="text">
19.          </TD>
20.        </TR>
21.        <TR>
22.          <TH ALIGN="left">Title</TH>
23.          <TD COLSPAN="5">
24.            <INPUT NAME="Title" SIZE="60" TYPE="text">
25.          </TD>
26.        </TR>
27.        <TR>
28.          <TH ALIGN="left">Address</TH>
29.          <TD COLSPAN=5>
30.            <INPUT NAME="Address" SIZE="60" TYPE="text">
31.          </TD>
32.        </TR>
33.        <TR>
34.          <TH ALIGN="left">City</TH>
35.          <TD><INPUT SIZE=20 TYPE="text" Name=City></TD>
36.          <TH ALIGN="left">State</TH>
37.          <TD><INPUT SIZE=10 TYPE="text" Name=State></TD>
38.          <TH ALIGN="left">Zip</TH>
39.          <TD><INPUT SIZE=15 TYPE="text" Name=Zip></TD>
40.        </TR>
41.        <TR>
42.          <TH ALIGN="left">Phone</TH>
43.          <TD><INPUT SIZE=20 TYPE="text" Name=Phone></TD>
44.          <TH ALIGN="left">Email</TH>
45.          <TD COLSPAN=3>
46.            <INPUT SIZE=20 TYPE="text" Name=Email>
47.          </TD>
48.        </TR>
49.        <TR>
50.          <TH ALIGN="left">How did you learn about us?</TH>
51.          <TD COLSPAN=5>
52.          <SELECT name="Learn">
53.          <OPTION VALUE="radio">Radio</OPTION>
```

```
54.          <OPTION VALUE="Television">Television</OPTION>
55.          <OPTION VALUE="Lycos">Lycos</OPTION>
56.          <OPTION VALUE="Yahoo">Yahoo</OPTION>
57.          <OPTION VALUE="InfoSeek">Infoseek</OPTION>
58.          <OPTION VALUE="other">Other</OPTION>
59.          </SELECT>
60.          </TD>
61.       </TR>
62.       <TR>
63.          <TH COLSPAN=6>
64.             Comments<BR>
65.             <TEXTAREA ROWS=5 COLS="60" NAME="Comments">
66.             </TEXTAREA>
67.          </TH>
68.       </TR>
69.    </TABLE>
70.    <INPUT NAME="EmailRegister"
71.          TYPE="Submit" VALUE="Register">
72.    <INPUT TYPE="Reset">
73.    </FORM>
74.  </BODY>
75. </HTML>
```

Your CGI program doesn't care how the data is entered on your HTML form. All data generated from your HTML form and sent via the HTTP POST method header is translated the same way. Each HTML input tag, text area, text box, radio button, or option list is converted into URL-encoded name/value pairs, which your CGI program must decode. The address of the CGI program to receive and decode the data is on line 7 of Listing 16.1:

```
<FORM METHOD=POST ACTION="http://www.practical-inet.com
➥/cgi-bin/perlBook/registerEmail.cgi">
```

When your web client selects the Register button (refer to lines 70–72 of Listing 16.1), the browser generates the correct HTTP request headers, URL-encodes the data, and ships it to the web server identified in the action field of the HTML <FORM> tag.

The CGI Program to Respond to the HTML Form

Listing 16.2 processes the input received from the HTML registration form in Listing 16.1 and returns the page shown in Figure 16.3. Returning a Thank You page is more than just a courtesy to your web client—your CGI program must respond to every HTTP request with a valid HTTP response. The simplest HTTP response is another HTML web page.

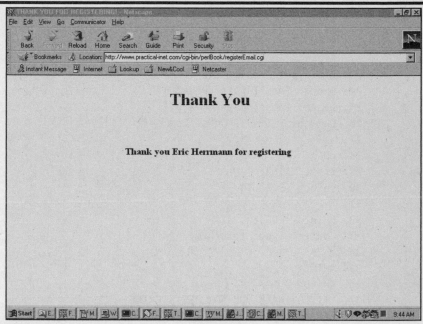

FIGURE 16.3:   E-mail Thank You web page

Listing 16.2: An E-Mail HTTP Response

```
1. #!/usr/bin/perl
2. require "readPostInput.cgi";
3.
4. %postInputs = readPostInput();
5. $time = scalar localtime();
6.
7. open (MAIL, "|/usr/sbin/sendmail -t") || return 0;
8.
9. select (MAIL);
10. print<<"EOF";
11. To: Eric.Herrmann\@assi.net
12. From: $postInputs{ 'email'}
13. Subject: Email Registration Received
14.
15. $time
```

```
16. Email Registration
17. Name: $postInputs{'Name'}
18. Email: $postInputs{'Email'}
19. Company Name: $postInputs{'Company'}
20. Street Address: $postInputs{'Address'}
21. City: $postInputs{'City'}
22. State : $postInputs{'State'}
23. Zip: $postInputs{'Zip'}
24. Phone: $postInputs{'Phone'}
25. Learn: $postInputs{'Learn'}
26. Comments: $postInputs{'Comments'}
27.
28. EOF
29. close(MAIL);
30. select (STDOUT);
31.
32. print<<"EOF";
33. Content-Type: text/html
34.
35. <HTML>
36. <HEAD>
37. <TITLE>THANK YOU FOR REGISTERING!</TITLE>
38. </HEAD>
39. <BODY>
40. <BR>
41. <CENTER>
42. <B>
43. <FONT SIZE=+3>Thank You</FONT>
44. <BR><BR>
45. <FONT SIZE=+1>
46. <P>Thank you $postInputs{'Name'} for registering</P>
47. </FONT>
48. </B>
49. </CENTER>
50. </BODY>
51. </HTML>
52. EOF
```

Listing 16.2 communicates with the Unix sendmail program, which you learned about at the beginning of this chapter. Line 4 of the listing reads the HTML POST input into the hash %postInputs:

```
%postInputs = readPostInput();
```

NOTE

The readPostInput subroutine was first introduced in Chapter 9, "Writing Your First Program." This subroutine uses a standard algorithm for decoding the URL-encoded data. The standard CGI.pm module also includes functionality for decoding the URL-encoded data.

The interface with the sendmail program begins on line 7:

```
open (MAIL, "|/usr/sbin/sendmail -t") || return 0;
```

Line 7 links the file handle with the sendmail program. If you want to communicate with a program, you open a pipe to it using the open function with the pipe symbol (|) instead of the file-input operator (<>). Line 9 selects the MAIL file handle as the default output handle to which print statements send their output.

The sendmail program requires the standard format, or e-mail headers, you see at the top of most e-mail messages. This format requires the To: and From: lines; the Subject: line is optional. The e-mail headers end with a blank line, which is then followed by the optional body of the e-mail message. You can send any information you want inside the body of the e-mail message. When the MAIL file handle is closed on line 29, your mail is sent via the sendmail program.

The HTML sent to the user, beginning at line 32, isn't sent until your communication with sendmail is completed. This can create a time delay between when the Register button is clicked and when the HTML Thank You page is received. You could write a CGI program that eliminates this delay by first sending the HTML Thank You page and then sending the e-mail message. However, depending on your web server's configuration, a CGI program may be considered to be operating improperly if it continues to process after responding to the HTML request. Because you rarely have control over where the final CGI program will be hosted, I recommend finishing your e-mail work before returning the HTTP response headers.

A Mailing List Application

Many word-processing programs, such as Microsoft Word, offer a mail merge feature that allows you to generate multiple personalized letters using a single letter template. You can write one form letter and send it to different people, with each person's name used in strategic places in your letter.

These days, many of us prefer to communicate via e-mail. Rather than producing multiple personalized letters, you can send e-mail to a lot of friends, relatives, or business clients by using the program in Listing 16.3.

Listing 16.3: Personalized E-Mail to a Contact List

```perl
1. #!/usr/bin/perl
2. if (@ARGV < 2){
3.   print "USAGE: $0 contact_list letter\n";
4.   exit 1;
5. }
6.
7. $contactFile = $ARGV[0];
8. $letterFile = $ARGV[1];
9.
10. open (CONTACTLIST, $contactFile)
11.   or die "Can't open $contactFile: $!\n";
12. @contacts = <CONTACTLIST>;
13. close (CONTACTLIST);
14.
15. open (LETTER, $letterFile)
16.   or die "Can't open $letterFile: $!\n";
17. @letter = <LETTER>;
18. close (LETTER);
19.
20. $count = 0;
21. for $contact (@contacts) {
22.   $count++;
23.
24.   ($companyName,$emailAddress,$FLName) =
                        split(/,/,$line);
25.   $emailAddress =~ s/\s+//g;
26.   $FLName =~ /\s*(\w+)\s+(\w+)/;
27.   ($firstName,$lastName) = ($1,$2);
28.
29.   open (MAIL, "|/usr/sbin/sendmail -t")
30.     or die "Can't open pipe to sendmail\n";
31.   select (MAIL);
32.
33.   $returnAddress = 'Eric.Herrmann@assi.net';
34.   print<<"EOF";
```

```
35. To: $emailAddress
36. From: $returnAddress
37. Subject: $companyName
38.
39. EOF
40.    for ( @letter ) {
41.       s/#companyName/$companyName/g;
42.       s/#firstName/$firstName/g;
43.       s/#lastName/$lastName/g;
44.       print;
45.    } # for
46.    close (MAIL);
47.    print STDOUT
            "Sent to $firstName $lastName at $companyName\n";
48. } # for $line
49.
50. print STDOUT "\nYou sent $count emails\n";
```

Listing 16.3 uses a contact list and a form letter to send personalized e-mail messages to a list of e-mail address and names. The program gets both filenames—for the contact list and the form letter files—from the command line. This is a Unix interface, but later in this chapter you'll learn how to use the Mail::Sender module, which allows you to create a Perl e-mail interface on both a Unix and Windows computer.

The contact list read in on line 10 of Listing 16.3 is formatted so that each line is made up of a company name, e-mail address, and recipient's name, all separated by commas. The contact name is expected to be a first and last name, separated by a space. The contact list is read into an array and then processed one line at a time. Here's a sample:

```
Petdance Industries,pcjc@petdance.com,Andy Lester
Microsoft,bill@microsoft.com,Bill Gates
```

The form letter file contains the text of the letter to be sent to the recipients. Any occurrences of the special strings #firstName, #lastName, and #companyName are replaced by the appropriate strings when the mail is sent. Here's a sample letter:

```
Dear #firstName,

How are things at your company, #companyName?

I hope all is well with the #lastName family.
```

Each time a new e-mail message is sent, a new connection is made to the `sendmail` program at line 29.

```
open (MAIL, "|/usr/sbin/sendmail -t")
    or die "Can't open pipe to sendmail\n";
```

Making a connection to a program always requires some extra processing time. Usually, it is faster to open a connection and keep it open as long as you are communicating with the other program. In the case of Listing 16.3, opening and closing a pipe to `sendmail` is slower than opening a connection and sending multiple e-mail messages through that one connection. If it is slow, why do it this way? You open and close a pipe to `sendmail` for two important reasons:

▶ You can start the program in Listing 16.3 and leave it running. You don't need to be concerned with whether it takes 10 minutes or 10 hours to run. It's not slowing your machine or your work. The time involved in running the program revolves around making a single connection to `sendmail` to send a single letter.

▶ Each mailing is an individual e-mail delivery, which keeps the e-mail message as personal as possible, considering it is a form letter. The letter may read like a form letter (depending on the author's writing skill), but it will look like an individual e-mail message because it is sent individually.

One alternative to this method of sending e-mail involves opening a connection to `sendmail` and sending a blast of e-mail messages with a lot of CC: or BCC: lines. But how personal would the e-mail message seem when its recipients see a lengthy CC: list?

The message is personalized on lines 33 through 37 of Listing 16.3:

```
$returnAddress = 'Eric.Herrmann@assi.net';
print<<"EOF";
To: $emailAddress
From: $returnAddress
Subject: $companyName
```

The subject line of each e-mail includes the recipient's company name. (If your recipients are like me, they will probably toss any e-mail that looks like a spam that has nothing to do with them.)

Lines 40 through 45 process each line of the letter, looking for the unique characters #companyName, #firstName, and #lastName. Each time one of these character strings is matched, all occurrences of those characters are replaced with the actual company name, first name, or last name retrieved from the contact list:

```
for ( @letter ) {
    s/#companyName/$companyName/g;
    s/#firstName/$firstName/g;
    s/#lastName/$lastName/g;
    print;
} # for
```

TIP

If you're going to send form letters, take the time to personalize them. Your recipients will appreciate the extra effort, and they are more likely to read the letter.

WINDOWS E-MAIL SOLUTIONS

Sending e-mail from a Perl program running on a Windows computer can be a pain in the neck if you don't have some type of interface to an SMTP server. As explained earlier in this chapter, opening up a Telnet session on port 25 to your Internet Service Provider's SMTP server is possible but not very practical. Here, you'll learn about two interfaces to SMTP servers. One is a freeware program, and the other is a module that provides a direct Perl–to–e-mail interface.

Blat: A Windows E-Mail Program

Originally intended as only a command-line interface, Blat became popular as a programming interface because it is the cheapest game in town. Blat is freeware, available from `http://www.interlog.com/~tcharron/blat.html`.

Blat is available in the public domain for you to use and/or modify. As is the case with all types of public domain programs, many people have helped to make Blat a useful and easy-to-install SMTP interface. The following sections explain how to install and use Blat.

Blat Installation

Current versions of Blat install easily. Copy the file `Blat.exe` to your `\WINNT\SYSTEM32` directory or to any other directory in your path. Then, install the configuration with this command:

```
blat -install mail.yourDomain.com yourName@yourDomain.com
```

Of course, substitute your SMTP server's name and your e-mail address in this example. If you don't know your SMTP server's name, look in your existing mail program's configuration setup. For example, my ISP's SMTP server is located at `mail.io.com`.

After you install Blat, when you send mail from the command line using Blat, it will try to connect to an SMTP server at `mail.yourDomain.com`. It will identify all e-mail messages as coming from `yourName@yourDomain.com`.

Blat in Action

Blat is designed as a command-line program for sending the contents of a file as the body of an e-mail message. You can also use Blat from within Perl programs.

To send a file as an e-mail message, use this syntax:

```
blat filename.txt -t yourName@yourDomain.com
```

This command sends the contents of the specified file to the specified e-mail address.

Blat version 1.9.4 (the current release at the time of this writing) has several command-line options that allow you to send binary files, send the same message multiple times, and read input from STDIN. These options are listed in Table 16.1.

TABLE 16.1: Common Blat Options

Option	Parameter	Description
-	None	For console input, end input with Ctrl+Z
-attach	*<file>*	Attach a binary file to the message (may be repeated)
-c	*<recipient>*	Carbon-copy recipient list (comma-separated)
-b	*<recipient>*	Blind carbon-copy recipient list (comma-separated)
-base64	None	MIME Base64 content transfer encoding
-f	*<sender>*	Override the default sender address (the new address must be known to server)
-h	None	Display help
-I	*<address>*	A From: address, not necessarily known to the SMTP server (*<address>* is included in the message header's Reply-to: and Sender: fields)

TABLE 16.1 continued: Common Blat Options

OPTION	PARAMETER	DESCRIPTION
-mime	None	MIME quoted printable content transfer encoding
-o	*<organization>*	Set Organization: to appear in the header fields
-p	*<profile>*	Use the stored profile for the -server, -sender, -try, and -port options
-port	None	Override the default port on the server
-q	None	Suppress all output
-s	*<subject>*	Subject line (if you do not include a subject line, the subject "contents of console input" will be sent)
-server	*<address>*	Override the default SMTP server to be used
-t	*<recipient>*	Recipient list (comma-separated)
-try	None	Set how many times Blat should try to send a message

The -q (suppress all output) and - (console input) options are important from a programmer's viewpoint. The -q option means your program doesn't have to worry about output from Blat appearing in the web page your user sees. The - option means your program can send data directly to the Blat program.

The programmer's interface to Blat can be finicky. Blat works flawlessly from the command line, but a misplaced switch or quote character stops the program without any helpful error messages. If you use Blat in your code, I suggest using one of the two subroutines in Listing 16.4; they make Blat a useful e-mail tool for Windows programmers.

Listing 16.4: The Blat Interface

```
 1. $msg = "Testing the Blat Interface\n";
 2. $blatexe = 'c:\winnt\system32\blat.exe';
 3.
 4. blatSTDIN( 'test@test.com', 'Eric@assi.net',
              "test blat", $msg);
 5. sub blatSTDIN {
 6.    my ($toName, $fromName, $subject, $message) = @_;
 7.    $blat = "$blatexe - -t $toName -s \"$subject\" -q";
 8.    open( MAIL, "| $blat -f \"$fromName\"" ) || die $!;
 9.    print MAIL $message;
10.    print MAIL "TESTING BLAT STDIN\n";
```

```
11.     close MAIL;
12. }
13.
14. blatFILE( 'test@test.com', 'Eric@assi.net',
            "test blat", $msg);
15. sub blatFILE {
16.     my ($toName, $fromName, $subject, $message) = @_;
17.     my $tmpfile = "tmp-$$";
18.     open( OUTFILE, ">$tmpfile" );
19.     print OUTFILE $message;
20.     print OUTFILE "Testing FILE interface\n";
21.     close( OUTFILE );
22.     system( "$blatexe $tmpfile -t $toName
        ➥-s \"$subject\" -q" );
23.     unlink( $tmpfile );
24. }
```

On line 7, the subroutine blatSTDIN uses the - (console input) option to force Blat to get its input from STDIN, or, in this case, from the open MAIL file handle. It also uses the -q (suppress all output) option. The blatSTDIN subroutine produces the e-mail message shown in Figure 16.4.

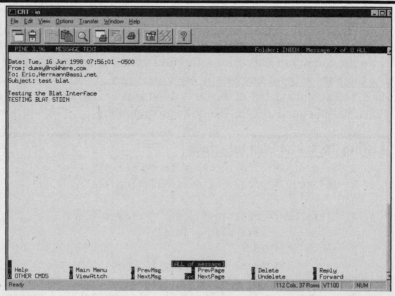

FIGURE 16.4:   Sending a Blat mail message from the open file handle

You might notice that Figure 16.4 uses a spoofed e-mail address (hiding the original address). Obviously, dummy@noWhere.com did not send this message. Blat allows you to change the From: e-mail address, but it always includes the registered e-mail address of the login process executing the Blat program in the Reply-to: header.

When you test Blat on your computer, expand the headers to show the entire path. You'll see the name of the SMTP server Blat connects to, the name of the computer that connected to the SMTP server, and the e-mail address of the person logged in to the computer that executed the Blat program. Blat is not a good tool if you are trying to hide the original sender's address.

NOTE

Blat uses an SMTP feature called *server relay*. This feature is often used to spoof e-mail addresses, hiding the original sender of the e-mail. My primary ISP does not allow this type of e-mail routing. It compares the address of the original message with the address of the sender, and if the address did not originate on my ISP's domain, the ISP does not relay the message. Check with your ISP to see how its servers are configured and to make sure that your e-mail sending doesn't violate any of the ISP's policies.

Lines 17 and 18 create an output file handle to a file whose name is based on the current process ID of the script:

```
my $tmpfile = "tmp-$$";
open( OUTFILE, ">$tmpfile" );
```

The process ID is guaranteed to be unique among all the processes currently executing, thereby creating a unique temporary filename. For example, if the process ID is 6789, you'll be using tmp-6789 as a filename. Note that it's possible (but not likely) that a file with the same filename already exists, in which case this program would overwrite it.

Lines 19 and 20 write your message to the file:

```
print OUTFILE $message;
print OUTFILE "Testing FILE interface\n";
```

Before you send your message, you must close your temporary file. Doing so makes sure the output buffers are flushed and any system file locks are released.

Line 22 uses the command-line interface of Blat to send the temporary file as an e-mail message (see Figure 16.5).

```
system( "$blatexe $tmpfile -t $toName  -s \"$subject\" -q" );
```

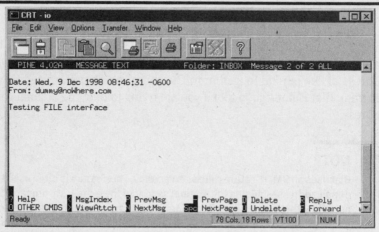

FIGURE 16.5:   Sending a Blat e-mail message from a file

Line 23 cleans up the temporary file, deleting it from your computer:

```
unlink ($tmpfile);
```

Mail::Sender: A Perl E-Mail Interface

In this section, you'll learn about Mail::Sender, a Perl module that provides a direct Perl interface to the SMTP server. The Mail::Sender module can be used on any platform that has a connection to an SMTP server. If you can send and receive e-mail, you probably can use Mail::Sender. The CPAN site includes an older module called Net::SMTP, which can also be used as a programmer's e-mail interface. However, I think Mail::Sender is easier to use—to send an e-mail, you only need to create a Sender object and call the MailMsg method.

In this section, you'll learn how easy it is to use Mail::Sender, and then you will progressively step into the methods that perform the actual connections to the SMTP server. When you are finished with this chapter, you'll know how to use Mail::Sender and why and how it works. If you decide to extend Mail::Sender or implement your own SMTP interface, you'll know how to proceed.

TIP

The Mail::Sender module was written by Jan Krynicky (Jenda@Krynicky .cz). She says this was her first module, and she had been writing Perl code for less than two years (as of the writing of this chapter). Congratulations are certainly in order; her code makes the interface to an SMTP server easier to understand. Mail::Sender and other modules by Jan are available from http://search.cpan.org/~jenda. Jan tells me she lives in the Czech Republic, which is east of Germany, south of Poland, and north of Austria. As far as I am concerned, Jan is at the end of the next e-mail message, only a click away. Country boundaries just don't matter any more!

Why do I like the Mail::Sender module so much? Listing 16.5 shows the reason.

Listing 16.5: The *Mail::Sender* Module

```
1.   use Mail::Sender;
2.   $sender = new Mail::Sender({ from => 'yawp@io.com',
3.                                smtp => 'mail.assi.net'} );
4.
5.   if (!(ref $sender) =~ /Sender/i){
6.     die $Mail::Sender::Error;
7.   }
8.
9.   $sender->MailMsg({ to =>'Eric.Herrmann@assi.net',
10.                     subject => 'Testing Sender',
11.                     msg => "An easy email interface?"} );
12.
13. if ( $sender >{'error'}) {
14.     print "ERROR: $Mail::Sender::Error\n";
15. }
16. else {
17.     print "Msg Sent Ok\n";
18. }
```

What could be easier? There are only two real lines of functional code in Listing 16.5; the rest of it is error-checking code. All that is required to send a mail message using Mail::Sender is initializing the $sender object with a From: address and a valid SMTP server to connect to. This is done on lines 2 and 3 (which contain just one Perl statement):

```
$sender = new Mail::Sender({ from => 'yawp@io.com',
                             smtp => 'mail.assi.net'} );
```

Then, all you need to do is call `MailMsg` method with your instance of a Sender object, providing the recipient address, subject line, and a message. This is done on lines 9 through 11 (which again contain only a single Perl statement):

```
$sender->MailMsg({ to =>'Eric.Herrmann@assi.net',
                   subject => 'Testing Sender',
                   msg => "An easy email interface?"} );
```

If you want to send a longer message, create a variable—either a scalar or an array of strings—and send the variable in the message field. To send a file or several files, use the `MailFile` syntax, as explained in the section *"Mail::Sender* Method Syntax."

Listing 16.5 uses several groups of Sender methods that work together to send an e-mail message. You'll learn more about using the Sender methods shortly. First, let's see how to use the lower-level and more direct methods of this module, which better illustrate the steps involved in communicating with the SMTP server.

Mail::Sender Communication with an SMTP Server

Rather than the code in Listing 16.5, you can use the more direct methods shown in Listing 16.6 to send an e-mail message. This example, which sends a binary file as an e-mail attachment, illustrates each of the steps you learned earlier in the section "SMTP Servers" to use an SMTP server through a Telnet connection. Listing 16.5 is more practical for everyday use, but it doesn't demonstrate the SMTP interface through `Mail::Sender` as well as Listing 16.6.

Listing 16.6: *Mail::Sender* **Module Lower-Level Methods**

```
1. use Mail::Sender;
2.
3. $sender = new Mail::Sender({
4.     from => 'yawp@io.com',
5.     smtp => 'chimpy.petdance.com'
6. } );
7. die $Mail::Sender::Error
8.     unless ref($sender) =~ /Mail::Sender/;
9.
10. $sender->OpenMultipart( {
11.     to =>'pcjc@petdance.com',
12.     subject => 'Testing Sender Direct I/F'
```

```
13. } );
14. $sender->SendFile({
15.     description => 'Chapter 16 image 2',
16.     ctype => 'image/tiff',
17.     encoding => 'Base64',
18.     disposition =>
19.         'attachment; filename="F0904.tif"; type="tiff"',
20.     file => 'F0904.tif',
21. } );
22. $sender->Close;
23.
24. if ( $sender->{'error'} < 0 ) {
25.     print "ERROR: $Mail::Sender::Error\n";
26. } else {
27.     print "Msg Sent Ok\n";
28. }
```

Listing 16.6 shows the steps required when communicating with the SMTP server. The SMTP communication works in the following order:

1. Connect.

2. Say hello.

3. Tell the server who is sending the e-mail.

4. Tell the server whom you are sending e-mail to.

5. Tell the SMTP server you are sending it data.

6. Send the mail headers.

7. Complete the OpenMultipart message headers line on line 11 by sending the body.

The remaining lines send the file attachment and then disconnect from the SMTP server.

The following section describes the syntax and use of the various methods. After you learn the complete syntax of the main methods of Mail::Sender, you'll step through the lower-level code that makes the connection to the SMTP server.

Mail::Sender Method Syntax

The Mail::Sender module uses object-oriented syntax. The module's new method initializes the Sender object so that the Sender methods listed in Table 16.2 can use the default values. Table 16.3 lists the default Sender method parameters. You can override each of the default parameters by explicitly passing the value in the appropriate method.

TABLE 16.2: Common Mail::Sender Methods

METHOD	DESCRIPTION
Body	Send the head of the multipart message body. You can specify the character set and the encoding. The default is "US- ASCII","7BIT".
Cancel	Cancel an opened message.
Close	Close and send the mail.
MailMsg(*msg*)	Send a message.
MailFile(*msg, file*)	Send one or more files by e-mail.
new	Prepare a Sender.
Open	Open a new message.
OpenMultipart	Open a multipart message.
Part	Print a part header for the multipart message. The undef or empty variables are ignored.
Send(@*strings*)	Print the strings to the socket. Don't add any end-of-line characters. Use \r\n as the end-of-line characters.
SendEnc(@*strings*)	Print the strings to the socket. Don't add any end-of-line characters. Use \r\n as the end-of-line characters. Encode the text using the selected encoding (Base64/Quoted-printable).
SendEx(@*strings*)	Print the strings to the socket. Don't add any end-of-line characters, but change all end-of-line characters to \r\n.
SendFile(*file*)	In multipart mode, send a file as a separate part of the mail message.
SendLine(@*strings*)	Print the strings to the socket. Add the end-of-line character at the end.
SendLineEnc(@*strings*)	Print the strings to the socket. Add the end-of-line character at the end. Encode the text using the selected encoding (Base64/Quoted-printable).
SendLineEx(@*strings*)	Print the strings to the socket. Don't add any end-of-line characters, but change all end-of-line characters to \r\n.

WARNING

Do not mix up SendEx and SendEnc or SendLineEx and SendLineEnc. SendEnc and SendLineEnc do some buffering necessary for correct Base64 encoding, and the Send method (which does the actual sending of the message) is not aware of that. Using SendLine and SendLineEx in non–7-bit parts is not recommended. In particular, if you use SendLine or SendLineEx to send several lines, eventually creating a single message, the data is likely to become corrupted.

TABLE 16.3: Default Sender Method Parameters

PARAMETER	DESCRIPTION
From	The address of the sender of the e-mail message
Replyto	The address at which the e-mail message should be replied to
To	The recipient's e-mail address
Smtp	The IP or domain address of the SMTP being connected to
Subject	The subject line of the e-mail message
Headers	Any additional headers sent before the body of the message
Boundary	The message boundary

The Mail::Sender methods return detailed failure information, as shown in Table 16.4. The method Mail::Sender::Error contains a textual description of the last error.

TABLE 16.4: Mail::Sender Method Failure Codes

CODE	MEANING
-1	SMTP host unknown
-2	Socket failed
-3	Connect failed
-4	Service not available
-5	Unspecified communication error
-6	Local user $to unknown on host $smtp

TABLE 16.4 continued: Mail::Sender Method Failure Codes

CODE	MEANING
-7	Transmission of message failed
-8	Argument $to empty
-9	No message specified in call to MailMsg or MailFile
-10	No filename specified in call to SendFile or MailFile
-11	File not found
-12	Not available in single-part mode

Most of the methods of Mail::Sender are straightforward and don't require a special explanation. The following are some of the more important methods or those that do not follow the default syntax.

new   This method is used to initialize a Sender object and must be called before any other Sender method. It initializes the default parameters listed in Table 16.3. You can set smtp, from, and other parameters here and then use the information in all messages.

The new method does not open a connection to the SMTP server. You must use $Sender->Open or $Sender->OpenMultipart to begin talking to the server. The parameters passed to the new method are used in subsequent calls to $Sender->Open and $Sender->OpenMultipart. Each call to a method with new default parameters, such as the to or from address, changes the variables initialized by the new method. If the new method is successful, it returns a reference variable to a Mail::Sender object. If a mail message in $sender is opened, it is closed and a new mail message is created and sent. $sender is then closed. The file parameter may be a filename, a list of filenames (separated by commas), or a reference to a list of filenames.

Close   Although this method does not require any parameters, it is important to note that the mail message being sent to the server is not processed until the Sender object is closed. The Close method should be called automatically when destroying the object, but you should call it yourself just to be sure—and you should do it as soon as possible to close the connection and free the socket.

Part   This method prints a part header for the multipart message. It accepts the following special parameters:

> ***ctype***   Defines the content type (MIME type) of this part. This parameter defaults to `"application/octet-stream"`.
>
> ***encoding***   Defines the encoding used for this part of message. This parameter defaults to `"7BIT"`.
>
> ***disposition***   Defines the type of e-mail as a message or an attachment. This parameter defaults to `"attachment"`.

SendFile   This method sends a file as a separate part of the e-mail message and operates only in multipart mode. `SendFile` accepts the same parameters as the `Part` method and, in addition, accepts the `file` parameter. The `file` parameter identifies the name of the file to send, a list of filenames, or a reference to a list of filenames. Each file will be sent as a separate part.

MailFile   This method lets you send a file or several files. For example, using the `MailFile` method, you can replace lines 10 through 21 of Listing 16.6 with this one simple call:

```
MailFile ({ msg=> "msg", file => 'f0904.tif'} );
```

MailMsg   This method sends the message. If a mail message in `$sender` is already open, it is closed, which sends the message, and a new mail message is then created and sent. `$sender` is then closed. The `MailMsg` method shows the exact sequence and syntax necessary for your program to communicate with the SMTP server. If you want to build your own interface to the SMTP server, you should study this method.

SUMMARY

When you learn how to program in Perl 5, you get to use and write some cool applications. In this chapter, you learned about coding Perl applications that use one of the earliest and most widely used tools of the Internet— e-mail. You can use the examples presented in this chapter as a starting point for your own HTML and e-mail programs.

Most e-mail programs on the Internet communicate through the `sendmail` daemon. The `sendmail` program, when run as a daemon, is frequently referred to as your SMTP server. The SMTP server is responsible for routing e-mail messages from domain to domain, across the network. Although it's more convenient to use an interface program to talk with your SMTP server, in this chapter you also learned the commands necessary to communicate with an SMTP server using a Telnet session.

After you learned about the `sendmail` program and SMTP servers, you saw an example of one of the more common CGI applications—reading an HTML registration form and sending an e-mail response. Then you learned more about the `sendmail` program through a Perl 5 interface program that sends form letters to a mailing list.

There is a growing demand for e-mail applications that run on a Windows computer. In this chapter, you learned about a Windows freeware program called Blat. Blat is an interface program to your SMTP server. To avoid problems with the Blat interface, you can use the two subroutines included in this section. The `blatSTDIN` subroutine sends e-mail messages directly through your program, and the `blatFILE` subroutine uses a file interface to send e-mail messages.

Finally, you learned about the `Mail::Sender` module. Perl 5 comes delivered with an SMTP interface module called `Net::SMTP`, but I think `Mail::Sender` is easier to use. With fewer than 20 lines of code and this module, you can send e-mail messages and attach files.

WHAT'S NEXT

In our next chapter, we'll put extra power into your Perl programs by allowing them to access databases. You'll learn about Perl's powerful set of DBI modules, as well as the SQL language, which allows flexible queries to get exactly the data your website needs.

Chapter 17

DATABASES AND THE WEB

Perl can do a lot more than just process form requests and send e-mail to the right person. You can use Perl together with many of the same facilities and systems you use for processing forms, to provide access to an external database.

If you think about a typical database application, there are really only four potential operations: listing, adding, updating, and deleting. If you can access the information in a database, then you can use Perl to format and display that data—in HTML, if necessary, if the data will be viewed on the Web. You already know you can create and process the contents of HTML forms, and a logical extension of that process is to take the information and update a database. You just need to interface to a database system and submit and update the records it stores. And if you can get that far, then deleting records should be easy.

Several things are required to do all this in Perl. Primarily, you need a database engine to store your data. In addition, you need a way of communicating with the engine from within Perl. You also have to know how to make the two talk to each other, and to your web browser.

● ●

Written for *Perl, CGI, and JavaScript Complete*
by Martin C. Brown
ISBN 0-7821-4213-3

In this chapter we'll look at installing and using the MySQL database system and the DBI toolkit that talks to MySQL. You will see how to create an application that uses all three plus HTML and a web browser to provide a web-based database management application.

Perl, MySQL, and DBI

Perl has a number of databases systems built in. The DBM-based systems, such as DBM, NDBM, and Berkeley DB, all provide a storage format that essentially matches the key/value pair system used by the internal hash variable type in Perl. Although this format is relatively flexible, it limits your options if you want to store more structured data. To store records that have a number of fields with different value types using DBM, you must jump through all sorts of hoops, not least of which is searching the database for the information you want. A much better solution is to use a proper database engine. You can then create tables that hold information stored in individual rows (or records) and rely on the database engine to search and retrieve the information you want.

In Perl, the main interface to any type of external database engine is called Database Interface (DBI). This is a generic API to all sorts of database engines. For our example, we'll use MySQL, which is probably the best open-source database engine available. You may even have it installed on your machine already.

Installing MySQL

MySQL is a relational database system that provides access to database tables using Structured Query Language (SQL). SQL is like any other language: You use a series of keywords to perform different operations. For example, in SQL you use the SELECT keyword to retrieve the rows of a table and the INSERT keyword to put data into a table.

MySQL is an open-source database solution, so you can use it on your machines without having to purchase the software. Because it's open-source, it's very reliable and supported on a wide variety of platforms. You can get MySQL for most flavors of Unix (including Linux, Solaris, and Mac OS X) and most Windows variants.

You can install MySQL using either the binary installation or the source-based installation. The former is the quickest way—you just download the corresponding binary package from the MySQL website (http://www.mysql.com) and follow the installation instructions to install it on your machine. If you choose the source-based installation, then you will need a C compiler to be able to build MySQL. Although this method takes slightly longer and is a bit more complicated, you have more flexibility over where you want to install the different MySQL components. Once the basic installation has completed, make sure you follow the additional instructions to set up an administration account and start your MySQL database engine.

With the database up and running, you need to create the database that will hold the tables for your application. MySQL allows you to set up an unlimited number of databases, and each database has a list of tables, indices, and other information. By using separate databases, you can limit and control access to sets of tables. In addition, this arrangement lets you migrate an individual database (and therefore all its tables) from one machine to another easily.

To create a new database, you use the mysqladmin command with the create option:

```
$ mysqladmin create property
```

This command creates a database called property. You can now connect to the property database using the command-line MySQL interpreter, mysql:

```
$ mysql property
Reading table information for completion of table and
  column names
You can turn off this feature to get a
  quicker startup with -A

Welcome to the MySQL monitor.  Commands end with ; or \g.
Your MySQL connection id is 5200 to server version: 3.23.36

Type 'help;' or '\h' for help. Type '\c' to clear the buffer

mysql>
```

If you want to protect your database so that a username and password are required to access it, then you need to use the GRANT SQL statement. Check the MySQL documentation for more information.

Installing DBI

The DBI toolkit is a generic interface to several database systems. The DBI element provides a consistent API to any database system from Perl—you can use the same functions to execute queries, retrieve rows, and update the database. Between DBI and the database is a database driver (DBD) that translates required operations for the functions you call in the DBI system into the necessary calls to the database engine to make the requests.

The benefit of the DBD system is that the main DBI API remains constant. Thus it's possible to use the same application with more than one database—MySQL, PostGreSQL, even text files—just by changing the way you connect to the database. All the methods used to access the information stored within the database once the connection has been made remain the same.

For the sample database, you need to install the DBI module and a suitable DBD for communicating with MySQL. It's easiest to use the CPAN module to install these modules into your Perl distribution for you. To use CPAN, in shell mode, type:

```
$ perl -MCPAN -e shell
cpan shell -- CPAN exploration and modules
   installation (v1.63)
ReadLine support available (try 'install Bundle::CPAN')

cpan>
```

NOTE
If you haven't already set up CPAN, you'll need to go through the initial configuration. In most cases, you can just press Return to use the default option; however, you will need to set the location of your nearest CPAN mirrors so CPAN knows where to download the modules from.

Once CPAN is set up, type the following to install the DBI bundle, including everything you need to use DBI with your Perl installation:

```
cpan> install Bundle::DBI
```

The configuration, compilation, and installation should occur automatically. Note that you need a C compiler in order to install the DBI system on your machine.

Install the MySQL database driver type as follows:

```
cpan> install Bundle::DBD::mysql
```

Follow the on-screen instructions. You'll be asked to provide the location of your MySQL installation (usually /usr/local/ under Unix/Linux) before the installation can complete.

Connecting Perl to MySQL

To open a connection to your MySQL database, you need to first load the DBI module and then use the connect() function to create a new database object. The argument to the connect() function is called the Data Source Name (DSN), and it defines which database driver you want to use and any additional database-specific options. Additional arguments to the function specify a username and password if required to access the database.

For example, to connect to a MySQL database, you might use a DSN like this:

```
use DBI;
my $dbh = DBI->connect("DBI:mysql:tv","myuser","mypw");
```

This command tells the DBI system to open a connection to a MySQL database called tv using a username and password.

The return value from the connect() function is a DBI object (called a *database handle*) that you use to communicate with the database. Additional methods to this object are used to send an SQL statement, create multirow queries, and receive and extract information from the database.

The connection is persistent—until you close it or until the script terminates, you can continue to use the database handle throughout your script. You do not need to continually open a new connection to the database. It's a good idea, therefore, to use a global variable in your script; or, if you are building a secondary interface to your database, it's wise to incorporate the database handle into your objects.

To close the connection, you use the disconnect() method on your database handle:

```
$dbh->disconnect();
```

QUICK SQL GUIDE

Before we go any further, let's look at the basics of the SQL language so you know how to write a simple query that requests or updates information in the database.

Syntax for *SELECT, INSERT, UPDATE,* and *DELETE* Statements

Essentially, four main SQL statements can be executed on an SQL database: SELECT, INSERT, UPDATE, and DELETE. You also use a fifth statement,

CREATE, which creates new objects (tables and indexes) within the database; of course, in most situations, you'll use CREATE only once.

SELECT

When you want to extract information from the database, you use the SELECT statement. The SELECT statement retrieves a set of rows and columns from the database, returning a dataset.

The basic format of the SELECT statement is

```
SELECT field [, field, ...]
FROM table
[WHERE condition]
ORDER BY field [ASC|DESC] [, field [ASC|DESC]]
```

The *field* is the name (or names) of the fields you want to select from the *table*. Because the SELECT statement allows you to specify the individual fields you want to extract from the table, you can avoid many problems normally associated with extracting data from a database. Instead of manually ignoring the fields you don't want to access, you can instead select only the fields you want. You can also specify an asterisk as the *field* name to select all fields in the table.

The WHERE condition allows you to specify the conditions under which a row should be extracted. For example, to extract a specific acronym from a database of acronyms, you might use:

```
SELECT Acronym FROM Acronyms WHERE Acronym = 'AAMOF'
```

The ORDER BY clause specifies which fields should be used to sort the information. You can select either ASC (ascending) or DESC (descending) order.

INSERT

The INSERT statement adds a row of information to a table. An INSERT statement has the following syntax:

```
INSERT INTO table
[(colname [, colname ] ... )]
VALUES (value [, value ] ... )
```

table is the name of a table into which the data will be inserted, and *colname* and *value* are the field names and corresponding values that you want to insert into the table. The field names and values should (obviously) match, to ensure that the information is inserted correctly;

alternatively, if you are inserting data into all the fields, you can omit the list of field names.

For example, to add a new record to the acronym database, you might use the following SQL statement:

```
INSERT INTO Acronyms (Acronym, Expansion)
VALUES ('PDQ', 'Pretty Darn Quick')
```

Because you are creating entries in both columns, you can simplify the statement:

```
INSERT INTO Acronyms VALUES ('PDQ', 'Pretty Darn Quick')
```

UPDATE

The UPDATE statement updates the information for one or more rows in a table. The syntax for the UPDATE statement is

```
UPDATE table
SET column=value
[, column=value ...]
[WHERE condition]
```

table is the name of the table in the database. *column* and *value* are the column names and values that you want to assign to those columns. If the WHERE keyword is included, then the statement updates only those columns that match *condition*. The condition uses the same operators and syntax as the SELECT statement. Note that if the condition matches multiple rows, all the rows will be updated with the given information.

For example, you can modify the entry for IIRC in the acronyms database as follows:

```
UPDATE Acronyms SET Expansion='If I Recall Correctly'
WHERE Acronym='IIRC'
```

Note that this statement updates all the IIRC entries in the table. You could supply a more specific statement to ensure you update the correct row:

```
UPDATE Acronyms SET Expansion='If I Recall Correctly'
WHERE Acronym='IIRC' AND Expansion='If I Remember Correctly'
```

DELETE

The DELETE statement is essentially identical to the SELECT statement, except that instead of returning a matching list of rows from a table, it deletes the rows from the database:

```
DELETE [FROM] table [WHERE condition]
```

table is the name of the table from which you want to delete rows, and *condition* is the expression to use to find the rows to be deleted. The FROM keyword is optional on some database drivers; check the documentation for more information.

For example, you can delete all the IIRC entries from the acronyms table as follows:

```
DELETE FROM Acronyms WHERE Acronym = 'IIRC'
```

You can also delete all the rows in a table by omitting the search condition:

```
DELETE FROM Acronyms
```

CREATE

If you are developing a database system, occasionally you'll need to build your tables pragmatically within Perl. One major benefit of creating databases this way is that you can transport an application to another machine and have the script create the tables it needs to operate. Not all databases support the creation of database tables. Many have some constraints or limitations on what can be done with a CREATE statement.

The basic format for a CREATE statement is as follows:

```
CREATE TABLE table
(field type[(size)]
[, field type[(size)] ...])
```

table is the name of the table to be created. *field* is the name of the field to be created in the table, and *type* and *size* define the field's type and width.

The valid data types depend on the underlying database you are using, but certain generic types work on most systems. Table 17.1 lists the base types that most drivers should translate into the local format.

TABLE 17.1: Basic SQL Field Types

DATA TYPE	SIZE SPECIFICATION	DESCRIPTION
Char (char or varchar)	(x)	A simple character field. The width is determined by the value of x.
Integer (int)	N/A	A field of whole numbers, positive or negative.

TABLE 17.1 continued: Basic SQL Field Types

DATA TYPE	SIZE SPECIFICATION	DESCRIPTION
Decimal (real)	(x,y)	A field of decimal numbers, where x is the number's maximum length in digits and y is the maximum number of digits after the decimal point.
Date (date)	N/A	A date field.
Logical	N/A	A field that can have only two values: true or false.

For example, you can use the following statement to create a table that holds the time information for a task:

```
CREATE TABLE tasktime (task int,
                       user int,
                       hours real,
                       work varchar(80),
                       note blob)
```

Notice that we've included a type called a blob (binary large object); this is a very large storage type provided by MySQL and many other databases. You can use the blob to store information that is too large to fit into a typical character array—for example, you can use it to store images or video, or as we've done here, just for text larger than 255 characters. MySQL offers a number of blob types, depending on the maximum size of data you want to store, from the tinyblob (which is just 256 bytes long) up to the longblob (which holds data up to 4GB in size).

Executing a Simple Query

If you have a simple query to execute—that is, one that does not require any response from the database, such as creating a table or index, or deleting rows from a table—then you can use the do() method to your database handle. For example, to create a table, you use the SQL CREATE command, which you can execute as follows:

```
$dbh->do("create table names (firstname varchar(20),
                              lastname varchar(20))");
```

The do() method does not return any information, so you can't use it to extract information from the database. To do that, you need to use one of the many extended query systems.

Executing Extended Queries

The SELECT statement in SQL retrieves information from a database. You need to use one of a special series of methods provided by the DBI toolkit to transfer the information from the database to your Perl script.

You begin by defining the query you want to run on the database and preparing a select table handler. This is a new object that is used to access the individual rows returned by the SELECT statement. You then call execute() on the statement, which sends the query to the database engine. For example:

```
my ($sth) = $dbh->prepare("select * from tv " .
                          "where title like " .
                          $dbh->quote("$title%") .
                          " order by date,time,channel");
$sth->execute();
```

To access the information returned by the query, you call one of the fetch functions in a while or other loop to extract each row of information from the query. For example:

```
while(my $row = $sth->fetchrow_hashref())
```

The fetchrow_hashref() method is probably the most practical, because it returns the row in the form of a hash reference. Each key is the name of a returned column, and the corresponding value is the value of the field. For example, you can extract the date and time as follows:

```
$date = $row->{date};
$time = $row->{time};
```

Other methods include fetchrow_array(), which returns an array of fields in the order they were specified in the SELECT statement, and fetchrow_arrayref(), which returns a reference to an array on the same basis.

Once you've read all the rows, you must call finish() on the select object ($sth in the previous examples) to complete the sequence and free up the query system.

Error Messages

All functions can return a true or false value based on the success or otherwise of the operation. You can extract the error message returned by the operation by accessing the errstr() method on the database handle. For example:

```
my $result = $dbh->do($query);
print $dbh->errstr(),"\n" unless ($result);
```

VIEWING AND UPDATING TABLES

Now that you know how to access the database and perform some simple queries, it's time to look at a real example that uses the DBI interface and a MySQL database. This example uses a simple database with just two tables. The first table, property, stores a list of personal items with a title, description, quantity, and value. Each item is also stored with its location. The location is a relation to the second table, location, which has two fields: an ID number and the description of the location.

To build the system you need three elements:

- ▶ A way of describing the database structure, so you can create the tables and so the application knows the structure when adding and updating the information in the tables. This is not a required element in all systems, but having the information available within our application means that we can use it to help validate data and structures.

- ▶ An interface to the database. Although the DBI system provides connectivity between Perl and MySQL, it does so on a very basic level. You need a more accessible system for adding, updating, and retrieving records from your database.

- ▶ The HTML interface you'll use to perform the updates. Assuming you get the database interface correct, the bulk of the HTML interface should be the HTML that builds the pages displayed to the user.

Creating the Database Structure

As you saw in the last section, you need to use the CREATE command to your MySQL database to create individual tables. Although you could just write a simple script that opens the connection to the database, calls the do() method, and sends the appropriate commands, I prefer a more structured method. There are two reasons: flexibility and usability. The flexibility comes from a definition that you can easily view, update, and, if necessary, modify, if you ever want to change the database structure or port the system to another database. The usability angle is related to the way you'll use the database structure information in the rest of the application (we'll cover that in more detail in the next section).

The system works by creating a module that holds the database definition. Scripts can load the module and use the information either to create the database structure or to use the structure information when accessing and using the database.

The module is object based and comes with three additional methods that return information about the tables in the database. These methods are table_list(), which provides a list of all the tables; table(), which returns the table definition for the specified table; and field_list(), which returns a list of the fields in a given table. You'll see all of these methods at work when you examine the complete code for this chapter, available for download from this book's page at www.sybex.com.

The individual tables are defined in a series of functions, and each function contains a complex hash object that defines the table parameters. You can see the table definition for the property table in Listing 17.1.

Listing 17.1: Table Definition for the *property* Table

```
sub deftable_property
{
    my $tablespec = {
        'description' => 'Property Record',
        'fields' => [
        {
            'opt' => 'auto_increment not null primary key',
            'type' => 'int',
            'field' => 'id',
        },
        {
            'type' => 'varchar',
            'size' => '80',
            'field' => 'shortdesc',
        },
        {
            'type' => 'blob',
            'field' => 'description',
        },
        {
            'opt' => 'NOT NULL',
            'type' => 'int',
            'field' => 'qty',
        },
```

```
        {
            'opt' => 'NOT NULL',
            'type' => 'int',
            'field' => 'location',
        },
        {
            'opt' => 'NOT NULL',
            'type' => 'real',
            'field' => 'value',
        },
        ],
    };

    return $tablespec;
}
```

The important part of this code is the fields block, which is an array of hashes. Each contained hash is the definition for just one field. For example, the first field has a name of id and a type of int. The options specify additional settings for this field. The auto_increment option tells MySQL to automatically increment the value of this field when a new record is added. This will automatically create a unique ID number for each record added. The not null option tells MySQL that an error should be generated if you ever try to add a record without this value set (which should be impossible, because MySQL is adding the value). The last option, primary key, tells MySQL to treat this field as the main lookup field for this database. The key setting is used by the indexing system to speed up lookups and relations.

To add another table to the database definition, you need only create a new function, change the function's name to match the name of the new table, and populate the hash the same way to define the individual fields.

By putting this information into a module called MyDBSpec, along with other table definitions and the methods that return the information, you will always have access to the database structure. In the database interface you'll build later in this chapter, you use the database specification to help build records and queries.

To show how you can use this table definition, Listing 17.2 shows the relevant portions of the createdb.pl script that create the tables in your database. (The complete `createdb.pl` script is included in the download-able code for this chapter.)

Listing 17.2: Creating a Table in the Database

```perl
sub create_tables
{
    my ($tables) = @_;
    foreach my $table (sort @{$tables})
    {
        my $tablespec = $dbh->{dbmeta}->table($table);
        my $query = "create table $table ";
        my @fieldspec;
        foreach my $fieldkey (@{$tablespec->{fields}})
        {
            my $fielddef;
            $fielddef = sprintf("%s %s",
                                $fieldkey->{field},
                                $fieldkey->{type});
            $fielddef .= "($fieldkey->{size})"
                if (exists($fieldkey->{size}));
            $fielddef .= " $fieldkey->{opt}"
                if (exists($fieldkey->{opt}));
            push(@fieldspec,$fielddef);
        }
        $query .= sprintf("(%s)",join(',',@fieldspec));
        print "Creating table $table...";
        $result = $dbh->do($query);
        print "Error: ",$dbh->{dbh}->errstr(),"\n"
            unless($result);
        print "Done\n";
    }
}
```

You already know that the CREATE SQL statement creates a new data-base, and you have the database definition. All you need to do is extract the table specification from your database definition system—done here by calling the `table()` method on the database handle's `dbmeta` attribute, which is an object from the definition class.

Armed with the table definition, you need to iterate over the field array, pulling out the relative field information such as the name, data type, and size, and then build your query. With the query in hand, you can submit the request to MySQL to create the table. The final query sent to MySQL from the script and definition looks like this:

```
create table property (id int auto_increment not null
      primary key,shortdesc varchar(80),description blob,
      qty int NOT NULL,location int NOT NULL,
      value real NOT NULL)
```

NOTE

The `createdb.pl` script automatically creates all the tables in the definition file by getting a list of tables using the `table_list()` method. The script does not drop tables before creating them, so you'll need to do that for yourself if you want to change the database structure. To export the data before you do this, try using the scripts in *XML Processing with Perl, Python, and PHP* (Sybex, 2001).

Creating an Interface to the Database

Although you can use the do() method directly on your database, as demonstrated in the preceding section, there's another way to go. Often it's better to create your own database interface, which allows you to set up various functions that suit your application and provide access to your specific database. This approach also lets you completely separate direct database access from the scripts that interface to the user.

For years, I have used a fairly basic suite of functions that provide generic access to most of my databases. Any application-specific functions are then added to the main database module, and I use a combination of the generic database functions and the application-specific functions in the script.

The interface is object based. You create a new database object, which holds the real database handle object, and an object that links you into the database specification system covered in the preceding section. Methods to the object provide access to the functions that update and retrieve information from the database.

The module presented here contains several methods, but we'll concentrate on just four: new_record(), get_generic_multi(), get_generic_single(), and add_generic().

NOTE

In all cases through the database interface, you work with references to hashes or arrays; you never return (or accept) an array or hash directly. If you don't understand references, you might want to view the perlref manual page.

The *new_record()* Method

Listing 17.3 shows the first method, new_record(). The method creates a new record according to a given table name. To do this, it creates a hash where the keys are the field names and the corresponding values are the field contents. The definition for a record from a given table is created by extracting the definition from the database specification. The method also accepts a hash containing record data, which is then directly assigned to the corresponding field in the final record.

Listing 17.3: Creating a Bare Record for a Table

```
sub new_record
{
    my ($self, $table, $recdata) = @_;

    my $tablespec = $self->{dbmeta}->table($table);

    my $record = {};

    foreach my $field (@{$tablespec->{fields}})
    {
        my $fieldname = $field->{field};
        if (exists($recdata->{$fieldname}))
        {
            $record->{$fieldname} = $recdata->{$fieldname};
        }
        else
        {
            $record->{$field->{field}} = ($field->{type}
                =~ m/(int|real)/ ? 0 : '');
        }
    }

    return $record;
}
```

To create a bare record for the property table, you can use the following:

```
my $properyrecord = $dbh->new_record('property');
```

The resulting hash has all the right fields and, more importantly, the right default values according to the table definition.

The *get_generic_multi()* Method

The get_generic_multi() method returns a hash of records returned from a query. Each hash key is a unique identifier, and each value is another hash of the individual field names and values. The unique identifier is the value of one of the fields—because the property table uses a unique ID, that ID makes an ideal identifier for the record data. The method also accepts an object containing the definition of the search criteria. This is either a hash specifying a simple matching list of fields and values (for example, id = 23 or location = 3) or an array with a more complex request. We won't go into the details; for more information, check the source code for this chapter.

As you can see in Listing 17.4, get_generic_multi() is made up of two parts. The first compiles an SQL query based on the requested table, fields, and search criteria, the second submits the query to the database and then uses a loop to build up the hash containing the record data.

Listing 17.4: Getting a List of Records from a Given Table

```perl
sub get_generic_multi
{
    my ($self,$table,$key,$criteria,$singlefield) = @_;

    my $query = sprintf('select %s from %s %s',
                        buildfieldlist($key,$singlefield),
                        $table,
                        $self->build_search_criteria($table,
                        $criteria)
                                                            );

    my $records = (defined($key) ? {} : []);

    my $sth = $self->{dbh}->prepare($query);
    $sth->execute();
    while(my $row = $sth->fetchrow_hashref())
    {
        if (defined($key))
        {
            if (defined($singlefield) &&
                ref($singlefield) eq '')
            {
                $records->{$row->{$key}}
                    = $row->{$singlefield}
            }
```

```
              else
              {
                  $records->{$row->{$key}}
                      = $row;
              }
          }
          else
          {
              if (defined($singlefield) &&
                  ref($singlefield) eq '')
              {
                  push @{$records},$row->{$singlefield}
              }
              else
              {
                  push @{$records},$row;
              }
          }
      }
      $sth->finish();

      return $records;
}
```

The first thing you should notice is that the method does a lot more than I've already described. Let's quickly cover the arguments and how to use the function, and you'll see how it all works.

The `$table` argument is the name of the table from which you're retrieving information. The `$key` argument is the name of the field from that table that you want to use as the unique identifier in the returned hash of records. If `$key` is not specified, the method returns an array of records rather than a hash of records.

`$criteria` is the hash or array specifying the search criteria. The last argument, `$singlefield`, changes the way information is returned. If `$singlefield` is defined, then the function returns a hash (or array) where the unique key (or each element of the array) is a single value. For example, the statement

```
my $records = $dbh->get_generic_multi('property','id',{});
```

puts all the records from the database that match our query into a hash, with each element of the hash identified by the unique ID from the property table, and the corresponding value containing a hash of the fields and values for each record.

This next statement, on the other hand, gets a list of all the values from the shortdesc field as an array:

```
my $records = $dbh->get_generic_multi('property',undef ,
                                    {},'shortdesc');
```

The *get_generic_single()* Method

The get_generic_single() method is identical to get_generic_multi(), except it returns a single record for a given table and search criteria. You can see the method definition in Listing 17.5.

Listing 17.5: Getting a Single Record from the Database

```
sub get_generic_single
{
    my ($self,$table,$criteria) = @_;

    my $fields = $self->{dbmeta}->getfieldlist($table);

    my $query = 'select ' .
                join(', ',@{$fields}) .
                " from $table " .
                $self->build_search_criteria($table,
                                        $criteria);

    my (@fielddata) = $self->{dbh}->selectrow_array($query);

    return undef unless(scalar @fielddata > 0);

    my $record = {};

    for(my $i=0;$i<scalar @fielddata;$i++)
    {
        $record->{$fields->[$i]} = $fielddata[$i];
    }
    return $record;
}
```

First, you get the list of fields from the database definition. This step is important because you need the list of fields in a fixed order so you know what the data means when you submit the query. Next, you build the query itself, using the specific list of fields.

Then you use `selectrow_array()` to execute the query. Unlike the previously discussed methods for getting data from the database, this method is designed to get just one row of information—it's perfect for obtaining a single record. As the function name suggests, it returns the information in the form of an array. You use this returned array in combination with your list of fields to produce a hash of a single record.

The *add_generic()* Method

The last method, add_generic(), shown in Listing 17.6, adds a record (supplied as a hash) to a specific table.

Listing 17.6: Adding a Record to the Database

```
sub add_generic
{
    my ($self, $table, $record) = @_;

    my (@fields,@values) = ((),());

    foreach my $field (sort keys %{$record})
    {
        next if ($field =~ m/^_/);
        push @fields,$field;
        push @values,$self->{dbh}->quote($record->{$field});
    }

    my $query = "insert into $table (" .
        join(', ',@fields) .
            ") values (" .
                join(', ',@values) .
                    ")";

    $self->{dbh}->do($query);

    return ($self->{dbh}->{mysql_insertid});
}
```

This method is fairly straightforward. You extract a list of fields from the supplied record, ignoring any fields that begin with a leading underscore character (so you can have private data in a record while you're processing it). There are two important elements to note, however: quote() and mysql_insertid.

The quote() method is defined by the DBI toolkit, although it's supplied by the corresponding DBD. It encapsulates data into a format suitable for submission to the database as part of an SQL statement. For example, it places text into quotes; it will even handle text containing quotes (of all types), according to the rules laid down by the database driver.

mysql_insertid is a property of the real database handle, and it contains the value of the field defined as auto_increment in the table definition. Although you won't need this value in the example application, it can be useful if you are creating related records as part of the same operation, when you need the automatically generated value for the other records.

You now have a working database interface that enables you to retrieve and add information to the database. Other functions exist in the module for updating records and for deleting them; check the scripts for this chapter for more information. Although it seems like a lot of additional work, you'll see in the next section how adding this extra layer simplifies working with the database.

Building the Web Interface

Because obtaining and updating information from the database is so easy, the script that provides the web interface is much simpler than you might first think. As with the database interface, I tend to use a fairly simple template for managing each table within the database. I use individual functions that provide a list of the values in a given table, another that provides the form for adding a record, and another for adding and modifying the records in the table.

I typically use the same script to provide access to a given database; or, if it's a particularly large database, I use individual scripts for a group of related tables. This approach makes it easier to manage and update the scripts. It also means that if necessary, I can split up the scripts through modules and Perl's AutoLoader system to help improve performance.

You can use parameters to help control the script's behavior. For example, the example script needs to handle management of two tables (the list of properties and the list of locations). To update the property table, you need to specify the mode (the parameter 'm') as 'property'. Then, a range of submodes tells the script whether you want a list or a form, or are updating the table.

Bypassing the typical preamble in the script, including the loading of the modules and the sending of the initial HTTP header, the first block is therefore the selection and execution of the correct function according to the supplied options. You can see this in action in the script in Listing 17.7.

Listing 17.7: Controlling the Script's Actions

```
if (param('m') eq 'property')
{
    property_list() if (param('sm') eq 'list');
    property_form() if (param('sm') eq 'form');
    property_add() if (param('sm') eq 'add');
    property_add() if (param('sm') eq 'update');
    property_delete() if (param('sm') eq 'delete');
    property_edit() if (param('sm') eq 'edit');
}
elsif (param('m') eq 'location')
{
    location_list() if (param('sm') eq 'list');
    location_form() if (param('sm') eq 'form');
    location_add() if (param('sm') eq 'add');
    location_add() if (param('sm') eq 'update');
    location_delete() if (param('sm') eq 'delete');
    location_edit() if (param('sm') eq 'edit');
}
else
{
    property_list();
}
```

This script shows the different types of functions. Those beginning with property relate to the property table. The list function lists data, form shows the form for a record, add updates the database (and is called whether you are in add or update mode), delete deletes records, and edit edits a record.

Because you use the same basic layout for all tables, you can repeat the same checks and function selections for specific tables—hence the location_*() functions for the location table. We'll look at each type of function individually, but not for both tables, because the two are largely identical.

Note that you have an exception—if the script is called without any arguments, as it will be when the page is first accessed, you just list the property records. This provides a way into the database without the user's selecting any additional options. It also avoids presentation of a blank screen when the user first visits the script online.

The first function is `property_list()`, which shows all the records in the `property` table. You can see a sample of the property listing screen in Figure 17.1. Listing 17.8 gives the function definition.

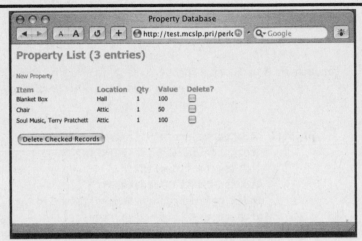

FIGURE 17.1: Viewing a list of property records

Listing 17.8: Listing the Records for a Table

```perl
sub property_list
{
    my $properties =
        $dbh->get_generic_multi('property','id',{});
    my $datacount = scalar keys %{$properties};
    my $locations =
        $dbh->get_generic_multi('location','id',{});

    print <<EOF;
<p class=pageheader>Property List ($datacount entries)</p>
<p>
<a href="index.cgi?m=property&sm=form">New Property</a>
</p>
<form method=POST action=index.cgi>
<input type=hidden name=m value=property>
<input type=hidden name=sm value=delete>
EOF
```

```perl
      print('<table border=0 cellpadding=0 cellspacing=0>',
            '<tr><th align=left>Item</th>',
            '<th width=15> </th>',
            '<th align=left>Location</th>',
            '<th width=15> </th>',
            '<th align=left>Qty</th><th width=15> </th>',
            '<th align=left>Value</th>',
            '<th width=15> </th>',
            '<th align=left>Delete?</th></tr>');

      foreach my $id (sort {$properties->{$a}->{shortdesc} cmp
                            $properties->{$b}->{shortdesc} }
                  keys %{$properties})
      {
          printf('<tr><td><a href="%s">%s</a></td>' .
                 '<td></td><td>%s</td><td></td>' .
                 '<td>%s</td><td></td>' .
                 '<td>%s</td><td></td>%s</tr>',
                 "index.cgi?m=property&sm=edit&id=$id",
                 $properties->{$id}->{shortdesc},
                 $locations->{$properties->{$id}->{location}}
                 ➥->{description},
                 $properties->{$id}->{qty},
                 $properties->{$id}->{value},
                 '<td><input type=checkbox name=delete
                 ➥value="' . $id . '"></td></tr>');
      }
    print '</table><br><input type=submit value="Delete
    ➥Checked Records"><br><br>';
}
```

You begin by getting a list of records in the property table using the
get_generic_multi() method. Although you don't specify any criteria
here, it would be relatively easy to add the necessary code to provide a
search form or similar interface and select the data using the criteria
argument. You then get a count of the entries, just for some additional user
information, and finally a list of all the locations, because you want to
display the location of each item in the list.

Next you create the HTML preamble to set up the page title, provide a
link for a creating a new item, and create the basis for the form you'll need
for the rest of the property list. The form is necessary because this list
will also provide the mechanism for deleting records from the database.

The final stage is to create a table and the table's header rows to describe the columns you'll print.

The bulk of the script, the `foreach` loop, iterates over the contents to display the relevant fields from each record in the set returned earlier. Although you could directly access the database handle and then iterate over the records as you retrieve them through `fetchrow_hashref()`, you gain a little flexibility by having the record set to play with first.

Although you don't need to do so in this instance, sometimes it's useful to post-process the data you retrieve, or to sort the information in a specific way. You can even sort and display the data on two different levels, perhaps split by both the location and the content description.

Two additional elements are added to the loop. First, you create a link that opens an edit window for a given item if its description is clicked on. Second, you create a check box to mark the item for deletion. The button at the end of the table activates the deletion using the list of ideas provided.

If the user clicks the New Property button or the description of one of the existing properties, they get the corresponding form—either blank or pre-filled with the current information. If the user was opening a new record, the script goes straight to the `property_form()` function. If the user is opening an existing record, the script first goes to the `property_edit()` function, shown in Listing 17.9.

Listing 17.9: Editing an Existing Item

```
sub property_edit
{
    my $propertyrecord =
        $dbh->get_generic_single('property',
                                   {'id' => param('id')});
    property_form($propertyrecord,'update');
}
```

The `property_edit()` function does just two things. First, it loads the existing record by specifying the criteria to the `get_generic_single()` method of the property record's ID number. Second, it calls the `property_form()` function, supplying the loaded record and specifying that you should be in `update` mode. The mode is required because it tells the form (and, later, the script) when the form is submitted how to handle the information it has been supplied.

The `property_form()` function is dual-purpose: It provides the form for creating a new record and also provides the form for editing an existing record. It does so by using an existing record (as supplied by the `property_edit()` function) or creating a new record containing all the fields in the `property` table (using the `new_record()` method in the database interface). If the form is for a new record, the contents are blank, so essentially you get a blank form. If the form is for an existing record, then it's filled with the existing information. You can see the form code in Listing 17.10.

Listing 17.10: Building a Data Entry Form

```perl
sub property_form
{
    my ($propertyrecord, $submode) = @_;

    $submode = 'add' unless defined($submode);
    $propertyrecord = $dbh->new_record('property')
        unless defined($propertyrecord);

    my $locations =
        $dbh->get_generic_multi('location','id',{});
    my $locoptions = '';
    foreach my $id (sort {
                        $locations->{$a}->{description} cmp
                        $locations->{$b}->{description} }
                    keys %{$locations})
    {
        $locoptions .=
            sprintf('<option value="%d"%s>%s</option>',
                    $id,
                    ($id == $propertyrecord->{location} ?
                     ' selected' : ''),
                    $locations->{$id}->{description});
    }

    print <<EOF;
<p class=pageheader>\u$submode Property</p>
<form method=POST action=index.cgi>
<input type=hidden name=m value=property>
<input type=hidden name=sm value=add>
<input type=hidden name=id value="$propertyrecord->{id}">
<table border=0 cellspacing=0 cellpadding=0>
<tr><td class=fieldlabel>Name<td width=10> </td>
    <td><input type=text name=shortdesc size=80
    ➥value="$propertyrecord->{shortdesc}"></td></tr>
```

```
<tr><td class=fieldlabel>Description<td width=10> </td>
    <td><textarea name=description rows=10
    ➥cols=80>$propertyrecord->{description}</textarea>
    </td></tr>
<tr><td class=fieldlabel>Quantity<td width=10> 
    </td><td><input type=text name=qty size=10
    ➥value="$propertyrecord->{qty}"></td></tr>
<tr><td class=fieldlabel>Value<td width=10> 
    </td><td><input type=text name=value size=10
    ➥value="$propertyrecord->{value}"></td></tr>
<tr><td class=fieldlabel>Location<td width=10> </td>
    <td><select name=location>$locoptions</select>
    </td></tr></table>
<input type=submit value="\u$submode Property"><BR>
EOF
}
```

One extra item to note is that you also build a list of HTML options for
a pop-up menu on the form—in this case, the pop-up menu of locations.
You set the selected option, if it's an existing record, by appending the text
'selected' to the relevant option.

Once you've done all that preamble and building, the last stage is to
dump out the form as HTML. You're using raw HTML here, although you
could use the HTML building functions provided by the CGI module.

The form incorporates some hidden fields. Two define the mode and
submode for the form when it's submitted—either add or update, according to whether you are adding or updating a record. You also embed the
record's unique ID into the list of fields supplied. If it's an existing record,
you know the record number to update. If the record is new, then the
record number is zero (because new_record() sets zero as the default value
for a numeric field). You'll need this information when the form is submitted
and the property_add() function has been called.

NOTE

Note that the title and submission buttons use the mode, either as supplied
from property_edit() or as defined in the first line of the function. This
eliminates another problem—how to title a page and button correctly. You just
use the information you already know.

Figure 17.2 showing us editing an existing record.

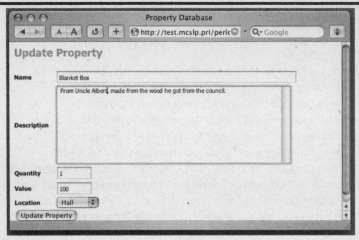

FIGURE 17.2:   Updating an existing record

Processing the Form and Adding a Record

Once the form has been submitted, the script calls the property_add()
function, shown in Listing 17.11. This function builds a record suitable
for supplying to your database interface, to either add to or update an
existing record.

Listing 17.11: Adding a Record to the Database

```
sub property_add
{
    my $propertyrecord =
        $dbh->new_record('property',
            { 'id' => param('id'),
              'shortdesc' => param('shortdesc') || '',
              'description' => param('description') || '',
              'qty' => param('qty') || 0,
              'value' => param('value') || 0,
              'location' => param('location') || 0,
              });

    if ($propertyrecord->{id} == 0)
    {
        $propertyrecord->{id} =
            $dbh->add_generic('property',$propertyrecord);
    }
```

```
else
{
    $dbh->update_generic_record('property',
                        { 'id' => $propertyrecord->{'id'} },
                                $propertyrecord);
}

property_list();
}
```

The first job is to build the record by collecting the field parameters from the form and applying them to a blank record for the corresponding table. You can do this by providing a hash reference to the field/value pairs to the new_record() method. Note that you also supply default options, using the || (OR) operator in case the values in the field are invalid.

Next, you determine whether this is a new record or an existing one. If it's new, its ID is zero, so you call add_generic(). Remember, you created the property table to automagically generate a new ID number each time a record is added. If you supply an ID number of zero when you add the record, the table still generates that number.

If the record has an ID, then you must be editing an existing record, so you call update_generic_record(). We didn't look at this function, but essentially it bonds the steps of loading an existing record (using the criteria supplied, in this case the ID number), merging the data, and then updating each individual field using a single SQL statement into one simple method. You merge, rather than update all the fields blindly, so that you can provide a simpler form that updates only specific fields.

Once you've finished adding or updating the records, you call property_list() to list the table records. Although there is no visual cue to say the record has been added, anybody entering information will probably spot the new record or changed record in the list. If you want to provide a visual confirmation, then remove the call to property_list() and instead display a simple page of HTML (but remember to provide a link to the listings page).

Deleting Existing Records

The last function, property_delete(), is the simplest of the lot and can be seen in Listing 17.12. This function iterates over the list of values provided by the delete parameter from the property list produced by the property_list() function. The CGI module automatically returns an array of values when the corresponding form provides a list of values with a single name (as in the case of a check box).

Listing 17.12: Deleting Records

```
sub property_delete
{
    foreach my $id (param('delete'))
    {
        $dbh->del_generic('property',{id => $id});
    }
    property_list();
}
```

Now all you have to do is delete each item, supplying the item's unique ID number as the criteria. When you're finished, you produce the list of property items again. As with adding and updating a record, you don't provide visual confirmation, or (more importantly in the case of deleting) any visual cue about what you're doing, but it would be easy to add the corresponding steps.

Extending the System

I've shown you how to build a simple database interface and an HTML script wrapper that provides a link between the database and the HTML used to display and edit it. Although I didn't include the source for manipulating the location table, the functions used to edit and list the various locations are almost identical to those used for the property table. By using the same structure and providing a suitable database interface, you can build extensive and complex sites using the techniques shown in this chapter.

To add another table to the system—including the code for manipulating that table—all you need to do is create the table definition, create the table itself, and then duplicate the function selector and functions, modifying them for the corresponding fields in the new table. This approach significantly reduces the amount of time required to build an interface to a table, and makes it easier to extend and expand the system without adding complexity.

WHAT'S NEXT

In addition to being a very capable text-processing language, Perl comprises an inline regular-expression engine and a strong, flexible object modeling system for building information trees. The next and final chapter, "XML Solutions in Perl," discusses the tools and modules in the Perl XML processing toolset.

Chapter 18
XML Solutions in Perl

As you've seen as you've worked through Chapters 14 through 17, Perl itself was based on some strong string and text processing tools, including awk, sed, and sort, to form a very capable text-processing language. In addition to all the normal text-processing facilities you would expect, it includes an inline regular expression engine and a strong but flexible object modeling system that is perfect for building the complex information trees that XML documents can develop into.

In this chapter, we'll look at the core modules that make up the Perl XML processing toolset. We'll also examine some of the lesser-known tools and modules that, although not vital to your processing, may be useful.

Adapted from *XML Processing with Perl, Python, and PHP*, by Martin C. Brown
ISBN 0-7821-4021-1

USING *XML::PARSER*

XML::Parser is built on top of the Expat XML processing library written by James Clark. XML::Parser is a vital component of XML processing under Perl, because most other modules within Perl use the facilities offered by XML::Parser to support their own processing.

XML::Parser is an event-based parser. Because it uses the Expat libraries, it also offers simple validation of your XML documents for well-formedness, although it doesn't validate your documents against a Document Type Definition (DTD).

The interface to the parser is simple: You create a new XML::Parser object and define a suite of functions that are called when the parser determines a start, end, or data portion in your XML document. For example, the code in Listing 18.1 builds a simple XML parser to output the start and end tags in a document.

Listing 18.1: A Simple XML Parser

```perl
use XML::Parser;

my $parse = new XML::Parser();

$parse->setHandlers(Start => \&handler_start,
                    End => \&handler_end,);

my $file = shift @ARGV or die "Must specify a file";
$parse->parsefile($file);

sub handler_start
{
    my ($parser, $element, %attr) = @_;
    print "Start: $element\n";
}

sub handler_end
{
    my ($parser, $element) = @_;
    print "End: $element\n";
}
```

Running this code on the following simple XML document results in the following output:

```
$ cat simple.xml
<simple>
<paragraph>
</paragraph>
</simple>

$ perl exxmlp.pl simple.xml
Start: simple
Start: paragraph
End: paragraph
End: simple
```

As you can see, the example outputs a list of the start and end tags. Since you "register" the functions you want to call when different elements are seen, the functions can be called anything you like. Note as well that the functions are supplied with the name of the tag that was found and the list of attributes for a given tag. You can use this information within the parsing process to be more explicit about the information you pass on.

Using *XML::Parser* to Convert to HTML

Being an event-based parser, the XML::Parser module is ideal in situations where you need to extract or convert elements into another form. A good example is converting an XML document into an HTML format for display on-screen.

Let's look at a CGI script I wrote on behalf of a client that wanted to convert XML documents into HTML for display on its website. The documents were a mixture of XML and some HTML components; you can see a sample in Listing 18.2.

Listing 18.2: A Sample Review Document

```
<video>
<main>
<title>Alien Resurrection</title>
<para>Sigourney Weaver, Winona Ryder</para>
<title>Witness the Resurrection</title>
<para>The review...</para>
</main>
<panel>
```

```
<paneltitle>Purchase</paneltitle>
<para><b>Amazon UK</b></para>
<para><azuk id="B00004CXQ6">Buy Alien Resurrection on
 Video</azuk></para>
<para><azuk id="B00004S8GR">Buy Alien Resurrection on
 DVD</azuk></para>
<para><azuk id="B00004CXR8">Buy the Alien Box Set on
 Video</azuk></para>
<para><azuk id="B00004S8K7">Buy the Alien Box Set on
 DVD</azuk></para>
<para><b>Amazon US</b></para>
<para><azus id="787987987">Buy Alien Resurrection on
 Video</azus></para>
<para><azus id="787987987">Buy Alien Resurrection on
 DVD</azus></para>
<para><azus id="787987987">Buy the Alien Box Set on
 Video</azus></para>
<para><azus id="787987987">Buy the Alien Box Set on
 DVD</azus></para>
<paneltitle>Related Items</paneltitle>
<para><realref id="video/alien.xml">Alien</realref></para>
<para><realref id="video/aliens.xml">Aliens</realref></para>
<para><realref id="video/alien3.xml">Alien3</realref></para>
<para><realref id="video/alien_boxset.xml">Alien Legacy Box
Set</realref></para>
<para>
<b>Also see</b>: <keyref id="Sci-Fi">Sci-Fi</keyref>,
<keyref id="Horror">Horror</keyref>,
<keyref id="Action">Action</keyref>
</para>
</panel>
</video>
```

The document contains both traditional XML data and some HTML-specific link information. For example, there are links to other review files and details on the ID and host information required to link to the items available for purchase on Amazon.

The script in Listing 18.3 translates the XML document into HTML. The script works by using a single hash that contains the HTML tags and attributes to output when a specific XML tag is seen. The handler_start() function identifies the tag and then builds the equivalent HTML tag.

Listing 18.3: An XML-to-HTML Converter

```perl
#!/usr/local/bin/perl -w
use strict;
use XML::Parser;

# The %elements hash holds the configuration information
# for the XML tags found by the parser. The tags output
# are HTML. Because an individual XML tag can generate
# multiple HTML tags, the base key links to a list.
# Within the list are individual hash references for
# each HTML tag, and the hash contains the tag and attribute
# information.
# For example, a <title> XML tag produces:
# <tr><td bgcolor="#000094" align="left">
# <font face="Arial, Helvetica" color="#ffffff"><b>

my %elements =
    (
      'video' => [ ],
      'title' => [{ tag => 'tr' },
                  { tag => 'td',
                    attr => {
                        'bgcolor' => '#000094',
                        'align' => 'left',
                    },
                },
                  { tag => 'font',
                    attr => {
                        'face' => 'Arial,Helvetica',
                        'color' => '#ffffff',
                    },
                },
                  { tag => 'b' },
                  ],
      'paneltitle' => [{ tag => 'tr' },
                       { tag => 'td',
                         attr => {
                             'bgcolor' => '#000094',
                             'align' => 'left',
                         },
                     },
                       { tag => 'font',
```

```
                               attr => {
                                    'face' => 'Arial,Helvetica',
                                    'color' => '#ffffff',
                               },
                     },
                  { tag => 'b' },
                  ],
   'stars' => [{ tag => 'tr' },
             { tag => 'td' },
             ],
   'description' => [{ tag => 'tr' },
                   { tag => 'td',
                     attr => {
                          'bgcolor' => '#000094',
                          'align' => 'left',
                     },
                   },
                  { tag => 'font',
                    attr => {
                          'face' => 'Arial,Helvetica',
                          'color' => '#ffffff',
                     },
                  },
                  { tag => 'b' },
                  ],
   'review' => [{ tag => 'tr' },
             { tag => 'td' },
             { tag => 'p' },
             ],
   'b' => [ { tag => 'b' }
        ],
   'br' => [ { tag => 'br' }
         ],
   'main' => [ { tag => 'td',
             attr => {
                  'width' => '66%',
                  'valign' => 'top',
             },
          },
            { tag => 'table',
             attr => {
                  'border' => '0',
                  'cellspacing' => '0',
```

```
                              'cellpadding' => '2',
                              'width' => '100%',
                         },
                    },
                    ],
        'para' => [ { tag => 'tr' },
                    { tag => 'td' },
                    ],
        'azus' => [ { tag => 'a',
                      href =>
'http://www.amazon.com/exec/obidos/ASIN/%%ID%%/myamzntag' },
                    ],
        'azuk' => [ { tag => 'a',
                      href =>
'http://www.amazon.co.uk/exec/obidos/
➡ASIN/%%ID%%/myamzntag' },
                    ],
        'keyref' => [ { tag => 'a',
                        href =>
                            '/cgi/reviews.cgi?t=k&d=%%ID%%' },
                    ],
        'realref' => [ { tag => 'a',
                         href =>
                             '/cgi/reviews.cgi?t=r&d=%%ID%%' },
                    ],
        'img' => [ { tag => 'img',
                     src => '/img/reviews/',
                     end => 0,},
                   ],
        'panel' => [{ tag => 'td',
                      attr => {
                          'width' => '34%',
                          'valign' => 'top',
                      },
                  },
                    { tag => 'table',
                      attr => {
                          'width' => '100%',
                          'border' => '0',
                          'cellspacing' => '0',
                          'cellpadding' => '2',
                      },
                  },
```

```
                    ],
        );

    # Because this is a CGI script we output the Content-type
    # http header before starting the parsing process.

    print "Content-type: text/html\n\n";
    print "<html><head></head><body>\n";
    show_review('alien_r.xml');
    print "</body></html>\n";


    # The main show_review() function formats a review on screen
    sub show_review
    {
        my $title = shift;


    # The review normally forms part of another page, so we
    # embed the whole thing into a table
        print <<EOF;
<table border=0 cellspacing=0 cellpadding=0 width=100%>
<tr>
EOF


    # Create the parser and pass it the XML document that
    # we want to process

        my $parse = new XML::Parser();

        $parse->setHandlers(Start => \&handler_start,
                            End => \&handler_end,
                            Char => \&handler_char,);



        $parse->parsefile($title);
    # Make sure we close off the table
        print "</tr></table>";


    }


    # the handler_start() function handles opening
    # tags. Because of the %elements structure
    # we need to extract the structure and parse
    # %elements to work out the HTML we need to produce
```

```perl
sub handler_start
{
    my ($parser, $element, %attr) = @_;


# First, we check that the XML tag we've just
# recognized has a matching element in the %elements
# hash.
    if (defined($elements{$element}))
    {
# Work through each of the HTML tags in the embedded
# array
        foreach my $tag (@{$elements{$element}})
        {
            print '<',$tag->{'tag'}
                if (exists($tag->{'tag'}));
# If there are ID attributes in the XML and a matching
# HREF element in %elements
# If we find them then we replace %%ID%% in the HREF
# from %elements with the ID supplied by the XML tag
            if (exists($attr{'id'}) &&
                exists($tag->{'href'}))
            {
                my $url = $tag->{'href'};
                $url =~ s/%%ID%%/$attr{'id'}/;
                print " href=\"$url\"";
                delete($attr{'id'});
            }
# Check if there are any HTML attributes we need to
# generate. If so, work through the attributes to build
# an array of the attribute text, and then join them
# together with spaces to make the actual attribute text
            if (exists($tag->{'tag'}) &&
                exists($tag->{'attr'}))
            {
                my @myattrlist = ();
                foreach my $attr (keys %{$tag->{'attr'}})
                {
                    push(@myattrlist,
                        sprintf('%s="%s"',
                            $attr,
                            $tag->{'attr'}->{$attr}));
                }
```

```perl
                       print " ", join(' ',@myattrlist);
                }
# Finally, add any other attributes defined in the XML
# to the HTML output.
                foreach my $attr (keys %attr)
                {
                        print " $attr=\"$attr{$attr}\"";
                }
# Print the closing tag
                print '>' if (exists($tag->{'tag'}));
# Output raw elements (which appear as normal text)
# if there are any
                print $tag->{'raw'} if (exists($tag->{raw}));
        }
    }
}


# The handler_end() has to output the HTML tags from the
# %elements hash, but in opposite order (to produce valid
# HTML) and as close tags.

sub handler_end
{
    my ($parser, $element) = @_;

    if (defined($elements{$element}))
    {
        foreach my $tag (reverse @{$elements{$element}})
        {
            if (exists($tag->{'tag'}))
            {
                print '</',$tag->{'tag'},'>'
                    unless (exists($tag->{end}));
            }
        }
    }
}


# Raw character data is just output verbatim
sub handler_char
{
    my ($parser,$data) = @_;
```

```
    print $data;
}
```

In Figure 18.1, you can see the result of running the script on the review document shown in Listing 18.3. Although this code was written for a specific solution, you can modify the %elements table to suit your own needs, and it will convert your XML documents into HTML.

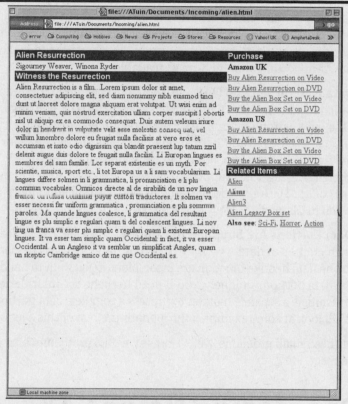

FIGURE 18.1:   An HTML version of an XML movie review document

XML::Parser Traps

The Expat libraries on which XML::Parser is based have a few small traps. Because XML::Parser is used by so many of the other modules within Perl, it's worth mentioning these problems before we go any further:

Errors Raise Exceptions   Although Expat is nonvalidating, it still checks the basic layout of your document to ensure that it's well formed. Unfortunately, this means any error in the basic structure of the document raises an exception. The only way to trap this exception is to embed your call to the parser within eval(). Luckily, a further call to the parser will allow parsing to continue from the position after the last error.

Expat Supplies All Data   Everything from the XML document is supplied back through one of the trigger functions you define for XML::Parser to use. Thus whatever function is used for handling character data must make decisions about what to do with characters beyond-normal text. Expat supplies linefeed/carriage return characters, spaces, and other characters to make the XML document more human readable.

Data Is Returned in UTF-8   Although Expat isn't strictly a Unicode parser, XML::Parser always returns UTF-8 strings. This isn't a problem for most English-sourced documents, because the UTF-8 and Latin-1 character sets are the same for the first 256 characters. For other Unicode strings—especially foreign languages not supported by the Latin-1 set—you can use Unicode::String; we looked at Unicode within Perl in more detail in Chapter 13, "Perl and Unicode."

Data Portions Are Supplied in Chunks   Because Expat deals with chunks of data, you may find that data portions passed to the data-handler function are incomplete. If you want to handle the data portions uniquely, you'll need to cache the information and initiate a separate handler to process a complete data portion. We'll look at some examples throughout the rest of this section.

Beyond these small problems, XML::Parser works pretty much as you would expect.

XML PROCESSING USING SAX

Many of the parser solutions for XML in Perl support a Simple API for XML (SAX) interface to enable you to communicate between different XML processors when reading a document. SAX parsers work in the same basic fashion as XML::Parser; as the document is parsed and different elements within the document are discovered, a function is called to process the entity.

A number of different SAX parsers are available, but the best is probably the XML::Parser::PerlSAX (PerlSAX) module. That module forms the basis of many others, including the XML::Grove module that provides a DOM-like interface for XML documents.

Unlike XML::Parser, which uses references to the functions that handle the entities, with PerlSAX you need to create a new class that defines the methods to use for parsing different XML tags—suitable methods are named according to the tag you want to process. Although this approach sounds more complex, it enables you to identify a number of different elements. The full SAX specification covers everything from basic document properties to specific elements.

For example, you can create a simple class to output the start and end tags from an XML document by creating a handler class like the one in Listing 18.4. You inherit from XML::Handler::Sample, which dumps the output for selected entities, and define two functions, start_element() and end_element(), which are called when the parser identifies start and end tags in the document.

Listing 18.4: *MyHandler.pm*: A Simple Handler Class for SAX Parsing

```perl
package MyHandler;

use XML::Handler::Sample;

our @ISA = qw/XML::Handler::Sample/;

sub new
{
    my $self = shift;
    my $class = ref($self) || $self;

    return bless {}, $class;
}

sub start_element
{
    my ($self, $info) = @_;

    print "Start Tag $info->{Name}\n";
}

sub end_element
```

```
{
    my ($self, $info) = @_;

    print "End Tag $info->{Name}\n";
}
```

To create the parser, create a new instance of your handler class and then a new instance of the XML::Handler::PerlSAX class, which does the actual processing. You can see the final parser script in Listing 18.5.

Listing 18.5: *PerlSAX* Parsing Script

```perl
#!/usr/local/bin/perl -w
use XML::Parser::PerlSAX;
use MyHandler;

my $file = shift @ARGV or die "You must specify a file";

$my_handler = MyHandler->new();

XML::Parser::PerlSAX->new->parse(Source =>
                                 { SystemId => $file },
                                 Handler => $my_handler);
```

If you run this script on a simple XML document, you'll get the following output:

```
$ cat simple.xml
<simple>
<paragraph>
</paragraph>
</simple>

$ perl perlsax-test.pl simple.xml
start_document
Start Tag simple
characters
Start Tag paragraph
characters
End Tag paragraph
characters
End Tag simple
end_document
```

SAX parsing is great for processing a document in sequence and can be useful for serializing a document into another format. You saw this with the XML::Parser solution earlier in this chapter, which converted a document to HTML.

XML PROCESSING USING DOM

The Document Object Model (DOM) for parsing an XML document is essentially a method of turning your XML document into an object tree. Because all XML documents are built like a tree, accessing an individual element by its branch seems to be a logical step.

Many different DOM parsers are supported under Perl, including XML::DOM, XML::Simple, and XML::Twig. My personal favorite is XML::Grove, written by Ken MacLeod. XML::Grove is not strictly a DOM parser—it doesn't adhere to W3C's DOM API, but it does provide a similar interface. For a genuine DOM parser, use the XML::DOM module.

The XML::Grove module provides an easy way to work with an entire XML document by loading it into memory and then converting it into a tree of objects that can be accessed like any other set of nested references. To demonstrate the tree format offered by XML::Grove, let's look at a sample XML document. It uses a contact entry within an address book, a structure most people are familiar with. If you think about a single record within a contact database, then the base of the XML document is the contact. The example uses a fictional version of me, as shown in Listing 18.6.

Listing 18.6: A Contact Record Written in XML

```
<contact>
  <name>Martin Brown</name>
  <address>
    <description>Main Address</description>
    <loc>The House, The Street, The Town</loc>
  </address>
  <address>
    <description>Holiday Chalet</description>
    <loc>The Chalet, The Hillside, The Forest</loc>
  </address>
</contact>
```

The grove.pl example script that comes with the XML::Grove module kit can convert this document into a textual tree. This version has been modified slightly so that it also outputs the array reference numbers of each branch. (You'll need this information in a later example.) The script is shown in Listing 18.7.

Listing 18.7: The *grove.pl XML::Grove* Sampler

```
#
# Copyright (C) 1998 Ken MacLeod
# See the file COPYING for distribution terms.
#
# $Id: grove.pl,v 1.4 1999/05/06 23:13:02 kmacleod Exp $
#

use XML::Parser::PerlSAX;
use XML::Grove;
use XML::Grove::Builder;

my $builder = XML::Grove::Builder->new;
my $parser = XML::Parser::PerlSAX->new(Handler => $builder);

my $doc;
foreach $doc (@ARGV) {
    my $grove = $parser->parse (Source =>
        { SystemId => $doc });

    dump_grove ($grove);
}


sub dump_grove {
    my $grove = shift;
    my @context = ();

    _dump_contents ($grove->{Contents}, \@context);
}

sub _dump_contents {
    my $contents = shift;
    my $context = shift;


    for my $item ( @$contents ) {
        if (ref ($item) =~ /::Element/) {
            push @$context, $item->{Name};
```

```
                    my @attributes = %{$item->{Attributes}};
                    print STDERR "@$context \\\\ (@attributes)\n";
                    _dump_contents ($item->{Contents}, $context);
                    print STDERR "@$context //\n";
                    pop @$context;
            } elsif (ref ($item) =~ /::PI/) {
                    my $target = $item->{Target};
                    my $data = $item->{Data};
                    print STDERR "@$context ?? $target($data)\n";
            } elsif (ref ($item) =~ /::Characters/) {
                    my $data = $item->{Data};
                    $data =~ s/([\x80-\xff])/
                    ➥sprintf "#x%X;", ord $1/eg;
                    $data =~ s/([\t\n])/sprintf "#%d;", ord $1/eg;
                    print STDERR "@$context || $data\n";
            } elsif (!ref ($item)) {
                    print STDERR "@$context !! SCALAR: $item\n";
            } else {
                    print STDERR "@$context !! OTHER: $item\n";
            }
        }
    }
}
```

The script works by recursively calling the _dump_contents() function on each branch of the tree. That function works through every element within a particular branch. Through each iteration, you prefix the output with the location of the current branch. The result of running the script on the sample XML document appears in Listing 18.8.

Listing 18.8: A Textual XML Tree of the Contact Document

```
contact \\ ()
contact || #10;
contact ||
contact name \\ ()
contact name || Martin Brown
contact name //
contact || #10;
contact ||
contact address \\ ()
contact address || #10;
contact address ||
contact address description \\ ()
contact address description || Main Address
```

```
contact address description //
contact address || #10;
contact address ||
contact address loc \\ ()
contact address loc || The House, The Street, The Town
contact address loc //
contact address || #10;
contact address ||
contact address //
contact || #10;
contact ||
contact address \\ ()
contact address || #10;
contact address ||
contact address description \\ ()
contact address description || Holiday Chalet
contact address description //
contact address || #10;
contact address ||
contact address loc \\ ()
contact address loc || The Chalet, The Hillside, The Forest
contact address loc //
contact address || #10;
contact address ||
contact address //
contact || #10;
contact //
```

Because you can access individual tags within a DOM-parsed XML document, DOM parsers are particularly useful when you want to update the contents of an XML document. Using SAX to process the document sequentially rather than using the tree model offered by a DOM parser is far from ideal, because it means reading in the content, identifying which bits you want to change as they are triggered, and then regenerating the result.

For example, if you wanted to update my Holiday Chalet address using SAX, you'd have to read in the content, identify first that you were in the address branch, and then be sure you were in the correct addressline branch. Then you could replace the information in the output.

Using DOM, you parse the entire document, update the address within the branch you want to update, and then dump the XML document back out again. Updating the branch is just a case of referencing the branch's location within the DOM structure.

XML::Grove converts an XML document into a series of nested arrays and hashes. The arrays contain a list of elements within the current branch, and the hashes are used to supply the element type, name, and data (if applicable) for that branch.

You can output the final version of the document using the following:

```
use XML::Grove::AsCanonXML;
print $grove->as_canon_xml();
```

GENERATING XML

The easiest way to generate XML information within Perl is to use print, probably in combination with a here document to make the process easier. Using print is an untidy solution, especially because it almost guarantees that you'll introduce errors and inconsistencies into the code that you generate, and debugging the output can be an absolute nightmare.

A much better solution is to output your XML tags by name in a structure format, just as if you were creating the XML tree yourself. You can do this using one of the modules that supports DOM parsing, because DOM allows you to build the XML document branch by branch and leaf by leaf.

However, it would be much better to use a tool such as the XML::Generator module. Instead of building the XML tags and objects and structure yourself, XML::Generator enables you to use functions to define the tag. Arguments to the functions create additional branches, leaves, and attributes. For example, you might populate a contact file using the following:

```
use XML::Generator;
my $gen = XML::Generator->new('escape' => 'always',
                              'pretty' => 2);
print $gen->contact($gen->name('Martin C Brown'),
                    $gen->email('mc@mcwords.com'));
```

The functions don't have to be predefined: XML::Generator creates the functions for you on-the-fly. The previous code generates the following XML document:

```
<contact>
  <name>Martin C Brown</name>
  <email>mc@mcwords.com</email>
</contact>
```

The module generates a raw XML document. To generate a DOM tree, which you could then separately parse and process using the techniques you saw earlier in this chapter, you can use the XML::Generator::DOM module:

```
use XML::Generator::DOM;
my $gen = XML::Generator::DOM->new();

my $domdoc = $gen->xml($gen->contact(
                          $gen->name('Martin C Brown'),
                          $gen->email('mc@mcwords.com')));

print $domdoc->toString();
```

OTHER XML MODULES

A host of other XML modules are available on CPAN. They're too numerous to mention in any detail here, but XML and Perl are developing all the time; if you want more information about any of the modules in Perl, check the CPAN XML page at http://www.perl.com/CPAN-local/modules/by-module/XML/.

DBIx::XML_RDB

Although there are lots of bits of Perl and XML that I really like, the DBIx::XML_RDB module is one of my favorites. It simplifies one of the more complicated and often convoluted processes when converting RDBMS information into an XML document. The DBIx::XML_RDB module makes an SQL query submitted to any database accessible through the DBI module into an XML document.

Using the module is straightforward—you create a new DBIx::XML_RDB object, supplying the datasource, driver, user ID, password, and database name:

```
my $sqlxml = DBIx::XML_RDB->new($datasource, $driver,
                                 $userid, $password, $dbname)
             || die "Failed to make new xmlout";
```

Submit an SQL statement:

```
$sqlxml->DoSql("SELECT * FROM $table ORDER BY 1");
```

Then print out the result:

```
print $sqlxml->GetData;
```

It's easier to demonstrate the effects using the sql2xml.pl and xml2sql.pl tools, which are installed when you install the module. These tools convert an SQL statement into an XML document and vice versa. For example, the following code dumps a table containing ISBN numbers to an XML file:

```
$ sql2xml.pl -sn books -driver mysql -uid mc -table isbn
-output hello.xml
```

You can see the resulting XML file in Listing 18.9.

Listing 18.9: The XML Result of an SQL Query Using DBIx::XML_RDB

```
<?xml version="1.0"?>
<DBI driver="bookwatch">
        <RESULTSET statement=
        ➥"SELECT * FROM isbn ORDER BY 1">
                <ROW>
                        <isbn>0002570254</isbn>
                        <title>Sony</title>
                        <author>John Nathan</author>
                        <followref>0</followref>
                </ROW>
                <ROW>

                        <isbn>0002570807</isbn>
                        <title>'Tis</title>
                        <author>Frank McCourt</author>
                        <followref>0</followref>
                </ROW>
    ...
    </RESULTSET>
    </DBI>
```

The xml2sql.pl script obviously does the reverse, converting an XML document following the same format as that in Listing 18.9 back into a series of SQL statements.

XML::RSS

If you use the Web to read the news and keep up-to-date with Perl, Python, Apache, and all the other cool stuff on the Internet, then you know how frustrating it is to have go to 10 or 20 different sites to pick your news. As a solution to this problem, many sites now export news and other regularly updated pieces through a Rich Site Summary (RSS) file. RSS files are really just XML documents conforming to a DTD that define a common format for news stories and how to link to the original items. For example,

Listing 18.10 shows a truncated version of the RSS file from CNN.com on
June 29, 2001.

Listing 18.10: A Sample RSS File from CNN.com

```
<?xml version="1.0"?>

<!DOCTYPE rss
   PUBLIC "-//Netscape Communications//DTD RSS 0.91//EN"
   "http://my.netscape.com/publish/formats/rss-0.91.dtd">

<rss version="0.91">

<channel>

<title>News from CNN.com</title>
<link>http://cnn.com/index.html</link>
<description>The world's news leader</description>
<language>en-us</language>

<image>
 <title>CNN.com</title>
 <url>http://cnn.com/images/1999/07/cnn.com.logo.gif</url>
 <link>http://CNN.com/index.html</link>
 <width>144</width>
 <height>34</height>
 <description>The world's news leader</description>
</image>

<item>
   <title>Retired grocery clerk claims $141 million
   ➥California lottery jackpot - June 29, 2001</title>
   <link>http://cnn.com/2001/US/06/29/lottery.winner.ap/
   ➥index.html</link>
</item>

<item>
   <title>Kmart pulling handgun ammunition from shelves in
   ➥wake of protests - June 29, 2001</title>

   <link>http://cnn.com/2001/US/06/29/kmart.guns.ap/
   ➥index.html</link>
</item>
...
```

How does RSS make reading news easier? Once you've downloaded the RSS files from a number of different sites, you can combine the information in each RSS file to aggregate the content into a single web page. Each item in the RSS file is a small outline of the full article. If you see something you like, you can go to the full page; otherwise, you can skip to the next story without going to multiple websites.

The XML::RSS module enables you to create and update your RSS files, usually from whatever source you use in your news service. Some people use the Slashcode (as used by slashdot.org and many other sites); in other instances, the RSS file is from the news database. You can also use RSS to convert an RSS file into HTML.

To get an idea of how RSS works, you might want to try the Meerkat service offered on the O'Reilly Network (http://www.oreillynet.com/meerkat/). If you want to play around with RSS in Perl and reap the benefits of reading all your news from a single web page, then check out AmphetaDesk. Ironically, AmphetaDesk doesn't use XML::RSS, but it does download, parse, and convert RSS documents into HTML. You can see a sample of AmphetaDesk in action in Figure 18.2. The package is available for Mac, Windows, and Unix from http://www.disobey.com/amphetadesk/.

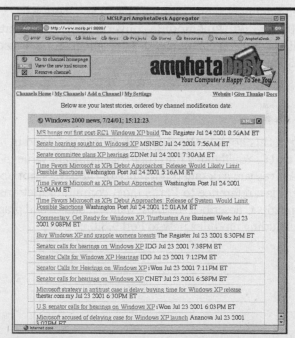

FIGURE 18.2:   AmphetaDesk, an RSS aggregator

SUMMARY

As with most problems in Perl, you can generally find a suitable solution in the CPAN archives. XML processing is no exception—a host of different modules are available for solving your XML processing and parsing problems using Perl.

For basic XML processing in Perl, we have the XML::Parser module. It provides a sequential method for calling a specific function when the different elements are identified within an XML document. XML::Parser is an ideal solution for converting the entire content of an XML document into another format, such as HTML. You saw a sample in this chapter.

For a more structured and ultimately expandable method of processing documents, we have the SAX interface in the form of the XML::Parser::PerlSAX module. The PerlSAX parser also provides the basis for a number of other modules, including a DOM-like parser in the form of XML::Grove. The XML::Grove module isn't a true DOM parser, but it does enable you to manipulate an XML document as if it were a DOM tree. If you want a full DOM implementation, you can use the XML::DOM and XML::Simple modules.

As if that weren't enough, many modules parse and work with XML documents. The DBIx::XML_RDB module converts XML documents to and from SQL statements. You can parse RSS documents for newsfeeds using the XML::RSS module.

WHAT'S NEXT

The final offering in this book is the three references provided in Appendixes A, B, and C. You'll likely find them of significant value in your work. Appendix A gives you a detailed reference of the JavaScript object model; Appendix B is a reference to Perl's most common functions and operators; and Appendix C describes the most handy modules and pragmas available in Perl, including modules new to Perl 5.8.0.

Appendix A
JavaScript Object Reference

This appendix provides an object reference manual for the JavaScript and JScript languages. It covers Navigator objects up to JavaScript 1.5 and Internet Explorer (IE) objects up to JScript 5.6. It identifies the properties, methods, and events of Navigator *and* IE objects, making it easier to select objects, properties, methods, and events that support cross-browser scripting.

Each object is presented in alphabetical order and includes a brief description and a listing of its properties, methods, and events. Properties and methods that are supported by both Navigator and IE are described. The earliest browser version that supports a particular property, method, and event is identified.

A (Anchor)

First Supported In: Navigator 2, IE 3

Represents a document-internal target of a hypertext link. An Anchor object is created for each A tag in the document that specifies a NAME attribute. These objects may be accessed from the anchors property of the document object. Anchor is referred to as the A object in Microsoft's documentation and is combined with the Netscape Link object.

Under Navigator, an Anchor object may also be a Link object if the A tag specifies the HREF attribute in addition to the NAME attribute. However, it's always recommended that you refer to objects by their most common name; doing so ensures maximal cross-platform support.

Properties

Supported by Both Navigator and IE: name (Navigator 4, IE 4); the anchor's NAME attribute

Other Properties: accessKey (IE 4), className (IE 4), charset (IE 6), coords (IE 6), dataFld (IE 4), dataSrc (IE 4), document (IE 4), hash (IE 4), host (IE 4), hostname (IE 4), href (IE 4), id (IE 4), innerHTML (IE 4), innerText (IE 4), isTextEdit (IE 4), lang (IE 4), language (IE 4), Methods (IE 4), offsetHeight (IE 4), offsetLeft (IE 4), offsetParent (IE 4), offsetTop (IE 4), offsetWidth (IE 4), outerHTML (IE 4), outerText (IE 4), parentElement (IE 4), parentTextEdit (IE 4), pathname (IE 4), port (IE 4), protocol (IE 4), recordNumber (IE 4), rel (IE 4), rev (IE 4), search (IE 4), sourceIndex (IE 4), style (IE 4), tabIndex (IE 4), tagName (IE 4), target (IE 4), text (Navigator 4), title (IE 4), type (IE 6), urn (IE 4), x (Navigator 4), y (Navigator 4)

Methods

Supported by Both Navigator and IE: None

Other Methods: blur (IE 4), click (IE 4), contains (IE 4), focus (IE 4), getAttribute (IE 4), insertAdjacentHTML (IE 4), insertAdjacentext (IE 4), removeAttribute (IE 4), scrollIntoView (IE 4), setAttribute (IE 4)

Events

onblur (IE 4), onclick (IE 4), ondblclick (Navigator 4, IE 4), ondragstart (IE 4), onerrorupdate (IE 4), onfilterchange (IE 4), onfocus (IE 4), onhelp (IE 4), onkeydown (IE 4), onkeypress (IE 4), onkeyup (IE 4), onmousedown (IE 4), onmousemove (IE 4), onmouseout (Navigator 3, IE 4), onmouseover (Navigator 2, IE 3), onmouseup (IE 4), onmousewheel (IE 6), onselectstart (IE 4), onselectstartonmousewheel (IE 6)

ACRONYM

First Supported In: IE 4

Provides access to the HTML ACRONYM tag.

Properties

Supported by Both Navigator and IE: None

Other Properties: className (IE 4), document (IE 4), id (IE 4), innerHTML (IE 4), innerText (IE 4), isTextEdit (IE 4), lang (IE 4), language (IE 4), offsetHeight (IE 4), offsetLeft (IE 4), offsetParent (IE 4), offsetTop (IE 4), offsetWidth (IE 4), outerHTML (IE 4), outerText (IE 4), parentElement (IE 4), parentTextEdit (IE 4), sourceIndex (IE 4), style (IE 4), tagName (IE 4), title (IE 4)

Methods

Supported by Both Navigator and IE: None

Other Methods: click (IE 4), contains (IE 4), getAttribute (IE 4), insertAdjacentHTML (IE 4), insertAdjacentText (IE 4), removeAttribute (IE 4), scrollIntoView (IE 4), setAttribute (IE 4)

Events

onclick (IE 4), ondblclick (IE 4), ondragstart (IE 4), onfilterchange (IE 4), onhelp (IE 4), onkeydown (IE 4), onkeypress (IE 4), onkeyup (IE 4), onmousedown (IE 4), onmousemove (IE 4), onmouseout (IE 4), onmouseover (IE 4), onmouseup (IE 4)

ActiveXObject

First Supported In: IE 4

Provides access to ActiveX objects via JavaScript. Has no defined properties, methods, or events.

Constructor

```
var newObject = new ActiveXObject("servername.typename"[,
    "location"])
```

Creates the `ActiveXObject` of the specified type from the specified server. The location can be used to specify the location of a remote server.

ADDRESS

First Supported In: IE 4

Provides access to the HTML ADDRESS tag.

Properties

Supported by Both Navigator and IE: None

Other Properties: `className` (IE 4), `document` (IE 4), `id` (IE 4), `inner-HTML` (IE 4), `innerText` (IE 4), `isTextEdit` (IE 4), `lang` (IE 4), `language` (IE 4), `offsetHeight` (IE 4), `offsetLeft` (IE 4), `offsetParent` (IE 4), `offsetTop` (IE 4), `offsetWidth` (IE 4), `outerHTML` (IE 4), `outerText` (IE 4), `parentElement` (IE 4), `parentTextEdit` (IE 4), `sourceIndex` (IE 4), `style` (IE 4), `tagName` (IE 4), `title` (IE 4)

Methods

Supported by Both Navigator and IE: None

Other Methods: `click` (IE 4), `contains` (IE 4), `getAttribute` (IE 4), `insertAdjacentHTML` (IE 4), `insertAdjacentText` (IE 4), `remove-Attribute` (IE 4), `scrollIntoView` (IE 4), `setAttribute` (IE 4)

Events

`onclick` (IE 4), `ondblclick` (IE 4), `ondragstart` (IE 4), `onhelp` (IE 4), `onkeydown` (IE 4), `onkeypress` (IE 4), `onkeyup` (IE 4), `onmousedown` (IE 4), `onmousemove` (IE 4), `onmouseout` (IE 4), `onmouseover` (IE 4), `onmouseup` (IE 4), `onmousewheel` (IE 6), `onselectstart` (IE 4), `onselect-startonmousewheel` (IE 6)

Applet

First Supported In: Navigator 3, IE 4

Represents a Java applet embedded in a web page. The `applets` property of the document object provides access to a list of `Applet` objects associated with the document. An applet is accessible to JavaScript only if the MAYSCRIPT attribute is supplied in the applet's APPLET tag.

For example, the following APPLET tag loads an applet that is accessible from JavaScript:

```
<APPLET CODE="myClassFile" MAYSCRIPT></APPLET>
```

Because the following APPLET tag does not include the MAYSCRIPT attribute, it cannot be accessed from JavaScript:

```
<APPLET CODE="myClassFile></APPLET>
```

The Applet object inherits all the public properties and methods of the Java applet it represents.

Properties

Supported by Both Navigator and IE: None

Other Properties: accessKey (IE 4), align (IE 4), altHTML (IE 4), className (IE 4), code (IE 1), codeBase (IE 4), dataFld (IE 4), dataSrc (IE 4), document (IE 4), height (IE 4), hspace (IE 4), id (IE 4), isText-Edit (IE 4), lang (IE 4), language (IE 4), name (IE 4), offsetHeight (IE 4), offsetLeft (IE 4), offsetParent (IE 4), offsetTop (IE 4), offset-Width (IE 4), outerHTML (IE 4), outerText (IE 4), parentElement (IE 4), parentTextEdit (IE 4), sourceIndex (IE 4), src (IE 4), style (IE 4), tagName (IE 4), title (IE 4), vspace (IE 4)

Methods

Supported by Both Navigator and IE: None

Other Methods: blur (IE 4), click (IE 4), contains (IE 4), focus (IE 4), getAttribute (IE 4), insertAdjacentHTML (IE 4), insert-AdjacentText (IE 4), removeAttribute (IE 4), scrollIntoView (IE 4), setAttribute (IE 4)

Events

onafterupdate (IE 4), onbeforeupdate (IE 4), onblur (IE 4), onclick (IE 4), ondataavailable (IE 4), ondatasetchanged (IE 4), ondataset-complete (IE 4), ondblclick (IE 4), onerrorupdate (IE 4), onfocus (IE 4), onhelp (IE 4), onkeydown (IE 4), onkeypress (IE 4), onkeyup (IE 4), onload (IE 4), onmousedown (IE 4), onmousemove (IE 4), onmouseout (IE 4), onmouseover (IE 4), onmouseup (IE 4), onreadystatechange (IE 4), onresize (IE 4), onrowenter (IE 4), onrowexit (IE 4)

Area

First Supported In: Navigator 3, IE 4

Defines an area of an image map. From a JavaScript perspective, Area is functionally identical to a Link object; it is associated with a URL. This URL is loaded when a user clicks on the area of the image map represented by the Area object.

Properties

Supported by Both Navigator and IE:

- ▶ hash (Navigator 2.02, IE 3)—The name of an anchor in the URL
- ▶ host (Navigator 2.02, IE 3)—A host name or IP address that represents the URL's host value
- ▶ hostname (Navigator 2.02, IE 3)—The host:port portion of the URL
- ▶ href (Navigator 2.02, IE 3)—The text of the entire URL
- ▶ pathname (Navigator 2.02, IE 3)—The pathname portion of the URL
- ▶ port (Navigator 2.02, IE 3)—The port value of the URL
- ▶ protocol (Navigator 2, IE 3.03)—The URL's protocol type
- ▶ search (Navigator 2, IE 3.03)—The value of any query string that is included in the URL
- ▶ target (Navigator 2, IE 3.03)—The value of the URL's TARGET attribute

Other Properties: alt (IE 4), className (IE 4), coords (IE 4), document (IE 4), id (IE 4), isTextEdit (IE 4), lang (IE 4), language (IE 4), noHref (IE 4), offsetHeight (IE 4), offsetLeft (IE 4), offsetParent (IE 4), offsetTop (IE 4), offsetWidth (IE 4), outerHTML (IE 4), outerText (IE 4), parentElement (IE 4), parentTextEdit (IE 4), sourceIndex (IE 4), style (IE 4), tabIndex (IE 4), tagName (IE 4), text (Navigator 4), title (IE 4), x (Navigator 4), y (Navigator 4)

Methods

Supported by Both Navigator and IE: None

Other Methods: blur (IE 4), click (IE 4), contains (IE 4), focus (IE 4), getAttribute (IE 4), handleEvent (Navigator 4), insertAdjacentHTML

(IE 4), `insertAdjacentText` (IE 4), `removeAttribute` (IE 4), `scrollIntoView` (IE 4), `setAttribute` (IE 4)

Events

`onblur` (IE 4), `onclick` (IE 4), `ondblclick` (Navigator 2, IE 3), `ondragstart` (IE 4), `onfilterchange` (IE 4), `onfocus` (IE 4), `onhelp` (IE 4), `onkeydown` (IE 4), `onkeypress` (IE 4), `onkeyup` (IE 4), `onmousedown` (IE 4), `onmousemove` (IE 4), `onmouseout` (Navigator 3, IE 4), `onmouseover` (Navigator 2, IE 3), `onmouseup` (IE 4), `onmousewheel` (IE 6), `onselectstart` (IE 4), `onselectstartonmousewheel` (IE 6)

Array

First Supported In: Navigator 3, IE 4

Represents a JavaScript array. Array was first introduced in JavaScript 1.1, but was modified in JavaScript 1.3 to ensure ECMA 262 compliance. It is supported in JScript 3 and later. It has no defined events.

Constructors

Arrays can be constructed in the following ways:

```
myArray = new Array()     // new empty array
myArray = new Array(10) // new Array(length)
myArray = new Array(100, 20, 40) // new Array(element_1, ...,
element_n)
myArray = [2, 4, 6, 8] // Assignment of array literal
```

The first form creates an empty array. The second causes an array of length 10 to be created. As with the first form, its elements are initially undefined. The third form creates an array of length 3, consisting of the values 100, 20, and 40. In the final form, the myArray variable is assigned an array literal that represents a four-element array consisting of the values 2, 4, 6, and 8.

If the constructor new Array(*n*), where *n* is a positive integer, is used with Navigator 4 or later and the script's LANGUAGE attribute is set to JavaScript1.2, then the constructor creates a one-element array consisting of the value *n*. This is a quirk that Netscape designed into JavaScript 1.2. This problem does not occur with IE or with Navigator when the LANGUAGE attribute is not set to JavaScript1.2.

Properties
Supported by Both Navigator and IE:

▶ `constructor` (Navigator 3, IE 4)—A reference to the object's constructor

▶ `length` (Navigator 3, IE 4)—The number of elements / size of the array

▶ `prototype` (Navigator 3, IE 4)—Used to define additional properties

Other Properties: `index` (Navigator 4), `input` (Navigator 4)

Methods
Supported by Both Navigator and IE:

▶ `concat(`*array1*`, `*array2*`, ..., `*array3*`)` (Navigator 4, IE 4)—Returns a new `Array` object that is the original array concatenated with the arrays identified as the method's arguments.

▶ `join(`*separator*`)` (Navigator 3, IE 4)—Joins the elements of the array together as a string. The *separator* is placed between the joined elements.

▶ `reverse()` (Navigator 3, IE 4)—Reverses the elements of the array.

▶ `slice(`*begin*`[,`*end*`])` (Navigator 4, IE 4)—Extracts and returns the array slice from *begin* (inclusive) to *end* (exclusive). If *end* is not supplied, then the slice continues to the end of the array.

▶ `sort(`*compareFunction*`)` (Navigator 3, IE 4)—Sorts the elements of the array using the specified compare function. If the compare function is omitted, then the elements are sorted in dictionary order. This method was updated to achieve ECMA 262 compliance in JavaScript 1.2.

▶ `toString()` (Navigator 3, IE 4)—Returns a string representation of the array. This method is compatible with `toSource()`.

▶ `valueOf()` (Navigator 3, IE 4)—Returns the primitive value of the array. For Boolean arrays, a Boolean value is returned. For number and data arrays, a number value is returned. For all other arrays, a string value is returned.

Other Methods: `pop` (Navigator 4), `push` (Navigator 4), `shift` (Navigator 4), `splice` (Navigator 4), `toSource` (Navigator 4.06), `unshift`

(Navigator 4), pop (IE 5.5+), push (IE 5.5+), shift (IE 5.5+), unshift (IE 5.5+), splice (IE 5.5+)

Attribute

First Supported In: IE 5

Encapsulates an attribute of an HTML element as an object. Has no defined events.

Properties

Supported by Both Navigator and IE: None

Other Properties: attributes (IE 6), childNodes (IE 6), cloneNode (IE 6), expando (IE 6), firstChild (IE 6), name (IE 6), nextSibling (IE 6), nodeName (IE 5), nodeType (IE 5), nodeValue (IE 5), parentNode (IE 6), previousSibling (IE 6), specified (IE 5)

Methods

Supported by Both Navigator and IE: None

Other Methods: appendChild (IE 6), createAttribute (IE 6), get-AttributeNode (IE 6), getNamedItem (IE 6), hasChildNodes (IE 6), insertBefore (IE 6), lastChild (IE 6), removeAttributeNode (IE 6), removeChild (IE 6), removeNamedItem (IE 6), replaceChild (IE 6), setNamedItem (IE 6)

B

First Supported In: IE 4

Provides access to the HTML B tag. **Note:** This tag is deprecated in the latest HTML specification, in favor of the Cascading Style Sheet (CSS) font-weight element.

Properties

Supported by Both Navigator and IE: None

Other Properties: className (IE 4), document (IE 4), id (IE 4), inner-HTML (IE 4), innerText (IE 4), isTextEdit (IE 4), lang (IE 4), language (IE 4), offsetHeight (IE 4), offsetLeft (IE 4), offsetParent (IE 4), offsetTop (IE 4), offsetWidth (IE 4), outerHTML (IE 4), outerText (IE 4), parentElement (IE 4), parentTextEdit (IE 4), sourceIndex (IE 4), style (IE 4), tagName (IE 4), title (IE 4)

Methods

Supported by Both Navigator and IE: None

Other Methods: click (IE 4), contains (IE 4), getAttribute (IE 4), insertAdjacentHTML (IE 4), insertAdjacentText (IE 4), removeAttribute (IE 4), scrollIntoView (IE 4), setAttribute (IE 4)

Events

onclick (IE 4), ondblclick (IE 4), ondragstart (IE 4), onfilterchange (IE 4), onhelp (IE 4), onkeydown (IE 4), onkeypress (IE 4), onkeyup (IE 4), onmousedown (IE 4), onmousemove (IE 4), onmouseout (IE 4), onmouseover (IE 4), onmouseup (IE 4), onmousewheel (IE 6), onselectstart (IE 4), onselectstartonmousewheel (IE 6)

BASE

First Supported In: IE 4

Provides access to the HTML BASE tag. Has no defined events.

Properties

Supported by Both Navigator and IE: None

Other Properties: className (IE 4), document (IE 4), href (IE 4), id (IE 4), isTextEdit (IE 4), lang (IE 4), outerHTML (IE 4), outerText (IE 4), parentElement (IE 4), parentTextEdit (IE 4), sourceIndex (IE 4), tagName (IE 4), target (IE 4), title (IE 4)

Methods

Supported by Both Navigator and IE: None

Other Methods: contains (IE 4), getAttribute (IE 4), removeAttribute (IE 4), setAttribute (IE 4)

BASEFONT

First Supported In: IE 4

Provides access to the HTML BASEFONT tag. Has no defined events. **Note:** This tag is deprecated in the latest HTML specification in favor of various CSS attributes, including font-size, font-name, font-style, and color.

Properties

Supported by Both Navigator and IE: None

Other Properties: className (IE 4), color (IE 4), document (IE 4), face (IE 4), id (IE 4), isTextEdit (IE 4), outerHTML (IE 4), outerText (IE 4), parentElement (IE 4), parentTextEdit (IE 4), size (IE 4), sourceIndex (IE 4), tagName (IE 4)

Methods

Supported by Both Navigator and IE: None

Other Methods: contains (IE 4), getAttribute (IE 4), removeAttribute (IE 4), setAttribute (IE 4)

BDO

First Supported In: IE 5

Provides the capability to control the reading order of a block of text.

Properties

Supported by Both Navigator and IE: None

Other Properties: accessKey (IE 5), canHaveChildren (IE 5), canHaveHTML (IE 5), className (IE 5), clientHeight (IE 5), clientLeft (IE 5), clientTop (IE 5), clientWidth (IE 5), contentEditable (IE 5), currentStyle (IE 5), dir (IE 5), disabled (IE 5), firstChild (IE 5), hasLayout (IE 5), hideFocus (IE 5), id (IE 5), innerHTML (IE 5), innerText (IE 5), isContentEditable (IE 5), isDisabled (IE 5), isTextEdit (IE 5), lang (IE 5), language (IE 5), lastChild (IE 5), nextSibling (IE 5), nodeName (IE 5), nodeType (IE 5), nodeValue (IE 5), offsetHeight (IE 5), offsetLeft (IE 5), offsetParent (IE 5), offsetTop (IE 5), offsetWidth (IE 5), outerHTML (IE 5), outerText (IE 5), parentElement (IE 5), parentNode (IE 5), parentTextEdit (IE 5), previousSibling (IE 5), readyState (IE 5), scopeName (IE 5), scrollHeight (IE 5), scrollLeft (IE 5), scrollTop (IE 5), scrollWidth (IE 5), sourceIndex (IE 5), tabIndex (IE 5), tagName (IE 5), tagUrn (IE 5), title (IE 5)

Methods

Supported by Both Navigator and IE: None

Other Methods: appendChild (IE 5), applyElement (IE 5), blur (IE 5), clearAttributes (IE 5), cloneNode (IE 5), componentFromPoint (IE 5), fireEvent (IE 5), focus (IE 5), getAdjacentText (IE 5), getElementsByTagName (IE 5), getExpression (IE 5), hasChildNodes (IE 5), insertAdjacentElement (IE 5), insertBefore (IE 5), mergeAttributes (IE 5), removeChild (IE 5), removeExpression (IE 5), removeNode (IE 5), replaceAdjacentText (IE 5), replaceChild (IE 5), replaceNode (IE 5), setActive (IE 5), setExpression (IE 5), swapNode (IE 5)

Events

onafterupdate (IE 5), onbeforecopy (IE 5), onbeforecut (IE 5), onbeforefocusenter (IE 5), onbeforefocusleave (IE 5), onbeforepaste (IE 5), onbeforeupdate (IE 5), onblur (IE 5), oncellchange (IE 5), onclick (IE 5), oncontextmenu (IE 5), oncontrolselect (IE 5), oncopy (IE 5), oncut (IE 5), ondblclick (IE 5), ondrag (IE 5), ondragend (IE 5), ondragenter (IE 5), ondragleave (IE 5), ondragover (IE 5), ondragstart (IE 5), ondrop (IE 5), onerrorupdate (IE 5), onfilterchange (IE 5), onfocus (IE 5), onfocusenter (IE 5), onfocusleave (IE 5), onhelp (IE 5), onkeydown (IE 5), onkeypress (IE 5), onkeyup (IE 5), onlosecapture (IE 5), onmousedown (IE 5), onmouseenter (IE 5), onmouseleave (IE 5), onmousemove (IE 5), onmouseout (IE 5), onmouseover (IE 5), onmouseup (IE 5), onpaste (IE 5), onpropertychange (IE 5), onreadystatechange (IE 5), onresizeend (IE 5), onresizestart (IE 5), onscroll (IE 5), onselectstart (IE 5)

BGSOUND

First Supported In: IE 4

Provides access to the HTML BGSOUND tag. Has no defined events. **Note:** This tag has never been a part of the formal HTML specification, and its support is expected to dwindle over time.

Properties

Supported by Both Navigator and IE: None

Other Properties: balance (IE 4), className (IE 4), document (IE 4), id (IE 4), isTextEdit (IE 4), loop (IE 4), offsetHeight (IE 4), offsetLeft (IE 4), offsetParent (IE 4), offsetTop (IE 4), offsetWidth (IE 4), outerHTML (IE 4), outerText (IE 4), parentElement (IE 4), parentTextEdit (IE 4), sourceIndex (IE 4), src (IE 4), style (IE 4), tagName (IE 4), title (IE 4), volume (IE 4)

Methods

Supported by Both Navigator and IE: None

Other Methods: contains (IE 4), getAttribute (IE 4), remove-Attribute (IE 4), setAttribute (IE 4)

BIG

First Supported In: IE 4

Provides access to the HTML BIG tag. **Note:** This tag is deprecated in the latest HTML specification in favor of the CSS attribute font-size.

Properties

Supported by Both Navigator and IE: None

Other Properties: className (IE 4), document (IE 4), id (IE 4), innerHTML (IE 4), innerText (IE 4), isTextEdit (IE 4), lang (IE 4), language (IE 4), offsetHeight (IE 4), offsetLeft (IE 4), offsetParent (IE 4), offsetTop (IE 4), offsetWidth (IE 4), outerHTML (IE 4), outerText (IE 4), parentElement (IE 4), parentTextEdit (IE 4), sourceIndex (IE 4), style (IE 4), tagName (IE 4), title (IE 4)

Methods

Supported by Both Navigator and IE: None

Other Methods: click (IE 4), contains (IE 4), getAttribute (IE 4), insertAdjacentHTML (IE 4), insertAdjacentText (IE 4), remove-Attribute (IE 4), scrollIntoView (IE 4), setAttribute (IE 4)

Events

onclick (IE 4), ondblclick (IE 4), ondragstart (IE 4), onfilterchange (IE 4), onhelp (IE 4), onkeydown (IE 4), onkeypress (IE 4), onkeyup (IE 4), onmousedown (IE 4), onmousemove (IE 4), onmouseout (IE 4), onmouseover (IE 4), onmouseup (IE 4), onmousewheel (IE 6), onselectstart (IE 4)

BLOCKQUOTE

First Supported In: IE 4

Provides access to the HTML BLOCKQUOTE tag. **Note:** This tag is deprecated in the latest HTML specification in favor of the CSS attributes margin-left and margin-right.

Properties

Supported by Both Navigator and IE: None

Other Properties: className (IE 4), document (IE 4), id (IE 4), inner-HTML (IE 4), innerText (IE 4), isTextEdit (IE 4), lang (IE 4), language (IE 4), offsetHeight (IE 4), offsetLeft (IE 4), offsetParent (IE 4), offsetTop (IE 4), offsetWidth (IE 4), outerHTML (IE 4), outerText (IE 4), parentElement (IE 4), parentTextEdit (IE 4), sourceIndex (IE 4), style (IE 4), tagName (IE 4), title (IE 4)

Methods

Supported by Both Navigator and IE: None

Other Methods: click (IE 4), contains (IE 4), getAttribute (IE 4), insertAdjacentHTML (IE 4), insertAdjacentText (IE 4), remove-Attribute (IE 4), scrollIntoView (IE 4), setAttribute (IE 4)

Events

onclick (IE 4), ondblclick (IE 4), ondragstart (IE 4), onfilterchange (IE 4), onhelp (IE 4), onkeydown (IE 4), onkeypress (IE 4), onkeyup (IE 4), onmousedown (IE 4), onmousemove (IE 4), onmouseout (IE 4), onmouseover (IE 4), onmouseup (IE 4), onmousewheel (IE 6), onselectstart (IE 4)

BODY

First Supported In: IE 4

Provides access to the HTML BODY tag.

Properties

Supported by Both Navigator and IE: None

Other Properties: accessKey (IE 4), aLink (IE 4), background (IE 4), bgColor (IE 4), bgProperties (IE 4), bottomMargin (IE 4), className (IE 4), clientHeight (IE 4), clientLeft (IE 4), clientTop (IE 4), clientWidth (IE 4), document (IE 4), filter (IE 4), id (IE 4), innerHTML (IE 4), innerText (IE 4), isTextEdit (IE 4), lang (IE 4), language (IE 4), leftMargin (IE 4), link (IE 4), noWrap (IE 4), offsetHeight (IE 4), offsetLeft (IE 4), offsetParent (IE 4), offsetTop (IE 4), offsetWidth (IE 4), outerHTML (IE 4), outerText (IE 4), parentElement (IE 4), parentTextEdit (IE 4), recordNumber (IE 4), rightMargin (IE 4), scroll (IE 4), scrollHeight (IE 4), scrollLeft (IE 4), scrollTop (IE 4), scrollWidth (IE 4), sourceIndex (IE 4), style (IE 4), tabIndex (IE 4), tagName (IE 4), text (IE 4), title (IE 4), topMargin (IE 4), vLink (IE 4)

Methods

Supported by Both Navigator and IE: None

Other Methods: click (IE 4), contains (IE 4), createTextRange (IE 4), getAttribute (IE 4), insertAdjacentHTML (IE 4), insertAdjacentText (IE 4), removeAttribute (IE 4), setAttribute (IE 4)

Events

onafterupdate (IE 4), onbeforeunload (IE 4), onbeforeupdate (IE 4), onchange (IE 4), onclick (IE 4), ondataavailable (IE 4), ondatasetchanged (IE 4), ondatasetcomplete (IE 4), ondblclick (IE 4), ondragstart (IE 4), onerrorupdate (IE 4), onfilterchange (IE 4), onhelp (IE 4), onkeydown (IE 4), onkeypress (IE 4), onkeyup (IE 4), onload (IE 4), onmousedown (IE 4), onmousemove (IE 4), onmouseout (IE 4), onmouseover (IE 4), onmouseup (IE 4), onmousewheel (IE 6), onrowenter (IE 4), onrowexit (IE 4), onscroll (IE 4), onselectstart (IE 4), onunload (IE 4)

Boolean

First Supported In: Navigator 3, IE 4

Provides an object representation of the primitive Boolean true and false values. It's important not to confuse Boolean objects with Boolean primitive values: Boolean objects always evaluate to true when used in place of a Boolean primitive value. The Boolean object has no associated events. It was introduced in JavaScript 1.1, but it was modified in JavaScript 1.3 to ensure ECMA 262 compliance. It is supported in JScript 3 and later.

Constructor

new Boolean(*value*)

The *value* used in the constructor creates an object that represents false if *value* is false, 0, "", NaN (not a number), null, or undefined, or if *value* is omitted. For any other *value*, an object is created that represents true.

Properties

Supported by Both Navigator and IE:

▶ constructor (Navigator 3, IE 4)—A reference to the object's constructor

▶ prototype (Navigator 3, IE 4)—Used to define additional properties

Methods
Supported by Both Navigator and IE:

- ▶ toString() (Navigator 3, IE 4)—Returns a string value of the object that is compatible with toSource()
- ▶ valueOf() (Navigator 3, IE 4)—Returns the object's primitive value

Other Methods: toSource (Navigator 4.06)

BR

First Supported In: IE 4

Provides access to the HTML BR tag. Has no defined events.

Properties
Supported by Both Navigator and IE: None

Other Properties: className (IE 4), clear (IE 4), document (IE 4), id (IE 4), isTextEdit (IE 4), language (IE 4), offsetHeight (IE 4), offset-Left (IE 4), offsetParent (IE 4), offsetTop (IE 4), offsetWidth (IE 4), outerHTML (IE 4), outerText (IE 4), parentElement (IE 4), parentTextEdit (IE 4), sourceIndex (IE 4), style (IE 4), tagName (IE 4), title (IE 4)

Methods
Supported by Both Navigator and IE: None

Other Methods: contains (IE 4), getAttribute (IE 4), insert-AdjacentHTML (IE 4), insertAdjacentText (IE 4), removeAttribute (IE 4), scrollIntoView (IE 4), setAttribute (IE 4)

Button

First Supported In: Navigator 2, IE 3

Provides access to the buttons of an HTML form. The basic Button object was introduced in JavaScript 1.0 and updated with JavaScript 1.1 and 1.2.

Properties
Supported by Both Navigator and IE:

- ▶ form (Navigator 2, IE 3)—Provides a reference to the form object that contains the button

- ► name (Navigator 2, IE 3)—The value of the button's NAME attribute

- ► type (Navigator 3, IE 4)—The value of the button's TYPE attribute

- ► value (Navigator 2, IE 3)—The value of the button's VALUE attribute

Other Properties: accessKey (IE 4), className (IE 4), dataFld (IE 4), dataFormatAs (IE 4), dataSrc (IE 4), disabled (IE 4), document (IE 4), id (IE 4), isTextEdit (IE 4), lang (IE 4), language (IE 4), offsetHeight (IE 4), offsetLeft (IE 4), offsetParent (IE 4), offsetTop (IE 4), offset-Width (IE 4), outerHTML (IE 4), outerText (IE 4), parentElement (IE 4), parentTextEdit (IE 4), readOnly (IE 4), recordNumber (IE 4), source-Index (IE 4), style (IE 4), tabIndex (IE 4), tagName (IE 4), title (IE 4)

Methods
Supported by Both Navigator and IE:

- ► blur() (Navigator 2, IE 3)—Removes input focus from the button

- ► click() (Navigator 2, IE 3)—Simulates clicking of the button

- ► focus() (Navigator 2, IE 3)—Moves input focus to the button

Other Methods: contains (IE 4), createTextRange (IE 4), get-Attribute (IE 4), handleEvent (Navigator 4), insertAdjacentHTML (IE 4), insertAdjacentText (IE 4), removeAttribute (IE 4), scrollIntoView (IE 4), select (IE 4), setAttribute (IE 4)

Events
onblur (Navigator 3, IE 4), onclick (Navigator 2, IE 3), ondblclick (IE 4), onfocus (Navigator 3, IE 4), onhelp (IE 4), onkeydown (IE 4), onkeypress (IE 4), onkeyup (IE 4), onmousedown (Navigator 2, IE 3), onmousemove (IE 4), onmouseout (IE 4), onmouseover (IE 4), onmouseup (Navigator 2, IE 3), onresize (IE 4), onselect (IE 4)

BUTTON

First Supported In: IE 4

Provides the capability to access buttons that contain HTML. **Note:** Buttons containing HTML are not supported in the latest HTML specification. Support for this object is expected to be eliminated over time.

Properties

Supported by Both Navigator and IE: None

Other Properties: accessKey (IE 4), className (IE 4), dataFld (IE 4), dataFormatAs (IE 4), dataSrc (IE 4), disabled (IE 4), document (IE 4), form (IE 4), id (IE 4), innerHTML (IE 4), innerText (IE 4), isTextEdit (IE 4), lang (IE 4), language (IE 4), name (IE 4), offsetHeight (IE 4), offsetLeft (IE 4), offsetParent (IE 4), offsetTop (IE 4), offsetWidth (IE 4), outerHTML (IE 4), outerText (IE 4), parentElement (IE 4), parentTextEdit (IE 4), sourceIndex (IE 4), status (IE 4), style (IE 4), tagName (IE 4), title (IE 4), type (IE 4), value (IE 4)

Methods

Supported by Both Navigator and IE: None

Other Methods: blur (IE 4), click (IE 4), contains (IE 4), createTextRange (IE 4), focus (IE 4), getAttribute (IE 4), insertAdjacentHTML (IE 4), insertAdjacentText (IE 4), removeAttribute (IE 4), scrollIntoView (IE 4), setAttribute (IE 4)

Events

onafterupdate (IE 4), onbeforeupdate (IE 4), onblur (IE 4), onclick (IE 4), ondblclick (IE 4), ondragstart (IE 4), onfilterchange (IE 4), onfocus (IE 4), onhelp (IE 4), onkeydown (IE 4), onkeypress (IE 4), onkeyup (IE 4), onmousedown (IE 4), onmousemove (IE 4), onmouseout (IE 4), onmouseover (IE 4), onmouseup (IE 4), onmousewheel (IE 6), onresize (IE 4), onrowenter (IE 4), onrowexit (IE 4), onselectstart (IE 4)

CAPTION

First Supported In: IE 4

Provides access to the HTML CAPTION tag.

Properties

Supported by Both Navigator and IE: None

Other Properties: align (IE 4), className (IE 4), clientHeight (IE 4), clientLeft (IE 4), clientTop (IE 4), clientWidth (IE 4), document (IE 4), id (IE 4), innerText (IE 4), isTextEdit (IE 4), lang (IE 4), language (IE 4), offsetHeight (IE 4), offsetLeft (IE 4), offsetParent

(IE 4), offsetTop (IE 4), offsetWidth (IE 4), outerText (IE 4), parent-Element (IE 4), parentTextEdit (IE 4), sourceIndex (IE 4), style (IE 4), tagName (IE 4), title (IE 4), vAlign (IE 4)

Methods
Supported by Both Navigator and IE: None

Other Methods: blur (IE 4), click (IE 4), contains (IE 4), focus (IE 4), getAttribute (IE 4), insertAdjacentHTML (IE 4), insertAdjacentText (IE 4), removeAttribute (IE 4), scrollIntoView (IE 4), setAttribute (IE 4)

Events
onafterupdate (IE 4), onbeforeupdate (IE 4), onblur (IE 4), onchange (IE 4), onclick (IE 4), ondblclick (IE 4), ondragstart (IE 4), onfilterchange (IE 4), onfocus (IE 4), onhelp (IE 4), onkeydown (IE 4), onkeypress (IE 4), onkeyup (IE 4), onmousedown (IE 4), onmousemove (IE 4), onmouseout (IE 4), onmouseover (IE 4), onmouseup (IE 4), onresize (IE 4), onrowenter (IE 4), onrowexit (IE 4), onscroll (IE 4), onselect (IE 4), onmousewheel (IE 6), onselectstart (IE 4)

CENTER

First Supported In: IE 4

Provides access to the HTML CENTER tag. **Note:** This tag is deprecated in the latest HTML specification.

Properties
Supported by Both Navigator and IE: None

Other Properties: className (IE 4), document (IE 4), id (IE 4), innerHTML (IE 4), innerText (IE 4), isTextEdit (IE 4), lang (IE 4), language (IE 4), offsetHeight (IE 4), offsetLeft (IE 4), offsetParent (IE 4), offsetTop (IE 4), offsetWidth (IE 4), outerHTML (IE 4), outerText (IE 4), parentElement (IE 4), parentTextEdit (IE 4), sourceIndex (IE 4), style (IE 4), tagName (IE 4), title (IE 4)

Methods
Supported by Both Navigator and IE: None

Other Methods: click (IE 4), contains (IE 4), getAttribute (IE 4), insertAdjacentHTML (IE 4), insertAdjacentText (IE 4), remove-Attribute (IE 4), scrollIntoView (IE 4), setAttribute (IE 4)

Events

onclick (IE 4), ondblclick (IE 4), ondragstart (IE 4), onfilterchange (IE 4), onhelp (IE 4), onkeydown (IE 4), onkeypress (IE 4), onkeyup (IE 4), onmousedown (IE 4), onmousemove (IE 4), onmouseout (IE 4), onmouseover (IE 4), onmouseup (IE 4), onmousewheel (IE 6), onselectstart (IE 4)

Checkbox

First Supported In: Navigator 2, IE 3

Provides access to the check boxes of an HTML form. The basic Checkbox object was introduced in JavaScript 1.0 and updated with JavaScript 1.1 and 1.2.

Properties
Supported by Both Navigator and IE:

▶ checked (Navigator 2, IE 3)—Provides the Boolean value of the check box's selection state

▶ defaultChecked (Navigator 2, IE 3)—The value of the check box's CHECKED attribute

▶ form (Navigator 2, IE 3)—Provides a reference to the form object that contains the check box

▶ name (Navigator 2, IE 3)—The value of the check box's NAME attribute

▶ type (Navigator 3, IE 4)—The value of the check box's TYPE attribute

▶ value (Navigator 2, IE 3)—The value of the check box's VALUE attribute

Other Properties: accessKey (IE 4), className (IE 4), dataFld (IE 4), dataSrc (IE 4), disabled (IE 4), document (IE 4), id (IE 4), indeterminate (IE 4), isTextEdit (IE 4), lang (IE 4), language (IE 4), offsetHeight (IE 4), offsetLeft (IE 4), offsetParent (IE 4), offsetTop (IE 4), offsetWidth (IE 4), outerText (IE 4), parentElement (IE 4), parentTextEdit (IE 4), recordNumber (IE 4), size (IE 4), source-Index (IE 4), status (IE 4), style (IE 4), tabIndex (IE 4), tagName (IE 4), title (IE 4)

Methods
Supported by Both Navigator and IE:

- ▶ blur() (Navigator 2, IE 3)—Removes input focus from the check box

- ▶ click() (Navigator 2, IE 3)—Simulates clicking of the check box

- ▶ focus() (Navigator 2, IE 3)—Moves input focus to the check box

Other Methods: contains (IE 4), getAttribute (IE 4), handleEvent (Navigator 4), insertAdjacentHTML (IE 4), insertAdjacentText (IE 4), removeAttribute (IE 4), scrollIntoView (IE 4), select (IE 4), setAttribute (IE 4)

Events

onafterupdate (IE 4), onbeforeupdate (IE 4), onblur (Navigator 3, IE 4), onchange (IE 4), onclick (Navigator 2, IE 3), ondblclick (IE 4), onerrorupdate (IE 4), onfilterchange (IE 4), onfocus (Navigator 3, IE 4), onhelp (IE 4), onkeydown (IE 4), onkeypress (IE 4), onkeyup (IE 4), onmousedown (IE 4), onmousemove (IE 4), onmouseout (IE 4), onmouseover (IE 4), onmouseup (IE 4), onresize (IE 4), onselect (IE 4)

CITE

First Supported In: IE 4

Provides access to the HTML CITE tag. **Note:** This tag is deprecated in the latest HTML specification in favor of the CSS margin attribute.

Properties
Supported by Both Navigator and IE: None

Other Properties: className (IE 4), document (IE 4), id (IE 4), innerHTML (IE 4), innerText (IE 4), isTextEdit (IE 4), lang (IE 4), language (IE 4), offsetHeight (IE 4), offsetLeft (IE 4), offsetParent (IE 4), offsetTop (IE 4), offsetWidth (IE 4), outerHTML (IE 4), outerText (IE 4), parentElement (IE 4), parentTextEdit (IE 4), sourceIndex (IE 4), style (IE 4), tagName (IE 4), title (IE 4)

Methods

Supported by Both Navigator and IE: None

Other Methods: `click` (IE 4), `contains` (IE 4), `getAttribute` (IE 4), `insertAdjacentHTML` (IE 4), `insertAdjacentText` (IE 4), `removeAttribute` (IE 4), `scrollIntoView` (IE 4), `setAttribute` (IE 4)

Events

`onclick` (IE 4), `ondblclick` (IE 4), `ondragstart` (IE 4), `onfilterchange` (IE 4), `onhelp` (IE 4), `onkeydown` (IE 4), `onkeypress` (IE 4), `onkeyup` (IE 4), `onmousedown` (IE 4), `onmousemove` (IE 4), `onmouseout` (IE 4), `onmouseover` (IE 4), `onmouseup` (IE 4), `onmousewheel` (IE 6), `onselectstart` (IE 4)

clientInformation

First Supported In: IE 5

Provides properties and methods that describe the browser that executes a script. Has no defined events.

Properties

Supported by Both Navigator and IE: None

Other Properties: `appCodeName` (IE 5), `appMinorVersion` (IE 5), `appName` (IE 5), `appVersion` (IE 5), `browserLanguage` (IE 5), `cookieEnabled` (IE 5), `cpuClass` (IE 5), `onLine` (IE 5), `platform` (IE 5), `systemLanguage` (IE 5), `userAgent` (IE 5), `userLanguage` (IE 5), `userProfile` (IE 5)

Methods

Supported by Both Navigator and IE: None

Other Methods: `javaEnabled` (IE 5), `taintEnabled` (IE 5)

clipboardData

First Supported In: IE 5

Provides access to the data saved in the Clipboard, if any. Has no defined properties or events.

Methods

Supported by Both Navigator and IE: None

Other Methods: `clearData` (IE 5), `getData` (IE 5), `setData` (IE 5)

CODE

First Supported In: IE 4

Provides access to the HTML CODE tag. **Note:** This tag is deprecated in the latest HTML specification in favor of the CSS attribute font-name.

Properties

Supported by Both Navigator and IE: None

Other Properties: className (IE 4), document (IE 4), id (IE 4), innerHTML (IE 4), innerText (IE 4), isTextEdit (IE 4), lang (IE 4), language (IE 4), offsetHeight (IE 4), offsetLeft (IE 4), offsetParent (IE 4), offsetTop (IE 4), offsetWidth (IE 4), outerHTML (IE 4), outerText (IE 4), parentElement (IE 4), parentTextEdit (IE 4), sourceIndex (IE 4), style (IE 4), tagName (IE 4), title (IE 4)

Methods

Supported by Both Navigator and IE: None

Other Methods: click (IE 4), contains (IE 4), getAttribute (IE 4), insertAdjacentHTML (IE 4), insertAdjacentText (IE 4), removeAttribute (IE 4), scrollIntoView (IE 4), setAttribute (IE 4)

Events

onclick (IE 4), ondblclick (IE 4), ondragstart (IE 4), onfilterchange (IE 4), onhelp (IE 4), onkeydown (IE 4), onkeypress (IE 4), onkeyup (IE 4), onmousedown (IE 4), onmousemove (IE 4), onmouseout (IE 4), onmouseover (IE 4), onmouseup (IE 4), onmousewheel (IE 6), onselectstart (IE 4)

COL

First Supported In: IE 4

Provides access to the HTML COL tag. Has no defined events.

Properties

Supported by Both Navigator and IE: None

Other Properties: align (IE 4), className (IE 4), document (IE 4), id (IE 4), isTextEdit (IE 4), parentElement (IE 4), parentTextEdit (IE 4), span (IE 4), style (IE 4), tagName (IE 4), title (IE 4), vAlign (IE 4), width (IE 4)

Methods

Supported by Both Navigator and IE: None

Other Methods: contains (IE 4), getAttribute (IE 4), remove-Attribute (IE 4), setAttribute (IE 4)

COLGROUP

First Supported In: IE 4

Provides access to the HTML COLGROUP tag. Has no defined events.

Properties

Supported by Both Navigator and IE: None

Other Properties: align (IE 4), className (IE 4), document (IE 4), id (IE 4), isTextEdit (IE 4), parentElement (IE 4), parentTextEdit (IE 4), span (IE 4), style (IE 4), tagName (IE 4), title (IE 4), vAlign (IE 4), width (IE 4)

Methods

Supported by Both Navigator and IE: None

Other Methods: contains (IE 4), getAttribute (IE 4), remove-Attribute (IE 4), setAttribute (IE 4)

COMMENT

First Supported In: IE 4

Provides access to the HTML COMMENT tag. Has no defined events.

Properties

Supported by Both Navigator and IE: None

Other Properties: className (IE 4), data (IE 6), document (IE 4), id (IE 4), isTextEdit (IE 4), lang (IE 4), length (IE 6), parentElement (IE 4), parentTextEdit (IE 4), sourceIndex (IE 4), tagName (IE 4), title (IE 4)

Methods

Supported by Both Navigator and IE: None

Other Methods: contains (IE 4), createComment (IE 6), getAttribute (IE 4), removeAttribute (IE 4), setAttribute (IE 4)

currentStyle

First Supported In: IE 5

Provides access to the current CSS style of an object. Has no defined methods or events.

Properties

Supported by Both Navigator and IE: None

Other Properties: backgroundAttachment (IE 5), backgroundColor (IE 5), backgroundImage (IE 5), backgroundPositionX (IE 5), backgroundPositionY (IE 5), backgroundRepeat (IE 5), borderBottomColor (IE 5), borderBottomStyle (IE 5), borderBottomWidth (IE 5), borderColor (IE 5), borderLeftColor (IE 5), borderLeftStyle (IE 5), borderLeftWidth (IE 5), borderRightColor (IE 5), borderRightStyle (IE 5), borderRightWidth (IE 5), borderStyle (IE 5), borderTopColor (IE 5), borderTopStyle (IE 5), borderTopWidth (IE 5), borderWidth (IE 5), bottom (IE 5), clear (IE 5), clipBottom (IE 5), clipLeft (IE 5), clipRight (IE 5), clipTop (IE 5), color (IE 5), cursor (IE 5), direction (IE 5), fontFamily (IE 5), fontSize (IE 5), fontStyle (IE 5), fontVariant (IE 5), fontWeight (IE 5), hasLayout (IE 5), height (IE 5), layoutFlow (IE 5), layoutGridChar (IE 5), layoutGridCharSpacing (IE 5), layoutGridLine (IE 5), layoutGridMode (IE 5), layoutGridType (IE 5), left (IE 5), letterSpacing (IE 5), lineHeight (IE 5), listStyleImage (IE 5), listStylePosition (IE 5), listStyleType (IE 5), margin (IE 5), marginBottom (IE 5), marginLeft (IE 5), marginRight (IE 5), marginTop (IE 5), overflow (IE 5), overflowX (IE 5), overflowY (IE 5), pageBreakAfter (IE 5), pageBreakBefore (IE 5), rectangular (IE 5), right (IE 5), scrollbar3dLightColor (IE 5), scrollbarArrowColor (IE 5), scrollbarBaseColor (IE 5), scrollbarDarkShadowColor (IE 5), scrollbarFaceColor (IE 5), scrollbarHighlightColor (IE 5), scrollbarShadowColor (IE 5), styleFloat (IE 5), tableLayout (IE 5), textAlign (IE 5), textDecoration (IE 5), textIndent (IE 5), textTransform (IE 5), textUnderlinePosition (IE 5), top (IE 5), unicodeBidi (IE 5), verticalAlign (IE 5), visibility (IE 5), width (IE 5), wordWrap (IE 5), writingMode (IE 5), zIndex (IE 5), zoom (IE 5)

custom

First Supported In: IE 5

Provides access to custom HTML tags.

Properties

Supported by Both Navigator and IE: None

Other Properties: accessKey (IE 5), canHaveChildren (IE 5), canHave-HTML (IE 5), className (IE 5), clientHeight (IE 5), clientLeft (IE 5), clientTop (IE 5), clientWidth (IE 5), contentEditable (IE 5), current-Style (IE 5), dir (IE 5), disabled (IE 5), document (IE 5), hasLayout (IE 5), hideFocus (IE 5), id (IE 5), innerHTML (IE 5), innerText (IE 5), isContentEditable (IE 5), isDisabled (IE 5), isTextEdit (IE 5), lang (IE 5), language (IE 5), offsetHeight (IE 5), offsetLeft (IE 5), offset-Parent (IE 5), offsetTop (IE 5), offsetWidth (IE 5), outerHTML (IE 5), outerText (IE 5), parentElement (IE 5), parentTextEdit (IE 5), ready-State (IE 5), recordNumber (IE 5), runtimeStyle (IE 5), scopeName (IE 5), scrollHeight (IE 5), scrollLeft (IE 5), scrollTop (IE 5), scroll-Width (IE 5), sourceIndex (IE 5), style (IE 5), tabIndex (IE 5), tagName (IE 5), tagUrn (IE 5), title (IE 5)

Methods

Supported by Both Navigator and IE: None

Other Methods: addBehavior (IE 5), applyElement (IE 5), attach-Event (IE 5), blur (IE 5), clearAttributes (IE 5), click (IE 5), componentFromPoint (IE 5), contains (IE 5), detachEvent (IE 5), do-Scroll (IE 5), fireEvent (IE 5), focus (IE 5), getAdjacentText (IE 5), getAttribute (IE 5), getBoundingClientRect (IE 5), getClientRects (IE 5), getElementsByTagName (IE 5), getExpression (IE 5), insert-AdjacentHTML (IE 5), insertAdjacentText (IE 5), mergeAttributes (IE 5), releaseCapture (IE 5), removeAttribute (IE 5), remove-Behavior (IE 5), removeExpression (IE 5), replaceAdjacentText (IE 5), scrollIntoView (IE 5), setActive (IE 5), setAttribute (IE 5), setCapture (IE 5), setExpression (IE 5)

Events

onafterupdate (IE 5), onbeforecopy (IE 5), onbeforecut (IE 5), onbeforeeditfocus (IE 5), onbeforefocusenter (IE 5), onbefore-focusleave (IE 5), onbeforepaste (IE 5), onbeforeupdate (IE 5), onblur

(IE 5), onclick (IE 5), oncontextmenu (IE 5), oncontrolselect (IE 5), oncopy (IE 5), oncut (IE 5), ondblclick (IE 5), ondrag (IE 5), ondragend (IE 5), ondragenter (IE 5), ondragleave (IE 5), ondragover (IE 5), ondragstart (IE 5), ondrop (IE 5), onerrorupdate (IE 5), onfilterchange (IE 5), onfocus (IE 5), onfocusenter (IE 5), onfocusleave (IE 5), onhelp (IE 5), onkeydown (IE 5), onkeypress (IE 5), onkeyup (IE 5), onlosecapture (IE 5), onmousedown (IE 5), onmouseenter (IE 5), onmouseleave (IE 5), onmousemove (IE 5), onmouseout (IE 5), onmouseover (IE 5), onmouseup (IE 5), onmousewheel (IE 6), onpaste (IE 5), onpropertychange (IE 5), onreadystatechange (IE 5), onresize (IE 5), onresizeend (IE 5), onresizestart (IE 5), onscroll (IE 5), onselectstart (IE 5)

dataTransfer

First Supported In: IE 5

Provides Clipboard support for drag-and-drop. Has no defined events.

Properties

Supported by Both Navigator and IE: None

Other Properties: dropEffect (IE 5), effectAllowed (IE 5)

Methods

Supported by Both Navigator and IE: None

Other Methods: clearData (IE 5), getData (IE 5), setData (IE 5)

Date

First Supported In: Navigator 2, IE 3

Provides access to basic date and time services. Date is a core object that has been standardized in ECMA 262. The basic Date object was introduced in JavaScript 1.0 and updated with JavaScript 1.1 and 1.3. It is supported in JScript 1 and later. It has no defined events.

Constructors

```
new Date()
```

Creates a Date object that represents the current (local) date and time.

```
new Date(milliseconds)
```

Creates a Date object that represents the time specified by the number of milliseconds since 12 A.M. 1 January 1970.

```
new Date(dateString)
```

Creates a Date object based on the date specified by *dateString*. The string should have a value that is recognized by the parse method of Date.

```
new Date(year, month, day[, hour, minute, second,
millisecond])
```

Creates a Date object with the specified year, month (0–11), day (1–31), hour (0–23), minute (0–59), second (0–59), and millisecond (0–999) values.

Properties
Supported by Both Navigator and IE:

▶ constructor (Navigator 3, IE 4)—A reference to the object's constructor

▶ prototype (Navigator 3, IE 4)—Used to define additional properties

Methods
Supported by Both Navigator and IE:

▶ getDate() (Navigator 2, IE 3)—Returns the day of the month as an integer between 1 and 31

▶ getDay() (Navigator 2, IE 3)—Returns the day of the week as an integer between 0 (Sunday) and 6 (Saturday)

▶ getFullYear() (Navigator 4.06, IE 4)—Returns the full value of a year

▶ getHours() (Navigator 2, IE 3)—Returns the current hours (local time) between 0 and 23

▶ getMilliseconds() (Navigator 4.06, IE 4)—Returns the current milliseconds (local time) between 0 and 999

▶ getMinutes() (Navigator 2, IE 3)—Returns the current minutes (local time) between 0 and 59

▶ getMonth() (Navigator 2, IE 3)—Returns the current month (local time) between 0 and 11

▶ getSeconds() (Navigator 2, IE 3)—Returns the current seconds (local time) between 0 and 59

- ▶ getTime() (Navigator 2, IE 3)—Returns the number of milliseconds since 1 January 1970 00:00:00

- ▶ getTimezoneOffset() (Navigator 2, IE 3)—Returns the current timezone offset in minutes between local time and Universal Coordinated Time (UTC; formerly Greenwich Mean Time [GMT])

- ▶ getUTCDate() (Navigator 4.06, IE 4)—Returns the current day of the month in UTC

- ▶ getUTCDay() (Navigator 4.06, IE 4)—Returns the current day of the week in UTC

- ▶ getUTCFullYear() (Navigator 4.06, IE 4)—Returns the current year in UTC

- ▶ getUTCHours() (Navigator 4.06, IE 4)—Returns the current hours in UTC

- ▶ getUTCMilliseconds() (Navigator 4.06, IE 4)—Returns the current milliseconds in UTC

- ▶ getUTCMinutes() (Navigator 4.06, IE 4)—Returns the current minutes in UTC

- ▶ getUTCMonth() (Navigator 4.06, IE 4)—Returns the current month in UTC

- ▶ getUTCSeconds() (Navigator 4.06, IE 4)—Returns the current seconds in UTC

- ▶ getYear() (Navigator 2, IE 3)—Returns the current year minus 1900

- ▶ parse(*dateString*) (Navigator 2, IE 3)—Returns the number of milliseconds in a date string since 12 A.M. 1 January 1970

- ▶ setDate(*dayOfMonth*) (Navigator 2, IE 3)—Sets the day of the month (local time)

- ▶ setFullYear(*year*[,*month*, *day*]) (Navigator 4.06, IE 4)—Sets the current year (local time)

- ▶ setHours(*hour*[,*minutes*, *seconds*, *milliseconds*]) (Navigator 2, IE 3)—Sets hours (local time)

- ▶ setMilliseconds(*milliseconds*) (Navigator 4.06, IE 4)—Sets the number of milliseconds (local time)

▶ setMinutes(*minutes*[,*seconds*, *milliseconds*]) (Navigator 2, IE 3)—Sets the minutes (local time)

▶ setMonth(*month*[,*day*]) (Navigator 2, IE 3)—Sets the month (local time)

▶ setSeconds(*seconds*[,*milliseconds*]) (Navigator 2, IE 3)—Sets the seconds (local time)

▶ setTime(*milliseconds*) (Navigator 2, IE 3)—Sets the date/time as the number of milliseconds since 12 A.M. 1 January 1970, local time)

▶ setUTCDate(*dayOfMonth*) (Navigator 4.06, IE 4)—Sets the day of the month (in UTC)

▶ setUTCFullYear(*year*[,*month*,*day*]) (Navigator 4.06, IE 4)—Sets the current year (in UTC)

▶ setUTCHours(*hours*[,*minutes*, *seconds*, *milliseconds*]) (Navigator 4.06, IE 4)—Sets the current hours (in UTC)

▶ setUTCMilliseconds(*milliseconds*) (Navigator 4.06, IE 4)—Sets the number of milliseconds (in UTC)

▶ setUTCMinutes(*minutes*[,*seconds*,*milliseconds*]) (Navigator 4.06, IE 4)—Sets the number of minutes (in UTC)

▶ setUTCMonth(*month*[,*day*]) (Navigator 4.06, IE 4)—Sets the current month (in UTC)

▶ setUTCSeconds(*seconds*[,*milliseconds*]) (Navigator 4.06, IE 4)—Sets the seconds value (in UTC)

▶ setYear(*year*) (Navigator 2, IE 3)—Sets the current year based on a year value between 0 and 99

▶ toGMTString() (Navigator 2, IE 3)—Converts a date to a string formatted according to UTC conventions (deprecated in favor of toUTCString())

▶ toLocaleString() (Navigator 2, IE 3)—Converts the date to a string using locale conventions

▶ toString() (Navigator 3, IE 4)—Converts the date to a string in local time

▶ toUTCString() (Navigator 4.06, IE 4)—Converts the date to a string in UTC

- ▶ UTC(*year*, *month*, *day*[, *hours*, *minutes*, *seconds*, *milli-seconds*]) (Navigator 2, IE 3)—Returns the number of milliseconds elapsed since 12 A.M. 1 January 1970 for the date specified by *year* through *milliseconds*; the *milliseconds* value was added in JavaScript 1.3

- ▶ valueOf() (Navigator 3, IE 4)—Returns the primitive value of the Date object, which is the number of milliseconds elapsed since 12 A.M. 1 January 1970

Other Methods: getVarDate (IE 4), toSource (Navigator 4.06)

DD

First Supported In: IE 4

Provides access to the HTML DD tag.

Properties
Supported by Both Navigator and IE: None

Other Properties: className (IE 4), document (IE 4), id (IE 4), inner-HTML (IE 4), innerText (IE 4), isTextEdit (IE 4), lang (IE 4), language (IE 4), offsetHeight (IE 4), offsetLeft (IE 4), offsetParent (IE 4), offsetTop (IE 4), offsetWidth (IE 4), outerHTML (IE 4), outerText (IE 4), parentElement (IE 4), parentTextEdit (IE 4), sourceIndex (IE 4), tagName (IE 4), title (IE 4)

Methods
Supported by Both Navigator and IE: None

Other Methods: click (IE 4), contains (IE 4), getAttribute (IE 4), insertAdjacentHTML (IE 4), insertAdjacentText (IE 4), remove-Attribute (IE 4), scrollIntoView (IE 4), setAttribute (IE 4)

Events
onclick (IE 4), ondblclick (IE 4), ondragstart (IE 4), onfilter-change (IE 4), onhelp (IE 4), onkeydown (IE 4), onkeypress (IE 4), onkeyup (IE 4), onmousedown (IE 4), onmousemove (IE 4), onmouseout (IE 4), onmouseover (IE 4), onmouseup (IE 4), onmousewheel (IE 6), onselect-start (IE 4)

DEL

First Supported In: IE 4

Provides access to the HTML DEL tag.

Properties
Supported by Both Navigator and IE: None

Other Properties: className (IE 4), document (IE 4), id (IE 4), inner-HTML (IE 4), innerText (IE 4), isTextEdit (IE 4), lang (IE 4), language (IE 4), offsetHeight (IE 4), offsetLeft (IE 4), offsetParent (IE 4), offsetTop (IE 4), offsetWidth (IE 4), outerHTML (IE 4), outerText (IE 4), parentElement (IE 4), parentTextEdit (IE 4), sourceIndex (IE 4), style (IE 4), tagName (IE 4), title (IE 4)

Methods
Supported by Both Navigator and IE: None

Other Methods: click (IE 4), contains (IE 4), getAttribute (IE 4), insertAdjacentHTML (IE 4), insertAdjacentText (IE 4), remove-Attribute (IE 4), scrollIntoView (IE 4), setAttribute (IE 4)

Events
onclick (IE 4), ondblclick (IE 4), ondragstart (IE 4), onfilter-change (IE 4), onhelp (IE 4), onkeydown (IE 4), onkeypress (IE 4), onkeyup (IE 4), onmousedown (IE 4), onmousemove (IE 4), onmouseout (IE 4), onmouseover (IE 4), onmouseup (IE 4)

DFN

First Supported In: IE 4

Provides access to the HTML DFN tag. **Note:** This tag is deprecated in the latest HTML specification in favor of CSS.

Properties
Supported by Both Navigator and IE: None

Other Properties: className (IE 4), document (IE 4), id (IE 4), inner-HTML (IE 4), innerText (IE 4), isTextEdit (IE 4), lang (IE 4), language (IE 4), offsetHeight (IE 4), offsetLeft (IE 4), offsetParent (IE 4),

offsetTop (IE 4), offsetWidth (IE 4), outerHTML (IE 4), outerText
(IE 4), parentElement (IE 4), parentTextEdit (IE 4), sourceIndex (IE 4),
style (IE 4), tagName (IE 4), title (IE 4)

Methods
Supported by Both Navigator and IE: None

Other Methods: click (IE 4), contains (IE 4), getAttribute (IE 4),
insertAdjacentHTML (IE 4), insertAdjacentText (IE 4), remove-
Attribute (IE 4), scrollIntoView (IE 4), setAttribute (IE 4)

Events
onclick (IE 4), ondblclick (IE 4), ondragstart (IE 4), onhelp (IE 4),
onkeydown (IE 4), onkeypress (IE 4), onkeyup (IE 4), onmousedown
(IE 4), onmousemove (IE 4), onmouseout (IE 4), onmouseover (IE 4),
onmouseup (IE 4), onmousewheel (IE 6), onselectstart (IE 4)

DIR

First Supported In: IE 4

Provides access to the HTML DIR tag. **Note:** This tag is deprecated in
the latest HTML specification.

Properties
Supported by Both Navigator and IE: None

Other Properties: className (IE 4), compact (IE 6), document (IE 4),
id (IE 4), innerHTML (IE 4), innerText (IE 4), isTextEdit (IE 4), lang
(IE 4), language (IE 4), offsetHeight (IE 4), offsetLeft (IE 4), offset-
Parent (IE 4), offsetTop (IE 4), offsetWidth (IE 4), outerHTML (IE 4),
outerText (IE 4), parentElement (IE 4), parentTextEdit (IE 4), source-
Index (IE 4), style (IE 4), tagName (IE 4), title (IE 4)

Methods
Supported by Both Navigator and IE: None

Other Methods: click (IE 4), contains (IE 4), getAttribute (IE 4),
insertAdjacentHTML (IE 4), insertAdjacentText (IE 4), remove-
Attribute (IE 4), scrollIntoView (IE 4), setAttribute (IE 4)

Events

onclick (IE 4), ondblclick (IE 4), ondragstart (IE 4), onfilterchange (IE 4), onhelp (IE 4), onkeydown (IE 4), onkeypress (IE 4), onkeyup (IE 4), onmousedown (IE 4), onmousemove (IE 4), onmouseout (IE 4), onmouseover (IE 4), onmouseup (IE 4), onmousewheel (IE 6), onselectstart (IE 4)

DIV

First Supported In: IE 4

Provides access to the HTML DIV tag.

Properties

Supported by Both Navigator and IE: None

Other Properties: align (IE 4), className (IE 4), clientHeight (IE 4), clientWidth (IE 4), dataFld (IE 4), dataFormatAs (IE 4), dataSrc (IE 4), document (IE 4), id (IE 4), innerText (IE 4), isTextEdit (IE 4), lang (IE 4), language (IE 4), offsetHeight (IE 4), offsetLeft (IE 4), offsetParent (IE 4), offsetTop (IE 4), offsetWidth (IE 4), outerText (IE 4), parentElement (IE 4), parentTextEdit (IE 4), scrollHeight (IE 4), scrollLeft (IE 4), scrollTop (IE 4), scrollWidth (IE 4), sourceIndex (IE 4), style (IE 4), tagName (IE 4), title (IE 4)

Methods

Supported by Both Navigator and IE: None

Other Methods: blur (IE 4), click (IE 4), contains (IE 4), focus (IE 4), getAttribute (IE 4), insertAdjacentHTML (IE 4), insertAdjacentText (IE 4), removeAttribute (IE 4), scrollIntoView (IE 4), setAttribute (IE 4)

Events

onafterupdate (IE 4), onbeforeupdate (IE 4), onblur (IE 4), onclick (IE 4), ondblclick (IE 4), ondragstart (IE 4), onfocus (IE 4), onhelp (IE 4), onkeydown (IE 4), onkeypress (IE 4), onkeyup (IE 4), onmousedown (IE 4), onmousemove (IE 4), onmouseout (IE 4), onmouseover (IE 4), onmouseup (IE 4), onmousewheel (IE 6), onresize (IE 4), onrowenter (IE 4), onrowexit (IE 4), onscroll (IE 4), onselectstart (IE 4)

DL

First Supported In: IE 4

Provides access to the HTML DL tag.

Properties
Supported by Both Navigator and IE: None

Other Properties: className (IE 4), compact (IE 4), document (IE 4), id (IE 4), innerHTML (IE 4), innerText (IE 4), isTextEdit (IE 4), lang (IE 4), language (IE 4), offsetHeight (IE 4), offsetLeft (IE 4), offset-Parent (IE 4), offsetTop (IE 4), offsetWidth (IE 4), outerHTML (IE 4), outerText (IE 4), parentElement (IE 4), parentTextEdit (IE 4), sourceIndex (IE 4), style (IE 4), tagName (IE 4), title (IE 4)

Methods
Supported by Both Navigator and IE: None

Other Methods: click (IE 4), contains (IE 4), getAttribute (IE 4), insertAdjacentHTML (IE 4), insertAdjacentText (IE 4), remove-Attribute (IE 4), scrollIntoView (IE 4), setAttribute (IE 4)

Events
onclick (IE 4), ondblclick (IE 4), ondragstart (IE 4), onfilter-change (IE 4), onhelp (IE 4), onkeydown (IE 4), onkeypress (IE 4), onkeyup (IE 4), onmousedown (IE 4), onmousemove (IE 4), onmouseout (IE 4), onmouseover (IE 4), onmouseup (IE 4), onmousewheel (IE 6), onselectstart (IE 4)

document

First Supported In: Navigator 2, IE 3

A fundamental object of client-side JavaScript. document provides access to a web page that is displayed in a browser window. It also provides properties and methods for accessing the objects that make up the document. The basic document object was introduced in JavaScript 1.0 and updated with JavaScript 1.1 and 1.2.

Properties
Supported by Both Navigator and IE:

▶ alinkColor (Navigator 2, IE 3)—Specifies the color of an active link (a link that has been clicked on [mouse down] before the mouse is released [mouse up]).

▶ anchors (Navigator 2, IE 3)—Provides access to the document's Anchor objects as an array. The array's elements are ordered according to how the objects appear in the document.

▶ applets (Navigator 3, IE 4)—Provides access to the applets associated with the document.

▶ bgColor (Navigator 2, IE 3)—Provides access to the document's background color.

▶ cookie (Navigator 2, IE 3)—Provides access to the HTTP cookies associated with the document.

▶ domain (Navigator 3, IE 4)—The domain name of the document server.

▶ embeds (Navigator 3, IE 4)—Provides access to the embedded media elements.

▶ fgColor (Navigator 2, IE 3)—Provides access to the document's foreground color.

▶ forms (Navigator 3, IE 4)—Provides access to the document's Form objects as an array. The array's elements are ordered according to how the objects appear in the document.

▶ images (Navigator 3, IE 4)—Provides access to the images defined in the document

▶ lastModified (Navigator 2, IE 3)—Identifies when the document was last modified based on information provided in its HTTP header.

▶ linkColor (Navigator 2, IE 3)—Specifies the normal color of all links contained in the document.

▶ links (Navigator 2, IE 3)—Provides access to the document's Link objects as an array. The array's elements are ordered according to how the objects appear in the document.

- ▶ plugins (Navigator 3, IE 4)—Provides access to the document's Plugin objects as an array. The array's elements are ordered according to how the objects appear in the document.

- ▶ referrer (Navigator 2, IE 3)—Identifies the URL of the document (if any) that provided the link to this document.

- ▶ title (Navigator 2, IE 3)—Provides access to the document's title.

- ▶ URL (Navigator 2, IE 3)—Provides access to the URL from which the document was loaded.

- ▶ vlinkColor (Navigator 2, IE 3)—Specifies the color of visited links.

Other Properties: activeElement (IE 4), body (IE 4), charset (IE 4), classes (Navigator 4), defaultCharset (IE 4), expando (IE 4), height (Navigator 4), ids (Navigator 4), layers (Navigator 4), linkColor (IE 4), location (IE 4), parentWindow (IE 4), readyState (IE 4), selection (IE 4), tags (Navigator 4), width (Navigator 4)

Methods
Supported by Both Navigator and IE:

- ▶ close() (Navigator 2, IE 3)—Closes output to the document object.

- ▶ open([*mimeType*, [*replace*]]) (Navigator 2, IE 3)—Creates and opens a new document of the specified MIME type. The *replace* argument specifies that the new document is to reuse the history entry of the previous document.

- ▶ write(*expr1*[, ..., *exprN*]) (Navigator 2, IE 3)—Writes the HTML expression(s) to the current document object.

- ▶ writeln(*expr1*[, ..., *exprN*]) (Navigator 2, IE 3)—Writes the HTML expression(s) to the current document object. A newline character is appended to the last expression.

Other Methods: captureEvents (Navigator 4), clear (IE 4), contextual (Navigator 4), createElement (IE 4), createStyleSheet (IE 4), elementFromPoint (IE 4), execCommand (IE 4), getSelection (Navigator 4), handleEvent (Navigator 4), queryCommandEnabled (IE 4), queryCommandIndeterm (IE 4), queryCommandState (IE 4), queryCommandSupported (IE 4), queryCommandText (IE 4), queryCommandValue (IE 4), releaseEvents (Navigator 4), routeEvent (Navigator 4), ShowHelp (IE 4)

Events

onafterupdate (IE 4), onbeforeupdate (IE 4), onclick (Navigator 2, IE 3), ondblclick (Navigator 4, IE 4), ondragstart (IE 4), onerrorupdate (IE 4), onhelp (IE 4), onkeydown (Navigator 4, IE 4), onkeypress (Navigator 4, IE 4), onkeyup (Navigator 4, IE 4), onmousedown (Navigator 4, IE 4), onmousemove (IE 4), onmouseout (IE 4), onmouseover (IE 4), onmouseup (Navigator 4, IE 4), onmousewheel (IE 6), onreadystatechange (IE 4), onrowenter (IE 4), onrowexit (IE 4), onselectstart (IE 4)

DT

First Supported In: IE 4

Provides access to the HTML DT tag.

Properties

Supported by Both Navigator and IE: None

Other Properties: className (IE 4), document (IE 4), id (IE 4), innerHTML (IE 4), innerText (IE 4), isTextEdit (IE 4), lang (IE 4), language (IE 4), offsetHeight (IE 4), offsetLeft (IE 4), offsetParent (IE 4), offsetTop (IE 4), offsetWidth (IE 4), outerHTML (IE 4), outerText (IE 4), parentElement (IE 4), parentTextEdit (IE 4), sourceIndex (IE 4), style (IE 4), tagName (IE 4), title (IE 4)

Methods

Supported by Both Navigator and IE: None

Other Methods: click (IE 4), contains (IE 4), getAttribute (IE 4), insertAdjacentHTML (IE 4), insertAdjacentText (IE 4), removeAttribute (IE 4), scrollIntoView (IE 4), setAttribute (IE 4)

Events

onclick (IE 4), ondblclick (IE 4), ondragstart (IE 4), onfilterchange (IE 4), onhelp (IE 4), onkeydown (IE 4), onkeypress (IE 4), onkeyup (IE 4), onmousedown (IE 4), onmousemove (IE 4), onmouseout (IE 4), onmouseover (IE 4), onmousewheel (IE 6), onselectstart (IE 4)

EM

First Supported In: IE 4

Provides access to the HTML EM tag. **Note:** This tag is deprecated in the latest HTML specification.

Properties
Supported by Both Navigator and IE: None

Other Properties: className (IE 4), document (IE 4), id (IE 4), inner-HTML (IE 4), innerText (IE 4), isTextEdit (IE 4), lang (IE 4), language (IE 4), offsetHeight (IE 4), offsetLeft (IE 4), offsetParent (IE 4), offsetTop (IE 4), offsetWidth (IE 4), outerHTML (IE 4), outerText (IE 4), parentElement (IE 4), parentTextEdit (IE 4), sourceIndex (IE 4), style (IE 4), tagName (IE 4), title (IE 4)

Methods
Supported by Both Navigator and IE: None

Other Methods: click (IE 4), contains (IE 4), getAttribute (IE 4), insertAdjacentHTML (IE 4), insertAdjacentText (IE 4), remove-Attribute (IE 4), scrollIntoView (IE 4), setAttribute (IE 4)

Events
onclick (IE 4), ondblclick (IE 4), ondragstart (IE 4), onfilterchange (IE 4), onhelp (IE 4), onkeydown (IE 4), onkeypress (IE 4), onkeyup (IE 4), onmousedown (IE 4), onmousemove (IE 4), onmouseout (IE 4), onmouseover (IE 4), onmousewheel (IE 6), onselectstart (IE 4)

EMBED

First Supported In: IE 4

Provides access to the HTML EMBED tag. **Note:** This tag is deprecated in the latest HTML specification.

Properties
Supported by Both Navigator and IE: None

Other Properties: accessKey (IE 4), align (IE 4), className (IE 4), document (IE 4), height (IE 4), Hidden (IE 4), id (IE 4), isTextEdit (IE 4), lang (IE 4), language (IE 4), offsetHeight (IE 4), offset-Left (IE 4), offsetParent (IE 4), offsetTop (IE 4), offsetWidth (IE 4), outerHTML (IE 4), outerText (IE 4), palette (IE 4), parentElement

(IE 4), parentTextEdit (IE 4), pluginspage (IE 4), sourceIndex (IE 4), src (IE 4), style (IE 4), tagName (IE 4), title (IE 4), units (IE 4), width (IE 4)

Methods

Supported by Both Navigator and IE: None

Other Methods: blur (IE 4), contains (IE 4), focus (IE 4), get-Attribute (IE 4), insertAdjacentHTML (IE 4), insertAdjacentText (IE 4), removeAttribute (IE 4), scrollIntoView (IE 4), setAttribute (IE 4)

Events

onblur (IE 4), onfocus (IE 4)

Enumerator

First Supported In: IE 4

An IE object used to iterate through a collection of objects. Has no defined properties or events.

Constructor

```
new Enumerator(collection)
```

Creates an Enumerator object from the *collection* argument.

Methods

Supported by Both Navigator and IE: None

Other Methods: atEnd (IE 4), item (IE 4), moveFirst (IE 4), move-Next (IE 4)

Error

First Supported In: IE 5

Provides information about errors that occur during the execution of a script. Has no defined methods or events.

Constructors

```
new Error()
```

Creates a new `Error` object with no error number or description.

```
new Error(number)
```

Creates a new `Error` object with the specified error number but no description.

```
new Error(number, description)
```

Creates a new `Error` object with the specified error number and description.

Properties

Supported by Both Navigator and IE: None

Other Properties: `description` (IE 5), `name` (IE 5.5), `number` (IE 5)

event

First Supported In: Navigator 4, IE 4

Used to encapsulate all events that can be handled by JavaScript. `event` is passed as an argument to an event handler and contains properties that describe the event. Has no defined methods.

Properties

Supported by Both Navigator and IE:

▶ `screenX` (Navigator 4, IE 4)—Identifies the cursor's horizontal position (in pixels) relative to the screen

▶ `screenY` (Navigator 4, IE 4)—Identifies the cursor's vertical position (in pixels) relative to the screen

▶ `type` (Navigator 4, IE 4)—The type of the event

▶ `x` (Navigator 4, IE 4)—Equivalent to the `layerX` property

▶ `y` (Navigator 4, IE 4)—Equivalent to the `layerY` property

Other Properties: `altKey` (IE 4), `button` (IE 4), `cancelBubble` (IE 4), `clientX` (IE 4), `clientY` (IE 4), `ctrlKey` (IE 4), `data` (Navigator 4), `fromElement` (IE 4), `height` (Navigator 4), `keyCode` (IE 4), `layerX` (Navigator 4), `layerY` (Navigator 4), `modifiers` (Navigator 4), `offsetX` (IE 4), `offsetY` (IE 4), `pageX` (Navigator 4), `pageY` (Navigator 4), `reason` (IE 4), `returnValue` (IE 4), `shiftKey` (IE 4), `srcElement` (IE 4), `srcFilter` (IE 4), `target` (Navigator 4), `toElement` (IE 4), `which` (Navigator 4), `width` (Navigator 4)

Events

Event handlers are defined for each event by type.

external

First Supported In: IE 4

Provides access to an external object model. Has no defined properties or events.

Methods

Supported by Both Navigator and IE: None

Other Methods: addChannel (IE 4), isSubscribed (IE 4)

FIELDSET

First Supported In: IE 4

Provides access to the HTML FIELDSET tag. **Note:** This tag is deprecated in the latest HTML specification.

Properties

Supported by Both Navigator and IE: None

Other Properties: accessKey (IE 4), align (IE 4), className (IE 4), clientHeight (IE 4), clientWidth (IE 4), document (IE 4), id (IE 4), innerHTML (IE 4), innerText (IE 4), isTextEdit (IE 4), lang (IE 4), language (IE 4), margin (IE 4), offsetHeight (IE 4), offsetLeft (IE 4), offsetParent (IE 4), offsetTop (IE 4), offsetWidth (IE 4), outerHTML (IE 4), outerText (IE 4), padding (IE 4), parentElement (IE 4), parentTextEdit (IE 4), recordNumber (IE 4), scrollHeight (IE 4), scrollLeft (IE 4), scrollTop (IE 4), scrollWidth (IE 4), sourceIndex (IE 4), style (IE 4), tabIndex (IE 4), tagName (IE 4), title (IE 4)

Methods

Supported by Both Navigator and IE: None

Other Methods: blur (IE 4), click (IE 4), contains (IE 4), focus (IE 4), getAttribute (IE 4), insertAdjacentHTML (IE 4), insertAdjacentText (IE 4), removeAttribute (IE 4), scrollIntoView (IE 4), setAttribute (IE 4)

Events

onafterupdate (IE 4), onbeforeupdate (IE 4), onblur (IE 4), onchange (IE 4), onclick (IE 4), ondblclick (IE 4), ondragstart (IE 4), onerror-update (IE 4), onfilterchange (IE 4), onfocus (IE 4), onhelp (IE 4), onkeydown (IE 4), onkeypress (IE 4), onkeyup (IE 4), onmousedown (IE 4), onmousemove (IE 4), onmouseout (IE 4), onmouseover (IE 4), onmouseup (IE 4), onmousewheel (IE 6), onresize (IE 4), onrowenter (IE 4), onrowexit (IE 4), onscroll (IE 4), onselect (IE 4), onselect-start (IE 4)

FileUpload (file)

First Supported In: Navigator 2, IE 4

Provides access to the file upload objects of an HTML form. These objects are INPUT tags with their TYPE attribute set to FILE. They provide the user with the capability to upload a file to your website. The basic FileUpload object was introduced in JavaScript 1.0 and updated with JavaScript 1.1 and 1.2. It is also referred to as a file object in the IE 4 documentation.

Properties
Supported by Both Navigator and IE:

- ▶ form (Navigator 2, IE 3)—Provides a reference to the form object that contains the file upload element

- ▶ name (Navigator 2, IE 3)—The value of the file upload's NAME attribute

- ▶ type (Navigator 3, IE 4)—The value of the file upload's TYPE attribute

- ▶ value (Navigator 2, IE 3)—The name of the file selected by the user

Other Properties: accessKey (IE 4), className (IE 4), default-Value (IE 4), disabled (IE 4), document (IE 4), id (IE 4), isTextEdit (IE 4), lang (IE 4), language (IE 4), offsetHeight (IE 4), offset-Left (IE 4), offsetParent (IE 4), offsetTop (IE 4), offsetWidth (IE 4), outerText (IE 4), parentElement (IE 4), parentTextEdit (IE 4), read-Only (IE 4), recordNumber (IE 4), sourceIndex (IE 4), style (IE 4), tabIndex (IE 4), tagName (IE 4), title (IE 4)

Methods

Supported by Both Navigator and IE:

- ▶ blur() (Navigator 2, IE 3)—Removes input focus from the file upload element
- ▶ focus() (Navigator 2, IE 3)—Moves input focus to the file upload element
- ▶ select() (Navigator 2, IE 3)—Selects (highlights) the input area of the file upload element

Other Methods: click (IE 4), contains (IE 4), getAttribute (IE 4), handleEvent (Navigator 4), insertAdjacentHTML (IE 4), insert-AdjacentText (IE 4), removeAttribute (IE 4), scrollIntoView (IE 4), setAttribute (IE 4)

Events

onblur (Navigator 3, IE 4), onchange (Navigator 3, IE 4), onfocus (Navigator 3, IE 4), onclick (IE 4), ondblclick (IE 4), onfilterchange (IE 4), onhelp (IE 4), onkeydown (IE 4), onkeypress (IE 4), onkeyup (IE 4), onmousedown (IE 4), onmousemove (IE 4), onmouseout (IE 4), onmouseover (IE 4), onmouseup (IE 4), onresize (IE 4), onselect (IE 4)

FONT

First Supported In: IE 4

Provides access to the HTML FONT tag. **Note:** This tag is deprecated in the latest HTML specification in favor of the CSS attributes font-size, font-name, font-style, and color.

Properties

Supported by Both Navigator and IE: None

Other Properties: className (IE 4), color (IE 4), document (IE 4), face (IE 4), id (IE 4), innerHTML (IE 4), innerText (IE 4), isText-Edit (IE 4), lang (IE 4), language (IE 4), offsetHeight (IE 4), offsetLeft (IE 4), offsetParent (IE 4), offsetTop (IE 4), offsetWidth (IE 4), outerHTML (IE 4), outerText (IE 4), parentElement (IE 4), parentText-Edit (IE 4), size (IE 4), sourceIndex (IE 4), style (IE 4), tagName (IE 4), title (IE 4)

Methods
Supported by Both Navigator and IE: None

Other Methods: click (IE 4), contains (IE 4), getAttribute (IE 4), insertAdjacentHTML (IE 4), insertAdjacentText (IE 4), removeAttribute (IE 4), scrollIntoView (IE 4), setAttribute (IE 4)

Events
onclick (IE 4), ondblclick (IE 4), ondragstart (IE 4), onfilterchange (IE 4), onhelp (IE 4), onkeydown (IE 4), onkeypress (IE 4), onkeyup (IE 4), onmousedown (IE 4), onmousemove (IE 4), onmouseout (IE 4), onmouseover (IE 4), onmouseup (IE 4), onmousewheel (IE 6), onselectstart (IE 4)

Form

First Supported In: Navigator 2, IE 3

Encapsulates an HTML form and provides access to the elements contained in a form. Form is used to handle user interactions with form elements and to perform form data validation prior to submission of form data to a web server. The basic Form object was introduced in JavaScript 1.0 and updated with JavaScript 1.1 and 1.2.

Properties
Supported by Both Navigator and IE:

▶ action (Navigator 2, IE 3)—Identifies the form's ACTION attribute

▶ elements (Navigator 2, IE 3)—An array containing all of the form's input elements in the order they appear in the form

▶ encoding (Navigator 2, IE 3)—Identifies the form's ENCTYPE attribute

▶ length (Navigator 2, IE 3)—Identifies the number of elements contained in the form (the length of the elements array)

▶ method (Navigator 2, IE 3)—Identifies the form's METHOD attribute

▶ name (Navigator 2, IE 3)—Identifies the form's NAME attribute

▶ target (Navigator 2, IE 3)—Identifies the form's TARGET attribute

Other Properties: className (IE 4), document (IE 4), id (IE 4), innerHTML (IE 4), innerText (IE 4), isTextEdit (IE 4), lang (IE 4), language

(IE 4), offsetHeight (IE 4), offsetLeft (IE 4), offsetParent (IE 4), offsetTop (IE 4), offsetWidth (IE 4), outerHTML (IE 4), outerText (IE 4), parentElement (IE 4), parentTextEdit (IE 4), sourceIndex (IE 4), style (IE 4), tagName (IE 4), title (IE 4)

Methods
Supported by Both Navigator and IE:

▶ reset() (Navigator 3, IE 3)—Reset the elements of a form

▶ submit() (Navigator 2, IE 3)—Submits the form's data

Other Methods: click (IE 4), contains (IE 4), getAttribute (IE 4), handleEvent (Navigator 4), insertAdjacentHTML (IE 4), insertAdjacentText (IE 4), removeAttribute (IE 4), scrollIntoView (IE 4), setAttribute (IE 4)

Events

onclick (IE 4), ondblclick (IE 4), ondragstart (IE 4), onfilterchange (IE 4), onhelp (IE 4), onkeydown (IE 4), onkeypress (IE 4), onkeyup (IE 4), onmousedown (IE 4), onmousemove (IE 4), onmouseout (IE 4), onmouseover (IE 4), onmouseup (IE 4), onmousewheel (IE 6), onReset (Navigator 3, IE 4), onselectstart (IE 4), onSubmit (Navigator 2, IE 3)

frame

First Supported In: Navigator 2, IE 3

Provides access to an HTML frame. frame is equivalent to a window object. Refer to the window object for a description of frame. Updated in JavaScript 1.1.

FRAMESET

First Supported In: IE 4

Provides access to the HTML FRAMESET tag.

Properties
Supported by Both Navigator and IE: None

Other Properties: border (IE 4), borderColor (IE 4), className (IE 4), cols (IE 4), document (IE 4), frameBorder (IE 4), frameSpacing

(IE 4), id (IE 4), isTextEdit (IE 4), lang (IE 4), language (IE 4), parentElement (IE 4), parentTextEdit (IE 4), rows (IE 4), sourceIndex (IE 4), style (IE 4), tagName (IE 4), title (IE 4)

Methods
Supported by Both Navigator and IE: None

Other Methods: contains (IE 4), getAttribute (IE 4), remove-Attribute (IE 4), setAttribute (IE 4)

Events
onbeforeunload (IE 4), onload (IE 4), onresize (IE 4), onunload (IE 4)

Function

First Supported In: Navigator 3, IE 4

Provides access to JavaScript functions as objects. Has no defined events. Updated in JavaScript 1.2 and 1.3.

Constructor
```
new Function ([arg1[, arg2[, ... argN]],] functionBody)
```

Creates a function that accepts arguments 1 through *N* with the specified function body (expressed as a string).

Properties
Supported by Both Navigator and IE:

- ▶ arguments (Navigator 3, IE 4)—Identifies the arguments that are passed to a function. Deprecated in the latest JavaScript specification in favor of the Arguments object.

- ▶ arguments.length (Navigator 3, IE 4)—Identifies the number of arguments passed to the function.

- ▶ caller (Navigator 4, IE 4)—Identifies the function that invoked this function.

- ▶ constructor (Navigator 3, IE 4)—Identifies the object's constructor.

- ▶ prototype (Navigator 3, IE 4)—Provides the capability to add new properties to the object.

Other Properties: arguments.callee (Navigator 4), arguments.caller (Navigator 3), arity (Navigator 4), caller (IE 4), length (Navigator 3)

Methods
Supported by Both Navigator and IE:

- ▶ toString() (Navigator 3, IE 4)—Returns a string representing the source code of the function

- ▶ valueOf() (Navigator 3, IE 4)—Returns a string representing the source code of the function

Other Methods: apply (Navigator 4.06), call (Navigator 4.06), toSource (Navigator 4.06)

Global

First Supported In: Navigator 2, IE 4

Identified in ECMAScript 1 as the Global object. Global has been supported in Navigator and IE since JavaScript 1.0 via top-level properties and methods. Additional properties and methods have been defined since JavaScript 1.0. In JavaScript 1.3, ECMA compliance was achieved in Navigator. Has no defined event handlers.

Properties
Supported by Both Navigator and IE:

- ▶ Infinity (Navigator 4.06, IE 4)—Represents infinity

- ▶ NaN (Navigator 4.06, IE 4)—Represents the value Not-a-Number

Other Properties: undefined (Navigator 4.06)

Methods
Supported by Both Navigator and IE:

- ▶ escape(*string*) (Navigator 2, IE 3)—Returns the URL-encoding of *string*

- ▶ eval(*string*) (Navigator 2, IE 3)—Evaluates the string as JavaScript code

- ▶ isFinite(*number*) (Navigator 4.06, IE 4)—Returns a Boolean value indicating whether *number* is finite

▶ isNaN(*value*) (Navigator 2, IE 3)—Returns a Boolean value indicating whether *value* is Not-a-Number

▶ parseFloat(*string*) (Navigator 2, IE 3)—Converts a string to a floating-point number

▶ parseInt(*string*[, *radix*]) (Navigator 2, IE 3)—Converts a string to an integer

▶ unescape(*string*) (Navigator 2, IE 3)—Converts the URL-encoded string to its value before encoding

Other Methods: Number (Navigator 4), String (Navigator 4), taint (Navigator 3), untaint (Navigator 3)

H1, H2, H3, H4, H5, H6

First Supported In: IE 4

Provide access to the HTML H1 through H6 tags. **Note:** These tags are deprecated in the latest HTML specification.

Properties

Supported by Both Navigator and IE: None

Other Properties: align (IE 4), className (IE 4), document (IE 4), id (IE 4), innerHTML (IE 4), innerText (IE 4), isTextEdit (IE 4), lang (IE 4), language (IE 4), offsetHeight (IE 4), offsetLeft (IE 4), offset-Parent (IE 4), offsetTop (IE 4), offsetWidth (IE 4), outerHTML (IE 4), outerText (IE 4), parentElement (IE 4), parentTextEdit (IE 4), source-Index (IE 4), style (IE 4), tagName (IE 4), title (IE 4)

Methods

Supported by Both Navigator and IE: None

Other Methods: click (IE 4), contains (IE 4), getAttribute (IE 4), insertAdjacentHTML (IE 4), insertAdjacentText (IE 4), remove-Attribute (IE 4), scrollIntoView (IE 4), setAttribute (IE 4)

Events

onclick (IE 4), ondblclick (IE 4), ondragstart (IE 4), onfilterchange (IE 4), onhelp (IE 4), onkeydown (IE 4), onkeypress (IE 4), onkeyup (IE 4), onmousedown (IE 4), onmousemove (IE 4), onmouseout (IE 4), onmouseover (IE 4), onmouseup (IE 4), onmousewheel (IE 6), onselectstart (IE 4)

HEAD

First Supported In: IE 4

Provides access to the HTML HEAD tag. Has no defined events.

Properties
Supported by Both Navigator and IE: None

Other Properties: className (IE 4), document (IE 4), id (IE 4), isTextEdit (IE 4), parentElement (IE 4), sourceIndex (IE 4), tagName (IE 4), title (IE 4)

Methods
Supported by Both Navigator and IE: None

Other Methods: contains (IE 4), getAttribute (IE 4), removeAttribute (IE 4), setAttribute (IE 4)

Hidden

First Supported In: Navigator 2, IE 3

Represents a hidden form field. Hidden form fields are INPUT tags with their TYPE attribute set to HIDDEN. They are used to store state information in forms. Updated in JavaScript 1.1.

Properties
Supported by Both Navigator and IE:

- ▶ form (Navigator 2, IE 3)—Provides a reference to the form object that contains the hidden field

- ▶ name (Navigator 2, IE 3)—The value of the hidden field's NAME attribute

- ▶ type (Navigator 3, IE 4)—The value of the hidden field's TYPE attribute

- ▶ value (Navigator 2, IE 3)—The value stored in the hidden field

Other Properties: className (IE 4), dataFld (IE 4), dataSrc (IE 4), disabled (IE 4), document (IE 4), id (IE 4), isTextEdit (IE 4), language (IE 4), parentElement (IE 4), parentTextEdit (IE 4), sourceIndex (IE 4), style (IE 4), tagName (IE 4)

Methods
Supported by Both Navigator and IE: None

   Other Methods: contains (IE 4), getAttribute (IE 4), remove-
Attribute (IE 4), setAttribute (IE 4)

Events
onafterupdate (IE 4), onbeforeupdate (IE 4), onerrorupdate (IE 4)

History
First Supported In: Navigator 2, IE 3

   Maintains information about the URLs the client has visited for a
particular window. Has no defined events. Updated in JavaScript 1.1.

Properties
Supported by Both Navigator and IE: length (Navigator 2, IE 3);
identifies the length of the history list

   Other Properties: current (Navigator 3), next (Navigator 3), previous
(Navigator 3)

Methods
Supported by Both Navigator and IE:

   ▶ back() (Navigator 2, IE 3)—Loads the previous URL in the
   history list

   ▶ forward() (Navigator 2, IE 3)—Loads the next URL in the
   history list

   ▶ go(*delta*) (Navigator 2, IE 3)—Loads a URL from the relative
   position in the history list specified by *delta*

   ▶ go(*location*) (Navigator 2, IE 3)—Loads a URL based on the
   partial URL specified by *location* by matching it with other
   URLs in the history list

   Other Methods: toString (IE 4)

HR
First Supported In: IE 4

   Provides access to the HTML HR tag.

Properties

Supported by Both Navigator and IE: None

    Other Properties: align (IE 4), className (IE 4), color (IE 4), document (IE 4), id (IE 4), isTextEdit (IE 4), lang (IE 4), language (IE 4), noShade (IE 4), offsetHeight (IE 4), offsetLeft (IE 4), offsetParent (IE 4), offsetTop (IE 4), offsetWidth (IE 4), outerHTML (IE 4), outerText (IE 4), parentElement (IE 4), parentTextEdit (IE 4), size (IE 4), sourceIndex (IE 4), style (IE 4), tagName (IE 4), title (IE 4), width (IE 4)

Methods

Supported by Both Navigator and IE: None

    Other Methods: blur (IE 4), click (IE 4), contains (IE 4), focus (IE 4), getAttribute (IE 4), insertAdjacentHTML (IE 4), insertAdjacentText (IE 4), removeAttribute (IE 4), scrollIntoView (IE 4), setAttribute (IE 4)

Events

onbeforeupdate (IE 4), onblur (IE 4), onclick (IE 4), ondblclick (IE 4), ondragstart (IE 4), onfilterchange (IE 4), onfocus (IE 4), onhelp (IE 4), onkeydown (IE 4), onkeypress (IE 4), onkeyup (IE 4), onmousedown (IE 4), onmousemove (IE 4), onmouseout (IE 4), onmouseover (IE 4), onmouseup (IE 4), onmousewheel (IE 6), onresize (IE 4), onrowenter (IE 4), onrowexit (IE 4), onselectstart (IE 4)

HTML

First Supported In: IE 4

    Provides access to the HTML HTML tag. Has no defined events.

Properties

Supported by Both Navigator and IE: None

    Other Properties: className (IE 4), document (IE 4), id (IE 4), isTextEdit (IE 4), language (IE 4), parentElement (IE 4), sourceIndex (IE 4), style (IE 4), tagName (IE 4), title (IE 4)

Methods

Supported by Both Navigator and IE: None

Other Methods: `contains` (IE 4), `getAttribute` (IE 4), `remove-Attribute` (IE 4), `setAttribute` (IE 4)

I

First Supported In: IE 4

Provides access to the HTML I tag. **Note:** This tag is deprecated in the latest HTML specification in favor of the CSS attribute `text-style`.

Properties
Supported by Both Navigator and IE: None

Other Properties: `className` (IE 4), `document` (IE 4), `id` (IE 4), `inner-HTML` (IE 4), `innerText` (IE 4), `isTextEdit` (IE 4), `lang` (IE 4), `language` (IE 4), `offsetHeight` (IE 4), `offsetLeft` (IE 4), `offsetParent` (IE 4), `offsetTop` (IE 4), `offsetWidth` (IE 4), `outerHTML` (IE 4), `outerText` (IE 4), `parentElement` (IE 4), `parentTextEdit` (IE 4), `sourceIndex` (IE 4), `style` (IE 4), `tagName` (IE 4), `title` (IE 4)

Methods
Supported by Both Navigator and IE: None

Other Methods: `click` (IE 4), `contains` (IE 4), `getAttribute` (IE 4), `insertAdjacentHTML` (IE 4), `insertAdjacentText` (IE 4), `remove-Attribute` (IE 4), `scrollIntoView` (IE 4), `setAttribute` (IE 4)

Events
`onclick` (IE 4), `ondblclick` (IE 4), `ondragstart` (IE 4), `onfilterchange` (IE 4), `onhelp` (IE 4), `onkeydown` (IE 4), `onkeypress` (IE 4), `onkeyup` (IE 4), `onmousedown` (IE 4), `onmousemove` (IE 4), `onmouseout` (IE 4), `onmouseover` (IE 4), `onmouseup` (IE 4), `onmousewheel` (IE 6), `onselectstart` (IE 4)

IFRAME

First Supported In: IE 4

Provides access to the HTML IFRAME tag. Has no defined events.

Properties
Supported by Both Navigator and IE: None

Other Properties: align (IE 4), className (IE 4), dataFld (IE 4), data-Src (IE 4), document (IE 4), frameBorder (IE 4), frameSpacing (IE 4), hspace (IE 4), id (IE 4), innerHTML (IE 4), innerText (IE 4), isTextEdit (IE 4), lang (IE 4), language (IE 4), marginHeight (IE 4), margin-Width (IE 4), offsetHeight (IE 4), offsetLeft (IE 4), offsetParent (IE 4), offsetTop (IE 4), offsetWidth (IE 4), outerHTML (IE 4), outer-Text (IE 4), parentElement (IE 4), parentTextEdit (IE 4), scrolling (IE 4), sourceIndex (IE 4), src (IE 4), style (IE 4), tagName (IE 4), title (IE 4), vspace (IE 4)

Methods
Supported by Both Navigator and IE: None

Other Methods: contains (IE 4), getAttribute (IE 4), insert-AdjacentHTML (IE 4), insertAdjacentText (IE 4), removeAttribute (IE 4), scrollIntoView (IE 4), setAttribute (IE 4)

image
First Supported In: IE 4

A form element that enables an image to be clicked to submit a form. It is not the same as the Image object supported by both Navigator and IE.

Properties
Supported by Both Navigator and IE: None

Other Properties: accessKey align (IE 4), alt (IE 4), border (IE 4), className (IE 4), complete (IE 4), disabled (IE 4), document (IE 4), dynsrc (IE 4), filter (IE 4), form (IE 4), height (IE 4), hspace (IE 4), id (IE 4), innerHTML (IE 4), isTextEdit (IE 4), language (IE 4), loop (IE 4), lowsrc (IE 4), name (IE 4), offsetHeight (IE 4), offsetLeft (IE 4), offset-Parent (IE 4), offsetTop (IE 4), offsetWidth (IE 4), outerHTML (IE 4), outerText (IE 4), parentElement (IE 4), parentTextEdit (IE 4), ready-State (IE 4), recordNumber (IE 4), sourceIndex (IE 4), src (IE 4), start (IE 4), style (IE 4), tabIndex (IE 4), tagName (IE 4), title (IE 4), type (IE 4), vspace (IE 4), width (IE 4)

Methods
Supported by Both Navigator and IE: None

Other Methods: `blur` (IE 4), `click` (IE 4), `contains` (IE 4), `focus` (IE 4), `getAttribute` (IE 4), `insertAdjacentHTML` (IE 4), `insertAdjacent-Text` (IE 4), `removeAttribute` (IE 4), `scrollIntoView` (IE 4), `select` (IE 4), `setAttribute` (IE 4)

Events

`onabort` (IE 4), `onafterupdate` (IE 4), `onbeforeupdate` (IE 4), `onblur` (IE 4), `onchange` (IE 4), `onclick` (IE 4), `ondataavailable` (IE 4), `ondatasetchanged` (IE 4), `ondatasetcomplete` (IE 4), `ondblclick` (IE 4), `onerror` (IE 4), `onerrorupdate` (IE 4), `onfocus` (IE 4), `onhelp` (IE 4), `onkeydown` (IE 4), `onkeypress` (IE 4), `onkeyup` (IE 4), `onload` (IE 4), `onmousedown` (IE 4), `onmousemove` (IE 4), `onmouseout` (IE 4), `onmouse-over` (IE 4), `onmouseup` (IE 4), `onresize` (IE 4), `onrowenter` (IE 4), `onrowexit` (IE 4), `onselect` (IE 4)

Image (IMG)

First Supported In: Navigator 3, IE 4

Represents an image that is loaded for the current document. The `images` property of the document object contains an array of all images loaded for that document. Updated in JavaScript 1.2. The `Image` object is also referred to as the `IMG` object in Microsoft's documentation.

Properties
Supported by Both Navigator and IE:

- ► `border` (Navigator 3, IE 4)—Identifies the value of the `BORDER` attribute

- ► `complete` (Navigator 3, IE 4)—Identifies whether the image's loading has been completed

- ► `height` (Navigator 3, IE 4)—Identifies the value of the `HEIGHT` attribute

- ► `hspace` (Navigator 3, IE 4)—Identifies the value of the `HSPACE` attribute

- ► `lowsrc` (Navigator 3, IE 4)—Identifies the value of the `LOWSRC` attribute

- ► `name` (Navigator 3, IE 4)—Identifies the value of the `NAME` attribute

- ▶ src (Navigator 3, IE 4)—Identifies the value of the SRC attribute
- ▶ vspace (Navigator 3, IE 4)—Identifies the value of the VSPACE attribute
- ▶ width (Navigator 3, IE 4)—Identifies the value of the WIDTH attribute

Other Properties: accessKey (IE 4), align (IE 4), alt (IE 4), class-Name (IE 4), dataFld (IE 4), dataFormatAs (IE 4), dataSrc (IE 4), document (IE 4), dynsrc (IE 4), fileCreatedDate (IE 4), fileModifiedDate (IE 4), fileSize (IE 4), fileUpdateDate (IE 4), filter (IE 4), href (IE 4), id (IE 4), innerHTML (IE 4), innerText (IE 4), isMap (IE 4), isText-Edit (IE 4), lang (IE 4), language (IE 4), loop (IE 4), mimeTypes (IE 4), offsetHeight (IE 4), offsetLeft (IE 4), offsetParent (IE 4), offset-Top (IE 4), offsetWidth (IE 4), outerHTML (IE 4), outerText (IE 4), parentElement (IE 4), parentTextEdit (IE 4), protocol (IE 4), ready-State (IE 4), scrollHeight (IE 4), scrollLeft (IE 4), scrollTop (IE 4), scrollWidth (IE 4), sourceIndex (IE 4), start (IE 4), style (IE 4), tab-Index (IE 4), tagName (IE 4), title (IE 4), useMap (IE 4)

Methods

Supported by Both Navigator and IE: None

Other Methods: blur (IE 4), click (IE 4), contains (IE 4), focus (IE 4), getAttribute (IE 4), handleEvent (Navigator 4), insertAdjacentHTML (IE 4), insertAdjacentText (IE 4), removeAttribute (IE 4), scroll-IntoView (IE 4), setAttribute (IE 4)

Events

onAbort (Navigator 3, IE 4), onafterupdate (IE 4), onbeforeupdate (IE 4), onblur (IE 4), onclick (IE 4), ondataavailable (IE 4), ondata-setchanged (IE 4), ondatasetcomplete (IE 4), ondblclick (IE 4), ondragstart (IE 4), onError (Navigator 3, IE 4), onfilterchange (IE 4), onfocus (IE 4), onhelp (IE 4), onkeydown (Navigator 4, IE 4), onkeypress (Navigator 4, IE 4), onkeyup (Navigator 4, IE 4), onLoad (Navigator 3, IE 4), onmousedown (IE 4), onmousemove (IE 4), onmouseout (IE 4), onmouseover (IE 4), onmouseup (IE 4), onmousewheel (IE 6), onresize (IE 4), onrowenter (IE 4), onrowexit (IE 4), onscroll (IE 4), onselectstart (IE 4)

INPUT

First Supported In: IE 4

Provides access to the HTML INPUT tag. Has no defined methods or events.

Properties
useMap (IE 6)

INS

First Supported In: IE 4

Provides access to the HTML INS tag.

Properties
Supported by Both Navigator and IE: None

Other Properties: className (IE 4), document (IE 4), id (IE 4), inner-HTML (IE 4), innerText (IE 4), isTextEdit (IE 4), lang (IE 4), language (IE 4), offsetHeight (IE 4), offsetLeft (IE 4), offsetParent (IE 4), offsetTop (IE 4), offsetWidth (IE 4), outerHTML (IE 4), outerText (IE 4), parentElement (IE 4), parentTextEdit (IE 4), sourceIndex (IE 4), style (IE 4), tagName (IE 4), titTe (IE 4)

Methods
Supported by Both Navigator and IE: None

Other Methods: click (IE 4), contains (IE 4), getAttribute (IE 4), insertAdjacentHTML (IE 4), insertAdjacentText (IE 4), remove-Attribute (IE 4), scrollIntoView (IE 4), setAttribute (IE 4)

Events
onclick (IE 4), ondblclick (IE 4), ondragstart (IE 4), onfilterchange (IE 4), onhelp (IE 4), onkeydown (IE 4), onkeypress (IE 4), onkeyup (IE 4), onmousedown (IE 4), onmousemove (IE 4), onmouseout (IE 4), onmouseover (IE 4), onmouseup (IE 4), onmousewheel (IE 6), onselectstart (IE 4)

ISINDEX

First Supported In: IE 5

Provides access to the HTML ISINDEX tag. **Note:** This tag is deprecated in the latest HTML specification.

Properties

Supported by Both Navigator and IE: None

Other Properties: accessKey (IE 5), canHaveHTML (IE 5), className (IE 5), clientHeight (IE 5), clientLeft (IE 5), clientTop (IE 5), client-Width (IE 5), contentEditable (IE 5), currentStyle (IE 5), disabled (IE 5), form (IE 6), hasLayout (IE 5), hideFocus (IE 5), id (IE 5), isContentEditable (IE 5), isDisabled (IE 5), lang (IE 5), language (IE 5), parentElement (IE 5), readyState (IE 5), scopeName (IE 5), scrollHeight (IE 5), scrollLeft (IE 5), scrollTop (IE 5), scroll-Width (IE 5), tabIndex (IE 5), tagUrn (IE 5)

Methods

Supported by Both Navigator and IE: None

Events

onbeforefocusenter (IE 5), onbeforefocusleave (IE 5), onblur (IE 5), oncontrolselect (IE 5), onfocus (IE 5), onfocusenter (IE 5), onfocusleave (IE 5), onreadystatechange (IE 5), onresize (IE 5), onresizeend (IE 5), onresizestart (IE 5)

java

First Supported In: Navigator 3

Provides access to objects in the java.* packages. Has no defined events. The java object is equivalent to Packages.java.

Properties

The java object does not define any properties of its own. It may be used to access the public properties of Java objects.

Methods

The java object does not define any methods of its own. It may be used to access the public methods of Java objects.

JavaArray

First Supported In: Navigator 3

Provides access to Java arrays. Has no defined events.

Properties

Supported by Both Navigator and IE: length (Navigator 3, IE 4); the number of elements in the Java array.

Other Properties: None

Methods

Supported by Both Navigator and IE: None

Other Methods: toString (Navigator 3)

JavaClass

First Supported In: Navigator 3

Provides access to a Java class. Has no defined events.

Properties

The static properties of the Java class being accessed.

Methods

The static methods of the Java class being accessed.

JavaObject

First Supported In: Navigator 3

An instance of a Java class that is created in or passed to JavaScript. Has no defined events.

Properties

Provides access to the public properties of the Java object being referenced.

Methods

Provides access to the public methods of the Java object being referenced.

JavaPackage

First Supported In: Navigator 3

Provides access to a Java package. Has no defined methods or events.

Properties

Provides access to the elements of the package as properties.

KBD

First Supported In: IE 4

Provides access to the HTML KBD tag. **Note:** This tag is deprecated in the latest HTML specification in favor of CSS.

Properties

Properties Supported by Both Navigator and IE: None

Other Properties: className (IE 4), document (IE 4), id (IE 4), inner-HTML (IE 4), innerText (IE 4), isTextEdit (IE 4), lang (IE 4), language (IE 4), offsetHeight (IE 4), offsetLeft (IE 4), offsetParent (IE 4), offsetTop (IE 4), offsetWidth (IE 4), outerHTML (IE 4), outerText (IE 4), parentElement (IE 4), parentTextEdit (IE 4), sourceIndex (IE 4), style (IE 4), tagName (IE 4), title (IE 4)

Methods

Methods Supported by Both Navigator and IE: None

Other Methods: click (IE 4), contains (IE 4), getAttribute (IE 4), insertAdjacentHTML (IE 4), insertAdjacentText (IE 4), removeAttribute (IE 4), scrollIntoView (InternetExplorer 4), setAttribute (IE 4)

Events

onclick (IE 4), ondblclick (IE 4), ondragstart (IE 4), onfilterchange (IE 4), onhelp (IE 4), onkeydown (IE 4), onkeypress (IE 4), onkeyup (IE 4), onmousedown (IE 4), onmousemove (IE 4), onmouseout (IE 4), onmouseover (IE 4), onmouseup (IE 4), onmousewheel (IE 6), onselectstart (IE 4)

LABEL

First Supported In: IE 4

Provides access to the HTML LABEL tag.

Properties

Properties Supported by Both Navigator and IE: None

Other Properties: accessKey (IE 4), className (IE 4), document (IE 4), form (IE 6), htmlFor (IE 4), id (IE 4), innerHTML (IE 4), innerText (IE 4), isTextEdit (IE 4), lang (IE 4), language (IE 4), offsetHeight (IE 4), offsetLeft (IE 4), offsetParent (IE 4), offsetTop (IE 4), offsetWidth (IE 4), outerHTML (IE 4), outerText (IE 4), parentElement (IE 4), parentTextEdit (IE 4), sourceIndex (IE 4), style (IE 4), tagName (IE 4), title (IE 4)

Methods

Methods Supported by Both Navigator and IE: None

Other Methods: click (IE 4), contains (IE 4), getAttribute (IE 4), insertAdjacentHTML (IE 4), insertAdjacentText (IE 4), removeAttribute (IE 4), scrollIntoView (IE 4), setAttribute (IE 4)

Events

onclick (IE 4), ondblclick (IE 4), ondragstart (IE 4), onfilterchange (IE 4), onhelp (IE 4), onkeydown (IE 4), onkeypress (IE 4), onkeyup (IE 4), onmousedown (IE 4), onmousemove (IE 4), onmouseout (IE 4), onmouseover (IE 4), onmouseup (IE 4), onmousewheel (IE 6), onselectstart (IE 4)

Layer

First Supported In: Navigator 4

Provides access to a layer of an HTML page. Layer is an object that is unique to Navigator and supports Navigator-specific DHTML (Dynamic HTML). Layer objects may also be created using the HTML DIV tag.

Properties

Properties Supported by Both Navigator and IE: None

Other Properties: above (Navigator 4), background (Navigator 4), below (Navigator 4), bgColor (Navigator 4), clip.bottom (Navigator 4),

clip.height (Navigator 4), clip.left (Navigator 4), clip.right
(Navigator 4), clip.top (Navigator 4), clip.width (Navigator 4),
document (Navigator 4), left (Navigator 4), name (Navigator 4), pageX
(Navigator 4), pageY (Navigator 4), parentLayer (Navigator 4), sibling-
Above (Navigator 4), siblingBelow (Navigator 4), src (Navigator 4),
top (Navigator 4), visibility (Navigator 4), window (Navigator 4),
x (Navigator 4), y (Navigator 4), zIndex (Navigator 4)

Methods
Methods Supported by Both Navigator and IE: None

Other Methods: captureEvents (Navigator 4), handleEvent
(Navigator 4), load (Navigator 4), moveAbove (Navigator 4), move-
Below (Navigator 4), moveBy (Navigator 4), moveTo (Navigator 4), move-
ToAbsolute (Navigator 4), releaseEvents (Navigator 4), resizeBy
(Navigator 4), resizeTo (Navigator 4), routeEvent (Navigator 4)

Events
onblur (Navigator 4), onfocus (Navigator 4), onLoad (Navigator 4),
onmouseout (Navigator 4), onmouseover (Navigator 4)

LEGEND
First Supported In: IE 4

Provides access to the HTML LEGEND tag.

Properties
Properties Supported by Both Navigator and IE: None

Other Properties: accessKey (IE 4), align (IE 4), className (IE 4),
clientHeight (IE 4), clientWidth (IE 4), document (IE 4), form (IE 6), id
(IE 4), innerHTML (IE 4), innerText (IE 4), isTextEdit (IE 4), lang (IE 4),
language (IE 4), margin offsetHeight (IE 4), offsetLeft (IE 4), offset-
Parent (IE 4), offsetTop (IE 4), offsetWidth (IE 4), outerHTML (IE 4),
outerText (IE 4), padding (IE 4), parentElement (IE 4), parentText-
Edit (IE 4), recordNumber (IE 4), scrollHeight (IE 4), scrollLeft
(IE 4), scrollTop (IE 4), scrollWidth (IE 4), sourceIndex (IE 4),
style (IE 4), tabIndex (IE 4), tagName (IE 4), title (IE 4)

Methods

Methods Supported by Both Navigator and IE: None

Other Methods: blur (IE 4), click (IE 4), contains (IE 4), focus (IE 4), getAttribute (IE 4), insertAdjacentHIML (IE 4), insert-AdjacentText (IE 4), removeAttribute (IE 4), scrollIntoView (IE 4), setAttribute (IE 4)

Events

onafterupdate (IE 4), onbeforeupdate (IE 4), onblur (IE 4), onclick (IE 4), ondblclick (IE 4), ondragstart (IE 4), onerrorupdate (IE 4), on-focus (IE 4), onhelp (IE 4), onkeydown (IE 4), onkeypress (IE 4), onkeyup (IE 4), onmousedown (IE 4), onmousemove (IE 4), onmouseout (IE 4), onmouseover (IE 4), onmouseup (IE 4), onmousewheel (IE 6), onresize (IE 4), onrowenter (IE 4), onrowexit (IE 4), onscroll (IE 4), onselect-start (IE 4)

LI

First Supported In: IE 4

Provides access to the HTML LI tag.

Properties

Properties Supported by Both Navigator and IE: None

Other Properties: className (IE 4), document (IE 4), id (IE 4), innerHTML (IE 4), innerText (IE 4), isTextEdit (IE 4), lang (IE 4), language (IE 4), offsetHeight (IE 4), offsetLeft (IE 4), offset-Parent (IE 4), offsetTop (IE 4), offsetWidth (IE 4), outerHTML (IE 4), outerText (IE 4), parentElement (IE 4), parentTextEdit (IE 4), sourceIndex (IE 4), style (IE 4), tagName (IE 4), title (IE 4), type (IE 4), value (IE 4)

Methods

Methods Supported by Both Navigator and IE: None

Other Methods: click (IE 4), contains (IE 4), getAttribute (IE 4), insertAdjacentHTML (IE 4), insertAdjacentText (IE 4), remove-Attribute (IE 4), scrollIntoView (IE 4), setAttribute (IE 4)

Events

onclick (IE 4), ondblclick (IE 4), ondragstart (IE 4), onfilterchange (IE 4), onhelp (IE 4), onkeydown (IE 4), onkeypress (IE 4), onkeyup (IE 4), onmousedown (IE 4), onmousemove (IE 4), onmouseout (IE 4), onmouseover (IE 4), onmouseup (IE 4), onmousewheel (IE 6), onselectstart (IE 4)

Link (A)

First Supported In: Navigator 2, IE 3

Represents a hypertext link. A Link object is created for each A tag in the document that specifies an HREF attribute. These objects may be accessed from the links property of the document object. The basic Link object was introduced in JavaScript 1.0 and updated with JavaScript 1.1 and 1.2. It is referred to as the A object in Microsoft's documentation. Under Navigator, a Link object may also be an Anchor object if the A tag specifies the NAME attribute in addition to the HREF attribute.

Properties

Properties Supported by Both Navigator and IE:

▶ hash (Navigator 2, IE 3)—The name of an anchor in the URL

▶ host (Navigator 2, IE 3)—A host name or IP address that represents the URL's host value

▶ hostname (Navigator 2, IE 3)—The host:port portion of the URL

▶ href (Navigator 2, IE 3)—The text of the entire URL

▶ pathname (Navigator 2, IE 3)—The pathname portion of the URL

▶ port (Navigator 2, IE 3)—The port value of the URL

▶ protocol (Navigator 2, IE 3)—The URL's protocol type

▶ search (Navigator 2, IE 3)—The value of any query string that is included in the URL

▶ target (Navigator 2, IE 3)—The value of the URL's TARGET attribute

Other Properties: accessKey (IE 4), className (IE 4), dataFld (IE 4), dataSrc (IE 4), document (IE 4), id (IE 4), innerHTML (IE 4), innerText (IE 4), isTextEdit (IE 4), lang (IE 4), language (IE 4), Methods (IE 4), offsetHeight (IE 4), offsetLeft (IE 4), offsetParent (IE 4), offsetTop (IE 4), offsetWidth (IE 4), outerHTML (IE 4), outerText (IE 4), parentElement (IE 4), parentTextEdit (IE 4), recordNumber (IE 4), rel (IE 4), rev (IE 4), sourceIndex (IE 4), style (IE 4), tabIndex (IE 4), tagName (IE 4), text (Navigator 4), title (IE 4), urn (IE 4), x (Navigator 4), y (Navigator 4)

Methods

Methods Supported by Both Navigator and IE: None

Other Methods: blur (IE 4), click (IE 4), contains (IE 4), focus (IE 4), getAttribute (IE 4), handleEvent (Navigator 4), insertAdjacent-HTML (IE 4), insertAdjacentText (IE 4), removeAttribute (IE 4), scrollIntoView (IE 4), setAttribute (IE 4)

Events

onblur (IE 4), onclick (Navigator 2, IE 3), ondblclick (Navigator 4, IE 4), ondragstart (IE 4), onerrorupdate (IE 4), onfilterchange (IE 4), onfocus (IE 4), onhelp (IE 4), onkeydown (Navigator 4, IE 4), onkey-press (Navigator 4, IE 4), onkeyup (Navigator 4, IE 4), onmousedown (Navigator 4, IE 4), onmousemove (IE 4), onmouseout (Navigator 3, IE 4), onmouseover (Navigator 2, IE 3), onmouseup (Navigator 4, IE 4), onmouse-wheel (IE 6), onselectstart (IE 4)

LINK

First Supported In: IE 4

Provides access to the HTML LINK tag. Has no defined events.

Properties

Properties Supported by Both Navigator and IE: None

Other Properties: charset (IE 6), className (IE 4), disabled (IE 4), document (IE 4), href (IE 4), id (IE 4), parentElement (IE 4), ready-State (IE 4), rel (IE 4), sourceIndex (IE 4), tagName (IE 4), title (IE 4), type (IE 6)

Methods

Methods Supported by Both Navigator and IE: None

Other Methods: contains (IE 4), getAttribute (IE 4), remove-Attribute (IE 4), setAttribute (IE 4)

LISTING

First Supported In: IE 4

Provides access to the HTML LISTING tag. **Note:** This tag is deprecated in the latest HTML specification in favor of CSS.

Properties

Properties Supported by Both Navigator and IE: None

Other Properties: className (IE 4), document (IE 4), id (IE 4), innerHTML (IE 4), innerText (IE 4), isTextEdit (IE 4), lang (IE 4), language (IE 4), offsetHeight (IE 4), offsetLeft (IE 4), offsetParent (IE 4), offsetTop (IE 4), offsetWidth (IE 4), outerHTML (IE 4), outerText (IE 4), parentElement (IE 4), parentTextEdit (IE 4), sourceIndex (IE 4), style (IE 4), tagName (IE 4), title (IE 4)

Methods

Methods Supported by Both Navigator and IE: None

Other Methods: click (IE 4), contains (IE 4), getAttribute (IE 4), insertAdjacentHTML (IE 4), insertAdjacentText (IE 4), removeAttribute (IE 4), scrollIntoView (IE 4), setAttribute (IE 4)

Events

onclick (IE 4), ondblclick (IE 4), ondragstart (IE 4), onfilterchange (IE 4), onhelp (IE 4), onkeydown (IE 4), onkeypress (IE 4), onkeyup (IE 4), onmousedown (IE 4), onmousemove (IE 4), onmouseout (IE 4), onmouseover (IE 4), onmouseup (IE 4), onmousewheel (IE 6), onselectstart (IE 4)

Location

First Supported In: Navigator 2, IE 3

Represents the URL of the document loaded into a window. The location property of the window object provides access to the window's Location object. Has no defined events. Updated in JavaScript 1.1.

Properties

Properties Supported by Both Navigator and IE:

► hash (Navigator 2, IE 3)—The name of an anchor in the URL

▶ host (Navigator 2, IE 3)—A host name or IP address that represents the URL's host value

▶ hostname (Navigator 2, IE 3)—The host:port portion of the URL

▶ href (Navigator 2, IE 3)—The text of the entire URL

▶ pathname (Navigator 2, IE 3)—The pathname portion of the URL

▶ port (Navigator 2, IE 3)—The port value of the URL

▶ protocol (Navigator 2, IE 3)—The URL's protocol type

▶ search (Navigator 2, IE 3)—The value of any query string that is included in the URL

Methods
Methods Supported by Both Navigator and IE:

▶ reload([*force*]) (Navigator 3, IE 4)—Reloads the current document. If the *force* argument is true, then the browser forces an HTTP GET, causing the document to be reloaded from the server instead of the browser's cache.

▶ replace(*url*) (Navigator 3, IE 4)—Loads the specified URL over the current document.

Other Methods: assign (IE 4)

MAP

First Supported In: IE 4

Provides access to the HTML MAP tag.

Properties
Properties Supported by Both Navigator and IE: None

Other Properties: className (IE 4), document (IE 4), filter (IE 4), id (IE 4), innerHTML (IE 4), innerText (IE 4), isTextEdit (IE 4), lang (IE 4), language (IE 4), name offsetHeight (IE 4), offsetLeft (IE 4), offsetParent (IE 4), offsetTop (IE 4), offsetWidth (IE 4), outer-HTML (IE 4), outerText (IE 4), parentElement (IE 4), parentTextEdit (IE 4), recordNumber (IE 4), sourceIndex (IE 4), style (IE 4), tagName (IE 4), title (IE 4)

Methods

Methods Supported by Both Navigator and IE: None

Other Methods: click (IE 4), contains (IE 4), getAttribute (IE 4), removeAttribute (IE 4), scrollIntoView (IE 4), setAttribute (IE 4)

Events

onafterupdate (IE 4), onbeforeupdate (IE 4), onclick (IE 4), ondataavailable (IE 4), ondatasetchanged (IE 4), ondatasetcomplete (IE 4), ondblclick (IE 4), ondragstart (IE 4), onerrorupdate (IE 4), onfilterchange (IE 4), onhelp (IE 4), onkeydown (IE 4), onkeypress (IE 4), onkeyup (IE 4), onmousedown (IE 4), onmousemove (IE 4), onmouseout (IE 4), onmouseover (IE 4), onmouseup (IE 4), onrowenter (IE 4), onrowexit (IE 4), onmousewheel (IE 6), onselectstart (IE 4)

MARQUEE

First Supported In: IE 4

Provides access to the HTML MARQUEE tag. **Note:** This tag is not a part of the HTML specification and is only supported in Microsoft IE.

Properties

Properties Supported by Both Navigator and IE: None

Other Properties: accessKey (IE 4), behavior (IE 4), bgColor (IE 4), className (IE 4), clientHeight (IE 4), clientWidth (IE 4), dataFld (IE 4), dataFormatAs (IE 4), dataSrc (IE 4), direction (IE 4), document (IE 4), height (IE 4), hspace (IE 4), id (IE 4), innerHTML (IE 4), innerText (IE 4), isTextEdit (IE 4), lang (IE 4), language (IE 4), loop (IE 4), offsetHeight (IE 4), offsetLeft (IE 4), offsetParent (IE 4), offsetTop (IE 4), offsetWidth (IE 4), outerHTML (IE 4), outerText (IE 4), parentElement (IE 4), parentTextEdit (IE 4), scrollAmount (IE 4), scrollDelay (IE 4), scrollHeight (IE 4), scrollLeft (IE 4), scrollTop (IE 4), scrollWidth (IE 4), sourceIndex (IE 4), style (IE 4), tagName (IE 4), title (IE 4), trueSpeed (IE 4), vspace (IE 4), width (IE 4)

Methods

Methods Supported by Both Navigator and IE: None

Other Methods: blur (IE 4), click (IE 4), contains (IE 4), focus (IE 4), getAttribute (IE 4), insertAdjacentHTML (IE 4), insert-AdjacentText (IE 4), removeAttribute (IE 4), scrollIntoView (IE 4), setAttribute (IE 4), start (IE 4), stop (IE 4)

Events

onafterupdate (IE 4), onblur (IE 4), onbounce (IE 4), onclick (IE 4), ondblclick (IE 4), ondragstart (IE 4), onfinish (IE 4), onfocus (IE 4), onhelp (IE 4), onkeydown (IE 4), onkeypress (IE 4), onkeyup (IE 4), onmousedown (IE 4), onmousemove (IE 4), onmouseout (IE 4), onmouseover (IE 4), onmouseup (IE 4), onmousewheel (IE 6), onresize (IE 4), onrow-enter (IE 4), onrowexit (IE 4), onscroll (IE 4), onselectstart (IE 4), onstart (IE 4)

Math

First Supported In: Navigator 2, IE 3

A core object that provides a set of static mathematical constants and functions. Has no defined events.

Properties
Properties Supported by Both Navigator and IE:

- ▶ E (Navigator 2, IE 3)—Euler's constant e
- ▶ LN10 (Navigator 2, IE 3)—The natural log of 10, $\log_e 10$
- ▶ LN2 (Navigator 2, IE 3)—The natural log of 2, $\log_e 2$
- ▶ LOG10E (Navigator 2, IE 3)—The base 10 log of e, $\log_{10} e$
- ▶ LOG2E (Navigator 2, IE 3)—The base 2 log of e, $\log_2 e$
- ▶ PI (Navigator 2, IE 3)—The mathematical constant pi
- ▶ SQRT1_2 (Navigator 2, IE 3)—The constant $1/\sqrt{2}$
- ▶ SQRT2 (Navigator 2, IE 3)—The square root of 2($\sqrt{2}$)

Methods
Methods Supported by Both Navigator and IE:

- ▶ abs(x) (Navigator 2, IE 3)—Returns the absolute value of x

- acos(x) (Navigator 2, IE 3)—Returns the arc cosine of x
- asin(x) (Navigator 2, IE 3)—Returns the arc sine of x
- atan(x) (Navigator 2, IE 3)—Returns the arc tangent of x
- atan2(y,x) (Navigator 2, IE 3)—Returns the arc tangent of y/x
- ceil(x) (Navigator 2, IE 3)—Returns the smallest integer that is greater than or equal to x
- cos(x) (Navigator 2, IE 3)—Returns the cosine of x
- exp(x) (Navigator 2, IE 3)—Returns e raised to the x power
- floor(x) (Navigator 2, IE 3)—Returns the largest integer that is less than or equal to x
- log(x) (Navigator 2, IE 3)—Returns the natural logarithm of x
- max(x,y) (Navigator 2, IE 3)—Returns the greater of x and y
- min(x,y) (Navigator 2, IE 3)—Returns the lesser of x and y
- pow(x,y) (Navigator 2, IE 3)—Returns x raised to the y power, x^y
- random() (Navigator 2, IE 3)—Returns a pseudo-random floating-point number between 0 and 1
- round(x) (Navigator 2, IE 3)—Returns the value of x rounded to the nearest integer
- sin(x) (Navigator 2, IE 3)—Returns the sine of x
- sqrt(x) (Navigator 2, IE 3)—Returns the square root of x
- tan(x) (Navigator 2, IE 3)—Returns the tangent of x

MENU

First Supported In: IE 4

Provides access to the HTML MENU tag. **Note:** This tag is deprecated in the latest HTML specification in favor of CSS.

Properties

Properties Supported by Both Navigator and IE: None

Other Properties: className (IE 4), compact (IE 6), document (IE 4), id (IE 4), innerHTML (IE 4), innerText (IE 4), isTextEdit (IE 4), lang (IE 4), language (IE 4), offsetHeight (IE 4), offsetLeft (IE 4), offsetParent (IE 4), offsetTop (IE 4), offsetWidth (IE 4), outerHTML (IE 4), outerText (IE 4), parentElement (IE 4), parentTextEdit (IE 4), sourceIndex (IE 4), style (IE 4), tagName (IE 4), title (IE 4)

Methods
Methods Supported by Both Navigator and IE: None

Other Methods: click (IE 4), contains (IE 4), getAttribute (IE 4), insertAdjacentHTML (IE 4), insertAdjacentText (IE 4), removeAttribute (IE 4), scrollIntoView (IE 4), setAttribute (IE 4)

Events
onclick (IE 4), ondblclick (IE 4), ondragstart (IE 4), onfilterchange (IE 4), onhelp (IE 4), onkeydown (IE 4), onkeypress (IE 4), onkeyup (IE 4), onmousedown (IE 4), onmousemove (IE 4), onmouseout (IE 4), onmouseover (IE 4), onmouseup (IE 4), onmousewheel (IE 6), onselectstart (IE 4)

META
First Supported In: IE 4

Provides access to the HTML META tag. Has no defined events.

Properties
Properties Supported by Both Navigator and IE: None

Other Properties: charset (IE 4), className (IE 4), content (IE 4), document (IE 4), httpEquiv (IE 4), id (IE 4), isTextEdit (IE 4), lang (IE 4), name (IE 4), parentElement (IE 4), parentTextEdit (IE 4), sourceIndex (IE 4), tagName (IE 4), title (IE 4), url (IE 4)

Methods
Methods Supported by Both Navigator and IE: None

Other Methods: contains (IE 4), getAttribute (IE 4), removeAttribute (IE 4), setAttribute (IE 4)

MimeType

First Supported In: Navigator 3

Represents a MIME type as handled by the browser. MIME types are used to define the type of information contained in a file or data stream. Has no defined methods or event handlers.

Properties

Properties Supported by Both Navigator and IE: None

Other Properties: description (Navigator 3), enabledPlugin (Navigator 3), suffixes (Navigator 3), type (Navigator 3)

navigator

First Supported In: Navigator 2, IE 3

Provides access to basic information about the browser that is executing the script. Has no defined events. The basic navigator object was introduced in JavaScript 1.0 and updated with JavaScript 1.1 and 1.2.

Properties

Properties Supported by Both Navigator and IE:

- ▶ appCodeName (Navigator 2, IE 3)—The browser's code name.

- ▶ appName (Navigator 2, IE 3)—The browser's name.

- ▶ appVersion (Navigator 2, IE 3)—The browser's version number.

- ▶ mimeTypes (Navigator 3, IE 4)—An array of MimeType objects supported by the browser. Value not substantiated in IE 4.

- ▶ platform (Navigator 4, IE 5)—The operating system the browser is running under.

- ▶ plugins (Navigator 3, IE 4)—An array of all Plugin objects supported by the browser.

- ▶ userAgent (Navigator 2, IE 3)—The user-agent header sent in the HTTP protocol by the browser to a web server.

Other Properties: appMinorVersion (IE 4), browserLanguage (IE 4), connectionSpeed (IE 4), cookieEnabled (IE 4), cpuClass (IE 4), language (Navigator 4), onLine (IE 4), systemLanguage (IE 4), userProfile (IE 4)

Methods
Methods Supported by Both Navigator and IE:

- ▶ javaEnabled() (Navigator 3, IE 4)—Returns True if Java is enabled by the browser.

- ▶ taintEnabled() (Navigator 3, IE 4)—Returns True if tainting is enabled. (Deprecated in the JavaScript 1.3 specification.)

Other Methods: plugins.refresh (Navigator 3), preference (Navigator 4), savePreferences (Navigator 4)

net∧cape
First Supported In: Navigator 3

Provides access to Java classes in the package netscape.*. Equivalent to the netscape property of the Packages object.

NEXTID
First Supported In: IE 4

Provides access to the HTML NEXTID tag. Has no defined events.

Properties
Properties Supported by Both Navigator and IE: None

Other Properties: className (IE 4), document (IE 4), id (IE 4), isTextEdit (IE 4), language (IE 4), parentElement (IE 4), parent-TextEdit (IE 4), sourceIndex (IE 4), tagName (IE 4), title (IE 4)

Methods
Methods Supported by Both Navigator and IE: None

Other Methods: contains (IE 4), getAttribute (IE 4), remove-Attribute (IE 4), setAttribute (IE 4)

NOBR
First Supported In: IE 5

Provides access to the HTML NOBR tag.

Properties

Properties Supported by Both Navigator and IE: None

Other Properties: canHaveHTML (IE 5), className (IE 5), client-
Height (IE 5), clientLeft (IE 5), clientTop (IE 5), clientWidth (IE 5),
contentEditable (IE 5), currentStyle (IE 5), dir (IE 5), disabled
(IE 5), hasLayout (IE 5), id (IE 5), innerHTML (IE 5), innerText (IE 5),
isContentEditable (IE 5), isDisabled (IE 5), isTextEdit (IE 5),
lang (IE 5), language (IE 5), offsetHeight (IE 5), offsetLeft (IE 5),
offsetParent (IE 5), offsetTop (IE 5), offsetWidth (IE 5), outer-
HTML (IE 5), outerText (IE 5), parentElement (IE 5), parentTextEdit
(IE 5), readyState (IE 5), recordNumber (IE 5), runtimeStyle (IE 5),
scopeName (IE 5), scrollHeight (IE 5), scrollLeft (IE 5), scrollTop
(IE 5), scrollWidth (IE 5), sourceIndex (IE 5), style (IE 5), tag-
Name (IE 5), tagUrn (IE 5), uniqueID (IE 5)

Methods

Methods Supported by Both Navigator and IE: None

Other Methods: addBehavior (IE 5), attachEvent (IE 5), click
(IE 5), componentFromPoint (IE 5), contains (IE 5), detachEvent (IE 5),
fireEvent (IE 5), getAttribute (IE 5), getBoundingClientRect
(IE 5), getClientRects (IE 5), getExpression (IE 5), insertAdjacent-
HTML (IE 5), insertAdjacentText (IE 5), releaseCapture (IE 5),
removeAttribute (IE 5), removeBehavior (IE 5), removeExpression
(IE 5), scrollIntoView (IE 5), setAttribute (IE 5), setCapture (IE 5),
setExpression (IE 5)

Events

onbeforecopy (IE 5), onbeforecut (IE 5), onbeforepaste (IE 5),
onclick (IE 5), oncontextmenu (IE 5), oncopy (IE 5), oncut (IE 5),
ondblclick (IE 5), ondrag (IE 5), ondragend (IE 5), ondragenter (IE 5),
ondragleave (IE 5), ondragover (IE 5), ondragstart (IE 5), ondrop
(IE 5), onhelp (IE 5), onkeydown (IE 5), onkeypress (IE 5), onkeyup (IE 5),
onlosecapture (IE 5), onmouseenter (IE 5), onmouseleave (IE 5),
onmousemove (IE 5), onmouseover (IE 5), onmouseup (IE 5), onmousewheel (IE 6), onpaste (IE 5), onpropertychange (IE 5), onreadystatechange (IE 5), onselectstart (IE 5)

NOFRAMES

First Supported In: IE 5

Provides access to the HTML NOFRAMES tag.

Properties

Properties Supported by Both Navigator and IE: None

Other Properties: canHaveHTML (IE 5), contentEditable (IE 5), disabled (IE 5), id (IE 5), isContentEditable (IE 5), isDisabled (IE 5), parentElement (IE 5), readyState (IE 5), scopeName (IE 5), tagUrn (IE 5)

Methods

Methods Supported by Both Navigator and IE: None

Other Methods: addBehavior (IE 5), componentFromPoint (IE 5), fireEvent (IE 5), removeBehavior (IE 5)

Event

onreadystatechange (IE 5)

NOSCRIPT

First Supported In: IE 5

Provides access to the HTML NOSCRIPT tag.

Properties

Properties Supported by Both Navigator and IE: None

Other Properties: canHaveHTML (IE 5), contentEditable (IE 5), disabled (IE 5), id (IE 5), isContentEditable (IE 5), isDisabled (IE 5), parentElement (IE 5), readyState (IE 5), scopeName (IE 5), tagUrn (IE 5)

Methods

Methods Supported by Both Navigator and IE: None

Other Methods: addBehavior (IE 5), componentFromPoint (IE 5), fireEvent (IE 5), removeBehavior (IE 5)

Event

onreadystatechange (IE 5)

Number

First Supported In: Navigator 3, IE 4

A core JavaScript object that is an object wrapper for number values. Has no defined events. Introduced in JavaScript 1.1 and updated with JavaScript 1.2 and 1.3.

Constructor

new Number(*value*)

Creates a number object with the specified value.

Properties

Properties Supported by Both Navigator and IE:

- ▶ constructor (Navigator 3, IE 4)—Identifies the object's constructor

- ▶ MAX_VALUE (Navigator 3, IE 4)—Identifies the largest number

- ▶ MIN_VALUE (Navigator 3, IE 4)—Identifies the smallest number

- ▶ NaN (Navigator 3, IE 4)—Represents the value Not-a-Number

- ▶ NEGATIVE_INFINITY (Navigator 3, IE 4)—Represents negative infinity

- ▶ POSITIVE_INFINITY (Navigator 3, IE 4)—Represents positive infinity

- ▶ prototype (Navigator 3, IE 4)—Provides the capability to define additional properties

Methods

Methods Supported by Both Navigator and IE:

- ▶ toString([*radix*]) (Navigator 3, IE 4)—Returns a string representation of the number

- ▶ valueOf() (Navigator 3, IE 4)—Returns the primitive value corresponding to the Number object

Other Methods: toSource (Navigator 4.06)

Object

First Supported In: Navigator 2, IE 4

The core JavaScript object that defines properties and methods inherited by all other objects. Has no defined events. The Object object was introduced in JavaScript 1.0 and updated with JavaScript 1.1, 1.2, and 1.3, and JScript 6.5.

Properties

Properties Supported by Both Navigator and IE: constructor (Navigator 3, IE 4); Refers to the object's constructor

Other Properties: alt (IE 6), body (IE 6), border (IE 6), useMap (IE 6)

Methods

Methods Supported by Both Navigator and IE:

- ► toString() (Navigator 2, IE 4)—Returns the string representation of the object

- ► valueOf() (Navigator 3, IE 4)—Returns the primitive value associated with the object

Other Methods: eval (Navigator 3), toSource (Navigator 4.06), unwatch (Navigator 4), watch (Navigator 4)

OBJECT

First Supported In: IE 4

Provides access to the HTML OBJECT tag.

Properties

Properties Supported by Both Navigator and IE: None

Other Properties: accessKey (IE 4), align (IE 4), altHTML (IE 4), classid (IE 4), className (IE 4), code (IE 4), codeBase (IE 4), codeType (IE 4), data (IE 4), dataFld (IE 4), dataFormatAs (IE 4), dataSrc (IE 4), document (IE 4), height (IE 4), hspace (IE 4), id (IE 4), isTextEdit (IE 4), lang (IE 4), language (IE 4), name (IE 4), object (IE 4), offsetHeight (IE 4), offsetLeft (IE 4), offsetParent (IE 4), offsetTop (IE 4), offsetWidth (IE 4), outerHTML (IE 4), outerText (IE 4),

parentElement (IE 4), parentTextEdit (IE 4), readyState (IE 4),
sourceIndex (IE 4), style (IE 4), tabIndex (IE 4), tagName (IE 4), title
(IE 4), type (IE 4), vspace (IE 4), width (IE 4)

Methods
Methods Supported by Both Navigator and IE: None

  Other Methods: blur (IE 4), click (IE 4), contains (IE 4), focus
(IE 4), getAttribute (IE 4), removeAttribute (IE 4), scrollInto-
View (IE 4), setAttribute (IE 4)

Events
onafterupdate (IE 4), onbeforeupdate (IE 4), onblur (IE 4), onclick
(IE 4), ondataavailable (IE 4), ondatasetchanged (IE 4), ondatasetcomplete (IE 4), ondblclick (IE 4), ondragstart (IE 4), onerror (IE 4),
onerrorupdate (IE 4), onfilterchange (IE 4), onfocus (IE 4), onmousewheel (IE 6), onreadystatechange (IE 4), onrowenter (IE 4), onrowexit
(IE 4), onselectstart (IE 4)

OL

First Supported In: IE 4

  Provides access to the HTML OL tag.

Properties
Properties Supported by Both Navigator and IE: None

  Other Properties: className (IE 4), document (IE 4), id (IE 4),
innerHTML (IE 4), innerText (IE 4), isTextEdit (IE 4), lang (IE 4),
language (IE 4), offsetHeight (IE 4), offsetLeft (IE 4), offset-
Parent (IE 4), offsetTop (IE 4), offsetWidth (IE 4), outerHTML (IE 4),
outerText (IE 4), parentElement (IE 4), parentTextEdit (IE 4),
sourceIndex (IE 4), start (IE 4), style (IE 4), tagName (IE 4), title
(IE 4), type (IE 4)

Methods
Methods Supported by Both Navigator and IE: None

  Other Methods: click (IE 4), contains (IE 4), getAttribute (IE 4),
insertAdjacentHTML (IE 4), insertAdjacentText (IE 4), remove-
Attribute (IE 4), scrollIntoView (IE 4), setAttribute (IE 4)

Events

onclick (IE 4), ondblclick (IE 4), ondragstart (IE 4), onfilter-change (IE 4), onhelp (IE 4), onkeydown (IE 4), onkeypress (IE 4), onkeyup (IE 4), onmousedown (IE 4), onmousemove (IE 4), onmouseout (IE 4), onmouseover (IE 4), onmouseup (IE 4), onmousewheel (IE 6), onselectstart (IE 4)

Option

First Supported In: Navigator 2, IE 3

Represents an option in the select field of a form. Has no defined events. The Option object was introduced in JavaScript 1.0 and updated with JavaScript 1.1.

Constructor

```
new Option([text[, value[, defaultSelected[, selected]]]])
```

Creates a new Option object with the specified text and (optionally) value. If the *defaultSelected* argument is supplied, then its value (Boolean) sets the default selection state of the option. If the *selected* argument is supplied, it determines the object's current selection state.

Properties

Properties Supported by Both Navigator and IE:

- ▶ defaultSelected (Navigator 3, IE 4)—Indicates whether an option is selected by default

- ▶ index (Navigator 2, IE 3)—Identifies the index of the option in the options array of the corresponding Select object

- ▶ length (Navigator 2, IE 3)—Identifies the length of the options array of the corresponding Select object

- ▶ selected (Navigator 2, IE 3)—Identifies the option's current selection state

- ▶ text (Navigator 2, IE 3)—Identifies the option's text

- ▶ value (Navigator 2, IE 3)—Identifies the option's value

Other Properties: None

Methods
Methods Supported by Both Navigator and IE: None

> **Other Methods:** contains (IE 4), getAttribute (IE 4), remove-Attribute (IE 4), scrollIntoView (IE 4), setAttribute (IE 4)

P

First Supported In: IE 4

Provides access to the HTML P tag.

Properties
Properties Supported by Both Navigator and IE: None

> **Other Properties:** className (IE 4), document (IE 4), id (IE 4), innerHTML (IE 4), innerText (IE 4), isTextEdit (IE 4), lang (IE 4), language (IE 4), offsetHeight (IE 4), offsetLeft (IE 4), offset-Parent (IE 4), offsetTop (IE 4), offsetWidth (IE 4), outerHTML (IE 4), outerText (IE 4), parentElement (IE 4), parentTextEdit (IE 4), source-Index (IE 4), style (IE 4), tagName (IE 4), title (IE 4)

Methods
Methods Supported by Both Navigator and IE: None

> **Other Methods:** click (IE 4), contains (IE 4), getAttribute (IE 4), insertAdjacentHTML (IE 4), insertAdjacentText (IE 4), remove-Attribute (IE 4), scrollIntoView (IE 4), setAttribute (IE 4)

Events
onclick (IE 4), ondblclick (IE 4), ondragstart (IE 4), onfilter-change (IE 4), onhelp (IE 4), onkeydown (IE 4), onkeypress (IE 4), onkeyup (IE 4), onmousedown (IE 4), onmousemove (IE 4), onmouseout (IE 4), onmouseover (IE 4), onmouseup (IE 4), onmousewheel (IE 6), onselectstart (IE 4)

Packages

First Supported In: Navigator 3

Provides access to Java packages from within JavaScript. Has no defined methods or events.

Properties
Properties Supported by Both Navigator and IE: None

Other Properties: className (Navigator 3), java (Navigator 3), netscape (Navigator 3), sun (Navigator 3)

Password

First Supported In: Navigator 2; IE 3

Represents a password field of an HTML form. Password fields are represented by INPUT tags with their TYPE attribute set to PASSWORD. Password objects allow a user to type a password without its contents being displayed. However, the password values are not encrypted and are transmitted in the clear from the user's browser to a web server via HTTP. The basic Password object was introduced in JavaScript 1.0 and updated with JavaScript 1.1.

Properties
Properties Supported by Both Navigator and IE:

- ▶ defaultValue (Navigator 2, IE 3)—The default value of the password field

- ▶ form (Navigator 2, IE 3)—Provides a reference to the form object that contains the password field

- ▶ name (Navigator 2, IE 3)—The value of the password field's NAME attribute

- ▶ type (Navigator 3, IE 4)—The value of the password field's TYPE attribute

- ▶ value (Navigator 2, IE 3)—The value entered by the user in the password field

Other Properties: accessKey (IE 4), align (IE 4), className (IE 4), dataFld (IE 4), dataSrc (IE 4), disabled (IE 4), document (IE 4), id (IE 4), isTextEdit (IE 4), lang (IE 4), language (IE 4), maxLength (IE 4), offsetHeight (IE 4), offsetLeft (IE 4), offsetParent (IE 4), offsetTop (IE 4), offsetWidth (IE 4), outerHTML (IE 4), outerText (IE 4), parentElement (IE 4), parentTextEdit (IE 4), readOnly (IE 4), size (IE 4), sourceIndex (IE 4), style (IE 4), tabIndex (IE 4), tagName (IE 4), title (IE 4)

Methods

Methods Supported by Both Navigator and IE:

- ► blur() (Navigator 2, IE 3)—Removes input focus from the password field

- ► focus() (Navigator 2, IE 3)—Moves input focus to the password field

- ► select() (Navigator 2, IE 3)—Selects (highlights) the input area of the password field

Other Methods: click (IE 4), contains (IE 4), getAttribute (IE 4), handleEvent (Navigator 4), insertAdjacentHTML (IE 4), insert-AdjacentText (IE 4), removeAttribute (IE 4), scrollIntoView (IE 4), setAttribute (IE 4)

Events

onblur (Navigator 3, IE 4), onfocus (Navigator 3, IE 4), onchange (IE 4), onclick (IE 4), ondblclick (IE 4), onhelp (IE 4), onkeydown (IE 4), onkeypress (IE 4), onkeyup (IE 4), onmousedown (IE 4), onmousemove (IE 4), onmouseout (IE 4), onmouseover (IE 4), onmouseup (IE 4), onresize (IE 4), onselect (IE 4)

PLAINTEXT

First Supported In: IE 4

Provides access to the HTML PLAINTEXT tag. **Note:** This tag is deprecated in the latest HTML specification in favor of CSS.

Properties

Properties Supported by Both Navigator and IE: None

Other Properties: className (IE 4), document (IE 4), id (IE 4), innerHTML (IE 4), innerText (IE 4), isTextEdit (IE 4), lang (IE 4), language (IE 4), offsetHeight (IE 4), offsetLeft (IE 4), offset-Parent (IE 4), offsetTop (IE 4), offsetWidth (IE 4), outerHTML (IE 4), outerText (IE 4), parentElement (IE 4), parentTextEdit (IE 4), sourceIndex (IE 4), style (IE 4), tagName (IE 4), title (IE 4)

Methods

Methods Supported by Both Navigator and IE: None

Other Methods: click (IE 4), contains (IE 4), getAttribute (IE 4), insertAdjacentHTML (IE 4), removeAttribute (IE 4), scrollIntoView (IE 4), setAttribute (IE 4)

Event

onclick (IE 4), ondblclick (IE 4), ondragstart (IE 4), onfilter-change (IE 4), onhelp (IE 4), onkeydown (IE 4), onkeypress (IE 4), onkeyup (IE 4), onmousedown (IE 4), onmousemove (IE 4), onmouseout (IE 4), onmouseover (IE 4), onmouseup (IE 4), onmousewheel (IE 6), onselectstart (IE 4)

Plugin

First Supported In: Navigator 3

Represents a browser plug-in. Plugin objects are accessed via the plugins property of the navigator object. Has no defined methods or events.

Properties

Properties Supported by Both Navigator and IE: None

Other Properties: description (Navigator 3), filename (Navigator 3), length (Navigator 3), name (Navigator 3)

PRE

First Supported In: IE 4

Provides access to the HTML PRE tag. **Note:** This tag is deprecated in the latest HTML specification in favor of CSS.

Properties

Properties Supported by Both Navigator and IE: None

Other Properties: className (IE 4), document (IE 4), id (IE 4), innerHTML (IE 4), innerText (IE 4), isTextEdit (IE 4), lang (IE 4), language (IE 4), offsetHeight (IE 4), offsetLeft (IE 4), offset-Parent (IE 4), offsetTop (IE 4), offsetWidth (IE 4), outerHTML (IE 4), outerText (IE 4), parentElement (IE 4), parentTextEdit (IE 4), sourceIndex (IE 4), style (IE 4), tagName (IE 4), title (IE 4)

Methods

Methods Supported by Both Navigator and IE: None

Other Methods: click (IE 4), contains (IE 4), getAttribute (IE 4), insertAdjacentHTML (IE 4), insertAdjacentText (IE 4), removeAttribute (IE 4), scrollIntoView (IE 4), setAttribute (IE 4)

Events

onclick (IE 4), ondblclick (IE 4), ondragstart (IE 4), onfilterchange (IE 4), onhelp (IE 4), onkeydown (IE 4), onkeypress (IE 4), onkeyup (IE 4), onmousedown (IE 4), onmousemove (IE 4), onmouseout (IE 4), onmouseover (IE 4), onmouseup (IE 4), onmousewheel (IE 6), onselectstart (IE 4)

Q

First Supported In: IE 4

Provides access to the HTML Q tag. **Note:** This tag is deprecated in the latest HTML specification in favor of CSS.

Properties

Properties Supported by Both Navigator and IE: None

Other Properties: className (IE 4), document (IE 4), id (IE 4), innerHTML (IE 4), innerText (IE 4), isTextEdit (IE 4), lang (IE 4), language (IE 4), offsetHeight (IE 4), offsetLeft (IE 4), offsetParent (IE 4), offsetTop (IE 4), offsetWidth (IE 4), outerHTML (IE 4), outerText (IE 4), parentElement (IE 4), parentTextEdit (IE 4), sourceIndex (IE 4), style (IE 4), tagName (IE 4), title (IE 4)

Methods

Methods Supported by Both Navigator and IE: None

Other Methods: click (IE 4), contains (IE 4), getAttribute (IE 4), insertAdjacentHTML (IE 4), insertAdjacentText (IE 4), removeAttribute (IE 4), scrollIntoView (IE 4), setAttribute (IE 4)

Events

onclick (IE 4), ondblclick (IE 4), ondragstart (IE 4), onfilterchange (IE 4), onhelp (IE 4), onkeydown (IE 4), onkeypress (IE 4), onkeyup (IE 4), onmousedown (IE 4), onmousemove (IE 4), onmouseout (IE 4), onmouseover (IE 4), onmouseup (IE 4), onmousewheel (IE 6), onselectstart (IE 4)

Radio

First Supported In: Navigator 2, IE 3

Form fields that support the selection of exactly one choice from a set of one or more choices. Radio buttons are INPUT elements that have their TYPE attribute set to RADIO. Radio buttons are grouped by setting their NAME attributes to the same values. The basic Radio object was introduced in JavaScript 1.0 and updated in JavaScript 1.1 and 1.2.

Properties
Properties Supported by Both Navigator and IE:

- ▶ checked (Navigator 2, IE 3)—Identifies via a Boolean value whether the radio button is checked or unchecked

- ▶ defaultChecked (Navigator 2, IE 3)—The value of the button's CHECKED attribute

- ▶ form (Navigator 2, IE 3)—Provides a reference to the form object that contains the button

- ▶ name (Navigator 2, IE 3)—The value of the button's NAME attribute

- ▶ type (Navigator 3, IE 4)—The value of the button's TYPE attribute

- ▶ value (Navigator 2, IE 3)—The value of the button's VALUE attribute

Other Properties: accessKey (IE 4), className (IE 4), dataFld (IE 4), dataSrc (IE 4), disabled (IE 4), document (IE 4), id (IE 4), isTextEdit (IE 4), lang (IE 4), language (IE 4), offsetHeight (IE 4), offsetLeft (IE 4), offsetParent (IE 4), offsetTop (IE 4), offsetWidth (IE 4), outerText (IE 4), parentElement (IE 4), parentTextEdit (IE 4), recordNumber (IE 4), size (IE 4), sourceIndex (IE 4), style (IE 4), tabIndex (IE 4), tagName (IE 4), title (IE 4)

Methods
Methods Supported by Both Navigator and IE:

- ▶ blur() (Navigator 2, IE 3)—Removes input focus from the button

- ▶ click() (Navigator 2, IE 3)—Simulates clicking of the button
- ▶ focus() (Navigator 2, IE 3)—Moves input focus to the button

Other Methods: contains (IE 4), getAttribute (IE 4), handle-Event (Navigator 4), insertAdjacentHTML (IE 4), insertAdjacentText (IE 4), removeAttribute (IE 4), scrollIntoView (IE 4), select (IE 4), setAttribute (IE 4)

Events

onafterupdate (IE 4), onbeforeupdate (IE 4), onblur (Navigator 3, IE 4), onchange (IE 4), onclick (Navigator 2, IE 3), ondblclick (IE 4), onerrorupdate (IE 4), onfocus (Navigator 3, IE 4), onhelp (IE 4), onkeydown (IE 4), onkeypress (IE 4), onkeyup (IE 4), onmousedown (IE 4), onmousemove (IE 4), onmouseout (IE 4), onmouseover (IE 4), onmouseup (IE 4), onresize (IE 4), onselect (IE 4)

RegExp (Regular Expreɑion)

First Supported In: Navigator 4, IE 4

A core object that encapsulates a regular expression and provides properties and methods for accessing the regular expression. Navigator recognizes a single RegExp object for all regular expressions. IE documents the RegExp object and a separate Regular Expression object that is created via the /pattern/flags constructor. Has no defined events. The basic RegExp object was introduced in JavaScript 1.2 and updated with JavaScript 1.3.

Constructors

```
/pattern/flags
```

(Navigator 4) Creates a RegExp object using the specified pattern and flags.

```
new RegExp("pattern"[, "flags"])
```

(Navigator 4) Creates a RegExp object using the specified pattern and flags.

Properties

Properties Supported by Both Navigator and IE:

- ▶ $1 through $9 (Navigator 4, IE 4)—Parenthesized substring matches

- ► input (Navigator 4, IE 4)—The string against which a regular expression is matched

- ► lastIndex (Navigator 4, IE 4)—The index at which to start the next match

- ► source (Navigator 4, IE 4)—The pattern to be matched

Other Properties: $+ (Navigator 4), $& (Navigator 4), $' (Navigator 4), $* (Navigator 4), $_ (Navigator 4), $` (Navigator 4), constructor (Navigator 4), global (Navigator 4), ignoreCase (Navigator 4), index (IE 4), lastMatch (Navigator 4), lastParen (Navigator 4), leftContext (Navigator 4), multiline (Navigator 4), prototype (Navigator 4), rightContext (Navigator 4)

Methods
Methods Supported by Both Navigator and IE:

- ► compile(*pattern*[, *flags*]) (Navigator 4, IE 4)

- ► Compiles the regular expression

- ► exec([*string*]) (Navigator 4, IE 4)—Executes the regular expression with the specified string

- ► test([*string*]) (Navigator 4, IE 4)—Tests the regular expression with the specified string

Other Methods: toSource (Navigator 4.06), toString (Navigator 4), valueOf (Navigator 4)

Reset

First Supported In: Navigator 2, IE 3

Form fields that reset form fields back to their original values. Reset buttons are INPUT elements that have their TYPE attribute set to RESET. The basic Reset object was introduced in JavaScript 1.0 and updated in JavaScript 1.1 and 1.2.

Properties
Properties Supported by Both Navigator and IE:

- ► form (Navigator 2, IE 3)—Provides a reference to the form object that contains the button

- ▶ name (Navigator 2, IE 3)—The value of the button's NAME attribute

- ▶ type (Navigator 3, IE 4)—The value of the button's TYPE attribute

- ▶ value (Navigator 2, IE 3)—The value of the button's VALUE attribute

Other Properties: accessKey (IE 4), className (IE 4), disabled (IE 4), document (IE 4), id (IE 4), isTextEdit (IE 4), lang (IE 4), language (IE 4), offsetHeight (IE 4), offsetLeft (IE 4), offsetParent (IE 4), offsetTop (IE 4), offsetWidth (IE 4), outerHTML (IE 4), outerText (IE 4), parentElement (IE 4), parentTextEdit (IE 4), recordNumber (IE 4), sourceIndex (IE 4), style (IE 4), tabIndex (IE 4), tagName (IE 4), title (IE 4)

Methods

Methods Supported by Both Navigator and IE:

- ▶ blur() (Navigator 2, IE 3)—Removes input focus from the button

- ▶ click() (Navigator 2, IE 3)—Simulates clicking of the button

- ▶ focus() (Navigator 2, IE 3)—Moves input focus to the button

Other Methods: contains (IE 4), getAttribute (IE 4), handleEvent (Navigator 4), insertAdjacentHTML (IE 4), insertAdjacentText (IE 4), removeAttribute (IE 4), scrollIntoView (IE 4), select (IE 4), setAttribute (IE 4)

Events

onblur (Navigator 3, IE 4), onclick (Navigator 2, IE 3), onfocus (Navigator 3, IE 4), ondblclick (IE 4), onfilterchange (IE 4), onhelp (IE 4), onkeydown (IE 4), onkeypress (IE 4), onkeyup (IE 4), onmousedown (IE 4), onmousemove (IE 4), onmouseout (IE 4), onmouseover (IE 4), onmouseup (IE 4), onresize (IE 4), onselect (IE 4)

RT

First Supported In: IE 5

Provides access to the Microsoft RT tag.

Properties

Properties Supported by Both Navigator and IE: None

Other Properties: accessKey (IE 5), canHaveHTML (IE 5), className (IE 5), contentEditable (IE 5), dir (IE 5), disabled (IE 5), hide-Focus (IE 5), id (IE 5), innerHTML (IE 5), innerText (IE 5), isContent-Editable (IE 5), isDisabled (IE 5), lang (IE 5), language (IE 5), name (IE 5), offsetHeight (IE 5), offsetLeft (IE 5), offsetParent (IE 5), offsetTop (IE 5), offsetWidth (IE 5), outerHTML (IE 5), outerText (IE 5), parentElement (IE 5), readyState (IE 5), scopeName (IE 5), tabIndex (IE 5), tagName (IE 5), tagUrn (IE 5), title (IE 5)

Methods

Methods Supported by Both Navigator and IE: None

Other Methods: addBehavior (IE 5), blur (IE 5), componentFromPoint (IE 5), fireEvent (IE 5), focus (IE 5), getExpression (IE 5), remove-Behavior (IE 5), removeExpression (IE 5), setActive (IE 5), set-Expression (IE 5)

Events

onafterupdate (IE 5), onbeforecut (IE 5), onbeforefocusenter (IE 5), onbeforefocusleave (IE 5), onbeforepaste (IE 5), onbefore-update (IE 5), onblur (IE 5), onclick (IE 5), oncontextmenu (IE 5), oncontrolselect (IE 5), oncut (IE 5), ondblclick (IE 5), ondragstart (IE 5), onerrorupdate (IE 5), onfilterchange (IE 5), onfocus (IE 5), onfocusenter (IE 5), onfocusleave (IE 5), onhelp (IE 5), onkeydown (IE 5), onkeypress (IE 5), onkeyup (IE 5), onmousedown (IE 5), onmouse-enter (IE 5), onmouseleave (IE 5), onmousemove (IE 5), onmouseout (IE 5), onmouseover (IE 5), onmouseup (IE 5), onmousewheel (IE 6), onpaste (IE 5), onreadystatechange (IE 5), onresizeend (IE 5), onresizestart (IE 5), onselectstart (IE 5)

RUBY

First Supported In: IE 5

Provides access to the Microsoft RUBY tag.

Properties

Properties Supported by Both Navigator and IE: None

Other Properties: accessKey (IE 5), canHaveHTML (IE 5), className (IE 5), contentEditable (IE 5), dir (IE 5), disabled (IE 5), hideFocus

(IE 5), id (IE 5), innerHTML (IE 5), innerText (IE 5), isContent-Editable (IE 5), isDisabled (IE 5), lang (IE 5), language (IE 5), name (IE 5), offsetHeight (IE 5), offsetLeft (IE 5), offsetParent (IE 5), offsetTop (IE 5), offsetWidth (IE 5), outerHTML (IE 5), outerText (IE 5), parentElement (IE 5), readyState (IE 5), recordNumber (IE 5), scope-Name (IE 5), tabIndex (IE 5), tagName (IE 5), tagUrn (IE 5), title (IE 5)

Methods

Methods Supported by Both Navigator and IE: None

Other Methods: addBehavior (IE 5), blur (IE 5), componentFrom-Point (IE 5), fireEvent (IE 5), focus (IE 5), getExpression (IE 5), removeBehavior (IE 5), removeExpression (IE 5), setActive (IE 5), setExpression (IE 5)

Events

onafterupdate (IE 5), onbeforecut (IE 5), onbeforefocusenter (IE 5), onbeforefocusleave (IE 5), onbeforepaste (IE 5), onbeforeupdate (IE 5), onblur (IE 5), onclick (IE 5), oncontextmenu (IE 5), oncontrol-select (IE 5), oncut (IE 5), ondblclick (IE 5), ondragstart (IE 5), onerrorupdate (IE 5), onfilterchange (IE 5), onfocus (IE 5), onfocus-enter (IE 5), onfocusleave (IE 5), onhelp (IE 5), onkeydown (IE 5), onkeypress (IE 5), onkeyup (IE 5), onmousedown (IE 5), onmouseenter (IE 5), onmouseleave (IE 5), onmousemove (IE 5), onmouseout (IE 5), onmouseover (IE 5), onmouseup (IE 5), onmousewheel (IE 6), onpaste (IE 5), onreadystatechange (IE 5), onresizeend (IE 5), onresize-start (IE 5), onselectstart (IE 5)

rule

First Supported In: IE 5

Provides access to rules that apply CSS attributes (styles that are applied to HTML elements on an HTML page). Has no defined methods or events.

Properties

Properties Supported by Both Navigator and IE: None

Other Properties: readOnly (IE 5), runtimeStyle (IE 5), selector-Text (IE 5), style (IE 5)

runtimeStyle

First Supported In: IE 5

Provides access to CSS styles that override global styles. Has no defined methods or events.

Properties

Properties Supported by Both Navigator and IE: None

Other Properties: background (IE 5), backgroundAttachment (IE 5), backgroundColor (IE 5), backgroundImage (IE 5), background-Position (IE 5), backgroundPositionX (IE 5), backgroundPositionY (IE 5), backgroundRepeat (IE 5), border (IE 5), borderBottom (IE 5), borderBottomColor (IE 5), borderBottomStyle (IE 5), borderBottom-Width (IE 5), borderColor (IE 5), borderLeft (IE 5), borderLeftColor (IE 5), borderLeftStyle (IE 5), borderLeftWidth (IE 5), border-Right (IE 5), borderRightColor (IE 5), borderRightStyle (IE 5), border-RightWidth (IE 5), borderStyle (IE 5), borderTop (IE 5), border-TopColor (IE 5), borderTopStyle (IE 5), borderTopWidth (IE 5), borderWidth (IE 5), bottom (IE 5), clear (IE 5), clip (IE 5), color (IE 5), cssText (IE 5), cursor (IE 5), direction (IE 5), filter (IE 5), font (IE 5), fontFamily (IE 5), fontSize (IE 5), fontStyle (IE 5), font-Variant (IE 5), fontWeight (IE 5), height (IE 5), layoutFlow (IE 5), layoutGrid (IE 5), layoutGridChar (IE 5), layoutGridCharSpacing (IE 5), layoutGridLine (IE 5), layoutGridMode (IE 5), layoutGrid-Type (IE 5), left (IE 5), letterSpacing (IE 5), lineHeight (IE 5), listStyle (IE 5), listStyleImage (IE 5), listStylePosition (IE 5), listStyleType (IE 5), margin (IE 5), marginBottom (IE 5), marginLeft (IE 5), marginRight (IE 5), marginTop (IE 5), overflow (IE 5), overflowX (IE 5), overflowY (IE 5), pageBreakAfter (IE 5), pageBreakBefore (IE 5), pixelBottom (IE 5), pixelHeight (IE 5), pixel-Left (IE 5), pixelRight (IE 5), pixelTop (IE 5), pixelWidth (IE 5), posBottom (IE 5), posHeight (IE 5), position (IE 5), posLeft (IE 5), pos-Right (IE 5), posTop (IE 5), posWidth (IE 5), rectangular (IE 5), right (IE 5), scrollbar3dLightColor (IE 5), scrollbarArrowColor (IE 5), scrollbarBaseColor (IE 5), scrollbarDarkShadowColor (IE 5), scroll-barFaceColor (IE 5), scrollbarHighlightColor (IE 5), scrollbar-ShadowColor (IE 5), styleFloat (IE 5), tableLayout (IE 5), textAlign (IE 5), textDecoration (IE 5), textDecorationLineThrough (IE 5), textDecorationNone (IE 5), textDecorationOverline (IE 5), text-DecorationUnderline (IE 5), textIndent (IE 5), textTransform (IE 5), textUnderlinePosition (IE 5), top (IE 5), unicodeBidi (IE 5), verticalAlign (IE 5), visibility (IE 5), width (IE 5), wordWrap (IE 5), writingMode (IE 5), zIndex (IE 5), zoom (IE 5)

S

First Supported In: IE 4

Provides access to the HTML S tag. **Note:** This tag is deprecated in the latest HTML specification in favor of CSS.

Properties
Properties Supported by Both Navigator and IE: None

Other Properties: className (IE 4), document (IE 4), id (IE 4), inner-HTML (IE 4), innerText (IE 4), isTextEdit (IE 4), lang (IE 4), language (IE 4), offsetHeight (IE 4), offsetLeft (IE 4), offsetParent (IE 4), offsetTop (IE 4), offsetWidth (IE 4), outerHTML (IE 4), outerText (IE 4), parentElement (IE 4), parentTextEdit (IE 4), sourceIndex (IE 4), style (IE 4), tagName (IE 4), title (IE 4)

Methods
Methods Supported by Both Navigator and IE: None

Other Methods: click (IE 4), contains (IE 4), getAttribute (IE 4), insertAdjacentHTML (IE 4), insertAdjacentText (IE 4), remove-Attribute (IE 4), scrollIntoView (IE 4), setAttribute (IE 4)

Events
onclick (IE 4), ondblclick (IE 4), ondragstart (IE 4), onfilter-change (IE 4), onhelp (IE 4), onkeydown (IE 4), onkeypress (IE 4), onkeyup (IE 4), onmousedown (IE 4), onmousemove (IE 4), onmouseout (IE 4), onmouseover (IE 4), onmouseup (IE 4), onmousewheel (IE 6), onselectstart (IE 4)

SAMP

First Supported In: IE 4

Provides access to the HTML SAMP tag. **Note:** This tag is deprecated in the latest HTML specification in favor of CSS.

Properties

Properties Supported by Both Navigator and IE: None

Other Properties: className (IE 4), document (IE 4), id (IE 4), innerHTML (IE 4), innerText (IE 4), isTextEdit (IE 4), lang (IE 4), language (IE 4), offsetHeight (IE 4), offsetLeft (IE 4), offset-Parent (IE 4), offsetTop (IE 4), offsetWidth (IE 4), outerHTML (IE 4), outerText (IE 4), parentElement (IE 4), parentTextEdit (IE 4), sourceIndex (IE 4), style (IE 4), tagName (IE 4), title (IE 4)

Methods

Methods Supported by Both Navigator and IE: None

Other Methods: click (IE 4), contains (IE 4), getAttribute (IE 4), insertAdjacentHTML (IE 4), insertAdjacentText (IE 4), remove-Attribute (IE 4), scrollIntoView (IE 4), setAttribute (IE 4)

Events

onclick (IE 4), ondblclick (IE 4), ondragstart (IE 4), onfilter-change (IE 4), onhelp (IE 4), onkeydown (IE 4), onkeypress (IE 4), onkeyup (IE 4), onmousedown (IE 4), onmousemove (IE 4), onmouseout (IE 4), onmouseover (IE 4), onmouseup (IE 4), onmousewheel (IE 6), onselectstart (IE 4)

screen

First Supported In: Navigator 4, IE 4

Provides access to the parameters of the user's display monitor. Has no defined methods or events.

Properties

Properties Supported by Both Navigator and IE:

► availHeight (Navigator 4, IE 5)—The available height of the screen

► availWidth (Navigator 4, IE 5)—The available width of the screen

► colorDepth (Navigator 4, IE 4)—The number of colors supported by the current color palette

▶ `height` (Navigator 4, IE 4)—The height of the screen

▶ `width` (Navigator 4, IE 4)—The width of the screen

Other Properties: `availLeft` (Navigator 4), `availTop` (Navigator 4), `bufferDepth` (IE 4), `pixelDepth` (Navigator 4), `updateInterval` (IE 4)

SCRIPT

First Supported In: IE 4

Provides access to the HTML SCRIPT tag.

Properties
Properties Supported by Both Navigator and IE: None

Other Properties: `charset` (IE 6), `className` (IE 4), `defer` (IE 4), `document` (IE 4), `event` (IE 4), `htmlFor` (IE 4), `id` (IE 4), `innerHTML` (IE 4), `innerText` (IE 4), `isTextEdit` (IE 4), `language` (IE 4), `parentElement` (IE 4), `parentTextEdit` (IE 4), `readyState` (IE 4), `sourceIndex` (IE 4), `src` (IE 4), `style` (IE 4), `tagName` (IE 4), `text` (IE 4), `title` (IE 4), `type` (IE 4)

Methods
Methods Supported by Both Navigator and IE: None

Other Methods: `contains` (IE 4), `getAttribute` (IE 4), `insertAdjacentHTML` (IE 4), `insertAdjacentText` (IE 4), `removeAttribute` (IE 4), `setAttribute` (IE 4)

Events
`onerror` (IE 4), `onload` (IE 4), `onreadystatechange` (IE 4)

Select

First Supported In: Navigator 2, IE 3

Provides an HTML menu of choices to users. The SELECT tags enclose zero or more OPTION tags. The OPTION tags specify the menu choices and are represented by OPTION objects in JavaScript. The basic Select object was introduced in JavaScript 1.0 and updated in JavaScript 1.1 and 1.2.

Properties

Properties Supported by Both Navigator and IE:

- ► form (Navigator 2, IE 3)—Provides a reference to the form object that contains the SELECT field.

- ► length (Navigator 2, IE 3)—Identifies the number of options.

- ► name (Navigator 2, IE 3)—The value of the select field's NAME attribute.

- ► options (Navigator 2, IE 3)—An array that identifies the Option objects of the select element. The objects appear in the same order that they do in the source HTML.

- ► selectedIndex (Navigator 2, IE 3)—Identifies (by index) the first selected option in the SELECT element. This property is set to 1 if no options are selected.

- ► type (Navigator 3, IE 4)—If the select field's MULTIPLE attribute is set, then type has the value select-multiple. Otherwise, it is set to select-one.

Other Properties: accessKey (IE 4), className (IE 4), dataFld (IE 4), dataSrc (IE 4), disabled (IE 4), document (IE 4), id (IE 4), isText-Edit (IE 4), lang (IE 4), language (IE 4), multiple (IE 4), offset-Height (IE 4), offsetLeft (IE 4), offsetParent (IE 4), offsetTop (IE 4), offsetWidth (IE 4), outerHTML (IE 4), outerText (IE 4), parent-Element (IE 4), parentTextEdit (IE 4), recordNumber (IE 4), size (IE 4), sourceIndex (IE 4), style (IE 4), tabIndex (IE 4), tagName (IE 4), value (IE 4)

Methods

Methods Supported by Both Navigator and IE:

- ► blur() (Navigator 2, IE 3)—Removes input focus from the field

- ► focus() (Navigator 2, IE 3)—Moves input focus to the field

Other Methods: add (IE 4), click (IE 4), contains (IE 4), get-Attribute (IE 4), handleEvent (Navigator 4), insertAdjacentHTML (IE 4), insertAdjacentText (IE 4), item (IE 4), remove (IE 4), remove-Attribute (IE 4), scrollIntoView (IE 4), setAttribute (IE 4), tags (IE 4)

Events

onafterupdate (IE 4), onbeforeupdate (IE 4), onblur (Navigator 2, IE 3), onChange (Navigator 2, IE 3), onclick (IE 4), ondblclick (IE 4), ondragstart (IE 4), onerrorupdate (IE 4), onfilterchange (IE 4), onfocus (Navigator 2, IE 3), onhelp (IE 4), onkeydown (IE 4), onkeypress (IE 4), onkeyup (IE 4), onmousedown (IE 4), onmousemove (IE 4), onmouseout (IE 4), onmouseover (IE 4), onmouseup (IE 4), onmousewheel (IE 6), onresize (IE 4), onrowenter (IE 4), onrowexit (IE 4), onselectstart (IE 4)

selection

First Supported In: IE 4

Provides access to text that is currently selected by the user. Has no defined events.

Property

Properties Supported by Both Navigator and IE: None

Other Properties: type (IE 4)

Methods

Methods Supported by Both Navigator and IE: None

Other Methods: clear (IE 4), createRange (IE 4), empty (IE 4)

SMALL

First Supported In: IE 4

Provides access to the HTML SMALL tag. **Note:** This tag is deprecated in the latest HTML specification in favor of CSS.

Properties

Properties Supported by Both Navigator and IE: None

Other Properties: className (IE 4), document (IE 4), id (IE 4), innerHTML (IE 4), innerText (IE 4), isTextEdit (IE 4), lang (IE 4), language (IE 4), offsetHeight (IE 4), offsetLeft (IE 4), offsetParent (IE 4), offsetTop (IE 4), offsetWidth (IE 4), outerHTML (IE 4), outerText (IE 4), parentElement (IE 4), parentTextEdit (IE 4), sourceIndex (IE 4), style (IE 4), tagName (IE 4), title (IE 4)

Methods
Methods Supported by Both Navigator and IE: None

Other Methods: click (IE 4), contains (IE 4), getAttribute (IE 4), insertAdjacentHTML (IE 4), insertAdjacentText (IE 4), removeAttribute (IE 4), scrollIntoView (IE 4), setAttribute (IE 4)

Events
onclick (IE 4), ondblclick (IE 4), ondragstart (IE 4), onfilter-change (IE 4), onhelp (IE 4), onkeydown (IE 4), onkeypress (IE 4), onkeyup (IE 4), onmousedown (IE 4), onmousemove (IE 4), onmouseout (IE 4), onmouseover (IE 4), onmouseup (IE 4), onmousewheel (IE 6), onselectstart (IE 4)

SPAN

First Supported In: IE 4

Provides access to the HTML SPAN tag.

Properties
Properties Supported by Both Navigator and IE: None

Other Properties: className (IE 4), dataFld (IE 4), dataFormatAs (IE 4), dataSrc (IE 4), document (IE 4), id (IE 4), innerText (IE 4), isTextEdit (IE 4), lang (IE 4), language (IE 4), offsetHeight (IE 4), offsetLeft (IE 4), offsetParent (IE 4), offsetTop (IE 4), offsetWidth (IE 4), outerText (IE 4), parentElement (IE 4), parentTextEdit (IE 4), scrollHeight (IE 4), scrollLeft (IE 4), scrollTop (IE 4), scrollWidth (IE 4), sourceIndex (IE 4), style (IE 4), tagName (IE 4), title (IE 4)

Methods
Methods Supported by Both Navigator and IE: None

Other Methods: blur (IE 4), click (IE 4), contains (IE 4), focus (IE 4), getAttribute (IE 4), insertAdjacentHTML (IE 4), insertAdjacentText (IE 4), removeAttribute (IE 4), scrollIntoView (IE 4), setAttribute (IE 4)

Events

onblur (IE 4), onclick (IE 4), ondblclick (IE 4), ondragstart (IE 4), onfilterchange (IE 4), onfocus (IE 4), onhelp (IE 4), onkeydown (IE 4), onkeypress (IE 4), onkeyup (IE 4), onmousedown (IE 4), onmousemove (IE 4), onmouseout (IE 4), onmouseover (IE 4), onmouseup (IE 4), onmousewheel (IE 6), onscroll (IE 4), onselectstart (IE 4)

STRIKE

First Supported In: IE 4

Provides access to the HTML STRIKE tag. **Note:** This tag is deprecated in the latest HTML specification in favor of CSS.

Properties

Properties Supported by Both Navigator and IE: None

Other Properties: className (IE 4), document (IE 4), id (IE 4), innerHTML (IE 4), innerText (IE 4), isTextEdit (IE 4), lang (IE 4), language (IE 4), offsetHeight (IE 4), offsetLeft (IE 4), offsetParent (IE 4), offsetTop (IE 4), offsetWidth (IE 4), outerHTML (IE 4), outerText (IE 4), parentElement (IE 4), parentTextEdit (IE 4), sourceIndex (IE 4), style (IE 4), tagName (IE 4), title (IE 4)

Methods

Methods Supported by Both Navigator and IE: None

Other Methods: click (IE 4), contains (IE 4), getAttribute (IE 4), insertAdjacentHTML (IE 4), insertAdjacentText (IE 4), removeAttribute (IE 4), scrollIntoView (IE 4), setAttribute (IE 4)

Events

onclick (IE 4), ondblclick (IE 4), ondragstart (IE 4), onfilterchange (IE 4), onhelp (IE 4), onkeydown (IE 4), onkeypress (IE 4), onkeyup (IE 4), onmousedown (IE 4), onmousemove (IE 4), onmouseout (IE 4), onmouseover (IE 4), onmouseup (IE 4), onmousewheel (IE 6), onselectstart (IE 4)

String

First Supported In: Navigator 2, IE 3

A core object that provides an object wrapper for string values. The basic String object was introduced in JavaScript 1.0 and updated in JavaScript 1.1, 1.2, and 1.3. Has no defined events.

Constructor

```
new String(string)
```

Constructs a String object from the *string* value.

Properties
Properties Supported by Both Navigator and IE:

► constructor (Navigator 3, IE 4)—References the constructor used to create the object

► length (Navigator 2, IE 3)—Identifies the length of the associated string

► prototype (Navigator 2, IE 4)—Provides the capability to define additional properties

Methods
Methods Supported by Both Navigator and IE:

► anchor(*name*) (Navigator 2, IE 3)—Creates an HTML anchor with the specified NAME attribute

► big() (Navigator 2, IE 3)—Renders a string using the BIG tags

► blink() (Navigator 2, IE 3)—Renders a string using the BLINK tags

► bold() (Navigator 2, IE 3)—Renders a string using the BOLD tags

► charAt(*index*) (Navigator 2, IE 3)—Returns the character at the specified index

► charCodeAt([*index*]) (Navigator 4, IE 4)—Returns a number corresponding to the Unicode character at the specified index

► concat(*string1*[,...,*stringN*]) (Navigator 4, IE 4)—Concatenates strings 1 through *N* to the current string

► fixed() (Navigator 2, IE 3)—Renders a string using the TT tags

- ► fontcolor(*color*) (Navigator 2, IE 3)—Displays the string with the specified color

- ► fontsize(*size*) (Navigator 2, IE 3)—Displays the string with the specified font size

- ► fromCharCode(*num1*,...,*numN*) (Navigator 4, IE 4)—Returns a string created from the Unicode value sequence

- ► indexOf(*searchValue*[,*index*]) (Navigator 2, IE 3)—Returns the index of the first occurrence of the search value

- ► italics() (Navigator 2, IE 3)—Renders a string using the I tags

- ► lastIndexOf(*searchValue*[,*index*]) (Navigator 2, IE 3)—Returns the index of the last occurrence of the search value

- ► link(*attribute*) (Navigator 2, IE 3)—Creates a hypertext link with the specified HREF attribute

- ► match(*regexp*) (Navigator 4, IE 4)—Matches the regular expression against the string

- ► replace(*regexp*, *newSubstring*) (Navigator 4, IE 4)—Matches the regular expression and replaces the matches with the new string

- ► search(*regexp*) (Navigator 4, IE 4)—Searches the string for the regular expression

- ► slice(*beginslice*[, *endSlice*]) (Navigator 2, IE 3)—Returns a slice of the string

- ► small() (Navigator 2, IE 3)—Renders a string using the SMALL tags

- ► split([*separator*][, *limit*]) (Navigator 3, IE 4)—Splits the string into an array of strings based on the specified separator

- ► strike() (Navigator 2, IE 3)—Renders a string using the STRIKE tags

- ► sub() (Navigator 2, IE 3)—Renders a string using the SUB tags

- ► substr(*start*[, *length*]) (Navigator 2, IE 3)—Returns a substring of the string

- ► substring(*indexA*, *indexB*) (Navigator 2, IE 3)—Returns a substring of the string starting at *indexA* until *indexB* (or the end of the string)

▶ sup() (Navigator 2, IE 3)—Renders a string using the SUP tags

▶ toLowerCase() (Navigator 2, IE 3)—Returns a lowercase version of the string

▶ toUpperCase() (Navigator 2, IE 3)—Returns an uppercase version of the string

▶ valueOf() (Navigator 3, IE 4)—Returns the primitive value corresponding to the object

Other Methods: replace (Navigator 4.06), toSource (Navigator 4.06)

STRONG

First Supported In: IE 4

Provides access to the HTML STRONG tag. **Note:** This tag is deprecated in the latest HTML specification in favor of CSS.

Properties

Properties Supported by Both Navigator and IE: None

Other Properties: className (IE 4), document (IE 4), id (IE 4), inner-HTML (IE 4), innerText (IE 4), isTextEdit (IE 4), lang (IE 4), language (IE 4), offsetHeight (IE 4), offsetLeft (IE 4), offsetParent (IE 4), offsetTop (IE 4), offsetWidth (IE 4), outerHTML (IE 4), outerText (IE 4), parentElement (IE 4), parentTextEdit (IE 4), sourceIndex (IE 4), style (IE 4), tagName (IE 4), title (IE 4)

Methods

Methods Supported by Both Navigator and IE: None

Other Methods: click (IE 4), contains (IE 4), getAttribute (IE 4), insertAdjacentHTML (IE 4), insertAdjacentText (IE 4), remove-Attribute (IE 4), scrollIntoView (IE 4), setAttribute (IE 4)

Events

onclick (IE 4), ondblclick (IE 4), ondragstart (IE 4), onfilter-change (IE 4), onhelp (IE 4), onkeydown (IE 4), onkeypress (IE 4), onkeyup (IE 4), onmousedown (IE 4), onmousemove (IE 4), onmouseout (IE 4), onmouseover (IE 4), onmouseup (IE 4), onmousewheel (IE 6), onselectstart (IE 4)

style

First Supported In: IE 4

Provides access to the inline style of an HTML element. Has no defined events.

Properties

Properties Supported by Both Navigator and IE: None

Other Properties: background (IE 4), backgroundAttachment (IE 4), backgroundColor (IE 4), backgroundImage (IE 4), backgroundPosition (IE 4), backgroundPositionX (IE 4), backgroundPositionY (IE 4), backgroundRepeat (IE 4), border (IE 4), borderBottom (IE 4), borderBottomColor (IE 4), borderBottomStyle (IE 4), borderBottomWidth (IE 4), borderColor (IE 4), borderLeft (IE 4), borderLeftColor (IE 4), borderLeftStyle (IE 4), borderLeftWidth (IE 4), borderRight (IE 4), borderRightColor (IE 4), borderRightStyle (IE 4), borderRightWidth (IE 4), borderStyle (IE 4), borderTop (IE 4), borderTopColor (IE 4), borderTopStyle (IE 4), borderTopWidth (IE 4), borderWidth (IE 4), clear (IE 4), clip (IE 4), color (IE 4), cssText (IE 4), cursor (IE 4), display (IE 4), filter (IE 4), font (IE 4), fontFamily (IE 4), fontSize (IE 4), fontStyle (IE 4), fontVariant (IE 4), fontWeight (IE 4), height (IE 4), left (IE 4), letterSpacing (IE 4), lineHeight (IE 4), listStyle (IE 4), listStyleImage (IE 4), listStylePosition (IE 4), listStyleType (IE 4), margin (IE 4), marginBottom (IE 4), marginLeft (IE 4), marginRight (IE 4), marginTop (IE 4), overflow (IE 4), paddingBottom (IE 4), paddingLeft (IE 4), paddingRight (IE 4), paddingTop (IE 4), pageBreakAfter (IE 4), pageBreakBefore (IE 4), pixelHeight (IE 4), pixelLeft (IE 4), pixelTop (IE 4), pixelWidth (IE 4), posHeight (IE 4), position (IE 4), posLeft (IE 4), posTop (IE 4), posWidth (IE 4), styleFloat (IE 4), textAlign (IE 4), textDecoration (IE 4), textDecorationBlink (IE 4), textDecorationLineThrough (IE 4), textDecorationNone (IE 4), textDecorationOverline (IE 4), textDecorationUnderline (IE 4), textIndent (IE 4), textTransform (IE 4), top (IE 4), verticalAlign (IE 4), visibility (IE 4), width (IE 4), zIndex (IE 4)

Methods

Methods Supported by Both Navigator and IE: None

Other Methods: getAttribute (IE 4), removeAttribute (IE 4), setAttribute (IE 4)

Style

First Supported In: Navigator 4

Forms the basis for Navigator's support of DHTML styles. Has no defined events.

Properties

Properties Supported by Both Navigator and IE: None

Other Properties: align (Navigator 4), backgroundColor (Navigator 4), backgroundImage (Navigator 4), borderBottomWidth (Navigator 4), borderColor (Navigator 4), borderLeftWidth (Navigator 4), borderRightWidth (Navigator 4), borderStyle (Navigator 4), borderTopWidth (Navigator 4), clear (Navigator 4), color (Navigator 4), display (Navigator 4), fontFamily (Navigator 4), fontSize (Navigator 4), fontStyle (Navigator 4), fontWeight (Navigator 4), lineHeight (Navigator 4), listStyleType (Navigator 4), marginBottom (Navigator 4), marginLeft (Navigator 4), marginRight (Navigator 4), marginTop (Navigator 4), paddingBottom (Navigator 4), paddingLeft (Navigator 4), paddingRight (Navigator 4), paddingTop (Navigator 4), textAlign (Navigator 4), textDecoration (Navigator 4), textIndent (Navigator 4), textTransform (Navigator 4), whiteSpace (Navigator 4), width (Navigator 4)

Methods

Methods Supported by Both Navigator and IE: None

Other Methods: borderWidths (Navigator 4), margins (Navigator 4), paddings (Navigator 4)

STYLE

First Supported In: IE 4

Allows a CSS style sheet to be specified for the current document.

Properties

Properties Supported by Both Navigator and IE: None

Other Properties: className (IE 4), disabled (IE 4), document (IE 4), id (IE 4), isTextEdit (IE 4), offsetHeight (IE 4), offsetLeft (IE 4), offsetParent (IE 4), offsetTop (IE 4), offsetWidth (IE 4), parentElement (IE 4), parentTextEdit (IE 4), readyState (IE 4), sourceIndex (IE 4), style (IE 4), tagName (IE 4), type (IE 4)

Methods

Methods Supported by Both Navigator and IE: None

   Other Methods: borderWidths (Navigator 4), click (IE 4), contains (IE 4), getAttribute (IE 4), insertAdjacentHTML (IE 4), insertAdjacentText (IE 4), scrollIntoView (IE 4), setAttribute (IE 4)

Events

onerror (IE 4), onload (IE 4), onreadystatechange (IE 4)

styleSheet

First Supported In: IE 4

   Provides access to a CSS style sheet. Has no defined events.

Properties

Properties Supported by Both Navigator and IE: None

   Other Properties: disabled (IE 4), href (IE 4), id (IE 4), owningElement (IE 4), parentStyleSheet (IE 4), readOnly (IE 4), type (IE 4)

Methods

Methods Supported by Both Navigator and IE: None

   Other Methods: addImport (IE 4), addRule (IE 4)

SUB

First Supported In: IE 4

   Provides access to the HTML SUB tag. **Note:** This tag is deprecated in the latest HTML specification in favor of CSS.

Properties

Properties Supported by Both Navigator and IE: None

   Other Properties: className (IE 4), document (IE 4), id (IE 4), innerHTML (IE 4), innerText (IE 4), isTextEdit (IE 4), lang (IE 4), language (IE 4), offsetHeight (IE 4), offsetLeft (IE 4), offsetParent (IE 4), offsetTop (IE 4), offsetWidth (IE 4), outerHTML (IE 4), outerText (IE 4), parentElement (IE 4), parentTextEdit (IE 4), sourceIndex (IE 4), style (IE 4), tagName (IE 4), title (IE 4)

Methods
Methods Supported by Both Navigator and IE: None

   Other Methods: click (IE 4), contains (IE 4), getAttribute (IE 4), insertAdjacentHTML (IE 4), insertAdjacentText (IE 4), removeAttribute (IE 4), scrollIntoView (IE 4), setAttribute (IE 4)

Events
onclick (IE 4), ondblclick (IE 4), ondragstart (IE 4), onfilterchange (IE 4), onhelp (IE 4), onkeydown (IE 4), onkeypress (IE 4), onkeyup (IE 4), onmousedown (IE 4), onmousemove (IE 4), onmouseout (IE 4), onmouseover (IE 4), onmouseup (IE 4), onmousewheel (IE 6), onselectstart (IE 4)

Submit

First Supported In: Navigator 2, IE 3

   A form field used to submit form values to a web server for processing. A submit button is an INPUT element that has its TYPE attribute set to SUBMIT. The basic Submit object was introduced in JavaScript 1.0 and updated in JavaScript 1.1 and 1.2.

Properties
Properties Supported by Both Navigator and IE:

▶ form (Navigator 2, IE 3)—Provides a reference to the form object that contains the button

▶ name (Navigator 2, IE 3)—The value of the button's NAME attribute

▶ type (Navigator 3, IE 4)—The value of the button's TYPE attribute

▶ value (Navigator 2, IE 3)—The value of the button's VALUE attribute

   Other Properties: accessKey (IE 4), className (IE 4), disabled (IE 4), document (IE 4), id (IE 4), isTextEdit (IE 4), lang (IE 4), language (IE 4), offsetHeight (IE 4), offsetLeft (IE 4), offsetParent (IE 4), offsetTop (IE 4), offsetWidth (IE 4), outerHTML (IE 4), outerText (IE 4), parentElement (IE 4), parentTextEdit (IE 4), recordNumber (IE 4), sourceIndex (IE 4), style (IE 4), tabIndex (IE 4), tagName (IE 4), title (IE 4)

Methods

Methods Supported by Both Navigator and IE:

- ► blur() (Navigator 2, IE 3)—Removes input focus from the button

- ► click() (Navigator 2, IE 3)—Simulates clicking of the button

- ► focus() (Navigator 2, IE 3)—Moves input focus to the button

Other Methods: contains (IE 4), getAttribute (IE 4), handle-Event (Navigator 4), insertAdjacentHTML (IE 4), insertAdjacentText (IE 4), removeAttribute (IE 4), scrollIntoView (IE 4), select (IE 4), setAttribute (IE 4)

Events

onblur (Navigator 3, IE 4), onclick (Navigator 2, IE 3), onfocus (Navigator 3, IE 4), ondblclick (IE 4), onfilterchange (IE 4), onhelp (IE 4), onkeydown (IE 4), onkeypress (IE 4), onkeyup (IE 4), onmousedown (IE 4), onmousemove (IE 4), onmouseout (IE 4), onmouseover (IE 4), onmouseup (IE 4), onresize (IE 4), onselect (IE 4)

ʌun

First Supported In: Navigator 3

A shorthand equivalent to the sun property of the Packages object.

SUP

First Supported In: IE 4

Provides access to the HTML SUP tag. **Note:** This tag is deprecated in the latest HTML specification in favor of CSS.

Properties

Properties Supported by Both Navigator and IE: None

Other Properties: className (IE 4), document (IE 4), id (IE 4), inner-HTML (IE 4), innerText (IE 4), isTextEdit (IE 4), lang (IE 4), offset-Height (IE 4), offsetLeft (IE 4), offsetParent (IE 4), offsetTop (IE 4), offsetWidth (IE 4), outerHTML (IE 4), outerText (IE 4), parent-Element (IE 4), parentTextEdit (IE 4), sourceIndex (IE 4), style (IE 4), tagName (IE 4), title (IE 4)

Methods
Methods Supported by Both Navigator and IE: None

Other Methods: click (IE 4), contains (IE 4), getAttribute (IE 4), insertAdjacentHTML (IE 4), insertAdjacentText (IE 4), removeAttribute (IE 4), scrollIntoView (IE 4), setAttribute (IE 4)

Events
onclick (IE 4), ondblclick (IE 4), ondragstart (IE 4), onfilterchange (IE 4), onhelp (IE 4), onkeydown (IE 4), onkeypress (IE 4), onkeyup (IE 4), onmousedown (IE 4), onmousemove (IE 4), onmouseout (IE 4), onmouseover (IE 4), onmouseup (IE 4), onmousewheel (IE 6), onselectstart (IE 4)

TABLE

First Supported In: IE 4

Provides access to the HTML TABLE tag.

Properties
Properties Supported by Both Navigator and IE: None

Other Properties: align (IE 4), background (IE 4), bgColor (IE 4), border (IE 4), borderColor (IE 4), borderColorDark (IE 4), borderColorLight (IE 4), cellPadding (IE 4), cellSpacing (IE 4), className (IE 4), clientHeight (IE 4), clientWidth (IE 4), cols (IE 4), dataFld (IE 4), dataPageSize (IE 4), dataSrc (IE 4), document (IE 4), frame (IE 4), height (IE 4), id (IE 4), innerText (IE 4), isTextEdit (IE 4), lang (IE 4), language (IE 4), offsetHeight (IE 4), offsetLeft (IE 4), offsetParent (IE 4), offsetTop (IE 4), offsetWidth (IE 4), outerText (IE 4), parentElement (IE 4), parentTextEdit (IE 4), rules (IE 4), scrollHeight (IE 4), scrollLeft (IE 4), scrollTop (IE 4), scrollWidth (IE 4), sourceIndex (IE 4), style (IE 4), tagName (IE 4), title (IE 4), width (IE 4)

Methods
Methods Supported by Both Navigator and IE: None

Other Methods: blur (IE 4), click (IE 4), contains (IE 4), focus (IE 4), getAttribute (IE 4), insertAdjacentHTML (IE 4), insertAdjacentText (IE 4), nextPage (IE 4), previousPage (IE 4), refresh (IE 4), removeAttribute (IE 4), scrollIntoView (IE 4), setAttribute (IE 4)

Events

onafterupdate (IE 4), onbeforeupdate (IE 4), onblur (IE 4), onclick (IE 4), ondblclick (IE 4), ondragstart (IE 4), onfocus (IE 4), onhelp (IE 4), onkeydown (IE 4), onkeypress (IE 4), onkeyup (IE 4), onmousedown (IE 4), onmousemove (IE 4), onmouseout (IE 4), onmouseover (IE 4), onmouseup (IE 4), onmousewheel (IE 6), onresize (IE 4), onrowenter (IE 4), onrowexit (IE 4), onscroll (IE 4), onselectstart (IE 4)

TBODY

First Supported In: IE 4

Provides access to the HTML TBODY tag.

Properties

Properties Supported by Both Navigator and IE: None

Other Properties: align (IE 4), bgColor (IE 4), className (IE 4), document (IE 4), id (IE 4), isTextEdit (IE 4), lang (IE 4), language (IE 4), offsetHeight (IE 4), offsetLeft (IE 4), offsetParent (IE 4), offsetTop (IE 4), offsetWidth (IE 4), parentElement (IE 4), parentTextEdit (IE 4), sourceIndex (IE 4), style (IE 4), tagName (IE 4), title (IE 4), vAlign (IE 4)

Methods

Methods Supported by Both Navigator and IE: None

Other Methods: click (IE 4), contains (IE 4), getAttribute (IE 4), removeAttribute (IE 4), scrollIntoView (IE 4), setAttribute (IE 4)

Events

onclick (IE 4), ondblclick (IE 4), ondragstart (IE 4), onfilterchange (IE 4), onhelp (IE 4), onkeydown (IE 4), onkeypress (IE 4), onkeyup (IE 4), onmousedown (IE 4), onmousemove (IE 4), onmouseout (IE 4), onmouseover (IE 4), onmouseup (IE 4), onmousewheel (IE 6), onselectstart (IE 4)

TD

First Supported In: IE 4

Provides access to the HTML TD tag.

Properties

Properties Supported by Both Navigator and IE: None

Other Properties: align (IE 4), background (IE 4), bgColor (IE 4), borderColor (IE 4), borderColorDark (IE 4), borderColorLight (IE 4), className (IE 4), clientHeight (IE 4), clientWidth (IE 4), colSpan (IE 4), document (IE 4), height (IE 4), id (IE 4), isTextEdit (IE 4), lang (IE 4), language (IE 4), noWrap (IE 4), offsetHeight (IE 4), offsetLeft (IE 4), offsetParent (IE 4), offsetTop (IE 4), offsetWidth (IE 4), parentElement (IE 4), parentTextEdit (IE 4), rowSpan (IE 4), sourceIndex (IE 4), style (IE 4), tagName (IE 4), title (IE 4), vAlign (IE 4), width (IE 4)

Methods

Methods Supported by Both Navigator and IE: None

Other Methods: blur (IE 4), click (IE 4), contains (IE 4), focus (IE 4), getAttribute (IE 4), insertAdjacentHTML (IE 4), insertAdjacentText (IE 4), removeAttribute (IE 4), scrollIntoView (IE 4), setAttribute (IE 4)

Events

onafterupdate (IE 4), onbeforeupdate (IE 4), onblur (IE 4), onclick (IE 4), ondblclick (IE 4), ondragstart (IE 4), onfilterchange (IE 4), onfocus (IE 4), onhelp (IE 4), onkeydown (IE 4), onkeypress (IE 4), onkeyup (IE 4), onmousedown (IE 4), onmousemove (IE 4), onmouseout (IE 4), onmouseover (IE 4), onmouseup (IE 4), onmousewheel (IE 6), onresize (IE 4), onrowenter (IE 4), onrowexit (IE 4), onselectstart (IE 4)

Text

First Supported In: Navigator 2, IE 3

A form field used to obtain a single line of text from the user. A text field is an INPUT element that has its TYPE attribute set to TEXT. The basic Text object was introduced in JavaScript 1.0 and updated in JavaScript 1.1 and 1.2.

Properties

Properties Supported by Both Navigator and IE:

▶ defaultValue (Navigator 2, IE 3)—The value of the field's VALUE attribute

▶ form (Navigator 2, IE 3)—Provides a reference to the form object that contains the field

▶ name (Navigator 2, IE 3)—The value of the field's NAME attribute

▶ type (Navigator 3, IE 4)—The value of the field's TYPE attribute

▶ value (Navigator 2, IE 3)—The text string value currently contained in the field

Other Properties: accessKey (IE 4), align (IE 4), className (IE 4), dataFld (IE 4), dataSrc (IE 4), disabled (IE 4), document (IE 4), id (IE 4), innerHTML (IE 4), isTextEdit (IE 4), lang (IE 4), language (IE 4), maxLength (IE 4), offsetHeight (IE 4), offsetLeft (IE 4), offsetParent (IE 4), offsetTop (IE 4), offsetWidth (IE 4), outerHTML (IE 4), outerText (IE 4), parentElement (IE 4), parentTextEdit (IE 4), readOnly (IE 4), recordNumber (IE 4), size (IE 4), sourceIndex (IE 4), style (IE 4), tabIndex (IE 4), tagName (IE 4), title (IE 4)

Methods
Methods Supported by Both Navigator and IE:

▶ blur() (Navigator 2, IE 3)—Removes input focus from the field

▶ focus() (Navigator 2, IE 3)—Moves input focus to the field

▶ select() (Navigator 2, IE 3)—Selects (highlights) the value of the text field

Other Methods: click (IE 4), contains (IE 4), createTextRange (IE 4), getAttribute (IE 4), handleEvent (Navigator 4), insertAdjacentHTML (IE 4), insertAdjacentText (IE 4), removeAttribute (IE 4), scrollIntoView (IE 4), setAttribute (IE 4)

Events
onafterupdate (IE 4), onbeforeupdate (IE 4), onblur (Navigator 2, IE 3), onchange (Navigator 2, IE 3), onclick (IE 4), ondblclick (IE 4), onerrorupdate (IE 4), onfilterchange (IE 4), onfocus (Navigator 2, IE 3), onhelp (IE 4), onkeydown (IE 4), onkeypress (IE 4), onkeyup (IE 4), onmousedown (IE 4), onmousemove (IE 4), onmouseout (IE 4), onmouseover (IE 4), onmouseup (IE 4), onresize (IE 4), onselect (Navigator 2, IE 3)

Textarea

First Supported In: Navigator 2, IE 3

A form field used to obtain multiple lines of text from the user. A text area field uses the TEXTAREA tags to surround lines of default text to be placed in the field. The basic Textarea object was introduced in JavaScript 1.0 and updated in JavaScript 1.1 and 1.2.

Properties

Properties Supported by Both Navigator and IE:

- ▶ defaultValue (Navigator 2, IE 3)—Identifies the default value of the text area field

- ▶ form (Navigator 2, IE 3)—Provides a reference to the form object that contains the field

- ▶ name (Navigator 2, IE 3)—The value of the field's NAME attribute

- ▶ type (Navigator 3, IE 4)—The value of the field's TYPE attribute

- ▶ value (Navigator 2, IE 3)—The text string value currently contained in the field

Other Properties: accessKey (IE 4), className (IE 4), clientHeight (IE 4), clientWidth (IE 4), cols (IE 4), dataFld (IE 4), dataSrc (IE 4), disabled (IE 4), document (IE 4), id (IE 4), innerText (IE 4), isTextEdit (IE 4), lang (IE 4), language (IE 4), offsetHeight (IE 4), offsetLeft (IE 4), offsetParent (IE 4), offsetTop (IE 4), offsetWidth (IE 4), outerText (IE 4), parentElement (IE 4), parentTextEdit (IE 4), readOnly (IE 4), rows (IE 4), scrollHeight (IE 4), scrollLeft (IE 4), scrollTop (IE 4), scrollWidth (IE 4), sourceIndex (IE 4), status (IE 4), style (IE 4), tabIndex (IE 4), tagName (IE 4), title (IE 4), wrap (IE 4)

Methods

Methods Supported by Both Navigator and IE:

- ▶ blur() (Navigator 2, IE 3)—Removes input focus from the field

- ▶ focus() (Navigator 2, IE 3)—Moves input focus to the field

- ▶ select() (Navigator 2, IE 3)—Selects (highlights) the value of the text field

Other Methods: click (IE 4), contains (IE 4), createTextRange (IE 4), getAttribute (IE 4), handleEvent (Navigator 4), insertAdjacent-HTML (IE 4), insertAdjacentText (IE 4), removeAttribute (IE 4), scrollIntoView (IE 4), setAttribute (IE 4)

Events

onafterupdate (IE 4), onbeforeupdate (IE 4), onblur (Navigator 2, IE 3), onchange (Navigator 2, IE 3), onclick (IE 4), ondblclick (IE 4), ondragstart (IE 4), onerrorupdate (IE 4), onfilterchange (IE 4), onfocus (Navigator 2, IE 3), onhelp (IE 4), onkeydown (Navigator 4, IE 4), onkeypress (Navigator 4, IE 4), onkeyup (Navigator 4, IE 4), onmouse-down (IE 4), onmousemove (IE 4), onmouseout (IE 4), onmouseover (IE 4), onmouseup (IE 4), onmousewheel (IE 6), onresize (IE 4), onrowenter (IE 4), onrowexit (IE 4), onscroll (IE 4), onselect (Navigator 2, IE 3), onselectstart (IE 4)

TextNode

First Supported In: IE 5

Provides access to a text node in a document object hierarchy (XML or HTML). Has no defined methods or events.

Properties

Properties Supported by Both Navigator and IE: None

Other Properties: data (IE 5), length (IE 5), nextSibling (IE 5), nodeName (IE 5), nodeType (IE 5), nodeValue (IE 5), previousSibling (IE 5)

TextRange

First Supported In: IE 4

Provides access to text contained in an HTML or XML element. Has no defined events.

Properties

Properties Supported by Both Navigator and IE: None

Other Properties: htmlText (IE 4), text (IE 4)

Methods

Methods Supported by Both Navigator and IE: None

Other Methods: collapse (IE 4), compareEndPoints (IE 4), duplicate (IE 4), execCommand (IE 4), expand (IE 4), findText (IE 4), getBookmark (IE 4), inRange (IE 4), isEqual (IE 4), move (IE 4), moveEnd (IE 4), moveStart (IE 4), moveToBookmark (IE 4), moveToElementText (IE 4), moveToPoint (IE 4), parentElement (IE 4), pasteHTML (IE 4), queryCommandEnabled (IE 4), queryCommandIndeterm (IE 4), query-CommandState (IE 4), queryCommandSupported (IE 4), queryCommand-Value (IE 4), scrollIntoView (IE 4), select (IE 4), setEndPoint (IE 4)

TextRectangle

First Supported In: IE 5

Provides access to a rectangular strip of text contained in a document element. Has no defined methods or events.

Properties

Properties Supported by Both Navigator and IE: None

Other Properties: bottom (IE 5), left (IE 5), right (IE 5), top (IE 5)

TFOOT

First Supported In: IE 4

Provides access to the HTML TFOOT tag.

Properties

Properties Supported by Both Navigator and IE: None

Other Properties: align (IE 4), bgColor (IE 4), className (IE 4), document (IE 4), id (IE 4), isTextEdit (IE 4), lang (IE 4), language (IE 4), offsetHeight (IE 4), offsetLeft (IE 4), offsetParent (IE 4), offsetTop (IE 4), offsetWidth (IE 4), parentElement (IE 4), parent-TextEdit (IE 4), sourceIndex (IE 4), style (IE 4), tagName (IE 4), title (IE 4), vAlign (IE 4)

Methods

Methods Supported by Both Navigator and IE: None

Other Methods: `click` (IE 4), `contains` (IE 4), `getAttribute` (IE 4), `removeAttribute` (IE 4), `scrollIntoView` (IE 4), `setAttribute` (IE 4)

Events

`onclick` (IE 4), `ondblclick` (IE 4), `ondragstart` (IE 4), `onfilter-change` (IE 4), `onhelp` (IE 4), `onkeydown` (IE 4), `onkeypress` (IE 4), `onkeyup` (IE 4), `onmousedown` (IE 4), `onmousemove` (IE 4), `onmouseout` (IE 4), `onmouseover` (IE 4), `onmouseup` (IE 4), `onmousewheel` (IE 6), `onselectstart` (IE 4)

TH

First Supported In: IE 4

Provides access to the HTML TH tag.

Properties

Properties Supported by Both Navigator and IE: None

Other Properties: `align` (IE 4), `background` (IE 4), `bgColor` (IE 4), `borderColor` (IE 4), `borderColorDark` (IE 4), `borderColorLight` (IE 4), `className` (IE 4), `colSpan` (IE 4), `document` (IE 4), `id` (IE 4), `isText-Edit` (IE 4), `lang` (IE 4), `language` (IE 4), `noWrap` (IE 4), `offsetHeight` (IE 4), `offsetLeft` (IE 4), `offsetParent` (IE 4), `offsetTop` (IE 4), `off-setWidth` (IE 4), `parentElement` (IE 4), `parentTextEdit` (IE 4), `rowSpan` (IE 4), `sourceIndex` (IE 4), `style` (IE 4), `tagName` (IE 4), `title` (IE 4), `vAlign` (IE 4)

Methods

Methods Supported by Both Navigator and IE: None

Other Methods: `click` (IE 4), `contains` (IE 4), `getAttribute` (IE 4), `removeAttribute` (IE 4), `scrollIntoView` (IE 4), `setAttribute` (IE 4)

Events

`onclick` (IE 4), `ondblclick` (IE 4), `ondragstart` (IE 4), `onhelp` (IE 4), `onkeydown` (IE 4), `onkeypress` (IE 4), `onkeyup` (IE 4), `onmousedown` (IE 4), `onmousemove` (IE 4), `onmouseout` (IE 4), `onmouseover` (IE 4), `onmouse-up` (IE 4), `onmousewheel` (IE 6), `onselectstart` (IE 4)

THEAD

First Supported In: IE 4

Provides access to the HTML THEAD tag.

Properties

Properties Supported by Both Navigator and IE: None

Other Properties: align (IE 4), bgColor (IE 4), className (IE 4), document (IE 4), id (IE 4), isTextEdit (IE 4), lang (IE 4), language (IE 4), offsetHeight (IE 4), offsetLeft (IE 4), offsetParent (IE 4), offsetTop (IE 4), offsetWidth (IE 4), parentElement (IE 4), parentTextEdit (IE 4), sourceIndex (IE 4), style (IE 4), tagName (IE 4), title (IE 4), vAlign (IE 4)

Methods

Methods Supported by Both Navigator and IE: None

Other Methods: click (IE 4), contains (IE 4), getAttribute (IE 4), removeAttribute (IE 4), scrollIntoView (IE 4), setAttribute (IE 4)

Events

onclick (IE 4), ondblclick (IE 4), ondragstart (IE 4), onfilterchange (IE 4), onhelp (IE 4), onkeydown (IE 4), onkeypress (IE 4), onkeyup (IE 4), onmousedown (IE 4), onmousemove (IE 4), onmouseout (IE 4), onmouseover (IE 4), onmouseup (IE 4), onmousewheel (IE 6), onselectstart (IE 4)

TITLE

First Supported In: IE 4

Provides access to the HTML TITLE tag. Has no defined events.

Properties

Properties Supported by Both Navigator and IE: None

Other Properties: className (IE 4), document (IE 4), id (IE 4), isTextEdit (IE 4), lang (IE 4), parentElement (IE 4), parentTextEdit (IE 4), sourceIndex (IE 4), tagName (IE 4), text (IE 4), title (IE 4)

Methods

Methods Supported by Both Navigator and IE: None

Other Methods: contains (IE 4), getAttribute (IE 4), remove-Attribute (IE 4), setAttribute (IE 4)

TR

First Supported In: IE 4

Provides access to the HTML TR tag.

Properties

Properties Supported by Both Navigator and IE: None

Other Properties: align (IE 4), bgColor (IE 4), borderColor (IE 4), borderColorDark (IE 4), borderColorLight (IE 4), className (IE 4), document (IE 4), id (IE 4), isTextEdit (IE 4), lang (IE 4), language (IE 4), offsetHeight (IE 4), offsetLeft (IE 4), offsetParent (IE 4), offsetTop (IE 4), offsetWidth (IE 4), parentElement (IE 4), parentTextEdit (IE 4), sourceIndex (IE 4), style (IE 4), tagName (IE 4), title (IE 4), vAlign (IE 4)

Methods

Methods Supported by Both Navigator and IE: None

Other Methods: blur (IE 4), click (IE 4), contains (IE 4), focus (IE 4), getAttribute (IE 4), removeAttribute (IE 4), scrollIntoView (IE 4), setAttribute (IE 4)

Events

onafterupdate (IE 4), onbeforeupdate (IE 4), onblur (IE 4), onclick (IE 4), ondblclick (IE 4), ondragstart (IE 4), onfilterchange (IE 4), onfocus (IE 4), onhelp (IE 4), onkeydown (IE 4), onkeypress (IE 4), onkeyup (IE 4), onmousedown (IE 4), onmousemove (IE 4), onmouseout (IE 4), onmouseover (IE 4), onmouseup (IE 4), onmousewheel (IE 6), onresize (IE 4), onrowenter (IE 4), onrowexit (IE 4), onselectstart (IE 4)

TT

First Supported In: IE 4

Provides access to the HTML TT tag. **Note:** This tag is deprecated in the latest HTML specification in favor of CSS.

Properties
Properties Supported by Both Navigator and IE: None

Other Properties: className (IE 4), document (IE 4), id (IE 4), inner-
HTML (IE 4), innerText (IE 4), isTextEdit (IE 4), lang (IE 4), language
(IE 4), offsetHeight (IE 4), offsetLeft (IE 4), offsetParent (IE 4),
offsetTop (IE 4), offsetWidth (IE 4), outerHTML (IE 4), outerText
(IE 4), parentElement (IE 4), parentTextEdit (IE 4), sourceIndex (IE 4),
style (IE 4), tagName (IE 4), title (IE 4)

Methods
Methods Supported by Both Navigator and IE: None

Other Methods: click (IE 4), contains (IE 4), getAttribute (IE 4),
insertAdjacentHTML (IE 4), insertAdjacentText (IE 4), remove-
Attribute (IE 4), scrollIntoView (IE 4), setAttribute (IE 4)

Events
onclick (IE 4), ondblclick (IE 4), ondragstart (IE 4), onfilterchange (IE 4), onhelp (IE 4), onkeydown (IE 4), onkeypress (IE 4),
onkeyup (IE 4), onmousedown (IE 4), onmousemove (IE 4), onmouseout
(IE 4), onmouseover (IE 4), onmouseup (IE 4), onmousewheel (IE 6),
onselectstart (IE 4)

U

First Supported In: IE 4

Provides access to the HTML U tag. **Note:** This tag is deprecated in the
latest HTML specification in favor of CSS. Additionally, some browsers
omit support for this tag; therefore, although it may appear as part of the
object hierarchy, the values therein might be ignored or unsubstantiated.

Properties
Properties Supported by Both Navigator and IE: None

Other Properties: className (IE 4), document (IE 4), id (IE 4), inner-
HTML (IE 4), innerText (IE 4), isTextEdit (IE 4), lang (IE 4), language
(IE 4), offsetHeight (IE 4), offsetLeft (IE 4), offsetParent (IE 4),
offsetTop (IE 4), offsetWidth (IE 4), outerHTML (IE 4), outerText
(IE 4), parentElement (IE 4), parentTextEdit (IE 4), sourceIndex (IE 4),
style (IE 4), tagName (IE 4), title (IE 4)

Methods
Methods Supported by Both Navigator and IE: None

   Other Methods: click (IE 4), contains (IE 4), getAttribute (IE 4), insertAdjacentHTML (IE 4), insertAdjacentText (IE 4), removeAttribute (IE 4), scrollIntoView (IE 4), setAttribute (IE 4)

Events
onclick (IE 4), ondblclick (IE 4), ondragstart (IE 4), onfilterchange (IE 4), onhelp (IE 4), onkeydown (IE 4), onkeypress (IE 4), onkeyup (IE 4), onmousedown (IE 4), onmousemove (IE 4), onmouseout (IE 4), onmouseover (IE 4), onmouseup (IE 4), onmousewheel (IE 6), onselectstart (IE 4)

UL

First Supported In: IE 4

   Provides access to the HTML UL tag.

Properties
Properties Supported by Both Navigator and IE: None

   Other Properties: className (IE 4), document (IE 4), id (IE 4), innerHTML (IE 4), innerText (IE 4), isTextEdit (IE 4), lang (IE 4), language (IE 4), offsetHeight (IE 4), offsetLeft (IE 4), offsetParent (IE 4), offsetTop (IE 4), offsetWidth (IE 4), outerHTML (IE 4), outerText (IE 4), parentElement (IE 4), parentTextEdit (IE 4), sourceIndex (IE 4), style (IE 4), tagName (IE 4), title (IE 4), type (IE 4)

Methods
Methods Supported by Both Navigator and IE: None

   Other Methods: click (IE 4), contains (IE 4), getAttribute (IE 4), insertAdjacentHTML (IE 4), insertAdjacentText (IE 4), removeAttribute (IE 4), scrollIntoView (IE 4), setAttribute (IE 4)

Events
onclick (IE 4), ondblclick (IE 4), ondragstart (IE 4), onfilterchange (IE 4), onhelp (IE 4), onkeydown (IE 4), onkeypress (IE 4), onkeyup (IE 4), onmousedown (IE 4), onmousemove (IE 4), onmouseout (IE 4), onmouseover (IE 4), onmouseup (IE 4), onmousewheel (IE 6), onselectstart (IE 4)

userProfile

First Supported In: IE 4

Provides access to user profile information. Has no defined properties or events.

Methods

Methods Supported by Both Navigator and IE: None

Other Methods: addReadRequest (IE 4), clearRequest (IE 4), doReadRequest (IE 4), getAttribute (IE 4)

VAR

First Supported In: IE 4

Provides access to the HTML VAR tag. **Note:** This tag is deprecated in the latest HTML specification in favor of CSS.

Properties

Properties Supported by Both Navigator and IE: None

Other Properties: className (IE 4), document (IE 4), id (IE 4), innerHTML (IE 4), innerText (IE 4), isTextEdit (IE 4), lang (IE 4), language (IE 4), offsetHeight (IE 4), offsetLeft (IE 4), offset-Parent (IE 4), offsetTop (IE 4), offsetWidth (IE 4), outerHTML (IE 4), outerText (IE 4), parentElement (IE 4), parentTextEdit (IE 4), source-Index (IE 4), style (IE 4), tagName (IE 4), title (IE 4)

Methods

Methods Supported by Both Navigator and IE: None

Other Methods: click (IE 4), contains (IE 4), getAttribute (IE 4), insertAdjacentHTML (IE 4), insertAdjacentText (IE 4), remove-Attribute (IE 4), scrollIntoView (IE 4), setAttribute (IE 4)

Events

onclick (IE 4), ondblclick (IE 4), ondragstart (IE 4), onfilter-change (IE 4), onhelp (IE 4), onkeydown (IE 4), onkeypress (IE 4), onkeyup (IE 4), onmousedown (IE 4), onmousemove (IE 4), onmouseout (IE 4), onmouseover (IE 4), onmouseup (IE 4), onmousewheel (IE 6), onselectstart (IE 4)

VBArray

First Supported In: IE 4

Provides access to a Visual Basic safe array. Has no defined properties or events.

Constructor

```
new VBArray(safeArray)
```

Creates a VBArray object from a safe array retrieved from an ActiveX object.

Methods

Methods Supported by Both Navigator and IE: None

Other Methods: dimensions (IE 4), getItem (IE 4), lbound (IE 4), toArray (IE 4), ubound (IE 4)

WBR

First Supported In: IE 5

Provides access to the HTML WBR tag. Has no defined events.

Properties

Properties Supported by Both Navigator and IE: None

Other Properties: canHaveHTML (IE 5), contentEditable (IE 5), currentStyle (IE 5), disabled (IE 5), hasLayout (IE 5), id (IE 5), isContentEditable (IE 5), isDisabled (IE 5), outerHTML (IE 5), outerText (IE 5), parentElement (IE 5), scopeName (IE 5), tagUrn (IE 5)

Methods

Methods Supported by Both Navigator and IE: None

Other Methods: addBehavior (IE 5), componentFromPoint (IE 5), fireEvent (IE 5), getAttribute (IE 5), removeAttribute (IE 5), removeBehavior (IE 5), scrollIntoView (IE 5), setAttribute (IE 5)

window

First Supported In: Navigator 2, IE 3

Encapsulates a browser window and provides access to the objects that are contained in the window. The basic window object was introduced in JavaScript 1.0 and updated in JavaScript 1.1 and 1.2.

Properties
Properties Supported by Both Navigator and IE:

- ▶ closed (Navigator 3, IE 4)—Identifies whether the window is closed

- ▶ defaultStatus (Navigator 2, IE 3)—The default status displayed in the bottom of the window

- ▶ document (Navigator 2, IE 3)—The document loaded in the window

- ▶ frames (Navigator 2, IE 3)—An array of frames contained in the current window

- ▶ history (Navigator 3, IE 4)—Provides access to the History object associated with the window

- ▶ length (Navigator 2, IE 3)—Identifies the length of the frames array property

- ▶ location (Navigator 2, IE 3)—Provides access to the Location object associated with the window

- ▶ name (Navigator 2, IE 3)—Identifies the window's name

- ▶ navigator (Navigator 3, IE 4)—Refers to the navigator object

- ▶ offscreenBuffering (Navigator 4, IE 4)—Identifies whether offscreen buffering is turned on

- ▶ opener (Navigator 3, IE 4)—Identifies the window object that caused the current window object to be opened

- ▶ parent (Navigator 2, IE 3)—Identifies the window's parent window

- ▶ screen (Navigator 3, IE 4)—Provides information about the screen

- ▶ self (Navigator 2, IE 3)—Refers to the current window

- ▶ status (Navigator 2, IE 3)—Provides access to the window's status display area

- ▶ top (Navigator 2, IE 3)—Provides access to the topmost browser window

- ▶ window (Navigator 2, IE 3)—Refers to the current window

Other Properties: `clientInformation` (IE 4), `crypto` (Navigator 4), `dialogArguments` (IE 4), `dialogHeight` (IE 4), `dialogLeft` (IE 4), `dialogTop` (IE 4), `dialogWidth` (IE 4), `event` (IE 4), `innerHeight` (Navigator 4), `innerWidth` (Navigator 4), `locationbar` (Navigator 4), menubar (Navigator 4), `navigator` (IE 4), `outerHeight` (Navigator 4), outer-Width (Navigator 4), pageXOffset (Navigator 4), pageYOffset (Navigator 4), personalbar (Navigator 4), `returnValue` (IE 4), screen (IE 4), screenX (Navigator 4), screenY (Navigator 4), `scrollbars` (Navigator 4), status-bar (Navigator 4), `toolbar` (Navigator 4)

Methods
Methods Supported by Both Navigator and IE:

▶ `alert(message)` (Navigator 2, IE 3)—Displays the alert message

▶ `blur()` (Navigator 2, IE 3)—Removes focus from the window

▶ `clearInterval(interval)` (Navigator 4, IE 4)—Clears the specified interval timer

▶ `clearTimeout(timeout)` (Navigator 2, IE 3)—Clears the specified timeout

▶ `close()` (Navigator 2, IE 3)—Closes the window

▶ `confirm(string)` (Navigator 2, IE 3)—Displays a confirmation message

▶ `focus()` (Navigator 3, IE 4)—Brings focus to the window

▶ `open(url, name[, features])` (Navigator 2, IE 3)—Opens a window with the specified name and features

▶ `prompt(string[,default])` (Navigator 2, IE 3)—Displays a prompt to the user

▶ `scroll(x,y)` (Navigator 3, IE 4)—Scrolls the window to the specified coordinates

▶ `setInterval(expression, milliseconds)` (Navigator 4, IE 4)—Sets an interval timer

▶ `setInterval(function, milliseconds[, arg1[, ..., argN]])` (Navigator 4, IE 4)—Sets an interval timer

▶ setTimeout(*expression*, *milliseconds*) (Navigator 2, IE 3)—
Sets a timeout

Other Methods: atob (Navigator 4), back (Navigator 4), btoa (Navigator 4), captureEvents (Navigator 4), crypto.random (Navigator 4), crypto.signText (Navigator 4), disableExternalCapture (Navigator 4), enableExternalCapture (Navigator 4), execScript (IE 4), find (Navigator 4), forward (Navigator 4), handleEvent (Navigator 4), home (Navigator 4), moveBy (Navigator 4), moveTo (Navigator 4), navigate (IE 4), print (Navigator 4), releaseEvents (Navigator 4), resizeBy (Navigator 4), resizeTo (Navigator 4), routeEvent (Navigator 4), scrollBy (Navigator 4), scrollTo (Navigator 4), setHotKeys (Navigator 4), setResizable (Navigator 4), setTimeout (Navigator 4), setZ-Options (Navigator 4), showHelp (IE 4), showModalDialog (IE 4), stop (Navigator 4)

Events

onbeforeunload (IE 4), onblur (Navigator 3, IE 4), ondragdrop (Navigator 4), onerror (Navigator 3, IE 4), onfocus (Navigator 3, IE 4), onhelp (IE 4), onload (Navigator 2, IE 3), onmove (Navigator 4), onresize (Navigator 4, IE 4), onscroll (IE 4), onunload (Navigator 2, IE 3)

XML

First Supported In: IE 5

Provides access to an XML data island.

Properties

Properties Supported by Both Navigator and IE: None

Other Properties: canHaveHTML (IE 5), contentEditable (IE 5), disabled (IE 5), id (IE 5), isContentEditable (IE 5), isDisabled (IE 5), parentElement (IE 5), readyState (IE 5), recordset (IE 5), scopeName (IE 5), src (IE 5), tagUrn (IE 5), XMLDocument (IE 5)

Methods

Methods Supported by Both Navigator and IE: None

Other Methods: addBehavior (IE 5), componentFromPoint (IE 5), fireEvent (IE 5), removeBehavior (IE 5)

Events

ondataavailable (IE 5), ondatasetchanged (IE 5), ondatasetcomplete (IE 5), onreadystatechange (IE 5), onrowenter (IE 5), onrowexit (IE 5), onrowsdelete (IE 5), onrowsinserted (IE 5)

XMP

First Supported In: IE 4

Provides access to the HTML XMP tag.

Properties

Properties Supported by Both Navigator and IE: None

Other Properties: className (IE 4), document (IE 4), id (IE 4), innerText (IE 4), isTextEdit (IE 4), lang (IE 4), language (IE 4), offsetHeight (IE 4), offsetLeft (IE 4), offsetParent (IE 4), offsetTop (IE 4), offsetWidth (IE 4), outerHTML (IE 4), outerText (IE 4), parentElement (IE 4), parentTextEdit (IE 4), sourceIndex (IE 4), style (IE 4), tagName (IE 4), title (IE 4)

Methods

Methods Supported by Both Navigator and IE: None

Other Methods: click (IE 4), contains (IE 4), getAttribute (IE 4), insertAdjacentHTML (IE 4), removeAttribute (IE 4), scrollIntoView (IE 4), setAttribute (IE 4)

Events

onclick (IE 4), ondblclick (IE 4), ondragstart (IE 4), onfilterchange (IE 4), onhelp (IE 4), onkeydown (IE 4), onkeypress (IE 4), onkeyup (IE 4), onmousedown (IE 4), onmousemove (IE 4), onmouseout (IE 4), onmouseover (IE 4), onmouseup (IE 4), onmousewheel (IE 6), onselectstart (IE 4)

Appendix B
PERL FUNCTIONS

The following functions, listed alphabetically by function name, are available in the standard installation of Perl (as of version 5.8.0). When you're using Perl on platforms other than Unix, some of the functions may operate partially—or not at all. Platform-dependent behavior is noted in an individual function's description.

-X (File Test Operators)

An easy shorthand for finding out information about files in the filesystem. For example, the -s operator returns the size of a file in bytes:

```
$filename = "summary.txt";
if ( -s $filename > 10_000 ) {
    print "10,000 characters is too big for a
        summary.\n";
}
```

If you're familiar with shell programming, these operators will probably look very familiar. In many cases, the Perl file test operators are the same as the shell version. Table B.1 shows the complete list.

TABLE B.1:   *-X* File Test Operators

OPERATORS	DEFINITION
-r/-w/-x/-o	File is readable/writable/executable/owned by effective userid/groupid
-R/-W/-X/-O	File is readable/writable/executable/owned by real uid/gid
-e	File exists
-s	File size in bytes
-z	File has zero size
-f	File is a plain file
-d	File is a directory
-l	File is a symbolic link
-p	File is a named pipe
-S	File is a socket
-b	File is a block special file
-c	File is a character special file
-t	Filehandle is opened to a tty; for example, to see if your program is being run interactively, check if (-t STDIN) { ... }
-u/-g	File has setuid/setgid bit set
-k	File has sticky bit set
-T	File seems to be an ASCII text file (Perl makes a rough guess)
-B	File is a binary file; opposite of -T
-M	Script start time minus file modification time, in days; effectively, the number of days since the file was changed

TABLE B.1 continued: –*X* File Test Operators

OPERATORS	DEFINITION
–A	Script start time minus access time, in days
–C	Script start time minus Unix inode change time, in days

abs $value

Returns the absolute value of its numeric argument. If $value is non-numeric, returns a value of 0. For example:

```
$value = -4;
print abs($value); # prints '4'
```

accept $new_socket, $old_socket

Analogous to the Unix accept() system call. Accepts a network connection, returning the packed address if successful or false if unsuccessful.

alarm $seconds

Sets a timer to have a SIGALRM delivered to this process after the approximate number of seconds has elapsed. There is a single global counter for alarm; if you call alarm a second time before the first call's timer has elapsed, the timer is reset to the $seconds specified in the last call, and the number of seconds remaining on the first call are returned. You can cancel the timer by calling alarm with $seconds set to 0.

NOTE

You should not use alarm and sleep in the same block of code, because their timer data structures can interact in undefined ways. The accuracy of the timer is effectively plus or minus one second.

atan2 $y, $x

Returns the arctangent of $y/$x in the range –pi to pi (radians).

To find a tangent, use Math::Trig::tan, or use the following function to obtain the tangent of $x:

```
$tangent = ( sin($x) / cos($x) );
```

bind $socket, $name

Binds a network address to a socket. Analogous to the bind() Unix system call. Returns true if successful or false if not. *$name* should be a packed address of the appropriate type for the socket specified in *$socket*.

binmode FILEHANDLE

Forces the file to be read or written in binary mode. This is meaningful only on operating systems that distinguish between binary and text files. binmode has no effect on many operating systems (notably Unix and MacOS); however, in MS-DOS and Windows, it is essential to prevent file corruption on writes. The *FILEHANDLE* can be an expression, in which case the value is taken as the name of the filehandle.

bless $reference

bless $reference, $classname

Causes the object referenced by *$reference* to be an object in the *$classname* package. If *$classname* is omitted, the current package is used. Use the two-argument version if the function doing the blessing might be inherited by a derived class; otherwise the wrong class may be used.

caller

caller $num_frames

Returns information about the current call stack. Useful for debugging and profiling. If the current block of code has been called as a function by some other block of code, you can use the following line:

```
($package, $filename, $line) = caller;
```

If the current block hasn't been called from elsewhere (the stack is empty), *$package*, *$filename*, and *$line* are set to undefined.

If you pass a number to caller(), that number indicates how many calls in the call stack to go back.

chdir $new_directory

Changes the working directory to *$new_directory*, if possible. If *$new_directory* is omitted, changes to the user's home directory (this in particular may be undefined on non-Unix systems). Returns true if successful or false if not. You should always check the result, and you may want to use die() or warn() to print the error message if false is returned.

chmod $mode, @filelist

Sets the permissions on a list of files. *$mode* should always be numeric; using a string will probably have unintended results. The value returned is the number of files successfully changed. For example:

```
# the following line sets filename.dat to be owner
# readable/writeable, and world-readable
$mode = 0644;   chmod $mode, 'filename.dat';
# this does the same thing... the string-to-octal
  # conversion is necessary
$mode = '0644'; chmod oct($mode), 'filename.dat';
# sets mode to -w--r-T, which is probably not what you want
$mode = '0644'; chmod $mode, 'filename.dat';
```

chomp

chomp @list

chomp $variable

Removes the trailing string if it corresponds to the current value of *$/* (which is probably "\n" unless you've set it to something else) and returns the total number of characters removed from all its arguments. Often used to remove the newline from the end of an input record. If *$variable* and *@list* are not used, the function chomps *$_*. For example:

```
while (<MYFILE>) {
   chomp;  # remove last \n from current value in $_
   @array = split(/:/);
   # now the last item in @array doesn't end with a \n
}
```

If you chomp a list, each element is chomped, and the total number of characters removed is returned.

chop

chop @list

chop $variable

Removes the last character of a string and returns the character chopped. Used primarily to remove the newline from the end of an input record, but chomp() is preferred because it is safer.

If you chop a list, each element is chopped. Only the value of the last chop() is returned.

chown $uid, $gid, @list_of_files

Changes the owner (and group) of a list of files. Returns the number of files successfully changed. Both $uid and $gid must be numeric, or they must evaluate to numbers. Depending on your operating system and its configuration, you may not be able to change $uid; so, if you use a value other than the one the file is currently set to, the call will fail.

chr

chr $number

Returns the ASCII character corresponding to $number in the character set. If $number is omitted, the current value of $_ is used. To find the number corresponding to an ASCII character, use ord(). For example:

```
$char = chr(65);
print $char; # prints 'A'
```

chroot

chroot $directory

Works similarly to the chroot() Unix system call. Makes the directory the new root directory for path names that begin with a slash (/). The current working directory is unaffected (use chdir() for that). For security reasons, chroot() is restricted to the superuser. If $directory is omitted, the current value of $_ is used.

close

close FILEHANDLE

Closes the file or pipe associated with the file handle, returning true if the system call to close the file, pipe, or socket succeeds. Closes the currently selected filehandle if the argument is omitted.

NOTE

You don't need to close FILEHANDLE if you are immediately going to do another open() on it, because open() will close it for you. However, using close() on an input file does reset the line counter $., and using the implicit close performed by open() does not.

closedir DIRHANDLE

Closes a directory opened by opendir(). Returns true if it succeeds.

connect $socket, $name

Analogous to the connect() Unix system call. Attempts to connect to a remote network socket. Returns true if successful or false if not. $name should be a packed address of the appropriate type for the socket.

cos $radians

Returns the cosine of $radians (a numeric value expressed in radians). If $radians is omitted, the value of $_ is used.

For the inverse cosine operation, you can use Math::Trig::acos() or the following:

```
$acos = atan2( sqrt(1 - $x * $x), $x ) }
```

crypt $plaintext, $salt

Performs *trapdoor* encryption via the crypt() Unix system call. To verify an existing encrypted string, you can use the encrypted text as the salt (for example, compare crypt *($plain, $crypted)* to the existing crypted string). This allows your code to work with the standard crypt() and with more exotic implementations.

defined

defined EXPR

Returns true if *EXPR* has a defined value or false if *EXPR* has the value undef. If *EXPR* is not present, $_ is checked. Note that undef is not the same as 0 or " ", which are both defined values, although all three evaluate to false in a Boolean context.

When used on a hash element, defined() tells you whether the value is defined. It does not tell you if the key itself exits in the hash. Use the exists() function for that.

To determine whether a subroutine exists, use defined *&myFuncName* without parentheses. Using defined() on hashes and arrays is deprecated.

delete EXPR

Deletes the specified key(s) and their associated values from a hash. Returns the deleted value(s) associated with the key(s), or returns the undefined value if there was no such key in the hash. Deleting from the environment variable hash $ENV{} modifies the environment in which

your program runs (deleting $ENV{'PATH'} would alter the directory
search path applied to any executed system commands).

For example:

```
# deletes the key 'something' and the value delete
# associated with it from the hash
$myHash{'something'};

# deletes everything from the hash
delete @myHash{keys %myHash};
```

However, the last statement is slower than just assigning the empty list to
the hash or undefining it, as shown in the following statements, respectively:

```
%myHash = ();
undef %myHash;
```

die $message

Prints *$message* to STDERR and stops execution of the program. If the
string in *$message* does not end with a newline character, the name of
the script and the line number stopped at are also printed. Including the
special variable *$!*, which in a string context carries a system-produced error
message, is frequently useful.

For example:

```
open MYFILE, "test.dat" or die "Can't open file: $!";
```

might produce

```
Can't open file: No such file or directory at test.pl line 5.
```

each %hash

Returns the key (and value) of the next element in *%hash*. In a list context,
returns a two-element list containing the key and value for the next element
of a hash. When called in a scalar context, returns just the key. Each successive call to each() on the same hash will iterate through the contents of that
hash, returning the *next* element(s). When the end of the hash is reached, a
null array (in list context) or undef (in scalar context) is returned. Another
call to each() on the same hash will return the *first* element again.

NOTE

You can't rely on the order of the keys and values returned (because the order may
change in future versions of Perl). You can, however, rely on the order returned by
the keys() or values() function being the same on the same, unmodified hash.

For example, the following code returns the keys and values of the current environment, and then prints them:

```
while (($key,$value) = each %ENV) {
    print "$key=$value\n";
}
```

See also keys(), values().

eof
eof()
eof FILEHANDLE

Returns 1 if the next read on *FILEHANDLE* will return end of file, or if *FILEHANDLE* is not open. *FILEHANDLE* may be an expression whose value gives the real filehandle. If *FILEHANDLE* is omitted, the last filehandle used is assumed. If eof() is called with empty parentheses, the pseudofile of files specified on the command line, accessed with the <> operator, is checked.

exists $array{$key}

Returns true if the key specified by the contents of *$key* exists in the hash *$array*. Note that the value of *$array{$key}* may be undef, and exists *$array{$key}* will still return true.

exit $status

Exits the program with a return code of *$status*. If *$status* is omitted, exits with status of 0 (no error). Typically, you use a status of 0 for a normal exit, and a status of 1 for an exit on error—although this may vary depending on your environment.

See also die().

exp
exp $power

Returns *e* (the natural logarithm base) to the power of *$power*. If *$power* is omitted, gives exp($_).

fcntl FILEHANDLE, FUNCTION, SCALAR

Implements the fcntl(2) Unix system function. To import the correct constant definitions, place

```
use Fcntl;
```

before the call to fcntl().

fcntl() will produce a fatal error if used on a machine that doesn't implement fcntl(2).

fileno FILEHANDLE

Returns the file descriptor for a filehandle. Returns undefined if the *FILEHANDLE* does not refer to an open file.

flock FILEHANDLE, $operation

Implements the flock(2) Unix system call to lock access to the file specified by *FILEHANDLE*. Depending on your system environment, Perl may use an emulation of Unix flock() to provide the same functionality. Returns true for success or false on failure. Produces a fatal error if the environment doesn't implement flock(2), fcntl(2) locking, or lockf(3). The file-locking mechanisms used are adhered to only if all other processes and programs accessing the file use flock().

$operation is defined as LOCK_SH, LOCK_EX, or LOCK_UN, possibly combined with LOCK_NB. To use these constants, you must place

```
use Fcntl;
```

before the call to flock(). LOCK_SH requests a shared lock, LOCK_EX requests an exclusive lock, and LOCK_UN releases a previously requested lock. LOCK_NB is used to prevent the call to flock() from blocking while waiting for the lock to be granted.

Recent versions of Perl flush *FILEHANDLE* before locking or unlocking it.

fork

Performs a fork(2) Unix system call to create a child process. Execution for the child process begins at the same point in the script at which the fork() call was made. It returns the process id (pid) of the child process to the parent, 0 to the child process, or undef if the call to fork() is unsuccessful.

NOTE

Not all system environments support fork().

format

Declares a picture format for use by the write() function.

getc FILEHANDLE

getc

Returns the next single character from the input file specified by
FILEHANDLE. Returns undef if *FILEHANDLE* is at the end of the file or if
there was an error. If *FILEHANDLE* is omitted, getc() reads from the
standard input.

getlogin

Implements the getlogin() Unix system call, which on most systems
returns the current login name—if there is one. In most cases, using
getpwuid($<) is preferable.

getpeername SOCKET

Returns the packed sockaddr address of the other end of the *SOCKET*
connection.

getpgrp $pid

For systems that implement or emulate the getpgrp() Unix system
call, returns the current process group for the specified pid. For a *$pid*
of 0, returns the current process group for the current process. If *$pid* is
omitted, returns the process group of the current process.

getppid

Returns the pid of the parent process.

getpriority $process_id

getpriority $uid

Returns the current priority for a process, a process group, or a user. If used
on a system that doesn't implement the getpriority() Unix system call,
raises a fatal exception.

glob

glob EXPR

Returns the value of *EXPR* with filename expansions as the standard Unix shell /bin/csh would do. If *EXPR* is omitted, *$_* is used. This function is implemented with the File::Glob extension. See its man page for more information.

gmtime EXPR

In a list context, converts a time as returned by the time() function to a nine-element array with the time localized for the standard Greenwich Mean Time (GMT):

```
#  0    1     2      3      4     5      6      7      8
($sec,$min,$hour,$mday,$mon,$year,$wday,$yday,$isdst)
  = gmtime(time);
```

Each array element is numeric and comes straight out of a struct tm (defined in /usr/include/time/h on Unix systems). The month value *$mon* has the range 0 through 11. The weekday *$wday* has the range 0 through 6, starting with Sunday as day 0. *$year* is the number of years since 1900; therefore, the *$year* for 2021 is 121.

If *EXPR* is omitted, the current system time is assumed.

goto LABEL

goto EXPR

goto &SUB

Causes execution to jump to the statement with the unique *LABEL* preceding it. You can also call goto *EXPR*, where *EXPR* is a string that evaluates to a label, as in the goto *LABEL* form; or goto *&SUB*, where *SUB* is a subroutine name. This function exits the current function and immediately calls *SUB*, and keeps the current function's *@_* parameters intact. Whatever form you use, it is not possible to jump into a subroutine or into the middle of a loop.

grep EXPR, @list

In a list context, returns a new list consisting of each element from *@list* for which *EXPR* evaluates to true. In a scalar context, returns the number of times the expression was true. For example:

```
# remove lines that begin with a '#'
@newlines = grep(!/^#/, @input_lines);
```

See also the map( ) function for an array composed of the results of *EXPR*.

hex

hex EXPR

Interprets *EXPR* as a hex string and returns the corresponding value. If *EXPR* is omitted, *$_* is used.

For example:

```
print hex '0xA'; # prints '10'
print hex 'aF';  # same
```

index $string, $substring

index $string, $substring, $position

Returns the position of the first occurrence of *$substring* in *$string* at or after *$position*. If *$position* is omitted, begins searching from the beginning of the string. The return value is the position, starting at 0, for the first character of *$string*. If the substring is not found, returns −1.

int

int EXPR

Returns the integer portion of *EXPR*, truncating any value after the decimal point. If *EXPR* is omitted, uses *$_*. Note that this function does not perform rounding. For example:

```
$a = int(5.94); # $a become '5'
```

ioctl FILEHANDLE, FUNCTION, SCALAR

Implements the ioctl( ) Unix system call. *See* the ioctl Unix man pages for details.

join EXPR, @list

Joins the separate strings of *@list* into a single string with fields separated by the value of *EXPR*, and returns that new string. For example:

```
$fullpath = join('/', $relative_path, $myfile);
```

See also split( ).

keys %hash

Returns an array whose members are all the keys of the named hash. For example:

```
%hash = ( 'fish' => 'yellowtail',
          'mammal' => 'dolphin' );

@types = keys(%hash); # @types contains 'fish' and 'mammal'
```

See also each(), values().

kill $signal, @list_of_processes

Sends a signal to a list of processes and returns the number of processes successfully signaled.

last

last LABEL

When used without *LABEL*, breaks out of the innermost loop being executed. If used with *LABEL*, jumps to the end of the block named by *LABEL*.

lc

lc $string

Returns the lowercase version of $string (or $_ if $string is omitted).

lcfirst

lcfirst $string

Returns the value of $string (or $_ if $string is omitted) with only the first character set in lowercase.

length

length $string

Returns the length in characters of the value of $string (or $_ if $string is omitted).

link OLDFILE, NEWFILE

Creates a new filename linked to the old filename. Returns true if successful or false if not.

listen SOCKET, QUEUESIZE

Implements the listen() Unix system call, accepting connections on a predefined *SOCKET*. Returns true if successful or false if not.

localtime EXPR

Similar to the gmtime() function, but uses the local time zone for the system rather than GMT.

log

log EXPR

Returns the natural logarithm of *EXPR* (or *$_* if *EXPR* is omitted). *See* exp() for the inverse operation.

lstat

lstat FILEHANDLE

lstat $filename

Similar to the stat() function (including setting the special '_' filehandle). However, in a symbolic link, it operates on the link itself instead of on the file to which the link points. If symbolic links are unimplemented on your system, a normal stat() is performed. If *$filename* is omitted, calls stat on $_ is performed.

m/PATTERN/cgimosx

/PATTERN/cgimosx

Searches a string for a pattern match between the slash delimiters. In a scalar context, returns true or false. In a list context, returns any matching groups specified. If no string is specified with a =~ operator, then *$_* is searched. The m in front of the first slash is not necessary, but if you use it, then you can use delimiters other than slashes.

The following are all identical:

```
if ( m/needle/ ) ...
if ( $_ =~ /needle/ ) ...
if ( $_ =~ m[needle] ) ...
if ( m!needle! ) ...
```

The m// operator takes a number of modifier functions. The most common is /i, for case-insensitive searches. Without it, the pattern will not ignore case:

```
if ( "PERL" =~ m/perl/i ) ... # matches
if ( "PERL" =~ m/perl/ ) ... # doesn't match
```

Table B.2 gives a complete list of options.

TABLE B.2:   Pattern Options

OPTION	DEFINITION
c	Do not reset the search position on a failed match when /g is in effect.
g	Find all occurrences globally. Repeated calls to m// for the string will find subsequent matches.
i	Perform case-insensitive matching.
m	Treat the string as multiple lines.
o	Compile the pattern once only. This option is meaningful only if the pattern is a variable.
s	Treat the string as a single line.
x	Use extended regexes. White space is ignored, and comments are allowed in the pattern. This makes it easier to document complex expressions.

See also the s/// operator.

map EXPR, @list

Evaluates *EXPR* for each element of @list and returns the list value. In a scalar context, returns the total number of elements generated. For example:

```
# returns the names in all uppercase
@uppercased = map(uc, @names);
```

mkdir $filename

mkdir $filename, $mode

Creates the directory specified by *$filename*, with permissions specified by *$mode* (as modified by umask). If *$mode* is omitted, then 0777 is used. If it succeeds, returns true. If it doesn't succeed, returns false and sets $! (errno).

next

next LABEL

Skips to the loop within the block named by *LABEL*. If *LABEL* is omitted, skips to the next iteration within the innermost loop.

oct

oct EXPR

Interprets *EXPR* as an octal string and returns the corresponding value. If *EXPR* begins with 0x, oct() interprets it as a hex string. If *EXPR* starts with 0b, it is interpreted as a binary string. If *EXPR* is omitted, *$_* is used.

open FILEHANDLE, $filename

open FILEHANDLE, $mode, $filename

Opens a file whose name is *$filename* and associates it with the *FILEHANDLE*. If the filename begins with < or nothing, the file is opened for input. If the filename begins with >, the file is created if necessary, truncated, and opened for output. If the filename begins with >>, the file is created if necessary and opened for appending. You can put a + in front of the > or < to indicate that you want both read and write access to the file. Therefore, +< is usually preferred for making read/write updates—the +> mode erases the file first. Normally, you can't use either read-write mode to update text files, because they have variable-length records.

If the filename begins with |, the filename is interpreted as a command to which output is to be piped. If the filename ends with |, the filename is interpreted as a command that pipes output to the invoking code.

The three-argument form of open() allows you to specify the mode separate from the filename. The following are equivalent:

```perl
open( FH, "> $filename" )
open( FH, ">", $filename )
```

You can also create lexical filehandle references on the fly. The following two snippets are identical:

```perl
open( FH, "> $filename" )
while (<FH>) { ... }

open( my $fh, "> $filename" )
while (<$fh>) { ... }
```

opendir DIRHANDLE, $directory_name

Opens a directory named *$directory_name* for processing by the `readdir()`, `telldir()`, `seekdir()`, `rewinddir()`, and `closedir()` functions. Returns true if successful.

ord

ord EXPR

Returns the numeric ASCII value of the first character of *EXPR*. Returns *$_* if *EXPR* is omitted. The `chr()` function performs the inverse operation.

pack $template, @list

Packs an *@list* into a binary structure determined by *$template*, returning a scalar string with the structure. *$template* is a sequence of characters that determine the order and type of values that are aggregated to construct the return value and consists of the character codes shown in Table B.3.

TABLE B.3: Codes for pack and unpack

CODE	MEANING
a	String with arbitrary binary data, will be null padded.
A	An ASCII string, will be space padded.
Z	Null-terminated ASCII string, will be null padded.
b	Bit string, ascending bit order, like vec().
B	Bit string, descending bit order.
h	Hex string (low nybble first).
H	Hex string (high nybble first).
c	Signed char value.
C	Unsigned char value.
s	Signed short value.
S	Unsigned short value (exactly 16 bits).
i	Signed integer value.
I	Unsigned integer value (at least 32 bits).
l	Signed long value.
L	Unsigned long value (exactly 32 bits).

TABLE B.3 continued: Codes for pack and unpack

CODE	MEANING
n	A short in network (big-endian) order (exactly 16 bits).
N	A short in network (big-endian) order (exactly 32 bits).
v	A short in VAX (little-endian) order (exactly 16 bits).
V	A short in VAL (little-endian) order (exactly 32 bits).
q	Signed quad (64-bit) value.
Q	Unsigned quad value (only on 64-bit integer capable systems).
f	Single-precision float in the native format.
d	Double-precision float in the native format.
p	Pointer to a null-terminated string.
P	Pointer to a structure (fixed-length string).
u	Uuencoded string.
w	A BER compressed integer. Its bytes represent an unsigned integer in base 128, most significant digit first, with as few digits as possible. Bit eight (the high bit) is set on each byte except the last.
x	A null byte.
X	Back up a byte.
@	Null fill to absolute position.

For example:

```
$foo = pack("CCCC",65,66,67,68);
# foo eq "ABCD"
$foo = pack("C4",65,66,67,68);
# same thing

$foo = pack("s2",1,2);
# "\1\0\2\0" on little-endian
# "\0\1\0\2" on big-endian

$foo = pack("a4","abcd","x","y","z");
# "abcd"

$foo = pack("aaaa","abcd","x","y","z");
# "axyz"

$foo = pack("a14","abcdefg");
# "abcdefg\0\0\0\0\0\0\0"
```

pop

pop @array

Removes and returns the last element from *@array*. The array is shortened by one element. Returns undef if *@array* is empty. If *@array* is not specified, the function uses the *@ARGV* array in the main program block or *@_* in a subroutine block.

pos

pos $scalar

Returns the offset position where the last matched search was performed on the *$scalar* variable. If *$scalar* is omitted, then *$_* is used.

print

print FILEHANDLE LIST

print LIST

Prints the contents of *LIST* as a string to the appropriate output. If *FILEHANDLE* is specified, sends the output to the file specified by *FILEHANDLE* (assuming the file is open and can be written to). If *FILEHANDLE* is omitted, the currently selected output device (STDOUT by default) is used. If *LIST* is omitted, the print() function prints the contents of *$_*. For example:

```
print MYFILE "save this for later\n";
print "i tried $count times to do it\n";
```

printf FILEHANDLE $format, LIST

printf $format, LIST

Analogous to the ANSI C language printf() function. Parses *$format* and substitutes the values of the variables in *LIST* in place of the % markers. The most common markers are %s for string and %d for integer. Many other options are possible; however, so refer to a C language reference for more detail.

As with print(), if *FILEHANDLE* is specified, the output goes to the file specified by *FILEHANDLE*. If *FILEHANDLE* is omitted, the output goes to the currently selected output device. In general, print() is more efficient than printf().

For example:

```
$count = 5;
$thing = "sorting";
printf "i tried %d times to do %s\n", $count, $thing;
```

push @array, LIST

Appends the elements in *LIST* to the end of the @*array*, returning the new number of elements in the array.

See also pop( ).

quotemeta

quotemeta $string

Returns a copy of $*string* with all the nonalphanumeric characters backslashed. If $*string* is omitted, $_ is used.

rand

rand $number

Returns a random fractional number between 0 and the value of $*number*. $*number* must be positive, and if it's omitted, 1 is used.

See also srand( ).

read FILEHANDLE, $scalar, $length

read FILEHANDLE, $scalar, $length, $offset

Reads $*length* bytes of data into variable $*scalar* from the *FILEHANDLE*. Returns the number of bytes actually read, or returns undef when there is an error. $*scalar* will grow or shrink to the length read. If no $*offset* is specified, it is assumed to be 0.

readdir DIRHANDLE

Returns the next directory entry for a directory opened by opendir( ). If used in a list context, returns the rest of the entries in the directory. If there are no more entries, returns undef in a scalar context or a null list in a list context.

readlink

readlink EXPR

If symbolic links are implemented, returns the value of a symbolic link. If symbolic links are not implemented, gives a fatal error. If there is a system error, returns the undefined value and sets $! (errno). If *EXPR* is omitted, $_ is used.

recv SOCKET, $scalar, $len, $flags

Receives a message on a socket. The data is read into the $scalar variable from the specified *SOCKET* filehandle up to $len bytes. The flags are defined in the recvfrom() Unix system call.

redo

redo LABEL

Restarts a loop block without reevaluating the conditional. The continue block, if there is one, is not executed. If *LABEL* is omitted, the command refers to the innermost enclosing loop.

ref

ref EXPR

Returns true if *EXPR* is a reference or false if not. If *EXPR* is not specified, $_ is used. If the value returned is true, it will vary based on the type of thing that is being referred to. The built-in types are SCALAR, ARRAY, HASH, CODE, REF, GLOB, and LVALUE. If *EXPR* refers to a blessed object, then the package name of that object is returned instead.

rename $oldname, $newname

Changes the name of the file $oldname to $newname. Returns true for success and false for failure. This function does not work across filesystem boundaries.

reset

reset EXPR

Clears the value of variables whose names begin with the letters in *EXPR*. More than one letter can be specified using ranges. If *EXPR* is not specified, uses the special variable ?? (two question marks). The reset() function always returns true. If you use

```
reset 'A-Z';
```

you will reset all of your environment variables ENV and ARGV, which is probably not what you want.

return

return EXPR

Returns the list of arguments at the end of a subroutine's execution. If no return statement is found, a subroutine always returns the result of the last expression in it.

reverse @list

reverse $string

Reverses the order of elements in @list, or reverses the order of characters in $string.

rewinddir DIRHANDLE

Resets the current position to the start of the directory for use with the readdir() function on DIRHANDLE.

rindex $str, $substring

rindex $str, $substring, $position

Gets the position of the last occurrence of $substring in $str. Starts the search from the end of $string unless a position has been specified. If a position is specified, the function starts the search at the position from the end of the string.

rmdir

rmdir $filename

Removes the directory specified by $filename, but only if the directory is empty. Uses $_ if $filename is not specified. Returns true on success or false on failure with the error code in $!.

s/PATTERN/REPLACEMENT/egimosx

Searches a string for *PATTERN* and replaces it with *REPLACEMENT*. Returns the number of replacements made, or a false value.

The s/// operator functions much like the m// operator. It operates on *$_* if some other variable isn't specified to its left with =~, and you can use different delimiters if you don't like slashes. Here are some examples:

```
# Replace first dogs with cats in $_
s/dogs/cats/;

# Replace all Python or PHP with Perl in $str
# regardless of case.
$str =~ s/P(ython|HP)/Perl/ig;
```

Table B.4 gives a complete list of options.

TABLE B.4:   Pattern Replacement Options

OPTION	DEFINITION
e	Evaluate *REPLACEMENT* as code.
g	Replace all occurrences in the string. Without /g, only the first match will be replaced.
I	Perform case-insensitive matching.
m	Treat the string as multiple lines.
o	Compile the pattern once only. This is meaningful only if the patterns are variables.
s	Treat the string as a single line.
x	Use extended regexes. White space is ignored, and comments are allowed in the pattern. This makes it easier to document complex expressions.

scalar EXPR

Forces the *EXPR* to be interpreted in a scalar context, and returns the value of *EXPR*.

seek FILEHANDLE, $position, $startingpoint

Similar to the seek() and fseek() Unix system calls; sets the file pointer for *FILEHANDLE*. The values for *$startingpoint* are 0 to set the position from the beginning of the file, 1 to set the position relative to the current location in the file, and 2 to set the position relative to the end of file. Returns 1 on success or 0 on failure.

seekdir DIRHANDLE, $position

Moves the current position for the readdir() routine on *DIRHANDLE* to *$position*, which must be a value returned by telldir().

select

select FILEHANDLE

If *FILEHANDLE* is specified, sets the currently selected filehandle to *FILEHANDLE*. If *FILEHANDLE* is omitted, returns the currently selected filehandle. The currently selected filehandle is the filehandle to which all write() and print() statements output if the filehandle isn't specified in the write() or print() statement.

send SOCKET, MSG, FLAGS

send SOCKET, MSG, FLAGS, TO

Sends a message on a *SOCKET* using the socket() Unix system call.

setpgrp $pid, $pgrpid

Sets the current process group for the specified *$pid*. Use a *$pid* of 0 to imply the current process. Works only if the underlying system supports the operation.

setpriority $process, $group, $user

Sets the current priority for a process, a process group, or a user, like the Unix system call setpriority(). Works only if the underlying system supports it.

shift

shift @array

Removes the first value from the front of *@array* and returns the value. The size of *@array* is reduced by one. If *@array* is empty, returns undef. If *@array* is not specified, *@_* is used.

See also pop(), push(), and unshift().

shmctl ID, CMD, ARG

shmget KEY, SIZE, FLAGS

Work just like the Unix System V IPC shared memory functions. *See* the Unix man pages for more detail.

sin

sin $radians

Returns a double-precision scalar with the sine of the value of *$radians*. If *$radians* is omitted, *$_* is used. For the inverse sine operation, you can use the Math::Trig::asin function, or this:

```
sub asin { atan2($_[0], sqrt(1 - $_[0] * $_[0])) }
```

sleep

sleep $seconds

Makes the process do nothing for the number of seconds specified. If *$seconds* is omitted or evaluates to NULL, the process sleeps forever. You should not mix calls to alarm() and sleep() in the same program.

socket SOCKET, DOMAIN, TYPE, PROTOCOL

socketpair SOCKET1, SOCKET2, DOMAIN, TYPE, PROTOCOL

Open a socket of the specified kind and attach it to filehandle *SOCKET*. In the case of socketpair(), two sockets are created. *DOMAIN*, *TYPE*, and *PROTOCOL* are specified the same as for the system call of the same name. For serious socket work, you may want to use the IO::Socket module.

sort BLOCK @list

sort @list

sort SUBNAME @list

Sorts *@list* and returns the sorted list value. Empty values in arrays are removed. The *SUBNAME* and code *BLOCK* are pointers to user-defined functions that take two arguments and return an integer value of 1, 0, or –1.

1 indicates that the first argument is greater than the second. 0 indicates that the arguments are equal. −1 indicates that the second argument is greater than the first.

splice @array, $offset

splice @array, $offset, $length

splice @array, $offset, $length, @list

Removes from the @array the elements at the position specified by the integer $offset and continuing for the number of items specified by $length and replaces them with the contents of @list. Returns the list of items removed from @array. @array grows or shrinks as needed. If @list is not provided, nothing is inserted. If $length is not provided, all the elements from $offset onward are removed.

split

split /PATTERN/

split /PATTERN/, $string

split /PATTERN/, $string, $limit

Returns an array derived from splitting $string into an array of strings of items equal to the number of elements in $limit. If $string is not provided, $_ is used. PATTERN may be more than one character long. If PATTERN is not specified, the function splits at white spaces after the leading white spaces have been removed. It returns the number of items up to the limit specified and leaves the remainder as one long list. A call to split() with no arguments is equivalent to a split(' ', $_) call. PATTERN can be a regular expression or a variable containing a regular expression.

sprintf FORMAT, LIST

Similar to the printf() function, but instead of sending the output to the currently selected output device, sends it to the return value of the function. For example:

```
$adjective = "nice";
$mystring = sprintf "this is %s", $adjective;
# now $mystring contains "this is nice"
```

sqrt

sqrt $value

Returns the square root of *$value*. If *$value* is omitted, *$_* is used.

srand

srand $seed

Seeds the random number generator for rand() using *$seed* as a number. Explicitly calling srand() is usually not necessary because it is called implicitly when the rand() operator is first used. However, this was not the case in versions of Perl before 5.004. Therefore, if your script will run under older Perl versions, it should explicitly call srand().

stat

stat FILEHANDLE

stat $filename

Returns a 13-element list giving the status information for either the file opened via *FILEHANDLE* or the file named by *$filename*. If *$filename* is omitted, *$_* is used. Returns a null list if it fails. For example:

```
($dev,$ino,$mode,$nlink,$uid,$gid,$rdev,$size
   $atime,$mtime,$ctime,$blksize,$blocks)
      = stat($filename);
```

Not all fields are supported on all filesystem types. The meanings of the fields by position in the returned array are shown in Table B.5.

TABLE B.5: Return Values from stat()

POSITION	NAME	MEANING
0	dev	Device number of filesystem
1	ino	Inode number
2	mode	File mode (type and permissions)
3	nlink	Number of hard links to the file
4	uid	Numeric user ID of file's owner
5	gid	Numeric group ID of file's owner
6	rdev	Device identifier (special files open)
7	size	Total size of file in bytes

TABLE B.5: continued: Return Values from stat()

Position	Name	Meaning
8	atime	Last access time since the epoch (1/1/1970)
9	mtime	Last modify time since the epoch
10	ctime	Inode change time (not creation time)
11	blksize	Preferred block size for file system I/O
12	blocks	Actual number of blocks allocated

substr $string, $offset

substr $string, $offset, $length

substr $string, $offset, $length, $replacement

Gets a substring from $string of up to $length characters and returns it. The first character to extract from $string is at position 0, unless a positive $offset is specified. If $offset is negative, the offset starts from the end of the string. If $length is not provided, everything up to the end of the string is returned. If $length is negative, the function leaves that many characters off the end of $string. Using $replacement allows you to replace parts of $string with the contents of $replacement, returning what was in $string before the replacement (like a call to splice()).

symlink $oldfile, $newfile

Creates a new filename symbolically linked to the old filename. Returns 1 for success or 0 for failure.

syscall LIST

Makes the system call, passing the remaining elements as arguments. Using unimplemented system calls will produce a fatal error. Strings are passed by reference, and numbers are passed as integers.

sysread FILEHANDLE, $scalar, $length

sysread FILEHANDLE, $scalar, $length, $offset

Reads $length bytes of data into variable $scalar from the specified FILEHANDLE using the read() Unix system call. Returns the number of bytes actually read. Returns undef in the case of an error. $scalar grows or shrinks to the length read. The offset is used to read data at some place other than the first bytes in $scalar.

system $program @arguments
Similar to exec(), but branches off and returns to the parent process when the child process is finished. Because system() and backticks block SIGINT and SIGQUIT, killing the program they are running won't interrupt your program.

syswrite FILEHANDLE, $scalar
syswrite FILEHANDLE, $scalar, $length
syswrite FILEHANDLE, $scalar, $length, $offset
Attempts to write $length bytes of data from variable $scalar to the specified FILEHANDLE using the Unix system call write(). Returns the number of bytes written. Returns undef when an error occurs. An $offset is used to place the read data at the number of $offset at the beginning of the string in $scalar.

tell
tell FILEHANDLE
Gets the current file position for FILEHANDLE. If no FILEHANDLE is specified, uses the last read file.

telldir DIRHANDLE
Returns the current position of the readdir() routines on DIRHANDLE. A value can be used with seekdir() to access a particular location in a directory.

time
Returns the number of non-leap seconds since the epoch (00:00:00 UTC, January 1, 1970). Used with gmtime() and localtime().

times
Returns a four-item array with the user and system times (in seconds) for this process and the children (if any) of this process. In scalar context, returns only the user time.

tr/SEARCHLIST/REPLACEMENTLIST/cds

Translates characters in a string. Returns the number of characters translated, or deleted if you use the /d flag.

The `tr///` operator is similar to `s///`, with one big difference: It operates on ranges and lists of characters, but not on regular expressions. The following converts a phone number that spells a word into its numeric version.

```
$phone = "1-900-USE-PERL";
print "$phone\n";
$phone =~ tr/ABCDEFGHIJKLMNOPRSTUVWXY/
➡222333444555666777888999/;
print "$phone\n";

# prints:
# 1-900-USE-PERL
# 1-900-873-7375
```

The optional flags are listed in Table B.6.

TABLE B.6: Flags for the tr/// Operator

FLAG	DEFINITION
c	Complements the searchlist: tr/A-Z//c replaces everything that is *not* an uppercase letter to a space.
d	Delete any characters that were matched but don't have corresponding values in the replacement list.
s	Squash repeated runs of the replaced characters. This option is useful, for example, if you're replacing invalid characters with spaces but don't want long runs of spaces.

As with `m//` and `s///`, you can change the delimiters if you don't like slashes, or to help readability.

truncate FILEHANDLE, $length

truncate $filename, $length

Truncates the file opened on *FILEHANDLE* (or the file specified by *$filename*) to the specified *$length*.

uc

uc $string

Returns an uppercased copy of $string (or $_ if $string is omitted).

ucfirst

ucfirst $string

Returns the value of $string (or $_ if $string is omitted) with the first character uppercased.

umask

umask $value

Sets the umask for the process to $value and returns the old value. If $value is omitted, returns the current umask.

If umask(2) is not implemented on your system and you are trying to restrict access for yourself (that is, (EXPR & 0700) > 0), umask produces a fatal error at runtime. If umask(2) is not implemented and you are not trying to restrict access for yourself, umask returns undef.

undef EXPR

Removes any definition of EXPR, which can be a scalar, array, hash, or subroutine. Note that undef $hash{$key} only changes the value of $hash{$key} to the undefined value. If you want to remove the value from the hash, use delete().

unlink

unlink LIST

Deletes the files named in LIST (or in $_ if no list is specified). Returns the number of files successfully deleted. Use rmdir() to remove a directory.

unpack $template, EXPR

Does the reverse of pack(): takes a string representing a structure and expands it, returning the array value. In a scalar context, returns the first value produced. $template has the same format as with the pack() function.

See also pack().

unshift @array, @list

Adds the contents of @list to the front of @array and returns the new number of elements in the array. It is the complement to shift(), just as push() is the complement to pop() at the end of an array.

utime $accesstime, $modificationtime, @files

Modifies the access and modification times on each file in a list of files. Returns the number of files successfully changed.

values %hash

Returns an array containing only the values of %hash. The order in which the values are returned may be assumed to be random—although it's the same order the keys() or each() function would produce on the same modified hash.

    See also keys().

wait

Waits for a child process to terminate and returns the pid of the deceased process. Returns −1 if there are no child processes. The status is returned in the $? special variable.

waitpid PID, FLAGS

Waits for a particular child process to terminate and returns the pid of the deceased process. Returns −1 if there is no such child process. The status is returned in $?.

wantarray

Returns true if the currently executing subroutine is looking for a list value, returns false if a scalar value is being looked for, and returns undef if no value is being looked for.

warn LIST

Produces a message on STDERR similar to die(), but doesn't exit or throw an exception.

write

write EXPR

write FILEHANDLE

Writes a formatted record to the specified file using the format associated with that file.

See also print().

y/SEARCHLIST/REPLACEMENTLIST/cds

See the identical tr/// operator.

Appendix C

STANDARD PERL MODULES

This appendix describes how to use the modules included with a standard Perl installation (as of version 5.8.0). These modules (listed alphabetically) represent a small fraction of the modules publicly available for Perl. If you can't find what you need here, visit the CPAN archives (http://www.cpan.org).

AutoLoader

This module allows you to load subroutines only on demand instead of preloading them before your program executes.

Synopsis

```
package Foo;
use AutoLoader 'AUTOLOAD';
# import the default AUTOLOAD subroutine

package Bar;
use AutoLoader;
# don't import AUTOLOAD, define our own
sub AUTOLOAD {
    ...
    $AutoLoader::AUTOLOAD = "...";
    goto &AutoLoader::AUTOLOAD;
}
```

Description

The AutoLoader module works with the AutoSplit module and the __END__ token to defer the loading of some subroutines until they are used instead of loading them all at once. To use AutoLoader, the author of a module must place the definitions of subroutines to be autoloaded after an __END__ token. (See the perldata man page.) You can manually run the AutoSplit module to extract the definitions into individual files, which will be named according to the convention auto/funcname.al.

AutoLoader implements an AUTOLOAD subroutine. When an undefined subroutine is called in a client module of AutoLoader, AutoLoader's AUTOLOAD subroutine attempts to locate the subroutine in a file with a name related to the location of the file from which the client module was read. As an example, if POSIX.pm is located in /usr/local/lib/perl5/POSIX.pm, AutoLoader looks for Perl subroutines Posix in /usr/local/lib/perl5/auto/POSIX/*.al, where the .al file has the same name as the subroutine, sans *package*. If such a file exists, AUTOLOAD reads and evaluates it, thereby (presumably) defining the needed subroutine. AUTOLOAD will then goto the newly defined subroutine. Once this process completes for a given function, it is defined, so future calls to the subroutine bypass the AUTOLOAD mechanism.

Subroutine Stubs

In order for object method lookup and/or prototype checking to operate correctly even when methods have not yet been defined, you need to *forward declare* each subroutine (as in sub *NAME*;). See the "Synopsis" section in the perlsub man page. Such forward declaration creates *subroutine stubs*, which are placeholders with no code.

The AutoSplit and AutoLoader modules automate the creation of forward declarations. The AutoSplit module creates an index file containing forward declarations of all the AutoSplit subroutines. When the AutoLoader module is used (run with use), it loads these declarations into its caller's package.

Because of this mechanism, it is important that AutoLoader is always used and not required (run with require). In order to use AutoLoader's AUTOLOAD subroutine, you must explicitly import it:

```
use AutoLoader 'AUTOLOAD';
```

Overriding *AutoLoader's AUTOLOAD* Subroutine

Some modules, mainly extensions, provide their own AUTOLOAD subroutines. They typically need to check for special cases (such as constants) and then fall back to AutoLoader's AUTOLOAD for the rest.

Such modules should *not* import AutoLoader's AUTOLOAD subroutine. Instead, they should define their own AUTOLOAD subroutines along these lines:

```
use AutoLoader;
use Carp;

sub AUTOLOAD {
  my $constname;
  ($constname = $AUTOLOAD) =~ s/.*:://;
  my $val = constant($constname, @_ ? $_[0] : 0);
  if ($! != 0) {
    if ($! =~ /Invalid/) {
    $AutoLoader::AUTOLOAD = $AUTOLOAD;
    goto &AutoLoader::AUTOLOAD;
    }
    else {
      croak "constant $constname is not defined";
    }
  }
}
```

```
    *$AUTOLOAD = sub { $val };
    # same as: eval "sub $AUTOLOAD { $val }";
    goto &$AUTOLOAD;
}
```

If any module's own AUTOLOAD subroutine has no need to fall back to the AutoLoader's AUTOLOAD subroutine (because it doesn't have any AutoSplit subroutines), then that module should not use AutoLoader.

Package Lexicals

Lexicals declared with my in the main block of a package using AutoLoader are not visible to autoloaded subroutines, because the given scope ends at the __END__ marker. A module using such variables as package globals will not work properly under the AutoLoader.

The vars pragma (see the section on vars in the perlmod man page) can be used in such situations as an alternative to explicitly qualifying all globals with the package namespace. Variables predeclared with this pragma are visible to any autoloaded routines (but are invisible outside the package, unfortunately).

AutoLoader versus *SelfLoader*

The AutoLoader is similar in purpose to SelfLoader: They both delay the loading of subroutines. SelfLoader uses the __DATA__ marker rather than __END__. Although this means you don't need to use a hierarchy of disk files and the associated open and close for each routine loaded, Self-Loader is slower when parsing the lines after __DATA__. Once the lines are parsed at startup, routines are cached. SelfLoader can also handle multiple packages in a file.

AutoLoader reads code only as it is requested. In many cases this should make it faster than SelfLoader; however, AutoLoader requires that a mechanism like AutoSplit be used to create the individual files. The ExtUtils::MakeMaker man page invokes AutoSplit automatically if AutoLoader is used in a module source file.

Caveats

Prior to Perl 5.002, AutoLoader had a slightly different interface. Any old modules that use AutoLoader should be changed to the new calling style. Typically, this means changing a require to a use, adding the explicit AUTOLOAD import, if needed, and removing AutoLoader from @ISA.

On systems with restrictions on filename length, the file corresponding to a subroutine may have a shorter name that the routine itself. This situation can lead to conflicting filenames. The AutoSplit package warns of these potential conflicts when used to split a module.

AutoLoader may fail to find the autosplit files (or may even find the wrong ones) when @INC contains relative paths and the program uses chdir.

See Also

The SelfLoader man page—an autoloader that doesn't use external files.

Benchmark

Benchmark provides ways to determine the amount of time needed to execute a block of code. It is useful for comparing different ways of doing the same thing and can help you optimize code:

Synopsis

```
timethis ($count, "code");

# Use Perl code in strings...
timethese($count, {
  'Name1' => '...code1...',
  'Name2' => '...code2...',
});

# ... or use subroutine references.
timethese($count, {
  'Name1' => sub { ...code1... },
  'Name2' => sub { ...code2... },
});

$t = timeit($count, '...other code...')
print "$count loops of other code took:",timestr($t),"\n";
```

Description

The Benchmark module encapsulates a number of routines to help you figure out how long it takes to execute code.

Methods

The following methods configure Benchmark for use.

new   new returns the current time. For example:

```
use Benchmark;
$t0 = new Benchmark;
# ... your code here ...
$t1 = new Benchmark;
$td = timediff($t1, $t0);
print "the code took:",timestr($td),"\n";
```

debug   The debug command enables or disables debugging by setting the $Benchmark::Debug flag:

```
debug Benchmark 1;
$t = timeit(10, ' 5 ** $Global ');
debug Benchmark 0;
```

Standard Exports

The following routines are available if you use the Benchmark module.

timeit (COUNT, CODE)   The *COUNT* argument is the number of times to run the loop, and *CODE* is the code to run. *CODE* may be either a code reference or a string to be evaluated; either way it runs in the caller's package. The routine returns a Benchmark object.

timethis (COUNT, CODE, [TITLE, [STYLE]])   The *COUNT* argument is the number of times to run the loop, and *CODE* is the code to run. *CODE* may be a string to evaluate or a code reference; either way *CODE* runs in the caller's package. Results are printed to STDOUT as *TITLE* followed by the times. If the *TITLE* argument is omitted, the title defaults to "timethis *COUNT*". *STYLE* determines the format of the output, as described for timestr().

If *COUNT* is negative, the number is interpreted to mean the *minimum number of CPU seconds* to run. A zero signifies the default of three seconds.

This example runs for at least 10 seconds:

```
timethis(-10, $code)
```

This runs two pieces of code tests for at least three seconds:

```
timethese(0, { test1 => '...', test2 => '...'})
```

CPU seconds are, in Unix terms, the user time plus the system time of the process itself, as opposed to the real-time (wall-clock time) and the time spent by the child processes. Less than 0.1 seconds is not accepted (for example, −0.01 as the count will cause a fatal runtime exception).

The CPU seconds is the minimum time. CPU scheduling and other operating system factors may complicate the attempt so that a little more time is spent. The benchmark output will, however, also list the number of $code runs/second, which should be a more interesting number than the actual seconds. This routine returns a Benchmark object.

timethese (COUNT, CODEHASHREF, [STYLE])   CODEHASHREF is a reference to a hash containing names as keys and either a string to evaluate or a code reference for each value. For each (*KEY, VALUE*) pair in *CODEHASHREF*, this routine calls timethis(*COUNT, VALUE, KEY, VALUE*). The routines are called in string comparison order of *KEY. COUNT* can be zero or negative.

See timethis().

timediff (T1, T2)   Timediff (*T1, T2*) returns the difference between two Benchmark times as a Benchmark object suitable for passing to timestr().

timesum (T1, T2)   This command returns the sum of two Benchmark times as a Benchmark object suitable for passing to timestr().

timestr (TIMEDIFF, [STYLE, [FORMAT]])   This routine returns a string that formats the times in the *TIMEDIFF* object in the requested *STYLE. TIMEDIFF* is expected to be a Benchmark object similar to the one returned by timediff().

STYLE can be all, noc, nop, or auto. The all command shows each of the five available times (wall-clock time, user time, system time, user time of children, and system time of children). The noc command shows all the available times except the two children times. The nop command shows only wall-clock time and the two children times. The auto command (the default) acts as all unless the children times are both zero, in which case it acts as noc.

FORMAT is the printf-style format specifier (without the leading %) used to print the times. It defaults to 5.2f.

Caveats

Comparing evaluated strings with code references will give you inaccurate results. A code reference shows a slower execution time than the equivalent evaluated string.

The real-time timing is performed using time(2) and the granularity is, therefore, only one second.

Short tests may produce negative figures because Perl can appear to take longer to execute the empty loop than it takes to execute a short test. For example, try:

```
timethis(100,'1');
```

The system time of the null loop might be slightly more than the system time of the loop with the actual code; therefore, the difference might end up being less than 0.

bytes

This pragma forces Perl to consider strings as bytes, rather than characters. This is important when working with Unicode data, where chr(400) is one character but two bytes:

```
my $x = chr(400);
print length($x); # 1, since it's one character
{
    use bytes;
    print length($x); # 2, since it's two bytes
}
```

See Also
Chapter 13, "Perl and Unicode."

Carp

This module writes error or diagnostic info, but with more context information than warn() or die() provides.

Synopsis
```
use Carp;
croak "We're outta here!";

use Carp qw(cluck);
cluck "This is how we got here!";
```

Description
The Carp routines are useful in your own modules because they act like die() or warn(); however, they report where the error was in the code from which they were called. If a routine Foo() has a carp() in it, the carp() reports the error as occurring where Foo() was called, not where carp() was called.

Forcing a Stack Trace   As a debugging aid, you can force Carp to treat a `croak` as a `confess` and treat a `carp` as a `cluck` across *all* modules. In other words, you can force a detailed stack trace to be performed. This can be very helpful when you are trying to understand why, or from where, a warning or error is being generated.

This feature is enabled as follows

```
perl -MCarp=verbose script.pl
```

or by including the string `MCarp=verbose` in the `PERL5OPT` environment variable.

Bugs

Currently, the Carp routines don't handle exception objects. If called with a first argument that is a reference, they simply call `die()` or `warn()`, as appropriate.

CGI::Carp

This module provides routines for writing error and diagnostic messages to an HTTPD web server's logs, rather than the standard error device.

Synopsis

```
use CGI::Carp;

die "dying because of fatal error.\n";

use CGI::Carp qw(cluck);
cluck "I wouldn't do that if I were you";

use CGI::Carp qw(fatalsToBrowser);
die "Fatal error messages are now sent to browser";
```

Description

CGI scripts have a nasty habit of leaving warning messages that are neither time stamped nor fully identified in the error logs. Tracking down the script that caused the error is a pain. CGI::Carp fixes the problem. Replace the usual

```
use Carp;
```

with

```
use CGI::Carp
```

The standard `warn()`, `die()`, `croak()`, `confess()`, and `carp()` calls are replaced automatically with functions that write nicely time-stamped messages to the HTTP server error log. For example:

```
[Fri Nov 17 21:40:43 1995] test.pl: I'm confused at test.pl
➥line 3.
[Fri Nov 17 21:40:43 1995] test.pl: Got an error message:
➥Permission denied.
[Fri Nov 17 21:40:43 1995] test.pl: I'm dying.
```

Redirecting Error Messages   By default, error messages are sent to STDERR. Most HTTPD servers direct STDERR to the server's error log. Some applications may keep private error logs, distinct from the server's error log, or they may direct error messages to STDOUT so that the browser will receive them.

The `carpout()` function is provided for this purpose. Because `carpout()` is not exported by default, you must import it explicitly by saying

```
use CGI::Carp qw(carpout);
```

The `carpout()` function requires one argument, which should be a reference to an open filehandle for writing errors. It should be called in a BEGIN block at the top of the CGI application so that compiler errors will be caught. For example:

```
BEGIN {
  use CGI::Carp qw(carpout);
  open(LOG, ">>/usr/local/cgi-logs/mycgi-log") or
    die("Unable to open mycgi-log: $!\n");
  carpout(LOG);
}
```

The `carpout()` command does not handle file locking on the log for you at this point.

The real STDERR is not closed. It is moved to SAVEERR. Some servers, when dealing with CGI scripts, close their connection to the browser when the script closes STDOUT and STDERR. SAVEERR is used to prevent this from happening prematurely.

You can pass filehandles to `carpout()` in a variety of ways, but the easiest is to pass a filehandle glob:

```
carpout(\*LOG);
```

`FileHandle` and other objects work, as well.

Using `carpout()` is not great for performance; however, using it for debugging or moderate-use applications is recommended. Perhaps a future version of this module will delay the redirection of STDERR until one of the CGI::Carp methods is called to prevent the performance hit.

Making Perl Errors Appear in the Browser Window   If you want to send fatal (`die`, `confess`) errors to the browser, ask to import the special `fatalsToBrowser` subroutine:

```
use CGI::Carp qw(fatalsToBrowser);
die "Bad error here";
```

Fatal errors are now echoed to the browser as well as to the log. CGI::Carp arranges to send a minimal HTTP header to the browser so that even errors that occur in the early compile phase will be seen. Nonfatal errors are directed only to the log file (unless redirected with `carpout`).

Changing the Default Message   By default, the software error message is followed by a note to contact the webmaster by e-mail with the time and date of the error. If you don't like this message, you can change it using the `set_message()` routine. This routine is not imported by default. You should import it on the `use()` line:

```
use CGI::Carp qw(fatalsToBrowser set_message);
set_message("It's not a bug, it's a feature!");
```

You can also pass a code reference to create a custom error message. At runtime, your code will be called with the text of the error message that caused the script to die. For example:

```
use CGI::Carp qw(fatalsToBrowser set_message);
BEGIN {
    sub handle_errors {
        my $msg = shift;
        print "<h1>Oh gosh</h1>";
        print "Got an error: $msg";
    }
    set_message(\&handle_errors);
}
```

In order to correctly intercept compile-time errors, you should call `set_message()` from within a BEGIN{} block.

CGI::Cookie

This module is a standard interface that provides reading, parsing, and writing of Netscape-style browser cookies.

Synopsis

```
use CGI qw/:standard/;
use CGI::Cookie;

# Create new cookies and send them
$cookie1 = new CGI::Cookie(-name=>'ID',-value=>123456);
$cookie2 = new CGI::Cookie(-name=>'preferences',
                           -value=>{ font => Helvetica,
                           size => 12 }
);
print header(-cookie=>[$cookie1,$cookie2]);

# fetch existing cookies
%cookies = fetch CGI::Cookie;
$id = $cookies{'ID'}->value;

# create cookies returned from an external source
%cookies = parse CGI::Cookie($ENV{COOKIE});
```

Description

CGI::Cookie is an interface to Netscape (HTTP/1.1) cookies. This innovation allows web servers to store information on the browser's side of the connection so that it persists across multiple client requests. Although CGI::Cookie is intended to be used in conjunction with CGI.pm (and is used by it internally), you can use this module independently.

For full information on cookies, see: http://www.ics.uci.edu/pub/ietf/http/rfc2109.txt.

Using *CGI::Cookie*   CGI::Cookie is object oriented. Each cookie object has a name and a value. The name is any scalar value. The value is any scalar or array value (associative arrays are also allowed). Cookies also have several optional attributes, including:

> **Expiration Date**   The expiration date tells the browser how long to hang onto the cookie. If the cookie specifies an expiration date in the future, the browser stores the cookie information in a disk file and returns it to the server every time the user reconnects

(until the expiration date is reached). If the cookie specifies an expiration date in the past, the browser removes the cookie from the disk file. If the expiration date is not specified, the cookie persists only until the user quits the browser.

Domain   This is a partial or complete domain name for which the cookie is valid. The browser returns the cookie to any host that matches the partial domain name. For example, if you specify a domain name of .capricorn.com, Netscape returns the cookie to web servers running on any of the machines named www.capricorn.com, ftp.capricorn.com, feckless.capricorn .com, and so on. Domain names must contain at least two periods to prevent attempts to match on top-level domains like .edu. If no domain is specified, the browser returns the cookie only to servers on the host from which the cookie originated.

Path   If you provide a cookie-path attribute, the browser checks it against your script's URL before returning the cookie. For example, if you specify the path /cgi-bin, the cookie is returned to each of the scripts /cgi-bin/tally.pl, /cgi-bin/order.pl, and /cgi-bin/customer_service/complain.pl, but not to the script /cgi-private/site_admin.pl. By default, path is set to backslash (/), which causes the cookie to be sent to any CGI script on your site.

Secure Flag   If the secure attribute is set, the cookie is sent to your script only if the CGI request is occurring on a secure channel, such as SSL.

Creating New Cookies

```
$c = new CGI::Cookie(-name    => 'foo',
                     -value   => 'bar',
                     -expires => '+3M',
                     -domain  => '.capricorn.com',
                     -path    => '/cgi-bin/database'
                     -secure  => 1
);
```

Create cookies from scratch with the new method. The -name and -value parameters are required. The name must be a scalar value. The value can be a scalar, an array reference, or a hash reference. (At some point in the future, cookies will support one of the Perl object serialization protocols for full generality.)

In addition to the required –name and –value parameters, the following optional parameters can be specified:

▶ expires accepts any of the relative or absolute date formats recognized by CGI.pm (for example, '+3M' for three months in the future). See CGI.pm's documentation for details.

▶ domain points to a domain name or to a fully qualified hostname. If not specified, the cookie is returned only to the web server that created it.

▶ path points to a partial URL on the current server. The cookie is returned to all URLs beginning with the specified path. If not specified, it defaults to /, which returns the cookie to all pages at your site.

▶ If set to a true value, secure instructs the browser to return the cookie only when a cryptographic protocol is in use.

Sending the Cookie to the Browser   Within a CGI script, you can send a cookie to the browser by creating one or more Set-Cookie: fields in the HTTP header. Here is a typical sequence:

```
my $c = new CGI::Cookie(-name    =>  'foo',
                        -value   =>  ['bar','baz'],
                        -expires =>  '+3M');

print "Set-Cookie: $c\n";
print "Content-Type: text/html\n\n";
```

To send more than one cookie, create several Set-Cookie: fields. Alternatively, you can concatenate the cookies with a semicolon and space (;) and send them in one field.

Internally, Cookie overloads the " " operator to call its as_string() method when incorporated into the HTTP header. The as_string() command turns the cookie's internal representation into an RFC-compliant text representation. You can call the as_string() command yourself if you prefer:

```
print "Set-Cookie: ",$c->as_string,"\n";
```

Recovering Previous Cookies

```
%cookies = fetch CGI::Cookie;
```

fetch returns an associative array consisting of all the cookies returned by the browser. The keys of the array are the cookie names. You can iterate through the cookies this way:

```
%cookies = fetch CGI::Cookie;
foreach (keys %cookies) {
    do_something($cookies{$_});
}
```

In a scalar context, fetch() returns a hash reference, which may be more efficient if you are manipulating multiple cookies. CGI.pm uses the URL escaping methods to save and restore reserved characters in its cookies. If you are trying to retrieve a cookie set by a foreign server, this escaping method may trip you up. Instead, use raw_fetch(), which has the same semantics as fetch(), but performs no unescaping.

You can also retrieve cookies that were stored in some external form using the parse() class method:

```
$COOKIES = `cat /usr/tmp/Cookie_stash`;
%cookies = parse CGI::Cookie($COOKIES);
```

Manipulating Cookies   Cookie objects have a series of accessor methods to get and set cookie attributes. Each accessor has a similar syntax. Called without arguments, the accessor returns the current value of the attribute. Called with an argument, the accessor changes the attribute and returns its new value.

See Also

The CGI::Carp man page and the CGI man page.

Class::Struct

Provides a mechanism for declaring struct and similar datatypes, while retaining Perl's notion of basic scalar, array, hash, and module types.

Synopsis

```
use Class::Struct;
# declare struct, based on array:
struct( CLASS_NAME => [ ELEMENT_NAME => ELEMENT_TYPE, ... ]);
# declare struct, based on hash:
struct( CLASS_NAME => { ELEMENT_NAME => ELEMENT_TYPE, ... });

package CLASS_NAME;
use Class::Struct;
```

```
# declare struct, based on array, implicit class name:
struct( ELEMENT_NAME => ELEMENT_TYPE, ... );

package Myobj;
use Class::Struct;
# declare struct with four types of elements:
struct( s => '$', a => '@', h => '%',
        c => 'My_Other_Class' );

$obj = new Myobj;                        # constructor

# scalar type accessor:
$element_value = $obj->s;                # element value
$obj->s('new value');                    # assign to element

# array type accessor:
$ary_ref = $obj->a;                      # reference to array
$ary_element_value = $obj->a(2);         # array element value
$obj->a(2, 'new value');                 # assign to array element

$hash_ref = $obj->h;                     # reference to whole hash
$hash_element_value = $obj->h('x');      # hash element value
$obj->h('x', 'new value');               # assign to hash element

# class type accessor:
$element_value = $obj->c;                # object reference
$obj->c->method(...);                    # call method of object
$obj->c(new My_Other_Class);             # assign a new object
```

Description

Class::Struct exports a single function: struct. Given a list of element names and types, and optionally a class name, struct creates a Perl 5 class that implements a data structure similar to struct. The new class is given a constructor method, new, for creating struct objects.

Each element in the struct data has an accessor method, which is used to assign to the element and to fetch its value. The default accessor can be overridden by declaring a sub of the same name in the package. Each element's type can be scalar, array, hash, or class.

constant

This pragma defines compile-time constants that cannot be changed.

Synopsis

```
use constant PI    => 3.14159;
$area = PI * $radius * $radius; # calculate circle area
PI = 4; # error!
```

Description

The constant pragma allows you to create values that cannot be changed during the course of the program. Trying to modify that constant generates an error at runtime.

Note that because constant is invoked in a use statement, and all use statements are evaluated at compile time, it doesn't make sense to define constants conditionally, as in:

```
# Warning! Won't do what you want!
if ( $month eq "January" ) {
    use constant DAYS => 31;
}
```

CPAN

This module automates the installation of Perl modules from the CPAN.

Summary

```
perl -MCPAN -eshell
perl -MCPAN -e'install modulename'
```

Description

The CPAN is the Comprehensive Perl Archive Network, the source for thousands of useful (and not so useful) modules for Perl. CPAN, the module, makes it easy for you to install these modules.

Usually, CPAN is used from the command line, either to install a single module or to run the interactive CPAN shell. The first time you use CPAN, you should run the shell like so:

```
perl -MCPAN -eshell
```

The CPAN module goes through setup with you interactively, asking questions about your system. After the setup has completed, you'll have a menu-driven shell that lets you search for modules, install them, and search for updated modules.

You can also install modules directly from the command line. To install the WWW::Mechanize module, run this from the command line:

```
perl -MCPAN -e'install WWW::Mechanize'
```

Caveats

For most installations, you must have root or administrator privileges in order to install modules.

See Also

The CPAN website at http://www.cpan.org. A searchable interface is available at http://search.cpan.org. A newer module called CPANPLUS is currently under development and will replace CPAN.

Cwd

This module allows you to determine the current working directory without performing a system() call.

Synopsis

```
use Cwd;
$dir = cwd;
$dir = getcwd;
$dir = fastgetcwd;

use Cwd 'chdir';
chdir "/tmp";
print $ENV{'PWD'};

use Cwd 'abs_path';
print abs_path($ENV{'PWD'});

use Cwd 'fast_abs_path';
print fast_abs_path($ENV{'PWD'});
```

Description

The abs_path() function takes a single argument and returns the absolute pathname for that argument. It uses the same algorithm as getcwd() (actually, getcwd() is abs_path(".")).

The fastcwd() function looks the same as getcwd(), but it runs faster. It's also more dangerous because it might chdir() you out of a directory that it can't chdir() you back into. If fastcwd encounters a problem, it returns undef; however, it will probably leave you in a different directory. For a measure of extra security, if everything appears to have worked, the fastcwd() function verifies that it leaves you in the same directory it started in. If the directory has changed, fastcwd() will die with the following message:

> Unstable directory path, current directory changed unexpectedly.
> That should never happen.

The fast_abs_path() function looks the same as abs_path(), but it runs faster and, like fastcwd(), is more dangerous.

The cwd() function looks the same as getcwd and fastgetcwd, but it is implemented using the most natural and safe form for the current architecture. For most systems, it is identical to pwd (but without the trailing line terminator). You should use cwd (or another *cwd() function) in *all* code to ensure portability.

If you ask to override your chdir() built-in function, your PWD environment variable will be kept up-to-date. It will be kept up-to-date only if all the packages that use chdir import it from cwd.

See Also
The "Overriding Built-in Functions" section in the perlsub man page.

Data::Dumper

This module takes a Perl data structure and provides a text representation, suitable for persistent storage of data or objects.

Synopsis

```
use Data::Dumper;

# simple procedural interface
print Dumper($foo, $bar);

# extended usage with names
print Data::Dumper->Dump([$foo, $bar], [qw(foo *ary)]);
```

```
# configuration variables
{
  local $Data::Dump::Purity = 1;
  eval Data::Dumper->Dump([$foo, $bar], [qw(foo *ary)]);
}

# OO usage
$d = Data::Dumper->new([$foo, $bar], [qw(foo *ary)]);
...
print $d->Dump;
...
$d->Purity(1)->Terse(1)->Deepcopy(1);
eval $d->Dump;
```

Description

Given a list of scalars or reference variables, Data::Dumper writes their contents in Perl syntax. The references can also be objects. The contents of each variable are output in a single Perl statement. Data::Dumper correctly handles self-referential structures. The return value can be evaluated to get back an identical copy of the original reference structure.

Any reference that is the same as one of those passed is named $VARn (where n is a numeric suffix). Other duplicate references to substructures within $VARn are appropriately labeled using arrow notation. You can specify names for individual values to be dumped if you use the Dump() method, or you can change the default $VAR prefix to something else. See $Data::Dumper::Varname and $Data::Dumper::Terse.

The default output of self-referential structures can be evaluated; however, the nested references to $VARn will be undefined, because a recursive structure cannot be constructed using one Perl statement. You should set the Purity flag to 1 to get additional statements that correctly fill these references.

In the extended usage form, the references to be dumped can be given user-specified names. If a name begins with an asterisk (*), the output describes the dereferenced type of the supplied reference for hashes and arrays, and coderefs. Where possible, output of names is avoided if the Terse flag is set.

In many cases, methods that are used to set the internal state of the object return the object itself, so method calls can be conveniently chained together.

Several styles of output are possible, all controlled by setting the Indent flag. See the "Configuration Variables or Methods" section for details.

Methods

This method returns a newly created `Data::Dumper` object:

```
*PACKAGE*->new(*ARRAYREF [*, *ARRAYREF]*)
```

The first argument is an anonymous array of values to be dumped. The optional second argument is an anonymous array of names for the values. The names do not need a leading $ sign, and they must be made up of alphanumeric characters. For ARRAY and HASH references, you can begin a name with an * to specify that the dereferenced type must be dumped instead of the reference itself. The prefix specified by $Data::Dumper::Varname is used with a numeric suffix if the name for a value is undefined.

`Data::Dumper` catalogs all references encountered while dumping the values. Cross-references (in the form of names of substructures in Perl syntax) are inserted at all possible points, preserving any structural interdependencies in the original set of values. Structure traversal is depth-first and proceeds in order from the first supplied value to the last.

The following code:

```
*$OBJ*->Dump  *or*  *PACKAGE*->Dump(*ARRAYREF [*,
       *ARRAYREF]*)
```

returns the string form of the values stored in the object (preserving the order in which they were supplied to new), subject to the following listed configuration options. In an array context, it returns a list of strings corresponding to the supplied values. The second form, for convenience, simply calls the new method on its arguments before immediately dumping the object.

```
*$OBJ*->Dumpxs  *or*  *PACKAGE*->Dumpxs(*ARRAYREF [*,
       *ARRAYREF]*)
```

This method is available if you were able to compile and install the XSUB extension to `Data::Dumper`. It is similar to the previous Dump method; however, it is four to five times faster, because it is written entirely in C.

```
*$OBJ*->Seen(*[HASHREF]*)
```

This code queries or adds to the internal table of already encountered references. You must use `Reset` to explicitly clear the table if needed. Such references are not dumped; instead, their names are inserted wherever they are encountered. This technique is useful for properly dumping subroutine references. This method expects an anonymous hash of name => value pairs. The same rules apply for names that apply for new. If no argument is supplied, it returns the "seen" list of name => value pairs, in an array context. Otherwise, it returns the object itself.

```
*$OBJ*->Values(*[ARRAYREF]*)
```

This code queries or replaces the internal array of values that are dumped. When called without arguments, it returns the values. Otherwise, it returns the object itself.

```
*$OBJ*->Names(*[ARRAYREF]*)
```

This code queries or replaces the internal array of user-supplied names for the values that are dumped. When called without arguments, it returns the names. Otherwise, it returns the object itself.

```
*$OBJ*->Reset
```

This code clears the internal table of "seen" references and returns the object itself.

Functions

This function returns the string form of the values in the list, subject to the following listed configuration options:

```
Dumper(*LIST*)
```

The values are named $VAR*n* in the output, where *n* is a numeric suffix. It returns a list of strings in an array context.

```
DumperX(*LIST*)
```

This function is similar to the Dumper() function; however, it calls the XSUB implementation. It is available only if you were able to compile and install the XSUB extensions in Data::Dumper.

Configuration Variables or Methods

You can use several configuration variables to control the kind of output generated when the procedural interface is used. These variables are usually localized (run with local) in a block so that other parts of the code are not affected by the change. These variables determine the default state of the object created by calling the new method, but they cannot be used to alter the state of the object thereafter. Instead, the equivalent method names should be used to query or set the internal state of the object.

The method forms return the object itself when called with arguments, so that they can be chained together:

```
$Data::Dumper::Indent  *or*  *$OBJ*->Indent(*[NEWVAL]*)
```

This method controls the style of indentation. It can be set to 0, 1, 2, or 3. Style 0 spews output without any newlines, indentation, or spaces between list items. It is the most compact format possible that can still be called valid Perl. Style 1 outputs a readable form with newlines but no fancy indentation (each level in the structure is simply indented by a fixed amount of whitespace). Style 2 outputs a very readable form, which considers the length of hash keys (so the hash values line up). Style 3 is similar to Style 2, but it also annotates the elements of arrays with their indexes (the comments have their own lines, so array output consumes twice the number of lines). Style 2 is the default.

```
$Data::Dumper::Purity  *or*  *$OBJ*->Purity(*[NEWVAL]*)
```

This method controls the degree to which the output can be evaluated to re-create the supplied reference structures. Setting it to 1 outputs additional Perl statements that correctly re-create nested references. The default is 0.

```
$Data::Dumper::Pad  *or*  *$OBJ*->Pad(*[NEWVAL]*)
```

This method specifies the string that is prefixed to every line of the output. Empty string is used by default if this method isn't used to specify something.

```
$Data::Dumper::Varname  *or*
      *$OBJ*->Varname(*[NEWVAL]*)
```

This method contains the prefix to use for tagging variable names in the output. The default is VAR.

```
$Data::Dumper::Useqq  *or*  *$OBJ*->Useqq(*[NEWVAL]*)
```

When set, this method enables the use of double quotes to represent string values. Whitespace other than space is represented as [\n\t\r], "unsafe" characters are backslashed, and unprintable characters are output as quoted octal integers. Because setting this variable imposes a performance penalty, the default is 0. The Dumpxs() method does not honor this flag yet.

```
$Data::Dumper::Terse  *or*  *$OBJ*->Terse(*[NEWVAL]*)
```

When set, Data::Dumper emits single, non-self-referential values as atoms/terms rather than statements. This means that the VARn$ names are avoided when possible; however, the output may not always be parseable by eval.

```
$Data::Dumper::Freezer  *or*
        $*OBJ*->Freezer(*[NEWVAL]*)
```

This variable can be set to a method name or to an empty string to disable the feature. Data::Dumper invokes that method via the object before attempting to make it into a string. This method can alter the contents of the object (if, for instance, it contains data allocated from C) and even rebless (reuse the command bless) it in a different package. The client is responsible for making sure the specified method can be called via the object and that the object ends up containing only Perl data types after the method has been called. It defaults to an empty string.

```
$Data::Dumper::Toaster  *or*
        $*OBJ*->Toaster(*[NEWVAL]*)
```

This variable can be set to a method name or to an empty string to disable the feature. Data::Dumper emits a method call for any objects that are to be dumped using the syntax bless(*DATA*, *CLASS*)->*METHOD*(). This means the method specified must perform any modifications required on the object (like creating a new state within it and/or reblessing it in a different package) and then return it. The client is responsible for making sure the method can be called via the object and that it returns a valid object. It defaults to an empty string.

```
$Data::Dumper::Deepcopy  *or*
        $*OBJ*->Deepcopy(*[NEWVAL]*)
```

This variable can be set to a boolean value to enable deep copies of structures. Cross-referencing is then performed only when absolutely essential (to break reference cycles). The default is 0.

```
$Data::Dumper::Quotekeys  *or*
        $*OBJ*->Quotekeys(*[NEWVAL]*)
```

This variable can be set to a boolean value to control whether hash keys are quoted. A false value prevents hash keys from being quoted when they look like a simple string. The default is 1, which always encloses hash keys in quotes.

```
$Data::Dumper::Bless  *or*  $*OBJ*->Bless(*[NEWVAL]*)
```

This variable can be set to a string that specifies an alternative to the bless built-in operator used to create objects. A function with the specified name should exist and should accept the same arguments as the built-in. The default is bless.

Examples

Run these code snippets to get a quick feel for the behavior of this module. When you are through with these examples, you may want to add or change the various configuration variables previously described to see their behavior. (See the test suite in the Data::Dumper distribution for more examples.)

```
use Data::Dumper;

package Foo;
sub new {bless {'a' => 1,
                'b' => sub { return "foo" }}, $_[0]};

package Fuz;          # a weird REF-REF-SCALAR object
sub new {bless \($_ = \ 'fu\'z'), $_[0]};

package main;
$foo = Foo->new;
$fuz = Fuz->new;
$boo = [ 1, [], "abcd", \*foo,
{1 => 'a', 023 => 'b', 0x45 => 'c'},
\\"p\q\'r", $foo, $fuz];

########
# simple usage
########

$bar = eval(Dumper($boo));
print($@) if $@;
print Dumper($boo), Dumper($bar);
# pretty print (no array indices)

$Data::Dumper::Terse = 1;    # omit names where feasible
$Data::Dumper::Indent = 0;   # turn off all pretty print
print Dumper($boo), "\n";

$Data::Dumper::Indent = 1;   # mild pretty print
print Dumper($boo);

$Data::Dumper::Indent = 3;   # pretty print with array indices
print Dumper($boo);

$Data::Dumper::Useqq = 1;    # print strings in double quotes
print Dumper($boo);

########
# recursive structures
########

@c = ('c');
$c = \@c;
$b = {};
$a = [1, $b, $c];
```

```perl
$b->{a} = $a;
$b->{b} = $a->[1];
$b->{c} = $a->[2];
print Data::Dumper->Dump([$a,$b,$c], [qw(a b c)]);

$Data::Dumper::Purity = 1;   # fill in the holes for eval
print Data::Dumper->Dump([$a, $b], [qw(*a b)]); # print as @a
print Data::Dumper->Dump([$b, $a], [qw(*b a)]); # print as %b

$Data::Dumper::Deepcopy = 1;# avoid cross-refs
print Data::Dumper->Dump([$b, $a], [qw(*b a)]);


$Data::Dumper::Purity = 0;   # avoid cross-refs
print Data::Dumper->Dump([$b, $a], [qw(*b a)]);


########
# object-oriented usage
########

$d = Data::Dumper->new([$a,$b], [qw(a b)]);
$d->Seen({'*c' => $c});        # stash a ref without printing it
$d->Indent(3);
print $d->Dump;
$d->Reset->Purity(0);          # empty the seen cache
print join "--\n", $d->Dump;

########
# persistence
########

package Foo;
sub new { bless { state => 'awake' }, shift }
sub Freeze {
  my $s = shift;
  print STDERR "preparing to sleep\n";
  $s->{state} = 'asleep';
  return bless $s, 'Foo::ZZZ';
}

package Foo::ZZZ;
sub Thaw {
  my $s = shift;
  print STDERR "waking up\n";
```

```
        $s->{state} = 'awake';
        return bless $s, 'Foo';
}

package Foo;
use Data::Dumper;
$a = Foo->new;
$b = Data::Dumper->new([$a], ['c']);
$b->Freezer('Freeze');
$b->Toaster('Thaw');
$c = $b->Dump;
print $c;
$d = eval $c;
print Data::Dumper->Dump([$d], ['d']);

########
# symbol substitution (useful for recreating CODE refs)
########

sub foo { print "foo speaking\n" }
*other = \&foo;
$bar = [ \&other ];
$d = Data::Dumper->new([\&other,$bar],['*other','bar']);
$d->Seen({ '*foo' => \&foo });
print $d->Dump;
```

Bugs

Due to the limitations of Perl subroutine call semantics, you cannot pass
an array or hash. Prepend it with a \ to pass its reference instead. This
limitation will be remedied with the arrival of prototypes in later versions
of Perl. For now, you need to use the extended usage form and prepend the
name with an asterisk (*) to output it as a hash or an array.

Data::Dumper cheats with CODE references. If a code reference is encountered in the structure being processed, an anonymous subroutine that
contains the string "DUMMY" is inserted in its place, and a warning is printed
if Purity is set. You can evaluate the result, but bear in mind that the
anonymous sub that is created is just a placeholder. Perhaps someday,
Perl will have a switch to cache-on-demand the string representation of a
compiled piece of code. If you know all the code refs your data structures
are likely to have, you can use the Seen method to precede the internal
reference table and make the dumped output point to them. See the previous "Examples" section.

DB_File

DB_File enables access to Berkeley DB version 1.x database files using tie() functions.

Synopsis

```
use DB_File ;

[$X =] tie %hash,
            'DB_File',
            [$filename, $flags, $mode, $DB_HASH] ;
[$X =] tie %hash,
            'DB_File',
            $filename, $flags, $mode, $DB_BTREE ;
[$X =] tie @array,
            'DB_File',
            $filename, $flags, $mode, $DB_RECNO ;

$status = $X->del($key [, $flags]) ;
$status = $X->put($key, $value [, $flags]) ;
$status = $X->get($key, $value [, $flags]) ;
$status = $X->seq($key, $value, $flags) ;
$status = $X->sync([$flags]) ;
$status = $X->fd ;

# BTREE only
$count = $X->get_dup($key) ;
@list  = $X->get_dup($key) ;
%list  = $X->get_dup($key, 1) ;
$status = $X->find_dup($key, $value) ;
$status = $X->del_dup($key, $value) ;

# RECNO only
$a = $X->length;
$a = $X->pop ;
$X->push(list);
$a = $X->shift;
$X->unshift(list);

untie %hash ;
untie @array ;
```

Description

DB_File is a module that allows Perl programs to use the facilities provided by Berkeley DB version 1.x. (If you have a newer version of DB, see the

"Using DB_File with Berkeley DB Version 2" section.) You should have a copy of the Berkeley DB manual pages at hand when you read this documentation. The interface defined here closely mirrors the Berkeley DB interface.

Berkeley DB is a C library that provides a consistent interface to a number of database formats. DB_File provides an interface to all three of the database types currently supported by Berkeley DB. The file types are as follows:

DB_HASH   Allows arbitrary key/value pairs to be stored in data files. This is equivalent to the functionality provided by other hashing packages like DBM, NDBM, ODBM, GDBM, and SDBM. Remember though, the files created using DB_HASH are not compatible with any of the other packages mentioned.

A default hashing algorithm, which is adequate for most applications, is built into Berkeley DB. If you need to use your own hashing algorithm, you can write it in Perl and have DB_File use it instead.

DB_BTREE   Allows arbitrary key/value pairs to be stored in a sorted, balanced binary tree. As with the DB_HASH format, you can provide a user-defined Perl routine to perform the comparison of keys. By default, though, the keys are stored in lexical order.

DB_RECNO   Allows both fixed-length and variable-length flat text files to be manipulated using the same key/value pair interface as in DB_HASH and DB_BTREE. In this case, the key consists of a record (line) number.

Using *DB_File* with Berkeley DB Version 2

Although DB_File is intended to be used with Berkeley DB Version 1, it can also be used with Version 2. In this case, the interface is limited to the functionality provided by Berkeley DB 1.*x*. Anywhere the Version 2 interface differs, DB_File arranges for it to work like Version 1. This feature allows DB_File scripts that were built with Version 1 to be migrated to Version 2 without any changes.

If you want to use the new features available in Berkeley DB 2.*x*, use the Perl module BerkeleyDB instead. Please read the "COPYRIGHT" section in the Berkeley DB distribution before using Version 2.*x* of Berkeley DB with DB_File.

Interface to Berkeley DB

DB_File allows access to Berkeley DB files using the tie() mechanism. This facility allows DB_File to access Berkeley DB files using either an associative array (for DB_HASH and DB_BTREE file types) or an ordinary array (for the DB_RECNO file type). In addition to using the tie() interface, you can also directly access most of the functions provided in the Berkeley DB API. See the "The API Interface" section.

Opening a Berkeley DB Database File

```
tie %array, 'DB_File', $filename, $flags, $mode, $DB_HASH;
```

The *filename, flags,* and *mode* parameters are the direct equivalent of their dbopen() counterparts. The final parameter ($DB_HASH) performs the function of both the *type* and *openinfo* parameters in dbopen().

In the previous example, $DB_HASH is a predefined reference to a hash object. DB_File has three of these predefined references: $DB_HASH, $DB_BTREE, and $DB_RECNO. The keys allowed in each of these predefined references are limited to the names used in the equivalent C structure. For example, the $DB_HASH reference allows only keys called bsize, cachesize, ffactor, hash, lorder, and nelem. To change one of these elements, just assign to it like this:

```
$DB_HASH->{'cachesize'} = 10000 ;
```

The three predefined variables $DB_HASH, $DB_BTREE, and $DB_RECNO are usually adequate for most applications. If you do need to create extra instances of these objects, constructors are available for each file type. Here are examples of the constructors and the valid options available for DB_HASH, DB_BTREE, and DB_RECNO:

```
$a = new DB_File::HASHINFO ;
$a->{'bsize'} ;
$a->{'cachesize'} ;
$a->{'ffactor'};
$a->{'hash'} ;
$a->{'lorder'} ;
$a->{'nelem'} ;

$b = new DB_File::BTREEINFO ;
$b->{'flags'} ;
$b->{'cachesize'} ;
$b->{'maxkeypage'} ;
$b->{'minkeypage'} ;
$b->{'psize'} ;
```

```
$b->{'compare'} ;
$b->{'prefix'} ;
$b->{'lorder'} ;

$c = new DB_File::RECNOINFO ;
$c->{'bval'} ;
$c->{'cachesize'} ;
$c->{'psize'} ;
$c->{'flags'} ;
$c->{'lorder'} ;
$c->{'reclen'} ;
$c->{'bfname'} ;
```

The values stored in the previous hashes are, for the most part, the direct equivalents of their C counterparts. Like their C counterparts, they are set to default values, meaning you don't have to set *all* the values when you only want to change one. Here is an example:

```
$a = new DB_File::HASHINFO ;
$a->{'cachesize'} =  12345 ;
tie %y, 'DB_File', "filename", $flags, 0777, $a ;
```

A few of the options need extra discussion here. When used, the C equivalent of the keys hash, compare, and prefix stores pointers to C functions. In DB_File, these keys are used to store references to Perl subs. Here are templates for each of the subs:

```
sub hash
{
    my ($data) = @_ ;
    ...
    # return the hash value for $data
    return $hash ;
}

sub compare
{
    my ($key, $key2) = @_ ;
    ...
    # return  0 if $key1 eq $key2
    #        -1 if $key1 lt $key2
    #         1 if $kcy1 gt $key2
    return (-1 , 0 or 1) ;
}

sub prefix
{
```

```
        my ($key, $key2) = @_ ;
        ...
        # return number of bytes of $key2 which are
        # necessary to determine that it is greater
        # than $key1
        return $bytes ;
    }
```

See the "Changing the BTREE Sort Order" section for an example of using the compare template. If you are using the DB_RECNO interface and you intend to use bval, you should check the "The bval Option" section.

Default Parameters   You can omit some or all of the final four parameters in the call to tie and let them take default values. Because DB_HASH is the most common file format used, the call

```
    tie %A, "DB_File", "filename" ;
```

is equivalent to:

```
    tie %A, "DB_File", "filename",
            O_CREAT|O_RDWR, 0666, $DB_HASH ;
```

You can also omit the *filename* parameter, so the call

```
    tie %A, "DB_File" ;
```

is equivalent to:

```
    tie %A, "DB_File", undef, O_CREAT|O_RDWR, 0666, $DB_HASH ;
```

In-Memory Databases   Berkeley DB allows the creation of in-memory databases by using NULL (that is, a (char *) 0 in C) in place of the filename. DB_File uses undef instead of NULL to provide this functionality.

DB_HASH

The DB_HASH file format is probably the most commonly used of the three file formats that DB_File supports. It is also very straightforward to use.

A Simple Example   This example shows how to create a database, add key/value pairs to the database, delete key/value pairs, and, finally, how to enumerate the contents of the database:

```
    use strict;
    use DB_File;
    use vars qw( %h $k $v );
```

```
tie %h, "DB_File", "fruit", O_RDWR|O_CREAT, 0640, $DB_HASH
            or die "Cannot open file 'fruit': $!\n";

# Add a few key/value pairs to the file
$h{"apple"} = "red";
$h{"orange"} = "orange";
$h{"banana"} = "yellow";
$h{"tomato"} = "red";

# Check for existence of a key
print "Banana Exists\n\n" if $h{"banana"} ;

# Delete a key/value pair.
delete $h{"apple"} ;

# print the contents of the file
while (($k, $v) = each %h)
  { print "$k -> $v\n" }

untie %h ;
```

Here is the output:

```
Banana Exists

orange -> orange
tomato -> red
banana -> yellow
```

Note that, like a Perl hash, the keys are retrieved in an apparently random order.

DB_BTREE

The DB_BTREE format is useful when you want to store data in a given order. By default, the keys are stored in lexical order; however, as you will see from the example shown in the next section, it is easy to define your own sorting function.

Changing the *BTREE* Sort Order   This script shows how to override the default sorting algorithm that BTREE uses. Instead of using the normal lexical ordering, a case-insensitive compare function is used:

```
use strict;
use DB_File;
```

```perl
my %h;

sub Compare
{
    my ($key1, $key2) = @_;
    "\L$key1" cmp "\L$key2";
}

# specify the Perl sub that will do the comparison
$DB_BTREE->{'compare'} = \&Compare;

tie %h, "DB_File",
        "tree", O_RDWR|O_CREAT, 0640, $DB_BTREE
    or die "Cannot open file 'tree': $!\n";

# Add a key/value pair to the file
$h{'Wall'}  = 'Larry';
$h{'Smith'} = 'John';
$h{'mouse'} = 'mickey';
$h{'duck'}  = 'donald';

# Delete
delete $h{"duck"} ;

# Cycle through the keys printing them in order.
# Note it is not necessary to sort the keys as
# the btree will have kept them in order
# automatically.
foreach (keys %h)
  { print "$_\n" }

untie %h ;
```

Here is the output from the previous code:

```
mouse
Smith
Wall
```

Bear the following points in mind if you want to change the order in a BTREE database:

▶ The new compare function must be specified when you create the database.

▶ You cannot change the order once the database has been created. Therefore, you must use the same compare function every time you access the database.

Handling Duplicate Keys   The BTREE file type optionally allows a single key to be associated with an arbitrary number of values. You enable this option by setting the flags element $DB_BTREE to R_DUP when you create the database.

Using the tied hash interface when you want to manipulate a BTREE database with duplicate keys can be difficult. Consider this code:

```
use strict;
use DB_File;

use vars qw($filename %h );

$filename = "tree";
unlink $filename;

# Enable duplicate records
$DB_BTREE->{'flags'} = R_DUP;

tie %h, "DB_File", $filename, O_RDWR|O_CREAT, 0640,
        $DB_BTREE
    or die "Cannot open $filename: $!\n";

# Add some key/value pairs to the file
$h{'Wall'} = 'Larry';
$h{'Wall'} = 'Brick'; # Note the duplicate key
$h{'Wall'} = 'Brick'; # Note duplicate key & value
$h{'Smith'} = 'John';
$h{'mouse'} = 'mickey';

# iterate through the associative array
# and print each key/value pair.
foreach (keys %h)
  { print "$_  -> $h{$_}\n" }

untie %h ;
```

Here is the output:

```
Smith    -> John
Wall     -> Larry
Wall     -> Larry
Wall     -> Larry
mouse    -> mickey
```

As you can see, three records have been successfully created with key Wall. The only problem is that when they are retrieved from the database, they *seem* to have the same value: Larry. The problem is caused by the way the associative array interface works. Basically, when the associative array interface is used to fetch the value associated with a given key, it retrieves only the first value.

Although it may not be immediately obvious from the previous code, the associative array interface can be used to write values with duplicate keys, but it cannot be used to read them back from the database. You can get around this problem by using the Berkeley DB API method called seq. This method allows sequential access to key/value pairs. See the "The API Interface" section for details about both the seq method and the API. Here is the previous script rewritten using the seq API method:

```
use strict;
use DB_File;

use vars qw($filename $x %h $status $key $value);

$filename = "tree";
unlink $filename;

# Enable duplicate records
$DB_BTREE->{'flags'} = R_DUP;

$x = tie %h, "DB_File", $filename, O_RDWR|O_CREAT,
                        0640, $DB_BTREE
    or die "Cannot open $filename: $!\n";

# Add some key/value pairs to the file
$h{'Wall'} = 'Larry';
$h{'Wall'} = 'Brick'; # Note the duplicate key
$h{'Wall'} = 'Brick'; # Note duplicate key & value
$h{'Smith'} = 'John';
$h{'mouse'} = 'mickey';

# iterate through the btree using seq
# and print each key/value pair.
$key = $value = 0;
for ($status = $x->seq($key, $value, R_FIRST);
     $status == 0;
     $status = $x->seq($key, $value, R_NEXT) )
  { print "$key -> $value\n" }

undef $x;
untie %h;
```

It will print the following:

```
Smith   -> John
Wall    -> Brick
Wall    -> Brick
Wall    -> Larry
mouse   -> mickey
```

This time you have all the key/value pairs, including the multiple values associated with the key Wall.

Utility Methods

To make life easier when dealing with duplicate keys, DB_File comes with a few utility methods.

The *get_dup()* Method   The get_dup method assists in reading duplicate values from BTREE databases. The method can take the following forms:

```
$count = $x->get_dup($key) ;
@list  = $x->get_dup($key) ;
%list  = $x->get_dup($key, 1) ;
```

In a scalar context, the method returns the number of values associated with the key $key. In a list context, it returns all the values that match $key. Note that the values are returned in an apparently random order.

In a list context, if the second parameter is present and evaluates true, the method returns an associative array. The keys of the associative array correspond to the values that matched in the BTREE, and the values of the array are a count of the number of times that particular value occurred in the BTREE.

Assuming the previously created database, you can use get_dup as in the following code:

```
my $cnt  = $x->get_dup("Wall") ;
print "Wall occurred $cnt times\n" ;

my %hash = $x->get_dup("Wall", 1) ;
print "Larry is there\n" if $hash{'Larry'} ;
print "There are $hash{'Brick'} Brick Walls\n" ;

my @list = $x->get_dup("Wall") ;
print "Wall =>      [@list]\n" ;
```

```
@list = $x->get_dup("Smith") ;
print "Smith =>     [@list]\n" ;

@list = $x->get_dup("Dog") ;
print "Dog =>       [@list]\n" ;
```

It prints the following:

```
Wall occurred 3 times
Larry is there
There are 2 Brick Walls
Wall =>       [Brick Brick Larry]
Smith =>      [John]
Dog =>        []
```

The *find_dup()* Method

```
$status = $X->find_dup($key, $value) ;
```

This method checks for the existence of a specific key/value pair. If the pair exists, the cursor is left pointing to the pair, and the method returns 0. Otherwise, the method returns a nonzero value.

Assuming the database from the previous example, consider the following code:

```
use strict ;
use DB_File ;

use vars qw($filename $x %h $found) ;

my $filename = "tree" ;

# Enable duplicate records
$DB_BTREE->{'flags'} = R_DUP ;

$x = tie %h, "DB_File", $filename, O_RDWR|O_CREAT,
            0640, $DB_BTREE
    or die "Cannot open $filename: $!\n";

$found = ( $x->find_dup("Wall", "Larry") == 0 ? ""
                                           : "not") ;
print "Larry Wall is $found there\n" ;

$found = ( $x->find_dup("Wall", "Harry") == 0 ? ""
                                           : "not") ;
print "Harry Wall is $found there\n" ;

undef $x ;
untie %h ;
```

It prints the following:

```
Larry Wall is there
Harry Wall is not there
```

The *del_dup()* Method

```
$status = $X->del_dup($key, $value) ;
```

This method deletes a specific key/value pair. It returns 0 if they exist and have been deleted successfully. Otherwise, the method returns a nonzero value.

Again, assume the existence of the tree database:

```
use strict;
use DB_File;

use vars qw($filename $x %h $found);

my $filename = "tree";

# Enable duplicate records
$DB_BTREE->{'flags'} = R_DUP;

$x = tie %h, "DB_File", $filename, O_RDWR|O_CREAT,
            0640, $DB_BTREE
    or die "Cannot open $filename: $!\n";

$x->del_dup("Wall", "Larry");

$found = ( $x->find_dup("Wall", "Larry") == 0 ? ""
                                              : "not");
print "Larry Wall is $found there\n";

undef $x;
untie %h;
```

This code prints the following:

```
Larry Wall is not there
```

Matching Partial Keys

The BTREE interface has a feature that allows partial keys to be matched. This functionality is available *only* when the seq method is used with the R_CURSOR flag. For example:

```
$x->seq($key, $value, R_CURSOR) ;
```

Here is the relevant quote from the dbopen man page, which defines the use of the R_CURSOR flag with seq: *"For the DB_BTREE access method, the returned key is not necessarily an exact match for the specified key. The returned key is the smallest key greater than or equal to the specified key, permitting partial key matches and range searches."*

In the following example script, the match sub uses this feature to find and print the first matching key/value pair given a partial key:

```perl
use strict;
use DB_File;
use Fcntl;

use vars qw($filename $x %h $st $key $value);

sub match
{
    my $key = shift;
    my $value = 0;
    my $orig_key = $key;
    $x->seq($key, $value, R_CURSOR);
    print "$orig_key\t-> $key\t-> $value\n";
}

$filename = "tree";
unlink $filename;

$x = tie %h, "DB_File", $filename, O_RDWR|O_CREAT,
            0640, $DB_BTREE
    or die "Cannot open $filename: $!\n";

# Add some key/value pairs to the file
$h{'mouse'} = 'mickey';
$h{'Wall'} = 'Larry';
$h{'Walls'} = 'Brick';
$h{'Smith'} = 'John';

$key = $value = 0;
print "IN ORDER\n";
for ($st = $x->seq($key, $value, R_FIRST);
     $st == 0;
     $st = $x->seq($key, $value, R_NEXT) )

   { print "$key -> $value\n" }

print "\nPARTIAL MATCH\n" ;
```

```
        match "Wa";
        match "A";
        match "a";

        undef $x;
        untie %h;
```

Here is the output:

```
IN ORDER
Smith -> John
Wall  -> Larry
Walls -> Brick
mouse -> mickey

PARTIAL MATCH
Wa -> Wall  -> Larry
A  -> Smith -> John
a  -> mouse -> mickey
```

DB_RECNO

DB_RECNO provides an interface to flat text files. Both variable-length and fixed-length records are supported. In order to make RECNO more compatible with Perl, the array offset for all RECNO arrays begins at 0 rather than 1, as in Berkeley DB. As with normal Perl arrays, a RECNO array can be accessed using negative indexes. The index −1 refers to the last element of the array, −2 the second to the last, and so on. Attempting to access an element before the start of the array will cause a fatal runtime error.

The *bval* Option   The operation of the bval option warrants some discussion. Here is the definition of bval from the Berkeley DB 1.85 recno manual page: *"The delimiting byte to be used to mark the end of a record for variable-length records, and the pad character for fixed-length records. If no value is specified, newlines ("\n") are used to mark the end of variable-length records and fixed-length records are padded with spaces."*

The second sentence is wrong. In fact, bval defaults to "\n" only when the openinfo parameter in dbopen is NULL. If a non-NULL openinfo parameter is used, the value that happens to be in bval is used. That means you must always specify bval when using any of the options in the openinfo parameter. This documentation error will be fixed in the next release of Berkeley DB.

Now that Berkeley DB is clarified, what about DB_File? The behavior defined in the previous quote is quite useful, so DB_File conforms to it.

You can specify other options (e.g., cachesize) and still have bval default to "\n" for variable-length records and default to space for fixed-length records.

A Simple Example   Here is a simple example that uses RECNO (if you are using a version of Perl prior to 5.004_57, this example won't work; see the "Extra *RECNO* Methods" section for a workaround):

```
use strict ;
use DB_File ;

my @h ;
tie @h, "DB_File", "text", O_RDWR|O_CREAT, 0640,
        $DB_RECNO
    or die "Cannot open file 'text': $!\n" ;

# Add a few key/value pairs to the file
$h[0] = "orange" ;
$h[1] = "blue" ;
$h[2] = "yellow" ;

push @h, "green", "black" ;

my $elements = scalar @h ;
print "The array contains $elements entries\n" ;

my $last = pop @h ;
print "popped $last\n" ;

unshift @h, "white" ;
my $first = shift @h ;
print "shifted $first\n" ;

# Check for existence of a key
print "Element 1 Exists with value $h[1]\n"
    if $h[1] ;

# use a negative index
print "The last element is $h[-1]\n" ;
print "The 2nd last element is $h[-2]\n" ;

untie @h ;
```

Here is the output from the script:

```
The array contains 5 entries
popped black
```

```
unshifted white
Element 1 Exists with value blue
The last element is green
The 2nd last element is yellow
```

Extra *RECNO* Methods   If you are using a version of Perl earlier than 5.004_57, the tied array interface is quite limited. In the previous example script, push, pop, shift, and unshift would not work with a tied array, nor would you be able to determine the array length of a tied array.

To make the interface more useful for older versions of Perl, a number of methods are supplied with DB_File to simulate the missing array operations. All these methods are accessed via the object returned from the tie call. Here are the methods:

```
$X->push(list);
```

Pushes the elements of list to the end of the array.

```
$value = $X->pop;
```

Removes and returns the last element of the array.

```
$X->shift
```

Removes and returns the first element of the array.

```
$X->unshift(list);
```

Pushes the elements of list to the start of the array.

```
$X->length
```

Returns the number of elements in the array.

Another Example   Here is a more complete example that uses some of the previously described methods. It also uses the API interface directly (see the "The API Interface" section).

```
use strict ;
use vars qw(@h $H $file $i) ;
use DB_File ;
use Fcntl ;

$file = "text" ;

unlink $file ;

$H = tie @h, "DB_File", $file, O_RDWR|O_CREAT,
               0640, $DB_RECNO
    or die "Cannot open file $file: $!\n" ;
```

```
# first create a text file to play with
$h[0] = "zero" ;
$h[1] = "one" ;
$h[2] = "two" ;
$h[3] = "three" ;
$h[4] = "four" ;


# Print the records in order.
#
# The length method is needed here
# because evaluating a tied
# array in a scalar context does
# not return the number of
# elements in the array.

print "\nORIGINAL\n" ;
foreach $i (0 .. $H->length - 1) {
    print "$i: $h[$i]\n" ;
}

# use the push & pop methods
$a = $H->pop ;
$H->push("last") ;
print "\nThe last record was [$a]\n" ;

# and the shift & unshift methods
$a = $H->shift ;
$H->unshift("first") ;
print "The first record was [$a]\n" ;

# Use the API to add a new record after record 2.
$i = 2 ;
$H->put($i, "Newbie", R_IAFTER) ;

# and a new record before record 1.
$i = 1 ;
$H->put($i, "New One", R_IBEFORE) ;

# delete record 3
$H->del(3) ;

# now print the records in reverse order
print "\nREVERSE\n" ;
for ($i = $H->length - 1 ; $i >= 0 ; - $i)
  { print "$i: $h[$i]\n" }
```

```
# same again, but use the API functions instead
print "\nREVERSE again\n" ;
my ($s, $k, $v) = (0, 0, 0) ;
for ($s = $H->seq($k, $v, R_LAST) ;
        $s == 0 ;
        $s = $H->seq($k, $v, R_PREV))
  { print "$k: $v\n" }

undef $H ;
untie @h ;
```

This is what it outputs:

```
ORIGINAL
0: zero
1: one
2: two
3: three
4: four

The last record was [four]
The first record was [zero]

REVERSE
5: last
4: three
3: Newbie
2: one
1: New One
0: first

REVERSE again
5: last
4: three
3: Newbie
2: one
1: New One
0: first
```

The API Interface

In addition to accessing Berkeley DB using a tied hash or array, you can also directly use most of the API functions defined in the Berkeley DB documentation. To do this you need to store a copy of the object returned from the tie:

```
$db = tie %hash, "DB_File", "filename" ;
```

Once you have done that, you can access the Berkeley DB API functions as DB_File methods directly like this:

```
$db->put($key, $value, R_NOOVERWRITE) ;
```

If you saved a copy of the object returned from tie, the underlying database file will *not* be closed until the tied variable is untied *and* all copies of the saved object are destroyed:

```
use DB_File ;
$db = tie %hash, "DB_File", "filename"
    or die "Cannot tie filename: $!" ;
...
undef $db ;
untie %hash ;
```

All the functions defined in the dbopen man page—except close() and dbopen()—are available. The DB_File method interface to the supported functions has been implemented to mirror the way Berkeley DB works whenever possible. In particular, note that:

▶ The methods return a status value. All methods return 0 on success. All methods return −1 to signify an error and set $! to the exact error code. The return code 1 generally (but not always) means the key specified did not exist in the database. Other return codes are defined. Refer to the following and to the Berkeley DB documentation for details. The Berkeley DB documentation should be used as the definitive source.

▶ When a Berkeley DB function returns data via one of its parameters, the equivalent DB_File method does exactly the same.

▶ If you are careful, you can mix API calls with the tied hash/array interface in the same piece of code. Although only a few of the methods used to implement the tied interface currently use the cursor, you should always assume that the cursor has been changed any time the tied hash/array interface is used. As an example, this code will probably not do what you expect:

```
$X = tie %x, 'DB_File', $filename, O_RDWR|O_CREAT, 0777,
        $DB_BTREE
    or die "Cannot tie $filename: $!" ;

# Get the first key/value pair and set the cursor
$X->seq($key, $value, R_FIRST) ;

# this line will modify the cursor
$count = scalar keys %x ;
```

```
# Get the second key/value pair.
# oops, it didn't, it got the last key/value pair!
$X->seq($key, $value, R_NEXT) ;
```

The previous code can be rearranged to get around the problem, like this:

```
$X = tie %x, 'DB_File', $filename, O_RDWR|O_CREAT, 0777,
        $DB_BTREE
    or die "Cannot tie $filename: $!" ;

# this line will modify the cursor
$count = scalar keys %x ;

# Get the first key/value pair and set the cursor
$X->seq($key, $value, R_FIRST) ;

# Get the second key/value pair.
# worked this time.
$X->seq($key, $value, R_NEXT) ;
```

All the constants defined in the dbopen man page for use in the flags parameters in the following defined methods are also available. Refer to the Berkeley DB documentation for the precise meaning of the flags values.

Here is a list of the methods available:

```
$status = $X->get($key, $value [, $flags]) ;
```

Given a key, reads the value associated with it from the database. The value read from the database is returned in the $value parameter. If the key does not exist, the method returns 1. No flags are currently defined for this method.

```
$status = $X->put($key, $value [, $flags]) ;
```

Stores the key/value pair in the database. If you use either the R_IAFTER or R_IBEFORE flag, the $key parameter has the record number of the inserted key/value pair set. Valid flags are R_CURSOR, R_IAFTER, R_IBEFORE, R_NOOVERWRITE, and R_SETCURSOR.

```
$status = $X->del($key [, $flags]) ;
```

Removes all key/value pairs with key $key from the database. A return code of 1 means the requested key was not in the database. R_CURSOR is the only valid flag at present.

```
$status = $X->fd ;
```

Returns the file descriptor for the underlying database.

```
$status = $X->seq($key, $value, $flags) ;
```

Allows sequential retrieval from the database. See the dbopen man page for full details. Both the *$key* and *$value* parameters are set to the key/value pair read from the database. The flags parameter is mandatory. The valid flag values are R_CURSOR, R_FIRST, R_LAST, R_NEXT, and R_PREV.

```
$status = $X->sync([$flags]);
```

Flushes any cached buffers to disk. R_RECNOSYNC is the only valid flag at present.

diagnostics

diagnostics tells Perl to give more-verbose, helpful error messages for help in debugging.

Synopsis

```
use warnings;
use diagnostics;
```

Description

The diagnostics pragma makes Perl give longer error messages. You won't usually have this pragma in production code, but it can be a blessing during debugging. For instance, the following code has an error that will be caught because of warnings (see the warnings pragma):

```
use warnings;
$name = "Larry";
print $nam;         # Oops, $nam instead of $name

Name "main::nam" used only once: possible typo at line 3.
Use of uninitialized value in print at line 3.
```

After adding the use diagnostics directive, the output is even more helpful:

```
Name "main::nam" used only once: possible typo at line 3
    (W once) Typographical errors often show up as unique
    variable names.  If you had a good reason for having
    a unique name, then just mention it again somehow to
    suppress the message.  The our declaration is provided
    for this purpose.
```

```
Use of uninitialized value in print at line 3
(W uninitialized) An undefined value was used as if
it were already defined.  It was interpreted as a ""
or a 0, but maybe it was a mistake.  To suppress this
warning assign a defined value to your variables.

To help you figure out what was undefined, perl tells
you what operation you used the undefined value in.
Note, however, that perl optimizes your program and the
operation displayed in the warning may not necessarily
appear literally in your program.  For example, "that
$foo" is usually optimized into "that " . $foo, and the
warning will refer to the concatenation (.) operator,
even though there is no . in your program.
```

Note that it's not necessary to modify your code to use the diagnostics pragma. You can use the -M command-line switch to invoke it as you run your program:

```
perl -Mdiagnostics myprogram.pl
```

Functions

The enable() and disable() functions allow you to enable and disable the expanded diagnostics at runtime.

Notes

Using the diagnostics pragma automatically enables Perl's warnings.

The no directive does not work with diagnostics.

See Also

The warnings and strict pragmas.

DirHandle

DirHandle is an alternative interface for accessing and reading filesystem directory information.

Synopsis

```
use DirHandle;
  $d = new DirHandle ".";
if (defined $d) {
```

```
    while (defined($_ = $d->read)) {
      something($_);
    }
    $d->rewind;
    while (defined($_ = $d->read)) {
      something_else($_);
    }
  undef $d;
  }
```

Description

The DirHandle method provides an alternative interface to the opendir(), closedir(), readdir(), and rewinddir() functions. The only objective benefit to using DirHandle is that it prevents namespace pollution by creating globs to hold directory handles.

English

English provides easy-to-read aliases for Perl's cryptic punctuation variables.

Synopsis

```
use English;
$str =~ /(Larry|Curly|Moe)/;
$stooge = $MATCH;
```

Description

Perl's punctuation variables can be confusing to read in your code. If you can't remember that $. is the number of lines you've read from a file, then the English module lets you rename the variable to $INPUT_LINE_NUMBER. Table C.1 lists some of the aliases created by the English module.

TABLE C.1:   Common English Aliases

Short	Use English	Meaning
$&	$MATCH	String matched by the last successful pattern match.
$`	$PREMATCH	String preceding the last successful pattern match.
$'	$POSTMATCH	String following the last successful pattern match.

TABLE C.1 continued: Common English Aliases

Short	Use English	Meaning
$+	$LAST_PAREN_MATCH	Text matched by the last bracket of the last successful search pattern.
$.	$NR $INPUT_LINE_NUMBER	Current line number for the last filehandle accessed.
$/	$RS $INPUT_RECORD_SEPARATOR	Input record separator. This is \n by default.
$|	$OUTPUT_AUTOFLUSH	If nonzero, doesn't buffer output to the currently selected filehandle.
$,	$OFS $OUTPUT_FIELD_SEPARATOR	String put between the elements of a print statement. Typically this is an empty string.
$\	$ORS $OUTPUT_RECORD_SEPARATOR	String put at the end of a print statement. Typically this is an empty string.
$?	$CHILD_ERROR	Status of the last external program, usually from a backtick command or the system() operator.
$!	$ERRNO $OS_ERROR	Error code from the last system or library call. It is meaningful only immediately after a failed call.
$@	$EVAL_ERROR	Perl syntax error message from the last eval() operator.
$$	$PID $PROCESS_ID	Process number of the script that's being run.
$0	$PROGRAM_NAME	Name of the program currently being run.
$^O	$OSNAME	Name of the operating system you're running under.
$^T	$BASETIME	Time at which the program started running, in seconds since the beginning of 1970.
$^W	$WARNING	Tells whether warnings are enabled.

Caveats

Using the English module can create severe inefficiencies with code that relies heavily on regular expressions. If your code is bottlenecked in regular expressions, you can tell English to not import $MATCH, $PREMATCH, and $POSTMATCH, which eliminates these inefficiencies. Invoke the English module like so:

```
use English '-no_match_vars';
```

Env

Using Env enables a more convenient and familiar way to reference environment variables.

Synopsis

```
use Env;
use Env qw(PATH HOME TERM);
```

Description

Perl maintains environment variables in a pseudo-hash named %ENV. When this access method is inconvenient, you can use the Perl module Env to treat environment variables as simple variables.

The Env::import() function ties environment variables with suitable names to global Perl variables with the same names. By default, it does so with all existing environment variables (keys %ENV). If the import function receives arguments, it treats them like a list of environment variables to tie; it's okay if they don't yet exist.

After an environment variable is tied, use it like a normal variable. You can access its value

```
@path = split(/:/, $PATH);
```

or modify it

```
$PATH .= ":.";
```

as you like. To remove a tied environment variable from the environment, assign it the undefined value:

```
undef $PATH;
```

File::Basename

This module provides ways to extract name and path information from complete file paths.

Synopsis

```
use File::Basename;

($name,$path,$suffix) = fileparse($fullname,@suffixlist)
fileparse_set_fstype($os_string);
$basename = basename($fullname,@suffixlist);
$dirname = dirname($fullname);

($name,$path,$suffix) =
    fileparse("lib/File/Basename.pm","\.pm");
fileparse_set_fstype("VMS");
$basename = basename("lib/File/Basename.pm",".pm");
$dirname = dirname("lib/File/Basename.pm");
```

Description

These routines allow you to parse file specifications into useful pieces using the syntax of different operating systems.

fileparse_set_fstype   You select the syntax via the routine fileparse_set_fstype(). If the argument passed to it contains one of the substrings VMS, MSDOS, MacOS, AmigaOS, or MSWin32, the file specification syntax of that operating system is used in future calls to fileparse(), basename(), and dirname(). If it contains none of these substrings, Unix syntax is used. The pattern matching is case-insensitive. If you selected VMS syntax and the file specification you pass to one of these routines contains a /, the routine assumes you are using Unix emulation and applies the Unix syntax rules instead—for that function call only. If the argument passed to it contains one of the substrings VMS, MSDOS, MacOS, AmigaOS, os2, MSWin32, or RISCOS, the pattern matching for suffix removal is performed without regard to case, because those systems are not case-sensitive when opening existing files (although some of them preserve case on file creation). If you haven't called fileparse_set_fstype(), the syntax is chosen by examining the built-in variable $^O according to these rules.

fileparse   The fileparse() routine divides a file specification into three parts: a leading path, a filename, and a suffix. The path contains everything up to and including the last directory separator in the input file specification. The remainder of the input file specification is then divided into name and suffix based on the optional patterns you specify in @*suffixlist*. Each element of this list is interpreted as a regular expression and is matched against the end of *name*. If this succeeds, the matching portion of *name* is removed and prepended to the suffix. By properly using @suffixlist, you can remove file types or versions for examination.

If you concatenate *path*, *name*, and *suffix* in that order, the result denotes the same file as the input file specification.

Here's an example of Unix file syntax:

```
($base,$path,$type) = fileparse('/virgil/aeneid/draft.book7',
                                '\.book\d+');
```

It yields the following:

```
$base eq 'draft'
$path eq '/virgil/aeneid/',
$type eq '.book7'
```

Similarly, here's an example of VMS syntax:

```
($name,$dir,$type) = fileparse('Doc_Root:[Help]Rhetoric.Rnh',
                               '\..*');
```

It yields:

```
$name eq 'Rhetoric'
$dir  eq 'Doc_Root:[Help]'
$type eq '.Rnh'
```

basename   The basename() routine returns the first element of the list produced by calling fileparse() with the same arguments, except that it always quotes metacharacters in the given suffixes. It is provided for program compatibility with the Unix shell command basename(1).

dirname   The dirname() routine returns the directory portion of the input file specification. When using VMS or MacOS syntax, the result of the routine is identical to the second element of the list produced by calling fileparse() with the same input file specification. (Under VMS, if there is no directory information in the input file specification, then the current default device and directory are returned.) When using Unix or MS-DOS syntax, the return value conforms to the behavior of the Unix shell command dirname(1). This is usually the same as the behavior of fileparse(), but it differs in some cases. For example, for the input file specification lib/, fileparse() considers the directory name to be lib/, and dirname() considers the directory name to be a dot (.).

The dirname command runs a variety of file-test checks on directory trees.

File::CheckTree

This module performs standard file-test operations on one or more files.

Synopsis

```
use File::CheckTree;

$warnings += validate( q{
    /vmunix                 -e || die
    /boot                   -e || die
    /bin                    cd
        csh                 -ex
        csh                 !-ug
        sh                  -ex
        sh                  !-ug
    /usr                    -d || warn "What happened
                            ➥to $file?\n"
});
```

Description

The validate() routine takes a single multiline string consisting of lines containing a filename plus a file test to try on it. (The file test may also be a cd, causing subsequent relative filenames to be interpreted relative to that directory.) After the file test you can put || die to make it a fatal error if the file test fails. The default is || warn. The file test can optionally have a ! prepended to test for the opposite condition. If you perform a cd and then list some relative filenames, you may want to indent them slightly for readability. If you supply your own die() or warn() message, you can use $file to interpolate the filename.

File tests can be bunched: -rwx tests for -r, -w, and -x. Only the first failed test of the bunch will produce a warning.

The routine returns the number of warnings issued.

File::Compare

This module tests two files to see if they are the same.

Synopsis

```
use File::Compare;
```

```
if (compare("file1","file2") == 0) {
    print "They're equal\n";
}
```

Description

The File::Compare::compare function compares the contents of two sources, each of which can be a file or a filehandle. It is exported from File::Compare by default.

File::Compare::cmp is a synonym for File::Compare::compare. It is exported from File::Compare only by request.

Returns

File::Compare::compare returns 0 if the files are equal, 1 if the files are unequal, or −1 if an error was encountered.

File::Copy

This module copies or moves a file specified using a string filename or a filehandle.

Synopsis

```
use File::Copy;

copy("file1","file2");
copy("Copy.pm",\*STDOUT);
move("/dev1/fileA","/dev2/fileB");

use POSIX;
use File::Copy cp;

$n=FileHandle->new("/dev/null","r");
cp($n,"x");
```

Description

The File::Copy module provides two basic functions: copy and move, which are useful for getting the contents of a file from one place to another. The copy function takes two parameters: a file from which to copy and a file to which to copy. Either argument can be a string, a FileHandle reference, or a FileHandle glob. Obviously, if the first argument is a filehandle, it will be read from. If it is a filename, it will be opened for reading. Likewise, the second argument will be created if necessary and written to.

NOTE

Passing files as handles instead of names may cause information to be lost on some operating systems. You should use filenames whenever possible. Files are opened in binary mode where applicable. To obtain consistent behavior when copying from a filehandle to a file, use `binmode` on the filehandle.

You can use an optional third parameter to specify the buffer size used for copying. This parameter is the number of bytes from the first file that are held in memory at any given time before being written to the second file. The default buffer size depends on the file, but it will generally be the whole file (up to 2MB) or 1KB for filehandles that do not reference files (such as sockets).

You can use the syntax use `File::Copy "cp"` to get at the cp alias for this function. The syntax is the same.

The move function also takes two parameters: the current name and the intended name of the file to be moved. If the destination is a directory that already exists and the source is not a directory, the source file is renamed into the directory specified by the destination.

If possible, move simply renames the file. Otherwise, it copies the file to the new location and deletes the original. If an error occurs during this copy-and-delete process, you may be left with a copy or possibly a partial copy of the file under the destination name. You can use the mv alias for this function the same way you use the cp alias for copy.

`File::Copy` also provides the syscopy routine, which copies the file specified in the first parameter to the file specified in the second parameter—preserving OS-specific attributes and file structure. For Unix systems, this is equivalent to the simple copy routine. For VMS systems, this calls the rmscopy routine. For OS/2 systems, this calls the syscopy XSUB directly.

Returns

All functions return 1 on success and 0 on failure. $! is set if an error was encountered.

File::DosGlob

This module implements DOS-like globbing with a few enhancements.

Synopsis

```
require 5.004;

# override CORE::glob in current package
use File::DosGlob 'glob';

# override CORE::glob in ALL packages
# (use with extreme caution!)
use File::DosGlob 'GLOBAL_glob';

@perlfiles = glob  "..\\pe?l/*.p?";
print <..\\pe?l/*.p?>;

# from the command line (overrides only in main::)
> perl -MFile::DosGlob=glob -e "print <../pe*/*p?>"
```

Description

This module is largely compatible with perlglob.exe (the M$ setargv
.obj version) in all but one respect: It understands wildcards in directory
components. For example, <..\\l*b\\file/*glob.p?> works as expected
(it will find something like ..\lib\File/DosGlob.pm). Note that all
path components are case-insensitive and that backslashes and forward
slashes are both accepted and preserved. You may have to double the
backslashes if you are putting them in literally, due to parsing of the pattern
by Perl.

Spaces in the argument delimit distinct patterns, so glob('*.exe
*.dll') globs all filenames that end in .exe or .dll. If you want to put
literal spaces in the glob pattern, you can escape them with either double
quotes or backslashes—for example, glob('c:/"Program Files"/*/*
.dll'), or glob('c:/Program\ Files/*/*.dll'). The argument
is tokenized using Text::ParseWords::parse_line(), so see the
Text::ParseWords man page for details of the quoting rules used.

File::Find

This module traverses a file tree, optionally depth-first, returning all
filenames that match a set of criteria.

Synopsis

```
use File::Find;
find(\&wanted, '/foo','/bar');
sub wanted { ... }
```

```
use File::Find;
finddepth(\&wanted, '/foo','/bar');
sub wanted { ... }
```

Description

The first argument to find() is either a hash reference describing the operations to be performed for each file, a code reference, or a string that contains a subroutine name. If the argument is a hash reference, the value for the key wanted should be a code reference. This code reference is called the wanted() function.

Currently the only other supported key for the previous hash is bydepth. When it is used, the directory walk-over is performed depth-first. Entry point finddepth() is a shortcut for specifying {bydepth = 1} in the first argument of find().

The wanted() function performs the actions you specify. It's called once for each file (including directories) that find() finds. Usually, you'll have the wanted() function store filenames in an outside array or hash, or print something about the file. $File::Find::dir contains the current directory name, and $_ contains the current filename within that directory. $File::Find::name contains $File::Find::dir/$_. The current working directory is changed to $File::Find::dir when the function is called. The function can set $File::Find::prune to prune the tree.

File::Find assumes that you don't alter the $_ variable. If you do alter it, make sure you return it to its original value before exiting your function.

This library is useful for the find2perl tool, which when fed

```
find2perl / -name .nfs\* -mtime +7 \
    -exec rm -f {} \; -o -fstype nfs -prune
```

produces something like this:

```
sub wanted {
    /^\.nfs.*$/ &&
    (($dev,$ino,$mode,$nlink,$uid,$gid) = lstat($_))
      &&
    int(-M _) > 7 &&
    unlink($_)
    ||
    ($nlink || (($dev,$ino,$mode,$nlink,$uid,$gid) =
      lstat($_))) &&
    $dev < 0 &&
    ($File::Find::prune = 1);
}
```

Set the variable $File::Find::dont_use_nlink if you're using AFS or NFS filesystems.

The finddepth command is similar to find, except that it performs a depth-first search.

Here's another interesting function. It finds all the symlinks that don't resolve:

```
sub wanted {
    -l && !-e && print "bogus link $File::Find::name\n";
}
```

Bugs

There is no way to make find or finddepth follow symlinks.

File::Path

This module creates or removes a series of directories.

Synopsis

```
use File::Path

mkpath(['/foo/bar/baz', 'blurfl/quux'], 1, 0711);

rmtree(['foo/bar/baz', 'blurfl/quux'], 1, 1);
```

Description

The mkpath function provides a convenient way to create directories—even if your mkdir kernel call won't create more than one directory level at a time. The mkpath command takes three arguments:

▶ The name of the path to create or a reference to a list of paths to create

▶ A boolean value, which if true causes mkpath to print the name of each directory as it is created (defaults to false)

▶ The numeric mode to use when creating the directories (defaults to 0777)

It returns a list of all directories (including intermediates determined using the Unix / separator) created.

Similarly, the rmtree function provides a convenient way to delete a subtree from the directory structure, much like the Unix command rm -r. The rmtree command takes three arguments:

▶ The root of the subtree to delete or a reference to a list of roots. All the files and directories below each root, as well as the roots themselves, are deleted.

▶ A boolean value, which if true causes rmtree to print a message (giving the name of the file and indicating whether it's using rmdir or unlink to remove it, or that it's skipping it) each time it examines a file. (Defaults to false.)

▶ A boolean value, which if true causes rmtree to skip any files to which you do not have delete access (if running under VMS) or write access (if running under another OS). In the future, this process will change when a criterion for delete permission under operating systems other than VMS is settled. (Defaults to false.)

It returns the number of files successfully deleted. Symlinks are treated as ordinary files.

NOTE

If the third parameter is not true, rmtree is not secure in the face of failure or interruption. Files and directories that were not deleted may be left with permissions reset to allow world read-and-write access. The occurrence of errors in rmtree is not apparent from the return value and can be determined only by trapping diagnostic messages using $SIG{__WARN__}. Therefore, it is best not to use rmtree($foo, $bar, 0) in situations where security is an issue.

File::Spec

File::Spec allows filenames to be constructed in way that preserves functionality on a number of different operating system platforms.

Synopsis

```
use File::Spec;

$x=File::Spec->catfile('a','b','c');
```

Returns 'a/b/c' under Unix.

Description

This module is designed to support operations commonly performed on file specifications (such as concatenating several directory and filenames into a single path or determining whether a path is rooted). Although `File::Spec` is usually called *filenames*, do not confuse it with the contents of a file or with Perl's filehandles. It is based on code taken directly from Make-Maker 5.17, which is code written by Andreas König, Andy Dougherty, Charles Bailey, Ilya Zakharevich, Paul Schinder, and others.

Because these functions are different for most operating systems, each set of OS specific routines is available in a separate module, including:

```
File::Spec::Unix
File::Spec::Mac
File::Spec::OS2
File::Spec::Win32
File::Spec::VMS
```

The module appropriate for the current OS is automatically loaded by `File::Spec`. Because some modules (like VMS) use OS-specific facilities, it may not be possible to load all modules under all operating systems.

Because `File::Spec` is object-oriented, subroutines should not be called directly, as in:

```
File::Spec::catfile('a','b');
```

They should be called as class methods:

```
File::Spec->catfile('a','b');
```

For a reference of the available functions, consult the `File::Spec::Unix` man page, which contains the entire set of functions, each of which is inherited by the modules for other platforms. For further information, see the `File::Spec::Mac` man page, the `File::Spec::OS2` man page, the `File::Spec::Win32` man page, or the `File::Spec::VMS` man page.

File::Spec::Mac

`File::Spec::Mac` is a subclass of `File::Spec`, which is used for handling file specifications on MacOS.

Synopsis

```
require File::Spec::Mac;
```

Description

These methods are for manipulating file specifications.

Methods

The following methods are available when `File::Spec::MacOS` is used.

canonpath On MacOS, there's nothing to be done. It returns what it's given.

catdir This command concatenates two or more directory names to form a complete path ending with a directory. Put a trailing colon (:) on the end of the complete path if there isn't one, as you would in MacPerl's environment.

The fundamental requirement of this routine is that

```
File::Spec->catdir(split(":",$path)) eq $path
```

Due to the nature of Macintosh paths, you can obtain reasonable results for some common situations by utilizing additional possibilities. Here are the rules:

▶ Each argument must have its trailing : removed.

▶ Each argument, except the first, must have its leading : removed.

▶ They must be joined by a :.

For example:

```
File::Spec->catdir("a","b") = "a:b:"
File::Spec->catdir("a:",":b") = "a:b:"
File::Spec->catdir("a:","b") = "a:b:"
File::Spec->catdir("a",":b") = "a:b"
File::Spec->catdir("a","","b") = "a::b"
```

To obtain a relative path (one beginning with :), begin the first argument with : or put "" as the first argument. If you don't want to worry about these rules, only allow a : at the beginning of the first argument. Never allow a : at the beginning or end of any other arguments.

An additional ambiguity exists under MacPerl. In the following code, does the programmer intend the code to be relative or absolute?

```
File::Spec->catfile("LWP","Protocol","http.pm")
```

There's no way to tell, except by checking for the existence of LWP: or :LWP. The user may mean a dismounted volume or a relative path in a different directory (like in @INC). Because those checks aren't performed here, this routine treats code as absolute.

catfile   This command concatenates one or more directory names and a filename to form a complete path ending with a filename. Because this command uses `catdir`, the same caveats regarding placement of colons apply. Note that the leading : is removed from the filename, so that

```
File::Spec->catfile($ENV{HOME},"file");
```

and

```
File::Spec->catfile($ENV{HOME},":file");
```

give the same answer, as you might expect.

curdir   This command returns a string representing the current directory.

rootdir   This command returns a string representing the root directory. Under MacPerl, it returns the name of the startup volume (because it's the closest in concept, although other volumes aren't rooted there). On any other platform, it returns " " (an empty string), because there's no common way to indicate the root directory across all Macs.

updir   This command returns a string representing the parent directory.

file_name_is_absolute   This command takes a path as its argument and returns true, if the path is an absolute path. When a name can be either relative or absolute (for example, a folder named HD in the current working directory on a drive named HD), relative wins. Use a : in the appropriate place in the path if you want to distinguish without ambiguity.

path   This command returns the null list for the MacPerl application, because the concept is usually meaningless under MacOS. If you're using the MacPerl tool under MPW, it gives back $ENV{Commands} suitably split, as is done in :lib:ExtUtils:MM_Mac.pm.

See Also
The File::Spec man page.

File::Spec::OS2

This module is a subclass of `File::Spec`, which is used for handling file specifications on OS/2.

Synopsis

```
use File::Spec::OS2; # Done by File::Spec if needed
```

Description

See `File::Spec::Unix` for documentation of the methods provided. This package overrides the implementation of these methods, not the semantics.

File::Spec::Unix

This module is a subclass of `File::Spec`, which is used for handling file specifications on Unix.

Synopsis

```
require File::Spec::Unix;
```

Description

These are methods for manipulating file specifications.

Methods

The following methods are available when using `File::Spec::Unix`.

canonpath   This command performs no physical check on the filesystem; however, it performs a logical cleanup of a path. On Unix, it eliminates successive slashes and successive / ..

catdir   This command concatenates two or more directory names to form a complete path ending with a directory. You should remove the trailing slash from the resulting string, because it doesn't look good, isn't necessary, and confuses OS/2. Of course, if this is the root directory, don't cut off the trailing slash.

catfile   This command concatenates one or more directory names and a filename to form a complete path ending with a filename.

curdir   This command returns a string representing the current directory—. on Unix.

rootdir   This command returns a string representing the root directory—/ on Unix.

updir   This command returns a string representing the parent directory—.. on Unix.

no_upwards   Given a list of filenames, this command strips out those that refer to a parent directory. (It does not strip symlinks; it strips only ., .., and equivalents.)

file_name_is_absolute   This command takes a path as its argument and returns true, if the path is an absolute path.

path   This command takes no argument. It returns the environment variable PATH as an array.

join   join is the same as catfile. It concatenates one or more directory names and a filename to form a complete path ending with a filename.

See Also
The File::Spec man page.

File::Spec::VMS

This module is a subclass of File::Spec, which is used for handling file specifications on VMS.

Synopsis
```
use File::Spec::VMS; # Done by File::Spec if needed
```

Description
See File::Spec::Unix for documentation of the methods provided. This package overrides the implementation of these methods, not the semantics.

Methods

The following methods are available when using `File::Spec::VMS`.

catdir   This command concatenates a list of file specifications, and it returns the result as a VMS-syntax directory specification.

catfile   This command concatenates a list of file specifications, and it returns the result as a VMS-syntax directory specification.

curdir (override)   This command returns a string representing the current directory.

rootdir (override)   This command returns a string representing the root directory.

updir (override)   This command returns a string representing the parent directory.

path (override)   This command translates the logical name DCL$PATH as a searchlist, rather than trying to split the string value of $ENV{ *'PATH'* }.

file_name_is_absolute (override)   This command checks for VMS directory specifications and Unix separators.

File::Spec::Win32

This is a subclass of `File::Spec` for handling file specifications on 32-bit Windows.

Synopsis

```
use File::Spec::Win32; # Done by File::Spec if needed
```

Description

See the `File::Spec::Unix` documentation for the methods provided. This package overrides the implementation of these methods, not the semantics.

Methods

The following methods are available when you use `File::Spec::Win32`.

catfile   This command concatenates one or more directory names and a filename to form a complete path ending with a filename.

canonpath   This command does not perform a physical check on the filesystem; however, it does perform a logical cleanup of a path. On Unix, successive slashes and successive / combinations are eliminated.

File::stat

This method is an alternative, object-oriented interface to Perl's built-in stat() function.

Synopsis

```
use File::stat;
$st = stat($file) or die "No $file: $!";
if ( ($st->mode & 0111) && $st->nlink > 1) ) {
    print "$file is executable with lotsa links\n";
}

use File::stat qw(:FIELDS);
stat($file) or die "No $file: $!";
if ( ($st_mode & 0111) && $st_nlink > 1) ) {
    print "$file is executable with lotsa links\n";
}
```

Description

This module's default exports override the core stat() and lstat() functions, replacing them with versions that return File::stat objects. This object has methods that return the similarly named structure field name from the stat(2) function—namely dev, ino, mode, nlink, uid, gid, rdev, size, atime, mtime, ctime, blksize, and blocks.

You can also import all the structure fields directly into your namespace as regular variables using the :FIELDS import tag. (This still overrides your stat() and lstat() functions.) Access these fields as variables named by putting st_ in front of their method names. Thus, $stat_obj->dev() corresponds to $st_dev if you import the fields.

To access this functionality without the core overrides, pass the use an empty import list, and then access functions with their full qualified names. The built-ins are still available via the CORE:: pseudo-package.

NOTE

Although this class currently is implemented using the Class::Struct module to build a class similar to struct, you shouldn't rely on this implementation.

File::Temp

This module conveniently and safely creates temporary files and directories.

Synopsis

```
use File::Temp qw( tempdir tempfile );
$dir = tempdir( "temp-XXXX" );
($fh,$filename) = tempfile( "work-XXXX", DIR=>$dir );
```

Description

File::Temp provides a convenient and, more importantly, safe way to create temporary files and directories. The easiest way is to use the functions tempfile() and tempdir(), respectively.

One of the security problems with the typical way of opening temporary files is that it's possible to have someone else open a file between the time you determine the filename and the time when you actually open the file. File::Temp alleviates this problem by returning both the name of the file and the open filehandle at one time.

File::Temp provides mktemp(), tmpnam(), and tempnam() for compatibility with older programs, but they are not as safe as tempdir() and tempfile().

Functions

tempfile   This is the basic function to create temporary files. Its most simple invocation is

```
($fh, $filename) = tempfile();
```

This creates a temporary file in the directory specified for temporary files by the tmpdir() function in File::Spec. $fh is an open filehandle to the file specified in $filename, so you do not need to open the file.

tempfile() can take many options:

```
my $template = "work-XXXX";
($fh, $filename) = tempfile($template);
```

This form creates a temporary file in the current directory, using the template as a guide. The trailing XXXX characters are replaced with random letters. In this example, the filename might be work-h4Fa. There must be at least four X characters. If you do not specify the template, one is generated for you automatically.

```
my $template = "work-XXXX";
($fh, $filename) = tempfile($template, SUFFIX => ".txt");
```

This form is the same as the previous form, but a suffix is added to the template after the X translation.

```
($fh, $filename) =
    tempfile($template, DIR => "/var/myapp/tmp" );
```

This form specifies the directory where the file should go.

```
($fh, $filename) = tempfile($template, UNLINK => 1);
```

With the UNLINK parameter, the file is automatically deleted at the end of the program.

Of course, all these options can be combined, as in the following:

```
($fh, $filename) =
    tempfile(
        "work-XXXX",
        DIR=>"/var/myapp/tmp",
        EXT=>".ext",
        UNLINK=>1,
    );
```

tempdir   This function creates a temporary directory, much like tempfile(). tempdir() creates the directory, but does not return a handle. Like tempfile(), tempdir() takes a template.

```
$dir = tempdir( "temp-XXXX" );
```

You can specify the directory in which the temporary directory is created by specifying the *DIR* parameter.

```
$dir = tempdir( "temp-XXXX", DIR => "/tmp" );
```

FileCache

This module provides a way to keep more files open than the operating system permits.

Synopsis

```
cacheout $path;
print $path @data;
```

Description

The cacheout function makes sure a filehandle (with the pathname you give it) is open and available for writing. It automatically closes and reopens files if you exceed your system file descriptor maximum.

Bugs

The system header file sys/param.h may have a NOFILE definition that is ignored on some systems, so you may have to set $FileCache::cacheout_ maxopen yourself.

FileHandle

This method is an alternative, object-oriented interface used to manipulate files via filehandles.

Synopsis

```
use FileHandle;

$fh = new FileHandle;
if ($fh->open("< file")) {
    print <$fh>;
    $fh->close;
}

$fh = new FileHandle "> FOO";
if (defined $fh) {
    print $fh "bar\n";
    $fh->close;
}

$fh = new FileHandle "file", "r";
if (defined $fh) {
    print <$fh>;
    undef $fh;      # automatically closes the file
}
```

```
$fh = new FileHandle "file", O_WRONLY|O_APPEND;
if (defined $fh) {
    print $fh "corge\n";
    undef $fh;      # automatically closes the file
}

$pos = $fh->getpos;
$fh->setpos($pos);

$fh->setvbuf($buffer_var, _IOLBF, 1024);

($readfh, $writefh) = FileHandle::pipe;

autoflush STDOUT 1;
```

Description

FileHandle::new creates a FileHandle, which is a reference to a newly created symbol (see the Symbol package). If it receives any parameters, they are passed to FileHandle::open. If the open fails, the FileHandle object is destroyed. Otherwise, it is returned to the caller.

NOTE
This class is a front-end to the IO::* classes.

FileHandle::new_from_fd creates a FileHandle similarly to way new creates one. It requires two parameters, which are passed to FileHandle::fdopen. If the fdopen fails, the FileHandle object is destroyed. Otherwise, it is returned to the caller.

FileHandle::open accepts one or two parameters. With one parameter, it is just a front-end for the built-in open function. With two parameters, the first parameter is a filename that can include whitespace or other special characters, and the second parameter is the open mode, optionally followed by a file permission value.

If FileHandle::open receives a Perl mode string (>, +<, and so on) or a Posix fopen() mode string (w, r+, and so on), it uses the basic Perl open operator.

If FileHandle::open is given a numeric mode, it passes that mode and the optional permissions value to the Perl sysopen operator. For convenience, FileHandle::import tries to import the O_XXX constants from the Fcntl module. If dynamic loading is not available, this import may fail, but the rest of FileHandle will still work.

FileHandle::fdopen is similar to open except that its first parameter is not a filename but rather a filehandle name, a FileHandle object, or a file descriptor number.

If the C functions fgetpos() and fsetpos() are available, then FileHandle::getpos returns an opaque value that represents the current position of the FileHandle, and FileHandle::setpos uses that value to return to a previously visited position.

If the C function setvbuf() is available, then FileHandle::setvbuf sets the buffering policy for the FileHandle. The calling sequence for the Perl function is the same as its C counterpart, including the macros _IOFBF, _IOLBF, and _IONBF, except that the buffer parameter specifies a scalar variable to use as a buffer.

WARNING

A variable used as a buffer by FileHandle::setvbuf must not be modified until the FileHandle is closed or until FileHandle::setvbuf is called again. If it is modified in any way, memory corruption may result.

See the perlfunc man page for complete descriptions of each of the following supported FileHandle methods, which are just front-ends for the corresponding built-in functions:

```
clearerr
close
eof
fileno
getc
gets
seek
tell
```

See the perlvar man page for complete descriptions of each of the following supported FileHandle methods:

```
autoflush
format_formfeed
format_line_break_characters
format_lines_per_page
format_lines_left
format_name
format_page_number
format_top_name
```

```
input_line_number
input_record_separator
output_field_separator
output_record_separator
```

For normal I/O, you might need the following methods.

$fh->print   See the "print" entry in the perlfunc man page.

$fh->printf   See the "printf" entry in the perlfunc man page.

$fh->getline   This method works similarly to <$fh>, which is described in the "I/O Operators" section in the perlop man page. However, it's more readable and can be safely called in an array context and still returns just one line.

$fh->getlines   This method works like <$fh> when it is called in an array context to read the remaining lines in a file; however, it's more readable. It will also croak() if accidentally called in a scalar context.

Many other functions are available, because FileHandle is descended from IO::File, IO::Seekable, and IO::Handle. Refer to those respective pages for documentation on more functions.

FindBin

This command is used to find the full path on the filesystem to the script that's currently running.

Synopsis

```
use FindBin;
use lib "$FindBin::Bin/../lib";
```

or

```
use FindBin qw($Bin);
use lib "$Bin/../lib";
```

Description

This method locates the full path to the script bin directory to allow the use of paths relative to the bin directory. This method allows a user to set up a directory tree for software with directories <root>/bin and <root>/lib. The previous example allows the use of modules in the lib directory without knowing where the software tree is installed. If perl is invoked using the -e option or the perl script is read from STDIN, then FindBin sets both $Bin and $RealBin to the current directory.

Exportable Variables

```
$Bin    - path to bin directory from where script was invoked
$Script - basename of script from which perl was invoked
$RealBin    - $Bin with all links resolved
$RealScript - $Script with all links resolved
```

Known Bugs

If perl is invoked as

```
perl filename
```

and *filename* does not have executable rights and a program called *filename* exists in the user's $ENV{PATH} (which satisfies both -x and -T), then FindBin assumes it was invoked via the $ENV{PATH}. The workaround invokes perl as:

```
perl ./filename
```

Hash::Util

This collection of utility functions helps prevent accidental modification of hashes.

Synopsis

```
$hash{name} = "Larry";
lock_hash( %hash );
$hash{name} = "Randal"; # error!
```

Description

Accidentally modifying hashes can introduce subtle bugs into your code. This is even more insidious when the hash is used as the base type for an object, as most objects do.

Functions

lock_keys(%hash)* and *unlock_keys(%hash)   This function locks and unlocks the set of keys defined in the hash. If the hash's keys are locked, then no keys can be added to the hash. Attempting to do so will throw an error.

lock_value(%hash, $key) **and** ***unlock_value(%hash, $key)***   This function locks and unlocks the value in *%hash* defined by *$key*.

lock_hash(%hash) **and** ***unlock_hash(%hash)***   `lock_hash()` locks an entire hash, making all keys and values read-only. No value can be changed, and no keys can be added or deleted. `unlock_hash()` is the opposite. All keys and values are made read/write. All values can be changed and keys can be added and deleted.

IO

This is a convenient class loader for some of the `IO::*` modules.

Synopsis

```
use IO;
```

Description

IO provides a simple mechanism to load some of the IO modules at once. Currently, it includes:

```
IO::File
IO::Handle
IO::Pipe
IO::Seekable
IO::Socket
```

For more information on any of these modules, refer to its respective documentation.

IO::File

This is an alternative, object-oriented interface used for accessing files. With the addition of autovivified filehandle references in Perl 5.6, this module isn't used as much.

Synopsis

```
use IO::File;
```

```
$fh = new IO::File;
if ($fh->open("< file")) {
    print <$fh>;
    $fh->close;
}

$fh = new IO::File "> file";
if (defined $fh) {
    print $fh "bar\n";
    $fh->close;
}

$fh = new IO::File "file", "r";
if (defined $fh) {
    print <$fh>;
    undef $fh;       # automatically closes the file
}

$fh = new IO::File "file", O_WRONLY|O_APPEND;
if (defined $fh) {
    print $fh "corge\n";

    $pos = $fh->getpos;
    $fh->setpos($pos);

    undef $fh;       # automatically closes the file
}

autoflush STDOUT 1;
```

Description

IO::File inherits from IO::Handle and IO::Seekable. It extends these classes with methods that are specific to filehandles.

Constructors

Either of following constructors may be used to create a new File::IO object.

```
new ([ ARGS ] )
```

This constructor creates an IO::File. If it receives any parameters, they are passed to the method open. If the open fails, the object is destroyed. Otherwise, it is returned to the caller.

```
new_tmpfile
```

This constructor creates an IO::File opened for read/write on a newly created temporary file. On systems where this is possible, the temporary file is anonymous (it is unlinked after creation, but held open). If the temporary file cannot be created or opened, the IO::File object is destroyed. Otherwise, it is returned to the caller.

Methods

The following methods are available when using IO::File.

open(FILENAME [,MODE [,PERMS]])   The open method accepts one, two, or three parameters. With one parameter, it is just a front-end for the built-in open function. With two parameters, the first parameter is a filename that can include whitespace or other special characters, and the second parameter is the open mode, optionally followed by a file permission value.

If IO::File::open receives a Perl mode string (>, +<, and so on) or a Posix fopen() mode string (w, r+, and so on), it uses the basic Perl open operator.

If IO::File::open is given a numeric mode, it passes that mode and the optional permissions value to the Perl sysopen operator. For convenience, IO::File::import tries to import the O_XXX constants from the Fcntl module. If dynamic loading is not available, this may fail, but the rest of IO::File will still work.

See Also

The perlfunc man page, the "I/O Operators" section in the perlop man page, the IO::Handle man page, and the IO::Seekable man page.

IO::Handle

This is an alternative, object-oriented interface for using filehandles.

Synopsis

```
use IO::Handle;

$fh = new IO::Handle;
if ($fh->fdopen(fileno(STDIN),"r")) {
    print $fh->getline;
    $fh->close;
}
```

```
$fh = new IO::Handle;
if ($fh->fdopen(fileno(STDOUT),"w")) {
    $fh->print("Some text\n");
}

use IO::Handle '_IOLBF';
$fh->setvbuf($buffer_var, _IOLBF, 1024);

undef $fh; # automatically closes the file if open

autoflush STDOUT 1;
```

Description

IO::Handle is the base class for all other IO handle classes. Objects of IO::Handle were not intended to be created directly; instead IO::Handle is inherited from several other classes in the IO hierarchy.

If you are looking for a replacement for the FileHandle package, refer to the documentation for IO::File.

An IO::Handle object is a reference to a symbol (see the Symbol package).

Constructors

Either of the following constructors can be used to create a new IO::Handle object:

```
new ()
```

This constructor creates a new IO::Handle object.

```
new_from_fd ( FD, MODE )
```

This constructor creates an IO::Handle similarly to the way new does. It requires two parameters, which are passed to the method fdopen. If the fdopen fails, the object is destroyed. Otherwise, it is returned to the caller.

IO::Pipe

This is an alternative, object-oriented interface used for handling pipes.

Synopsis

```
use IO::Pipe;
```

```
$pipe = new IO::Pipe;

if($pid = fork()) { # Parent
    $pipe->reader();

    while(<$pipe> {
        ....
    }

}
elsif(defined $pid) { # Child
    $pipe->writer();

    print $pipe ....
}

or

$pipe = new IO::Pipe;

$pipe->reader(qw(ls -l));

while(<$pipe>) {
    ....
}
```

Description

IO::Pipe provides an interface for creating pipes between processes.

Constructor

The following constructor is used to create a new IO::Pipe object:

```
new ( [READER, WRITER] )
```

The resulting IO::Pipe is a reference to a newly created symbol (see the Symbol package). IO::Pipe::new optionally takes two arguments, which should be objects blessed into IO::Handle or a subclass thereof. These two objects are used for the system call to pipe. If no arguments are given, the method handles is called on the new IO::Pipe object. These two handles are held in the array part of the glob until either reader or writer is called.

Methods

The following methods are available when using IO::Pipe.

reader ([ARGS])   The object is reblessed into a subclass of IO::Handle, and it becomes a handle at the reading end of the pipe. If *ARGS* are given, fork is called and *ARGS* are passed to exec.

writer ([ARGS])   The object is reblessed into a subclass of IO::Handle, and it becomes a handle at the writing end of the pipe. If *ARGS* are given, fork is called and *ARGS* are passed to exec.

handles ()   This method is called during construction by IO::Pipe:: new on the newly created IO::Pipe object. It returns an array of two objects blessed into IO::Pipe::End, or a subclass thereof.

IO::Seekable

This is a class that supplies seek-based methods to other objects based on IO::Handle.

Synopsis

```
use IO::Seekable;
package IO::Something;
@ISA = qw(IO::Seekable);
```

Description

IO::Seekable does not have a constructor of its own, because it is intended to be inherited by other objects based on IO::Handle. It provides methods that allow seeking of the file descriptors.

If the C functions fgetpos() and fsetpos() are available, then IO:: File::getpos returns an opaque value that represents the current position of the IO::File, and IO::File::setpos uses that value to return to a previously visited position.

See the perlfunc man page for complete descriptions of each of the following supported IO::Seekable methods (which are just front-ends for the corresponding built-in functions):

```
seek
tell
```

IO::Select

This is an object-oriented interface to the select() system call.

Synopsis

```
use IO::Select;

$s = IO::Select->new();

$s->add(\*STDIN);
$s->add($some_handle);

@ready = $s->can_read($timeout);

@ready = IO::Select->new(@handles)->read(0);
```

Description

The IO::Select package implements an object approach to the system select function call. It allows the user to see what IO handles (see the IO::Handle man page) are ready for reading, ready for writing, or have an error condition pending.

Constructor

The following constructor is used to create a new IO::Select object:

```
new ( [ HANDLES ] )
```

It creates a new object and optionally initializes it with a set of handles.

Methods

The following methods are available when using IO::Select.

add (HANDLES)   This method adds the list of handles to the IO::Select object. These values are returned when an event occurs. IO::Select keeps these values in a cache, which is indexed by the fileno of the handle; therefore, if more than one handle with the same fileno is specified, only the last one is cached. Each handle can be an IO::Handle object, an integer, or an array reference where the first element is an IO::Handle or an integer.

remove (HANDLES)   This method removes all the given handles from the object. It also works by using the fileno of the handles. The exact handles that were added do not need to be passed; only handles that have an equivalent fileno need to be passed.

exists (HANDLE) This method returns a true value (actually the handle itself) if the handle is present. It returns undef if the handle does not exist.

handles This method returns an array of all registered handles.

can_read ([TIMEOUT]) This method returns an array of handles that are ready for reading. *TIMEOUT* is the maximum amount of time to wait before returning an empty list. If *TIMEOUT* is not given and any handles are registered, then the call blocks.

can_write ([TIMEOUT]) This is similar to can_read. It also checks for handles that can be written to.

has_error ([TIMEOUT]) This is similar to can_read. It also checks for handles that have an error condition, for example EOF.

count () This method returns the number of handles that the object checks for when one of the can_ methods is called or the object is passed to the select static method.

bits() This method returns the bit string suitable as an argument to the core select call.

select (READ, WRITE, ERROR [, TIMEOUT]) The select method is a static method (that is, you call it with the package name like new). *READ, WRITE,* and *ERROR* are either undef or IO::Select objects. *TIMEOUT* is optional and has the same effect as the core select call.

The result is an array of three elements, each a reference to an array that holds the handles that are ready for reading, are ready for writing, or that have error conditions. Upon error, an empty array is returned.

Example

This short example shows how IO::Select could be used to write to a server that communicates with several sockets while also listening for more connections on a listen socket:

```
use IO::Select;
use IO::Socket;

$lsn = new IO::Socket::INET(Listen => 1,
                            LocalPort => 8080);
```

```
$sel = new IO::Select( $lsn );

while(@ready = $sel->can_read) {
    foreach $fh (@ready) {
        if($fh == $lsn) {
            # Create a new socket
            $new = $lsn->accept;
            $sel->add($new);
        }
        else {
            # Process socket

            # Maybe we have finished the socket
            $sel->remove($fh);
            $fh->close;
        }
    }
}
```

List::Util

This module provides handy routines for common operations with lists.

Synopsis

```
$hightemp = max @temperatures;
$buyprice = min @prices;
```

Description

The utility functions in List::Util arc simple enough that you could probably write them yourself, but it's bettcr to use well-tested code rather than reinvent your own.

Functions

first BLOCK LIST   This function finds the first value in a list that matches some criterion specified in the block. The following finds the first code in the list that is higher than 5000:

```
my @codes = qw( 2112 5150 90125 );
my $biggie = first { $_ > 5000 } @codes;
```

Another great use of first is with objects. For instance, the following finds the first manager in a list of employee objects:

```
$manager = first { $_->is_manager() } @employees;
```

max LIST and min LIST   These functions find the largest and smallest value, respectively, within the list. The comparison is done with numeric comparisons. If the list is empty, they return undef:

```
$price = min @prices; # Find the lowest price
```

maxstr LIST and minstr LIST   These functions find the largest and smallest value, respectively, within the list. The comparison is done with string comparisons. If the list is empty, they return undef:

```
$end_of_the_line = maxstr @names;
```

reduce BLOCK LIST   This function iterates over *LIST* by calling *BLOCK* multiple times. The value returned is the value of *BLOCK* the final time it is called. If the list is empty, undef is returned. If the list has one item, that is returned without having called *BLOCK*.

The first call to *BLOCK* is with $a and $b set to the first two elements of the list. Each subsequent call, $a will have the previous result of the block, and $b will be the next value in the list. For example, to calculate the factorial of 5 ($5 \times 4 \times 3 \times 2 \times 1$), use this:

```
$factorial = reduce { $a*$b } 1..5;
```

shuffle LIST   This function returns the elements of *LIST* in a random order. For example, here's a simple way to do a holiday gift swap:

```
my @givers = qw( Mom Dad Grandma Grandpa Sister Brother );
my @recipients = shuffle @givers;

while ( @givers ) {
    print  shift @givers, " gives to ",
           shift @recipients, "\n";
}
```

sum LIST   This function returns the sum of all the elements in *LIST*:

```
$foo = sum 1..10;   # 55
$total_bill = sum @line_item_prices;
```

Math::BigFloat

This method offers a way to use floating-point numerals of arbitrary length.

Synopsis

```
use Math::BigFloat;
$f = Math::BigFloat->new($string);
```

```
$f->fadd(NSTR) return NSTR              addition
$f->fsub(NSTR) return NSTR              subtraction
$f->fmul(NSTR) return NSTR              multiplication
$f->fdiv(NSTR[,SCALE]) returns NSTR     division to SCALE
places
$f->fneg() return NSTR                  negation
$f->fabs() return NSTR                  absolute value
$f->fcmp(NSTR) return CODE              compare
undef,<0,=0,>0
$f->fround(SCALE) return NSTR           round to SCALE digits
$f->ffround(SCALE) return NSTR          round at SCALEth
place
$f->fnorm() return (NSTR)               normalize
$f->fsqrt([SCALE]) return NSTR          sqrt to SCALE places
```

Description

All basic math operations are overloaded if you declare your big floats as follows:

```
$float = new Math::BigFloat
         "2.12312312312312312312312312312312";
```

Number Format   Canonical strings have the form /[+-]\d+E[+-]\d+/. Input values can have embedded whitespace.

Error Returns *NaN*   An input parameter was Not-a-Number, or an attempt was made to divide by zero or take the square root of a negative number.

Division is computed to max($div_scale, length(dividend)+length (divisor)) digits by default. This method is also used for default sqrt scale.

Math::BigInt

This method offers a way to use integers of arbitrary size.

Synopsis

```
use Math::BigInt;
$i = Math::BigInt->new($string);

$i->bneg return BINT                        negation
$i->babs return BINT                        absolute value
$i->bcmp(BINT) return CODE                  compare numbers
(undef,<0,=0,>0)
$i->badd(BINT) return BINT                  addition
$i->bsub(BINT) return BINT                  subtraction
$i->bmul(BINT) return BINT                  multiplication
$i->bdiv(BINT) return (BINT,BINT)           division (quo,rem) just
quo if scalar
$i->bmod(BINT) return BINT                  modulus
$i->bgcd(BINT) return BINT                  greatest common divisor
$i->bnorm return BINT                       normalization
```

Description

All basic math operations are overloaded if you declare your big integers as follows:

```
$i = new Math::BigInt '123 456 789 123 456 789';
```

The actual math is done in an internal format consisting of an array whose first element is the sign (/^[+-]$/) and whose remaining elements are base 100,000 digits with the least significant digit first. The string NaN is used to represent the result when input arguments are not numbers; it is also used to represent the result of dividing by zero.

Math::Complex

This package lets you create and manipulate complex numbers.

Synopsis

```
use Math::Complex;

$z = Math::Complex->make(5, 6);
$t = 4 - 3*i + $z;
$j = cplxe(1, 2*pi/3);
```

Description

By default, Perl limits itself to real numbers; however, an extra use statement brings full support for complex numbers, along with a full set of mathematical functions typically associated with and/or extended to complex numbers.

To create a complex number, use either

```
$z = Math::Complex->make(3, 4);
```

or

```
$z = cplx(3, 4);
```

if you know the Cartesian form of the number. You can use

```
$z = 3 + 4*i;
```

if you like. To create a number using the polar form, use either

```
$z = Math::Complex->emake(5, pi/3);
```

or

```
$x = cplxe(5, pi/3);
```

The first argument is the modulus, and the second is the angle (in radians; the full circle is 2*pi). (Remember that *e* is used as a notation for complex numbers in the polar form.)

You could write:

```
$x = cplxe(-3, pi/4);
```

but that will be silently converted into [3,-3pi/4], because the modulus must be nonnegative (it represents the distance to the origin in the complex plane).

You could also have a complex number as the argument of either make or emake. The appropriate component of the argument is used:

```
$z1 = cplx(-2, 1);
$z2 = cplx($z1, 4);
```

Here are some examples:

```
use Math::Complex;

$j = cplxe(1, 2*pi/3);  # $j ** 3 == 1
print "j = $j, j**3 = ", $j ** 3, "\n";
print "1 + j + j**2 = ", 1 + $j + $j**2, "\n";

$z = -16 + 0*i;                  # Force it to be a complex
print '"sqrt($z) = '", sqrt($z), "\n";
```

```
$k = exp(i * 2*pi/3);
print '"$j - $k = '", $j - $k, "\n";

$z->Re(3);                    # Re, Im, arg, abs,
$j->arg(2);                   # (the last two aka rho, theta)
                              # can be used also as mutators.
```

Net::hostent

This is an alternative, object-oriented interface to Perl's built-in gethost-
byname() and gethostbyaddr() functions.

Synopsis
```
use Net::hostent;
```

Description

This module's default exports override the core gethostbyname() and
gethostbyaddr() functions, replacing them with versions that return
Net::hostent objects. This object has methods that return the similarly
named structure field name from the C's hostent structure from netdb.h.
These methods are name(), aliases(), addrtype(), length(), and
addr_list(). The aliases and addr_list methods return array reference;
the rest return scalars. The addr method is equivalent to the zero placed
element in the addr_list array reference.

You can also import all the structure fields directly into your namespace
as regular variables using the :FIELDS import tag. (Note that this still
overrides your core functions.) You access these fields as variables named
with a preceding h_. Therefore, $host_obj->name() corresponds to
$h_name if you import the fields. Array references are available as regular
array variables; for example, @{$host_obj->aliases()} would be simply
@h_aliases.

The gethost() function is a simple front-end that forwards a numeric
argument to gethostbyaddr() by way of Socket::inet_aton and forwards
the rest of the arguments to gethostbyname().

To access this functionality without the core overrides, pass the empty
import list to the use, and then access functions with their full qualified
names. On the other hand, the built-ins are still available via the CORE::
pseudo-package.

Examples

```perl
use Net::hostent;
use Socket;

@ARGV = qw( netscape.com ) unless @ARGV;

for $host ( @ARGV ) {
    unless ($h = gethost($host)) {
        warn "$0: no such host: $host\n";
        next;
    }

    printf "\n%s is %s%s\n",
        $host,
        lc($h->name) eq lc($host) ? "" : "*really* ",
        $h->name;

    if ( @aliases = @{$h->aliases} ) {
        print "\taliases are ", join( ", ", @aliases), "\n";
    }

    if ( @{$h->addr_list} > 1 ) {
        my $i;
        for $addr ( @{$h->addr_list} ) {
            printf "\taddr #%d is [%s]\n",
                    $i++, inet_ntoa($addr);
        }
    } else {
        printf "\taddress is [%s]\n", inet_ntoa($h->addr);
    }

    if ($h = gethostbyaddr($h->addr)) {
        if (lc($h->name) ne lc($host)) {
            printf "\tThat addr reverses to host %s!\n",
                    $h->name;
            $host = $h->name;
            redo;
        }
    }
}
```

NOTE

Although this class is currently implemented using the Class::Struct module to build a class of struct and similar datatypes, you should not rely on this.

Net::netent

This module provides an alternative, object-oriented interface to Perl's
getnetbyname() and getnetbyaddr() functions.

Synopsis

```
use Net::netent qw(:FIELDS);
getnetbyname("loopback")            or die "bad net";
printf "%s is %08X\n", $n_name, $n_net;

use Net::netent;

$n = getnetbyname("loopback")       or die "bad net";
{ # there's gotta be a better way, eh?
    @bytes = unpack("C4", pack("N", $n->net));
    shift @bytes while @bytes && $bytes[0] == 0;
}
printf "%s is %08X [%d.%d.%d.%d]\n", $n->name,
  $n->net, @bytes;
```

Description

This module's default exports override the core getnetbyname() and
getnetbyaddr() functions, replacing them with versions that return
Net::netent objects. This object has methods that return the similarly
named structure field name from the C's netent structure from netdb.h.
These methods are name(), aliases(), addrtype(), and net(). The
aliases() method returns an array reference; the rest of the methods
return scalars.

You can also import all the structure fields directly into your namespace
as regular variables using the :FIELDS import tag. (Note that this still
overrides your core functions.) You access these fields as variables named
with a preceding n_. Therefore, $net_obj->name() corresponds to $n_name
if you import the fields. Array references are available as regular array
variables—for example, @{$net_obj->aliases()} would be simply
@n_aliases.

The getnet() function is a simple front-end that forwards a numeric
argument to getnetbyaddr() and forwards the rest of the arguments to
getnetbyname().

To access this functionality without the core overrides, pass an empty
import list to use, and then access functions with their full qualified

names. On the other hand, the built-ins are still available via the CORE::
pseudo-package.

Examples

The getnet() functions perform the following in the Perl core:

```
sv_setiv(sv, (I32)nent->n_net);
```

The gethost() functions perform the following in the Perl core:

```
sv_setpvn(sv, hent->h_addr, len);
```

This means the address comes back in binary for the host functions
and as a regular Perl integer for the net functions. This seems to be a bug,
but here's how to deal with it:

```perl
use strict;
use Socket;
use Net::netent;

@ARGV = qw( loopback ) unless @ARGV;

my($n, $net);

for $net ( @ARGV ) {

    unless ($n = getnetbyname($net)) {
        warn "$0: no such net: $net\n";
        next;
    }

    printf "\n%s is %s%s\n",
            $net,
            lc($n->name) eq lc($net) ? "" : "*really* ",
            $n->name;

    print "\taliases are ", join(", ", @{$n->aliases}), "\n"
                if @{$n->aliases};

    {
        my @a = unpack("C4", pack("N", $n->net));
        shift @a while @a && $a[0] == 0;
        printf "\taddr is %s [%d.%d.%d.%d]\n", $n->net, @a;
    }

    if ($n = getnetbyaddr($n->net)) {
        if (lc($n->name) ne lc($net)) {
```

```
        printf "\tThat addr reverses to net %s!\n", $n->name;
            $net = $n->name;
            redo;
        }
    }
}
```

NOTE

Although this class is currently implemented using the Class::Struct module to build a class of struct and similar datatypes, you shouldn't rely on this.

Net::Ping

This package provides a way to check the reachability of remote host over a network connection.

Synopsis

```
use Net::Ping;

$p = Net::Ping->new();
print "$host is alive.\n" if $p->ping($host);
$p->close();

$p = Net::Ping->new("icmp");
foreach $host (@host_array)
{
    print "$host is ";
    print "NOT " unless $p->ping($host, 2);
    print "reachable.\n";
    sleep(1);
}
$p->close();

$p = Net::Ping->new("tcp", 2);
while ($stop_time > time())
{
    print "$host not reachable ",
        scalar(localtime()), "\n"
        unless $p->ping($host);
    sleep(300);
}
undef($p);
```

```
# For backward compatibility
print "$host is alive.\n" if pingecho($host);
```

Description

This module contains methods to test the ability to reach remote hosts on a network. A ping object is created with optional parameters, a variable number of hosts may be pinged multiple times, and then the connection is closed.

You can choose one of three different protocols to use for the ping. With the tcp protocol, the ping() method attempts to establish a connection to the remote host's echo port. If the connection is successfully established, the remote host is considered reachable. No data is actually echoed. This protocol does not require any special privileges, but it has a higher overhead than the other two protocols.

Specifying the udp protocol causes the ping() method to send a udp packet to the remote host's echo port. If the echoed packet is received from the remote host and the received packet contains the same data as the packet that was sent, the remote host is considered reachable. This protocol does not require any special privileges.

If the icmp protocol is specified, the ping() method sends an icmp echo message to the remote host, which is what the Unix ping program does. If the echoed message is received from the remote host and the echoed information is correct, the remote host is considered reachable. Specifying the icmp protocol requires that the program be run as root or that the program be setuid to root.

Functions

The following functions are available when using Net::Ping.

Net::Ping->new([$proto [, $def_timeout [, $bytes]]]);   This function creates a new ping object. All the parameters are optional. The $proto command specifies the protocol to use when doing a ping. The current choices are tcp, udp, and icmp. The default is udp.

If a default timeout ($def_timeout) in seconds is provided, it is used when a timeout is not given to the ping() method (see the following listing). The timeout must be greater than 0; the default, if not specified, is five seconds.

If the number of data bytes ($bytes) is given, that many data bytes are included in the ping packet sent to the remote host. The number of data bytes is ignored if the protocol is tcp. The minimum (and default) number of data bytes is 1 if the protocol is udp; it is 0 if the protocol is not udp. The maximum number of data bytes that can be specified is 1,024.

***$p->ping($host [, $timeout]);***   This function pings the remote host and waits for a response. *$host* can be either the hostname or the IP number of the remote host. The optional timeout must be greater than 0 seconds and defaults to whatever was specified when the ping object was created. If the hostname cannot be found or there is a problem with the IP number, undef is returned. Otherwise, 1 is returned if the host is reachable and 0 if it is not. For all practical purposes, undef and 0 can be treated as the same case.

$p->close();   This function closes the network connection for this ping object. The network connection is also closed by undef $p. The network connection is automatically closed if the ping object goes out of scope (for example, $p is local to a subroutine and you leave the subroutine).

pingecho($host [, $timeout]);   To provide backward compatibility with the previous version of Net::Ping, a pingecho() subroutine is available with the same functionality as before. The pingecho() command uses the tcp protocol. The return values and parameters are the same as described for the ping() method. This subroutine is obsolete and may be removed in a future version of Net::Ping.

NOTE

The pingecho() command and a ping object with the tcp protocol use alarm() to implement the timeout. Therefore, don't use alarm() in your program while you are using pingecho() or a ping object with the tcp protocol. The udp and icmp protocols do not use alarm() to implement the timeout.

There will be less network overhead (and less efficiency in your program) if you specify either the udp or the icmp protocol. The tcp protocol generates 2.5 times or more traffic for each ping than either udp or icmp. If many hosts are pinged frequently, you may want to implement a small wait (25 milliseconds or more) between each ping to avoid flooding your network with packets.

The icmp protocol requires that the program be run as a root or that it be setuid to a root. The tcp and udp protocols do not require special privileges; however, not all network devices implement the echo protocol for tcp or udp.

Local hosts normally should respond to pings within milliseconds. However, on a very congested network, it may take up to three seconds or longer to receive an echo packet from the remote host. If the timeout is set too low under these conditions, it will appear that the remote host is not reachable (which is almost the truth).

Being able to be reached doesn't necessarily mean the remote host is functioning beyond its ability to echo packets.

Because of a lack of anything better, this module uses its own routines to pack and unpack ICMP packets. It would be better for a separate module that understands all the different kinds of ICMP packets to be written.

Net::protoent

This method provides an alternative, object-oriented interface to Perl's built-in getprotoent(), getprotobyname(), and getnetbyport() functions.

Synopsis

```
use Net::protoent;
$p = getprotobyname(shift || 'tcp') || die "no proto";
printf "proto for %s is %d, aliases are %s\n",
    $p->name, $p->proto, "@{$p->aliases}";

use Net::protoent qw(:FIELDS);
getprotobyname(shift || 'tcp') || die "no proto";
print "proto for $p_name is $p_proto, aliases are
    @p_aliases\n";
```

Description

This module's default exports override the core getprotoent(), getprotobyname(), and getnetbyport() functions, replacing them with versions that return Net::protoent objects. They take default second arguments of tcp. This object has methods that return the similarly named structure field name from C's protoent structure from netdb.h. These methods are name(), aliases(), and proto(). The aliases() method returns an array reference; the rest of the methods return scalars.

You can also import all the structure fields directly into your namespace as regular variables using the :FIELDS import tag. (Note that this still overrides your core functions.) You access these fields as variables named with a preceding p_. Therefore, $proto_obj->name() corresponds to $p_name if you import the fields. Array references are available as regular array variables. For example, @{$proto_obj->aliases()} would be simply @p_aliases.

The getproto() function is a simple front-end that forwards a numeric argument to getprotobyport() and forwards the rest of the arguments to getprotobyname().

To access this functionality without the core overrides, pass an empty list to the use, and then access functions with their full qualified names. On the other hand, the built-ins are still available via the CORE:: pseudo-package.

NOTE

Although this class is currently implemented using the Class::Struct module to build a class of struct and similar datatypes, you shouldn't rely on this.

Net::servent

This is an alternative, object-oriented interface to Perl's built-in getservent(), getservbyname(), and getnetbyport() functions.

Synopsis

```
use Net::servent;
$s = getservbyname(shift || 'ftp') ||
        die "no service";
printf "port for %s is %s, aliases are %s\n",
    $s->name, $s->port, "@{$s->aliases}";

use Net::servent qw(:FIELDS);
getservbyname(shift || 'ftp') || die "no service";
print "port for $s_name is $s_port, aliases are
    @s_aliases\n";
```

Description

This module's default exports override the core getservent(), get-servbyname(), and getnetbyport() functions, replacing them with versions that return Net::servent objects. They take default second arguments of `tcp`. This object has methods that return the similarly named structure field name from C's `servent` structure from `netdb.h`. These methods are `name()`, `aliases()`, `port()`, and `proto()`. The `aliases()` method returns an array reference; the rest of the methods return scalars.

You can also import all the structure fields directly into your namespace as regular variables using the `:FIELDS` import tag. (Note that this still overrides your core functions.) You access these fields as variables named with a preceding n_. Therefore, `$serv_obj->name()` corresponds to `$s_name` if you import the fields. Array references are available as regular array variables; for example, `@{$serv_obj->aliases()}` would be simply `@s_aliases`.

The `getserv()` function is a simple front-end that forwards a numeric argument to `getservbyport()`, and forwards the rest of the arguments to `getservbyname()`.

To access this functionality without the core overrides, pass an empty import list to the `use`, and then access functions with their full qualified names. On the other hand, the built-ins are still available via the `CORE::` pseudo-package.

Examples

```
use Net::servent qw(:FIELDS);

while (@ARGV) {
    my ($service, $proto) = ((split m!/!, shift),
        'tcp');
    my $valet = getserv($service, $proto);
    unless ($valet) {
        warn "$0: No service: $service/$proto\n";
        next;
    }
    printf "service $service/$proto is port %d\n",
      $valet->port;
    print "alias are @s_aliases\n" if @s_aliases;
}
```

Safe

The Safe extension module allows the creation of compartments in which Perl code can be evaluated.

Synopsis

```
use Safe;
$compartment = new Safe;
$compartment->permit(qw(time sort :browse));
$result = $compartment->reval($unsafe_code);
```

Description

Each compartment has a new namespace and an operator mask. The root of the namespace (such as main::) is changed to a different package. The code evaluated in the compartment cannot refer to variables outside this namespace, even with runtime glob lookups and other tricks.

The code, which is compiled outside the compartment, can place variables into (or *share* variables with) the compartment's namespace. Only that data is visible to code evaluated in the compartment.

By default, the only variables shared with compartments are the underscore variables $_ and @_ (and, technically, the less frequently used %_, the _ filehandle, and so on). If variables other than these were shared, the Perl operators that default to $_ would not work, nor would the assignment of arguments to @_ on subroutine entry.

Each compartment has an associated *operator mask*. Recall that Perl code is compiled into an internal format before execution. Evaluating Perl code (such as via eval or do 'file') causes the code to be compiled into an internal format and then, provided there was no error in the compilation, executed. Code evaluated in a compartment compiles the subject to the compartment's operator mask. Attempting to evaluate code in a compartment that contains a masked operator causes the compilation to fail with an error. The code is not executed.

The default operator mask for a newly created compartment is the :default optag.

Make sure you read the Opcode(3) module documentation for more important information, especially the detailed definitions of opnames, optags, and opsets.

Because the operator mask applies only at the compilation stage, you can control access to potentially unsafe operations by having a handle to a wrapper subroutine (written outside the compartment) placed into the compartment. For example:

```
$cpt = new Safe;
sub wrapper {
    # vet arguments and perform potentially
```

```
            # unsafe operations
        }
        $cpt->share('&wrapper');
```

Search::Dict, Look

This method allows case-dependent or case-independent searching in a dictionary file.

Synopsis

```
        use Search::Dict;
        look *FILEHANDLE, $key, $dict, $fold;
```

Description

This method sets the file position in *FILEHANDLE* to be the first line greater than or equal (stringwise) to *$key*. It returns the new file position or −1 if an error occurs.

The flags specify dictionary order and case folding:

▶ If *$dict* is true, search by dictionary order (ignore everything except word characters and whitespace).

▶ If *$fold* is true, ignore case.

SelectSaver

SelectSaver provides a way to save and restore filehandles.

Synopsis

```
        use SelectSaver;

        {
            my $saver = new SelectSaver(FILEHANDLE);
            # FILEHANDLE is selected
        }
        # previous handle is selected

        {
            my $saver = new SelectSaver;
            # new handle may be selected, or not
        }
        # previous handle is selected
```

Description

A SelectSaver object contains a reference to the filehandle that was selected when it was created. If its new method gets an extra parameter, then that parameter is selected; otherwise, the selected filehandle remains unchanged. When a SelectSaver is destroyed, it reselects the filehandle that was selected when it was created.

SelfLoader

SelfLoader allows functions to be loaded only when they are used, not when the script is loaded for execution.

Synopsis

```
package FOOBAR;
use SelfLoader;

... (initializing code)

__DATA__
sub {....
```

Description

This module tells its users that functions in the FOOBAR package are to be autoloaded from after the __DATA__ token. See also the "Autoloading" section in the perlsub man page.

The __DATA__ Token

The __DATA__ token tells the Perl compiler that the Perl code has finished compiling. Everything after the __DATA__ token is available for reading via the filehandle *FOOBAR*::DATA (where *FOOBAR* is the name of the current package when the __DATA__ token is reached). This works the same way that __END__ does in the main package—except the data from the modules after __END__ is not automatically retrievable, whereas data after __DATA__ is automatically retrievable. The __DATA__ token is not recognized in versions of Perl prior to 5.001m.

If a package is split across multiple files and more than one of those files contains a __DATA__ token, the last __DATA__ token encountered is the one that is accessible by the filehandle. Further, the __DATA__ token of an included package supersedes the __END__ tag of the main program, because the included package is encountered later in the compilation process. .

SelfLoader Autoloading

To make the SelfLoader work, the user places the __DATA__ token *after* the Perl code that needs to be compiled and run at require time and *before* the subroutine declarations that can be loaded later—usually because they may never be called. The SelfLoader reads from the *FOOBAR*::DATA filehandle to load the data after __DATA__ and loads any subroutine when it is called. The costs are the one-time parsing of the data after __DATA__ and a load delay for the _first_ call of any autoloaded function. The benefits include a speeded up compilation phase, with no need to load functions that are never used.

The SelfLoader stops reading from __DATA__ if it encounters the __END__ token—just as you would expect. If the __END__ token is present and is followed by the token DATA, then the SelfLoader leaves the *FOOBAR*::DATA filehandle open on the line after that token.

The SelfLoader exports the AUTOLOAD subroutine to the package using the SelfLoader, and this loads the called subroutine when it is first called.

There is no advantage to putting subroutines that will always be called after the __DATA__ token.

SelfLoader and *AutoLoader*

The SelfLoader can replace the AutoLoader. You just need to change use AutoLoader to use SelfLoader. (Note that the SelfLoader exports the AUTOLOAD function and the __END__ token to __DATA__. If you have your own AUTOLOAD and are using the AutoLoader too, you probably know what you're doing. There is no need to inherit from the SelfLoader.)

The SelfLoader works similarly to the AutoLoader, but it picks up the subs from after the __DATA__ instead of picking them up from the lib/auto directory. You achieve a maintenance gain because you do not need to run AutoSplit on the module at installation, and you achieve a runtime gain because you do not need to keep opening and closing files to load subs. You do accept a runtime loss from parsing the code after the __DATA__. Details of the AutoLoader and another view of these distinctions can be found in that module's documentation.

Socket, sockaddr_in, sockaddr_un, inet_aton, inet_ntoa

This module is just a translation of the C socket.h file.

Synopsis

```
use Socket;

$proto = getprotobyname('udp');
socket(Socket_Handle, PF_INET, SOCK_DGRAM, $proto);
$iaddr = gethostbyname('hishost.com');
$port = getservbyname('time', 'udp');
$sin = sockaddr_in($port, $iaddr);
send(Socket_Handle, 0, 0, $sin);

$proto = getprotobyname('tcp');
socket(Socket_Handle, PF_INET, SOCK_STREAM,
        $proto);
$port = getservbyname('smtp', 'tcp');
$sin = sockaddr_in($port,inet_aton("127.1"));
$sin = sockaddr_in(7,inet_aton("localhost"));
$sin = sockaddr_in(7,INADDR_LOOPBACK);
connect(Socket_Handle,$sin);

($port, $iaddr) =
    sockaddr_in(getpeername(Socket_Handle));
$peer_host = gethostbyaddr($iaddr, AF_INET);
$peer_addr = inet_ntoa($iaddr);

$proto = getprotobyname('tcp');
socket(Socket_Handle, PF_UNIX, SOCK_STREAM,
        $proto);
unlink('/tmp/usock');
$sun = sockaddr_un('/tmp/usock');
connect(Socket_Handle,$sun);
```

Description

Unlike the old mechanism, which required a translated socket.ph file, this mechanism uses the h2xs program (see the Perl source distribution material) and your native C compiler. This means Perl has a far better chance of getting the numbers right—including all the commonly used pound-defines like AF_INET, SOCK_STREAM, and so on—because the C compiler includes the header files from your particular system.

Some common socket newline constants are provided, including CR, LF, and CRLF, as well as $CR, $LF, and $CRLF, which map to \015, \012, and \015\012. If you do not want to use the literal characters in your programs, then use the constants provided here. They are not exported by default, but they can be imported individually and with the :crlf export tag, as shown here:

```
use Socket qw(:DEFAULT :crlf);
```

In addition, some structure manipulation functions are available.

inet_aton HOSTNAME   This command takes a string giving the name of a host, and it translates that string to the four-byte string (structure). It takes arguments of both the rtfm.mit.edu type and the 18.181.0.24 type. If the hostname cannot be resolved, it returns undef. For multihomed hosts (hosts with more than one address), the first address found is returned.

inet_ntoa IP_ADDRESS   This command takes a four-byte IP address (as returned by inet_aton()) and translates it into a string of the form *d.d.d.d*, where the *d*'s are numbers less than 256 (the normal readable four-dotted number notation for Internet addresses).

INADDR_ANY   INADDR_ANY returns a packed string and does not return a number. It returns the four-byte wildcard IP address, which specifies any of the hosts' IP addresses. (A particular machine can have more than one IP address, each address corresponding to a particular network interface. This wildcard address allows you to bind to all of them simultaneously.) Normally, it is equivalent to inet_aton('0.0.0.0').

INADDR_BROADCAST   INADDR_BROADCAST does not return a number, but it returns a packed string. It returns the four-byte this-lan IP broadcast address. This can be useful for some protocols to solicit information from all servers on the same LAN cable. It is normally equivalent to inet_aton('255.255.255.255').

INADDR_LOOPBACK   INADDR_LOOPBACK returns the four-byte loopback address and does not return a number. Normally, it is equivalent to inet_aton('localhost').

INADDR_NONE INADDR_NONE returns the four-byte invalid IP address and does not return a number. Normally, it is equivalent to inet_aton ('255.255.255.255').

sockaddr_in PORT, ADDRESS

sockaddr_in SOCKADDR_IN In an array context, this command unpacks its *SOCKADDR_IN* argument and returns an array consisting of (*PORT*, *ADDRESS*). In a scalar context, it packs its (*PORT*, *ADDRESS*) arguments as a *SOCKADDR_IN* and returns it. If this is confusing, use pack_sockaddr_in() and unpack_sockaddr_in() explicitly.

pack_sockaddr_in PORT, IP_ADDRESS This command takes two arguments: a port number and a four-byte *IP_ADDRESS* (as returned by inet_aton()). It returns the sockaddr_in structure with those arguments packed with AF_INET filled. For Internet domain sockets, this structure is normally what you need for the arguments in bind(), connect(), and send(), and it is also returned by getpeername(), getsockname(), and recv().

unpack_sockaddr_in SOCKADDR_IN This command takes a sockaddr_in structure (as returned by pack_sockaddr_in()) and returns an array of two elements: the port and the four-byte IP address. It croaks if the structure does not have AF_INET in the right place.

sockaddr_un PATHNAME

sockaddr_un SOCKADDR_UN In an array context, this command unpacks its *SOCKADDR_UN* argument and returns an array consisting of (*PATHNAME*). In a scalar context, it packs its *PATHNAME* arguments as a *SOCKADDR_UN* and returns it. If this is confusing, use pack_sockaddr_un() and unpack_sockaddr_un() explicitly. They are supported only if your system has <sys/un.h>.

pack_sockaddr_un PATH This command takes one argument, a pathname. It returns the sockaddr_un structure with that path packed with AF_UNIX filled. For Unix domain sockets, this structure is normally what you need for the arguments in bind(), connect(), and send(). It is also returned by getpeername(), getsockname(), and recv().

unpack_sockaddr_un SOCKADDR_UN   This command takes a
sockaddr_un structure (as returned by pack_sockaddr_un()) and
returns the pathname. It croaks if the structure does not have AF_UNIX
in the right place.

strict

The strict pragma prevents you from doing a number of unsafe things
in Perl, most of them left over from older versions. There are three different
flavors of stricture, listed in this section. A simple use strict sets all
three of them on.

use strict 'refs'   A common trick in Perl is to use symbolic references,
where variables define other variables to use. For example:

```
$var = "foo";
$$var = 3; # Same as $foo=3
print $foo; # prints "3"
```

The use strict 'refs' pragma prevents this.

use strict 'vars'   The vars stricture prevents you from using variables
that you have not defined or package variables that are not fully qualified.
For example, it's common to accidentally mistype a variable name, like so:

```
my $name = "Larry Wall";
print $nmae;  # oops, $nmae instead of $name
```

In this case, $nmae has not been used, and so print will print nothing, but
not generate an error. With use strict 'vars' in place, Perl will complain
that $nmae has not been used before, potentially saving you from debugging
hassles.

use strict 'subs'   This stricture disables the "poetry" optimization,
which is rarely used in current programs. With subs in effect, Perl generates
a compile-time error if you try to use a bareword identifier that's not a
subroutine, unless it appears in curly braces or on the left hand side of
the => symbol.

Symbol

Symbol provides different ways for you to manipulate Perl's symbol table.

Synopsis

```
use Symbol;

$sym = gensym;
open($sym, "filename");
$_ = <$sym>;
# etc.

ungensym $sym;        # no effect

print qualify("x"), "\n";                    # "Test::x"
print qualify("x", "FOO"), "\n"              # "FOO::x"
print qualify("BAR::x"), "\n";               # "BAR::x"
print qualify("BAR::x", "FOO"), "\n";        # "BAR::x"
print qualify("STDOUT", "FOO"), "\n";        # "main::STDOUT"
print qualify(\*x), "\n";                    # returns \*x
print qualify(\*x, "FOO"), "\n";             # returns \*x

use strict refs;
print { qualify_to_ref $fh } "foo!\n";
$ref = qualify_to_ref $name, $pkg;

use Symbol qw(delete_package);
delete_package('Foo::Bar');
print "deleted\n" unless exists $Foo::{'Bar::'};
```

Description

Symbol::gensym creates an anonymous glob and returns a reference to it. This glob reference can be used as a file or directory handle.

For backward compatibility with older implementations that didn't support anonymous globs, Symbol::ungensym is also provided. However, it doesn't do anything.

Symbol::qualify turns unqualified symbol names into qualified variable names (for example, myvar -> MyPackage::myvar). If it is given a second parameter, qualify uses it as the default package; otherwise, it uses the package of its caller. Regardless, global variable names (such as STDOUT, ENV, and SIG) are always qualified with main::.

Qualification applies only to symbol names (strings). References are left unchanged under the assumption that they are glob references, which are qualified by their nature.

Symbol::qualify_to_ref is similar to Symbol::qualify, except that it returns a glob reference rather than a symbol name; therefore, you can use the result even if use strict 'refs' is in effect.

Symbol::delete_package wipes out a whole package namespace. This routine is not exported by default; therefore, you may want to import it explicitly.

Sys::Hostname

This module tries every conceivable method to get the system's hostname.

Synopsis

```
use Sys::Hostname;
$host = hostname;
```

Description

This module attempts several methods to get the system hostname and then caches the result. It tries syscall(SYS_gethostname), `hostname`, `uname -n`, and the file /com/host. If all these attempts fail, it croaks. All NULLs, returns, and newlines are removed from the result.

Sys::Syslog

This is a Perl interface to the Unix syslog(3) calls, which are used for logging error and diagnostic information to syslogd.

Synopsis

```
# all except setlogsock, or:
use Sys::Syslog;
# default set, plus setlogsock
use Sys::Syslog qw(:DEFAULT setlogsock);

setlogsock $sock_type;
openlog $ident, $logopt, $facility;
syslog $priority, $format, @args;
$oldmask = setlogmask $mask_priority;
closelog;
```

Description

Sys::Syslog is an interface to the Unix syslog() system call. You can call syslog() with a string priority and a list of printf() args just like you call syslog().

Syslog provides the following functions.

openlog $ident, $logopt, $facility $ident is prepended to every message. $logopt contains zero or more of the following words: pid, ndelay, cons, and nowait. $facility specifies the part of the system. Note that openlog now takes three arguments, just like openlog(3).

syslog $priority, $format, @args If $priority permits, this command logs ($format, @args) similarly to the way printf(3V) would print it, except that %m is replaced with $! (the latest error message).

setlogmask $mask_priority This command sets log mask $mask_priority and returns the old mask.

setlogsock $sock_type (added in 5.004_02) This command sets the socket type to be used for the next call to openlog() or syslog(). It returns true on success and undef on failure.

A value of unix connects to the Unix domain socket returned by _PATH_LOG in syslog.ph. A value of inet connects to an INET socket returned by getservbyname(). Any other value croaks. The INET socket is used by default.

closelog closelog closes the log file.

Examples

```
openlog($program, 'cons,pid', 'user');
syslog('info', 'this is another test');
syslog('mail|warning', 'this is a better test: %d',time);
closelog();

syslog('debug', 'this is the last test');

setlogsock('unix');
openlog("$program $$", 'ndelay', 'user');
syslog('notice', 'fooprogram: this is really done');
```

```
setlogsock('inet');
$! = 55;
syslog('info', 'problem was %m'); # %m == $! in syslog(3)
```

Dependencies

Sys::Syslog needs syslog.ph, which can be created with h2ph.

See Also

The Unix syslog(3) man page.

Term::Cap

This module provides an interface to the terminal capabilities (termcap) database.

Synopsis

```
require Term::Cap;
$terminal = Tgetent Term::Cap {
                        TERM => undef,
                        OSPEED => $ospeed };
$terminal->Trequire(qw/ce ku kd/);
$terminal->Tgoto('cm', $col, $row, $FH);
$terminal->Tputs('dl', $count, $FH);
$terminal->Tpad($string, $count, $FH);
```

Description

These are low-level functions to extract and use capabilities from a terminal capability (termcap) database. The Tgetent function extracts the entry of the specified terminal type TERM (defaults to the environment variable TERM) from the database.

It looks in the environment for a TERMCAP variable. If one is found and the value does not begin with a slash and the terminal type name is the same as the environment string TERM, the TERMCAP string is used instead of reading a termcap file. If it does begin with a slash, the string is used as a pathname of the termcap file to search. If TERMCAP does not begin with a slash and the name is different from TERM, Tgetent searches the files $HOME/.termcap, /etc/termcap, and /usr/share/misc/termcap, in that order—unless the environment variable TERMPATH exists, in which case it specifies a list of file pathnames (separated by spaces or colons) to be searched instead. Whenever multiple files are searched and a tc field occurs in the requested entry, the entry it names must be found in the same file or one of the succeeding files. If there is a ":tc=...:" in the TERMCAP environment variable string, the function continues the search in the files as previously described.

OSPEED is the terminal output bit rate (often mistakenly called the baud rate). OSPEED can be specified as either a Posix termios/SYSV termio speed (where 9600 equals 9600) or an old BSD-style speed (where 13 equals 9600).

Tgetent returns a blessed object reference, which the user can then use to send the control strings to the terminal using Tputs and Tgoto. It calls croak on failure. Tgoto decodes a cursor addressing string with the given parameters.

The output strings for Tputs are cached for counts of 1 for performance. Tgoto and Tpad do not cache. $self->{ xx} is the raw termcap data, and $self->{xx} is the cached version. Tgoto, Tputs, and Tpad return the string and also output the string to $FH if specified. The extracted termcap entry is available in the object as $self->{TERMCAP}.

Examples

```
# Get terminal output speed
require POSIX;
my $termios = new POSIX::Termios;
$termios->getattr;
my $ospeed = $termios->getospeed;

# Old-style ioctl code to get ospeed:
#     require 'ioctl.pl';
#     ioctl(TTY,$TIOCGETP,$sgtty);
#     ($ispeed,$ospeed) = unpack('cc',$sgtty);

# allocate and initialize a terminal structure
$terminal = Tgetent Term::Cap {
    TERM => undef, OSPEED => $ospeed };

# require certain capabilities to be available
$terminal->Trequire(qw/ce ku kd/);

# Output Routines, if $FH is undefined
# these just return the string

# Tgoto does the % expansion stuff with
# the given args
$terminal->Tgoto('cm', $col, $row, $FH);
```

```
# Tputs doesn't do any % expansion.
$terminal->Tputs('dl', $count = 1, $FH);
```

Term::Complete

This routine provides word completion on the list of words in the array (or array reference).

Synopsis

```
$input = Complete('prompt_string', \@completion_list);
$input = Complete('prompt_string', @completion_list);
```

Description

Complete provides word completion on a specified list of words. The tty driver is put into raw mode using the system command stty raw - echo and restored using stty -raw echo.

The following command characters are defined:

<tab>	Attempts word completion. Cannot be changed.
^D	Prints a completion list. Defined by *$Term::Complete::complete*.
^U	Erases the current input. Defined by *$Term::Complete::kill*.
<del>, <bs>	Erases one character. Defined by *$Term::Complete::erase1* and *$Term::Complete::erase2.

Diagnostics

A bell sounds when word completion fails.

Bugs

The completion character <tab> cannot be changed.

Term::ReadLine

This module provides a coherent front-end interface to various Readline packages. If no real package is found, it substitutes stubs instead of basic functions.

Synopsis

```
use Term::ReadLine;
$term = new Term::ReadLine 'Simple Perl calc';
$prompt = "Enter your arithmetic expression: ";
$OUT = $term->OUT || STDOUT;
while ( defined ($_ = $term->readline($prompt)) ) {
  $res = eval($_), "\n";
  warn $@ if $@;
  print $OUT $res, "\n" unless $@;
  $term->addhistory($_) if /\S/;
}
```

Description

This package is just a front-end to some other packages. At the time of this writing, the only such package is Term-ReadLine, which is available on CPAN. The real target of this stub package is to set up a common interface to whatever Readline emerges with time.

It supports a minimal set of functions. All the supported functions should be called as methods either as

```
$term = new Term::ReadLine 'name';
```

or as

```
$term->addhistory('row');
```

where $term is a return value of Term::ReadLine->Init.

ReadLine   This command returns the actual package that executes the commands. Possible values include: Term::ReadLine::Gnu, Term::ReadLine::Perl, and Term::ReadLine::Stub Exporter.

new   This command returns the handle for subsequent calls to following functions. The argument is the name of the application. As an option, it can be followed by two arguments for IN and OUT filehandles. These arguments should be globs.

readline   This command gets an input line, *possibly* with actual Readline support. The trailing newline is removed. It returns undef on EOF.

addhistory   This command adds a line to the input history, from where it can be used if the actual Readline is present.

IN, $OUT   If Readline input and output cannot be used for Perl, this command returns the filehandles for input and output or undef.

MinLine   If an argument is specified, MinLine specifies the minimum size line to be included in the history. If no argument is specified, nothing should be included in the history. MinLine returns the old value.

findConsole   This command returns an array with two strings that give the most appropriate names for files for input and output using the conventions "<$in" and ">out".

Attribs   This command returns a reference to a hash that describes the internal configuration of the package. The names of keys in this hash conform to standard conventions with the leading rl_ stripped.

Features   This command returns a reference to a hash with keys that are present in the current implementation. Several optional features are used in the minimal interface:

- ► appname should be present if the first argument to new is recognized.

- ► minline should be present if the MinLine method is not a dummy.

- ► autohistory should be present if lines are put into history automatically (autohistory may be subject to MinLine).

- ► addhistory should be present if the addhistory method is not a dummy.

If the Features method reports that the feature attribs is present, the method Attribs is not a dummy.

Additional Supported Functions

Term::ReadLine can use some other package that supports a richer set of commands. All these commands are callable via a method interface, and they have names that conform to standard conventions with the leading rl_ stripped. The stub package included with the Perl distribution material allows these additional methods: tkRunning and ornaments. You can check to see whether the currently loaded ReadLine package supports these methods by checking for the corresponding Features.

tkRunning   This method makes the Tk event loop run while waiting for user input (during the Readline method).

ornaments This method makes the command line stand out by using termcap data. The argument to ornaments should be 0, 1, or a string of the form "*aa,bb,cc,dd*". The four components of this string should be names of terminal capacities. The first two are issued to make the prompt standout; the last two are issued to make the input line standout.

newTTY This command takes two arguments: input filehandle and output filehandle. The default input and output filehandles are switched to use these filehandles.

Test

Test provides a simple framework for writing test scripts. If your testing requirements are more complex, take a look at Test::More.

Synopsis

```
use strict;
use Test;

# use a BEGIN block so we print our plan
# before MyModule is loaded
BEGIN { plan tests => 14, todo => [3,4] }

# load your module...
use MyModule;

ok(0); # failure
ok(1); # success

ok(0); # ok, expected failure (see todo list, above)
ok(1); # surprise success!

ok(0,1);              # failure: '0' ne '1'
ok('broke','fixed'); # failure: 'broke' ne 'fixed'
ok('fixed','fixed'); # success: 'fixed' eq 'fixed'
ok('fixed',qr/x/);   # success: 'fixed' =~ qr/x/

ok(sub { 1+1 }, 2);  # success: '2' eq '2'
ok(sub { 1+1 }, 3);  # failure: '2' ne '3'
ok(0, int(rand(2)));  # (just kidding :-)

my @list = (0,0);
ok @list, 3, "\@list=".join(',',@list); # diagnostics
```

```
ok '.segmentation fault', '/(?i)success/';  # regex match
skip($feature_is_missing, ...);
#do platform specific test
```

Description

The Test::Harness module expects to see particular output when it executes tests. This module aims to make writing proper test scripts a little easier (and less error prone).

Test Types   You can choose among three different test types: normal, skip, and todo. Normal tests are expected to succeed. If they don't, something's wrong. skip is used for tests that may or may not be able to run, depending on the availability of platform specific features. The first argument should evaluate to true (think "yes, please skip") if the required feature is not available. After the first argument, skip works the same way normal tests do.

todo tests are designed to maintain an executable todo list. These tests are expected to fail. If a todo test does succeed, the feature in question should not be on the todo list. Packages should *not* be released with successful todo tests. As soon as a todo test begins working, it should be promoted to a normal test, and the newly working feature should be documented in the release notes or change log.

Return Value

In a scalar context, both ok and skip return true if their test succeeds or false if it doesn't.

onfail

```
BEGIN { plan test => 4, onfail =>
    sub { warn "CALL 911!" } }
```

Although test failures should be enough, extra diagnostics can be triggered at the end of a test run. An array ref of hash refs that describe each test failure is passed to onfail. Each hash contains at least the following fields: package, repetition, and result. (The file, line, and test number are not included because their correspondence to a particular test is tenuous.) If the test has an expected value or a diagnostic string, it is also included.

The optional onfail hook can be used to print the version of your package and/or how to report problems. It can also be used to generate sophisticated diagnostics for a particularly bizarre test failure. However, it's not a panacea. Core dumps and other unrecoverable errors prevent the onfail hook from running. (It is run inside an END block.) Besides, onfail is probably overkill in most cases. (Your test code should be simpler than the code it is testing.)

Text::ParseWords

This module parses text into an array of tokens or an array of arrays.

Synopsis

```
use Text::ParseWords;
@lists = &nested_quotewords($delim, $keep, @lines);
@words = &quotewords($delim, $keep, @lines);
@words = &shellwords(@lines);
@words = &parse_line($delim, $keep, $line);
@words = &old_shellwords(@lines); # DEPRECATED!
```

Description

The &nested_quotewords() and &quotewords() functions accept a delimiter (which can be a regular expression) and a list of lines. They break those lines into a list of words (ignoring delimiters that appear inside quotes). &quotewords() returns all the tokens in a single long list. &nested_quotewords() returns a list of token lists corresponding to the elements of @lines. &parse_line() tokenizes a single string. The &*quotewords() functions call &parse_lines(); so if you're splitting only one line, you can call &parse_lines() directly and save a function call.

The $keep argument is a Boolean flag. If true, the tokens are split on the specified delimiter, but all other characters (quotes, backslashes, and so on) are kept in the tokens. If $keep is false, the &quotewords() functions remove all quotes and backslashes that are not themselves backslash-escaped or inside single quotes (&quotewords() tries to interpret these characters just like the Bourne shell). These semantics are significantly different from the original version of this module shipped with Perl 5.000 through 5.004. As an additional feature, $keep may be the keyword delimiters, which causes the functions to preserve the delimiters in each string as tokens in the token lists—in addition to preserving quote and backslash characters.

&shellwords() is written as a special case of &quotewords(), and it does token parsing with whitespace as a delimiter—similar to most Unix shells.

Examples

Here's the sample program:

```
use Text::ParseWords;
@words = &quotewords('\s+', 0,
    q{this   is "a test" of\ quotewords \"for you});
$i = 0;
foreach (@words) {
    print "$i: <$_>\n";
    $i++;
}
```

Here is the program's output:

```
0: <this>
1: <is>
2: <a test>
3: <of quotewords>
4: <"for>
5: <you>
```

The previous program demonstrates the following:

```
0
a simple word
1
multiple spaces are skipped because of our $delim
2
use of quotes to include a space in a word
3
use of a backslash to include a space in a word
4
use of a backslash to remove the special meaning of a
double-quote
5
another simple word (note the lack of effect of the
backslashed double-quote)
Replacing '&quotewords('\s+', 0, q{this is...})' with
'&shellwords(q{this is...})' is a simpler way to
accomplish the same thing.
```

Text::Soundex

This is an implementation of the Soundex algorithm as described by Donald Knuth.

Synopsis

```
use Text::Soundex;

$code = soundex $string;  # get soundex code for a string
@codes = soundex @list;   # get list of codes for list of
                          # strings

# set value to be returned for strings without soundex code

$soundex_nocode = 'Z000';
```

Description

This module implements the Soundex algorithm as described by Donald Knuth in *The Art of Computer Programming, Volume 3* (Addison-Wesley Publishing, 1998). The algorithm is intended to hash words (in particular surnames) into a small space using a simple model that approximates the sound of the word when spoken by an English speaker. Each word is reduced to a four-character string, the first character being an uppercase letter and the remaining three characters being digits.

If there is no Soundex code representation for a string, the value of $soundex_nocode is returned. This is initially set to undef, but many people seem to prefer an unlikely value like Z000 (how unlikely this is depends on the data set being used). Any value can be assigned to $soundex_nocode.

In a scalar context, soundex returns the Soundex code of its first argument. In an array context, a list is returned in which each element is the Soundex code for the corresponding argument passed to soundex. For example,

```
@codes = soundex qw(Mike Stok);
```

leaves @codes containing ('M200', 'S320').

Examples

Knuth's examples of various names and the Soundex codes they map to are listed here:

```
Euler, Ellery -> E460
Gauss, Ghosh -> G200
Hilbert, Heilbronn -> H416
Knuth, Kant -> K530
Lloyd, Ladd -> L300
Lukasiewicz, Lissajous -> L222
```

The following lines show the scalar and list use of soundex:

```
$code = soundex 'Knuth';  # $code contains 'K530'
@list = soundex qw(Lloyd Gauss);
# @list contains 'L300', 'G200'
```

Limitations

Because the Soundex algorithm was originally used a long time ago in the United States, it considers only the English alphabet and pronunciation. Because it is mapping a large space (arbitrary length strings) onto a small space (single letter plus three digits), no inference can be made about the similarity of two strings that end up with the same Soundex code. For example, both Hilbert and Heilbronn end up with a Soundex code of H416.

Text::Tabs

Text::Tabs provides a Perl interface to the Unix expand() and unexpand() utilities.

Synopsis

```
use Text::Tabs;

$tabstop = 4;
@lines_without_tabs = expand(@lines_with_tabs);
@lines_with_tabs = unexpand(@lines_without_tabs);
```

Description

Text::Tabs does about what the Unix utilities expand(1) and un-expand(1) do. Given a line with tabs in it, expand replaces the tabs with the appropriate number of spaces. Given a line with or without tabs in it, unexpand adds tabs when it can save bytes by doing so.

Bugs

Expand doesn't handle newlines very quickly. Do not feed an entire document to it in one string. Instead, feed it an array of lines.

Text::Wrap

Text::Wrap provides simple word wrapping to format paragraphs within a string.

Synopsis

```
use Text::Wrap

print wrap($initial_tab, $subsequent_tab, @text);
print fill($initial_tab, $subsequent_tab, @text);

use Text::Wrap qw(wrap $columns $huge);

$columns = 132;
$huge = 'die';
$huge = 'wrap';
```

Description

Text::Wrap::wrap() is a very simple paragraph formatter. It formats a single paragraph at a time by breaking lines at word boundaries. Indentation is controlled for the first line ($initial_tab) and all subsequent lines ($subsequent_tab) independently.

Lines are wrapped at $Text::Wrap::columns columns. $Text::Wrap::columns should be set to the full width of your output device. When words longer than $columns are encountered, they are broken up. Previous versions of wrap() died (used die()). To restore the old (dying) behavior, set $Text::Wrap::huge to die.

Text::Wrap::fill() is a simple multiparagraph formatter. It formats each paragraph separately and then joins them together when it's done. It destroys any whitespace in the original text. It breaks text into paragraphs by looking for whitespace after a newline. In other respects, it acts like wrap().

Example

```
print wrap("\t","","This is a bit of text that forms a
➥normal book-style paragraph");
```

Tie::Array

This module provides methods for array-tying classes.

Synopsis

```
package NewArray;
use Tie::Array;
@ISA = ('Tie::Array');
```

```
# mandatory methods
sub TIEARRAY { ... }
sub FETCH { ... }
sub FETCHSIZE { ... }

sub STORE { ... }
# mandatory if elements writeable
sub STORESIZE { ... }
# mandatory if elements can be added/deleted

# optional methods - for efficiency
sub CLEAR { ... }
sub PUSH { ... }
sub POP { ... }
sub SHIFT { ... }
sub UNSHIFT { ... }
sub SPLICE { ... }
sub EXTEND { ... }
sub DESTROY { ... }

package NewStdArray;
use Tie::Array;

@ISA = ('Tie::StdArray');

# all methods provided by default

package main;

$object = tie @somearray,Tie::NewArray;
$object = tie @somearray,Tie::StdArray;
$object = tie @somearray,Tie::NewStdArray;
```

Description

The Tie::Array module provides methods for array-tying classes. See the
perltie man page for a list of the functions required in order to tie an
array to a package. The basic Tie::Array package provides stub DELETE
and EXTEND methods and provides implementations of PUSH, POP, SHIFT,
UNSHIFT, SPLICE, and CLEAR in terms of basic FETCH, STORE, FETCHSIZE,
and STORESIZE.

The Tie::StdArray package provides efficient methods required for
tied arrays that are implemented as blessed references to an inner Perl array.
It inherits from Tie::Array and should cause tied arrays to behave exactly
like standard arrays, allowing for the selective overloading of methods.

For developers wanting to write their own tied arrays, the required methods are briefly defined here. See the `perltie` man page section for a more detailed description and example code.

TIEARRAY classname, LIST   The class method is invoked by the command `tie @array, classname`. It associates an array instance with the specified class. *LIST* represents additional arguments (along the lines of the AnyDBM _File man page and compatriots) needed to complete the association. The method should return an object of a class that provides the methods listed in the following text.

STORE this, index, value   This method stores datum *value* into *index* for the tied array associated with object *this*. If this makes the array larger, then the class's mapping of undef should be returned for new positions.

FETCH this, index   This method retrieves the datum in *index* for the tied array associated with object *this*.

FETCHSIZE this   This method returns the total number of items in the tied array associated with object *this*. (It is equivalent to `scalar(@array)`.)

STORESIZE this, count   This method sets the total number of items in the tied array associated with object *this* to be *count*. If this makes the array larger, then the class's mapping of undef should be returned for new positions. If the array becomes smaller, then entries beyond count should be deleted.

EXTEND this, count   This is an informative call that the array is likely to grow to have *count* entries. It can be used to optimize allocation. This method need do nothing.

CLEAR this   This command clears (removes, deletes) all values from the tied array associated with object *this*.

DESTROY this   This is the normal object destructor method.

PUSH this, LIST   This command appends elements of *LIST* to the array.

POP this   This command removes the last element of the array and returns it.

SHIFT this   This command removes the first element of the array (shifting other elements down) and returns it.

UNSHIFT this, LIST   This command inserts *LIST* elements at the beginning of the array, moving existing elements up to make room.

SPLICE this, offset, length, LIST   This command perform the equivalent of `splice` on the array. *offset* is optional and defaults to 0; negative values count back from the end of the array. *length* is optional and defaults to the rest of the array. *LIST* may be empty. It returns a list of the original *length* elements at *offset*.

Caveats

At present, `tied` @ISA is unsupported. There is a potential conflict between magic entries needed to flag a modification to @ISA, and those needed to implement `tie`.

Very little consideration has been given to the behavior of a tied array when $[is not set to default value of 0.

Tie::Handle

This module provides some skeletal methods for handle-tying classes.

Synopsis

```
package NewHandle;
require Tie::Handle;

@ISA = (Tie::Handle);

sub READ { ... }       # Provide a needed method
sub TIEHANDLE { ... }  # Overrides inherited method

package main;

tie *FH, 'NewHandle';
```

Description

The `Tie::Handle` module provides skeletal methods for handle-tying classes. See the `perltie` man page for a list of the functions required to tie a handle to a package. The basic `Tie::Handle` package provides a new method, as well as methods TIESCALAR, FETCH, and STORE. The new method is provided as a means of grandfathering for classes that forget to provide their own TIESCALAR method.

For developers wanting to write their own tied-handle classes, the methods are summarized in the following text. The perltie man page section documents these methods and has sample code:

TIEHANDLE classname, LIST   This method is invoked by the command tie *glob, classname. It associates a new glob instance with the specified class. LIST represents additional arguments (along the lines of the AnyDBM_File man page and compatriots) needed to complete the association.

WRITE this, scalar, length, offset   This method writes length bytes of data from scalar starting at offset.

PRINT this, LIST   This method prints the values in LIST.

PRINTF this, format, LIST   This method prints the values in LIST using format.

READ this, scalar, length, offset   This method reads length bytes of data into scalar starting at offset.

READLINE this   This method reads a single line.

GETC this   This method gets a single character.

DESTROY this   This method frees the storage area associated with the tied handle referenced by this. This method is rarely needed, because Perl manages its memory quite well. But the option exists, should a class need to perform specific actions upon the destruction of an instance.

Tie::Hash and Tie::StdHash

These modules provide some skeletal methods for hash-tying classes.

Synopsis

```
package NewHash;
require Tie::Hash;
```

```
@ISA = (Tie::Hash);

sub DELETE { ... }      # Provides needed method
sub CLEAR  { ... }      # Overrides inherited method


package NewStdHash;
require Tie::Hash;

@ISA = (Tie::StdHash);

# All methods provided by default, define only
# those needing overrides
sub DELETE { ... }

package main;

tie %new_hash, 'NewHash';
tie %new_std_hash, 'NewStdHash';
```

Description

These modules provide skeletal methods for hash-tying classes. See the perltie man page for a list of the functions required to tie a hash to a package. The basic Tie::Hash package provides a new method, as well as the methods TIEHASH, EXISTS, and CLEAR. The Tie::StdHash package provides most methods required for hashes in the perltie man page. It inherits from Tie::Hash and causes tied hashes to behave exactly like standard hashes, allowing for selective overloading of methods. The new method is provided as grandfathering in case a class forgets to include a TIEHASH method.

For developers wanting to write their own tied hashes, the required methods are briefly defined in the following sections. See the perltie man page section for a more detailed description, as well as example code.

TIEHASH *classname, LIST*   This is the method invoked by the command tie %hash, classname. It associates a new hash instance with the specified class. *LIST* represents additional arguments (along the lines of the AnyDBM_File man page and compatriots) needed to complete the association.

STORE *this, key, value*   This method stores the datum *value* into *key* for the tied hash *this*.

FETCH this, key This method retrieves the datum in *key* for the tied hash *this*.

FIRSTKEY this This method returns the (*key*, *value*) pair for the first key in the hash.

NEXTKEY this, lastkey This method returns the next key for the hash.

EXISTS this, key This method verifies that *key* exists with the tied hash *this*.

DELETE this, key This method deletes the key *key* from the tied hash *this*.

CLEAR this This method clears all values from the tied hash *this*.

Caveats
The perltie man page documentation includes a method called DESTROY as a necessary method for tied hashes. Neither Tie::Hash nor Tie::StdHash defines a default for this method. This is a standard for class packages, but it may be omitted in favor of a simple default.

More Information
The packages relating to various DBM-related implementations (DB_File, NDBM_File, and so on) show examples of general tied hashes, as does the Config man page module. Although they do not utilize Tie::Hash, they serve as good working examples.

Tie::RefHash

This module provides the ability to use references as hash keys.

Synopsis
```
require 5.004;
use Tie::RefHash;
tie HASHVARIABLE, 'Tie::RefHash', LIST;

untie HASHVARIABLE;
```

Description

The Tie::RefHash module provides the ability to use references as hash keys if you first tie the hash variable to this module. It is implemented using the standard Perl TIEHASH interface. See the tie entry in perl-func(1) and perltie(1) for more information.

Example

```
use Tie::RefHash;
tie %h, 'Tie::RefHash';
$a = [];
$b = {};
$c = \*main;
$d = \"gunk";
$e = sub { 'foo' };
%h = ($a => 1, $b => 2, $c => 3, $d => 4, $e => 5);
$a->[0] = 'foo';
$b->{foo} = 'bar';
for (keys %h) {
    print ref($_), "\n";
}
```

Tie::Scalar and Tie::StdScalar

These modules provide some skeletal methods for scalar-tying classes.

Synopsis

```
package NewScalar;
require Tie::Scalar;

@ISA = (Tie::Scalar);

sub FETCH { ... }        # Provides a needed method
sub TIESCALAR { ... }    # Overrides inherited method


package NewStdScalar;
require Tie::Scalar;

@ISA = (Tie::StdScalar);

# All methods provided by default,
# so define only what
# needs be overridden
sub FETCH { ... }
```

```
package main;

tie $new_scalar, 'NewScalar';
tie $new_std_scalar, 'NewStdScalar';
```

Description

See the perltie man page for a list of the functions required to tie a scalar to a package. The basic Tie::Scalar package provides a new method as well as the methods TIESCALAR, FETCH, and STORE. The Tie::StdScalar package provides all the methods specified in the perltie man page. It inherits from Tie::Scalar and causes scalars tied to it to behave exactly like the built-in scalars, allowing for selective overloading of methods. The new method is provided as a means of grandfathering for classes that forget to provide their own TIESCALAR method.

For developers wanting to write their own tied-scalar classes, the methods are summarized in the following sections. The perltie man page section documents these and has sample code as well:

TIESCALAR *classname*, *LIST* This is the method invoked by the command tie $*scalar*, *classname*. It associates a new scalar instance with the specified class. *LIST* represents additional arguments (along the lines of the AnyDBM_File man page and compatriots) needed to complete the association.

FETCH *this* This method retrieves the value of the tied scalar referenced by *this*.

STORE *this*, *value* This method stores data *value* in the tied scalar referenced by *this*.

DESTROY *this* This method frees the storage associated with the tied scalar referenced by *this*. This method is rarely needed, because Perl manages its memory quite well. But the option exists, should a class want to perform specific actions upon the destruction of an instance.

The perltie man page section uses a good example of tying scalars by associating process IDs with priority.

Tie::SubstrHash

This module provides fixed-table-sized, fixed-key-length hashing functions.

Synopsis

```
require Tie::SubstrHash;

tie %myhash,
    'Tie::SubstrHash',
    $key_len,
    $value_len,
    $table_size;
```

Description

The Tie::SubstrHash package provides a hash-table-like interface to an array of determinate size, with constant key size and record size. Upon tying a new hash to this package, you must specify the size of the keys that will be used, the size of the value fields the keys will index, and the size of the overall table (in terms of key-value pairs, not size in hard memory). *These values will not change for the duration of the tied hash.* The newly allocated hash table may now have data stored and retrieved.

Efforts to store more than $table_size elements will result in a fatal error—as will efforts to store a value not exactly $value_len characters in length or efforts to reference through a key not exactly $key_len characters in length. Although these constraints may seem excessive, the result is a hash table that uses much less internal memory than an equivalent freely allocated hash table.

Caveats

Because the current implementation uses the table and key sizes for the hashing algorithm, there is no means by which to dynamically change the value of any of the initialization parameters.

Time::gmtime

This module provides an alternative, object-oriented interface to Perl's built-in gmtime() function.

Synopsis

```
use Time::gmtime;
$gm = gmtime();
printf "The day in Greenwich is %s\n",
  (qw(Sun Mon Tue Wed Thu Fri Sat Sun))[ gm->wday() ];
```

```
use Time::gmtime w(:FIELDS;
printf "The day in Greenwich is %s\n",
 (qw(Sun Mon Tue Wed Thu Fri Sat Sun))[ gm_wday() ];

$now = gmctime();

use Time::gmtime;
use File::stat;
$date_string = gmctime(stat($file)->mtime);
```

Description

This module's default exports override the core gmtime() function, replacing it with a version that returns Time::tm objects. This object has methods that return the similarly named structure field name from C's tm structure from time.h. These methods are sec(), min(), hour(), mday(), mon(), year(), wday(), yday(), and isdst().

You can also import all the structure fields directly into your namespace as regular variables using the :FIELDS import tag. (Note that this still overrides your core functions.) You access these fields as variables named with a preceding tm_ in front their method names. Therefore, $tm_obj->mday() corresponds to $tm_mday if you import the fields.

The gmctime() function provides a way of getting at the scalar sense of the original CORE::gmtime() function.

To access this functionality without the core overrides, pass an empty import list to the use, and then access functions with their full qualified names. On the other hand, the built-ins are still available via the CORE:: pseudo-package.

Time::Local

This module provides ways to efficiently compute time from local time and GMT.

Synopsis

```
$time = timelocal($sec,$min,$hours,$mday,$mon,$year);
$time = timegm($sec,$min,$hours,$mday,$mon,$year);
```

Description

These routines are quite efficient, and yet they are always guaranteed to agree with localtime() and gmtime(). The most notable points are that the year is *the year minus 1900* and the month is *a number from 0 to 11.* You manage this by caching the start times of any months you've seen before. If you know the start time of the month, you can always calculate any time within the month. The start times themselves are guessed by successive approximation starting at the current time, because most dates seen in practice are close to the current date. Unlike algorithms that do a binary search (calling gmtime once for each bit of the time value, resulting in 32 calls), this algorithm calls it at most six times—and usually only once or twice. If you hit the month cache, of course, it doesn't call it at all.

Timelocal is implemented using the same cache. You just assume that you're translating a GMT time, and then fudge it when you're done for the timezone and daylight savings arguments. The timezone is determined by examining the result of localtime(0) when the package is initialized. The daylight savings offset is currently assumed to be one hour.

Both routines return –1 (negative one) if the integer limit is hit (for dates after the January 1, 2038 on most machines).

Time::localtime

This module provides an alternative, object-oriented interface to Perl's built-in localtime() function.

Synopsis

```
use Time::localtime;
printf "Year is %d\n", localtime->year() + 1900;

$now = ctime();

use Time::localtime;
use File::stat;
$date_string = ctime(stat($file)->mtime);
```

Description

This module's default exports override the core localtime() function, replacing it with a version that returns Time::tm objects. This object has methods that return the similarly named structure field name from C's tm structure from time.h. These methods are sec(), min(), hour(), mday(), mon(), year(), wday(), yday(), and isdst().

You can also import all the structure fields directly into your namespace as regular variables using the :FIELDS import tag. (Note that this still overrides your core functions.) You access these fields as variables named with a preceding tm_ in front their method names. Therefore, $tm_obj->mday() corresponds to $tm_mday if you import the fields.

The ctime() function provides a way of getting at the scalar sense of the original CORE::localtime() function.

To access this functionality without the core overrides, pass an empty import list to the use, and then access function functions with their full qualified names. On the other hand, the built-ins are still available via the CORE:: pseudo-package.

NOTE

Although this class is currently implemented using the Class::Struct module to build a class of struct and similar datatypes, you shouldn't rely on this.

User::grent

This module provides an alternative, object-oriented interface to Perl's built-in getgrent(), getgruid(), and getgrnam() functions.

Synopsis

```
use User::grent;
$gr = getgrgid(0) or die "No group zero";
if ( $gr->name eq 'wheel' && @{$gr->members} > 1 ) {
    print "gid zero name wheel, with other members";
}

use User::grent qw(:FIELDS;
getgrgid(0) or die "No group zero";
if ( $gr_name eq 'wheel' && @gr_members > 1 ) {
    print "gid zero name wheel, with other members";
}

$gr = getgr($whoever);
```

Description

This module's default exports override the core getgrent(), getgruid(), and getgrnam() functions, replacing them with versions that return User::grent objects. This object has methods that return the similarly named structure field name from C's passwd structure from grp.h. These methods are name(), passwd(), gid(), and members() (not mem). The first three methods return scalars; the last method returns an array reference.

You can also import all the structure fields directly into your namespace as regular variables using the :FIELDS import tag. (Note that this still overrides your core functions.) You access these fields as variables named with a preceding gr_. Therefore, $group_obj->gid() corresponds to $gr_gid if you import the fields. Array references are available as regular array variables, so @{$group_obj->members()} is simply @gr_members.

The getpw() function is a simple front-end that forwards a numeric argument to getpwuid() and forwards the rest of the arguments to getpwnam().

To access this functionality without the core overrides, pass an empty import list to the use, and then access functions with their full qualified names. On the other hand, the built-ins are still available via the CORE:: pseudo-package.

User::pwent

This module provides an alternative, object-oriented interface to Perl's built-in getpwent(), getpwuid(), and getpwnam() functions.

Synopsis

```
use User::pwent;
$pw = getpwnam('daemon') or die "No daemon user";
if ( $pw->uid == 1 && $pw->dir =~ m#^/(bin|tmp)?$# ) {
    print "gid 1 on root dir";
}

use User::pwent qw(:FIELDS);
getpwnam('daemon') or die "No daemon user";
if ( $pw_uid == 1 && $pw_dir =~ m#^/(bin|tmp)?$# ) {
    print "gid 1 on root dir";
}

$pw = getpw($whoever);
```

Description

This module's default exports override the core getpwent(), getpwuid(), and getpwnam() functions, replacing them with versions that return User::pwent objects. This object has methods that return the similarly named structure field name from C's passwd structure from pwd.h—namely name, passwd, uid, gid, quota, comment, gecos, dir, and shell.

You can also import all the structure fields directly into your name-space as regular variables using the :FIELDS import tag. (Note that this still overrides your core functions.) Access these fields as variables named with a preceding pw_ in front their method names. Therefore, $passwd_obj->shell() corresponds to $pw_shell if you import the fields.

The getpw() function is a simple front-end that forwards a numeric argument to getpwuid() and forwards the rest of the arguments to getpwnam().

To access this functionality without the core overrides, pass an empty import list to the use, and then access functions with their full qualified names. On the other hand, the built-ins are still available via the CORE:: pseudo-package.

warnings

This pragma enables Perl's warnings for some of the more common programming problems.

Description

The most common way to get runtime warnings is with the -w command-line switch. The warnings pragma allows finer control over when warnings are available.

One of the most common warnings occurs when Perl warns you about using a variable that has not yet been defined. For example, consider the following code:

```
use warnings;
my $name;
print "name is $name\n";
```

It generates this output:

```
Use of uninitialized value in concatenation (.) or
string at line 3.
name is
```

Like most pragmas, you can reverse the meaning by using the no keyword, which turns off warnings until the end of the block.

```
use warnings;
my $name;
```

```
{
    no warnings;
    print "name is $name\n";
}
# warnings are back on
```

Warnings fall into the following categories:

```
closure
deprecated
exiting
glob
io
misc
numeric
once
overflow
pack
portable
recursion
redefine
regexp
severe
signal
substr
syntax
taint
threads
uninitialized
unpack
untie
utf8
void
y2k
```

You can use these categories to achieve fine control over which warnings are enabled or disabled. In the previous example, you could turn off only certain categories of warnings:

```
use warnings;
my $name;
{
    no warnings "uninitialized";
    print "name is $name\n";
}
# warnings are back on
```

This way, you limit your exposure to unexpected problems.

INDEX

Note to the reader: Throughout this index **boldfaced** page numbers indicate primary discussions of a topic. *Italicized* page numbers indicate illustrations.

E

O

X

Y

Z

About the Contributors

Some of the best—and best-selling—Sybex authors have contributed chapters from their books to *Perl, CGI, and JavaScript Complete, 2nd Edition.*

Martin C. Brown has written several books on Perl, as well as on Python programming, the iMac, and the BeOS operating system. He has more than 15 years of multi-platform programming experience in Perl, C/C++, Java, JavaScript, VBScript, and more. He writes regular columns for *Linux-Programming.com* and *ApacheToday.com* and helped start one of the UK's largest ISPs.

Eric C. Herrmann is president of Application Software Solutions, Inc. (ASSI), which builds business Internet solutions in Perl, JavaScript, and other languages. The author of the best-selling *Teach Yourself CGI Programming with Perl 5 in a Week*, he has an MS in computer science and more than 10 years of programming experience.

James Jaworski used to write the "SuperScripter" column for *Builder.com*, CNET's leading website for webmasters. He led the development of multilevel secure networks for the Department of Defense. He has written numerous books on Java and JavaScript.

Deborah S. Ray and Eric J. Ray are the award-winning coauthors of more than 10 computer books. They have also published a variety of articles and conducted HTML- and Internet-related training courses. Eric is a senior technical writer at Sun. Deborah is the lead author/editor for *Technical Communications Journal.*

Joseph Schmuller, a senior systems analyst at Barnett Technologies, is the author of *ActiveX: No experience required.*, also from Sybex. Editor-in-chief of *PC AI Magazine* from 1991 through 1997, he has written numerous articles and reviews on advanced computing technology. He is a partner in Adcomtec, a firm specializing in website design for mass media organizations, and is an adjunct professor at the University of North Florida.

Erik Strom herds computers and their users as an assistant managing editor at *The Denver Post*. He was a freelance writer, editor, and systems consultant in his previous life.

TELL US WHAT YOU THINK!

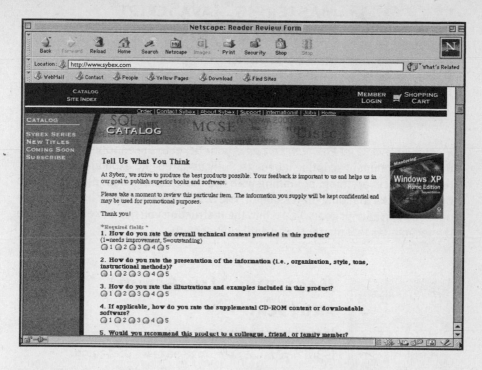

Your feedback is critical to our efforts to provide you with the best books and software on the market. Tell us what you think about the products you've purchased. It's simple:

1. Go to the Sybex website.
2. Find your book by typing the ISBN number or title into the Search field.
3. Click on the book title when it appears.
4. Click **Submit a Review.**
5. Fill out the questionnaire and comments.
6. Click **Submit.**

With your feedback, we can continue to publish the highest quality computer books and software products that today's busy IT professionals deserve.

www.sybex.com

SYBEX Inc. • 1151 Marina Village Parkway, Alameda, CA 94501 • 510-523-8233

MASTERING™ JAVASCRIPT®
PREMIUM EDITION™
JAMES JAWORSKI
ISBN: 0-7821-2819-X   1,136 pages   US $49.99

Mastering JavaScript Premium Edition is your ticket to the enormous power of the Web's dominant scripting language. Fully updated and expanded, this book teaches you everything, beginning with the basics and culminating with the tips and tricks that only professionals know. Regardless of your experience or particular JavaScript goals, you'll find the instruction you need to quickly master the techniques that matter to you and your website.

MASTERING™ JAVASCRIPT®
AND JSCRIPT™
JAMES JAWORSKI
ISBN: 0-7821-2492-7   928 pages   US $39.99

Mastering JavaScript and JScript is aimed at savvy HTML users who want to take the next step and learn to write JavaScript programs that will make their websites come alive! This is the most comprehensive tutorial and reference available. The book starts with everything beginners need to know and then moves on to more advanced topics, such as scripting ActiveX components, working with plug-ins, building multimedia applications, and interfacing with CGI programs. The companion website offers all the sample code from the book, which readers can drop into their own programs, and a complete JavaScript command reference.